I0642407

Letters of H. P. *Lovecraft*

LETTERS TO RHEINHART KLEINER AND OTHERS

Rheinhart Kaufmann [i.e., Kleiner]

H. P. LOVECRAFT

LETTERS TO RHEINHART KLEINER AND OTHERS

EDITED BY S. T. JOSHI AND DAVID E. SCHULTZ

Hippocampus Press

New York

Copyright © 2020 by Hippocampus Press
Introduction and editorial matter copyright © 2020
by S. T. Joshi and David E. Schultz

H. P. Lovecraft's letters published with the permission of Lovecraft
material used by permission of Lovecraft Holdings, LLC, Robert C. Harrall,
Administrator, and John Hay Library, Brown University.

Published by Hippocampus Press
P.O. Box 641, New York, NY 10156.
www.hippocampuspress.com

All rights reserved. No part of this work may be reproduced in any form
or by any means without the written permission of the publisher.

Cover design and Hippocampus Press logo by Anastasia Damianakos.
Cover production by Barbara Briggs Silbert.

First Edition
1 3 5 7 9 8 6 4 2

ISBN 978-1-61498-312-5

Contents

Introduction

Over his lifetime H. P. Lovecraft acquired cadres of friends, colleagues, correspondents, and associates. These individuals largely fell into several broad categories—the amateur journalism movement (first phase extending from 1914 to 1925; second phase from 1930 to 1937); the Kalem Club, the band of friends he fraternized with during his New York years (1924–26); professional writers of weird fiction, many of them focused around the pulp magazine *Weird Tales;* young fans and devotees of weird fiction in the 1930s, who saw in Lovecraft a pioneering figure in the field; and so on. While some individuals fell into more than one category, for the most part these groups were discrete. In this volume two of these categories are represented: amateur journalists (Rheinhart Kleiner, Arthur Harris, James Larkin Pearson, Winifred Virginia Jackson) and the Kalem Club (Rheinhart Kleiner and Arthur Leeds). Jackson is of added interest in being a woman with whom Lovecraft may or may not have carried on a mild romance.

It would be helpful if we knew more about Rheinhart John Kleiner (1893–1949) than we do, for he was not only one of the earliest but also one of the most enduring of Lovecraft's friends and colleagues. Kleiner has already suffered the indignity of having his first name misspelled throughout the first two volumes of Lovecraft's *Selected Letters,* and—despite an abundance of his own writings (mostly poetry) surviving in the amateur press, along with a succession of provocative memoirs on Lovecraft—he remains a shadowy figure. His greatest celebrity, perhaps, derives from his being a founding member of the Kalem Club, the informal group of writers that had been organized even before Lovecraft's own entry, and whose last names mostly began with the letters K, L, or M, during Lovecraft's New York years (1924–26); but even so, he lives chiefly in the vivid pages of Lovecraft's own correspondence rather than in the few articles he wrote years after the Kalems' dissolution. A solitary letter by Kleiner to Lovecraft survives; otherwise, we must rely on Lovecraft's letters to him, and information buried in amateur journals of nearly a century ago, for a picture of this sophisticated Brooklynite.

Kleiner was born in New York City in 1893, one of four children of Charles and Elizabeth Kaufmann. His mother was born in Germany. Charles Kaufmann was his stepfather. His father's name is not known. The *National Amateur* for January 1914 reports his name-change to Kleiner with the following explanation from Kleiner: "Kaufmann was the name of my step-father and I have used it almost as long as I can remmber [*sic*], but I shall be twenty-one in January and intend to assume my own name at that time." Kleiner, three years younger than Lovecraft, had joined amateurdom before Lovecraft's own entrance in April 1914, although the exact date of his entry has not been determined. His sporadic amateur journal, the *Piper,* first began publication in November 1914, but he came in touch with Lovecraft only when Lovecraft issued the first number of his *Conservative* in March 1915 (the issue, dated April, was distributed at least a month prior to the cover date). Kleiner has testified to the striking impression the *Conservative* made upon its first readers: "Its critical pronouncements were relished by some and resented by others, but there was no doubt of the respect with which they were held by all." It is not known whether Kleiner at the time belonged to the United Amateur Press Association (UAPA) or the National Amateur Press Association (NAPA). It is likely that he was a member of both (just as Lovecraft, initially a staunch UAPA man, would join the NAPA in 1917), with perhaps a slight leaning toward the NAPA.

One of the most controversial aspects of Lovecraft's early issues of the *Conservative* was its forthright emphasis on Teutonism and Anglo-Saxondom— to put it bluntly, its overt racism. The early letters of the two colleagues manifestly discussed this sensitive issue also, and we would give much to know Kleiner's responses. As it is, we can only infer that, genial and accommodating as Kleiner appears to have been, he did not allow Lovecraft to expound the issue without challenge. Lovecraft comments in passing, in a letter of 6 December 1915, "I hardly wonder that my racial ideas seem bigoted to one born and reared in the vicinity of cosmopolitan New York."

Fortunately, there were other subjects on which the two were in greater accord, chief among them poetry. To be sure, Kleiner was not a devotee of the eighteenth century as was Lovecraft, and his delightfully witty *vers de société* was in many senses an antipodal contrast to Lovecraft's heavy-handed Georgianism. But Lovecraft was quick to appreciate Kleiner's mastery of light verse, and it was not long before Kleiner's influence on Lovecraft's own poetic output became evident. Their mutual love of films led Kleiner to write "To Mary of the Movies," on Mary Pickford, to which Lovecraft responded, in the fall of 1915, with "To Charlie of the Comics," on Charlie Chaplin. This was the first of a succession of poems by Kleiner to which Lovecraft replied with verses of his own. In the course of these whimsical works—and in the numerous poems Lovecraft either dedicated or directly addressed to Kleiner—we can detect Lovecraft's gradual emergence from an eighteenth-century poetic fossil to one who could see at least a few merits in the poetic output of the nineteenth and even the twentieth centuries. Kleiner would laud Lovecraft's verse—singling out his satirical poetry as the pinnacle of his output—in the first critical article ever written on Lovecraft, "A Note on Howard P. Lovecraft's Verse" (*United Amateur,* March 1919).

In the summer of 1916 the relationship between the two men took a new turn, with the establishment of the Kleicomolo. This round-robin correspondence cycle involving the amateurs Maurice W. Moe and Ira A. Cole (the name derives from the first syllables of each member's name—*Klei*ner, *Co*le,

*Mo*e, *Lo*vecraft), was (as Lovecraft admits in a letter to Kleiner of 4 June 1916) Moe's idea, but Lovecraft enthusiastically embraced it. The three surviving letters of the Kleicomolo—as well as those from a later group, comprising Alfred Galpin, Lovecraft, and Moe—will be included in a subsequent volume of this series.

Kleiner's departure from the round-robin correspondence groups did not imply any secession of correspondence—or, indeed, of personal encounters—with Lovecraft. Lovecraft continued to write directly to Kleiner even during the heyday of the Kleicomolo, using this correspondence as a means of conveying his sentiments in a less pontifical manner than what he chose to do in the Kleicomolo. His astonishing autobiographical letter of 16 November 1916 tells us more about his early life and attitudes than a volume of reminiscences could; his attempt to enlist in the Rhode Island National Guard is chronicled in several letters of 1917;[1] and his listing of amateur poetry, embodied in a letter of 1918, is a bibliographically invaluable document.

By this time Lovecraft and Kleiner had become genuine friends, not merely correspondents. In 1916 Kleiner had been one of a handful of amateurs who had fleetingly met Lovecraft at the Providence train station on their way to the NAPA convention of that year. In 1917 Kleiner took occasion to make a personal visit to Lovecraft, and his various memoirs contain some marvelously affecting details: how Lovecraft's mother and aunts interrupted their discussions to make Lovecraft drink a glass of milk; how uncomfortable Lovecraft felt when venturing to a local restaurant for a meal; how Lovecraft's mother, seeing Kleiner take a pipe from his pocket, expressed the wish that her son might take up pipe smoking. What emerges in this whole encounter—especially when contrasted with Lovecraft's meeting with the amateur writer and publisher W. Paul Cook, who also came to Providence in the summer of 1917—is the class-consciousness of Lovecraft's mother and aunts: for them, the debonair and sophisticated Kleiner was exactly the sort of friend they would have wanted for Lovecraft, whereas the unkempt Cook came close to being sent away with a flea in his ear until Lovecraft intervened on his behalf. Kleiner visited Lovecraft again, apparently fleetingly, in 1918, although it was sufficient for Kleiner to write the charming poem "At Providence in 1918," published in Lovecraft's *Conservative*.

By 1919 the correspondence took another turn. Until then, the two men had been linked by their interest in poetry, film, and amateur affairs (Lovecraft had become President of the UAPA for the 1917–18 term; Kleiner succeeded him for the 1918–19 term). Now, Lovecraft's early love, weird fiction, suddenly re-emerged. Kleiner does not appear to have been in any sense responsive to the weird (Lovecraft wrote in 1920 with some exasperation,

---

1. Kleiner filled out his own registration report on 5 June 1917, which stated that at the time he was a collector working for the Fairbanks Company in New York City.

"Your recent indifference to cosmical ideas is actually puzzling to me"), but there is sufficient evidence that he appreciated Lovecraft's own ventures in that regard, or at least provided a sympathetic ear when Lovecraft chose to discourse on the subject in letters. Kleiner's lack of interest may account for the otherwise curious fact that, although the two met in Boston in October 1919 (at which time they teamed up to write a cycle of flippant poems on fellow amateurs, "On Collaboration"), Kleiner did not accompany Lovecraft and others to Copley Plaza to hear a lecture by Lovecraft's new idol, Lord Dunsany. In any case, the correspondence of 1919–20 is full of weird tidbits, and shows how Lovecraft's imagination was shifting from poetry and *belles lettres* to the supernatural. We find a highly truncated account of the dream of December 1919 that led to the writing of "The Statement of Randolph Carter"; we find other accounts of highly bizarre dreams, including the one that inspired the prose-poem "Nyarlathotep"; and we learn of Lovecraft's commencing his commonplace book, a repository of weird ideas and images that would serve as an inexhaustible mine for his weird fiction for the remainder of his life.

Lovecraft and Kleiner next met at the NAPA convention in Boston in July 1921. It was there that Kleiner made the fateful gesture of introducing Lovecraft to Sonia H. Greene, the woman who would become his wife. Lovecraft was immediately captivated—at least, by Sonia's generosity to the amateur cause (she contributed an unprecedented $50 to the Official Organ Fund for the printing of the *United Amateur*) and her excellent amateur journal, the *Rainbow*, the first issue of which (October 1921) had contributions by, and photographs of, both Lovecraft and Kleiner. Kleiner's exquisite description of first hearing of Lovecraft's marriage in March 1924—"it was while riding in a taxi with Mr. and Mrs. Houtain that the startling news of the Lovecraft–Greene marriage was imparted to me. At once, I had a feeling of faintness at the pit of my stomach and became very pale. Houtain laughed uproariously at the effect of his announcement, but agreed that he felt much as I did"—leaves very little to be said. Nevertheless, Kleiner was gracious enough to write a pretty poem on the marriage of his two friends, "Epistle to Mr. and Mrs. Lovecraft."

Lovecraft met Kleiner again on his two visits to New York in 1922 (April and September), although the surviving letters say little about it. The extant correspondence ceases in the spring of 1923, even though he did not move to Brooklyn until a year later. It was, of course, the period of 1924–26 that represented the summit of their involvement, as they met nearly weekly as members of the Kalem Club, along with Samuel Loveman, James F. Morton, Everett McNeil, Frank Belknap Long, Arthur Leeds, and others. This period is too rich in incident for detailed description here; we can get a representative glimpse of what the endless round of cafeteria-loafing among these bachelors (for Lovecraft, especially with Sonia's departure for the Midwest in late 1924, in essence resorted to bachelorhood for the duration of his New York stay) must have been like by reading Kleiner's poem "The Four of Us!," written at the Double-R

Coffee House on 15 February 1925. (Two weeks earlier, Lovecraft had written a similar poem on, and at, the coffee house.[2]) One of the surprising activities in which the two engaged was hiking, especially in the lovely wooded regions of the New Jersey Palisades. Kleiner commemorated these events in such poems as "Hiking at Plainfield" and "The June Meeting on the Palisades." Kleiner and other amateurs in the Blue Pencil Club called their hiking group the Hika-Walkas. On one of these hikes, in Long Island (Lovecraft apparently was not present), on 19 June 1925, Kleiner was struck by a recklessly driven automobile, suffering serious injuries, although he would fully recover. The incident led Lovecraft to write a whimsical poem condemning the heedless driver. The two men were also regulars of the Blue Pencil Club, a NAPA group that met in Brooklyn. It is not entirely clear whether Lovecraft was an actual member, but Kleiner was, and his contributions in the club's paper, the *Brooklynite,* are extensive.

For most of the period of his association with Lovecraft, Kleiner lived in Brooklyn. In a letter of late 1925 Lovecraft reports that Kleiner worked for the "Fairbanks Scale Co."[3] The Fairbanks Scales Company was a branch of E. & T. Fairbanks Company, an industrial manufacturing company established in Vermont in 1824. In the 1860s it opened offices in Boston and New York. In 1916, Charles Hosmer Morse acquired ownership of the company, and it was renamed the Fairbanks Morse Company. In early 1926, Lovecraft reports that Kleiner "has lost his position with the old reliable Fairbanks Scale Co., & is looking for a new berth as accountant or bookkeeper!"[4] It is not known what employment Kleiner subsequently obtained, although a photograph of him in *Selected Letters II* shows an elderly figure standing adjacent to a sign that reads "Kleiner's Hollow [/] Justice of the Peace [/] Notary Public," apparently at his home in Chester, NJ.

Lovecraft's departure from the New York area in April 1926 appears to have signaled a nearly decade-long cessation in their correspondence but not with their association. In 1928, when he returned to Brooklyn for several weeks to help Sonia set up a hat shop, he reported that "Kleiner has virtually dropped out of everybody's sight save for the Paterson Sunday hikes."[5] In 1930, as Lovecraft was passing through New York in the course of one of his increasingly lengthy travels to the South, he wrote:

> It was good to see old Kleiner again—& I am told that he is slowly drifting back to contact with the old crowd after a long period of invisibility. He even says he may get around to Providence one of these days! He does not age visibly except that his hair is rapidly turning grey—even greyer than my

---

2. See "[On the Double-R Coffee House]" (*AT* 163–64), written 1 February 1925.
3. HPL to Lillian D. Clark, 13 December 1925; *LFF* 507.
4. HPL to Lillian D. Clark, 12 February 1926; *LFF* 552.
5. HPL to Lillian D. Clark, 3 May 1928; *LFF* 643–44.

own few remaining spears. Otherwise he is still the same lean, languid Kleiner of other days.[6]

Kleiner, for his part, continued his amateur activity: he attended the NAPA convention in Boston in 1932 and he was secretary of the Blue Pencil Club for the period 1935–37. Lovecraft met Kleiner, along with many other of his New York colleagues, during his regular visits to the area in the Christmas seasons of 1931–35, but their correspondence apparently resumed only in early 1936, at which point it became evident that they did not have a great deal to say to each other.

Nevertheless, Kleiner was among the first to pay homage to Lovecraft's memory, writing the affecting memoir "Howard Phillips Lovecraft" for the Summer 1937 issue of the *Californian*. It was the first of numerous reminiscences he would write; the best of these, "Some Lovecraft Memories," published only in 1990, is manifestly Kleiner's original version of the memoir published (with some modifications by August Derleth) as "A Memoir of Lovecraft" in *Something about Cats and Other Pieces* (1949). Kleiner also commemorated Lovecraft with the touching poem "H. P. L." in the Autumn 1940 issue of Edward H. Cole's *Olympian*, which featured exemplary memoirs by Cole, James F. Morton, and Ernest Edkins.

Of Kleiner's remaining years we have only fleeting glimpses. He became Official Editor of the NAPA for 1937–38. He appears to have severed relations with the Blue Pencil Club in the mid-1940s, but then, surprisingly, married a former BPC member, Ruth Pietchman, in 1946. By then Kleiner had at last abandoned Brooklyn to reside in Chester, New Jersey, where BPC members met occasionally in the later 1940s. Kleiner only sent his Lovecraft letters to Arkham House for transcription in June 1945. At the time he estimated he had more than 150 letters—considerably more than the number included herein. He also gave Derleth an unidentified story manuscript. In the fall of 1948 Kleiner suffered a stroke, dying the following year.[7]

Rheinhart Kleiner emerges—from the pages of Lovecraft's correspondence as well as from his own poetry and prose—as a poet of admirable technical skill with a flair for pungent wit and satire but, more significantly, as a warm, non-judgmental boon companion whose sophistication and worldly wisdom may have played a role in Lovecraft's transformation from a social misfit to a genial friend who could feel comfortable in social settings of widely different sorts. In some senses, their early correspondence does not reveal Lovecraft in a positive light: he comes off as racist, bookish, and dogmatic. Kleiner's response to Lovecraft's eccentricities was, clearly, not censorious disapproval, but kindly tolerance and a quiet offering of contrary views. That dynamic appears to have had its influence in inciting Lovecraft to question

---

6. HPL to Lillian D. Clark, 27–28 May 1930; *LFF* 855.
7. See further James Guinane, *Rheinhart Kleiner: A Memoir* (New Town, Tasmania: James Guinane, 1951).

his own certitudes and to initiate a process of self-questioning that would lead him to wholesale revisions in his philosophy, his politics, and his relations with others. Kleiner had the privilege of knowing Lovecraft for the better part of twenty-five years, and he could take his share of the credit—along with such other longtime friends as W. Paul Cook and Frank Belknap Long—for bringing Lovecraft out of his shell and making him the warm, kindly, generous human being he became in the last decade of his life.

Arthur Harris (1893–1966) was an amateur journalist living in Llandudno, Wales. He published one of the longest-running British amateur journals, *Interesting Items,* which ran from March 1904 (as *Llandudno's Weekly*) to April 1964, each issue usually consisting only of four to eight small pages. His large collection of amateur journals was estimated (in 1962) to include 15,000 items. It is not certain how Lovecraft came to correspond with him, and even to have some of his earliest published work in British amateur journals. Harris published "1914," "The Crime of Crimes," and, years later, two sonnets of *Fungi from Yuggoth.* He also published "The Crime of Crimes" as a pamphlet in 1915, thereby making it Lovecraft's first separate publication, of which only three copies are known now to exist. Lovecraft continued to correspond with Harris for the entirety of his life, although as early as 1918 his letters numbered no more than one or two a year. His surviving letters to others contain no mentions of Harris. The news of Lovecraft's passing reached Harris swiftly, for the May 1937 issue of *Interesting Items* contained his heartfelt reminiscence of Lovecraft, in which he acknowledged "no one has ever written me such interesting and lengthy letters."[8] Harris's name was in Lovecraft's address book, but it does not seem that Arkham House approached him to borrow Lovecraft's letters to him for transcription.

James Larkin Pearson (1879–1981) was a poet and newspaper publisher in North Carolina. For most of his adult life, he lived on his farm, called "Fifty Acres," in Boomer. In 1910, he was president of the Southern Amateur Journalists' Association. He published a satirical newspaper called *The Fool-Killer* (1910–17, 1919–35), named for a story by O. Henry, another writer from North Carolina. One of his amateur publications was *Pearson's Pet.*

It is not known how he came to correspond with Lovecraft; their earliest letters date to just a year after Lovecraft's advent in the UAPA. At first they pertained to amateur affairs, but in time Lovecraft's letters grew more substantial. They corresponded sporadically. Pearson dropped out of the UAPA not long thereafter, but eventually rejoined. He printed and published his book *Pearson's Poems* in 1924.

Perhaps the most that is known of their association is Lovecraft's record

---

8. "More Regrettable Passings," in Joshi and Schultz, *Ave atque Vale* 445.

of an exercise he unwillingly engaged in with James F. Morton and Rheinhart Kleiner in November 1925—the evaluation and selection of the best poems in a lengthy manuscript submitted for that purpose:

> Howsumever—even if I don't get frozen stiff I sure am bored stiff, & your fellow-Iacobus of Boomer is the cause. I've put in damn near a whole day on the ——— ————— thing, & have drawn up the accompanying body of verdicts & revisions. Maybe I'm blunted by the allopathic dose of 400 pages of quasi-goodenoughery, but I didn't see much that could be notably asterisked as high spots . . . . . although you may take all of my Class A selections as the equivalents. These are really very good poems, & do Jacobus Larcinius genuine credit. The B. items aren't at all bad for amateur work, & where they most conspicuously sag I've tried to tighten 'em up a bit. But most of the residual truck does The Fool-Killer no credit, & I wouldn't advise its inclusion in any future volume. I'm curious to see how well my lists coincide with what you drew up & what Kleiner will draw up. If Pearson doesn't pay us for this Bush-whacking I move we all go on strike—indeed, Loveman flatly refused to bind himself to the toil, as Sonny also probably will. But I always was a facile goat. I'll take the book to the meeting Wednesday & heave a sigh of relief—if I don't freeze to death in the damned interim.[9]

In *Poet's Progress,* Pearson's autobiography, he acknowledged that Lovecraft "had something to do with editing my third book" (302), *Fifty Acres and Other Selected Poems* (1937), which did not appear until more than ten years after Lovecraft had examined and revised the manuscript. It is not known if the book contains any poems revised by Lovecraft. Since Lovecraft revised only those that "conspicuously sag[ged]," it may well be that Pearson did not include any of them.

Lovecraft's last letter to Pearson went unanswered. Pearson's letter to him of 12 September 1926 seems to be his last, and since his name was not recorded in Lovecraft's address book from late in life, they undoubtedly fell out of touch the decade before Lovecraft died. Pearson later served as North Carolina Poet Laureate from 1953 until his death in 1981 at the age of 101, the second poet to hold the title.

Winifred Virginia Jackson (1876–1959) occupies a curious place among Lovecraft's friends, colleagues, and correspondents: aside from Sonia H. Greene, whom he married, Jackson is perhaps the only woman who could be said to have conducted a romance with Lovecraft.

At the time when Lovecraft first became acquainted with her, she was known as Winifred Virginia Jordan, the wife of Horace Jordan, whom she had married in 1915. She lived in the Boston area. An avid amateur writer, she submitted several poems to Lovecraft's *Conservative* in 1916; a total of seven of her poems appeared in the issues of January, April, and October 1916.

---

9. HPL to James F. Morton, November 1925; *Letters to James F. Morton* 85–86.

Lovecraft later borrowed some elements of one of these—"Insomnia"—for his own lengthy story-in-verse, "Psychopompos" (written in 1917–18). Two poems by Lovecraft, "The Unknown" (*Conservative,* October 1916) and "The Peace Advocate" (*Tryout,* May 1917), actually appeared under Jordan's pseudonym "Elizabeth Berkeley." Lovecraft later admitted that this was done "in an effort to mystify the [amateur] public by having widely dissimilar work from the same nominal hand."[10]

Jordan was elected second vice-president at the UAPA convention of 1917 (an office she held for three consecutive years); Lovecraft himself was elected president at that event, serving until the summer of 1918. Jordan and Lovecraft continued to collaborate in various ways in the amateur press. They and others jointly issued three issues of the *United Co-operative* (December 1918, June 1919, and April 1921). She published the first of Lovecraft's birthday odes to Jonathan E. Hoag ("To Jonathan E. Hoag, Esq., on His 87th Birthday: February 10, 1918") in her amateur journal, *Eurus* (February 1918). About a year later, Lovecraft wrote a flattering piece on Jordan, "Winifred Virginia Jordan: Associate Editor" (*Silver Clarion,* April 1919). As the official editor of the United Women's Press Club of Massachusetts, Jordan served as the editor of the paper's official organ, the *Bonnet.* Only one issue (June 1919) is known to have appeared; but it contained an unsigned editorial, "Trimmings," undoubtedly by Lovecraft, as well as a poem, "Helene Hoffman Cole: 1893–1919: The Club's Tribute." He later wrote another effusive essay on her, "Winifred Virginia Jackson: A 'Different' Poetess" (*United Amateur,* March 1921).

The most significant way in which the two writers collaborated was in the stories "The Green Meadow" and "The Crawling Chaos." The former was written in 1918–19, the latter in 1920–21. Lovecraft notes in letters that both stories were based on dreams that Jackson had; Lovecraft claims that the "Green Meadow" dream was "exceptionally singular in that I had one exactly like it myself—save that mine did not extend so far. It was only when I had related my dream that Miss J. related the similar and more fully developed one. The opening paragraph of 'The Green Meadow' was written for my own dream, but after hearing the other, I incorporated it into the tale which I developed therefrom."[11] Elsewhere Lovecraft says that Jackson supplied "a *map*" of the scene of "The Green Meadow," and that he added the "quasi-realistic . . . introduction from my own imagination."[12] The story was not published until it appeared in the final issue of W. Paul Cook's amateur journal, the *Vagrant* (Spring 1927). "The Crawling Chaos"—whose title, Lovecraft admitted, was taken from the prose poem "Nyarlathotep," where it is used in reference to Nyarlathotep—was published in their jointly edited

---

10. HPL, letters to the Gallomo (12 September 1923), 108.
11. HPL to RK, [April 1920]; see p. 164.
12. HPL to Frank Belknap Long, 4 June 1921; *SL* 1.136.

publication *United Co-operative* for April 1921.

All this suggests no more than that Jordan and Lovecraft were close col-leagues in the amateur press. But there appears to have been considerable gos-sip at the time that there was a romantic involvement between the two. Evidence for such an involvement is exceedingly sparse and indirect. On 4 July 1920, Lovecraft did pay a visit to a home at 20 Webster Street in the Boston suburb of Allston, then jointly occupied by Jordan, Laurie A. Sawyer, and Edith Miniter. Evidently she had divorced Horace Jordan in 1919, whereupon she presumably resumed her maiden name.[13] It is certainly of some interest that Lovecraft, in one of his few extant letters to Jackson—a charming (and per-haps mildly flirtatious) letter on Christmas Day, 1920—had enclosed a poem he had written: "On Receiving a Portraiture of Mrs. Berkeley, yᵉ Poetess."

Otherwise, evidence for the romance is based upon hearsay. Willametta Keffer, an amateur of a somewhat later period, purportedly told George T. Wetzel that (and here Wetzel is paraphrasing a letter by Keffer) "everybody in Amateur Journalism thought Lovecraft would marry Winifred Jordan"; Kef-fer herself stated to Wetzel, "A long time member of NAPA who knew and met both HPL and Winifred Virginia told me of the 'romance.'"[14] A photo-graph was taken at some point by Lovecraft (probably in 1921) of Jackson at the seaside; and Lovecraft's wife Sonia Greene told R. Alain Everts in 1967 that "I stole HPL away from Winifred Jackson."

But there are reasons to doubt there was a genuine romance. According to research by Wetzel and Everts, Horace Jordan was an African American.[15] Given Lovecraft's abhorrence of "miscegenation" and racial intermixing, it would presumably have been difficult for him to associate with Winifred Jor-dan if he had known the racial status of her husband—but perhaps he did not know. Moreover, Jackson later carried on a long-time affair with William Stanley Braithwaite (1878–1962), a prominent critic and editor who was con-sidered African American (he won the Spingarn Award of the NAACP in 1918), even though he was only one-eighth black.[16] Braithwaite included her poems in several volumes of his *Anthology of Magazine Verse* (1913–39). He founded a publishing firm, B. J. Brimmer in 1922, and Jackson was his busi-ness partner. Bizarrely, a book published in 1921 intended to promote racial

---

13. George T. Wetzel and R. Alain Everts, *Winifred Virginia Jackson—Lovecraft's Lost Romance* [Madison, WI: R. Alain Everts, 1976].

14. Ibid.

15. Charles Tromblee of winifredvjackson.blogspot.com disputes this.

16. His father, originally from British Guiana, was of mixed racial heritage, and his mother the daughter of a mulatto ex-slave. HPL once referred to him as an "octo-roon" (*Letters to Maurice W. Moe and Others* 497). One extant letter from HPL to Braithwaite (dated 7 February 1930; ms., JHL) survives, in which he mentions "the continued progress of Miss Jackson, whose work gave me such an instant impression of authentic genius a decade ago."

pride among African Americans names Jackson as among the "foremost writers the race has produced during the past few years."[17]

The fact that this "romance" (if it was that) blossomed exactly at the time when Lovecraft's mother, Sarah Susan ("Susie") Lovecraft, had to be hospitalized (beginning in March 1919), is of some interest. She remained in the hospital for the duration of her life, dying on 24 May 1921. Lovecraft wrote a somewhat stiff letter to Jackson in which he maintained that Susie "may be reckoned among the earliest and most enthusiastic admirers of your work." Otherwise, their extant correspondence deals largely with amateur matters. One wonders if their friendship ended, seemingly abruptly, when Lovecraft remarked that he wished to name a black kitten that visited him William Stanley Braithwaite, around the time he learned that Braithwaite was of mixed racial background. His comment now seems stunningly tone-deaf, and one imagines Jackson found very little reason to be amused.

Among the members of the Kalem Club, we know the least about Arthur Leeds (1882–1952?). Leeds had a varied career: as a boy he worked in a traveling circus, he was a volunteer with the Canadian Army in World War I, and in the 1920s he was a columnist for *Writer's Digest*. In the 1930s he worked at the New Deal Book Store in New York City. He wrote also several short stories for various fiction magazines. In the decade before he became acquainted with Lovecraft, Leeds appears to have made something of a career by writing "photoplays" (that is, screenplays) for the burgeoning motion picture industry. The database IMDb.com lists only three silent films whose screenplays Leeds wrote: *Don't Let Mother Know; or, The Bliss of Ignorance* (1913); *Through Another Man's Eyes* (1913); and *A Pearl of Greater Price* (1917). All appear to be short films. Given that many silent films do not survive or are poorly documented, there were probably many more films on which Leeds worked. A contemporary treatise states:

> Arthur Leeds is another of the younger men who have succeeded in the photoplay world. His produced photoplays, "Sun, Sand and Solitude," "Through Another Man's Eyes," "The Heart of a Jew," "A Pearl of Greater Price," "In the Country God Forgot," "Without Reward," "The Germinal Element," "The Man Who Mocked," and many other feature films, have placed him in the front rank of photo playwrights.
>
> His experience as an actor and in many other branches of theatrical work, fitted him in many ways for his future work, and he is also another newspaper product who has taken up photoplay work. He is the author of a book on *Writing the Photoplay*, is editor of *The Photoplay Author*, and is generally

---

17. William Henry Harrison, Jr., *Colored Girls and Boys' Inspiring United States History: and a Heart to Heart Talk about White Folks* ([Allentown, PA]: [Searle & Dressler Co.], 1921), 183.

well known and liked among the photoplay authors of the country.[18]

Aside from *Through Another Man's Eyes* and *A Pearl of Greater Price*, IMDb.com does not list any of the films named above.[19]

Leeds co-wrote *Writing the Photoplay* with J. Berg Esenwein (1867–1946), published in 1913 by the Home Correspondence School (Springfield, MA).[20] A revised edition appeared in 1919. The magazine cited by Smith, the *Photoplay Author,* was published in 1913–14 by the Home Correspondence School. It was renamed *Photoplay Author and Writer's Monthly* (January–June 1915), and as *Writer's Monthly* (1915–51). Leeds is listed as editor for the 1913–14 issues, but Esenwein took over the editorship thereafter; Leeds, however, continued to contribute extensively to the periodical.

The Home Correspondence School was one of numerous such organizations that catered to those who (like Lovecraft in the years after his dropping out of high school in 1908) could not attend college. Lovecraft reports sending away for chemistry courses from the International Correspondence Schools of Scranton, Pennsylvania, in 1909. As for Leeds, Lovecraft notes that "an inveterate geographer & student of far-away life (also a story writer & critic—formerly connected with the Home Correspondence School) is Belknap's & my old friend Arthur Leeds, 2736 W. 16th St., Brooklyn, N.Y."[21]

Lovecraft does not appear to have made Leeds's acquaintance during his two visits to New York in 1922, but he was already a fixture in Lovecraft's circle in the summer of 1924, after Lovecraft's marriage to Sonia Greene on 3 March 1924, and his move into Sonia's apartment at 259 Parkside Avenue, Brooklyn. Leeds enjoyed accompanying Lovecraft on long walks (sometimes in the middle of the night) throughout the New York area. But the Kalem Club suffered a rift when the ever-impecunious Leeds was slow in repaying a debt ($8.00) owed to another member, the elderly writer Everett McNeil.[22] As a result, separate "Leeds" and "McNeil" meetings began to be

---

18. Russell E. Smith, "The Authors of the Photoplay," *Book News Monthly* 33, No. 7 (March 1915): 331.

19. The database lists a film titled *The Heart of a Jewess* (1913), but Leeds is not credited as having written the screenplay. It lists *The Country That God Forgot* (1916), but again Leeds is not credited with the screenplay. *Without Reward* (1913) is listed, but with no information about the cast, so Leeds may have written this screenplay.

20. It is of interest to note that one of the two books that HPL purchased around the time he was resuming the writing of fiction in 1917 after a nine-year hiatus was Esenwein's *Writing the Short-Story: A Practical Handbook on the Rise, Structure, Writing, and Sale of the Modern Short-Story* (New York: Hinds, Hayden & Eldredge, 1918; *LL* 320).

21. HPL to E. Hoffmann Price, 18 September 1934 (ms., JHL).

22. See HPL to PJC, 2 March 1927: "Leeds is always broke & in debt. He was a very congenial member of our old gang in New York, & went to Chicago about the time I came home to Providence. Let him talk—but don't let him borrow any cash of you. He *means* to pay back—in fact, he never ceases to mean!" (p. 356)

held; the former were much more popular with the other Kalems, as many of them did not find McNeil a stimulating conversationalist.

One of the more curious instances of Leeds's association with Lovecraft was his introducing the Providence writer to Jean Libbera (1884–1946), a human oddity exhibited at Hubert's Museum, with which Leeds was at one time associated. Libbera had a miniature twin growing from his body. Its rudimentary head was embedded in Libbera's torso, and since it had a nervous system, Libbera could feel when it was touched. Of Libbera, Lovecraft had written "Clothed, he looked merely like a somewhat 'pot-bellied' individual."[23] Sometime in 1925 Leeds wanted to introduce Lovecraft to him because Libbera enjoyed Lovecraft's fiction. Leeds himself had written but not sold a story about Libbera.[24] Lovecraft did meet Libbera, and subsequently wrote an entry in his commonplace book that reflects the encounter: "Man has miniature shapeless Siamese twin—exhib. in circus—twin surgically detached— disappears—does hideous things with malign life of his own" (entry 133). Lovecraft passed on the plot-germ to Henry S. Whitehead, who used it as the basis of his story "Cassius" (*Strange Tales,* November 1931). He never wrote up a story based on this idea, but in describing Wilbur Whateley of "The Dunwich Horror," he must have had Libbera in mind: "the torso and lower parts of the body were teratologically fabulous, so that only generous clothing could ever have enabled it to walk on earth unchallenged or uneradicated" (*CF* 2.439).

In the spring of 1925, Leeds urged Lovecraft to do freelance work for a man named Yesley in writing advertising copy; Lovecraft wrote several pieces (R. H. Barlow gave them the collective name "Commercial Blurbs"), but the venture came to nothing. It is unclear how closely Lovecraft kept in touch with Leeds following his return to Providence in April 1926; clearly Leeds was on Lovecraft's list of recipients for the postcards he would write on his increasingly wide travels during the final decade of his life, but few actual letters are extant. However, there must have been far more correspondence than what survives today, since Lovecraft reports that in 1932 Leeds had spoken to a friend of his who was an editor at Vanguard (formerly Macy-Masius) about publishing Lovecraft's work. Vanguard wanted a novel, but Lovecraft (having already repudiated *The Dream-Quest of Unknown Kadath* and *The Case of Charles Dexter Ward* and evidently not considering *At the Mountains of Madness* a true novel) said he had none at hand. Nevertheless, the firm did ask to see some of his short stories, so Lovecraft sent them "Pickman's Model," "The Dunwich Horror," "The Rats in the Walls," and "The Call of Cthulhu." The stories were eventually rejected.

---

23. HPL to Duane W. Rimel, 12 September 1934; *Letters to F. Lee Baldwin, Duane W. Rimel, and Nils Frome* 217.
24. Frank Belknap Long, *Howard Phillips Lovecraft: Dreamer on the Nightside* (Sauk City, WI: Arkham House, 1975), 62.

The close contact Lovecraft established with Leeds in the 1924–26 period is clearly reflected in the informality and collegiality of the extant correspondence. And yet, Leeds—who apparently lost touch with the other members of the Kalem Club after Lovecraft's death and also did not seem to have much contact with Lovecraft's publisher August Derleth[25]—was one of the few colleagues who did not write a memoir of Lovecraft. He could no doubt have shed additional light on that critical period of Lovecraft's life.

Paul Jonas Campbell, Jr. (1884–1945) of Georgetown, Illinois, was a farmer by trade. He inherited from his grandfather a 537-acre farm, along with a considerable amount of money, when he was a young man. He also owned a printing company in Danville, which he purchased with his inheritance. The census for 1910 and 1920 identified his occupation as farm manager or farmer, and his operation was known as Ridgefarm. He was a member of the Prairie Queen Grange. The census does not mention the printing business, because it failed before 1919. Because Campbell badly injured his right leg in 1906 on the way to the print shop, the physical labor required for farming was difficult for him.

> The fall which resulted at long last in the amputation of my leg wasn't much of a tumble. In getting off a street car before it came to a full stop, I jumped on a small puddle of ice in the uneven brick pavement, spun half way around, lost my balance and came down on my right knee. This twisting fall dislocated the innominate where it fastens to the spine. I did not discover this for many months and then declined to give up walking for a while to allow the stretched ligaments to contract. Consequently I had much trouble with the hip.[26]

In the next nine years he fell twice more, reinjuring the leg. He realized in 1915 when he was about thirty that his leg would have to be amputated and that he would need a wooden prosthesis. Lovecraft knew of Campbell's disability, for he wrote James F. Morton that "Campbell is down & out—& with his only ankle broken,"[27] clearly aware that Campbell had only one ankle.

Campbell's chief aspiration, however, was to write—including the proverbial Great American Novel—but he stayed with the farm until the 1920s. He entered the world of amateur journalism in June 1902, when he was a seventeen-year-old "farm boy with a yen to write."[28] As a youngster, Campbell made "lead pencil publications for family circulation, before I went to school,"[29] much as Lovecraft hectographed youthful scientific "journals" for his family. Just like Lovecraft in his early days in amateur journalism, Campbell eagerly

---

25. Only two letters by HPL to Leeds are in the Arkham House transcripts.
26. PJC, "Adventures in Appreciation," *Courage* No. 21 (April–May 1943): [13].
27. HPL to James F. Morton, 9 March 1933; *Letters to James F. Morton* 315.
28. "Adventures in Appreciation" 463.
29. Ibid.

absorbed the publications of numerous like-minded individuals, and he soon was issuing his own papers. He noted that "for the next three years, amateur journalism was the most important thing in the world to me."[30] He participated in the NAPA campaign of 1903. In 1904, he attended Amateur Journalists' Day in St. Louis, where he met and made friends with many other amateurs. He attended his first NAPA convention in Cleveland in July 1905, and as part of his travels he visited the Massachusetts Agricultural College through which he had taken a correspondence course in agriculture. Lovecraft learned much about Campbell's early days in amateur journalism, thanks to Campbell's generosity in lending material to the new recruit:

> Pres. Campbell recently favoured me with the loan of many books & papers touching upon the older days of amateur journalism [. . .] Another matter of interest in the collection lent me, is the career of Pres. Campbell himself, as exhibited by a complete file of his various publications. He joined both associations [i.e., NAPA and UAPA] in 1902, at the age of 17, and commenced issuing a miserable sheet called *The Ideal Politician*. The first number contained a "poem" entitled "You Can't Convince a Scotchman", which is one of the most wretched metrical misfits ever inflicted upon amateurdom. Quite naturally, this crude paper excited much ridicule and sarcasm from the older members, and Campbell began to attack his critics with great vigour. This controversial practice improved his bad English; and his second paper, *The Scottish Highlander*, reveals very plainly that mental keenness which was later to distinguish Campbell's work. At one time this enterprising amateur published two papers at a time; *The Scottish Highlander* for the National, and *The Prairie State Journal* for the United; meanwhile acting as associate editor of *The Reflector*, which was issued by L. M. Starring of Tennessee. In 1905 he commenced his most famous enterprise, *The Scotchman*,[31] and by that time he had educated himself from complete crudity to a condition of enviable distinction as an essayist. His controversy of 1907–08 with the Gotham Club was exceedingly bitter, and enabled him to exhibit some of the sharpest and cleverest personal satire ever known to the amateur world.[32]

Campbell soon was official editor for the NAPA during Timothy Burr Thrift's administration as president. His volume of the *National Amateur* (1905), the third largest ever, made him famous, but as Campbell wryly noted, "I made a record in two ways, I did publish a volume of 120 pages which placed me in the upper brackets for quantity, and I perpetuated more typographical errors in my volume, perhaps, than had ever been perpetrated in the official organ in the previous years of its existence."[33] James Larkin Pearson

---

30. "Adventures in Appreciation" 469.
31. The *Scotchman* ran from Vol. 1, No. 1 (January 1905) to Vol. 3, No. 4 (June 1908), twelve issues totaling 312 pp.
32. HPL to John T. Dunn, 17 December 1916; *Letters to Alfred Galpin and Others* 173–74.
33. "Adventures in Appreciation" 469.

said that he printed Campbell's various publications from 1902 to 1906. He remarked that "Campbell was a young man with a lot of money and a great ambition to be a writer. As I remember, he never learned the printer's trade (or at least was not working at it) but always hired his printing work done."[34] Campbell had the *National Amateur* published locally in Danville, Illinois, eventually purchasing the News Printing Company with his inheritance and running it for two years, before he was forced to sell it. He then ran an automobile agency until 1912, when the reinjury of his leg laid him up for three years.

Campbell said that he published 354 separate articles in the amateur press in 1906.[35] At the 1906 NAPA convention in Philadelphia, he sidestepped being elected NAPA president, the usual follow-on position for the official editor, but was awarded a silver loving cup for distinguished services to NAPA. In his acceptance speech, Campbell "paid tribute to Amateur Journalism [. . .] for what it had done for me, and I like to think that the sentiments I voiced then had been shared by many."[36] Lovecraft's own essay "What Amateurdom and I Have Done for Each Other" comes to mind. Campbell had hoped to elope with fellow amateur and actress Amanda Eunice Frees ("Freezette"; b. 1883) after the convention, but she quietly dropped him and instead married Tim Thrift (1882–1947).[37]

Campbell was a dedicated recruiter for UAPA. In March 1920 alone he sent out ninety-eight recruiting letters. Just as Edward F. Daas recruited Lovecraft in 1914 when he read Lovecraft's ongoing letter battle in the *Argosy*, Campbell recruited Frank Belknap Long into the UAPA around 1919, when he took note of an essay Long published in the *Boy's World* magazine. Long's first published story, "Dr. Whitlock's Price," appeared in the *United Amateur* in March 1920, and his pastiche of Edgar Allan Poe, "The Eye Above the Mantel" (March 1921), caught Lovecraft's attention. The two became lifelong friends.

Lovecraft and Campbell probably began corresponding as early as mid-1914. As Lovecraft became more involved in amateur journalism, references in his columns to Campbell were fairly frequent and favorable. Besides generously lending Lovecraft numerous amateur journals of the previous generation, Campbell exercised various other influences on Lovecraft. "It is to a poem quoted by Mr. P. J. Campbell that I owe my introduction to [Alan] Seeger and his verse, an introduction for which I cannot sufficiently thank our esteemed President."[38] He acknowledged gratitude for being able to read a

---

34. *Poet's Progress* 227.

35. "Adventures in Amateur Journalism" 471. But note that that number differs wildly from that given here on p. 25.

36. "Adventures in Appreciation" 471.

37. The two continued to publish *Lucky Dog* into the 1940s.

38. HPL, letters to the Kleicomolo (April 1917), 103.

powerful tale by Ernest A. Edkins—"Phantasus"—in a collection of amateur stories loaned him by Campbell.[39]

Soon after induction, just as in Campbell's case, Lovecraft became active in the administrative aspects of the organization. Lovecraft was on the ballot for president in the UAPA election of July 1916. He lost to Campbell by a vote of 38–2, and to Andrew F. Lockhart for official editor by a vote of 28–1. Lovecraft had been appointed Chairman of the Department of Public Criticism in November 1914 by President Dora M. Hepner, and was reappointed by President Leo Fritter in September 1915 and by Campbell in August 1916. In the election for September 1917 Lovecraft himself was elected president, and he appointed Rheinhart Kleiner Chairman of the Department of Public Criticism. In September 1918 President Kleiner appointed Lovecraft as Chairman; this was Lovecraft's last term in the office. Lovecraft served as official editor for 1920–22 and 1924–25.

When he published "A Request" in the *Conservative* in January 1917, asking that amateur journalists provide personal information for the UAPA's yearbook for 1916–17,[40] he used an entry for Campbell for the purpose of illustration. The actual text may have been written by Campbell himself, since "the biographical dictionary or 'Who's Who' of the more prominent members of the Association . . . is due to the fertile brain of Pres. Campbell":

> The Conservative, as Chairman of the United's Year-Book Committee, will deem it a favour of great magnitude if every recipient of this paper will send him, as soon as possible, a set of autobiographical notes for use in the forthcoming annual. A complete biographical dictionary of amateurs is planned as a feature of that publication. The following specimen may serve as a guide to what is desired:
>
> 647c CAMPBELL, PAUL J., Farmer, Printer, Journalist. Born Georgetown, Ill., Nov. 8, 1884. Public School Education. Joined June, 1902, recommended by Ira E. Seymour. Published Ideal Politician, Scottish Highlander, Prairie State Journal, Illinoian, Scotchman, and Invictus. Contributed 59 articles to the amateur press in 1906, his most active year. Elected Director in 1908, Treasurer in 1915, President in 1916. Interested in Literature, Religion, History, Philosophy, and Free Thought. (*CE* 1.138–39)

Campbell married three times. He wrote that when he was just twenty-one, he was "romantically inclined and seeking a sympathetic help-mate to

---

39. HPL to RK, 17 July 1917 (p. 87).
40. The volume was never published, presumably for lack of funds, although the ms. was apparently completed (see "President's Message" [November 1917]; *CE* 1.173).

share my dream of life and the literary distinction which I meant to win."[41] He said that his mother was trying to hitch him up with one Helen Baird, but it seems he resisted that, even though they remained friends. He had his eye on many women. He was smitten by Myrtle Almedia "Tommy" Thomas, an amateur from St. Louis, but she married someone else. After he was jilted by Freezette, he immediately married Ada Clara Parkhurst (b. 1882) on the re-bound, but the marriage did not last. In 1915, he married Agnes Westwater (b. 1887). About that marriage, Lovecraft wrote:

> Regarding Campbell's second sacrifice upon the cruel altar of Hymen, I must say that he has my complete sympathy—though it seems as if previous experience might have forewarned him. According to my view, the best thing which a man may have betwixt himself and the fair, is *distance*. As P.J.C. related the catastrophe to me, his second venture was a "spite marriage"; due to the injured feelings which resulted from his heartless & summary jilting by a fair, frivolous & flirtatious amateuress of Piqua, Ohio.[42] This calculating and fickle damsel, to whom he was engaged in the spring of 1915, decided to re-locate her affections after Campbell underwent his hospital ordeal—and the Sage of Georgetown, smarting under the slight, thought his engagement ring too good to be wasted; so placed it upon the finger of one whom he now lovingly describes as a "crass red nurse". [. . .] The nurse, an illiterate coal-miner's daughter, proved uncongenial as a life partner; so has been allowed to drift away into the dim corridors of unpleasant memories.[43]

That marriage also ended in divorce, and Campbell unsurprisingly did not even write about it. Lovecraft rued his own "sacrifice upon the cruel altar of Hymen" and was happy to "return to the proud & independent estate of celibacy."[44] Campbell seems to be one of only a very few correspondents to whom Lovecraft confided the circumstances of his "divorce."

Campbell's third marriage—the one that "rang the bell," as Lovecraft said[45]—was to Eleanor J. Barnhart (born c. 1895; died after 1959), an amateur journalist from Minneapolis, in 1918. Lovecraft had previously written a biographical sketch of Barnhart.[46] The Campbells had two sons: Paul Marion (b.

---

41. "Adventures in Appreciation" 470. See also "Reminiscences of Romances," *Library News* No. 9 (December 1941): [1], which discusses PJC's account and what became of his early romantic interests.
42. Dora M. Hepner (1888–1968) of Piqua married Anthony F. Moitoret (1892–1979) in 1917. They later divorced. Both were bitter foes of HPL.
43 HPL to Maurice W. Moe, 30 May 1917; *Letters to Maurice W. Moe and Others* 64.
44. HPL to PJC, 17 September 1930 (p. 363).
45. HPL to Maurice W. Moe, 2 July 1929; *Letters to Maurice W. Moe and Others* 207.
46. "Little Journeys to the Homes of Prominent Amateurs: V. Eleanor J. Barnhart" (*United Amateur*, July 1917; *CE* 1.165–69).

1923)[47] and Donald James (1926–2012?). Campbell's sister-in-law, Elizabeth Barnhart, another amateur,[48] lived with the Campbells. Soon after meeting Sonia Greene in July 1921, Lovecraft wrote to Rheinhart Kleiner: "I hope Mrs. Campbell will not later blame me if the enterprising recruit [Greene] captures P. J. C.'s mutable heart & replaces her as #IV!"[49]

Campbell "persuaded Clarence Darrow to be the judge [of a NAPA Laureate Contest]. He came down to the Atlantic hotel a month later when our convention was in session [in Chicago], and made his report in an excellent talk. That was in July 1917."[50] The outcome of the event may seem a bit dubious. About it, Lovecraft wrote: "The delayed report of Clarence S. Darrow, Judge of Essays, has been received. He assigns the highest award to Paul J. Campbell for 'The Age of Accuracy' and Honourable Mention to Helene Hoffman Cole for 'The Epic of the Poor'."[51]

In October 1919, Lovecraft asked Campbell to bring up to date an unpublished history of the UAPA that W. Paul Cook had written in 1915, which only went down to 1912. Campbell extended the history only to 1915, and again, the enlarged history was not published. Lovecraft was not entirely satisfied with the result and told the editor of the *Californian*, "some day I may carry this on to the suspension of our branch in 1926–7." He did not complete the proposed extension and finally submitted the article as written for publication.

> As you may see, P J C blandly glossed over the issue which Cook refused to handle—not even admitting the existence of another United. . . . Therefore I've had to insert a short passage regarding the 1912 convention, indicating how matters really stood. In case Campbell (if indeed he still recalls having written the thing!) objects to such a gratuitous liberty, you might add a footnote that the original 1915 copy required editing in the light of subsequent developments.[52]

Campbell acquired his own printing press and (badly pied) type from Edward F. Daas. Campbell soon became editor and printer of *Corona, Invictus: An Organ of Individuality,* and the *Liberal.* Regarding *Invictus,*[53] Lovecraft wrote:

> In the first issue of *Invictus* Mr. Paul J. Campbell has set a standard for the

---

47. Death date unknown. He married for the third time in 1988.
48. HPL wrote three spoofs for PJC's sister-in-law for an anti-Woodbee paper. If such a publication appeared, it has not been found.
49. HPL to RK, 11 August 1921 (p. 185).
50. "Adventures in Appreciation" 463.
51. "President's Message," *United Amateur* 17, No. 1 (September 1917): 12–13 (*CE* 1.173).
52. HPL to Hyman Bradofsky: 24 November 1936 (ms., JHL). The issue was the split of the UAPA into two rival factions that occurred in 1912 as the result of a disputed election.
53. *Invictus* means *unconquerable*, a sentiment PJC espoused on account of his handicap. The first issue appeared around the time of his amputation.

strictly individual paper which few other amateurs will ever attain. One cannot become too enthusiastic in speaking of this inspired brochure. As a philosophical essayist Mr. Campbell probably has no superior in the United, and his three brilliant homilies, "The Impost of the Future", "The Sublime Ideal", and "Whom God Hath Put Asunder", are notable additions to amateur literature.[54]

It would seem that the *Liberal* was meant to be a genial foil to Lovecraft's *Conservative*. For it, Lovecraft wrote "A Confession of Unfaith" (February 1922). His piece emerged as part of an "Experience Meeting" conducted by Campbell, "wherein amateurs are invited to state their theories of the universe." James F. Morton's "My Intellectual Evolution" was a part of the series.[55] The *Liberal* first appeared as Lovecraft's *Conservative* (1915–1923) was ending its run. An early issue contained the following item: "The event of the season is the appearance of my good friend Howard P. Lovecraft, who has 'never tasted alcoholic liquor,' as a conspicuous contributor to the 'makin's' of *Home Brew!*"[56] The extent to which Campbell followed publication of Lovecraft's professional work is unknown. He may only have known that Lovecraft appeared in *Home Brew,* and not read Lovecraft's "Herbert West—Reanimator." Still, we read elsewhere that "P. J. Campbell of Ridgefarm, Illinois, declares the same story [i.e., "Dagon"] 'is a little masterpiece of its kind'."[57]

Campbell and his wife built a house on the farm around 1923, "in which there was a den for the amateur papers and press."[58] Not long afterward, Lovecraft wrote that Campbell "has been exceedingly busy with agricultural pursuits during the past year, but has found time to make several highly interesting motor trips, and to complete the manuscript of the novel, 'The Pursuit of Happiness', on which he had long been working."[59] Unfortunately, the Campbells' house burned in April 1927, and Campbell lost his novel (which he hoped to rewrite) and many of his amateur papers. Just as Campbell provided Lovecraft with many amateur journals years before, Lovecraft now provided duplicates to Campbell to help restore his collection.

It was probably around this time that Campbell looked for a new livelihood. He wrote in 1930 that since 1925, he had drilled twenty-three oil wells and also undertaken some wildcatting ventures. His printed stationery identi-

---

54. Untitled note, *Conservative* 1, No. 1 (April 1915); *CE* 1.36.

55. *CE* 5.145. Morton's piece (*Liberal,* February 1923) is now included in *Letters to James F. Morton* 425–26.

56. "The Event of the Season," *Liberal* 1, No. 2 (February 1922): 36.

57. [Letter to the Eyrie,] *Weird Tales* 2, No. 4 (December 1923–January 1924): 86.

58. "Adventures in Appreciation" 472.

59. "News Notes," *United Amateur* 24, No. 1 (July 1925): 11 (*CE* 1.357). PJC had previously written an essay titled "The Pursuit of Happiness" (1916). He spent three years writing the novel.

fies him as a "drilling contractor." In 1929 alone he drove 27,500 miles in pursuit of productive wells. Lovecraft knew this, referring to it as Campbell's "oleaginous profession" and saying that he hoped it would prove successful. That same year, Campbell put an old but reliable revision client, David Van Bush, back in touch with Lovecraft; but because Bush wanted work done at no cost, Lovecraft declined.

Following the fire, Campbell had fallen out of amateur journalism, but as he once observed, "Once an amateur always an amateur." In 1930 Charles W. Smith persuaded him to reenlist. Campbell soon was getting back in touch with fellow amateurs, but he had an ulterior motive. "Paul J. Campbell is alas a Chicagoan now. Still in the oil-drilling business, & wants me to make a fortune by putting 200 bucks into some new project. What a pity I haven't the spare cash. I would so enjoy sudden affluence!"[60] He may have known Lovecraft fairly well, but he seems oblivious to his friend's perpetual state of penury. Campbell also contacted other amateur associates to drum up funds to finance an oil-drilling project that he called "my A. J. Oil Co." He does not seem to have been especially successful overall, especially in light of the travel he undertook looking for profitable wells, but he stuck at it for at least eighteen years.

Because Campbell was in the oil business, Lovecraft thought that he might be able to contribute colorful copy to Wilfred B. Talman, editor of the *Texaco Star,* a trade magazine for the oil company. Talman published Campbell's piece, "The Joke Was on the White Man." Campbell intended to write a piece about southwest tourist camps, but it appears he did not. He did, however, take advantage of Talman's approaching him for an article as an opportunity to try to get Talman to invest in his project.

In 1931, W. Paul Cook, amateur journalist, printer, and friend of both Lovecraft and Campbell, was down on his luck. Campbell offered to try to find work for Cook in Oklahoma. Either Cook demurred or Campbell couldn't find anything for him. In 1935 he still was looking for work, and Campbell again tried to help out.

It is not clear just what transpired regarding the business venture in East St. Louis. Of it Lovecraft wrote: "He [Cook] has had a vague offer of a printing job from [. . .] Paul J. Campbell—now connected with a neighbourhood newspaper venture [. . .] As yet the matter still hangs in the balance. It's a poor looking proposition, & I rather hope W P C won't go."[61] About it Campbell himself wrote that he began "10 years ago [i.e., 1933] writing subscriptions and advertising for, and wound up owning,"[62] the *Canteen News,* a weekly neighborhood newspaper. Other evidence suggests that in September

60. HPL to Maurice W. Moe, [17 September 1930]; *Letters to Maurice W. Moe and Others* 515.

61. HPL to R. H. Barlow, [11? May 1935]; *OFF* 258.

62. "Paul J. Campbell, the Legal Guardian . . ." 6.

1935, at the age of fifty-one, he took over editorship of a newspaper, enlisting Cook, still out of work. Lovecraft wrote:

> Cook [. . .] has produced a 200% improvement in the aspect of the *Canteen Township News*. Campbell has given him the whole bungalow at 5720 Westmoreland Place, & taken his own household to another roost nearby. The erstwhile Recluse is not merely a printer, but an associate editor as well—having just written the News's feature article . . . an exposé of conditions at the St. Clair Co. gaol.[63]

Nevertheless, Lovecraft disparaged the undertaking, referring to Campbell as a "notoriously irresponsible plunger."[64] He described the Campbell family as "down & out."[65] In late November 1936, he declared that "the poor old *Canteen News* has flopped at last"[66] and that Cook was now looking for work in East St. Louis. It is not known why Lovecraft came to this conclusion. He may have based his comment on information received from Cook, who left the paper after a year. But the *Canteen News* did not "flop." Campbell was still working on it in 1943, and probably did so until his death in 1945.[67] The paper continued to be published until 1973. Campbell also remained somewhat active in the oil business. He surely had more than his share of setbacks in his lifetime, and even if he never grew wealthy, he at least was employed and provided for his family.

After twenty-four years of wearing his prosthesis and musing about a way to bring together and offer support to amputees, Campbell and Augusta Belle Weaver (1898?–?) of Sapulpa, Oklahoma, another amputee, organized the "Fraternity of the Wooden Leg" in 1939, with Campbell as the president of the organization. He stated: "My mother used to repeat the phrase, 'Fraternity of the Wooden Leg,' as though she liked it—as though it was a distinction of which one might be proud. And the more I think about it, the more I am convinced that it is a distinction that justifies greater pride than wearing false teeth or horn-rimmed glasses or carrying a cane."[68] The couple began publishing a bi-monthly magazine for and about amputees titled *Courage: Official Magazine of the Fraternity of the Wooden Leg* (June 1940). This occurred even as Campbell was still involved with both the *Canteen News* and more oil speculating. It is sadly ironic that six months after Campbell launched *Courage*, his elder son was injured in a car collision with his motor-

---

63. HPL to R. H. Barlow, 21 October 1935; *OFF* 300.
64. HPL to R. H. Barlow, [11? May 1935]; *OFF* 258.
65. HPL to R. H. Barlow, 30 November 1936; *OFF* 370.
66. HPL to R. H. Barlow, 30 November 1936; *OFF* 370.
67. Interviewer Virginia Irwin wrote that he "makes a nice living publishing [. . .]"'"The Canteen News.'"
68. "Founding of the Fraternity Wooden Leg" (p. 482).

cycle, resulting in the loss of his left leg. *Courage* carried on for twenty-three years after Campbell died, ceasing publication in 1968. As editor, Campbell could write on any subject he wished for his regular column, "Adventures in Appreciation," including his experience in amateur journalism. H. P. Lovecraft has been mentioned in all manner of unusual publications, but perhaps none more unusual than the journal of the Fraternity of the Wooden Leg.

Campbell said that his correspondence with Lovecraft was "long and interesting," and so the few surviving letters are not at all indicative of how many they actually exchanged. The fire that destroyed Campbell's amateur papers may well have taken many of Lovecraft's letters. Campbell's letters from Lovecraft arrived at Arkham House somewhat late, after the vast bulk of letters to others had been transcribed.[69] Only sixteen missives survive. The John Hay library holds only five complete letters. The Arkham House transcripts contain only seven edited letters, and only four fugitive postcards have been seen. One of these is among the four Lovecraft sent him in 1934 during his trip in the South.

The surviving whole letters suggest that Lovecraft and Campbell corresponded quite a bit, as Lovecraft's statements suggest that Campbell was readily familiar with the individuals and situations mentioned. It was Campbell who guided the eager neophyte into amateur journalism, and it is regrettable that we have so little first-hand documentation of that period of indoctrination.

—S. T. JOSHI
DAVID E. SCHULTZ

A Note on the Texts

The manuscripts of Lovecraft's letters to Rheinhart Kleiner do not appear to survive. Thus, the texts of the letters in this volume derive mainly from the Arkham House transcripts of Lovecraft's letters preparatory to editing *Selected Letters* and from a few paragraphs published nowhere else save in Kleiner's "By Post from Providence," which appeared shortly after Lovecraft's death. Since the content of "By Post from Providence" consists of brief extracts only, it is difficult to know the proper placement of these extracts in relation to the portions preserved in the Arkham House transcripts. In some cases, the transcripts contain material not found in "By Post from Providence," and vice versa. Thus, the organization of such reconstituted letters is conjectural. Obvious transcriptional errors have been silently corrected. The Arkham House transcripts contained among them transcripts of various of Lovecraft's ama-

---

69. The last of Clark Ashton Smith's letters from HPL (volume 36 of 39) arrived at Arkham House in May 1944. Campbell's letters from HPL (volume 38) may have been received after Campbell's death in August the following year.

teur works; some appear to be tearsheets of pages from the *Conservative*. It is not clear that these were actually enclosures to letters 5, 38, and 41, and so they are not reproduced herein, though the titles of such items are noted. All may be found in *The Ancient Track* (2013).

The John Hay Library owns all the letters to Arthur Harris. Wilkes Community College (Wilkesboro, NC) owns the letters to James Larkin Pearson. The letters to Winifred Virginia Jackson derive from partial typescripts made by R. H. Barlow in 1938 for the purpose of providing them to August Derleth and Donald Wandrei for possible inclusion in a book of Lovecraft's letters, even as they were busy transcribing other letters obtained from other recipients. The letters to Arthur Leeds and Paul J. Campbell are few. They derive primarily from the Arkham House transcripts, although the John Hay Library owns a few of each.

The editors and publisher are grateful to Robert C. Harrall, of Lovecraft Holdings LLC, for permission to publish the letters by Lovecraft contained in this book. They are also grateful to Derrick Hussey, Kenneth W. Faig, Jr., and Mike Horvat for assistance in obtaining copies of Kleiner's writings, to Umesh Amtey, Victor A. Berch, Donovan K. Loucks, Christopher M. O'Brien, and J.-M. Rajala for assistance in annotating the letters, and to Martin Andersson for his assiduous proofreading.

Abbreviations

AT	*The Ancient Track: Complete Poetical Works*
CE	*Collected Essays* (5 vols.)
CF	*Collected Fiction* (4 vols.)
LL	S. T. Joshi & David E. Schultz, *Lovecraft's Library: A Catalogue,* 4th ed.
SL	*Selected Letters* (5 vols.)
WT	*Weird Tales*

AHT	Arkham House transcripts
ALS	autograph letter, signed
ANS	autograph note, signed
JHL	John Hay Library, Brown University (Providence, RI)
NAPA	National Amateur Press Association
Post	Kleiner, "By Post from Providence" (*Californian,* Summer 1937)
UAPA	United Amateur Press Association

AH	Arthur Harris
HPL	H. P. Lovecraft
JLP	James Larkin Pearson
PJC	Paul J. Campbell
RK	Rheinhart Kleiner

Rheinhart Kleiner

Letters to Rheinhart Kleiner

[1]   [Post; AHT]

598 Angell St.,
Providence, R.I.
March 28, 1915

My dear Mr. Kleiner:—

[. . .]

[Post:] You are the first to acknowledge receipt of *The Conservative*, 210 copies of which I mailed last Wednesday night. I must ask pardon from all the members for the crude appearance of the issue, since a cheap printer has made such an utter failure of it. The second number is already planned, & I hope to have it done by a far more reliable typographical artist.[1]

[AHT:] I am certainly a relic of the 18th century both in prose & in verse. My taste in poetry is really defective, for I love nothing better than the resounding couplets of Dryden & Pope, unless it be the stately phraseology of Thomson's "Seasons".[2] In prose, I have read less of the novelists than of the essayists & historians. I suppose I picked up my peculiar style from Addison, Steele, Johnson, & Gibbon.

I have absolutely no use for modern forms & tendencies, & am firmly of opinion that the English language has done nothing but decline since the formal school of composition disappeared. The romantic movement in poetry is a vague unreality to me. I admire the later poets because they are considered admirable & I am supposed to admire them; but inwardly I cannot be weaned away from my old-fashioned couplets. You will soon see in Daas's forthcoming paper, "Here & There", a specimen of my earlier, rougher verse, written in the style of Dryden, with many rhymes which are merely allowable, & with a free use of triplets & Alexandrines.[3]

[Post:] Speaking of amateur verse, have you ever read the exquisite work of Samuel Loveman? This poet was active in the National about eight years ago, & is in many respects unsurpassed. It is only recently that I had an opportunity to see his verse, but what I have seen makes me an enthusiastic admirer. Loveman was a thorough archaist, going back to the era of Queen Elizabeth for his inspiration; & his ruggedness of metre was the ruggedness of a Shakespeare, not of a modern. His images and expressions were of classic purity, and wholly apart from the present trend. He is said to have received much hostile criticism, but this was probably aroused by the very thing which makes me fond of his work—his complete possession by the spirit of a former age.

I wish you would put your epigrams into heroic couplets, as I suggested in *The Conservative*.[4] This form is peculiarly the medium of pointed antithesis, and seems never brighter than in satire or epigram. I have occasionally tried epigram, the following being one of my old attempts:

> Thy lyrics, gifted Browning, charm the ear,
> And ev'ry mark of classic polish bear.
> With subtile raptures they enchain the heart;
> To soul & mind a mystic thrill impart:
> Yet would their rhythmic magic be more keen,
> If we could but discover what they mean![5]

[. . .]
I remain

Very sincerely yours,
H P Lovecraft

Notes

1. The first issue of HPL's *Conservative* was apparently printed by a local printer in Providence. Albert A. Sandusky, an amateur journalist in Cambridge, MA, printed the next four under his imprint, The Lincoln Press.

2 James Thomson (1700–1748), *The Seasons* (1726–30), rpt. in *The Seasons; with The Castle of Indolence* (1819).

3. Edward F. Daas recruited HPL into amateur journalism in April 1914 and was editor of the *Lake Breeze*. The poem HPL refers to is "New England Fallen" (1912). For the "allowable rhyme" see HPL's essay of that title.

4. See *Conservative* 1, No. 1 (April 1915): [6]; in *CE* 1.36.

5. Now published as "[On Robert Browning]." This may possibly have been part of a nonextant "essay on the modern poets" that HPL says in "In a Major Key" (*Conservative*, July 1915; *CE* 1.56) was "written several years ago."

[2]   [AHT]

June 29, 1915

Dear Mr. Kleiner:—

I am glad that you have secured the National Convention for your city, but scarcely believe I could attend, since my health is so poor that I am very little of a traveller. In fact, in all my life I have never been beyond the limits of the three states of Rhode Island, Massachusetts, & Connecticut. However, I appreciate your invitation, & assure you that I will take advantage of it *next year*, when the convention is in Boston, for that is a city within an hour's ride of Providence, & I frequently go thither to visit my young cousin in Cambridge. This same cousin, by the way, is the son of an old time amateur, & may possibly become interested in amateur journalism himself.[1] I am hoping to get him interested in the United. Frankly, I believe that the United has greater possibilities than the National, & I do not encourage the recruits to whom I write to join the older body. I often wish that you were an exclusively United man, but suppose that is well-nigh impossible in such a hotbed of Nationalism as Brooklyn.

Sincerely,

H P Lovecraft

Notes

1. Phillips Gamwell (1898–1916), son of Edward F[rancis] Gamwell (1869–1936) and Annie E. Phillips Gamwell (1866–1941). Edward was editor of the *Cambridge* (MA) *Tribune,* which published HPL's "Elegy on Phillips Gamwell, Esq." [as "An Elegy"] (13 January 1917): 5. HPL did not in fact attend the 1916 NAPA convention.

[3]   [AHT]

July 31, 1915

My dear Kleiner:—

[. . .]

But there is another type of "poet" which is amusing, even though the very antithesis of this class. I recently received an attempt called "A Prayer for Universal Peace", by Rev. Robert L. Selle,[1] D.D., Little Rock, Arkansas. This man is the author of innumerable popular theological books & hymns, & is considered quite a leader of thought in his primitive community. He is a possible recruit of Mrs. Renshaw's, & had sent her this "poem" for "frank criticism". She requested me to perform this task instead, but I am at a loss what to do, since anything like frankness would offend Dr. Selle unpardonably. In a word, he is a relic of that age of American literature which Charles Francis Adams has called the "theologico-glacial period."[2] He has the poetical technique of a child of seven, & the style of a narrow old Puritan. I cannot conceive of him as any such personage as his numerous book advertisements picture him, yet I am assured of his prominence & popularity by Mrs. Renshaw. Not daring to go too far, I have asked advice from her as to how he would take advice from one exactly half his age, & whether he would feel insulted at a revised version by me for an example. Here are two specimen stanzas of his work, & of my revisions. Notice that his metre, while apparently merely an internally rhymed tetrameter, is really double dimeter, like the old New-England Primer alphabet which used to run: "In Adam's fall, we sin-ned all", &c.

> "Give thou to us O Lord give us,
>   Instead of war revivals four—
>   Agriculture, Education,
>   Temperance & Christian religion."

Would you believe that a prominent clergyman wrote the foregoing? Yet such is the case. Here is my revision:

> "Give Thou to us, O Mighty Lord of Lords,
> The boons that Peace, not bloody War affords:
> Let teeming fields of golden grain arise,
> Whilst Education clears our blinded eyes:
> Let Rum, the noxious demon, be no more,
> And Christian Majesty above us soar!"

I could not retain his metre, since it seems so manifestly unfit for a poem of any length. Here is another of his stanzas:

> "Revive, Revive, O Lord, revive,
> For every man throughout the land
> The things that'll make for home & state
> Conditions right for man's best plight."

What kind of work is this! The following is the best I can do with it:

> "Revive, Almighty Lord, throughout the lands,
> The laws whereon domestic virtue stands.
> Teach ev'ry man to hold his peaceful place,
> And show'r Thy Heav'nly blessings on his race."

I remain

> Very sincerely yours,
> H P Lovecraft

Notes

1. Robert L. Selle (1865–1929), author of *Old Time Religion* (Louisville, KY: Pentecostal Pub. Co., 1900?) and *Which Church Would Jesus Join?* (Louisville, KY: Pentecostal Pub. Co., 1915?). HPL gave cordial nods to Selle in his "Department of Public Criticism" for August and September 1916, but in "Idle Lines on a Poetick Dunce" (c. 1920), he named Selle (along with David V. Bush and J. Morris Widdows) one of "Three fools of diff'ring grade." "A Prayer for Universal Peace" appeared in *Apples of Gold in Pictures of Silver* (Louisville, KY: Pentecostal Publishing Company, 1917), 50–53. *AT* contains both HPL's revision and part of Selle's original.

2. See Charles Francis Adams (1835–1915), *Massachusetts: Its Historians and Its History* (Boston: Houghton Mifflin, 1893), 59f. Adams was referring to the 150-year period following the Cambridge Synod of 1637, in which American society slowly emerged from the influence of Puritan theocracy.

[4]   [AHT]

August 10, 1915

My dear Kleiner:—

From your hint regarding Isaacson[1] I imagine that my reply will differ *very much* from the apologetic form! A Jew is capable of infinite nastiness when he seeks revenge, & I believe I shall have ample grounds for making this particular Israelite the hero of a spirited Dunciad.[2] I can almost predict his line of attack. He will call me superficial, crude, barbaric in thought, imperfect in education, offensively arrogant & bigoted, filled with venomous prejudice, wanting in good taste, &c. &c. &c. But what I can and will say in reply is also violent & comprehensive. He will ask why I am an advocate of war, yet am not at this moment in the British army. I shall not stoop to explain that I am an invalid who would certainly be fighting under the Union Jack if able, but shall have plenty to say about the decadent cowardice responsible for the propagation of peace ideas. Peace is the ideal of a dying nation; a broken race. Isaacson belongs to a stock wholly broken & emasculated by two thousand years of cringing at the feet of Aryan masters. But I, thank the Gods, am an Aryan, & can rejoice in the glorious victory of T. Flavius Vespasianus,[3] under whose legions the Jewish race & their capital were trodden out of national existence! I am an anti-Semitic by nature, but thought I had concealed my prejudice in my remarks concerning Isaacson. I showed him every consideration in my article, carefully saying that I attacked not the man, but the ideas. However, if Jerusalem wishes to start trouble, he will find in me a new Titus, eager to inscribe on my eagles the triumphant legend IVDAEA CAPTA! I might here remark that my anti-Semitism is not entirely due to blind prejudice. The Jews are fundamentally Orientals, whilst the rising civilization of the world is Western—Teutonic—Anglo-Saxon. The struggle between the East & the West dates back to Marathon & Salamis, & it is the West which has ever represented progress & superior culture. The Jew is an adverse influence, since he insidiously degrades or Orientalizes our robust Aryan civilization. The intellect of the race is indisputably great, but its nature is not such that it may be safely employed in forming Western political & social ideas. Oppressive as it seems, the Jew must be muzzled. Wherefore Isaacson has reason to expect a warfare of the bitterest kind if he uses his revengeful sarcasm on me. I shall not utter the first word, but shall hold the CONSERVATIVE until the serpent strikes. Then—LET HIM BEWARE. Like old Marcus Fabius on his mission to Carthage, I come with folded toga, ready for peace or war.

  I remain

    Very sincerely yours,

     H P Lovecraft

Notes

1. Charles D. Isaacson (1891–1936), amateur journalist and author of *Face to Face with Great Musicians* (1918–21; 2 vols.). In "Concerning the Conservative," *In a Minor Key* No. 2 [1915]: [10–11], Isaacson had strongly criticized HPL's comments on Jews and on Walt Whitman as expressed in HPL's article "In a Major Key" (*Conservative*, July 1915; *CE* 1.56–58). HPL met Isaacson on 1 July 1916 as RK, Isaacson, and others passed through Providence on the way to the NAPA convention in Boston.

2. HPL refers to Alexander Pope's satire *The Dunciad* (1728; rev. 1742), chiefly an attack upon many of Pope's enemies, specifically the Shakespearean scholar Lewis Theobald (1688–1744), from whom HPL derived his pseudonym "Lewis Theobald, Jun." Around this time HPL wrote a *Dunciad*-like screed, "The Isaacsonio-Mortoniad," attacking both Isaacson and James F. Morton, but did not publish it.

3. I.e., Vespasian, emperor of Rome (69–79 C.E.). In 67–68 he quelled the Jewish rebellion in Palestine.

[5]   [AHT]

Sept. 14, 1915

My dear Kleiner:—

        Impromptu verse, or "poetry" to order, is easy only when approached in the coolly *prosaic* spirit. Given something to say, a *metrical mechanic*[1] like myself can easily hammer the matter into technically correct verse, substituting formal poetic diction for real inspiration of thought. For instance, I lately received a post-card bearing the picture of swans on a placid stream. Desiring to reply in appropriate verse, I harked back to the classic myth of Phaëthon and Cygnus, handling it as follows:

On Receiving a Picture of Swans

> With pensive grace, the melancholy Swan
> Mourns o'er the tomb of luckless Phaëthon;
> On grassy banks the weeping poplars wave,
> And guard with tender care the wat'ry grave.
> Would that I might, should I too proudly claim
> An Heav'nly parent, or a God-like fame;
> When flown too high, and dash'd to depths below,
> Receive such tribute as a Cygnus' woe!
> The faithful bird, that dumbly floats along,
> Sighs all the deeper for his want of song.

(This required about 10 minutes for composition.)
    I remain
        Your obt. Servt.
            H P Lovecraft

[Here AHT includes "The Isaacsonio-Mortoniad."]

Notes

1. HPL signed himself "Metrical Mechanic" when he published "A Mississippi Autumn" in *Ole Miss'* (December 1915).

[6]   [AHT]

Sept. 30, 1915

My dear Kleiner:—

Your "Mary of the Movies"[1] is delightful—so much so that it has inspired me to compose the following companion-poem, dedicated to another illustrious screen entertainer:

To Charlie of the Comics[2]

You trip and tumble o'er the sheet
That holds your lifelike image.
You shuffle your prodigious feet
Through love-scene, chase, or scrimmage.
As, gazing on each comic act,
I stare at your perfection,
I find it hard to face the fact
That you're a mere projection.

I've seen you as an artist rare,
With brush and paint-smear'd palette;
I've seen you fan the empty air
With ill-intention'd mallet.
I've watch'd you woo a winsome fay,
(You must a dream to her be)
But ne'er have caught you in a play
Without that cane and derby!

Dear lad, I trust your happiness
May be like that you give us;
And since ripe years the mirthful bless,
That you may long outlive us.
May you the smiles of Fortune see,
Nor know what want of cash is,
And may your times of trouble be
As short as your moustaches!

I'd like to meet you, Charles, old chap,
Though vast the space dividing;
Yet I must merely sit and clap
At your fantastic gliding.
But though you're far away, we know,
You still have pow'r to rouse us;
Your films can pack a picture show
That's roomy as your trousers!

How is this for a 15-minute impromptu? You need not criticise the "rouse us"–"trousers" rhyme—it is not meant to be perfect—merely *allowable*. By the way, this Charles is not the one I meant in the previous lines: "As Charles' return chang'd gloom to gay relief."[3] I then referred to his Majesty—the Merry Monarch who succeeded the prim parliament in 1660. Glorious Restoration!

[. . .]

I remain

Very sincerely yours

H P Lovecraft

[Enclosure:]

UNDA;
Or, THE BRIDE OF THE SEA.

Respectfully Dedicated without Permission to
MAURICE WINTER MOE, Esq.

A Dull, Dark, Drear, Dactylic Delirium in Sixteen Silly, Senseless, Sickly Stanzas

---

([*sic*]$5000.00 Reward for the Apprehension, Alive or Dead,
of the Person or Persons who can prove that This is the Work of

HOWARD PHILLIPS LOVECRAFT
—-o—-o—-
"Ego, canis, lunam cano".[4]
MAEVIUS BAVIANUS.[5]
—-o—-o—-o—-o—-o—-o—-o—-o—-o—-

Dark loom the crags of the uplands behind me.
Dark are the sands of the far-stretching shore.
Dim are the pathways and rocks that remind me
Sadly of years in the lost nevermore.

Soft laps the ocean on wave-polish'd boulder;
Sweet is the sound and familiar to me.
Here, with her head gently bent to my shoulder,
Walk'd I with Unda, the Bride of the Sea.

Bright was the morn of my youth when I met her,
Sweet as the breeze that blew in o'er the brine.
Swift was I captur'd in Love's strongest fetter,
Glad to be hers, and she glad to be mine.

Never a question ask'd I whence she wander'd,
Never a question ask'd she of my birth:
Happy as children, we thought not nor ponder'd,
Glad with the bounty of ocean and earth.

Once when the moonlight play'd soft 'mid the billows,
High on the cliff o'er the waters we stood.
Bound was her hair with a garland of willows,
Pluck'd by the fount in the bird-haunted wood.

Strangely she gaz'd on the surges beneath her,
Charm'd by the sound, or entranc'd by the light.
Then did the waves a wild aspect bequeath her,
Stern as the ocean and weird as the night.

Coldly she left me, astonish'd and weeping,
Standing alone 'mid the regions she bless'd:
Down, ever downward, half gliding, half creeping,
Stole the sweet Unda in oceanward quest.

Calm grew the sea, and tumultuous beating
Turn'd to a ripple, as Unda the fair
Trod the wet sands in affectionate greeting,
Beckon'd to me, and no longer was there!

Long did I pace by the banks where she vanquish'd:
High climb'd the moon, and descended again.
Grey broke the dawn till the sad night was banish'd,
Still ach'd my soul with its infinite pain.

All the wide world have I search'd for my darling,
Scour'd the far deserts and sail'd distant seas.
Once on the wave while the tempest was snarling,
Flash'd a fair face that brought quiet and ease.

Ever in restlessness onward I stumble,
Seeking and pining, scarce heeding my way,
Now have I stray'd where the wide waters rumble,
Back to the scene of the lost yesterday.

Lo! the red moon from the ocean's low hazes
Rises in ominous grandeur to view,
Strange is its face as my tortur'd eye gazes
O'er the vast reaches of sparkle and blue.

Straight from the moon to the shore where I'm sighing
Grows a bright bridge, made of wavelets and beams,

Frail may it be, yet how simple the trying;
Wand'ring from earth to the orb of sweet dreams.

What is yon face in the moonlight appearing;
Have I at last found the maiden that fled?
Out on the beam-bridge my footsteps are nearing
Her whose sweet beckoning hastens my tread.

Currents surround me, and I drowsily swaying,
Far on the moon-path I seek the sweet face.
Eagerly hasting, half panting, half praying,
Forward I reach for the vision of grace.

Murmuring waters about me are closing,
Soft the sweet vision advances to me:
Done are my trials; my heart is reposing
Safe with my Unda, the Bride of the Sea.

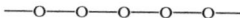

(Gentle Maurice, if thy longing be sated,
If my sad stanzas appeal to thy taste,
Let me at once as a poet be rated;
Then to heroics again I may haste.)

                                        H. P. L.

Notes

1. The poem is about Mary Pickford. See Appendix.
2. Sir Charles Chaplin (1889–1977), the celebrated English-born actor.
3. "The Introduction" l. 31, referring to Charles II, king of England.
4. "I, a dog, sing at the moon," a parody of Virgil's line, *Arma virumque cano*.
5. An invented name, derived from the names of two poetasters, Maevius and Bavius, mentioned in Virgil's *Eclogues* (3.19).

[7]   [AHT]

                                                    Nov. 19, 1915
My dear Kleiner:—
            Theobald, of course, is the original hero of the Dunciad,
& the butt of Pope's most brilliant ridicule.
    I remain
                Yours very sincerely,
                    H P Lovecraft

[8]   [AHT]

Nov. 25, 1915

My dear Kleiner:—

Isaacson's predilection for obscenity has robbed him of all the delicacy inherent in real white men, & he views Nature without its beauty & its refining adornments. It is a mistake to allow Jews to mingle with Aryans as social equals. I have never been forced to do this, & at high school I drew the colour line at Jews as well as negroes, though of course there is no racial comparison between the two classes of undesirables. How diabolically Isaacson tries to compare different classes of prejudices, & trace to one source those arising from race, religion & politics. As fellow sufferers with himself he groups races both above & beneath him; he calls everyone "persecuted", from the masterful Aryan German, representative of the world's highest racial stock, to the bestial nigger, link between man & the apes! If this be radicalism, let me thank heaven I am a conservative!

Morton is a problem.[1] I can feel the more wholesome nature of his work—with him I can come to grips as man to man—there is no slimy Jewry or Orientalism there—while Isaacson defies analysis with his shifty Asiatic caprices. Morton is harsh, insolent, overbearing, but not nasty. He has doubtless been criticised very roughly himself, and thereby made bitter toward men of conservative ideas. I understand that he overstudied in Harvard, taking a Master's degree in the same time that most young men take only Bachelor's honours. He has taught too much—overreached sane human limitations. I respect James F. Morton, Jr., no matter how much he reviles, for his has been a life of conscientious research and unceasing mental endeavour. His "Fragments of a Mental Autobiography" in LIBRA justify his erratic views,[2] & impose kindness on his critics. He is to be tolerated gently, & his declining years must not be vexed with any more criticism than is demanded by the self-defence of his victims. I can sympathise with Morton in many ways. I am not an orthodox disciple of religion, but I deem it dangerous to tamper with any system so manifestly beneficial to morality.[3] Whatever may be the faults of the church, it has never yet been surpassed or nearly equalled as an agent for the promotion of virtue. And the same thing applies to our present social system. It has its defects, but is evidently a natural growth, and better fitted to preserve an approximate civilization than any Utopian scheme conjured up over night by some artificially thinking radical. As to races, I deem it most proper to recognise the divisions into which Nature has grouped mankind. Science shows us the infinite superiority of the Teutonic Aryan over all others, and it therefore becomes us to see that his ascendancy shall remain undisputed. Any racial mixture can but lower the result. The Teutonic race, whether in Scandinavia, other parts of the continent, England, or America, is the cream of humanity, and its wanton or deliberate adulteration with baser material is even more repulsive to consider than the elaborately staged racial suicide now being conducted, wherein Germanic and Britannic Teutons are striving to annihilate each other instead of uniting against the Mongol-tainted Slav or menacing Oriental.

But radicals are "above" all truth & science, so let them rave on—Nature is too strong to be hurt seriously by their mistakes!

I suppose you think me altogether too vindictive about the Jew; but remember, that Dr. Johnson liked a *good hater*. I look upon Izzy much as the Doctor looked on the Ossianic faker—Macpherson.[4]

Race is a strange thing. Sometimes I think of racial combinations as chemical reactions; for instance, I believe that certain stocks have greater assimilative powers than others. The Gallo-Basque stock with Latin infusion, which constitutes the bulk of the French population, is much more receptive to alien blood than is our colder and more Northern Teutonic stock. That is, the French type seems more easily attainable by inferiors than is the straightforward Teutonic type. This is probably because France is more mongrelized to start with. Many eminent French have the Israelitish taint without apparent detraction from the Occidentalism of their mental type—Sarah Bernhart [*sic*] owns the touch of Judaea—so does Henri Bernstein,[5] the dramatist. But among English, Germans, & Americans, a Jew is a Jew, & is in no wise to be confounded with the dominant people amongst whom he dwells.

I remain

Sincerely and fraternally,
H P Lovecraft

Notes

1. James F. Morton had also attacked HPL in "'Conservatism' Run Mad," *In a Minor Key* No. 2 [1915]: [15–16].

2. *Libra* was an amateur journal edited by Morton beginning in 1907. His "Fragments of a Mental Autobiography" ran in successive numbers of the journal. Parts IV and V appeared in *Libra* 1, Nos. 5 and 6 (October and December 1907). The essay is reprinted in HPL's *Letters to James F. Morton.*

3. At this time Morton was an evangelical atheist, and HPL pokes fun at this stance in "The Isaacsonio-Mortoniad." Later Morton converted to the Bahá'i faith.

4. The Scottish poet James Macpherson attempted to pass off some poetry he had written as translations of the fragments of the ancient Scottish poet "Ossian." The chief works he produced were *Fingal* (1762) and *Temora* (1763). The hoax, initially criticized by Samuel Johnson, was definitively exploded in the early 19th century.

5. Sarah Bernhardt (born Henriette-Rosine Bernard, 1844–1923), the premier stage actress of her time. Her mother was a Dutch Jew. Henri Bernstein (1876–1953), French dramatist of Jewish descent whose plays dominated the Paris stage from 1900 to 1917.

[9]   [AHT]

Dec. 6, 1915

My dear Kleiner:—

I hardly wonder that my racial ideas seem bigoted to one born & reared in the vicinity of cosmopolitan New York, but you may better understand my repulsion to the Jew when I tell you that until I was fourteen years old I do not believe I ever spoke to one or saw one knowingly. My section of the city is what is known as the "East Side" (nothing like New York's "East Side"!!!) & it is separated from the rest of the town by the precipitous slope of College Hill, at the top of which is Brown University. In this whole locality, there are scarcely two or three families who are not of original Yankee Rhode Island stock— the place is as solidly Anglo-American as it was 200 years ago. Over on the "West Side", it is very cosmopolitan, but the East Side child might as well be in the heart of Old England so far as racial environment is concerned. Slater Avenue school was near my home,[1] & the only non-Saxons were niggers whose parents work for our families or cart our ashes, & who consequently know their place. Imagine, then, my feeling on entering high-school & being confronted with the offscourings of Judaea! True, some of the Jews were intelligent; in fact there were some very brilliant scholars among them; but how could a child used to other children like himself find anything in common with hook-nosed, swarthy, guttural-voiced aliens? Repulsion was instinctive—I never denied the mental capacity of the Jew; in fact I admire the race & its early history at a distance; but association with them was intolerable. Just as some otherwise normal men hate the sight or presence of a cat, so have I hated the presence of a Jew. Then, all apart from this instinctive feeling, I very soon formed a conviction that the Oriental mind is but ill adapted to mingle with the Aryan mind—that the glory of Israel is by itself. Oil & water are both desirable, but they will not mix. And the more I study the question, the more firmly am I convinced that the one supreme race is the Teuton. Observe the condition in the British Isles. The English are wholly Teutonic, and therefore dominant. The southern Scotch and Eastern Irish are also of that blood—they certainly surpass their fellows to the north and west. The Welsh, who have no Teutonic blood, are of little account. Had it not been for the Teutonic infusion at the beginning of the Dark Ages, southern Europe would have been lost. Who were these early "French" kings and heroes that founded French civilisation? Teutons, to a man! It was the Teutonic might of Charles Martel that drove the Saracen Semite out of Gaul. Who were the Normans? Teutons of the North. It is pitiful to me to hear apostles of equality pipe out that other races can equal this foremost of all—this successor to the Roman race in power and virility.

As you surmise, I am a devotee of the motion picture, since I can attend shows at any time, whereas my ill health seldom permits me to make definite engagements or purchase real theatre tickets in advance. Some modern films are really worth seeing, though when I first knew moving pictures their only value was to destroy time. Chaplin is infinitely amusing—too good for the rather vulgar films he used to appear in—and I hope he will in future be an exponent of more refined comedy. I saw the film "Trilby",[2] but it seemed incomplete to me because I have seen the actual play,[3] and have attached so much importance to the deep, fiendishly insinuating *voice* of Svengali. And here is a coincidence! Within reach of my hand is a clipping of that old speaking Svengali! It was five years ago that I cut this from the paper, but my room is full of ancient refuse. I enclose it, but it need not be returned.

Your work of art is indeed creditable. I knew who the subject was as soon as I saw it; without looking on the back. Have you ever taken lessons in drawing? I always wanted to be able to draw, but I have no talent, and in one of my pictures you cannot tell a cow from a locomotive. But spurred on by your example, I have just been trying my hand and fountain pen in an endeavour to represent myself just as I would like to be—a poet of two centuries ago, periwig and all. As you will note, I have adopted the old frontispiece engraving style, with little Pegasuses beneath me, and Apollo, Pan, and my family crest above me. How would that look facing the title page of a book of heroic verse? I should really feel at ease in that garb, for my spirit seems actually to be living in 1715 rather than 1915. I am almost tempted to have a cut made of that sketch, & use it in THE CONSERVATIVE as an illustration of the prevailing spirit of antiquity.[4] The only trouble would be that no one could detect the resemblance! Here is another much idealized picture of me—as I hie me to London & explore the bookstalls of Grub-Street. The resemblance is here even less, but the environment is indeed true to life—I spend much of my time amid the dust & mold of forgotten volumes in second-hand shops. The fact is, I was born 200 years too late—that is why Morton & your Semitic friend find so much to object to in me!

With best wishes, I remain, Sir,

Your most ob[t] humble serv[t],

H Lovecraft.

Notes

1. Now destroyed, Slater Avenue School was located at the northeast corner of Slater Avenue and University Avenue, where "School One" now stands.

2. There were at least three silent films called *Trilby* (based on the 1894 novel by George Du Maurier) released up to this time: one directed by Harold Shaw (London Film Co., 1914), one directed by Maurice Tourneur (World Film Corp., 1915), and one with an unknown director (Equitable Film Co., 1915).

3. *Trilby* was adapted as a play by Paul M. Potter (1853–1921); it premiered at the Garden Theatre, New York, on 15 April 1895.

4. HPL did not in fact publish the drawing in the *Conservative*.

[10] [AHT]

Jan. 20, 1916

My dear Kleiner:—

Regarding early reading, I am able to say that our tastes in childhood were even more similar than you imagine. When I was about twelve I became greatly interested in science, specialising in geography, (later to be displaced by astronomy), & being a Verne enthusiast. In those days I used to write fiction, & many of my tales showed the literary influence of the immortal Jules. I wrote one story about that side of the moon which is forever turned away from us—using, for fictional purposes—the Hansen theory that air & water still exist there as the result of an abnormal centre of gravity in the moon.[1] I hardly need add that the theory is really exploded—I even was aware of that fact at the time—but I desired to compose a "thriller". Some day I may take up fiction in the amateur press—revealing a side of my nature hitherto concealed from the United. When I write stories, Edgar Allan Poe is my model. I never choose normal subjects, & frequently deal with the supernatural. Only four persons in the association have seen any of my fiction—these being Misses Ballou & Hepner, & Messrs. Fritter & Geo. Schilling.[2] The story they saw is my unpublished credential—"The Alchemist," which, having been sent to Miss Ballou, then Secretary, was shown to Miss Hepner & Mr. Fritter. Later I sent Schilling a revised copy for publication in a paper he was finally forced to abandon. The tale was written 11 years ago, yet is my latest attempt at fiction.[3]

I believe you are correct in stating that modern children care less for fairy tales than we did. Children are too over-sophisticated nowadays—too prosaic—they lack refinement of imagination, & continually dwell upon the flaws & inconsistencies in legendary matter. It is the same instinct that impels college students to choose scientific instead of classical courses.

With sentiments of the most enduring esteem, & with desire to hear from you at no distant date, I remain,

Sir, yr most ob^t humble serv^t

H Lovecraft

Notes

1. Peter Andreas Hansen (1795–1874), Danish astronomer whose most important work was the improvement of the theories and tables of the orbits of the principal bodies in the solar system. At Altona Observatory, he assisted in measuring the arc of meridian (1821). He became director (1825) of Seeberg Observatory, which was removed to Gotha in a new observatory built for him (1857). He worked on theoretical geodesy, optics, and the theory of probability. The work in celestial mechanics for which he is best known are his theories of motion for comets, minor planets, and the moon, and his lunar tables (1857), in use until 1923. He published his lunar theory in *Fundamenta* (*Foundation*) in 1838, and *Darlegung* (*Explanation*) in 1862–64.

2. HPL refers to the amateur journalists Elizabeth M. Ballou, Dora M. Hepner, Leo Fritter, and George S. Schilling. Hepner (1888–1968) once served as UAPA President; in 1914 she appointed HPL chairman of the UAPA's Department of Public Criticism. Fritter (1878–1948) was a lawyer and member of the Woodbee Press Club. HPL supported Fritter's campaign to be President of the UAPA (1915), which Fritter won. (HPL was First Vice-President.)

3. In fact, the story was written in 1908.

[11] [AHT]

Feb. 2, 1916

My dear Kleiner:—

Mrs. Renshaw is so imbued with nonsense concerning "Poetic Spontaneity", that I doubt if her work will ever appeal to many. A rather famous poetess & friend of my mother—Miss Louise Imogen Guiney of Auburndale, Mass., is afflicted with much the same delusion. *It is said* that her "verses" mean something, but I have never taken the time & trouble to find out just what! Yet Dr. Oliver Wendell Holmes once predicted a bright future for her. She has written many books, & has an entrée to the best magazines, but I doubt if posterity will ever accord her a place even nearly approaching that of Dr. Holmes himself. It is through a long visit to her home in 1893 that I met Dr. Holmes, when I was only 2½ years old. He was a frequent visitor there. I was scarce old enough to be poetically influenced, yet I seem to have chosen the same model as the good Doctor—he was a devotee of Pope, & has been called "The Modern Pope". But Miss Guiney followed vaguer literary deities, of whom the Miltonic spirit *Chaos* seems to be the leader. And Mrs. Renshaw appears to be a sister-worshipper at the same shrine![1]

I wish that I might have read "The Electric Horse", for I am sure it must have contained some delightful passages.[2] I used to write detective stories very often, the works of A. Conan Doyle being my model so far as plot was concerned. But Poe was my God of Fiction. I used to love the horrible & the grotesque—much more than I do now—& can recall tales of murderers, spirits, reincarnations, metempsychoses, & every shudder-producing device known to literature!

One long-destroyed tale was of twin brothers—one murders the other, but conceals the body, & tries to *live the life of both*—appearing in one place as himself, & elsewhere as his victim. (Resemblance had been remarkable.) He meets sudden death (lightning) when posing as the dead man—is identified by a scar, & the secret finally revealed by his diary.[3] This, I think, antedates my 11th year. For fun, I have a great mind to write a story again from this plot, publish it without signature, & await the contemptuous laughter of the amateur critics!! I still have a copy of "The Beast in the Cave"—man lost in Mammoth Cave—hears strange animal in the darkness—fatally wounds it with sharp stone—guides enter with torches, & find dying animal to be a snowy-white ape-like, thing—beast gives dying gasp, turns over, & *SPEAKS!!* Then expires.

It had been a *MAN,* long ago lost in the cave, & mentally & physically metamorphosed by perpetual darkness, perpetual silence, & perpetual solitude! How is that for a "dime novel"?

Cole[4] is a born prig—a real grown-up boy prodigy—but even *he* was compelled to recognise your extraordinary merit. As most of my correspondents say, he is the least human of any amateur journalist. Of kindness, pity, toleration, or consideration he knows nothing. If he praises anything, it is *absolutely on its merits*—a commendation affected by none of the natural impulses whereby a normal man must needs favour a friend or shew coldness to a foe. And taking into account the fact that Cole *really possesses* the marvellous critical faculty about which he is so conceited, I think you need never again doubt the excellence of what you write. I observe that this mighty Olympian Zeus[5] manages to introduce a covert & very nasty sneer at my own style—in the sentence where he praises you for using modern methods. Some day I shall "get" him for that slur. I caught him in an historical error a year ago—he admitted it, & I have his letter to prove it. But the admission seems to have pained him so, that he became a subtle enemy. He never acknowledged *The Conservative,* so I did not send him the last two numbers. I will take his honest criticisms—even though he tears my work to pieces—for I recognise & respect his ability—but I *will not* accept his underhanded flings without ultimate reprisal.

[. . .] The Motion Picture magazine[6] declined them, but instead of returning them, sent them on to Chaplin himself, who wrote me a brief note, inquiring if he might keep the copy. I replied affirmatively, since I had a good carbon copy for Sandusky.

With best wishes, I remain, Sir,
　　　Your most ob^t humble serv^t
　　　　　H. P. Lovecraft

Notes

1. Louise Imogen Guiney (1861–1920), poet and essayist; Oliver Wendell Holmes (1809–1894), celebrated man of letters. HPL's family apparently stayed the winter of 1892–93 with the Guineys in Auburndale, MA. At the Guineys, HPL was often in the presence of noted literary figures (though he did not remember them) such as Holmes, who dandled HPL upon his knee.

2. HPL refers to one of the many dime novels written by Luis Senarens (1863–1939), many of which deal with "electric" devices of various sorts. See *The Electric Horse* (New York: Frank Tousey, 1888) or *Jack Wright and His New Electric Horse* (New York: Frank Tousey, 1895).

3. *The Case of Charles Dexter Ward* (1927) may have had its roots in the early tale. The notion of twins figures prominently in "The Dunwich Horror" (1928) and in the entry in HPL's commonplace book that Henry S. Whitehead used for his story "Cassius." HPL still contemplated the idea as late as 12 September 1934 (see *Letters to F. Lee Baldwin* 215–17).

4. Edward H. Cole.

5. The *Olympian* was one of Cole's amateur journals.

6. *Motion Picture Magazine* (Brooklyn, NY, 1911–51), later *Motion Picture and Television Magazine.* HPL had apparently submitted "To Charlie of the Comics" to the magazine.

[12]   [AHT]

Feb. 19, 1916

My dear Kleiner:—

[. . .]

As to celebrities—one experience of mine had to do with an *astronomical* instead of a poetical giant; namely, Percival Lowell, the brother of Pres. Lowell of Harvard, & the widely known observer of Mars—whose observatory is in Flagstaff, Arizona.[1] He lectured in this city in 1907, when I was writing for the *Tribune,* and Prof. Upton[2] of Brown introduced me to him before the lecture in Sayles' Hall. Now here is the amusing part—I never had, have not, & never will have the slightest belief in Lowell's speculations; & when I met him I had just been attacking his theories in my astronomical articles with my characteristically merciless language.[3] With the egotism of my 17 years, I feared that Lowell had read what I had written! I tried to be as noncommittal as possible in speaking, and fortunately discovered that the eminent observer was more disposed to ask me about my telescope, studies, &c., than to discuss Mars. Prof. Upton soon led him away to the platform, & I congratulated myself that a disaster had been averted!

With the customary Expressions of Esteem,

I beg, Sir,

to remain

Yr most oblig'd, obt,

humble Servt

H P Lovecraft

Notes

1. Percival Lowell (1855–1916), older brother of A. Lawrence Lowell (1856–1943), the president of Harvard University (1909–33), founded the Lowell Observatory at Flagstaff, AZ, in 1894.

2. Winslow Upton (1853–1914), astronomer and professor at Brown University. HPL owned his *Star Atlas* (Boston: Ginn & Co., 1896; *LL* 990).

3. HPL expressed tentative acceptance of Lowell's theories regarding the Martian canals in some of his early astronomy columns. In "Is Mars an Inhabited World?" (*Pawtuxet Valley Gleaner,* 7 September 1906), HPL refers to Lowell's theories as "not only possible, but even probable." There is no specific discussion of Lowell in the astronomy columns in the *Providence Tribune* (1906–08), but HPL frequently refers to the "Martian canals" without expressing any skepticism. Only in 1915, in "Mysteries of the Heavens: VII. Mars and the Asteroids" (*Asheville Gazette-News,* 9 March 1915), does HPL dismiss Lowell's speculations as "baseless."

[13]   [AHT]

March 2, 1916

My dear Kleiner:—

It is not remarkable that I should turn with particular relish to the art of pen printing, since in this manner I issued papers of various kinds for over ten years, in the decade 1897–1907, thus accustoming my hand quite completely to the formation of printed characters. Indeed, this recent printing & illustrating mania of mine, aroused by your portrait of me, is in reality only a sort of reminiscent reversion to childhood experiences. I used to be a water-colour fiend, & some day I may paint a picture or two for your amusement (& my own), for I still possess the painting materials that gave me so much harmless pleasure in happier days. I used to delight in marine subjects with the brush, just as with the pen I chose landscapes. Possibly this was because my first outfit had an extra plentiful supply of blue paint! My favourite type of view was a rural mead, & a promontory, with a forest in the background, the sea to one side, & a cottage or manor house in the foreground near the shore. I generally managed to find space for a lighthouse & a ship of ancient pattern.

[. . .]

With expressions of regard & esteem,

I am, Sir,

Yr most oblig'd,

humble, & obt Servt,

H P Lovecraft

[14]   [AHT]

March 9, 1916

My dear Kleiner:—

But returning to the subject of accents—I believe there is nothing worse or more incomprehensible than that of an English provincial peasant. A year or two ago we had a Yorkshire specimen doing some repairing hereabouts, & what he said was in a dialect best understood by himself. These inhabitants of the Northern counties have *words* & *idioms* peculiar to their localities, & it is credibly asserted that the humble denizens of certain districts cannot understand the churls of neighbouring localities without close attention. Russell,[1] of the United, asserts that the English of the Edinburgh district of Scotland, is better than that of Northern England, as spoken by the masses. It amuses me to hear Irishmen praise their ancestral Gaelic, & try to revive its use. They fail to appreciate that we have too many tongues already, without the forced resurrection of a barbaric jargon which was never the language of a developed civilisation. Celtic forms seem now limited to the inaccessible wastes of remote Scotland, Ireland, & Wales. The Cornish speech was declared extinct in the 18th century, & a monument was erected to an old woman, who was the last person ever to use it as a living language. Dunn & McManus are both

Gaelic enthusiasts,[2] but I should advise them to master their one living language before delving into Hibernian archives for any more!

> Yr most oblig'd obt Servt
>
> H Lovecraft

Notes

1. John Russell, a English-born amateur journalist who resided in Tampa, FL. He and HPL had feuded in the pages of the *Argosy* in 1913–14, leading to HPL's joining the UAPA. Russell also joined, although a bit later.

2. John T[homas] Dunn (1889–1983), an Irish-American living in North Providence who came in touch with HPL in late 1914 as a member of the Providence Amateur Press Club and corresponded with him for the period 1915–17. He assisted HPL in editing two issues of the *Providence Amateur* (June 1915, February 1916). Peter J. MacManus was also a member of the Providence Amateur Press Club; he contributed the article "The Irish and the Fairies" (*Providence Amateur*, February 1916), prefaced by an editorial note by HPL.

[15]   [ALS]

United Activity;
or, Why yᵉ Conſervative Doth
Not always anſwer his Letters
With Promptneſs.

31ſt March 1916
598 Angell-St

R Kleiner Eſq.,   Providence, in
Moſt Eſteem'd Sir: New-England
   'Twas yᵉ cuſtom of primitive Mankind, before Cadmus did
invent yᵉ Art of Writing, to expreſs Thought in Pictures, a Practice which ſtill
exiſteth amongſt savage Tribes, Though I be neither of yᵉ Times before
Cadmus, nor yet, I do truſt, a Savage; I will none yᵉ leſs uſe a Picture to shew
you a condition that hath kept me long from

[*Balance missing.*]

[16] [AHT]

June 14, 1916

My dear Kleiner:—
  The Providence Journal has virtually declared war on Germany, and
has well-nigh exhausted Roget's Thesaurus in looking for adjectives where-
with to denounce th' embattled Goth; but the editor scarce dares breathe a
word against the slippery sons of Saint Patrick who violate American neutrality just as flagrantly as any German ever did, and who have been consistently
doing so for the past century. These migrated Micks have not scrupled to use
the United States so far as they can as a weapon against their lawful King and
Empire, and the "Sinn Fein", "Finn Stein" or "Feinstein" revolt is not the
only one financed largely with American-gathered capital. (That name of
theirs sounds more Hebraic than Hibernian!) I regard the Celts as an inferior
race, but little better than Mexicans, & but little more capable of self-
government. They could never maintain an orderly existence save under the
domination of some branch of the Teutonic master-race—if they could leave
England, they would have to take Germany as a master; in fact, I am not sure
but that they *need* a few Prussian methods to curb their ebullient & seditious
emotions. They would like to secure German aid in a rebellion—& then trick
& cheat Germany as badly as they have tried to trick & cheat England! Ireland has produced some notable *individuals,* but the *aggregate* population is a
miserable mass of treachery & drunkenness. Savages—confound 'em.[1]
  Mr. Moe has recently outlined a plan for a rather unique sort of rotating
correspondence between four congenial United members. He proposes to
have a letter constantly going around in definite order, each member of the

chosen circle addressing the *three* others as he writes; & when the letter comes around to him again, taking out what he wrote before and substituting a fresh epistle. He proposed Ira A. Cole for membership, & asked me to name the fourth party. I named you, & shall, if you care to participate, start off the enterprise by sending you a letter written to you, Cole, & Moe. You will then add to this a letter addressed to Cole, Moe, & me, sending same to Cole. Cole will add a letter for Moe, myself, & you, & Moe one to me, you, & Cole; which, when I receive it, I shall deprive of my former letter, adding a fresh one to you, Cole, & Moe. Of course, when you receive it again, you will take out your old letter, adding another to Cole, Moe & me. And so on, till death breaks the continuity of the circle, or quadrangle. Moe has named this band after its members, thus! Klei(ner) Co(le) Mo(e) Lo(vecraft)—or "The Kleicomoloes"; When I write, I shall address my letter: "Dear Kleicomo", omitting my own part of the name. You will say "Dear Comolo"; Cole, "Dear Kleimolo"; & Moe, "Dear Kleicolo"! What a nomenclature! As Moe said to me, if you deem this idea too childish, you need not feel at all obliged to bother with it; but it has its interesting side, & Moe seems to have expended no little thought in devising it. He says that a similar sort of letter goes on its perpetual round through the hands of various separated members of his family; in fact, it was from this family letter that he derived his "Kleicomolo" inspiration. If he had arranged the names in a slightly different manner, "Kleimo*loco*", some astute Spanish scholar might fancy he could detect an etymological significance, & vow we were all *muy loco!* I suppose that literary topics of interest ought to form the principal contents of these epistles. If you join the circle, I will soon send you a "Kleicomo" letter, though I may not see your reply for many months, since Moe admits that his busy life may cause the missive to remain long unanswered each time it reaches him. He is a valued but sadly infrequent correspondent. My worst lapses & delays are trivial as compared with his average tactics.

But since I am becoming inconsequential in my epistolary style, I believe I will bring this missive to a conclusion, & subscribe myself,

    Sir,

        Your most humble obt. Servt.,

        H. P. Lovecraft

[Enclosure: "Ye Ballade of Patrick von Flynn."]

Notes

1. HPL elaborates upon this theme in the section "The Loyal Coalition" in "Lucubrations Lovecraftian," *United Co-operative* 1, No. 3 (April 1921): 8–11 (*CE* 1.277–80).

[17]   [AHT]

Aug. 23, 1916

My dear Kleiner:—

   I have lately been amusing myself by a perusal of some of the "Imagist" nonsense of the day.[1] As a species of pathological phenomena it is interesting. The authors are evidently of approximately harmless characteristics, since so far as I know, they are all at large; but their work indicates that most of them are dangerously near the asylum gates—uncomfortably close to the padded cell. There is absolutely no artistic principle in their effusions; ugliness replaces beauty, & chaos supplies the vacant chair of sense. Some of the stuff, though, would mean something if neatly arranged and read as prose. Of the major portion no criticism is necessary, or even possible. It is the product of hopelessly decayed taste, & arouses a feeling of sympathetic sadness, rather than of mere contempt. Since "Imagism" has no relation at all to poesy, I think no lover of the Muse need entertain apprehension for his art from this quarter.

   As to my lack of erudition in modern volumes of Georgian lore, I may remark that my aim is to avoid an objective view of my beloved age. I love to fuse myself into the old times—to become an actual part of them with all the strength of a not entirely inactive imagination. I love to look at the black body of this fountain pen & see a trusty grey goose quill instead! There is an indefinable charm in reading ancient volumes *as a contemporary;* to accept the language & statements of the old writers not as "quaint" antiques, but at their own face value. I firmly believe that Pope is more of a *living man* to me, than to the average reader.

   I am Sir,

     Ever yr most obt Servt

     H Lovecraft

Notes

1. Imagism was a poetic movement espoused chiefly by American poet Amy Lowell (1874–1925), who contributed to the first Imagist anthology, *Des Imagistes* (1914), and edited three volumes of *Some Imagist Poets* (1915–17). Its focus was to capture seemingly random "images" impinging upon the poet's mind without any attempt at coherence or logical structure. HPL attacked the movement in "The Vers Libre Epidemic."

[18]   [AHT]

Sept. 25, 1916

My dear Kleiner:—

   I also saw that refin'd comedy intitul'd "The Count", enacted by Mr. Charles Chaplin.[1] Mr. Chaplin hath indeed an unique charm of manner; the more marked when unobscured by the coarseness & crudity of the film wherein he is acting. I was much delighted with the film preceding "The Count"—"One A. M.",[2] in which Chaplin is the *only character,* with the exception of a hackney-coachman in the fore part of the play. Charles, in this film, is labouring beneath "The Power of Wine".[3] He also makes another escape from his traditional costume, appearing as once before in immaculate evening garb. At least, it is immaculate when the film *begins.* Charlie, though he might not shine in a comedy of wit & repartee, is indeed an enemy to melancholy! He has his own particular place in the world. I can even forgive him for being a Jew![4]

Trusting to receive a reply at yr Convenience,

I am, Sir,

Ever yr most humble

Obt Servt

H P Lovecraft

Notes

1. *The Count* (Lone Star Corp., 1916), directed by Charlie Chaplin; starring Charlie Chaplin, Eric Campbell, and Edna Purviance.

2. *One A.M.* (Lone Star Corp., 1916), directed by Charlie Chaplin; starring Charlie Chaplin and Albert Austin.

3. HPL alludes to his own poem of that title.

4. Although Chaplin himself frequently claimed to be part Jewish, there has been no verification of any Jewish strain in his immediate or remote ancestry.

[19]   [AHT]

Nov. 16, 1916

My dear Kleiner:—

As to my youthful limitations, I must admit that they were very real. At the time, I thought myself a much wronged genius; but later years have enabled me to view my childhood with more sense & cynicism, & less sympathy & self-pity. I believe it was Mr. De Quincey who complained of never being able to finish anything he commenced.[1] This is & was my own difficulty. Surrounded by those whose accomplishments were real & considerable, I was a dabbler in everything, & well versed in nothing. On the maternal side I inherited a love of art. My mother is a landscape painter of no little skill, whilst my eldest aunt[2] is still more expert in this direction, having had canvases hung in exhibition at the Providence Art Club—yet despite *their* genius, *I* could not draw anything better than the junk you have so often beheld in my letters. I tried my best, but the gift was *absolutely wanting.* With music I made a corresponding fiasco. My rhythmic tendencies led me into a love of melody, & I was forever whistling & humming in defiance of convention & good breeding. I was so exact in time & tune, & showed such a semi-professional precision & flourish in my crude attempts, that my plea for a violin was granted when I was seven years of age, & I was placed under the instruction of the best violin teacher for children in the city—Mrs. Wilhelm Nauck.³ For two years I made such progress that Mrs. Nauck was enthusiastic, & declared that I should adopt music as a career—**but,** all this time the tedium of practicing had been wearing shockingly on my always sensitive nervous system. My "career" extended until 1899, its summit being a public recital at which I played a solo from Mozart before an audience of considerable size. Soon after that, my ambition & taste alike collapsed like a house of cards (to use a trite simile). I began to detest classical music, because it had meant so much painful labour to me; & I positively *loathed* the violin! Our physician, knowing my temperament, advised an immediate discontinuance of music lessons, which speedily ensued. Is this not one of the most typical failures on record? In art, I lacked *talent;* but in music, I lacked *ambition & ability.* Twenty years ago I criticised Verdi & Wagner, & sat rapt with childish adoration at the strains of Beethoven—today I hum & whistle the stuff you despise so much as played on your relative's phonograph, that is, except "nigger laughing songs", & a few weeks ago I attended with delight that modern "classic" opera called "Katinka"!⁴ If this be not *backwardness & dulness,* what *do* you call it? But the climax is *yet to come!!* Three or four years ago I picked up my little neglected violin, tuned it after purchasing new strings, & thought I would amuse myself with its sound, even though I did no better than a rustic village fiddler. I drew my bow across the strings, when *lo!* I discovered that I had forgotten how to play as much as a single note! *It was as if I had never touched a violin before!!!!*

What can account for so complete an effacement of that which had been drilled into me for two laborious years? With *languages* I had failed equally. Latin is the only speech I have succeeded in mastering to an extent even mentionable. *Nervous exhaustion* always intervenes betwixt me & success, save in matters where a strong personal predilection aids the assimilation of knowledge. My love of Roman antiquities & of the power & majesty of the Eternal City is what helped me with Latin. But concerning my linguistic failures, the case is not so bad as that with music. I *do not forget* what I learn in the domain of letters. Mathematics is a melancholy word in my vocabulary. Having resolved at the age of twelve to become an astronomer, I of course deemed it needful to perfect myself in algebra, geometry, trigonometry & calculus; but discovered in high-school that my old hatred of *arithmetic* extended even into the loftier regions of mathematical research. The first year I barely passed in algebra, but was so little satisfied with what I had accomplished, that I voluntarily repeated the last half of the term. After three years I thought I had learnt something of algebra & geometry, but after my general nervous breakdown of 1908–1909 I must have allowed my knowledge to slip away, for when I tried to act as a tutor to my cousin last year, I found that I had no better command of the subjects than he! What a dunce I must be! Between

1909 & 1912 I tried to perfect myself as a chemist, conquering inorganic chemistry & qualitative analysis with ease, since they had been favourite pastimes of my youth. But in the midst of *organic* chemistry, with its frightfully dull theoretical problems, & involved cases of isomerism of hydrocarbon radicals—the benzene ring—&c., &., &c.—I found myself so wretched bored that I positively could not study for more than fifteen minutes without acquiring an excruciating headache which prostrated me completely for the rest of the day. I became rather thoroughly convinced that I was cursed with that most agonising combination of conflicting elements—an insatiable desire for knowledge & achievement, coupled with an intellect & constitution incapable of material progress toward the goal. What a mixture—the aspirations of a poet & philosopher beset by the mental limitations of a butcher or a bricklayer! In literature itself my faults are clearly shewn. I am master of no more than I happen to fancy. What I *do not* know of XIXth & XXth century prose & verse, is more than I would care to tell! All I know is, that I detest the stuff!

After this chronicle of disaster I fear you will not care to peruse such an autobiography as you suggested, for the intimate annals of life's failures seldom command interest. However, that fluency, which afflicts everyone when talking or writing of his own affairs, impels me to proceed. I am giving this bit of literature here, rather than in the Kleicomolo; since Moe & I have already exchanged ponderous autobiographies,[5] & Cole would hardly be pleased with such a tale of eccentricity, nervousness, & artificial living. He is too much the child of Nature to be tolerant of the victims of civilisation & their vagaries. But I hope your own story *will* be in the Kleicomolo, for I am sure you were never such an odd bundle of nerves as the young Conservative!

I was born on the 20th of August, 1890, at No. 454 (then numbered 194) Angell Street, in the city of Providence. This was the home of my mother's family; my parents' actual residence at the time being in Dorchester, Mass. My father was the son of an Englishman who came from Devonshire to the state of New York in 1847 on account of a loss of fortune. This British grandfather I never saw in person, though he is well known to me through daguerreotypes & photographs. He was the first of his line to adopt a remunerative occupation & American residence, & he remained British in spirit even unto death—even to the extent of a single eyeglass. He made, as I am told, every effort to avoid acquiring an American accent, which is not identical with the speech of cultivated London. My father, his youngest child & only son, was naturally something of an Englishman himself, though born in Rochester, N. Y. His later residence was in Mt. Vernon, N. Y., with an office in New York City. Still later, after his marriage, he transferred commercial interests to Boston, & lived successively in Dorchester & Auburndale. My father's mother was an Allgood of Northumberland, living in N. Y., descended from a British officer who remained in America after the disastrous Revolution.

On my mother's side, I am a complete New-England Yankee, coming from Phillipses, Places, & Rathbones. Of these stocks, the Rathbone is probably the best; this name having been borne by barons in England. The peerage, however, was not in direct line, & is extinct, though my maternal grandfather once attempted to establish heirship of property when the estates reverted to the crown. My mother has a double portion of Rathbone blood, her parents having been first cousins, the children of two Rathbone sisters, one of whom married a Phillips; the other, a Place. My grandfather, during my mother's childhood, lived in Greene, R. I., a village built entirely on his own land & named by him. Its former name was "Coffin's Corners", whose undertakerish sound perhaps introduced the pessimistic taint into my heredity!!

In the mid-seventies, my grandfather[6] transferred all his interests to Providence (where his offices had always been) & erected one of the handsomest residences in the city—to me, *the* handsomest—my own beloved birthplace! The spacious house, raised on a high green terrace, looks down upon grounds which are almost a park, with winding walks, arbours, trees, & a delightful fountain. Back of the stable is the orchard, whose fruits have delighted so many of my sad (?) childish hours. The place is sold now, & many of the things I have described in the present tense, ought to be described in the *past* tense. The house has been sold to one purchaser; the stable & orchard to another; & an ugly garage now smells to high heaven where once the crystal waters of the fountain played! Such degeneracy! Why could not the purchaser have kept his car elsewhere, & suffered the ancient fount to sparkle as of yore? But enough of this!

When I was two years old—or rather, a year & a half old—my parents moved to Auburndale, Mass., sharing a house with a family of the well known poetess, Miss Louise Imogen Guiney, whose verses you have probably seen, & who has been considered one of the foremost poets of the Massachusetts circle. Miss Guiney had been educated in Providence, where she met my mother years before.

At the home of Miss Guiney I probably saw more celebrated persons than I have ever seen since; for her poetical standing is very high. Dr. Oliver Wendell Holmes was a not infrequent caller. And now comes the personal element, for it is there, in Auburndale, amidst the most poetic of poetic auspices, that consciousness first came to my infant mind. I distinctly recall the quiet, shady suburb as I saw it in 1892—& it is a rather curious psychological fact that at this early age I was impressed most of all with the railway bridge & the four-tracked Boston & Albany road which extended beneath it. The trains fascinated me, & to this day I have a love for everything pertaining to railways. (Except the Adamson Law!!)[7] Miss Guiney kept a most extraordinary collection of St. Bernard dogs, all named after authors and poets. A shaggy gentleman by the classic name of Brontë was my particular favourite & companion, being ever in attendance on my chariot as my mother wheeled that vehicle through the streets & avenues. Brontë would permit me to place my fist in his mouth without biting me, & would snarl protectingly if any stranger approached me.

As an infant, I had been restless & prone to cry; now, when able to talk & walk, my temperamental excitability veered in the opposite direction, & I was nicknamed "Little Sunshine" by Mrs. Guiney, mother of the poetess. (Imagine the sour old Conservative being called *"Little Sunshine"*!!!!—Shades of Schopenhauer!!!!!) Mrs. Guiney was a delightfully cultured lady, the widow of a General of Mass. Volunteers, who had carried a bullet in his skull for ten years after the Civil War, when death finally released him from pain.[8] In appearance, I was vastly different then. My hair was yellow, & allowed to curl over my shoulders in ringlets much like those periwigs I am so fond of drawing. This golden mane was another cause of the nickname.

About this time I began to display a precocity which ought to have warned my parents of that mediocre older life which too often follows such an infancy. At the age of two I was a rapid talker, familiar with the alphabet from my blocks & picture-books, & (which will interest you) absolutely *metremad!* I could not read, but would repeat any poem of simple sort with unfaltering cadence. Mother Goose was my principal classic, & Miss Guiney would continually make me repeat parts of it; not that my rendition was necessarily notable, but because my age lent uniqueness to the performance. My father, (who was a lover of things military, & who in youth gave up an appointment to West Point only to please his mother) liked me to attain a martial key, & taught me "Sheridan's Ride"[9]—which I declaimed in a manner that brought loud applause—& painful egotism. My nervous utterance was rather well adapted to warlike numbers, & I am told that I put much fire into the lines. My mother innocently helped to swell my self-esteem by recording all my "cute" childish sayings, until I began to make these "naive" remarks *on purpose* to draw attention. (Observe the future Georgian—with his *artificial* wit!!) Miss Guiney would often ask of me: "Whom do you love"? And I would invariably pipe out the stereotyped reply: "Louise Imogen Guiney"! (Today I cannot say as much for her verse—she is too much a disciple of the Browning school, with all its obscurity.) Another "cute" observation & act of mine was to approach my father (whom I barely remember as a handsome figure in black coat & waistcoat & striped grey trousers) & slap him sharply on both knees; crying out, apropos of nothing, "Papa, you look just like a young man"! Since he had not passed his middle thirties, my remark was not exactly incorrect, after all.[10]

Such are the fragments of an early life too far remote for continuous remembrance. In April, 1893, my father was stricken with a complete paralysis resulting from a brain overtaxed with study & business cares. He lived for five years at a hospital, but was never again able to move hand or foot, or to utter a sound.[11] This tragedy dissolved all plans for permanent settlement in

Auburndale, & caused the sale of the property recently acquired there. Permanently stricken with grief, my mother took me to the Phillips household, thereby causing me to grow up as a complete Rhode-Islander. At the age of three, my memories crystallize definitely & connectedly for the first time. Both of my maternal grandparents were then living, & my beloved grandfather, Whipple Van Buren Phillips, became the centre of my entire universe. A man of culture & extensive travel, he had accumulated a fund of cosmopolitan lore which never ceased to delight me. His acquaintance with all the wonders of Europe, which he had seen at first hand, made me feel almost as if I had seen them myself. It was from him that I acquired my love of Rome. He had loved to muse amidst the ruins of the ancient city, & had brought from Italy a wealth of mosaics, (not the kind that Moe calls my verse!)[12] paintings & other objets d'art whose theme was more often classically *Roman* than *Italian*. He always wore a pair of mosaics in his cuffs for buttons—one of a view of the Coliseum (so *tiny* yet so *faithful*); the other of the Forum. I wear them now—for I still adhere to the old-style round cuff that most have discarded in favour of the modern "link". My grandmother[13] was a serene, quiet lady of the old school, & she did her best to correct my increasingly boorish deportment—for my nervousness made me a very restless & uncontrollable child. She was a devoted student of astronomy, & though she did not personally direct my gaze to the heavens, it was through her library of astronomical books that I first became interested in that direction. My two aunts presented rather a contrast. The elder was (& still is) a devotee of science & literature. She was a potent influence, I think, in turning my fancy toward the classics, while my old love of chemistry also arises from her remarks on that science. She was (though she has ceased to paint now) an artist of great power. When she married Dr. Clark,[14] she proved the means of introducing me to the most substantial classic element of all! My other aunt[15] was yet a very young lady when I first began to observe events around me. She was rather a favourite in the younger social set, & brought the principal touch of gayety to a rather conservative household. To the sprightly conversation & repartee of this younger generation, I owe my first lessons in the school of Pope. I could sense the artificiality of the atmosphere, & often strove to ape the airs & affectations of those whom I observed & studied. I extracted not a little celebrity & egotism from my mimicry of various types of callers; particularly one Edward F. Gamwell,[16] who next to my grandfather was my ideal male. I was infinitely delighted when this individual (then a Brown student) decided upon a lasting affiliation with the family. The engagement of my aunt & Mr. Gamwell, & the customary levity of the younger set in their good-natured raillery of the two, imparted to me a curiously worldly cynicism regarding sentimental matters, & forever turned my Muse from the field which you so gracefully adorn.

In 1894 I was able to read fluently, & was a tireless student of the dictionary; never allowing a word to slip by me without ascertaining its meaning.

It was then that the mellowed tomes of the family library became my complete world—at once my servants & my masters. I flitted hither & thither amongst them like a fascinated moth, taking supreme joy in the old English volumes of the Lovecrafts, sent to my mother for me when my father was paralysed, since I had become the only male representative of this family. I read everything, understood a little, & imagined more. Grimm's Fairy Tales were my truly representative diet, & I lived mostly in a mediaeval world of imagination. And now began my Britannic predilection, which had already been indicated in vague ways. I always had the impression of being English, & when my grandfather told me of the American Revolution, I shocked everyone by adopting a dissenting view. Though only 4 years old, I had a firm & to me invincible line of reasoning, something like this:

Grandpa: "And in 1776 our forefathers threw off the load of oppression, & founded our country."

Howard: "But didn't *they* come from England?"

Grandpa: "Yes, but England was cruel to them."

Howard: "But they were *still English,* weren't they?"

Grandpa: "Of course, in *blood,* but this was a new country."

Howard: "But if it hadn't been for England, there wouldn't have been any country, would there?"

Grandpa: "Why, our forefathers made this nation *themselves.*"

Howard: "But England made *them,* didn't it?"

Grandpa: "Oh, but they had the right to separate, as free men."

Howard: "But didn't you say that the 'rebels' of '61 had *no right* to secede?"

Grandpa: "Oh! but that was different—they seceded from *our country— our union!*"

Howard: "But wasn't *England our country* at first?"

Grandpa: "Oh! but the southerners weren't oppressed—they fought for slavery of human beings."

Howard: "But didn't they have a right to have slaves? And niggers aren't really like us. And we used to sell slaves here in Providence, 'way back before 1790—"

And so it went on without end! At length, in the interests of amity, we ceased to discuss the matter. But I had permanently come to feel myself an *outsider.* Grover Cleveland was grandpa's ruler, but Her Majesty, Victoria, Queen of Great Britain & Ireland & Empress of India commended my allegiance. "God Save the Queen!" was a stock phrase of mine.

In January, 1896, the death of my grandmother plunged the household into a gloom from which it never fully recovered. The black attire of my mother & aunts terrified & repelled me to such an extent that I would surreptitiously pin bits of bright cloth or paper to their skirts for sheer relief. They had to make a careful survey of their attire before receiving callers or going out! And then it was that my former high spirits received their damper. I began to have nightmares of the most hideous description, peopled with *things* which I called "night-gaunts"—a compound word of my own coinage. I used to draw them after waking (perhaps the idea of these figures came from an edition de luxe of "Paradise Lost" with illustrations by Doré, which I discovered one day in the east parlour). In dreams they were wont to whirl me through space at a sickening rate of speed, the while fretting & impaling me with their detestable tridents. It is fully fifteen years—aye, more—since I have seen a "night-gaunt", but even now, when half asleep & drifting vaguely along over a sea of childhood thoughts, I feel a thrill of fear—something like that in Mrs. Jordan's poem "The Pool"—& instinctively *struggle to keep awake.* That was my one prayer back in '96—each night—to *keep awake* & ward off the night-gaunts![17]

You will notice that I have made no reference to childish friends & playmates—I had none! The children I knew disliked me, & I disliked them. I was used to adult company & conversation, & despite the fact that I felt shamefully dull beside my elders, I had nothing in common with the infant train. Their romping & shouting puzzled me. I hated mere play & dancing about—in my relaxations I always desired *plot.* My mother once tried to place me in a children's dancing class, but I abhorred the thought. My reply to her suggestion sheds a light on the nature of my bookish browsings in about the year '98. I said: "Nemo fere saltat sobrius, nisi forte insanit!" Which is from Cicero's oration against Catiline.[18] It was in the sombre period of 1896 that I first became a temperance enthusiast. Somewhere I discovered an old copy of John B. Gough's "Sunshine & Shadow", & read & re-read it, backward & forward. From that time to this, I have never been at a loss for something to say against liquor! My reading now centred upon classical mythology, to which I had progressed from Grimm. I admired & emulated the poetical quotations so liberally interspersed through the pages of Bulfinch's "Age of Fable", & in 1897 produced my first formal "poem", entitled "The New Odyssey; or, the Adventures of Ulysses."[19] From 1894 to 1896 I had used only *printed* letters, but I now began to write in script. All this time my spirits were dampened by a vague sensation of impending calamity. I was not blind to a waning of the family fortune, as evidenced by a decrease in the number of servants & closing of the stables. I sadly missed Kelly, the coachman, who was an indisputable authority on all matters pertaining to Hibernian dialect, & who had the forbearance to listen placidly to my laudation of Mother England. By the time of his departure I had acquired a beautiful brogue, which I occasionally aired for the amusement of myself & those about me— particularly Miss Norah _____ (last name forgotten!) who presided over the culinary department. Religious matters likewise fretted me. *I never had the slightest shadow of belief in the supernatural,* but pretended to believe, because it was deemed the proper thing in a Baptist household. Sunday school so much depressed me, that I was soon relieved of that care. Later on my views were tolerated in silence, though not in secrecy.

It was in the winter of 1896 that I first became acquainted with the theatre, which has furnished my life with the only real relaxation it has ever had. The family were still in mourning for my grandmother, but we were acquainted with Mr. Morrow,[20] lessee & manager of Providence's chief theatre—The Providence Opera House—(he lived directly across the street) so that it was not thought too shocking to let my aunt take me to see something besides gloom. The play—the first I ever beheld—was one of Denman Thompson's minor efforts—"The Sunshine of Paradise Alley"[21]—& had a slum setting which rather enraptured me, since I had never beheld real slums. My memory of that play is yet more vivid than of any of last season's offerings! Act I— The slum home of Nellie O'Grady, nicknamed "The Sunshine of Paradise Alley." Act II—The Brooklyn Bridge by night—the lights of New York—the "wharf rats"—blear-eyed vagabonds lurking beneath the abutments of the bridge—the stage moon—rising upon a scene of mingled squalor & splendour—. Act III—A wretched courtyard in the tenement districts—a real hand organ & monkey—the underworld at a glance. Act IV—A political picnic in Harlem—the oddly loud apparel of the "ladies" & "gents"—the quaint Bowery dialect—the fascinating *scenery!* All this I recall as yesterday, though I have not even seen a programme of it for *twenty years*. It was an introduction to a new world—a world of *sham* & *artifice*, which blended well with my always artificial taste. From then on, I acted "plays" innumerable in the library at home, to the music of my own whistling—substitute for the enthralling orchestra at the Opera House. The best of my plays was Elizabethan—"The Tragicall Historie of yᵉ Emperour Caracalla".[22] I rather shocked everyone by my ferocious delineation of the murder of Geta, the Emperor's brother. Geta was a wonderful actor, composed inwardly of pillows, & outwardly of a toga (or sheet). My final death scene (of course I was the leading man, portraying Caracalla) was extremely powerful & pathetic!

It was in 1898 that I first attempted to attend school. Hitherto it had been deemed unwise to subject so irritable & sensitive a child to discipline of any sort. I entered the highest grade of primary school, but soon found the instruction quite useless, since I had picked up most of the material before. However, I do not regret the venture, since it was in dear old Slater Avenue (alas—to be abandoned next year!) that I made my only childhood friendship—that with Chester & Harold Munroe, the former of whom is in the United.[23]

The Spanish War excited me intensely.[24] For the first time I was in sympathy with those about me; for I sided with the States against a nation which had anciently been England's foe, & whose Armada Drake had destroyed. I longed to participate, but was denied that privilege. It was then that I acquired that admiration for T. R. which still animates me.

By 1899 my poetical outbursts had become quite numerous, one collection being still in my mother's possession. It is a book made of cheap pad paper, bound with pins, & is entitled "Poemata Minora". It contains an ode to the moon, regrets on the passing away of the pagan religion, musings on the downfall of Rome, & such like things![25]

I had also dabbled much in fiction, delighting mainly in the most exciting & horrible things a child's fancy can conceive of. I enclose an actual manuscript of this period—a short story written at the age of 8, whose conclusion contains a violent death—as did most of my stories. I wonder if you can decipher my childish handwriting? I will also enclose a less dismal tale than "The Secret Cave"—a juvenile attempt at humour entitled "The Little Glass Bottle". These things, as I read them over, reveal to me the fact that my skill in prose was not so great during childhood as I had imagined. We are all prone to overrate our early feats; & I see, in reality, that these 1898 stories were not at all remarkable in structure.

My taste in the drama was vastly improved in 1897, when I saw for the first time a Shakespearian play! This offering was "Cymbeline", with Margaret Mather,[26] a favourite artiste of a generation ago, as Imogen. It came to the Opera House during Christmas week, & I witnessed the Christmas (Saturday) matinee. It is needless to remark that I was absolutely enraptured with the glamour of the production, & the beauty of the blank verse, which I had never previously heard on the stage. My little toy theatre at home became resplendent with Shakespearian scenery—hand painted by the proprietor—& for weeks afterward I played nothing but "Cymbeline". I still have the set of pasteboard performers, in faithful costume, which I drew & cut out for this miniature production. For childish work, they are rather surprisingly faithful to the early British & Roman costumes, though much allowance must necessarily be made for the age of the designer. I followed my presentation of "Cymbeline" with other Shakespearian plays, though for these I had no actual model from life. Richard III was my favourite, & I also tried to act out parts of this myself, (in the Cibber version) throwing the household into terror with my wild snarling in the tent scene, where the guilty monarch starts from his troubled sleep with the famous passage beginning:

> "Give me another horse! Bind up my wounds!
> Have mercy, Jesu! Soft—I did but dream."[27]

The tower scene (properly part of King Henry VI) also formed a prominent piece in my classic repertoire. How I loved to stab poor Henry with my wooden sword, the while declaiming:

> "If any spark of life be yet remaining,
> Down, down to Hell, & say I sent thee thither!"[28]

All this was contemporaneous with my disastrous efforts to acquire musical proficiency. Of my failure in that direction, I can speak only with humiliation. My mother has a well-nigh professional skill both with voice & piano—but I did not inherit her ability for studious application, & proved an utter and ignominious failure with the violin.

In 1899 a new interest of mine began to gain ascendancy.[29] My predilection for natural science, fostered by my Aunt Lillian, took form in a love of chemistry. A friend of ours is Prof. John Howard Appleton, the venerable professor of chemistry at Brown, & author of many books on the subject. He presented me with his own book for beginners—"The Young Chemist", & before many months had elapsed, I was deep in experimental research, having a well equipped laboratory in the cellar, which my grandfather had fitted up for me. In March, 1899, I began to publish a chemical daily paper called "The Scientific Gazette", of which I made four carbon copies for "circulation". How I managed to keep this thing in existence for seven years, as I did, is still a mystery to me. However, it soon degenerated into a weekly!

About 1900 I became a passionate devotee of geography & history, & an intense fanatic on the subject of Antarctic exploration. The Borchgrevink expedition, which had just made a new record in South Polar achievement, greatly stimulated this study.[30] I wrote many fanciful tales about the Antarctic Continent, besides composing "learned" treatises on the real facts. This pursuit of science gave me something of a contempt for art & literature, & my progress in English style was somewhat retarded. I became quite indifferent to verse for a while; using it only in occasional satires. But my prose developed in spite of itself, since my omnivorous reading could not but help it on toward greater fluency.

In 1902 I again attempted school; & singularly enough, I went to the same old Slater Avenue edifice, which had now acquired a grammar department in addition to the primary grades. Here again I was brought into contact with other children, but my attitude toward them was now different. I had read enough idyllic verse to understand that childhood is a golden age in the life of man; never to be regained when once lost; so I tried to interest myself in the affairs of other boys with some degree of success. I joined the "Slater Avenue Army", whose wars were waged in the neighbouring woods, & though my dramatic suggestions were not always accepted with perfect tolerance, I managed to get along with my "fellow-soldiers" fairly well. One of these boys—named Manton Mitchell—later became a *real* soldier; attending West Point & being now a 1st Lieutenant of the U. S. Infantry. (He was with Pershing's Mexican expedition,[31] but is now home on furlough.) At school I was considered a bad boy, for I would never submit to discipline. When censured by my teacher for disregard of rules, I used to point out to her the essential emptiness of conventionality, in such a satirical way, that her patience must have been quite severely strained; but withal she was remarkably kind, considering my intractable disposition. Her name is Abbie A. Hathaway,[32] called "Abbie" behind her back by the boys. She is now retired on a pension, having been rather elderly even in my time. She still takes an interest in my work, & I chat pleasantly with her (more pleasantly than of yore) whenever I meet her. I managed to excel in studies at Slater Avenue, which perhaps reconciled her to my outrageous deportment. In history classes we used to have thunderous debates, for while "Abbie" was the daughter of a Union veteran, the Munroe boys & I were Confederate sympathizers. How we used to annoy her with our "compositions"—all flaming with love & glorification of the South! I subjoin some verses which I once placed upon her desk. I have the original copy, for I composed them on the back of a half-tone illustration in Montgomery's "American History"—a book still on my shelves.[33] Note the fact that I had then fallen completely into my present old-fashioned style.

C. S. A.

1861–1865

To the Starry Cross of the SOUTH.

When first this warlike Banner was unfurl'd
A noble cause was born into the World;
No purer Flag hath e'er defy'd the Wind
Proclaiming high the Rights of Human kind.
The cruel YANKEE, midst ignoble Fight,
Stood aw'd, or fled in Panick at the Sight;
And though the South by Treachery's o'erthrown,
The Mem'ry of past Valour ne'er is gone:
Midst Ruin vast, and overwhelming Loss,
All Southrons true revere the STARRY CROSS!

H. P. Lovecraft. (1902)

Of course, you will object to the "Wind–humankind" & "o'erthrown–gone" rhymes—but remember that the author was just turned twelve, & had too little artistic conscience to reject these makeshifts!

On graduation day—in June, 1903—occurred a rather interesting incident. I had affected a great contempt for ceremony of every sort, & had absolutely refused to deliver a "speech" from the platform, according to custom. But after the exercises began, I suddenly resolved to say something after all. I heard so much applause bestowed upon compositions which I felt to be mediocre, that I determined to surpass my fellow scholars by an impromptu address. Accordingly I ceased to pay attention to the speakers, but seized upon pad & pencil, & began to write an essay on the life of Sir William Herschel, the astronomer.[34] It was against all maxims of courtesy to commence scribbling in the midst of a publick ceremony, but I was ever disregardful of the amenities. When I had finished, I quietly stole up to "Abbie's" desk, & informed her in a dictatorial whisper that I would, in spite of my previous refusal, read a paper at the conclusion of the programme. She did not take offence at the eccentric manner in which I prepared my eleventh-hour oration, but announced me at the proper time. I mounted the platform with a sublime scorn of everyone & everything about me, & began in a very condescending & professional manner to address the assembled multitude of parents & children. I employed my best Georgian mode of speech, beginning in this fashion:

"Ladies and gentlemen: I had not thought to trespass upon your time & patience today, but when the Muse impels, it becomes a man but ill to stifle her demand. When I speak of the Muse, I do not mean to say that I am about to inflict my bad verses upon you—far be that from my intention. My Muse this day is Clio, who presides over affairs of history; & my subject, a very revered one to me, is the career of one who rose from the most unfortunate condition of insignificance to the utmost height of deserved eminence—Sir William Herschel, who from an Hanoverian peasant became the greatest astronomer of England, & therefore of the World!"

I think these are nearly the words I used. I kept them long in memory (through egotism) though I have not a copy beside me now. If this version be incorrect, it is because there are not enough long words present. I was a veritable pocket edition of Dr. Johnson for Latinated language. Much to my concern, this offering elicited smiles, rather than attention, from the adult part of my audience; but after I had done, I received a round of applause which well compensated for my trouble, & sent me off the platform with the self-satisfied glow of a triumphant Garrick.[35] Good old Miss Hathaway still relates this anecdote. My selection of Dr. Herschel as a hero for my extemporaneous panegyric, is an index of my latest predilection. Astronomy had seized me in its spell in the winter of 1902–03; & when speaking of the Muses, I should not have mentioned Clio alone, but should have included Urania as well![36] In the summer of 1903 my mother presented me with a 2½″ astronomical telescope, & thenceforward my gaze was ever upward at night. The late Prof. Upton of Brown, a friend of the family, gave me the freedom of the college observatory, (Ladd Observatory) & I came & went there at will on my bicycle. Ladd Observatory tops a considerable eminence about a mile from the house. I used to walk up Doyle Avenue hill with my wheel, but when returning would have a glorious coast down it. So constant were my observations, that my neck became affected by the strain of peering at a difficult angle. It gave me much pain, & resulted in a permanent curvature perceptible today to a close observer. My body has ever been unequal to the demands of an active career.

It was about this time that Dr. Franklin Chase Clark, a distant relative who had become a closer kin through marriage to my aunt, began to influence my intellectual development. He was a man of vast learning—a graduate of Brown, Harvard Medical School, & Columbia College, bearing the degree of A.M. besides his ordinary A.B. & professional M.D. He was an author of medical treatises, & an authority on medical ethics; but besides all this there was another separate side to his life—the classical side. He translated Homer, Virgil, Lucretius, & Statius into excellent English verse, & composed reams of original matter.[37] *Purely by coincidence,* he was an old-fashioned poet of my own beloved school, & he did much to correct & purify my faulty style. He likewise worked wonders with my prose. I regarded, & still regard, his level as unattainable by myself; but I was so desirous of his approbation, that I would labour hours with my work to win a word of praise from his lips. I hung upon his conversation as Boswell hung upon Dr. Johnson's; yet was ever oppressed by a sense of hopeless inferiority. His historical attainments were likewise immense. After his death last year, the R. I. Historical Society took over his unpublished manuscripts.

My other uncle-in-law, Mr. Gamwell, was a Cambridge man, hence my converse with him was less frequent; but I made the most of every opportunity. He had taught me to rattle off the Greek alphabet when I was six years old; a feat which made Greek much easier for me in high school. In 1903 he was owner & editor of the Cambridge Tribune, & stimulated my editorial tendencies to such an extent that I founded the *Rhode Island Journal of Astronomy,* to replace the almost defunct *Scientific Gazette.* (I conducted both simultaneously in 1903–04.) Mr. Gamwell's only son—my cousin Phillips—inherits his genius, & is now a very scholarly youth of 18—rather an authority on the French language & literature.[38]

In 1903–4 I had private tutors, but in the autumn of 1904 I mingled with the world once more—to the extent of entering Hope St. High School. Here I was confronted for the first time with cosmopolitanism. Slater Avenue school is public, but it is rather a neighbourhood affair, with most of its pupils drawn from the old families. But Hope Street is near enough to the "North End" to have a considerable *Jewish* attendance. It was there that I formed my ineradicable aversion to the Semitic race. The Jews were brilliant in their classes—calculatingly & schemingly brilliant—but their ideals were sordid & their manners coarse. I became rather well known as an anti-Semitic before I had been at Hope Street many days. Knowing of my ungovernable temperament, & of my lawless conduct at Slater Avenue, most of my friends (if friends they may be called) predicted disaster for me, when my will should conflict with the authority of Hope Street's masculine teachers. But a disappointment of the happiest sort occurred. The Hope Street preceptors quickly *understood* my disposition as "Abbie" had never understood it; & by *removing all restraint,* made me apparently their comrade & equal; so that I ceased to think of discipline, but merely comported myself as a gentleman among gentlemen. I had nothing but the pleasantest of relations with the Hope Street faculty during my four years' stay there. Declining health greatly interfered with my course at High School, but I managed to attend intermittently from 1904 to

1908. I was allowed to enter & leave classes at any hour without notice or excuse; a privilege which was absolutely necessary, though it gave me a reputation of being something of a "teacher's pet". At the time I was fonder of science than of English, though I always received the highest marks in the latter as well as the former. My English teacher was an old lady named Mrs. Blake, who had a pleasant though slightly cynical disposition. She annoyed me with a certain doubt of the *originality* of my compositions. One day she called me to her desk & asked me if a certain essay of mine, on the planet Mars (or the moon—I forget which!), were not copied from a magazine article; to which I replied, that I had taken it *verbatim* from a rural paper! Upon her waxing wroth, I produced the clipping—with the prominently printed heading "By H. P. Lovecraft"!!! After that, Mrs. Blake was somewhat less sceptical of my original literary powers.[39]

Mention of my early printed articles leads me to speak of my first experiences with the press. A "letter to the editor" in the *Prov. Sunday Journal* of June 3, 1906, was my debut before the publick.[40] In August, 1906, I began my series of regular monthly astronomical articles in the newly founded *Providence Tribune,* a series which was later transferred to the *News,* which allows me all the space I desire.[41] During 1906, 1907, & 1908 I flooded the *Pawtuxet Valley Gleaner* with my prose articles.[42] This rural paper was the oracle of that section of the country from which my mother's family had originally come, & was taken for old times' sake in our household. The name "Phillips" is a magic word in Western Rhode Island, & the *Gleaner* was more than willing to print & feature anything from Whipple V. Phillips' grandson. Only the failure of the *Gleaner* put an end to my activity in its columns.

But my progress had received its severest blow in the spring of 1904. On March 28th of that year my beloved grandfather passed away as the result of an apoplectic stroke, & I was deprived of my closest companion. I was never afterward the same. His death brought financial disaster besides its more serious grief. As President of the Owyhee Land & Irrigation Co., an Idaho corporation with Providence offices, he had struggled hard to achieve vast success in the reclamation of Western lands. He had weathered many calamities such as the bursting of his immense dam on Snake River; but now that he was gone, the company was without its brains. He had been a more vital & important figure than even he himself had realised; & with his passing, the rest of the board lost their initiative & courage. The corporation was unwisely dissolved at a time when my grandfather would have *persevered*—with the result that others reaped the wealth which should have gone to its stockholders. My mother & I were forced to vacate the beautiful estate at 454 Angell Street, & to enter the less spacious abode at #598, three squares eastward. The combined loss of grandfather & birthplace made me the most miserable of mortals. My grandfather was a cheerful man, whose conversation always brightened me; but it was to be heard no more. My home had been my ideal of Paradise & my source of inspiration—but it was to be profaned & altered by other hands. Life from that day has held for me but one ambition—to regain the old place & reëstablish its glory—a thing I fear I can never accomplish. For twelve years I have felt like an exile.

In 1908 I was about to enter Brown University, when my health completely gave way—causing the necessary abandonment of my college career.[43] Of my non-university education, I never cease to be ashamed; but I know, at least, that I could not have done differently. I busied myself at home with chemistry, literature, & the like; composing some of the weirdest & darkest fiction ever written by man! I was a close disciple of Poe, & a diligent delver into the regions of the "grotesque & arabesque" to quote his own phrase. It was in this period that I wrote "The Alchemist", my U.A.P.A. credential, which will appear in *The United Amateur* for December. I shunned all human society, deeming myself too much of a failure in life to be seen socially by those who had known me in youth, & had foolishly expected such great things of me. From then to now, I have been practically unknown save to a very few old acquaintances. I am a complete disappointment, having accomplished absolutely nothing during my 26 futile years of existence. In 1912 my first bit of published *verse* appeared in *The Evening Bulletin*. It is a 62-line satire in the usual heroic couplet, ridiculing a popular movement on the part of the Italians of the Federal Hill slums to change the name of their main street from "Atwells' Avenue" to "Columbus Avenue". I pictured Providence in 2000 A.D., with *all* the English names changed to foreign appellations. This piece received considerable notice of a minor sort, I am told, though I doubt if it had much effect in silencing the Italians' clamour. The idea was so foolish that it probably died of its own weakness.[44]

In 1913 I had formed the reprehensible habit of picking up cheap magazines like *The Argosy* to divert my mind from the tedium of reality. One of the authors in that periodical so much excited my contempt, that I wrote a letter to the editor in quaint Queen-Anne prose, satirising the offending novelist. This letter, which was printed in the September number, aroused a veritable tempest of anger amongst the usual readers of the magazine. I was assailed & reviled by innumerable letters, which appeared in the editorial department. Among these hostile compositions was a piece of tetrameter verse by one John Russell, of Tampa, Fla., which had in it so much native wit, that I resolved to answer it. Accordingly I sent *The Argosy* a 44-line satire in the manner of Pope's "Dunciad." This was duly printed in January, 1914, & it created an immense sensation (of hostile character) amongst the *Argosy* readers. The editorial department had nothing but anti-Lovecraft letters the following month! And then I composed *another* satire, flaying all my tormentors in a stinging pentameter. This, too, was printed, till the storm of fury waxed high. Russell's replies were all rather clever, & well worth answering. Finally I sent Russell a personal communication which led to an ultimate peace—a peace established just in time, for T. N. Metcalf, the editor of *The Argosy* had intimated that the poets' war must soon end, since correspondents were complaining of the prominence of our verses in their beloved magazine. They feared we were usurping all the extra space! So Russell & I officially closed the affair with a composite poem—my part of which was in heroics; his in anapaest. This farewell to *The Argosy* took place in October, 1914, & I have never since beheld that worthy organ of popular literature.[45] Here is my part of the farewell.

The Critics' Farewell
To the Editor of THE ARGOSY:

> Indulgent Sir, pray spare an inch or two,
> And print the carping critics' joint adieu.
> So long it is since we began the fray
> That readers swear we've filched your Log* away!
> Forgive, we beg, the sinners that presume
> To fill with venomed verse such precious room.
> Inflam'd by war, and in a martial rage,
> We held a while the centre of the stage
> Till, blinded by each other's furious fire,
> We battled on, forgetting to retire.
> But fiercest feuds draw sometimes to their ends,
> And ancient foemen live to meet as friends:
> So do we now, conjoin'd in lasting peace,
> Lay down our pens, and mutual slander cease.
> What sound is this? 'Tis but a joyous yell
> From thankful thousands, as we say farewell!

Amateur journalism has many eyes, & long before this momentous conflict passed into history it was being watched by no less a celebrity than Hon. Edward F. Daas of Milwaukee, Wis. This gentleman, then official editor, communicated with Russell & with me in March, 1914, which resulted in my advent to the United on April 6. Russell tarried, & was brought in later as my own recruit. Subsequent events in my career are well known to you.

Such is the life history of an eccentric & egotistical character who proves the assertion that children of phenomenal precocity too often attain ultimate mediocrity or failure. Told of a real genius, the foregoing pages would be of interest; told of me, they are merely tedious & silly. It is pathetic, almost, to analyse the career & temperament of one whose oddities are not those of artistic genius, but merely those of feeble eccentricity. For my poor attainments I have so great a contempt, that I am almost moved to disavow the quality of *egotism*, & to consider my interest in my own affairs the result of mere selfish-

---

*The letters column was called "The Log-Book."

ness. Looking at myself objectively, I find merely a queer, sickly old fool at whom to sneer & laugh. I am of no use to anyone, least of all to myself. It would be better if I had the fatalism to do

>"What Cato did, & Addison approv'd."[46]

But let me end this painful chronicle!
>With sincerest wishes,
>>I am, Sir,
>>>Yr most oblig'd & obt Servt
>>>>H Lovecraft

P. S. I really did not intend to write such a horribly detailed autobiography. It is twenty times longer than I gave Moe, but when I recall childhood, a million memories lend wings to my pen. Childhood was to me the zenith of life, & the thread with the present is unbroken.

Notes

1. Thomas De Quincey (1785–1859), English essayist best known for *Confessions of an English Opium-Eater* (1822).

2. Lillian D. Clark (1856–1932).

3. Abbie C. Shepardson-Nauck (1857–1939) taught at the Slade Mansion Select School, 547 Elmwood Avenue (later at 169 and still later 387 Angell Street).

4. *Katinka* (1915), a musical play in three acts; lyrics by Otto Hauerbach, music by Rudolf Friml. A comic melodrama about star-crossed lovers at the Russian Embassy in Vienna. It ran for 220 performances on Broadway (1915–16) and toured widely.

5. See HPL's letter to Moe dated 1 January 1915 (*Letters to Maurice W. Moe* 43–47).

6. Whipple Van Buren Phillips (1833–1904).

7. The Adamson Act of 1916 mandated an eight-hour day for the four operating unions of railroad workers at the same pay as the previous ten-hour day. Challenged in the courts, it was upheld by the Supreme Court on 19 March 1917.

8. Brigadier-General Patrick (1835–1877) and Janet Margaret Doyle.

9. Thomas Buchanan Read (1822–1872), "Sheridan's Ride" (1865), a 63-line poem on an incident in the Civil War.

10. Winfield S. Lovecraft (b. 1853) was 37 the year HPL was born.

11. Winfield Scott Lovecraft (1853–1898) was not paralyzed at all but was hospitalized in 1893 because of dementia resulting from tertiary syphilis. HPL may have been told he was paralyzed as an excuse for not being allowed to visit his father in the hospital.

12. See HPL, "Department of Public Criticism" (April 1916): "Mr. Maurice W. Moe, the distinguished Private Critic, lately gave us the following opinion of our verse. 'You are,' he writes, 'steeped in the poetry of a certain age; an age, by the way, which cut and fit its thought with greater attention to one model than any other age before or since; and the result is that when you turn to verse as a medium of expression, it is just as if you were pressing a button liberating a perfect flood of these perfectly good but stereotyped for-

mulae of expression. The result is very ingenious, but just because it is such a skillful mosaic of Georgian "rubber-stamp" phrases, it must ever fall short of true art'" (*CE* 1.108).

13. Robie Alzada Place Phillips (1827–1896).

14. Dr. Franklin Chase Clark (1847–1915) married Lillian D. Phillips in 1902.

15. Annie E[meline] P[hillips] Gamwell (1866–1941).

16. 1869–1936. The Gamwells separated in 1916.

17. HPL wrote the sonnet "Night-Gaunts" c. January 1930 as part of *Fungi from Yuggoth*. He also incorporated night-gaunts into his novel *The Dream-Quest of Unknown Kadath* (1926–27).

18. "Scarcely any sober person dances, unless by chance he is insane." The sentence comes from Cicero's *Pro Mureno* 13, not the Catilinarian orations.

19. Actually, "The Poem of Ulysses, or, The Odyssey."

20. Robert Morrow managed the Providence Opera House from 1885 until his death in 1898. He owned 455 ("directly across the street") and 463 Angell Street.

21. Denman Thompson (1833–1911), American actor and playwright. *The Sunshine of Paradise Alley* premiered at Haverly's 14th Street Theatre in New York on 11 May 1896.

22. Marcus Aurelius Severus Antoninus, known as Caracalla (188–217), Roman emperor. He became joint ruler in 211 with his brother Geta, whom he caused to be murdered in 212, thereby becoming sole emperor. He was himself slain in the neighborhood of Carrhae in Mesopotamia.

23. Chester Pierce Munroe (1889–1943) and Harold Bateman Munroe (1891–1966) were HPL's closest friends in grammar and high school. See "Introducing Mr. Chester Pierce Munroe," in which HPL welcomes Chester into the UAPA.

24. HPL wrote a nonextant treatise entitled "An Historical Account of Last Year's War with SPAIN" (c. 1899). It is cited among the list of works at the end of *Poemata Minora, Volume II* (1902).

25. HPL appears to make several errors. *Poemata Minora,* Volume I (nonextant), apparently dates to 1901. The dedication of *Poemata Minora, Volume II* (1902) reads: "To the Gods, Heroes, & Ideals of the Ancients This Volume Is Affectionately Dedicated by a Great Admirer." It contains "Ode to Selene or Diana," "To the Old Pagan Religion," "On the Ruin of Rome," "To Pan," and "On the Vanity of Human Ambition."

26. Margaret Mather (1862?–1898), American stage actress who came out of retirement to play Imogen in *Cymbeline* but died while on tour.

27. Shakespeare, *Richard III* 5.3.177–78. Colley Cibber's version (*The Tragical History of King Richard III*) appeared in 1700.

28. Shakespeare, *Henry VI* 5.6.66–67.

29. In a letter to Alfred Galpin (29 August 1918) and in other documents, HPL dates his interest in chemistry to 1898 (see *Letters to Alfred Galpin and Others* 209–11).

30. Carsten Egeberg Borchgrevink (1864–1934), a Norwegian explorer, undertook the first major expedition to the Antarctic since the 1840s. Sailing from England in August 1898, he established the first camp on actual Antarctic soil in February 1899 and stayed all through the long Antarctic night (May–July 1899). On 19 February 1900 he walked on the Ross Ice Shelf. He returned to England that summer.

31. Manton Campbell Mitchell (1887–1929) was a Lieutenant-Colonel in the U.S. Army. General John J. Pershing (1860–1948) led a punitive expedition into Mexico to avenge Pancho Villa's raid on Columbus, NM, in March 1916. Pershing's force remained in Mexico until February 1917, and, although it never captured Villa, the relentless pursuit shattered his power.

32. Abbie Anna Hathaway (1852–1917), the principal of Slater Avenue School, lived at 97 Blackstone Boulevard.

33. Probably Montgomery's *The Leading Facts of American History* (1890).

34. William Herschel (1738–1822), German-born English astronomer and probably the most famous astronomer of the 18th century, discovered Uranus as well as many new nebulae, stars clusters, and binary stars.

35. I.e., David Garrick (1717–1779), perhaps the most famous actor of the 18th century and a close friend of Samuel Johnson.

36. Clio was the Muse of history, Urania of astronomy.

37. See Clark's *Susan's Obituary,* ed. Kenneth W. Faig, Jr. (Glenview, IL: Moshassuck Press, 1996), for a bibliography of his writings.

38. Phillips Gamwell died of tuberculosis on 31 December, at the age of 18.

39. The article in question was "Can the Moon Be Reached by Man?," in the *Pawtuxet Valley Gleaner* (12 October 1906).

40. HPL refers to "No Transit of Mars," *Providence Sunday Journal* (3 June 1906) but he had a letter published ("Long Distance Predictions: Weather Guessers Willing to Take Any Sort of Chances and Trust to Providence") in the *Amsterdam* [NY] *Evening Recorder and Daily Democrat* 27, No. 14 (6 September 1905): 3; rpt. LA No. 5 (2011): 111 [HPL quotation only].

41. HPL's astronomy articles in the Providence *Tribune* had ended in June 1908, and the articles that he wrote for the *Evening News* in January 1914 had nothing to do with the *Tribune* series.

42. Only the *Gleaner* articles for 1906 have come to light, as issues of the paper in 1907 and 1908 do not appear to be extant.

43. Actually, HPL never finished high school.

44. "Providence in 2000 A.D."

45. The poem was published in *Argosy* (September 1914). HPL submitted "The Rats in the Walls" to editor Robert H. Davis in 1923, but it was rejected.

46. The suicide note of Eustace Budgell (1686–1737), English man of letters, read: "What Cato did, and Addison approved, / Cannot be wrong." Budgell was, with Sir Richard Steele and Joseph Addison, a writer for the *Tatler.* He was also a contributor to the *Spectator* and the *Guardian.* Budgell refers to Addison's play, *Cato* (1713).

[20] [Post; AHT]

Dec. 27, 1916

My dear Kleiner:—

How much of my Heliconian fire was kindled at the Guiney hearth, I have never sought to calculate with exactitude. I should dislike to blame either this environment, or mine own heredity, for the crimes I perpetrate each day in the name of poesy! The poet of this family is *Miss* not *Mrs.* Guiney, as you have written it—though your rendering may be the archaic usage of "Mrs." which covers both cases! Mrs. Guiney was a very highly cultivated old lady, but not a poet. It is her spinster daughter who has progressed so far in the ascent of Parnassus. Miss Guiney is of the eccentric type of genius, & was a child of phenomenal precocity. It was impossible to educate her at home, so she was placed at a very early age in the convent school of Elmhurst, in Providence.[1] Here she was a perpetual trial for the "sisters" or teachers, (they were Popish nuns) who pronounced her wholly ungovernable. At the age of seven she was continually writing verses, but deeming it hurtful to her regular education, these "Sisters" forbade her to compose more; whereupon she would write secretly, & bury her effusions in the grounds of the school! Her career began so early, that it will prove a long one. She used to cause her mother much anxiety through disregard of health—going out without rubbers in the rain, or refusing sometimes to eat her meals. Mrs. Guiney once said to my mother, that she was proud of "Lou", (as she called her poet offspring) but that geniuses were very difficult persons to live with!

I was interested in your favourable mention of "Inspiration", because this is the first "poem" of mine selected for publication by *The National Magazine*. It appears in the November number under my own name. In the December number is another effort of mine, which you have never seen, but which I will herewith copy for your perusal:

Brotherhood

In prideful scorn, I watch'd the farmer stride
With step uncouth o'er road and mossy lane;
How could I help but distantly deride
The churlish, callous'd, coarse-clad country swain?

Upon his lips a mumbled ballad stirr'd
The evening air with dull cacophony;
In cold contempt, I shudder'd as I heard,
And held myself no kin to such as he.

But as he leap'd the stile and gain'd the field
Where star-fac'd blossoms twinkled thro' the hay,
His lumb'ring footfalls oftentimes would yield,
To spare the flow'rs that bloom'd along the way.

And while I gaz'd, my spirit swell'd apace;
With the crude swain I own'd the human tie;
The tend'rest impulse of a noble race
Had prov'd the boor a finer man than I!

It seems almost comical to me to have trash like this printed in a real illustrated professional magazine, with my name on the page of contents! It does not require a very strong sense of humour to see the essentially maudlin quality of "poetry" like "Brotherhood"—in fact, it was composed more in levity than in lyrical rage. But I am glad the National is willing to accept my junk—it makes me feel almost like an author! I wonder when they will print "The Bride of the Sea"?[2] If they will "stand for" that, they will take anything! By the way— "Brotherhood" will appear in the coming Tryout, signed "Theobald". Smith[3] does not yet know the secret of this gentleman's identity!

Like you, I perused "Tarzan of the Apes" with a most unliterary & uncritical interest, but I felt impelled to write the editor that the author had placed a *tiger* in *Africa*—& also, that the youthful Tarzan is made to *write out* several names (of his jungle companions) *before* he has learnt the relation betwixt oral sounds & written letters!! These are bad mistakes—but I enjoyed the tale none the less, & have read every one of its many sequels! What a confession for a would-be critic!!! By the way—the original Tarzan appeared not in *The Argosy* but *The All-Story*. The author, then using the nom de plume of "Norman Bean" now uses real name—Edgar Rice Burroughs.[4] He is a clever writer of imaginative fiction, but is of course subject to the usual limitations of his kind. In his stories of the planet Mars he made a gross astronomical error (he spoke of the year as having 687 Martian days. This is not so. The Martian year is 687 days long by *our* reckoning, but the Martian day is over half an hour longer than ours, giving 668⅔ to one Martian year.), which I detected & exposed in the Log Book (or whatever corresponds to that column) of the *All-Story*.[5]

[Post:] Campbell has loaned me a vast number of old books & papers treating of the earlier days of amateur journalism. Harrison's "Career" (1883) well illustrates the first decade of amateurdom, being a veritable mass of bad grammar.[6] The amateur world was then almost wholly given over to crude & half-educated youths, more famous for quantity than for quality. Then comes Nixon's "History of the N.A.P.A." (1900), which describes not only the dim grey dawn, but the succeeding noon of prosperity. The period of 1885–1890 seems to contain the best years of amateur history, though even then some of the more gifted Nationalities were dissatisfied, & sought to establish a better & more exclusive "Literary Lyceum". The failure of this "Lyceum" offers a discouraging precedent for similar reform efforts of the present! But the most interesting amateur book of all is Spencer's "Cyclopedia of the Literature of Amateur Journalism" (1891). This is a large work of 512 pages, & recalls the fact that many writers of great talent have adorned the amateur ranks in the past; indeed, to such an extent that nothing today seems comparable. Not that we have no authors of equal attainments; but we have so pitiably few!

I remain

Yr most Obedient Servt

Lewis Theobald, Jun.

Notes

1. Elmhurst Academy at the Convent of the Sacred Heart in Providence.

2. The poem did not appear in the *National Magazine*.

3. Charles W. "Tryout" Smith, editor/publisher of the *Tryout*. HPL published numerous poems in *Tryout* under pseudonyms.

4. The pen name of Edgar Rice Burroughs (1875–1950) was supposed to be "Normal Bean"—indicating he was an average individual—but was published as "Norman" for the serialization of the first John Carter of Mars story, "Under the Moons of Mars" (*All-Story* 22, No. 2 [February 1912], not for "Tarzan of the Apes" (*All-Story* 24, No. 2 [October 1912], which appeared under Burroughs's own byline.

5. HPL's comments on Burroughs's inaccuracies are found in his letter to the *All-Story Weekly* (7 March 1914); *Miscellaneous Writings* 497. HPL similarly wrote the magazine regarding a scientific error in A. Merritt's "The Moon Pool."

6. HPL discusses Thomas G. Harrison (1860–1911), sixth president of the National Amateur Press Association, in *Looking Backward* (1920; *CE* 1.247–50).

[21]   [AHT; Post]

Jan. 31, 1917

My dear Kleiner:—

Your comparison of Gerner[1] with the perpetrators of modern cinema serials, reminds me that I have just profited to the extent of $25.00 from some remarks on a very crude motion picture. Last week a local emporium of amusement known as Fay's Theatre offered a cash prize of $25.00 for the best essay or review concerning a "feature" picture displayed by them—a widely advertised picture entitled "The Image-Maker of Thebes" (Thanhouser–Pathé release.)[2] Having something of a critical nature, I resolved to witness the great five-reel film spectacle, & to participate in the competition. The picture was even poorer than I expected—a rough-hewn amateurish affair dealing with reincarnation in a pitifully feeble & hackneyed manner, containing not the slightest subtlety or technical skill in plot, directing, or acting. It was a hopeless relic of the time-honoured "10–20–30" melodrama. I gave up all hope of winning the prize, since I thought nothing but a favourable critique would be acceptable; but in a spirit of semi-humour I sent the management a *genuine* criticism covering four typewritten pages—an essay in my customary U.A.P.A. manner—which would, in colloquial parlance, be designated as a "roast"! Imagine, then, my surprise at receiving yesterday a cheque for $25.00 as winner of the prize—a cheque accompanied by a letter of exceedingly flattering nature!! Which goes to show that the best method of eliciting praise from a motion-picture exhibitor is to ridicule, satirise, & condemn the pictures he displays!! If you should chance to have seen this picture, I will send you a copy of my "prize-winning review."

Ah, me! how strange & how much past finding out is the elusive spirit of Youth. The gamin of the streets is old & hard ere he turns ten—he has lived through all the possibilities of his sort of life before he is fifteen, & he is weazened & aged at twenty. And yet—how swiftly slip the unnoticed years over the head of the recluse! But yesterday we were children of seven, scrawling our first idle rhymes. Before we have time to lift the pencil we are grown to manhood; yet scrawling as before, & wondering why the world calls us grown, when but a moment before it called us children. Then, after a few more paragraphs are written, they tell us we are no longer young men! But what is this middle life we are entering? We feel the same—see the same sun & stars, feel the same breezes, & enjoy the same verdant vistas. We even see the same children—like ourselves—& yet! After all, they are *not* the *same* children! They are the children of those who were children with us—& we are children still, though exiled from our kind by the absurd notion of the world that we are growing old! And pray, why should we grow old? What is the reward of age, if it be not death? Verily, such things baffle the understanding! It is better not to seek the underlying truths of life. Let us glide o'er the surface on a summer wind, & sink to our last sleep before we shall ever have awakened to the repellent realities of sordid existence. But pardon the philosophising!! I must be on the brink of *second* childhood!

[. . .]

[Post:] I note your interest in the amateur matter loaned to me by Campbell, & have asked him for permission to "sub-lend" Harrison's book to you, on account of your expressed desire to see it. It is sadly crude, & treats of an era before amateurdom assumed its fullest splendour. But for those who take a minute interest in amateur history, independently of its literary development, the "Career & Reminiscences" may be recommended as the most ingenuously veracious & detailed of all accounts of the boyish friendships, quarrels, & occasional publications which mark the pre-Halcyon days of the hobby.

I am most Sincerely yours,
H. P. Lovecraft

Notes

1. Nita Edna (Gerner) Smith (1881–1969), amateur journalist, wife of Edwin Hadley Smith (1869–1944), editor of the *Passing Show,* and "an enthusiast on all matters pertaining to the theatre" ("Department of Public Criticism," May 1915; *CE* 1.41).

2. *The Image Maker* (Thanhouser, 1917), directed by Eugene Moore; starring Valda Valkyrien, Harris Gordon, Inda Palmer, and Morgan Jones.

[22]   [AHT]

From THE KLEILO
Providence, R.I., May 23, 1917
Vol. XYZ No. ZYX

Some time ago, impressed by my entire uselessness in the world, I resolved to attempt enlistment despite my almost invalid condition. I argued that if I chose a regiment soon to depart for France; my sheer nervous force, which is not inconsiderable, might sustain me till a bullet or piece of shrapnel could more conclusively & effectively dispose of me. Accordingly I presented myself at the recruiting station of the R. I. National Guard & applied for entry into whichever unit should first proceed to the front. On account of my lack of technical or special training, I was told that I could not enter the Field Artillery, which leaves first; but was given a blank of application for the Coast Artillery, which will go after a short preliminary period of defence service at one of the forts of Narragansett Bay. The questions asked me were childishly inadequate, & so far as physical requirements are concerned, would have admitted a chronic invalid. The only diseases brought into discussion were specific ailments from which I had never suffered, & of some of which I had scarce ever heard. The medical examination related only to major organic troubles, of which I have none, & I soon found myself (as I thought) a duly enrolled private in the 9th Co. R.I.N.G.! As you may have deduced, I embarked upon this desperate venture without informing my mother; & as you may also have deduced, the sensation created at home was far from slight. In fact, my mother was almost prostrated with the news, since she knew that only by rare chance could a weakling like myself survive the rigorous routine of camp life. Her activities soon brought my military career to a close for the present. It required but a few words from our family physician regarding my nervous condition to annul the enlistment, though the army surgeon declared that such an annulment was highly unusual & almost against the regulations of the service. The fact is, I had really gotten the best of that astute medicus; for without making a single positive misstatement I had effectively concealed the many & varied weaknesses which have virtually blasted my career. Fortune had sided with me in causing no attack of blurred eyesight to come upon me during the physical examination. But my final status is that of a man "Rejected for physical disability." On the appointed day I shall register for conscription, but I presume my services will not be desired. My mother has threatened to go to any lengths, legal or otherwise, if I do not reveal all the ills which unfit me for the army. If I had realised to the full how much she would suffer through my enlistment, I should have been less eager to attempt it; but being of no use to myself it was hard for me to believe I am of use to anyone else. Still, I might have known that mothers are always solicitous of their offspring, no matter how worthless said offspring may happen to be! And so I am still in civil life, scribbling as of old, & looking with envious eye upon the Khaki-clad men who are now so frequently seen upon the streets of the business section & in the cars everywhere. I envy your half-brother his position as a soldier of the N.Y.N.G. During the past week I have been quite prostrated with a cold & with frequent spells of bad vision. Had my enlistment matured successfully, I wonder how I should have kept up! And yet—I will wager that I *would* have kept up some way or other. Now that death is about to become the fashion, I wish that I might meet it in the most approved way, "Somewhere in France". The army doctor pronounced me so sound organically, that I fear I have many weary years to drag out, unless the draft comes to my relief by taking me in spite of medical & maternal protests! *I* shall not protest on mine own account!

Before leaving the subject of the *res militaria*, I must add an item concerning Alan Seeger which has just come to my notice. A recent rumour declares that the young poet did not die directly from his wounds, but shot himself in the temple after having been injured so direfully that death was only a few hours off. It accords with his notions of bodily pleasure & enjoyment of life, that he should end his existence when no more potentialities of bliss or glory remained. He was a strange youth, a pagan & a Sybarite whose martial experience was a joyously accepted part of the full life he worshipped & sought to live. Though I am intensely fond of his poetical technique (aside from his few bad rhymes & the like), I cannot respect him as a man so much as Rupert Brooke,[1] whose character was so much less sordid, materialistic, & sophisticated. Brooke was the greater, higher, less animal man in every respect. As he predicted, his lonely island grave is indeed "forever ENGLAND".

Your experience at the tabernacle of the Rev. W. Sunday[2] is one which interested me very much. He is indeed a strange character, & one who will be long remembered either as a great religious leader or as a curiosity. I have never heard any of his harangues, but am aware of his remarkable & semi-hypnotic power over certain psychological types. I doubt if he could affect me greatly, since I have an acute consciousness of the flimsy base on which his discourses rest; but I should surely not listen without respect, for I agree thoroughly with his ethical as distinguished from his theological tenets, & admire him for the practical good he has undoubtedly done. I fancy that I should not need much "converting" save upon points of dogma; for my life & morals are surely conventional enough to suit the most exacting of evangelists. But on pure religion, I have a vague though certain feeling that Sunday & I should differ more or less. In fact, I fear our argument would soon develop into a fist fight!

I remain as ever

Yr. most oblig'd, humble, & obedient Serv[t]

H P Lovecraft

Notes

1. See RK 33n2.
2. Billy Sunday (1862–1935), itinerant evangelical preacher.

[23]   [AHT]

June 22, 1917

My dear Kleiner:—

I am feeling desolate & lonely indeed as a civilian. Practically all my personal acquaintances are now in some branch of the service, mostly Plattsburg[1] or R.I.N.G. Yesterday one of my closest friends entered the Medical (not as a doctor, but as an assistant—carrying stretchers, driving ambulances, &c. &c.) Corps of the regular army. The physical tests for this corps are very light, & in spite of my previous rejection for Coast Artillery I would try to enter, were it not for the almost frantic attitude of my mother; who makes me promise every time I leave the house that I will not make another attempt at enlistment! But it is disheartening to be the one noncombatant among a profusion of proud recruits. The one fellow-sufferer with whom I can condole is a youth just discharged from Plattsburg on the ground that *homesickness* was making him ill. These are stirring times indeed! Rhode-Islanders are more partial to the army than the navy—probably because familiarity breeds contempt. Newport, long a naval base & the seat of a training station, has made drunken & dissipated sailors a common sight; so that olive-drab is more appealing than navy-blue in these parts.

Your anecdote of the literary darky who claimed Solomon as a racial brother was very entertaining. But after all, many are puzzled by the old-fashioned use of the word "black" in describing a dark Caucasian. I am sending the latest & perhaps most amusing of Brudder Evans' advertisements. Uncle Justus is gittin' to be a great prophet, even though he be "common in looks"![2] What, I wonder, goes on inside those thick, wool-clad skulls? The negro is obviously a link betwixt apedom & man; though all species do not show equal affinity to the beast. The Bantu of Central & Western Africa (The Guinea Coast nigger) is the most gorilla-like; whilst the tribes of Eastern & Southern Africa are more or less permeated with blood from other races. The Bantu is undoubtedly the purest negro type—the ape-man in all his sweet simplicity. Canoe migrations from India & the Indies have probably given the Hottentot his superior qualities; while a steady trickling of Jewish & Arabic blood is doubtless responsible for the good traits of the East Coast blacks. There is no doubt but that Semitic whites once had colonies far down the African coast—along the Red Sea & Indian Ocean.

I was properly shocked at your account of amateur Bohemianism in New-York, as exemplified by your recent *spree* wherein you failed to reach home till morning. I should be more shocked if I were not writing these words at the unholy hour of 3 a.m. To tell the truth, I am the most nocturnal of mortals—though there is doubtless a distinction betwixt being *out* late, & merely being *up* late. I love to pore over ancient volumes or scribble letters & bad verse when all the world is wrapp'd in silence & gloom. In spirit I am lingering at Will's Coffee-House with those congenial companions who died a century & a half ago.

I am, Sir, yr most oblig'd & Obedient Servt

H Lovecraft

Notes

1. Plattsburg (now spelled Plattsburgh), a city in northeastern New York State, is the site of the United States Military Reservation. In 1916 it became one of five camps in the eastern U.S. for the rapid training of officers to serve in the army in the event of American entry into World War I.

2. See HPL to Maurice W. Moe (30 May 1917): "speaking of eccentric theories, my sense of humour impels me to enclose for your perusal & amusement a *negro* advertisement which appears each day in the *Providence News*. Behold! from the humblest of races springs the greatest of prophets—Justus J. Evans, D.G., The Founder, Constructor, and Archbishop of the Only & Original 'Almighty Church'—modestly described by himself as 'the WISEST TEACHER that there is now in creation, so far as man is concerned.' Yea, verily, the African is a peculiar animal! I suppose Evans is a typical black 'exhorter' who has saved up enough money to break into print—and he has certainly 'broken in' with commendable vigour! The negro mind is a singular thing—a centre of grotesquely distorted ideas & extravagant conceptions that would brand any Caucasian brain as idiotic or insane. I wonder how even so plebeian a paper as the *News* can bring itself to accept such ludicrous advertising. Rev. W. Sunday must look to his laurels, now that this ebony victim of megalomania & exaggerated ego hath dawned above the theological horizon!" (*Letters to Maurice W. Moe* 63).

[24]   [Post]

July 17, 1917

Concerning C. W. Smith—I had heard of his retiring disposition, but had no idea of the extent of the latter quality. He once sent me a photograph of his "office", as well as of his two mascots—Annette & the "Tryout Cat".[1] Characteristically enough, he failed to send a picture of himself! He is an ardent stamp collector, & has acquired an enormous number of uncancelled postals & stamped envelopes of ancient vintage, which he sometimes uses. A short time ago, he used an 1880 envelope in writing me. A card I received from him yesterday is a relic of the nineties. I find Smith a very interesting person, since his character renders him almost a living incarnation of the conventional types of pastoral poetry. As he roams the fields & woods with his diminutive mascot, I fancy he is much like the old poets' conception of some Sicilian or Arcadian Damoetas,[2] who spent the day in innocent sport, & danced to the homely melody of the oaten reed. He reminds me of the old "post-boy" in the drama "Rosemary"[3]—whose seventy winters rested but lightly upon him, & who would frequently declare that he was still "a boy at 'eart!"

I hear you are contributing to Cook's *Vagrant*. Cook is a faithful amateur, & displays an enthusiasm which deserves recognition. I may meet him next month, for he will pass through Providence on a trip. He will use a short story of mine in December—a bit of horror entitled "The Tomb".[4] This is a Poe-like analysis of a gruesome case of monomania. But I am—if possible—a poorer fictioneer than poet. As in the case of my verses, I falter in chagrin when I peruse a really good amateur story. After reading Ernest A. Edkins' ghastly tale "Phantasus" in a collection of amateur stories loaned me by Campbell,[5] I realise how inefficient I am in this province. Amateur Journalism at first makes a man egotistical, but no man can read Spencer's "Cyclopaedia" or other works of that period, without swiftly learning his place and recognising his own inferiority. Edkins was a phenomenal writer—something of real, stark terror sweeps through certain passages both of his prose & verse.

Notes

1. The cat was named Sir Thomas Tryout. HPL wrote an elegy ("Sir Thomas Tryout") when the cat died in 1921.
2. A conventionalized shepherd in the pastoral poetry of Theocritus, Virgil, and other ancient poets.
3. Louis N. Parker (1852–1944) and Murray Carson (1865–1917), *Rosemary,* first staged in London and New York in 1896 and revived in 1915. It is a sentimental romance about a man who ages fifty years in the course of the play.
4. Written 1917, but not published until 1922. It is not clear why the story took so long to appear in print. Around 1919 or 1920 HPL thought it might be published in Cook's *Monadnock Monthly,* but it did not appear there.
5. Ernest A. Edkins (1867–1946), celebrated amateur writer of the late 19th and early 20th centuries. HPL came in direct contact with him only in 1932. Edkins's weird tale "Phantasus" appeared in *The Sheik and Other Stories* [no editor given] (Chicago: Walter C. Chiles, 1906), 85–114.

[25] [AHT]

The Deanery, St. Angell's, July 24, 1717

My dear Kleiner:—

I fear I was vague in referring to Mr. Florenz Ziegfeld[1] of the United. He is not a *new* recipient of the Story Laureateship, but has been Story Laureate during the year just closing. He is not a very studious young man, I fancy; for his prize-winning story was a simple & frothy (albeit clever) piece. But considering the dearth of fiction last year, he is entitled to whatever distinction he received. Despite his name, his story cannot be ranked amongst the downright "Follies of 1916"!

With customary expressions of Esteem,

I am, Sir,

Ever your most ob^t Servt
H. Lovecraft

Notes

1. Florenz Ziegfeld (1867–1932), impresario. His brother, Arthur F. Ziegfeld, edited the amateur journal *Ziegfeld's Follies,* to which Florenz contributed. The title of the journal is a play on the Ziegfeld Follies, an annual theatrical revue on Broadway from 1907 to 1931 arranged by Florenz Ziegfeld.

[26] [AHT; Post]

The Deanery, St. Angell's, 27th Aug., 1917

My dear Kleiner:—

Your experience in the toils of conscription is quite interesting, & reveals a general inefficiency & stupidity on the part of the examiners which is quite the rule throughout the nation. In this city, a *one-eyed* man, exempted by the first doctor, had to pass on to a second physician for full examination—whilst another young man, who had already enlisted in the navy, was called up through a mistake, & subjected to the whole routine before being exempted as a member of his country's forces. I am not sure whether or not I shall undergo examination. The examining physician of my ward is a friend of the family, & I think that possibly a statement from the National Guard physician who rejected me will be sufficient. The Guard examination was somewhat less clumsy than that which you underwent. It was conducted in an office whose privacy was absolute, & whose floor & temperature were both suitable. The physician who conducted this examination, Maj. Augustus W. Calder,[1] has just been rejected himself by the Federal surgeons as physically unfit. He is receiving the same treatment he finally gave me! If my mother had not interfered, I should certainly have slipped by, & would now be with my company (9th Coast Artillery) at Fort Standish, in Boston Harbour. It would have been an interesting experience, & would have either killed or cured me by this time.

[. . .]

[Post:] I had wholly forgotten about the story "The Secret Cave", which you returned. I was a persistent fiction-writer in youth, & turned out rubbish of that sort by the bushel. A large proportion is still in my possession, hence one tale was scarcely to be missed. The next time I visit the attic I will bring down two or three "thrillers" of the vintage of 1899 or 1900—which I will send you for your amusement. I revelled in tragedy & sudden death, & had a marked partiality for graveyards & ghosts. When I took up fiction again, a month or two ago, I found that my tastes had changed but little. My two latest, "The Tomb" & "Dagon", are enough to turn your hair white—or would be, if written more skilfully. They will appear in print some time next year; one in *The Vagrant* & the other in *The Phoenician*.[2] Both are analyses of strange monomania, involving hallucinations of the most hideous sort. Well may the shade of the late Mr. Poe of Baltimore turn green through jealously!

[. . .]

I am Sir, Ever yr most

    Oblig'd, humble, & ob^t Servt

        Lewis Theobald, Jun.

Notes

1. Augustus Woodbury Calder, Sr. (1869–1936), a Brown graduate (class of 1891) who gained his M.D. (1895) from Harvard. He practiced medicine at 184 Angell Street in Providence (1898–1918). In 1911 he was named chief surgeon of the R.I.N.G.
2. For "The Tomb" see RK 23n3.

[27]   [AHT; Post]

                                Sept. 24, 1917

My dear Kleiner:—

[AHT:] I have never beheld a "poem" from the pen of Mr. Lindsay,[1] though I may look him up some day at the library. As I think I have intimated before, I do not read the new "poetry", save when I skim over a typical collection by Amy Lowell, Ezra Pound, or some equally notorious dunce, for the purpose of obtaining material for a satire. There is nothing in this radicalism—it is all so arrantly nonsensical & foolishly futile! What do the poor fools want, anyway? I wish they'd might all be chloroform'd & put out of their misery. The other day Campbell sent me a copy of *The Seven Arts*, a magazine almost as radical in its way as the late but little lamented *Bruno's Weekly*.[2] It opens with a treasonable anti-war essay whose classic, fluent prose contains not a single sound idea or tenable theory; continues with a silly piece of Sinn Fein raving by the Irish author Padraic Colum; has a flagrantly disloyal **editorial in vers libre** by James Oppenheim[3]—an editorial whose outré verbiage at first gives no meaning whatever, but which boils down to a plea for a pacifist revolution when deciphered into respectable English; & contains in addition as choice a mess of soft-headed literary garbage as one might wish to behold. And what is it all for? Probably not even the editor & contributors know—yet the sport of juggling with words, ideas, & phantasies probably pleases them just as such frivolous things as games, sports, & vaudeville sometimes please us. But they carry their nonsense too far, & take it so absurdly seriously! Poor creatures!

Just a week ago, I enjoyed the honour of a personal call from W. Paul Cook, amateur of eminence & editor of *The Vagrant*. I was rather surprised at his appearance, for he is rather more rustic & carelessly groomed than I had expected a man of his celebrity to be. In fact, his antique derby hat, unpressed garments, frayed cravat, yellowish collar, ill-brushed hair, & none too immac-

ulate hands made me think of my old friend Sam Johnson; another great literary man who was somewhat negligent as to personal appearance & the like.
But Cook's conversation makes up for whatever outward deficiencies he may
possess. Though not overwhelmingly bookish, he has a keen mind, dry humour, & an infinite & quite encyclopaedic knowledge of the events & per-
sonages of amateur journalism past & present. I cannot see how one head can
hold such a mass of amateur history & anecdote. He is opinionated to a considerable degree, & has scant love for any existing amateur press association;
but his love of the general cause is so great, that he is ever willing to oblige
any amateur irrespective of association affiliations. He is to print the September *United Amateur*, though he will not accept a regular appointment as Official Publisher. His coming *Vagrant* promises to be an ample & notable issue,
having, I believe, 56 pages. I think I shall have Cook print *The Conservative* in
future, for he underbids all competitors. His low rates are a philanthropic favour to amateurdom, & are based upon a complete sacrifice of personal profit. He is so anxious to establish a revival of amateur journalism, that he is
doing the work absolutely at cost. His rates are as follows:

> 300 copies 5 × 7—per page—$0.85
> 300 copies 6 × 9—per page—$1.05
> 300 copies 7 × 10—per page—$1.25

[Post:] I was greatly pleased with Cook for he is interesting, high-minded,
& intellectual in tastes. He takes amateur journalism with phenomenal seri-
ousness—it is his world, so to speak; & its history & institutions are sacred to
him. It seems strange to meet my fellow-amateurs face to face, & discuss
orally those topics which I have been accustomed to write in my letters. As it
is, Cook makes only the third amateur with whom I have had a good talk;
Stoddard & Edward H. Cole being the others.[4]

I appreciate your remarks regarding my metrical effusions, as represented
by "The Rhyming Critic" & "Sophia Simple" pieces.[5] I have ever had a certain hesitancy in shewing my humorous attempts to the public, since in no
field is the amateur bard so liable to make a complete fool of himself, as in
that of levity & jocundity. When the average amateur would fain grow witty,
'tis a matter of doubt whether to laugh with, or at, him!

It has been remarked of that celebrated non-professional bard, Arthur H.
Goodenough, that much of his reputation is due to his consistent avoidance
of humour; wherein his dignity might have been lost, & his fame made cheap.
However, I may some time permit Mr. Theobald to air his flippancy.

Regarding those bards whom we have chosen as our respective poetic
models, I must admit that you are probably more familiar with my favourites
than I am with yours! With the death of Dr. Johnson, a veil seems to come
across my literary vista, nor have I read extensively in any of your chosen poets save Dr. Holmes. Holmes was personally known to many members of my

family, & was once seen by me (the year before his death); which circumstances, coupled with the Doctor's admitted archaism (he has been called the 'American Pope'), gave me a marked prejudice in his favour. I admire, but do not love, Longfellow, have respect for Bryant, & toleration for Whittier—but, in general, dislike the nineteenth-century bards save Dr. Holmes. Emerson rather bores me, for he is too speculative & philosophical. The more I observe mankind, the less sense I see in trying to reduce his species to philosophic systems. We are at best but creatures of an hour, unworthy of the grave attention bestowed upon us by owlish analysts & serious-minded pedants. I deem that poet best, who has the most courtly & pleasing polish; who can divert & enliven the mind with the smoothest numbers & most agreeable images; nor do I think that any soul-searching rhapsodist deserves so well of the public, as a plain man of sense or an honest humourist. As I wrote some time ago in a piece published in *The Tryout:*

> In search of Truth the hopeful zealot goes,
> But all the sadder turns, the more he knows![6]

[. . .]
    I remain
        As ever yr. humble Servant
          L Theobald, Jun.

Notes

1. Vachel Lindsay (1879–1931), a leading American poet of the period.

2. *Bruno's Weekly* (1915–16; later *Bruno's* [1917]) an avant-garde magazine edited by Guido Bruno (1884–1942), a New York intellectual known as the "Pope of Greenwich Village."

3. *Seven Arts* 2 (September 1917): Randolph Bourne, "A War Diary" (535–47); Padraic Colum, "Youngest Ireland" (608–23); James Oppenheim, "Editorial" (624–26). Bourne (1886–1918) was a leading American literary and social critic. Colum (1881–1972) was a prominent Irish poet and playwright. Oppenheim (1882–1932) was an American poet, novelist, and essayist.

4. HPL had met William B. Stoddard, a Brooklyn amateur, sometime in 1914 at the Crown Hotel in Providence. He had met Edward H. Cole at a meeting of the Providence Amateur Press Club in November 1914.

5. "On the Death of a Rhyming Critic" and "To Mistress Sophia Simple, Queen of the Cinema." RK must have read the latter poem in ms.; it is a reply to a poem by RK himself, "To a Movie Star" (see Appendix), published next to HPL's on the same page of the *United Amateur.*

6. "Fact and Fancy," ll. 11–12.

[28]   [AHT]

Oct. 14, 1917

My dear Kleiner:—

Like you, I have not so far seen a Goldwyn motion picture;[1] & form my judgment from newspaper accounts alone. In time, I believe the best pictures will attain a level entitling them to serious artistic consideration & criticism; though I scarcely think that they can bear comparison with the spoken drama. Drama, in order to mount the heights, seems to me to require the full expression of the characters, including voice. In recalling dramatic climaxes, I find that at least in my case the most effective impression comes through the ears. Rhetoric is a wonderful thing, & a passage of Shakespeare's verse well uttered can move an audience as no pantomime possibly could. Hamlet without his lines would be a mere shadow. A voiceless Richard III would be a clown. In comedy the lack of dialogue is irreparable. How Sheridan would have groaned to see his "School for Scandal" robbed of that scintillating succession of epigrams which only conversation can convey![2] I saw the Kalem version[3] several years ago, & doubt if Mr. Garrick would have thought it worth writing a prologue for, as he so kindly did for Mr. Sheridan in 1777, when the piece first came upon the town. But the fact that the motion picture possesses certain limitations, should not cause it to be lightly estimated. It is certainly capable of vast development, and can be made to convey artistic expression of the very first quality. Its ease of distribution is likely to make it a potent instrument in the diffusion of culture & good taste. To me a good motion picture is vastly more acceptable than a poor or poorly acted drama, & I am a regular patron of the Strand Theatre, whose management have placed me on their mailing list for advance notices of films. Chaplin has been greatly hampered in the past by the execrable taste of his directors. Not one in ten of the old "Keystone" comedies could be witnessed without disgust; & after the comedian graduated from them, their traditions could not help but cling slightly to him. Time will enable him to assert his individuality more completely above the commonplace conventions of cinematographic buffoonery. Fairbanks,[4] as you say, doubtless has much less of actual genius. I am fond of watching his pictures because there is a certain wholesomeness present, which the Chaplin type sometimes lacks. The atmosphere of squalor too often clouds the merit of the Chaplin plays. After a time, the fastidious eye tires of looking at rags & dirt; & turns gratefully to the breezy, captivating antics of the more human if less artistic Fairbanks. It is an old maxim in fiction & the drama, that a hero should be such that every man in the audience can imagine himself in that character. Fairbanks might well represent any virile young American, but what spectator could fancy himself a Chaplin? Both have their place, & the loss of either would subtract sadly from the gaiety of nations. Fairbanks, content to please in his own way, doubtless recognises the superior endowments of the clever little cockney Jew without enjoying that inimitable personality in the least!

Cook's visit was indeed a memorable event; an event which gives me a sense of closer kinship with the amateur world. His mind is the direct antithesis of his attire—brilliant, well-ordered, & possessed of excellent taste. I presume that amateurs do vary somewhat in the degree of care they bestow upon their appearance—in fact, I recall that you mentioned a certain youth at the National convention as being groomed in particularly faultless style *for an amateur*. However—it must take courage to face the world with a frayed tie, shiny elbows, & baggy knees. I should prefer to attain Johnsonian eminence before adopting Johnsonian negligence. There are degrees in all things. I am surely no fop, with my black cravats & plain garments, but there is such a thing as an aesthetic sensitiveness which imposes limits.

I am, my dear Sir,

     Ever yr. most oblig'd, humble, & obedient Servant,

        L. Theobald, Junr.

Notes

1. Samuel Goldwyn Pictures, a company established in 1916 by Samuel Goldwyn (born Samuel Goldfish, 1879–1974) and Archibald Selwyn after Goldwyn resigned as chairman of the board of Paramount. In 1924 it became Metro-Goldwyn-Mayer (MGM).

2. *Richard III* was released as a silent film four times between 1908 and 1919, *Hamlet* six times between 1907 and 1921, and *The School for Scandal* twice in 1914 and 1923.

3. The Kalem film company was founded in 1907 by George Kleine, Samuel Long, and Frank Marion, the name derived from the first letters of the last names of the three co-owners. This coinage may have influenced the formation of the Kalem Club, HPL's cadre of literary associates in New York City in 1924–26, whose name was formed on the same principle.

4. Douglas Fairbanks, Sr. (1883–1939), American stage and film actor who became famous for swashbuckling roles, especially with Mary Pickford (whom he married in 1920).

[29]   [AHT; Post]

                                      Nov. 8, 1917

My dear Kleiner:—

[AHT:] Loveman has become reinstated in the United through me. Jew or not, I am rather proud to be his sponsor for the second advent to the Association. His poetical gifts are of the highest order, & I doubt if the amateur world can boast his superior. The Laureateship, should he enter his work, rests betwixt him & Lowrey.[1] His variety of ideas, facility of expression, & background of classical & antiquarian knowledge, place him in the front rank.

What you & Loveman say of Austin Dobson[2] makes me somewhat desirous of re-reading him; & I think I shall give him some attention in the near future. Possibly I shall emerge from obscurity some day as the only genuine light poet in amateurdom. Since other amateur bards seem to be unable to achieve success in this medium, I shall perhaps aim for distinction in a field so little occupied, & hitherto neglected by me save for occasional effusions.

My latest efforts are of a somewhat varied nature. "Autumn", which I enclose, is about what might be expected of me. I take infinite pleasure in these venerable heroics, for to me Nature shines most brightly through the lenses of pastoral imagery. I can never think of natural beauty, but in the terms of the eighteenth century. If I see a pleasing prospect of a distant town, I think of it as

> The cluster'd spires and roofs that gaily gleam
> Across the verdant plain & glist'ning stream.

If I am struck with some idyllic vistas of tilled land & cottages, I see

> The bending corn that in profusion grows
> Where rural virtue earns its calm repose.

If a tangled brake or cluster of trees moves my fancy, I think of

> The twining thicket & the shady grove
> Where supple Fauns in artless pleasure move.[3]

Even the *allowable rhyme* suggests itself!

Another recent production of mine, which I will enclose, has a very different metre & appeal. I think I shall send this piece—"Nemesis"—to *The Vagrant,* since Cook seems fond of the unusual. It was written in the sinister small hours of the black morning after Hallowe'en, which may account for the colouring & atmosphere! It presents the conception, tenable to the orthodox mind, that nightmares are the punishment meted out to the soul for sins committed in previous incarnations—perhaps millions of years ago! The hybrid metre, a cross betwixt that of Poe's "Ulalume" & Swinburne's "Hertha", ought to satisfy the couplet-hating souls of yourself & Mo!

[Post:] Anent *The Vagrant,* & Cook's editorials, I cannot but marvel at the patient accuracy with which he delves into the minutiae of amateur history. He chronicles the trivialities of a convention as faithfully as most men would record an historical assemblage of statesmen. I am sure my endurance would be quite exhausted, should I endeavour to preserve in full the data of the associations—including those dreary intervals when literature was at a low ebb, & nothing occupied the stage but the low bickerings & cheap festivities of very mediocre individuals. Such I believe to have been the condition of the United about fifteen or twenty years ago, until the original assortment of members became supplanted by better material. I believe, from what I have seen of old papers, that the superiority may have rested with the National in those days—surely the prosy & plebeian politicians cannot have claimed equality with the really brilliant minds of amateurdom. And yet, I suppose it is well to have records of everything—so Cook is doubtless to be congratulated on his patience.

At the repeated solicitation of many persons who declared that my aloofness from the National was a barrier to inter-associational harmony, I sent in an application for membership about a week ago. My connexion, however, will be purely nominal; as I gave the Nationalites very clearly to understand. I have time & strength only for my own association, yet was willing to have my name on the National's list if it would help any. I bear no ill will toward the present Martin[4] administration, which is quite different from the former conditions which so strongly repelled me. There was an unscholarly & blustering quality about certain political rings which I could not help loathing. Daas will be furious at my recognition of the National, but personally, I deemed it best to respond to what seem to be genuinely friendly overtures on the part of the older association. Should the National presume to treat the United with disrespect again, I shall be the first to resent the act. My exhibition of good will is based upon Edward H. Cole's statement that he has induced Graeme Davis to abandon his anti-United campaign. If Davis will be so good, so will I!

I remain, Sir, ever yr most oblig'd, humble, obedient Serv[t]
Ludovicus Theobaldus, Jun[r.]

Notes

1. Perrin Holmes Lowrey (1886–1971), English professor and amateur poet. HPL frequently discusses his work in various "Department of Public Criticism" columns of the period.
2. [Henry] Austin Dobson (1840–1921), English essayist and poet in light verse. Like HPL, he imitated the 18th-century poets in much of his poetry. HPL owned volume 2 of his *Poems on Several Occasions* (New York: Dodd, Mead, 1895; *LL* 270).
3. HPL is apparently the author of these verses.
4. Harry E. Martin (1887–1972), president of the NAPA (1917–18).

[30]   [AHT]

Nov. 27, 1917

My dear Kleiner:—

I enclose a pseudo-Poe piece composed a day or so ago as an illustration.[1] The vagueness & mysticism are not at all natural—the weirdness is merely "laid on" as with a whitewash brush, in imitation of modern obscurity. The thought, of course, is something like that of my "Ἀλήθεια Φρικώδης" in The Kleicomolo.[2] The allusion to "Israfel" is made simply because Poe is fond of that allusion. The word "Cacodaemon" (or *cacodemon*, to use a more modern spelling) is employed for no other reason than that it is a big word which will send the admiring reader to the dictionary. If the public cannot understand what I say at the first glance, they will deem me deep & exclusive—a true exponent of modern culture. There is nothing like being *recherché* in these degenerate days! But when in a serious vein, I do not write for the modern public. They would not read my work even if I did—so I have the independence & advantages of obscure mediocrity. I do not "try to revive" taste for the simple ornaments & well-known Graeco-Roman allusions of yore—I merely ignore taste. Writing for my own pleasure, I care not how my readers may regard the result. If they relish it, well & good. If not, perusal is not compulsory! I do, however, resent the Boeotian[3] indifference to classical beauty which the majority exhibit today. The old images & allusions may be trite indeed, yet they are at least superior to the studied sterility of modern verse. They have the insuperable advantage of calling up unnumbered trains of thought which delight the mind, & of invoking a multiplicity of beautiful & fanciful associations. I do not think the modern public are so much ignorant of, as indifferent to, the charms of the classics. If they be indeed ignorant of these things, then they are not entitled to consideration as an intelligent publick at all. They are, in such a case, a mere *canaille* to be shunned. But I care little either way. I live in the past, & spin my antique couplets in serene indifference to the seething world about me.

I am yr. most obedient humble Serv[t]

H Lovecraft

Notes

1. "Astrophobos." Israfel is mentioned in l. 18; cacodaemons in l. 35.
2. The central section ("The Frightful Truth") of "The Poe-et's Nightmare" (1916). The entire poem was included in a letter to the Kleicomolo (April 1917), 92–99.
3. Boeotia, a region of Greece, developed a reputation in antiquity for the intellectual slowness of its citizens.

[31] [AHT]

December 23, 1917

My dear Kleiner:—

What you say about your painstaking habits of composition interests me exceedingly. Your case is both like, & opposite, my own—paradoxical statement! As with you, prolonged effort exhausts me completely—but unlike your case, letter-writing or verse composition is not effort for me. That is why my verses are so bad & my letters so careless. If I tried to stop & think what I am writing, I would be unable to continue. I work when the inspiration or mood takes me, & dash off whatever I have to write with great speed—then I am generally too indolent to polish what I have written, & so inflict it upon a patient publick in the rough. Of course, there are many exceptions to this, but curiously enough, those pieces which I have revised most, have generally been received with the least favour. There is always some vague couplet floating about in my head, & once I set it to paper, others seem naturally to follow—so long as I stick to familiar Georgian ground. My whole interest seems wrapped up in the eighteenth century—I preserve as much of its spirit as possible in the furnishing of my room, & always think of myself in breeches & full-bottomed periwig. It is when I attempt verse revision that I encounter really prostrating labour. This task, unless it be of Mr. Hoag's quaintly ancient lines, is exceedingly distressful to me; & an hour of Bush work[1] is enough to set my head throbbing in agony. As to letters, my case is peculiar. I write such things exactly as easily & as rapidly as I would utter the same topics in conversation; indeed, epistolary expression is with me largely replacing conversation, as my condition of nervous prostration becomes more & more acute. I cannot bear to talk much now, & am becoming as silent as the Spectator himself! My loquacity expends itself on paper. This habit gives to my letters a certain careless atmosphere & lack of rhetorical precision which I fear make an unfavourable impression upon my more scholarly correspondents; but these gentlemen I would admonish to regard my communications not as studied letters, but as fragments of discourse, spoken with the negligence of oral intercourse rather than the formal correctness of literary correspondence. A purist might easily pick an hundred flaws in any page of my letters, but I trust they do not interfere with the right understanding of what I say.

My questionnaire arrived yesterday, & I discussed it with the head physician of the local draft board—who happens to be a family friend & even a remote relative.[2] I wished, if possible, to place myself in class I, so that I might help in a clerical way as much as I could—as typist, clerk, or something of the sort. But he knew too much of my constitutional ailments, & directed me to class myself in Class V. Div. G.—totally & permanently unfit. This will be later acted upon by himself & his two associate physicians, but he does not think a reversal very likely; so that I fear whatever service I give the government must be unofficial & strictly voluntary. As he pointed out, my lack of physical endurance would make me a hindrance rather than a help in any work requiring schedule & discipline; also, my manifold weaknesses make me unable to endure any conditions of living except those of a comfortable home. Any work under military auspices would require my presence at camps & various places to which a physician would be loth to consign one of my condition. It is not flattering to be reminded of my utter uselessness twice within the space of six months, but the war is a great exposer of human failings & inefficiency. Had not my mother disturbed my ambitious effort of last May, in which I utilised my absurdly robust-looking exterior as a passport to martial glory in the National Guard, I should now be digging trenches, drilling, & pounding a typewriter at Fort Standish in Boston Harbour, where the 9th Co. R.I. Coast Artillery is placed at present. I wonder if a strictly amateur writer would be in any way acceptable to "The Vigilantes", of whom so much is heard lately.[3] Theirs is a worthy work, & a very necessary one in view of the subtle anti-government propaganda which remains to be combatted. You may be able to render valuable service in time—I believe you are a trained accountant or something of the sort. There is much need of skilful clerical assistance in various governmental departments.

As to the general situation, it seems very discouraging just now. It may take a second war to adjust things properly. I tremble to think of the possibilities of the Russian collapse—which may open the resources of a vast country to the enemy. If the predicted Western drive of the Huns succeeds, the war is virtually lost. There is something the matter with the morale of the more polished nations—they need a little more brutality of the ancient Teutonic sort. No army can win without a certain savage lust of combat, & this spirit is being undermined with the current cant about democracy, idealism, & all that sort of rot. The issues should be made clearer—the fight is not in the interests of a coming millennium of social reform; it is for hearth & home—for existing institutions against a perilous invasion of an unnatural culture. Racial factors are also against us. For all our Roman civilisation, the enemy has the preponderance of superior blood. If all the Allied nations were as thoroughly Teutonic as Prussia, the end would be nearer & happier. Nothing can withstand the might of the Teuton—he is logical successor of the Roman in power. Teutonic blood snatched Britain from the Celt & made England the greatest force in all civilisation. Teutonic blood conquered the Western wilderness & gave America an instant place amongst the great nations of the globe. But this blood has become so extensively & tragically diluted, that the non-German Teutons may well look with concern to their future. The grotesque fallacy of the "Great American Melting Pot" may yet be brought home to the people in one of the most tear-stained pages of their history. Germany herself has set a truer valuation on the importance of unmixed blood, but may yet come to grief through the absorption of Slavic elements. The course of Germany during the last half-century has been one of curiously mixed merit. Certain scientific & philosophical developments have been marvellous, yet they have been conjoined to a brutality & narrowness of vision which threaten the development of civilisation. The pan-Germanic ideal, attainable only by a complete & amicable coöperation between Anglo-Saxon & Germanic races, has been fallaciously subordinated to a petty pan-Germanic ideal which is bringing about the virtual suicide of the Teutonic race, & driving Anglo-Saxons & Germans into equally unnatural alliances with alien races. The Saxon has his Hindoos & Moors, & the German his Turks. Progress is at a standstill, & everything human is lost in a mad scramble for a material victory. Even a recurrence of the Dark Ages is not impossible—a recurrence which will leave the Teutonic race so depleted numerically that the world's future is seriously threatened. Wilhelm, Wilhelm! What hast thou wrought?

I remain,

Most sincerely yours,

H. P. Lovecraft

Notes

1. I.e., revising the work of his client, the poet and lecturer David Van Bush (1882–1959).
2. After being rejected by the R.I.N.G., HPL applied for the regular draft (as he was legally obliged to do) on 5 June 1917. The "family friend" is unidentified.
3. The Vigilantes was a group of writers devoted to the production of pro-American and anti-German propaganda. One of its leaders was Samuel Hopkins Adams.

[32] [AHT]

Feby. 9, 1918

My dear Kleiner:—
            I wish I possessed that book about 18th century Bath.[1] How well I recall the days when my Irish friend R. B. Sheridan liv'd there. 'Twas but four miles thence, at Kingsdown, that I beheld his second rencontre with that odious scoundrel Capt. Mathews, in which he received a severe array of wounds. Let me see—when was that? Ah, I remember! 'Twas the first of July, in 1772, the year before I visited Scotland with Dr. Johnson & Bozzy.[2] Sheridan was a good-hearted fellow, but monstrous wild! After this duel, one of the Bath papers printed a vicious libel about his courage in the affair—but 'twas wholly false. Sheridan had Woodfall copy the calumny in his paper, intending to reply most vigorously; but after going to the trouble of circulating the libel, his native indolence caused him to forget the matter, & to leave it after all unanswer'd!³ A curious wit & a gay dog was Richard, but hang him, I'd lik'd him despite all his failings! Pardon, I pray you, the ramblings of a very old man—but mention of Bath does bring back the good old days!
            I enclose my latest "freak" composition—an attempt in a style which I believe neither you nor I have ever tried before—the rugged Kipling style. In a temperance paper, *The National Enquirer,* there lately appeared a rough piece of verse entitled "Only A Volunteer"—in which the writer, an army Sergeant, complained of the neglect shewn by the publick to the volunteer forces, whilst the conscripts are feted & extolled to the skies. I was rather touched, & yet reflected that the element of courage & individual responsibility in the volunteer really places him on a level so much higher, that he really does not need the ostentatious pomp wherewith the spirits of the drafted men are sustained. I framed these reflections into verse as nearly like the original in metre as possible—only adding certain internal rhymes which my artistick conscience demanded. Nothing repels me more than the obvious concession to technical difficulties involved in unrhymed alternate lines. I think I succeeded in achieving the bold, crude, manner of this sort of verse—as you may see by comparing original & answer. I detest this style, & it is very unlikely that I shall ever employ it again. This answer will be printed in *The National Enquirer,* as a flattering letter from the Associate Editor informs me. I also had both

original & answer printed in parallel columns in the patient & obliging *Providence News*. I may let the equally patient & obliging (& equally misprintful) *Tryout* have the honour of printing these lines.

ONLY A VOLUNTEER
(From THE NATIONAL ENQUIRER)

Why didn't I wait to be drafted,
    And be led to the train by a band,
Or put in a claim for exemption,
    Oh, why did I hold up my hand?
Why didn't I wait for the banquets,
    Why didn't I wait to be cheered,
For the drafted man gets the credit,
    While I only volunteered?

For no one gave me a banquet,
    No one said just one kind word;
A puff of the engine, a grind of the wheels,
    Were all the goodbye that I heard;
Then off to a camp I was hustled,
    To be trained for the next half year,
In the shuffle I was forgotten—
    I was only a volunteer!

I have builded the others their barracks,
    While roasting alive in a tent;
I have cleaned off a dozen parade grounds
    For the fellows that "only were sent".
Then along came the National Army,
    And to me it was made very clear
That the honour goes to the drafted man
    And the work to the volunteer!

I have waded the mud in Texas,
    I have frozen in Canada cold;
I've walked my posts in the moonlight
    Till this army is getting old;
But I'm not on their roll of honour,
    And though someone may shed a tear,
By all the rest I'm forgotten,
    For I'm only a volunteer.

And I dreamed that in far-off Flanders,
    On that bloody field of hate,

I went over the top—by a bullet was stopped,
    Then I knocked at the pearly gate.
And I heard Saint Peter saying,
    "We've no room for your kind here,
We're reserved for the National Army—
    Hell was made for the volunteer."

And perhaps some day in the future,
    When my little boy sits on my knee,
And asks what I did in the great war
    As he looks up at me,
I will have to look into those eyes
    That at me so trustingly peer,
And tell him I was not drafted—
    I was only a volunteer!

Sergt. HAYES R. MILLER, 17th Aero Squadron, U.S.A.

THE VOLUNTEER
A Reply to the Lines of Sergt. Miller in THE NATIONAL ENQUIRER

Though today all the bands are playing
    For the fellow who had to go;
For the man of faint heart, who needed a start,
    And was caught in the current's flow;
Never think that we're scorned or slighted,
    Or that ever we hold less dear
The hero we raise above all common praise—
    The valorous volunteer!

In the turmoil of black disaster,
    When the nations totter and reel,
When our soft, fat race start awake to face
    The mad monster of blood and steel;
Then our hearts are tried in the furnace,
    And our souls are sounded for fear,
And while pity must go to the weak and the slow,
    We worship the volunteer!

We honour the ranks of the conscripts,
    For we know they are average men—
The plumber and clerk snatched up from their work
    To be thrown in the dragon's den;
They are bearing their fate rather nobly,
    Who is perfect enough to sneer?

But the laurels of fame and the patriot's name
  Go first to the volunteer!

'Tis not easy to leave all we cherish,
  To lose half our hope of life;
To suffer more than we dreamed of before,
  And conquer our dread of strife;
So we grudge none the pomp and the music
  That are needed to hearten and cheer;
There's just one in the throng who can fight without song—
  The man who can volunteer!

For his heart is the heart of our fathers,
  Who knew how to conquer or die,
Who could offer their all at their country's call,
  And knew never a tremor or sigh;
He has given himself to the ages,
  He has soared to a godlike sphere;
What honour needs he, but to feel and to be
  A Liberty Volunteer?

So when victory breaks through the war-clouds,
  And peace comes to bless us once more,
And each man on the roll searches deep in his soul
  For the thoughts of the conflict before,
Who can hold up his heart to the daylight
  With a conscience so joyous and clear
As the fellow who fought uncompelled and unsought—
  The chivalrous volunteer?

     Gen. LEWIS THEOBALD, JUN., 13th Battalion,
     Stay-at-Home Inf., Wilson Machine-Gun Div.

I am ever yr. most obedient Serv[t]
  Humphry Littlewit, Gent.

Notes

1. Possibly Mowbray A. Green, *The Eighteenth Century Architecture of Bath* (Bath: G. Gregory, 1904).

2. Samuel Johnson and James Boswell visited Scotland in 1773. See Johnson's *A Journey to the Western Islands of Scotland* (1775) and Boswell's *Journal of a Tour to the Hebrides* (1785).

3. English playwright Richard Brinsley Sheridan (1751–1816) moved to Bath in 1770. There he befriended a sixteen-year-old girl named Elizabeth Ann Linley, who was being pursued by a married man, Capt. Thomas Mathews. Sheridan fought two duels with Mathews, in the second of which he was seriously injured. Mathews wrote a

scurrilous attack on Sheridan in the *Bath Chronicle,* and Sheridan asked William Wood-fall, publisher of the *Chronicle,* to allow the attack to be reprinted in London papers, so that he might refute it; but he never did so. The source of this anecdote is Thomas Moore's *Memoirs of the Life of the Rt. Hon. Richard Brinsley Sheridan* (1825).

[33]   [AHT]

Feby. 23, 1918

My dear Kleiner:—

Your New York draft boards seem to be festooned with liberal amounts of red tape. I duly filled out a questionnaire some time ago, referring the medical authorities to National Guard rejection records if they should prove curious about my physical condition. They seem to have been satisfied, for they placed me as disabled—Class V Div. G. without the formality of an examination. One of the board, who is acquainted with the family, told my mother I could never have gotten so far with him as I did with poor Major Calder of the R.I.N.G. That was an artistic piece of lying—my most extensive misdemeanour in the art of untruthfulness! But I hated to be left out if there was any chance of volunteering. The company I would have been in was a splendid one, (9th C.A.C.) whose Captain chatted with the enlisted men just as though an unbreakable barrier were not supposed to exist between him & them! This company, now in Federal Service as the 55th Co., made a trip to Providence lately & gave an entertainment in the Strand Theatre. It made me feel so—shut out—left behind—that I could not bear to attend! It has developed into a fine company now, the group photograph shewing a splendid array of virile young men. If my health could have borne me along, I half believe I should have been at least a non-commissioned officer by this time, for I intended to study hard indeed. I half thought, that if I could hold out long enough, I might obtain even a commission. I should like one very much, since a clear majority of my friends now have them. But I suppose, as the doctor said, that I have no real idea of what a soldier has to undergo physically in even the smoothest of camp or barrack life. At any rate, he decided that a man who cannot stay up all day as a civilian, is not exactly a General in the making. So here I sit scribbling, & here I seem likely to sit indefinitely. I am almost ashamed to write war verse, so unmartial is my environment; yet occasionally I have to burst out with something like "The Volunteer". I trust the numerous boards may soon succeed in placing you somewhere definitely. In all probability eyes like yours would not be suitable even for limited service. By the way—our mutual friend & fellow-bard Samuel Loveman is in Class I Div. A., expecting to be called for active duty.[1] In the first draft he was exempted for poor vision, but the requirements are now less strict. If I were Loveman I should enlist. I have no patience at all with a strong man sans dependents who deliberately stays home till dragged out from under the bed. Loveman admits he is "unpoetically robust" & that his sight is not at all seriously impaired. But Jews will be Jews, & I will judge neither harshly nor hastily. He is certainly a very pleasant & exceedingly gifted person, & now that he is subject to call, shews no sign of timidity or unrest. I trust his career may be honourable, & that he will meet with an easier fate than the other soldier-poets, Brooke, Seeger, Ledwidge,[2] et al. He is contributing three beautiful stanzas to the March United Amateur,[3] though his best work is being saved for book publication.

Galpin will surely please you—though you may find him as provokingly philosophical in places as L. Theobald. He tells me he thinks he resembles me in many ways, as indeed I think myself. He is what I might have been, had my wit been a trifle (?) sharper, & my health a trifle (?) better. I hope he may not "peter out" like the friend you describe. This is his own earnest hope, for he is regretfully & apprehensively aware of the fate of the average "prodigy". I lately had a letter from his father—who is as interesting in his way as the son! In the first place, Galpin Sr. is *77* years of age, & a veteran of the Civil War![4] This was to me a great surprise, for I expected to find the parent of a 16-year old child a relatively young man. He is odd & abrupt in style, & brutally frank in opinions; his hatred for religion being intense. He says it stultified his own intellectual development sixty years ago, & is determined it shall not affect his son's. His learning is vast & encyclopaedic—I shall have to visit the public library in order to answer his letter! He seems to have read omnivorously all his long life. During the war he was detailed on Hospital duty after one year of active service, & while in the medical corps was finally converted from Christianity. He read Darwin & Huxley when first these sages began to attract general attention. Galpin enlisted in 1861, aged 20, & regrets that he did not have four years of active fighting instead of only one. I hope we have many young men like him today! His opinion of our colleague Mo is unjustly low—Moe's orthodoxy doubtless angers him. He says: "I do not know the man by sight, but have seen some of his lucubrations; & while I can admire his vocabulary, I unconsciously recall to mind hearing the 'Braying Jackass of the Platte', sometimes called Wm. J. Bryan. Moe's articles appear to me as very unfinished—lacking in intellectual conviction." Pray do not repeat this to Mo—though I fancy the dislike is mutual. Mo calls Galpin (Sr.) a "ranting, bigoted atheist". For mine own part, I like them both! Galpin is exceedingly (& justly) proud of "the boy", as he calls our new colleague. It is evident that Alfred Jr. has claimed a large place in his world, & is regarded with the traditional fondness which aged parents bestow upon their belated offspring. You will recall that Dr. Johnson once remarked to Mrs. Thrale, that "an old man's child leads much such a life . . . as a little boy's dog; teazed with awkward fondness, & forced, perhaps, to 'set up & beg', as we call it, to divert a company; who at last go away complaining of their disagreeable entertainment."[5] Johnson was himself an old man's son, & was often embarrassed by the ostentation with which his father displayed his infant genius. But Galpin Sr. is more scientific in his affection, & has guided his son's mind with minute care. He flatters himself that he has a slight share in bringing out A. G. Jr.'s brilliancy. Galpin says of his son: "When, in his early boyhood, he began to ask questions, I counted on him to *think,* & never grew out of patience with him." Galpin Sr. has much contempt for his own very conventional education in the 'forties & 'fifties. He was a schoolteacher—a very young one—before the war; hence I fancy he was something of a prodigy himself. It is easy to see that Galpin *pere* has greatly influenced the doctrines & ideas of Galpin *fils*—the two are as alike as two peas, despite the sixty-one years' difference in their ages. As to my dark doctrines of Ἀλήθεια Φρικῶδης—pray do not deem ordinary Greek letters as "mystic characters"! The Roman equivalents are *Aletheia Phrikodes*—signifying "Horrible Truth", & forming the title of my hideous blank verse piece in the latest Kleicomolo to reach you. This philosophy of the infinite & eternal interests Galpin Sr. Your philosophy is a very sensible sort to have—& in the end I suppose is not so remote from mine. What does it all amount to, anyway? In a few million years there will be no human race at all. Man, at best, is but an incident—& a very trifling incident—in the limitless history of Nature. I am inclined to think that all entity evolves in cycles—that sooner or later everything occurs practically all over again. Not that all details are necessarily alike—but that general forms & principles are repeated. Planets are born, die, & are born again—& so on without end. It really makes one quite dizzy to think of such expanded matters! Possibly it is better to be near-sighted & orthodox like Mo, trusting all to a Divine Providence, R. I.

GREEK ALPHABET

Αα—alpha	a	Νν—nu	n
Ββ—beta	b	Ξξ—xi	X
Γγ—gamma	c	Οο—omicron	O
Δδ—delta	d	Ππ—pi	P
Εε—epsilon	e	Ρϱ—rho	R
Ζζ—zeta	f	Σσ—sigma	S
Ηη—eta	long e	Ττ—tau	T
Θθ—theta	th	Υυ—upsilon	u or y
Ιι—iota	i	Φφ—phi	ph
Κϰ—kappa	k	Χχ—chi	ch (hard)
Λλ—lambda	l	Ψψ—psi	ps
Μμ—mu	m	Ωω—omega	long o

I doubt not but that Milton had philosophy in mind, when penning the lines you quote. The w. k. Khayyam–Fitzgerald reference to philosophy seems to shew an under-appreciation of the pure joy of argument.[6] However—the genial maker of tents was not one to appreciate anything truly intellectual in a detached way.

> Yr obedient & humble Serv[t]
> H Lovecraft

Notes

1. Loveman spent most of 1918–19 in Camp Gordon, GA, and did not serve overseas.

2. Rupert Brooke (1887–1915) was an English poet who died of blood-poisoning while the British Army was proceeding to the Dardanelles. Alan Seeger (1888–1916) was a minor American poet who joined the Foreign Legion and gained brief celebrity following his death in World War I. In his honor, HPL composed the poem "To Alan Seeger." Francis Ledwidge (1891–1917) was an Irish farmer whose poetry Lord Dunsany championed. He was killed in action in Flanders.

3. "Quatrains," *United Amateur* 17, No. 4 (March 1918): 61.

4. Alfred Galpin, Sr. (1841–1924) served in the First Wisconsin Infantry Regiment and other units in Tennessee, Kentucky, and Alabama.

5. Hester Lynch Thrale (later Mrs. Piozzi) (1741–1821), *Anecdotes of the Late Samuel Johnson* (Dublin: Moncrieffe, 1786), 11–12.

6. HPL probably alludes to stanza 27 of the *Rubaiyat of Omar Khayyam*, translated by Edward FitzGerald (1859): "Myself when young did eagerly frequent / Doctor and Saint, and heard great argument /About it and about: but evermore / Came out by the same door as in I went."

[34]   [AHT; Post]

April 4, 1918

My dear Kleiner:—

[Post:] Regarding your qualifications for office in the United, pray do not think that the regular publication of a paper is essential to recognition. This is not the National—with us, literary standing is the prime consideration. I dread the thought of a second Presidential term. In the first place, I am unable to administer the office as I should; & in the second place, it is a source of worry & nervous strain, even when I do not try to be as active as I might wish.[1]

Just now, the laureateship question is distracting me. The Lehr Amendment,[2] passed under the expectation of increased activity, has proved impracticable under present conditions; so that only by conscious effort can we ensure the granting of full awards. Full awards, as you know, cannot be made unless ten persons compete in each class. It will be necessary to urge all authors to make entries—&, even then, awards in the story & "study" classes are unlikely.[3]

I am also perplexed about choosing the Laureate Judges. The formation of next year's ticket will be a matter of extreme difficulty. I would accept the presidency if absolutely no one else could be found—but I hope I discover someone at least half capable. Miss McGeoch suggests Mrs. Campbell,[4] who is not only quite capable herself, but has Paul J. in the background as counselor & prime minister. I rather wish Campbell himself could take the office again.

The official organ outlook is very dark. Cook may not be able to act as publisher again—& I cannot think of anyone to serve as editor. This office seems to require financial as well as scholastic qualifications. I thank you for your offer to edit & distribute campaign matter—& were I at all disposed to run once more, I should avail myself of it. No one could be much worse than I, as an executive, unless perhaps some of the "roughneck" element of third-rate old-timers.

I feel that it will be enough if we can seat some harmless, conservative person who can tide the association smoothly, albeit inactively, over the present war period. More cannot be expected. To survive, is all we may well ask. Really competent persons, such as Cook, Campbell, Miss McGeoch, etc., all express either inability or extreme disinclination to serve. My general position in regard to the presidency is just one step short of Cook's. He declares he would not serve even if elected. I would—but I would not voluntarily permit such an election except as a last resort. I wish amateurdom could get along without officers or politics—but Russia's case proves that such a thing "can't be did"!!!

[AHT:] Verse of H. P. Lovecraft, published in amateur press from 1914 to 1918.

1914

"On a Modern Lothario"—*Blarney-Stone,* Jul.–Aug.
    Acrostic-satire on article by W. E. Griffin.
"To the Pinfeather Club"—*Pinfeather,* November.[5]
"To the Rev. Jas. T. Pyke"—*United Official Quarterly,* Nov.
"To Gen. Villa"—*Blarney-Stone,* Nov.–Dec.

1915

"1914"—Interesting Items, March.
"March"—United Amateur, March.
"The Simple Speller's Tale"—Conservative, April.
    Versified version of epigram from Piper—Conservative, April.[6]
"Elegy on Rev. F. C. Clark"—Prov. News, April 29.[7]
"Quinsnicket Park"—Badger, June.
"To the U.A.P.A. from the P.A.P.C."—Providence Amateur, June.[8]
"On the Bay-Stater's Policy"—Bay Stater, June.[9]
"On a N.E. Village Seen by Moonlight"—Trail, Summer.
"The Crime of Crimes"—Interesting Items, July.
"Fragment on Whitman"—Conservative, July.
"The Magazine Poet"—United Amateur, October.
"The State of Poetry"—Conservative, October.

"Gems from In a Minor Key"—Conservative, October.

"The Isaacsonio-Mortoniad"—unpublished.

"On the Cowboys of the West"—Plainsman, December.

"To Sam¹. Loveman, Esq."—Bearcat, December.

"A Mississippi Autumn" (versified from prose by Mrs. Renshaw)—Ole Miss., Dec.

1916

"A Rural Summer Eve"—*Trail,* January.

"On Receiving a Picture of Swans"—*Conservative,* January.

"An American to Mother England"—*Poesy,* January.

"The Bookstall"—*United Official Quarterly,* January.

"The Teuton's Battle-Song"—*United Amateur,* February.

"To the Late J. H. Fowler, Esq."—*Scot*—March.

"Temperance Song"—*Dixie Booster,* Spring.

"The Power of Wine"—*Tryout,* April.

"R. Kleiner, Laureatus, in Heliconem"—*Conservative,* April.

"Content"—*United Amateur,* June.

"The Beauties of Peace"—*Prov. News*—June 27.

"Respite"—*Conservative,* October.

"The Rose of England"—*Scot,* October.

"Brumalia"—*Tryout,* December.

By Lewis Theobald, Jun.

"The Bride of the Sea"—*Providence Amateur,* February.

"Ye Ballade of Patrick von Flynn"—*Conservative,* April.

"Inspiration"—*Conservative,* October.

"Brotherhood"—*Tryout,* December.

Anonymously Published

"To Charlie of the Comics"—*Providence Amateur,* February.

1917

"Elegy on Phillips Gamwell, Esq."—*Prov. News,* Jan. 5.

"On Gen¹. Robert Edward Lee"—*Coyote,* January.[10]

"Futurist Art"—*Conservative,* January.

"Fact and Fancy"—*Tryout,* February.

"On Receiving a Picture of the Marshes at Ipswich"—*Merry Minutes*—March.

"Percival Lowell"—*Excelsior,* March.

"To A. F. Lockhart"—*Tryout,* March.[11]

"Britannia Victura"—*Inspiration,* April.

"Iterum Conjunctae"—*Tryout,* May.

"To Templeton and Mount Monadnock"—*Vagrant,* June.[12]

"Prologue" (to Mr. Hoag's poem)—*Tryout*, July.
"Ode for July 4, 1917"—*United Amateur*, July.
"On the Death of a Rhyming Critic"—*Toledo Amateur*, July.
"The Smile"—*Little Budget*, September.
"Autumn"—*Tryout*, November.
"To Greece"—*Vagrant*, November.
"An American to the British Flag"—*Little Budget*, December.
"25th Anniv. Evening News"—*Tryout*, December.[13]

by Lewis Theobald, Jun.

"The Rutted Road"—*Tryout*, January.
"The Nymph's Reply"—*Tryout*, February.
"Pacifist War Song"—*Tryout*, March.
"The Poet of Passion"—*Tryout*, June.
"Sunset"—*Tryout*, December.

ascribed to the traitor John T. Dunn[14]

"On Graduation from R. I. Hospital School of Nurses"—*Tryout*, February.[15]

Anonymous

"To M. W. M."—*United Amateur*, July.
"To the Nurses of the Red Cross"—unpublished.

1918

"The Volunteer"—*Prov. News*, Feby. 1.
"A Winter Wish"—*Tryout*, February.
"To Jonathan Hoag, Esq."—*Eurus*, February.
"April"—*Tryout*, March.
"Ver Rusticum"—*Vagrant*, to appear soon.
"A Garden"—*Vagrant*, to appear soon.
"Nemesis"—*Vagrant*, to appear soon.
"The Poe-et's Nightmare"—*Vagrant*, to appear soon (written 1916).
"Ad Britannos, 1918"—*Little Budget*, to appear soon.

By Ward Phillips

"Astrophobos"—*United Amateur*, January.

By Ames Dorrance Rowley

"Laeta; A Lament"—*Tryout*, February.

What a mess of mediocre & miserable junk. He hath sharp eyes indeed, who can discover any trace of merit in so worthless an array of bad verse.

I remain
yr most obt humble Servt
H Lovecraft

Notes

1. HPL was president of the UAPA for the 1917–18 term, RK for the 1918–19 term.

2. The plan proposed by Mary Henrietta Lehr is described in HPL's "President's Message," *United Amateur* 17, No. 1 (September 1917): 12–13 (*CE* 1.172). It calls for a third and fourth vice-president to recruit amateurs in colleges and high schools, respectively.

3. HPL refers to the laureate awards, bestowed each year upon the best story, poem, essay, and editorial in the UAPA official year.

4. HPL refers to Verna McGeoch (Official Editor of the UAPA, 1917–19) and Eleanor B. Campbell, amateur journalist in Ridgefarm, IL, and wife of Paul J. Campbell.

5. I.e., "To the Members of the Pin-Feathers . . ."

6. See "[On Slang]" in the Bibliography.

7. Franklin C. Clark was a physician, not a clergyman.

8. I.e., "To the Members of the United . . ."

9. I.e., "The Bay-Stater's Policy."

10. I.e., "Lines on Gen. Robert Edward Lee."

11. I.e., "To Mr. Lockhart, on His Poetry."

12. I.e., "On Receiving a Picture of yᵉ Towne of Templeton . . ."

13. I.e., "Lines on the 25th. Anniversary . . ."

14. Dunn, who protested the United States' entry into World War I in April 1917, refused to register for the draft and was sentenced to twenty years in the Atlanta Federal Prison. He was released shortly after the end of the war.

15. I.e., "Lines on Graduation . . ."

[35]   [Post; AHT]

May 5, 1918

My dear Kleiner:—

[Post:] Mrs. Jordan's recovery has not been as rapid as one might wish, but a copy of *The London Daily Mail* lately came from her, addressed in her own handwriting instead of her nurse's, hence I assume she is much improved. In the last letter she dictated, she related an amusing recruiting incident. One of the "prospectives" to whom she had written—a man named Jones, whose book of poetry, according to a newspaper account, had passed through several editions—desired to answer in person instead of by letter, & accordingly trudged up to the door of 57 Morton St., with a volume of his verse (yclepted *Selected Gems!*) under his arm.[1]

Mrs. Jordan was unable to receive him, of course, but the nurse proved an equally acceptable victim, & the gentleman (who is a farmer, ex-foundryman, etc., given to raising prize vegetables—& inventor of a tree-spraying solution to kill gypsy moths—a very versatile gentleman!) proceeded to expatiate upon his own genius for her benefit, quoting liberally & voluminously from his own works, & recounting one of his masterpieces (entitled

"Father Tierney & Me") entire. He was dislodged with difficulty, & insisted on leaving his precious book of verses for further perusal. Mrs. Jordan had the nurse tell him to write me for additional information, but so far he has not honoured me with a missive—or called!

Speaking of recruiting incidents—here is a rather unusual coincidence. Not long ago, I received from our old friend, Albert A. Sandusky, a very puzzled letter, asking "how on earth I ever chanced to discover the new name & address of his married sister, Mrs. Clara Bamberg, & send her a copy of my paper"! This would have been all Sanscrit to me, had Sandusky not ventured a guess—that the name was derived from *The Boston Post* list of prize-winners. Then it came to me. I had not sent any paper to her, but one of the recruiters must have done so, since I gave Mrs. Jordan a large number for such use. Yet no one had any idea that the Mrs. Bamberg addressed, is a sister of Sandusky! But this is not the strangest part. The prize-winning story which led to the publication of Mrs. Bamberg's name, was written by Sandusky himself! He had let his sister send it as hers just for fun. I thought the coincidence quite singular. A letter or paper sent to an apparent stranger, evokes a reply from a well-known amateur, who turns out to be the real author of the story which led to the sending of the letter or paper.

[. . .]

I am grateful for your suggestions regarding Laureate Judges. I now have enough hints from various members to begin trying my luck with the literati in question. I presume the "Vachel Lindsay" you mention is Nicholas V. Lindsay, minus his first name. Some persons have a singular aversion to the honest appellations their parents bestow upon them—look at (Thomas) Woodrow Wilson, (James Beau)Champ Clark,[2] &c. I had Brander Matthews in mind, as a possible judge, sometime ago. I like everything about him but his spelling—which I "thoroly" detest. I wonder if Harriet Monroe is not too much in favour of modern pseudo-poesy?[3] I must get to work writing these celebrities ere long, but I wish I could transfer the job to someone else.

[. . .]

Cook's latest *Vagrant* is assuredly a marvel. The literary standard is this time even higher than before, I think. The esthetic Elsa Gidlow's outburst could undoubtedly be a great deal worse, as free verse is reckoned. Of the "two lovers that woo her unceasingly", I advise her to choose oblivion. That is the best way for all *vers-libristes*. Her colleague, Rossy George, tangles himself all up in some words & phrases, in which a trace of metre is observable. His spasms, however, are less definite in thought (if, indeed, there be any definiteness in imagistical chaos!) & less meritorious altogether.[4]

Cook attended the banquet of the "Fossils" in New York on April 27, & stopped off at Providence Monday on his way home. He was very tired after his trip, but had enjoyed himself immensely. He shewed me a programme bearing the signatures of all the prominent amateurs of the past. He thinks the "Fossils" are becoming less hostile toward contemporary amateurdom. Dr. Swift gave him a bound volume of his celebrated *Weekly*,[5] which Cook left here for my perusal. He has also left me a copy of Truman J. Spencer's famous farewell *Investigator*, which some kind "Fossil" gave him.[6]

[AHT:] Speaking of poetical reviewers—I have not yet recovered from the shock the newspaper gave me last night! At the First Baptist Church in this city, on Friday evening, there occurred the annual ceremony of the award of the "Spingarn Medal",[7] which is given to that member of the *negro race* who achieves the most notable success in 'any field of elevated or honourable human endeavour' during the year. At these impressive exercises, Gov. Beeckman of Rhode Island[8] gracefully awarded the badge of African supremacy to the Boston poet, critic, & literary editor—**William Stanley Braithwaite**!!!!!!!!!!!![9] Think of it—chew upon it—let it sink into your astonished & outraged consciousness—the great *Transcript* dictator, the little czar of the *Poetry Review*, is a **nigger**—a low-born, mongrel, semi-ape!—Ye gods—I gasp—I can say no more! Aid me, ye benign elves & daemons of anticlimax! So this—this—is the fellow who hath held the destinies of nascent Miltons in his sooty hand; this the sage who hath set the seal of his approval on *vers libre* & amylowellism—a miserable mulatto! To think of the years I have taken this nigger seriously, reading his critical dicta as though he were a Bostonian & a white man! I could kick myself! William's picture is printed in the *Bulletin* beside the news item, & from the likeness given I can deduce no visible sign of his black blood. A heavy moustache droops down over what may be thick negroid lips. But after all—I suppose he has only a slight taint of the beast. No nigger blacker than a quadroon would be likely to attain the intellectual level he has undoubtedly reached. I am not minimising what the fellow knows, but I think it monstrous bad taste for the *Transcript* to foist a black upon its literary readers!

Yr obt humble Servt

HLovecraft

Notes

1. It appears that RK (or Hyman Bradofsky, editor of the *Californian*) changed the name of the poet, Patrick James Pendergast (1850–?) to "Jones" so as not to offend him, should he see the letter in print.

2. Champ Clark (1850–1921), US representative (1893–95, 1897–1921) from Missouri and one of the leading Democratic politicians of his day.

3. Brander Matthews (1852–1929), literary critic and proponent of simplified spelling. HPL skewers him at the end of the poem "The Simple Speller's Tale" (1915). Harriet Monroe (1860–1936), poet and editor of the landmark magazine *Poetry* (1912f.).

4. HPL refers to the amateur writers Elsa A. Gidlow (1898–1986) and Roswell George Mills (1896–1966), later editors of *Les Mouches Fantastiques* (see HPL's *"Les Mouches Fantastiques"* [1918; *CE* 1.203–4]). Both were homosexuals. Elsa Alice Gidlow, "Two Lovers," *Vagrant* No. 7 (June 1918): 95–96. The poem begins "I have two lov-

ers who woo me unceasingly" and concludes, ". . . they are Life and Death. Which shall I take?" Mills's poem is "Once," *Vagrant* No. 7 (June 1918): 79–80.

5. Edwin B. Swift, amateur journalist and editor of *Swift's Weekly* (1905–09).

6. The Fossils is an association of amateur journalist alumni.

7. The Spingarn Medal, instituted in 1914 by literary critic Joel Elias Spingarn (1875–1939), is awarded annually by the National Association for the Advancement of Colored People for outstanding achievement by an African American. Recipients have included Charles Gilpin, Jackie Robinson, Rosa Parks, and Lena Horne.

8. R[obert] Livingston Beeckman (1866–1935), governor of Rhode Island (1915–21).

9. William Stanley Braithwaite (1878–1962), editor of *Anthology of Magazine Verse*, book reviewer for the *Boston Transcript,* and one of the leading African-American literary figures of his time. He was editor of the short-lived journal *Poetry Review of America* (May 1916–February 1917). HPL corresponded with him briefly in 1930. He was in fact of mixed racial heritage.

[36]   [Post; AHT]

June 5[, 1918]

My dear Klei:—

[Post:] I shall be glad to see you next month—when I trust no relentlessly scheduled train may interrupt our conversation. Let me know a day or so in advance when you can come, then notify me by telephone upon your arrival in the city.[1]

[AHT:] Now as to directions for reaching Castle Theobald. Upon emerging from Union Station you will face south. Go down the right hand (west) approach to the town, & keep straight ahead (through Dorrance Street) till you attain the corner of Dorrance & Weybosset Streets, which is adorned & distinguished by a pharmaceutical emporium—that is, commonly speaking, a drug-store. This is the southeast corner—where you wait for the local stage-coach, or street-car, as such things are called nowadays. The car, which will bear on its front sign either BUTLER AVE. or BUTLER AVE. & SWAN POINT, & on the dasher the sign TUNNEL, will approach you from the south—from the unknown, unexplored, & dismal lower reaches of Dorrance St. Board it before it turns the corner into Weybosset St. securing as good a seat as possible. Then remain seated for some time. The cumbersome vehicle will glide sonorously through the prosaic & curving stretches of the financial district, past our highest near-skyscraper, the Turk's Head (This is a name after my own heart. The original shop on this spot, built during the reign of His Majesty George II & demolished only a few years ago, bore the sign of the Turk's Head—a carven replica of which adorns the new edifice.) Building, whose sixteen stories are an object of wonder in this un-metropolitan village, & upon the spacious & sunlit expanse of Market Square, once the business centre of the town. Here you will behold the old "Market Building", a genuine relic of Colonial times. The clock which adorns it is not so old, though so far as its time-keeping qualities are concerned, it might as well be. The confounded thing *loses!* Southward you will glimpse the harbour, once a forest of masts, & even now a port of prominence. In September 1815, Market Square was temporarily transformed to a raging sea—the terrible gale of that month driving large full-rigged ships high over the bridge. A good-sized brig was left stranded on Westminster Street when the mad waters subsided. After a couple of turns North Main Street is encountered—an old thoroughfare yclept "Cheapside" in the good Georgian days. Ahead, & at your left as you approach it, stands the First Baptist Church, completed in 1775, & designed after St. Martin's-in-the-Fields in London, which I believe was a product of Chr. Wren, Esq. This is the oldest church building in Providence, & houses the oldest congregation in the state—the *original* Baptist congregation of Mr. Williams, established in 1636 when the colony was planted. This is also distinguished by being the Theobald family church—though for reasons made obvious in the *Kleicomolo,* the last of the Theobalds is far from being a faithful communicant!!!! Up the hill against which the church stands, you will obtain pleasing vistas—though your pleasure may be mixed with pity for the poor wretch who has to climb this nearly perpendicular obstacle. But your lot is more fortunate. Directly before you yawns a gruesome cave, ominously labelled with a date which history will record in letters of dripping blood—1914! The meaning is not so sinister as it appears, since it merely refers to the completion of the East Side Tunnel, through which the rail-bound chariot may glide with ease to the promised land beyond, without the exhausting climb suggested by your previous glance. Prior to the Year of Years, East Side cars ran on the north side of Market Square, & were dragged up the hill on College Street by means of a counterweight cable arrangement; but those days are forever gone, & College Street rears its precipitous slope in apparently pristine innocence of any such thing as a car track. In a way, the traveller is a loser by reason of the change, for though in the old days he would not have seen the Church, he would, instead, have been treated to a complete & beautiful view of the celebrated Brown University.

To a hardened New-York subway habitué, the tunnel will present nothing new or interesting, though to local villagers it came as a godsend. The hill, which residents bless as an exclusive barrier betwixt the residential & commercial sections, was a frightful impediment to rapid transit—cars being annoyingly delayed in waiting for the valiant little "grip cars" which ushered them up & down the walls of the abyss. But now we tarry not for cable or grip, but sail proudly & majestically into the darkness under our own power. (I mean the R. I. Co's power—but I must be poetical at any cost!) The darkness, however, is only relative; frequent electric bulbs affording a subdued & agreeable radiance. If you sit on the front seat of an open car, your poetic meditation & your new straw hat may be interrupted & spotted, respectively, by vagrant drops of muddy water which fall occasionally from the concrete arching roof. Said roof seems not wholly impermeable to // the dewy nectar of the hillside springs. // (Notice the unconscious heroic—my weakness is innate & automatic!!) Ere your eyes become accustomed to the faint illumination, you are once more dazzled by the light of day—the wire-borne chariot wheeling out upon the sunlit & delightful reaches of Thayer Street in the residential district. To the southwest the traveller beholds the rear campus (Lincoln Field) & some of the buildings of the University. The nearest one, on the corner of Thayer & Waterman Streets, is the Biological Laboratory. Once more we wheel—this time at almost a right angle to the east, into the shaded regions of Waterman Street. This is one of the two oldest & prettiest thoroughfares of the residential district—the other being my own native & beloved Angell Street. Angell & Waterman run east & west from the Seekonk River to the hill—Angell going half way down & Waterman all the way down. Waterman curves on the hill—for this is the selfsame street up which you looked as you entered the tunnel. It was then on your left, beside the Church. (Cars run east on Waterman & west on Angell. When you return down street you will spend a long time riding along my native pave.) As you glide eastward along Waterman Street, many of the prettiest estates in the city will unfold themselves to your view. The section is a beautiful one indeed, though the walled & parked palaces of the four or five supremely wealthy families lie off the car route, somewhat to the south. Sumptuous glimpses may be obtained by looking southward along Hope & Cooke Streets as you pass them. At Wayland Avenue the car turns north for two blocks, then entering Wayland Square, one of those neighbourhood semi-commercial districts on a small scale, like Harvard Square in miniature. Here may be found a pharmacy, a tailor's shop, & a neat little grocery. A tiny branch of the First Baptist Church—Wayland Chapel—once reared its little red spire toward Heaven from the southeast corner of Wayland Avenue—but it rears it no more—having given way to a neat Doctor's residence. (The adjective qualifies *residence,* but I am sure it can be applied to the *physician* with equal accuracy!) Thus does science ever supplant blind superstition in this progressive age! (Vide *Kleicomolo.*) Glancing to the west, (your left) along Angell Street, you may espy through the vista of verdure another street corner—Elmgrove Avenue—with a good-sized (now) yellow house perched upon a pleasing terrace. (N.W. corner.) This is not my present residence, but to me it is earth's most precious spot—my birthplace & childhood home! #454 Angell Street—magic name! When you return to the business section you will ride directly by this blessed edifice, obtaining glimpses of the (once) lovely park-like yard, stable, trees, & shrubbery. Today the place is unkempt—shamefully so—but once upon a time!!! Where now a prosaic garage stands, once played a beautiful fountain, in whose sparkling waters my childish fancy could discern many a Naiad or water-god. (What matter'd it to me that a pipe—not a divine spring—fed it?) But one sign of former tenancy lingers about the place. Upon the sunken horse-block before the stable door is graven a single initial—P— *Phillips!* Here my grandfather planned for the future of his race—how vain are the fondest designs of mankind! Of his last generation the brightest scion is no more—& the only surviving scion, last of his race, is a weak scribbler of bad verse! The house was in my day brown in colour, & adorned with many attractive mouldings about the windows, which have been removed by the present owner. It is today but a shadow of its former self in beauty—the dwelling place of a bustling young physician who knows not the House of Phillips nor the traditions of the roof & walls that enclose him. The vacant lot to the west of this estate was anciently owned by my grandfather, though now a separate property. Here, in the old semi-rural days when no houses existed to the north, was the family "farm" & vegetable garden, where wav'd the tassel'd corn, or rov'd the family cow—a beloved possession reminiscent of the prehistoric Greene days ere my grandfather became an urban dweller. In my own time, this Elysian mead was my playground & classic fairyland. Near the gate, against the high board fence, stood my juvenile "village" of huts—& here was enacted many a childish mimic fray or dramatic episode. (This lot is now an enclosed artificial skating rink for the young.) But I digress, & ramble of the past with the loose & trivial tongue of old age! Let us return to the journey, which is now nearly over.

At Wayland Square the car turns east into Angell Street on the last lap of our journey. On the N.E. corner of Angell & Wayland stands the widely known though not ancient or precisely aristocratic "Banigan Mansion".[2] The Banigans of Providence are rich Irish descendants of an honest fellow named Joseph Banigan who came from the Ould Sod in the '40's & through native wit became the millionaire "Rubber King" of America. He had the luck—or the shrewdness—to marry a native American lady of good stock, thereby giving himself a semblance of social position to match his very new millions. Shortly before his death he erected this picturesque "poem in brick & stone"—though he lived not long enough to enjoy it. He was a good man, Irish though he was, & I am not ashamed to number his younger grandsons Joseph, Richard, & John amongst the closest of my childhood companions.[3] They lived just across Elmgrove Avenue from my birthplace. Richard—who is three months my senior—lives a little nearer you now, at Camp Upton, on your native island. He was chosen as a—er—*volunteer* (?) in the latest large R. I. increment. But as the car sweeps past "Banigan Turnout" (even the car-track feels the Celtic breath, according to railway nomenclature) we arrive at a more Anglo-Saxon realm. In a region of rather pretty houses & lawns, the only very large building being the apartment house which bears the name "Buena Vista" to match its dignified Spanish architecture, (Do not confuse this with Mr. Hoag's Vista-Buena-on-the-Battenkill!)[4] we turn north into Butler Avenue—& having completed the turn, alight from the car! We glance about us at the four corners, & on each behold something architecturally different. To the northwest the paradoxical "Buena Vista" effectually cuts off the vista with its handsome expanse. To the southwest the eye feasts on an exquisite new house in pseudo-Elizabethan style. To the southeast is a pretty though modern residence. And to the northwest is a verdant tree-shaded lawn, lying between a large mid-Victorian grey house which fronts Butler Avenue, & a smaller yellow & white structure fronting Angell Street. On the nearest corner of the latter edifice you will probably see a tiny piazza shaded with not unattractive awnings. Stepping closer, you may discover upon the corner post of the piazza some figures—less portentious [*sic*] than those you saw upon the entrance of the tunnel, yet fairly familiar to the United fraternity—the three modest figures—598! Your journey is indeed o'er, & your pull of the bell will in all probability bring before you the ungainly form & pasty face of the Demon Critick—the Boeotian Ogre—Ludovicus Theobaldus II, whose welcome will be sincere & glowing indeed!

Doubtless you will desire to be ushered at once into the inner cave—that frightful chamber where rests upon miscellaneous shelves the lore of the ages—literary, historical, & scientific—much more wisdom (let me whisper in confidence) than ever was or will be in the owner's cranium! Here you may espy volumes of every sort, mostly unprepossessing of aspect—which comprise the works I consult most frequently, & which constitute possibly a third of the total number of books in the house—all rooms up to the attic considered. Doubtless many tomes you deem indispensable will be found missing—likewise there will be many in which you will find nothing of merit—pompous Erasmus Darwin, for instance, who clothes Botanick Science in pastoral garb, & who uses *o'er* with lamentable frequence. (However, you may be interested in the singularly simplified spelling in this book, which was imprinted at New-York, & publish'd by D. Longworth, At the Dramatic Repository, Shakspeare-Gallery, 1805.) But think of the other wonders!! The scrapbook & collected amateur journals containing the prose & poesie of the people's premier poet—popular publick pest—Pythagoras Ptolemaeus Pindaricus—alias L. Theobald! What a rich treasure-house of data for the biographer & the reviewer! I might even *consent* to let you read my latest masterpiece—a tale in *rhyme* 304 lines long—which stamps its author as a very long-tal'd animal indeed. And, too, a Christmas poem written last winter, totalling 332 lines![5] But lest I deter you from making the visit, let me assure you that I speak but in jest. I shall not inflict all this concentrated dulness upon you! Should your visit occur on a pleasant afternoon, we might wander afield, where I cou'd shew you some of the natural beauties which inclin'd my infant mind to compositions of the pastoral sort. Scarce a stone's throw from the house lie the nearest parts of that beautiful rustick reservation known as "Blackstone Park"—wherein I have been wont to wander some twenty or more years. Here Nature unadorn'd displays a multiplicity of agreeable phases; ravines, groves, brooklets, thickets, & Arcadian stretches of river-bank—for the park borders on the wide & salty Seekonk. The Seekonk is call'd a river, but in truth 'tis but a bay or inlet. The river proper doth not begin till four miles to the north, where (changing its name successively to the Pawtucket & the Blackstone) its fresh streams flow over the mill dam at the Great Bridge of the city of Pawtucket. How beauteous indeed is untainted Nature as beheld in so idyllick a spot as Blackstone Park! Here in early youth & later, oft

> "I sat me down to watch upon a bank
> With ivy canopy'd, & interwove
> With flaunting honeysuckle, & began,
> Wrapt in a pleasing fit of melancholy,
> To meditate my rural minstrelsy
> Till Fancy had her fill—"[6]

I think this park would explain why such a born & bred town man shou'd possess such a taste for rural musings & Arcadian themes!

But shou'd your town taste rebel at so great a dose of rusticity, I cou'd remove the effect by a pleasing digression, & shew you one of our quiet streets near my home, which pleases me unutterably on account of its extremely Georgian atmosphere. This street—Orchard Avenue—is one of the newer thoroughfares, & possesses none but the most beautiful dwellings. Those on the north side have all been erected within the last fifteen years, & in consequence all conform to the prevailing *imitation Colonial* style, both in architecture, interior, & grounds. For some distance there is not a single break in the chronological harmony, so that a section of the street is a veritable living breath from my favourite century. It is even more vivid than a really old street with its architectural relics, since the very *newness* of the houses imparts that vitalising charm which suggests the *real living presence* of the Georgian age, in all its first freshness & splendour. In the twilight the illusion is particularly haunting & delightful—the intrusion into the picture of any mortal without a well powder'd periwig is a shock! Verily, I have within reach much to sustain equal charms—but there is nothing like one's native heath! To me, any conception of Elysium must needs embody more than a few features of Providence scenery!

Pardon all this descriptive rot—the typical ebullition of a confirmed stay-at-home who knows but one locality on the face of the globe, but knows & loves every inch of that locality!

Ever yr most oblig'd obt Serv[t]

L Theobald Jun[r]

Notes

1. RK did indeed visit HPL later in the year; see his poem "At Providence in 1918" (Appendix).

2. Joseph Banigan (1839–1898) was a poor Irish immigrant who founded the Woonsocket Rubber Company in 1866, and by 1890 was one of the country's leading rubber manufacturers. In 1897, Banigan replaced the 2½-story house he had erected at the corner of Angell Street and Wayland Avenue in 1875 (now standing at 9 Orchard Avenue) by a larger stone house, now replaced by Wayland Manor (500 Angell Street).

3. Joseph Banigan (1888–1962), Richard Davis Banigan (1890–1973), and John Joseph Banigan (1894–1967).

4. See Winifred Virginia Jackson, "Our Dedication": "We take delight in being able to head these pages with one of Mr. Hoag's longest and most spirited compositions, 'To the Falls of Dionondawa,' which preserves in song the fame of a beautiful and legend-haunted cataract of the Battenkill River, close to Vista Buena, the author's pleasant Greenwich estate." *The Poetical Works of Jonathan E. Hoag* 60. The book was edited by HPL. Jackson's piece originally appeared in *Eurus* (February 1918).

5. The "tale in rhyme" was "Psychopompos" (312 lines), the other poem "Old Christmas" (322 lines).

6. John Milton, *Comus* (1637), ll. 543–48.

[37]   [AHT]

June 27, 1918

My dear Klei:—

[. . .]

My *Hesperia* will be critical & educational in object, though I am "sugar-coating" the first number by "printing" a conclusion of the serial "The Mystery of Murdon Grange." I will shew it to you when you call. It is outwardly done on the patchwork plan as before—each chapter bears one of my different *aliases*—Ward Phillips—Ames Dorrance Rowley—L. Theobald, &c.[1] It was a rather good diversion to write it. Really, I think I could have been a passable dime novelist if I had been trained in that noble calling! British amateurdom is reacting after its war depression. The first shock is over, & the war accepted as a permanent thing. I believe we are in for a fairly Napoleonic era of continuous fighting. It seems to me unlikely that we shall see the end in less than ten or fifteen years. Of course, this may be an extreme estimate, but I am on my guard against the undue optimism which caused men to laugh at the late Lord Kitchener when he opined that it would last *as long as* three years. If Germany can control Russia, she will have gained access to a source of infinite supplies. Like one of her own mediaeval "robber barons" she can hold out for ages, preying at will on her neighbours till sheer fatigue in so empty an enterprise shall cause her to collapse. The only possible ray of hope is the weakness of Austria. Austria is a mistake—an ethnological paradox. The masses of turbulent Slavs she seeks to control will prove her undoing some day. The best thing Austria could do is to seek cover inside the German Empire. Perhaps she will if all her Slavic & Magyar parts are removed by the war. But pardon the digression!

Hoping to see you a week from Monday, I am, Sir, Ever yr. most
oblig'd obedient Servt
Lo

Notes

1. *Hesperia* was a manuscript magazine that HPL circulated in Great Britain. "The Mystery of Murdon Grange" appears to have been a round-robin story written by various amateurs: chapters by Joseph Parks, Beryl Mappin, Benjamin Winskill, and Ernest Lionel McKeag (1896–1976) were published in McKeag's amateur journal *Spindrift* (see HPL's discussions in "Department of Public Criticism," January, March, and May 1918; *CE* 1.180, 188, 195). No segments written by HPL, whether in *Hesperia* or elsewhere, have been found.

[38]   [AHT]

July 14, 1918

My Dear Kleiner:—

I am glad you like the sonnet by "Wilfred Kemble"— (W. F. Pelton) for my own judgment told me it was worthy of a place at the head of the contents.[1] I think I told you that Mr. Pelton is author of a work on poetical technique, the manuscript of which is in Miss Hyde's possession. I advise you to ask her to let you read it—you would find it interesting. Pelton is having some difficulty in finding a publisher. I arranged purposely to have "The Despised Pastoral" come directly after "The Spirit of Summer"— as a sort of justification.[2] I am willing to *explain* my style, but not to *alter* it. If the publick relish not my pastorals, they need not peruse them—but no power on earth can stop me from writing them! I have an idea of writing some *absolutely conventional* pastorals soon—just as a sort of symbol of my defiance of modern criticks. By this I mean the old-fashion'd dialogues betwixt Damon, Menalcas, Colin, Damaetas, Meliboeus, &c., &c. about rustic themes— Strephon's complaint that he hath lost his sheep, or the lyrical contest betwixt Amyntas & Mopsus, at which old Tityrus awards the prize—a young lamb— to Mopsus, for his praise of Amaryllis, as sung to the accompaniment of a rustick lyre.[3] I shall probably begin something like this:

> Whilst you, Menalcas, feed your tender goats,
> And calm your restless herds with Dorick notes,
> In pensive strains amongst the mountain rocks,
> I tell the Oreads of my absent flocks—&c. &c.

I note your objections to "On Shore". I deemed the piece fairly well expressive of its subject—the grim, ugly, forbidding New-England sea-coast, with its wildness, danger, & desolation. In treating of New-England, Mrs. Jordan chooses aspects I seldom touch upon. She is affected by its bleaker features, whilst I pass over these, & dwell upon those things which resemble *Old* England. But I have a wholesome respect for her rugged marine pieces—even though I should not be likely to parallel them in my own metrical efforts. I think her "Song of the North Wind" was a tremendously powerful poem—an opinion spontaneously given by several persons who have read it. About the "Pollock's Rip bell"—I have an idea that this line alludes to some actual geographical locality.[4]

Your obt humble Serv[t]

L. Theobald, Jun[r].

[Here AHT includes "On a Battlefield in France."]

Notes

1. Wilfrid Kemble, "Lord Kitchener," *Conservative* 4, No. 1 (July 1918): 1.
2. "The Spirit of Summer," *Conservative* 4, No. 1 (July 1918): 1; "The Despised Pastoral," 2 (*CE* 2.22–23).
3. All these figures are stock characters mentioned in the pastoral poems of Theocritus, Bion, Virgil, and other ancient poets, as well as their British imitators.
4. Winifred Virginia Jackson, "On Shore": "I can but be praying, / 'Neath wind and sea's flaying, / And shut from my ears / The Pollock's Rip bell!" (ll. 13–16). The bell was a sea buoy at the entrance to Nantucket Sound.

[39] [AHT]

DAMON AND DELIA; A Pastoral by EDWARD SOFTLY—(Familiarity with *The Tatler* will explain this new pen-name of mine. I always choose dunces—historical, amateurical, or hypothetical—as the sources of my fictitious titles!)[1]

Dept. of Publick Criticism, Office of y[e] Chairman
Will's Coffee-House, Russell-Street, Covent-Garden, London

August 25, 1718

Revered Executive:—

Concerning a local American tone in the contents & decoration of a library, I confess I share not your scruples. I cannot feel any real difference betwixt the States & the Motherland, & believe there ought not to be. As you doubtless know, I do not favour the Colonial side of the Revolution, & should have stood by the King had I been alive in 1776. I am part & parcel of an age when Anglo-Saxondom was one & undivided—& I do not feel very wicked or abnormal when I say that I would give my life quite as freely for the old flag as for the new. It was in August, 1914, that my spirit "entered the war"—for King & Empire! Reckoning Anglo-Saxondom as a unit, I disregard recent political boundaries in choosing favourite authors. Of my prime favourites one (A. Pope) was of the old land, & another (E. A. Poe) of the new. I am not an Anglomaniac to the point of anti-Americanism—I am merely a Colonial Tory of the *ancien regime,* loving my native town of Providence, my native colony of Rhode-Island, & my ancestral & all-including circle of civilisation—Britannia's! I live in the vague hope of a reunion some day—& could not by any process of reasoning convince myself inwardly that I am not a loyal Englishman & faithful subject of H. M. George V. In early childhood, even, I used to insist to my somewhat shocked grandfather that the real super-ruler was Queen Victoria. I am no traitor to the States, but there never was a more thorough, ingrained, & absolute Queen-Anne British Colonial than L. Theobald Jun$^{r.}$! God save Y^e King!

In the non-personal family library we have a large number of American books, against which I hold no prejudice, & some of which I have read. But my partiality for 18th century work of course makes my reading preponderantly of the old land. I like the novels of J. Fenimore Cooper & of N. Hawthorne, & the verse of O. W. Holmes. The critical dissertations of J. R. Lowell likewise gratify my taste. Recently my discussion with Galpin hath led me to look over the essays of R. Emerson, Esq., of Concord, (Galpin sent me an exquisite little gift book de luxe for a birthday present last Tuesday—Emerson's Essay on Culture.) whose work I had previously dismissed after a mere skimming over. On second perusal, I find Mr. Emerson not altogether wanting in good sense, tho' I much prefer my older friend Mr. Addison. In enumerating American authors, I nearly forgot my early favourite Mr. Irving, of New-York, since I think of him half as an Englishman. Him do I admire vastly, both in themes & style, & deem his prose a masterpiece of harmony & model of elegance.

Then I have my pet detestations amongst the later English. Chas. Dickens I cannot bear, & R. Kipling I can only tolerate. A. Tennyson fatigues me, & after a time W. Thackeray induceth drowsiness. It seems to me that A. C. Swinburne was the only real poet either in England or America since the death of Mr. Poe. Decidedly, I find something missing in literature later than Dr. Johnson's day! 'Twou'd shock you monstrously, no doubt, were I to tell you that of L^d. Byron's verse, I enjoy "English Bards & Scotch Reviewers" *most!*

Ever yr. most oblig'd, most obt.

humble Servt.

Edw. Softly

Notes

1. The pseudonym derives from Addison's *Tatler* No. 163 (25 April 1710), where Ad-

dison pretends to praise a poem, "To Mira on Her Incomparable Poems," by "Ned Softly." See HPL's letter to the NAPA Bureau of Critics (*National Amateur,* January 1919; *CE* 1.214–16), as by "Ned Softly and Ward Phillips."

[40] [AHT]

Sept. 22, 1918

My dear Field-Marshal Klei:—

And by the way—under his pseudonym of "Crossman" (Do not reveal this pseudonym publicly. Cook likes to guard it.), Cook has written a most vivid & dramatic short story called "The Ends of the Law" about a Western Sheriff & his prisoner in the midst of a desert. The suspense, incidents, & development stamp Cook as a gifted fictionist. All the revision I made was to remove three split infinitives—Cook's favourite vice. You will laugh when you see *my* fictional attempt—the conclusion of "Murdon Grange". It is a typical dime novel—with all the time-worn appurtenances of its type! *Hesperia* ought to reach you in less than a month. I am circulating it on a geographical basis, & it will tour New York State after New England is covered. It will go to one Canadian amateur, John R. Nicol of Saskatchewan—who was in Scotland when the A.P.C. was organised, & to whom I sent *The Conservative* last July. His copy arrived too late, but followed him back across the Atlantic, & he now writes for information concerning the U.A.P.A. I may "land" him as a recruit.

I am, Sir, Ever
Yr most oblig'd obt Servt.
Lo

[41] [AHT]

Novr. 25, 1918

My dear Kleiner:—

"Col. Linkaby Didd", to whom the lines are inscribed, is an *imaginary* character figuring frequently in the local *Journal*.[1] Like Sir Roger de Coverly[2] [*sic*] he is supposed to be an odd rural character, residing at "Nooseneck Hill, in the town of Exeter"—the most desolate & remote spot conceivable in Rhode Island. "Col. Didd" always takes the *wrong* side of public questions, arguing picturesquely & illiterately, with many comic blunders & perversions of the Malaprop variety. These satirical "Didd" articles are generally thought to be the work of Mr. Rathom, editor of the *Journal*. In the recent political campaign, the greatest heat was engendered by the attempt of George F. O'Shaunessy, an Irish Wilson-Democratic congressman, formerly of the New York Tammany machine, to defeat for reëlection Senator Le Baron Bradford Colt, a statesman of honourable distinction, & a Rhode-Island Republican gentleman of ancient ancestry. O'Shaunessy based his campaign on lies; claiming that he has voted to increase soldiers' pay, when as a matter of fact he had voted *against* the increase. His vote to increase pay was at a *previous* time. He also charged Colt with deficient patriotism in voting down the old shipping bill, whereby the U.S. would have *paid* Germany for the interned vessels which were later *seized.* Wilson, of course, was duped, & sponsored the bill; but Colt could not be fooled so readily. As the campaign grew more bitter, O'Shaunessy became still more ridiculous, dragging in local issues such as street railway fares, & calling Colt every ill name imaginable, such as "Wall Street henchman", & kindred designations. The *Journal* satirised this wholesale demagoguery very effectively in the "Didd" articles, by *pretending* to praise O'Shaunessy & to denounce Colt. The paper also resurrected another fictitious comic character— "*Edward Leland Strong,* The Plumber-Poet of Pawtucket"—an intentional "D. V. Bush" whose bad verse on the wrong side of public questions stirred the general mirth a decade or two ago.[3] (Rathom is said to write this doggerel as well as the "Didd" stuff.) Now all this display of satire quite naturally excited my own satiric soul, hence on Novr. 1 I perpetrated the enclosed effusion, dating it from "Pascoag",[4] a comically obscure village, & signing my Theobald pseudonym. With high hope, I sent it to the *Journal,* only to meet with a cold rebuff. I later sent the carbon to Galpin, who appended a very frank criticism as you will see. It remains only to be added, that O'Shaunessy was very properly defeated by a vast majority. This state has had enough of Wilsonian masked autocracy, & will elect no more rubber-stamps to the Senate for T. Woodrow's private use. Now that the war is won, the nation is prepared to see that the present administration's arbitrary usurpations of power be ended. No more governmental control of utilities, restrictions upon the press, & restraints of individual liberty, can be tolerated. Each of the several war measures was doubtless necessary during belligerency, but T. Woodrow must be made to understand that with the coming of peace, the old constitution must again be enthroned!

　　Most sincerely yours,
　　　　HPLovecraft

[Here AHT includes "Oceanus" and "Clouds."]

Notes

1. "To Col. Linkaby Didd," unpublished in HPL's lifetime. The author of the articles was John Revelstoke Bunbury Roberts Rathom (1868–1923), editor of the *Journal* from 1912 until his death. The poem concerns the 1918 campaign for election to the US Senate from Rhode Island between the Republican LeBaron Colt (1846–1924), favored by HPL, and the Democrat George O'Shaunessy (1868–1934). Colt won the election and served until his death.

2. Sir Roger de Coverley is a recurring character in various papers by Addison, Steele, and others in the *Spectator.*

3. HPL mentions Strong in "To Col. Linkaby Didd," l. 114.
4. Part of "The Horror at Red Hook" takes place in Pascoag.

[42]   [AHT; Post]

Dec. 4[, 1918]

My dear Klei:—

MOTHER EARTH

One night I wander'd down the bank
Of a deep valley, hush'd and dank,
Whose stagnant air possess'd a taint
And chill that made me sick and faint.
The frequent trees on ev'ry hand
Loom'd like a ghastly goblin band,
And branches 'gainst the narrowing sky
Took shapes I fear'd—I knew not why.
Deeper I plung'd, and seem'd to grope
For some lost thing as joy or hope,
Yet found, for all my searchings there,
Naught save the phantoms of despair.
The walls contracted as I went
Still farther in my mad descent,
Till soon, of moon and stars bereft,
I crouch'd within a rocky cleft
So deep and ancient that the stone
Breath'd things primordial and unknown.
My hands, exploring, strove to trace
The features of the valley's face,
When midst the gloom they seem'd to find
An outline frightful to my mind.
Not any shape my straining eyes,
Could they have seen, might recognise;
For what I touch'd bespoke a day
Too old for man's fugacious sway.
The clinging lichens, moist and hoary,
Forbade me read the antique story;
But hidden water, trickling low,
Whisper'd the tales I should not know.
"Mortal, ephemeral and bold,
"In mercy keep what I have told,
"Yet think sometimes of what hath been,
"And sights these crumbling rocks have seen;

"Of sentience old ere thy weak brood
"Appear'd in lesser magnitude,
"And living things that yet survive,
"Tho' not to human ken alive.
"I AM THE VOICE OF MOTHER EARTH,
"FROM WHENCE ALL HORRORS HAVE THEIR BIRTH."

I share most emphatically your regret at the distance between 278 Grove & 598 Angell, & wish we both lived in Old London, within walking distance of Will's & of each other's homes. Like you I am absolutely devoid of actual friends outside of correspondence. Those whom I knew in youth are all active & successful now—one a Major in the Regular Army, another a lawyer, another an Episcopal clergyman, another a librarian of the R. I. Historical Society, &c., with any number of "rising young businessmen"—if I may employ a "rubber-stamp phrase". With such, a sickly recluse can have little or nothing in common;—their virile success & bustling prosperity but emphasise the melancholy of one whose active career ended at eighteen—if indeed it ever existed in more than a nominal sense. The only persons who could now be real friends, are those who never knew me in my days of high hope & expansive ambition; & who therefore expect no more from me than I am able to furnish. To them, I should exhibit no such ignominious decadence as I must to those who, from early acquaintance, took it for granted that I would go normally through the university, achieve a professorship, & by this time be a real person with a recognised place in the social & academic world, instead of a nonentity with absolutely nothing of real worth to justify existence. The other day, I saw a featured article in *The New York Tribune* by one whose compositions I used to correct at Hope Street High School! Could irony be greater? How are the tables turned! I may only thank the Fates that I am not embittered by the failure which my invalidism has brought upon me. I do not hate or envy my old acquaintances—I merely wish to sink out of their sight if I cannot shew some achievements to match theirs. Nor am I like my old friend Dean Swift, embittered with all humanity. I see no cause to blame society or any individual; but simply prefer to have intimacy with those who have never known me, save at my worst—which is now. I no more visit the Ladd Observatory or various other attractions of Brown University. Once I expected to utilise them as a regularly entered student, & some day perhaps control some of them as a faculty member. But having known them with this "inside" attitude, I am today unwilling to visit them as a casual outsider & non-university barbarian & alien.

Having finished this melancholiac spasm—for which I entreat your pardon—allow me to express my interest in your library, as at present arranged. I note that you are partial to epistolary collections; in which department your library easily excels mine. I have few letters save those of Mr. Pope, Mr.

Thomson, Mr. Cowper, Mr. Gray, & some others scatter'd about in various volumes. Those of Mr. Cowper are of a singular felicity & naturalness, & especially interesting to me because of Mr. Cowper's state of health; which, aside from his religious mania, is so much like my own. Cowper & I differ (aside from questions of merit) in that his writings reflect his tame domesticity & languor; whilst I strive to maintain a spirited & classical style which may accord better with the vigorous atmosphere of the coffee-house, than with the languid precincts of the sick-room or shelter'd study. Ld. Byron called Cowper a "coddled poet", & a recent writer remarks that there is a "suspicion of gruel & dressing-gowns about him."[1] I, however, should be the last to sneer at this. As I pen these lines, *I* am attired in a dressing-gown, & my latest meal, taken two hours ago, consists solely of a liquid food for invalids! All in all, I fancy the melancholy William & I are brothers in spirit, save where theology is concerned. Nevertheless, I dislike his tame subjects & weak spiritlessness—he shews the decline of the classical spirit. He is like the moderns—afraid to burst out in honest homely satire. Solemnity, which is never far from hypocrisy, has for the last century characterised literary censure of folly & evil. No such thing is needed—the bard should come forth with plain sarcastic vehemence; putting on no cloak of loftiness, but saying what he thinks!

I note the abundance of Lamb books in your library, & rejoice that you have assembled so much lore concerning your favourite. Some day I shall enlarge my knowledge of Lamb, tho' I fear I shall never come to know him so well as the wits of Will's or the circle of Sam: Johnson. With several of your poets—the more recent ones—I am not as well acquainted as I shou'd be. Matt: Arnold, Mr. Praed,[2] Mr. Stevenson (as a *poet*), Mr. Kipling, Mr. Dobson, Mr. Locker, &c. are but superficially known to me—or let me amplify in the interests of candour: I know not Locker *at all!*[3] I envy you Drayton, Prior, & Wither—with whom I have only a publick-library (albeit a thorough) acquaintance. Burns, Arnold, Tennyson, &c. are in the household library, but not in the personal collection in my room. And all this conversation reminds me that I must soon redeem my resolution to lend you *Oldham.*[4] Your description of your *walls* fills me with humility. I could never summon up the aesthetick energy to put my room in sightly order, or remove the heterogeneous "decorative" scheme of boyhood days. I am, aesthetically, all visions—I never find inclination to materialise my ideals of harmony—which, by the way, are constantly changing. Sometimes I desire a perfect Queen-Anne room, with every ornament & *objet d'art* in consonance; again I am filled with a passion for classical antiquity, with Grecian sculptures & bas-reliefs on every hand, & severely simple furniture. (In early childhood, I had an *Oriental* fad, & tried to fit up a corner of my room—at the old house—in true Saracen style, a la the Arabian Nights). And amidst all this dreaming I dwell in the unorderly room which you yourself beheld—a cross betwixt a small boy's nursery & the *Tryout* office!!! Verily, such cramped quarters must have taken all the furnishing ambition out of me!

> Yr obt hble Servt:
>> Lo

Notes

1. Byron's comment comes from a letter to John Murray (20 May 1820). The other comment is from Henry A. Beers (1847–1926), *An Outline Sketch of English Literature* (New York: Chautauqua Press, 1886), 211.

2. Winthrop Mackworth Praed (1802–1839), English politician and poet.

3. HPL must later have become acquainted with the English poet Frederick Locker-Lampson (1821–1895), as two editions of his *London Lyrics* (1884, 1891) are found in his library (*LL* 576–77).

4. No edition of John Oldham's poetry has been found for HPL's library. See, however, RK's poem "John Oldham: 1653–1683" (Appendix) and HPL's "John Oldham: A Defence," both published on the same page of the *United Co-operative* (June 1919).

[43]   [AHT]

Decr. 16, 1918

My dear Klei:—

Speaking of Morton—I like him more & more as I become further acquainted with him. Despite my antipodal differences on most matters, his absolute sincerity concerning all things appeals to me strongly. Most radicals are affected poseurs, but it did not take E. H. Cole's recent article to convince me that J. F. M. Jr.'s zeal is of the genuine & serious variety.[1] He maintains an open attitude in discussing poetick imagism, & I am going to ask Mo to lend me the *Kleicomolo* instalment containing the latter's lucid discussion of this theme; as well as the inimitable burlesque; to send along with my next instalment of the argument. Mo is an old opponent of Morton's, & will no doubt be glad to help me out!

> I beg to subscribe my self as yr most oblig'd, most obt.
>> & most Humble Servt:
>>> Ward Phillips

Notes

1. Edward H. Cole, "'Other Days,'" *National Amateur* 41, No. 2 (November 1918): 68–76 (a long article about four prominent amateur journalists: Edwin Booth Swift, James F. Morton, Jr., Edith Miniter, and Frank Austin Kendall). The Morton portion was reprinted with another piece as "James Ferdinand Morton, Jr.," *Ghost* No. 5 (July 1947): 11–15; rpt. in *Letters to James F. Morton* 435–38.

[44]   [AHT]

1/18/19

Honourable Sir:—

My mother, feeling no better here, has gone on a visit to my elder aunt for purposes of complete rest; leaving my younger aunt as autocrat of this dwelling. My aunt does splendidly—but you above all others can imagine the effect of maternal illness & absence. I cannot eat, nor can I stay up long at a time. Pen-writing or typewriting nearly drives me insane. But my nervous system seems to find its vent in feverish & incessant scribbling with a pencil. I have written a great deal, though perhaps the results shew the effects of my condition. I am assured, however, that my mother's state is not dangerous; that the apparent stomach trouble is neurotic & not organic. She writes optimistic letters each day, & I try to make my replies equally optimistic; though I do not find it possible to "cheer up", eat, & go out, as she encourages me to do. Such infirmity & absence on her part is so *unprecedented*, that it cannot but depress me, despite the brightest bulletins of her physician—whom, by the way, she writes that she is now well enough to dismiss.

Morton has just sent a new (but unconvincing) instalment of our friendly nigger argument.[1] He is so loftily humanitarian that he cannot see the plain facts. The whole U.S. negro question is very simple. (1) *Certainly* the negro is vastly the biological inferior of the Caucasian. (2) Therefore if racial amalgamation were to occur, the net level of American civilisation would perceptibly fall, as in such mongrel nations as Mexico—& several South American near-republics. (3) Amalgamation would undoubtedly take place if prejudice were eradicated, beginning with the lowest grades of Jews & Italians & eventually working upward until the whole country would be poisoned, & its culture & progress stunted. (4) Therefore the much-abused "colour line" is a self-protective measure of the white American people to keep the blood of their descendants pure, & the institutions & greatness of their country unimpaired. The colour line *must be maintained* in spite of the ranting & preaching of fanatical & ill-informed philanthropists. The genius of a few individuals is never an index of collective racial capacity. In spite of all the Booker Washingtons & Dunbars[2] we can see that the negro as a whole has never made any progress or founded any culture. We cannot judge a man sociologically by his own individual qualities; we have the future to think of. Two persons of different races, though equal mentally & physically, may have a vitally different sociological value, *because one will certainly produce an incalculably better type of descendants than the other*. We must see that *the best* retain social & political supremacy, in order that our *best* traditions may be preserved. Therefore, to me, racial prejudice is *not* irrational or unexplainable; nor in any way unjustifiable. It has awkward phases, but its benefits immeasurably outweigh its disadvantages.

Yr. oblig'd obt Servant

Lo

Notes

1. See Morton's pamphlet *The Curse of Race Prejudice* (1906?).
2. Booker T. Washington (1856–1915), African-American author and educator; Paul Laurence Dunbar (1872–1906), African-American poet and novelist.

[45]   [AHT]

2/19/19

Most Esteemed Klei:—

      Things hereabouts go evenly, albeit distressingly slowly. I am up & about, & go to call on my mother each day. She considers herself improving, as does her physician; yet the tardiness of the process is most trying to me, as it must be to her. So far as exact mental labour is concerned, I am quite useless for the time being. Melancholy at times seems oppressive, & tends to inspire effusions like the following, which is my latest:

DESPAIR

by Ward Phillips

O'er the midnight moorlands crying,
Thro' the cypress forests sighing,
In the night-wind madly flying,
    Hellish forms with streaming hair;
In the barren branches creaking,
By the stagnant swamp-pools speaking,
Past the shore-cliffs ever shrieking,
    Damnèd daemons of despair.

Once, I think I half remember,
Ere the grey skies of November
Quench'd my youth's aspiring ember,
    Liv'd there such a thing as bliss;
Skies that now are dark were beaming,
Gold and azure, splendid seeming
Till I learn'd it all was dreaming—
    Deadly drowsiness of Dis.

But the stream of Time, swift flowing,
Brings the torment of half-knowing—
Dimly rushing, blindly going
    Past the never-trodden lea;
And the voyager, repining,
Sees the grisly death-fires shining,

Hears the wicked petrel's whining
    As he helpless drifts to sea.

Evil wings in aether beating;
Vultures at the spirit eating;
Things unseen forever fleeting
    Black against the leering sky.
Ghastly shades of bygone gladness,
Clawing fiends of future sadness,
Mingle in a cloud of madness
    Ever on the soul to lie.

Thus the living, lone and sobbing,
In the throes of anguish throbbing,
With the loathsome Furies robbing
    Night and noon of peace and rest.
But beyond the groans and grating
Of abhorrent Life, is waiting
Sweet Oblivion, culminating
    All the years of fruitless quest.

April Dawn
by L. Theobald, Junr.

I love to watch the meadow-lands awake
    Beneath the breezes of an April dawn,
When o'er the stone-wall'd hill the sunbeams break,
    And tremble on the tender-tufted lawn.

When vernal tints of earth and heaven fuse
    Into one placid mist of morning light,
And the still landscape's intermingled hues
    Paint the high crests, and make the valleys bright.

The red-gold sun, reluctant to ascend,
    Lingers a moment o'er the velvet mound;
Mead, grove, and garden their faint fragrance blend,
    And matin skylarks thrill with crystal sound.

The fresh-turn'd furrows, damp with dew and haze,
    Breathe out a message of resurgent life;
Each shrub and tree receives increasing rays,
    And splendid shines, with joy and vigour rife.

Say you a barren vista strikes the eye;
    That no wild grace adorns the rolling green?

Say you that here unlovely pastures lie,
  And awkward cottage-roofs impair the scene?

Not so the sentient poet-glance can see
  The gentle glory of the sun-gilt slope;
A million Aprils from eternity
  Gleam in this one, and sing a world's fair hope!

  I am ever
    Yr Obt Humble Servt
      L. Theobald Jun[r.]

[46] [AHT]

March 19, 1919

My dear Klei:—

      My mother, showing no signs of recovery, has gone to a hospital, where she is receiving the most expert care which medical science can afford. I strongly hope the change will benefit her. It has a good chance to do so, since many features of diet & regimen which the physicians are prescribing, are directly opposite to those prescribed by the previous practitioner. She herself seems satisfied with the treatment, & is more optimistic than at any time for a month before. My own energy is spasmodic. For days at a time I can do nothing—but I wrote an entire March critical report one evening recently[1] & I am this morning able to write letters after having been up all night.

      I beg the honour to subscribe myself as your

      Most humble, most ob[t] Serv[t]

        Lo

Notes

1. "Department of Public Criticism," *United Amateur* 18, No. 4 (March 1919): 79–82 (*CE* 1.222–27). The issue was published at least a month after its cover date.

[47] [AHT]

March 30, 1919

My dear Klei:—

      I wish I could report equal improvement in my mother's case, but her condition is distressingly stationary. She has now gone to the best sanitarium in this state,[1] where every curative agency known to science, & every phase of expert nursing, care, & diet, may be hers. Her sojourn there, however, will have to be of great duration; & I am obliged to look forward to a long & dreary interval wherein home will be but half a home for want of its dominant figure. The prospect is not a pleasing one; but I shall be thankful if any procedure, however protracted, can restore my mother to normal or nearly normal health. My nerve strain seems now to be manifesting itself in my vision—I am frequently dizzy, & cannot read or write long without a blurring of sight or a severe headache. Existence seems of little value, & I wish it might terminate!

I am ever Yr most humble, most ob^t Servt

Lo

Notes

1. Butler Hospital (345 Blackstone Blvd.), a psychiatric hospital where she would die on 24 May 1921. It was the same hospital where her husband, Winfield Scott Lovecraft, was placed from 1893 until his death in 1898.

[48] [AHT]

4/16/19

My dear Klei:—

It is with the utmost delight that I hear of your proposed New-England trip, during which you certainly must not fail to give Providence's "hidden ways & quaint old places"[1] a liberal share of your time. The pleasure I experienced on that memorable July 6, 1918, has not since been equalled; & I can but look forward with eagerness to a similar delight. This time we can inspect wonders untasted last year. Whilst we then viewed some imitation Colonial architecture, we can next time behold some typical Georgian *interiors* by visiting the "Pendleton House" on Benefit Street.[2] This house is a typical Colonial edifice, furnished magnificently with the richest Georgian furniture, as if the owner were still in possession & the calendar indeed turned back to my beloved XVIIIth century. It is in fact a museum, belonging to the Rhode Island School of Design; but the home atmosphere is sedulously maintained in order to give the visitor a faithful picture of Georgian interiors as they really were. Such a place should have power to evoke some poesy from your Muse. We might also visit my favourite rural hunt, Quinsnicket Park, which is a bit of 18th century countryside surviving to this day. It contains houses dating as far back as 1670, & bits of farmland unchanged since the reign of the third George. For scenic effects it is unsurpassed, as I tried to point out in my lines on the subject—which you probably read four years ago.[3]

My mother is slightly improved in general physical condition, but not so far as nerves are concerned. Her sojourn at the sanitarium seems destined to be of long duration, & you will probably find my aunt still in domestic control here when you come. The one relieving factor is to know that my mother's condition is not one of actual danger. I have little incentive to do anything, & can appreciate, more than before, the effect of your bereavement.

I remain ever

> Yr most obt Servt
>
> Lo

1. From RK's poem "At Providence in 1918," l. 5.
2. HPL refers to the Colonial House, adjoining the Rhode Island School of Design Museum at 224 Benefit Street, containing the Pendleton Collection of antique furniture and china.
3. "Quinsnicket Park" (written in 1913).

[49]   [AHT]

> Prime-Minister's Chambers
> 6/17/19

To H. M. Rinarto I[1]
King of the United

Sire:—

My mother's health remains so stationary that I fear present arrangements must be considered as semi-permanent. The only hopeful thing is the assurance that she is organically well, & therefore in no danger of growing worse. It will probably be harder for her to recover from this breakdown than from that which she sustained in youth, but no physician seems to take anything but an ultimately optimistic view of the case. Nerves have always been the bane of the Phillips family.

With customary good wishes & assurances of esteem,

> I am, Sir, every y^r most
> ob^t humble Servt
> Jonathan Swift

Notes

1. Rinarto, manifestly based on RK, is a character in *Alfredo: A Tragedy* (14 September 1918).

[50]   [AHT]

> 7/9/19

Esteem'd Ex-President:—[1]

Speaking of Colonial houses, I could curse my stupidity at not taking you to 135 Benefit Street, the home of some friends of ours, where my elder aunt is staying for a few months during the absence of the family.[2] She would have been delighted to meet you, & the house is almost as good as a museum. It is over 140 years old, & has been inhabited continuously by the same family. Most of the original furniture is there—& what additions have been made are not obtrusively different. However—in a way it shews its age, & is therefore not as good as the Pendleton House in displaying Colonial magnificence *just as it was* in the old days. We must remember that in Colonial times all these old houses were bright, fresh, & new—just like those on Orchard Avenue where we took the pictures. Whilst it is in the ancient streets that we are most magically transported to the past, it is in the new fac-simile estates that we behold most faithfully the colonial scenery as it actually looked in its prime.

Yr most hble Ob^t Servt
L:Theobald

Notes

1. RK's term as president of the UAPA had ended in early July 1919, with the election of Mary Faye Durr as president for 1919–20.
2. This is the location of the celebrated "shunned house" of HPL's story and the poem in letter RK 51. The house was then occupied by Mrs. C. H. Babbit. Lillian D. Clark is listed as a resident of the house in the 1920 US census.

[51]   [AHT; Post]

July 16, 1919

Honour'd St. John:[1]—
                  [. . .]

Anent the political situation—hades has broken loose!! At the convention, our entire ticket went through, save for next year's convention seat, & the Moitoret petition was denied on grounds which appeared adequate to the delegates. But now the Clevelandites intend to frame another petition, signed by ten members, & in the event of its denial—which is almost certain—to conduct what they call an "appeal to the membership at large". This, I presume, means a campaign of reckless innuendo. I did not return Moitoret's petition—according to him, of course, the election was illegal—but sent a very candid reply which evoked a five-page letter from him. He expresses his determination to "kill off" the "highbrow" element if he can. Opinions vary as to Moitoret, but Daas likes him. Moitoret claims that no ballots reached Cleveland—but candidly, I think they did. Even the distant Appleton members were able to vote on time. Future procedure is rather doubtful, because Miss McGeoch, in her anxiety lest a strain rest upon the present administration, favours the idea of a second election as demanded by Cleveland. Perhaps full reports from the convention will cause her to change her mind. If Daas, Miss Durr, & Mrs. Renshaw are satisfied of the legality of the election, the rest of us ought not to find fault. Moitoret says that Dowdell *did* join the United *before* announcing his candidacy, which makes one statement in my

Conservative editorial inaccurate. He demands that I make a public retraction—or else, as he says, I am a "tricky knave!!" I am preparing the desired retraction, but I wonder how Moitoret thinks I could have known of Dowdell's reinstatement when no announcement of it appeared? It looks as if distressing & exciting times are ahead in amateurdom![2]

[. . .]

THE HOUSE

'Tis a grove-circled dwelling
    Set close to a hill,
Where the branches are telling
    Strange legends of ill;
Over timbers so old
    That they breathe of the dead,
Crawl the vines, green and cold,
    By strange nourishment fed;
And no man knows the juices they suck from the depths of their dank slimy bed.

In the gardens are growing
    Tall blossoms and fair,
Each pallid bloom throwing
    Perfume on the air;
But the afternoon sun
    With its red slanting rays
Makes the picture loom dun
    On the curious gaze,
And above the sweet scent of the blossoms rise odours of numberless days.

The rank grasses are waving
    On terrace and lawn,
Dim memories sav'ring
    Of things that have gone;
The stones of the walks
    Are encrusted and wet,
And a strange spirit stalks
    When the red sun has set,
And the soul of the watcher is fill'd with faint pictures he fain would forget.

It was in the hot Junetime
    I stood by that scene,
When the gold rays of noontime
    Beat bright on the green.
But I shiver'd with cold,
    Groping feebly for light,

As a picture unroll'd—
And my age-spanning sight
Saw the time I had been there before flash like a fulgury out of the night.

WARD PHILLIPS

Y^r Most Obt Servt

Ward Phillips

Notes

1. HPL frequently referred to RK as Randolph St. John, as if he were a relative of Henry St. John, Viscount Bolingbroke (1678–1751), English statesman and man of letters. A character in "The Hound" (October 1922), obviously based on RK, is named St. John. In letter RK 97, HPL uses the variant "Sinjin," reflecting the British pronunciation of the name.

2. HPL refers to Anthony F. Moitoret, an amateur journalist in Cleveland, who was apparently petitioning for a new election for Official Editor of the UAPA. In the recent election, Anne Tillery Renshaw had defeated William J. Dowdell of Cleveland. See HPL's editorial, "For Official Editor—Anne Tillery Renshaw" (*Conservative*, July 1919; *CE* 1.237–38), in which HPL falsely asserted that Dowdell "has not been in the United for a period of more than two years."

[52] [Post]

July 30[, 1919]

L'affaire Moitoret presents the appearance of a calm before a storm. As Daas clearly shews, Cleveland has no real ground for protesting. His presence on our side is very fortunate; since he is an experienced politician, & able to combat shrewdly all the subtleties of the Cleveland group. The main charge of the Clevelandites that they received no ballots at all, is not proved; & Cook is perfectly certain that all proxies were dispatched on the early morning of the 28th of June.

[53] [AHT]

August 12, 1919

Gifted St. John:—

That derby hat picture of me always makes my mother smile. I was never really young, & always strove for elderly, sedate effects in attire. I will wager that when I was nineteen most persons took me for thirty at least. However, a derby was so egregiously unbecoming to my long face that I soon abandoned it for the not less dignified fedora which now constitutes my winter headgear. Whenever I buy a suit or other article of attire, I am careful to impress upon the reluctant salesman that I do not desire anything youthful or ultra-fashionable!

In order to shew that I was sedate & middle-aged even before donning long trousers, I am going to enclose—subject to return—a picture of myself at the age of 12½—taken in March, 1903, in my room at the old house, #454 Angell Street. The book in which I am immersed is Hansen's treatise on the moon, property of the Prov. Publick Library.[1] And whilst I am about it, I will enclose one other view—Theobaldus in the year of our Lord 1894—when R. St. John was a docile infant of about 1½!! This is the first picture of me taken after the shearing of my infantile curls, (a shearing performed by the *selfsame barber* who now trims my rapidly whitening locks! Some conservatism!!!), & you can rely upon it that I felt monstrously proud & manly. I remember *perfectly* when the view was taken—on afternoon in a studio in the "Arcade"— that Parthenon-like building on Westminster Street which I think I pointed out to you as a specimen of the "classic period" of American architecture.[2]

You may be interested to hear of the new professional literary partnership of Molo, just entered into. Mo has long been urging me to try professionalism, but I have been reluctant on account of my variation from the tastes of the period. Now, however, Mo has proposed a plan for collaboration in which his modern personality will be merged with my antique one. I am to write the material—mainly fiction—because I am the more fertile in plots; whilst he is to revise to suit the market, since he is the more familiar with contemporary conditions. He will do all the business part, also; since I detest commercialism. Then, IF he is able to "land" anything with a remunerative magazine, we shall "go halves" on the spoils of victory.

The pseudonym under which we shall offer our composite wares for sale, is a compound of our own full names: *Horace Philter Mocraft.* This is Mo's own invention. I trust that we may be able to earn a farthing or two in this way, though I am hardly indulging in any Alnaschar's Dream[3] of how I shall spend my vast coming wealth!!! Of course, it is understood that this arrangement shall not interfere with amateur work. I shall continue to send my matter unaltered to the amateur press, merely letting Moe have carbon copies for mutilation & marketing. The real ego Theobaldus will not bow to any reviser, & will not own or assume responsibility for the mangled "Mocraft" material. (Possibly you know that the late George Meredith (a Liberal) wrote articles commercially for the Conservative Press—against his own doctrines!) This Mocrafty business is merely a side-line & by-product; a harmless means of turning an honest penny if possible. Probably Moe obtained that "Mocraft" idea from the "Goldwyn" (Goldfish–Selwyn) combination.[4] If I should withdraw from the dual alliance after it became famous, he might do as Goldfish did—change his name legally to "Mocraft" in order to capitalise on the celebrity of the enterprise! At any rate, if you ever see a tale signed "Mocraft" in the *Atlantic, Century,* or *Scribner's,* you will now know who wrote it!

Your sensation of being *altered* in a subtle way is rather singular, though not incomprehensible psychologically. Such a thing might not be an inappropriate subject for introspective, meditative verse. The oddest impression I ever possess, is of the tremendously rapid rush of time—which seems to slip by me alarmingly. Events of ten or fifteen years ago seem as but yesterday, & the mere fact of being grown up is at times incredible to me, as I glance over some book particularly associated with my boyhood. At such times it is the present world which seems the more unreal & fantastic—I half expect to wake up & find the world of 1903 or thereabouts encircling me. This retrospective cast of mind, operating in various other channels, is probably what inclines me toward Graeco-Romanism & the Georgian Age.

I remain

Yr most humble & Ob^t Servant,

L. Theobald, Jun.

Notes

1. For Hansen see RK 10n1. The book in question has not been identified.

2. The Westminster Arcade is a historic shopping center at 130 Westminster Street and 65 Weybosset Street in downtown Providence, built in 1828. Its columns are the largest monoliths in the world, except for those in the Cathedral of St. John the Divine in New York.

3. In the *Spectator* No. 525 (13 November 1712), Joseph Addison tells a tale (which he found in Antoine Galland's French translation of the *Arabian Nights*) of Alnaschar, a petty merchant who deals in glassware. One day Alnaschar became so involved in a daydream about attaining fantastic wealth from his business that he inadvertently kicked over his glassware, shattering it and destroying its value.

4. See RK 28n1.

[54]   [AHT]

8/21/19

Sir Godfrey Kneller,[1] London,

Honourable Sir:—

[. . .]

But I am gradually getting through with amateur journalism. What I have done for it has brought me only slights & insults, except from an intensely appreciated few to whom I shall ever be fervently grateful. I shall always cling to the Kleicomolo & Gallomo circle, & shall always be glad to help any writer who wishes me to do so; but with the organisation I am done—unless the majority of publishers shew their disapproval of Cleveland by publicly rebuking the *Sun*, (for its coming campaign of slander & ridicule).[2] I cannot remain active in an association which does not wish me to do so, & toleration of the *Sun* group would imply this. The United may choose between me & the Dowdell–Moitoret band of thieves & blusterers.

[. . .]

I shall be slow about composing it; avoiding the heat of my naturally quick & violent temper, & waiting to think of really biting, cutting things to say in a frigid way.[3]

With best wishes, Ever y[r] obt Humble Servt,

Timon Coriolanus, Esqr.

Notes

1. Godfrey Kneller (1646–1723), German/English painter of the Baroque era.
2. HPL refers to the *Cleveland Sun,* the amateur paper edited by William J. Dowdell.
3. HPL apparently refers to a sharp rebuttal of attacks on the UAPA by Dowdell, but he does not appear to have written any such article at this time.

[55]   [AHT]

Castle Theobald, 9/14/19

Esteem'd but Desolated St. John:—

To begin with, let me extend the sincerest commiserations on the general state of your mind & interests, which is indeed not at all unlike my own. As you are aware, I have never been able to soothe myself with the sugary delusions of religion; for these things stand convicted of the utmost absurdity in the light of modern scientific knowledge. With Nietzsche, I have been forced to confess that mankind as a whole has no goal or purpose whatsoever, but is a mere superfluous speck in the unfathomable vortices of infinity & eternity. Accordingly, I have hardly been able to experience anything which one could call real happiness; or to take as vital an interest in human affairs as can one who still retains the hallucination of a "great purpose" in the general plan of terrestrial life. All this you know through my contributions to "The Kleico-molo". However, I have never permitted these circumstances to react upon my daily life; for it is obvious that although I have "nothing to live for", I certainly have just as much as any other of the insignificant bacteria called human beings. I have thus been content to observe the phenomena about me with something like objective interest, & to feel a certain tranquillity which comes from perfect acceptance of my place as an inconsequential atom. In ceasing to care about most things, I have likewise ceased to suffer in many ways. There is a real restfulness in the scientific conviction that nothing matters very much; that the only legitimate aim of humanity is to minimise acute suffering for the majority, & to drive whatever satisfaction is derivable from the exercise of the mind in the pursuit of truth.

If I were to criticise your present philosophy, it would be that you demand too much *emotion*—which is, after all, a distinctly inferior form of psychic activity. It may, of course, be pleasant & desirable in a way; but it involves the play of nervous tissue far less evolved than that wherein true intellection resides. It is a link with the instinct of lower creation, & consequently is not to be fostered or encouraged as a supreme goal of human endeavour. What man should seek, is the pleasure of non-emotional imagination—the pleasure of pure reason, as found in the perception of truths. It will always be more or less accompanied by secondary or vestigial emotional phenomena, but these phenomena will be of a rarefied type dependent on reason & imagination. Now that poetry no longer enchants you, I should advise your choice of philosophy as a substitute. Having failed to derive satisfaction from contemplating yourself as a highly organised centre of impressions & sensations, try contemplating yourself as a speck of dust in the midst of infinite creation, whose depths hold vast secrets for your solution. There is excitement & life in the thought. In place of Lamb, Keats, Shelley, or Tennyson, try Darwin, Huxley, Tyndall, Spencer, & Haeckel. Be a scientist instead of a litterateur.

Utter happiness, in the romantic sense, is in most cases an unattainable impossibility. Remember that the goal of the great Epicurus was not an earthy ἡδονή, or pleasure, but a lofty ἀταραξία, or freedom from cares & trivial thoughts. Consider yourself an impersonal observer without emotions, & have as your aim in life the tranquil observation & classification of the facts about you. I am sure that I, who hardly know what an emotion is like (outside of a few bursts of honest *anger* once in a while!), am far less vexed than he who is constantly straining after new sensations. (cf. my lines on "Content" in answer to your "Another Endless Day".) Before formulating any definite new philosophy of life, pray read Haeckel's "Riddle of the Universe", wherein a sane natural order, without the childish fantasies of religion, is expounded.

Far be it from me to laugh at your pursuit of the fair, resulting as it does from such a melancholy cause. My amusement at the callow romances of persons like Alfredus, Lady Myrrha, & McDonald,[1] is due largely to the fact that these effervescent young folk are really not in the least serious or in need of diversion. I doubt not but that many cases of affection are quite enduring, & fairly wholesome & beneficial to the persons concerned. I am indeed a friend & encourager of matrimony, since it is the foundation of normal family life & the source of such idyllick happiness as that of Baucis & Philemon.[2] When I say that *keen* happiness is largely an illusion, I do not mean to deny the possibility of much genuine domestick felicity. It is without the least trace of my accustom'd satire that I express the hope that you may win your nymph, settling down to a lifelong enjoyment of connubial contentment. Such is the ordinary course of mankind, & your enjoyment of this limited bliss will not prevent you from seeking the more ethereal delights of science described earlier in this epistle. In taking your contemplated step, you have the reassuring evidence of Mo's matrimonial happiness to sustain you; & you may feel certain that I shall welcome with delight the announcement of your engagement or wedding. I shall even be so generous as to refrain from composing an Augustan epithalamium, if such would seriously mar the harmoniousness of the nuptial festivities!

But here I must close, subscribing myself most cheerfully & philosophically yours,

    H. Paget Lowe
    (my latest pseudonym)

Notes

1. HPL refers to Alfred Galpin (whose schoolboy crushes HPL mocked in his many poems about "Damon," as well as in *Alfredo*); one of Galpin's lady loves ("Myrrha") to whom HPL addressed "Hylas and Myrrha: A Tale" and "Myrrha and Strephon"; and Philip B. McDonald (1888–1959), professor of Engineering English at the University of Colorado and amateur journalist.

2. The story of Baucis and Philemon—a married couple in Phrygia who graciously received Jupiter and Mercury (disguised as mortals) and in return were granted the boon of dying in old age at the same moment—is recounted in Ovid's *Metamorphoses* 8.624–724.

[56]   [AHT]

             Angell-St., East of Y^e Great Bridge,[1] in Providence
                       27th Sept^r., N.S. 1919

Laurell'd Bard:—

        Speaking of R. I. matters, it may interest you to know that the celebrated Cardinal Mercier[2] will sleep tomorrow night on Angell Street, only four houses west of the Theobald Mansion. His hosts will be the Catholic McElroys, who occupy the large Gothick "Banigan Mansion" on the corner of Angell Street & Wayland Avenue—which I believe I pointed out to you last summer. Mrs. McElroy is a daughter of the late Joseph Banigan, & is a person of such cultivation that the old stock of this locality do not scorn her acquaintance—in fact, all the Banigan heirs are cultivated & well received in the community. They are not "climbers", but their innate good qualities have won for them spontaneous regard & respect. My aunt may attend the reception which Mrs. McElroy will give to the Cardinal tomorrow afternoon, but I shall not—for you can imagine how the bustle & excitement would prostrate one who is hardly able to sit up at all this week. All the spacious lawn around the Banigan home is fenced off by means of a temporary rampart of wire netting, for vast crowds are expected to flock about in the hope of glimpsing the illustrious prelate. It will be one of the most exciting events known in this quiet neighbourhood for several years! I suppose all the Catholic scum of the city will flock around to obtain a glimpse of the Cardinal—to say nothing of non-Catholics who admire his brave conduct during Belgium's captivity.

    Returning to the subject of Grove Street melancholy & matrimony—I concede the logick & desirability of your present course. A year or two's wait before the ceremony is to be understood—I took all that for granted when speaking of an "immediate" union. Of course, I am unfamiliar with amatory phenomena save through cursory reading. I always assumed that one waited till he encountered some nymph who seemed radically different to him from the rest of her sex, & without whom he felt he could no longer exist. Then, I fancied, he commenced to lay siege to her heart in businesslike fashion, not desisting till either he won her for life, or was blighted by rejection. Of seeking affection for affection's sake—without any one special fair creature in mind—I was quite ignorant! Pardon, I pray you, the dulness of one but imperfectly instructed in the details of Paphian emotion.[3]

I have never perused the epistles of M. Mérimée, nor indeed, anything else of that gentilhomme's![4] My reading of publish'd letters hath largely been confined to those of 18th century British authors, & of Romans such as M. Tullius Cicero, T. Pomponius Atticus,[5] & C. Plinius Caecilius Secundus. I agree that epistles have much interest, those of Mr. Cowper being perhaps the most interesting of all.[6] However, I can hardly agree that those pertaining to the fair are especially or even ordinarily entertaining. The whole subject of the fair is so overworked & done to death by authors great & small, that to me it seems somewhat trite & boresome. Anything else is a relief! Yet as you say, or rather, as you quote, the influence of females upon the superficial conventions of society is perhaps not inconsiderable. I probably underestimate it, since my poor health has ever kept me within a home wherein my mother & aunts have wielded influence. Were I to observe an exclusively masculine society, such as that of an army camp, I might note a repugnant coarseness alien to the atmosphere of home. The epistles of Mr. Swinburne must be interesting, & I trust you may enjoy their perusal.

My interest in Lord Dunsany continues, & I have obtained a biography of him.[7] He is the 18th Baron of his line; an intellectual-looking person of *Galpinian* build—6 ft. 2 in. in height, & very thin. He is called the "worst dressed man in Ireland". Dunsany is 41 years old, & has a son of 13. He was wounded in the 1916 Dublin rioting. I am now perusing a book of his dramatick productions, entitled "Plays of Gods & Men". A considerable part of *The Kleicomolo* will be devoted to Dunsany, & I shall quote at length from his works for the benefit of Kleicomogal.

As to that dream of mine—it is but one of countless nocturnal fantasies which I experience. Only its coherence & continuity are unusual. I am forever dreaming of strange barren landscapes, cliffs, stretches of ocean, & deserted cities with towers & domes. In the "Kleicomolo" I am relating a dream of gruesome nature, induced by a reading of some of Ambrose Bierce's horror stories. I shall also repeat my abyss dream in the K.—if you will pardon the repetition. I want Comogal to hear it. All this dreaming comes without the stimulus of *cannabis indica*. Should I take that drug, who can say what worlds of unreality I might explore?

I beg to subscribe my self ever

> Yr most obt humble Servt
> H. Paget Lowe

Notes

1. The Great Bridge spanned the Providence River, connecting downtown Providence with the East Side. In its day it was the widest river bridge in the world; however, recently much of it was removed to uncover more of the river.

2. Désiré Joseph Mercier (1851–1926), Belgian theologian and philosopher. He became Archbishop of Mechelen in 1906 and thus leader of the Catholic church in Belgium. He was a staunch resister of the German occupation of 1914–18 during World War I.

3. By "Paphian emotion" HPL alludes to Paphos, a city in Cyprus that featured a celebrated temple to Aphrodite.

4. Prosper Mérimée (1803–1870), French novelist and playwright. HPL would later read his horror tale "The Venus of Ille" and comment on it in "Supernatural Horror in Literature" (1927). RK was probably referring HPL to Mérimée's *Letters to an Unknown*, tr. Henri Pène du Bois (New York: Brentano's, 1897).

5. There are no surviving letters by T. Pomponius Atticus (110–32 B.C.E.). Cicero, however, was a voluminous correspondent of his, and Atticus apparently edited Cicero's *Letters to Atticus*.

6. William Cowper (1731–1800) was a English poet and hymnodist. His letters had appeared in several editions beginning in 1835, most notably in a two-volume edition of the *Letters of William Cowper*, with commentary by Sir James George Frazer (London: Macmillan, 1912).

7. Edward Hale Bierstadt, *Dunsany the Dramatist*. More a critical study of Dunsany's plays than a biography.

[57] [AHT]

October 14, 1919

Admirable St. John:—

I celebrated Columbus Day by one of my cherished solitary rambles through the agrestic recesses of Quinsnicket Park. The day was as delightful as October can produce, & I had the most congenial of companions—a pocket telescope, & a century-old copy of Thomson's "Seasons"[1]—which Alfredus despises so bitterly. As is my custom, I read those parts which possessed a particular bearing on the season—including the episode of Lavinia, where Mr. Pope inserted several lines of his own when criticising Thomson's rough MS. The time was late afternoon, & it was delightful to penetrate the primeval country after leaving behind the alienised suburbs where reigns Hebrew, Italian, & French-Canadian squalor. As I mounted the slope which leads to the most delightful portion of the forest, the sun was cut off from me, & was visible shining on the plains & villages below in such a manner that the scene suggested a beautiful picture rather than actual landskip. As I bade farewell to the meadows at set of sun, I regretted the absence of my camera; for truly, few sights are more lovely than that of the harvest fields by twilight, walls, hedges, stubble, sheaves, & all, blending into a delicious whole. Verily, I cannot comprehend the psychology of a town poet who can fail to succumb to the spell! And as if to complete the enchantment, I heard the mellow voices of distant swains in simple melody. True, they were probably town youths on an outing; but I preferred to think of them as the scions of that contented pleasantry of old, who happy stirr'd the glebe.

Yr most Obt humble Servt,

H. Paget Lowe

Notes

1. See RK 1n2.

[58]   [AHT]

Same Old Address
11/9/19

Lothario Chimney, Esqr.[1]
Brooklyn, in New-York

Philandering & Nicotinical Sir:—

Anent tobacco—I fancy you will be tired of it ere long. Lest you assign to me an excess of credit for conscious asceticism, let me say that perhaps the chief factor in my abstinence from the beguiling weed is that I detest the d——d stuff most cordially! Its fumes are disgusting to me, hence though I smoked when about twelve years old—just to seem like a grown man—I left off as soon as I acquired long trousers; which formed a substitute symbol of independent adulthood. I cannot see yet what anyone finds attractive about the habit of imitating a smokestack! I hope you may not take to drink—which reminds me of a friend of mine who was visiting in North Carolina last month.[2] He was very intent on absorbing all the local colour, & arranged at his brother's club to sample some of the moonshine whiskey or "white licker" of the mountaineers. Some one obligingly poured him out a thimbleful, & he caught the *odour!*—Then & there he decided to let his education in Tar Heel local colour remain incomplete!! He says it reminded him of castor oil more than anything else.

As you know, I take the Confederate side of all discussions involving North & South! At 7:00 a party consisting of Miss H., her aunt, young Lee,[3] & L. Theobald set out for the great event. Arriving early at the Copley-Plaza, we obtained front seats; so that during the address I sat directly opposite the speaker, not ten feet from him. Dunsany entered late, accompanied & introduced by Prof. George Baker of Harvard.[4] He is of Galpinian build—6 ft. 2 in. in height, & very slender. His face is fair & pleasing, though marred by a slight moustache. In manner he is boyish & a trifle awkward; & his smile is winning & infectious. His hair is light brown. His voice is mellow & cultivated, & very clearly British. He pronounces *were* as *wair*, &c. Dunsany first touched upon his ideals & methods; then hitched a chair up to his reading table, seated himself, crossed his long legs, & commenced reading his short play, "The Queen's Enemies." This is based very obviously upon the anecdote of Nitocris in the second book of Herodotus; but Dunsany averred that he had purposely avoided reading details or even learning the names of the characters in the story, for fear his original imaginative work on the play might be hampered or impaired. I advise you to read it for yourself—it is in "Plays of Gods & Men", which every well-regulated library has or ought to have on the shelves. Later Dunsany read selections from other works of his, including a masterly burlesque on his own style—"Why the Milkman Shudders when he Sees the Dawn".[5] As he read this, he could not repress his own smiles & incipient chuckles! The audience was large, select, & appreciative; & after the lecture Dunsany was encircled by autograph-seekers. Egged on by her aunt, Miss Hamlet almost mustered up courage enough to ask for an autograph, but weakened at the last moment. Of this more anon. For mine own part, I did not seek a signature; for I detest fawning upon the great. Dunsany himself has written a piece ("Fame & the Poet", in the August *Atlantic*)[6] which shews his contempt for the flatterers of genius. To some of those with whom he shook hands, Dunsany remarked that he had a severe headache. I could sympathise; for although I had stood the day of unusual exertion remarkably well, my poor cranium was pounding & reeling most lamentably— the pain having begun about half way through the lecture. Still, I was able to keep up & navigate my course through the maze of now disarranged chairs in the vast ballroom where the address was delivered. We saw Dunsany enter his cab & drive off; then repaired to the nearest white post for my South Stationward car. Of course, I could have taken the Prov. train at the adjacent Back Bay, but I hate that bleak barn, & wished to get in the train as soon as it was made up; ensconcing myself in a seat & beginning to read Dunsany's "The Gods of Pegāna", which Miss H. had kindly lent me. The H.'s invited me to stay all night, but I am a home-seeking soul & the hour was not late. So, after promising to call again—though I may never be able to do so—I boarded a car for the subway, & after one change reached the station & the 11:00 train. Opening the book, I was dead to the world & forgot my headache till the brakeman's cry of *"Pawtucket!"* reminded me of home—& of *P. D. S.!*[7] I donned my overcoat in time to alight at Providence at 12:35—& damn[8] it all, I missed the last Swan Point car home! (12:40) but I took the 1:10 Red Bridge car, & finally made #598 at 1:30—exhausted but not prostrated. The nervous reaction was less than I expected—I was able to get down the next evening & buy a *Boston Transcript* with an (unsatisfactory!) account of the lecture. Altogether it was a most remarkable & highly enjoyable experience for me in these latter days of valetudinarian retirement. I had not been in Boston before since Jan. 1916—& not in Cambridge since *1910*.[9] To see & hear a favourite author is something rare indeed for one whose favourites lie so largely in the past! With you, Mocrates, & little Galpinius there, my pleasure would have been compleat!

The one sequel to the lecture does not concern me, but deserves narration (an unconsciously egotistical sentence!). Miss H. could not quite give up the idea of an autograph, so on the following day wrote a letter to Dunsany, enclosing several tokens of esteem for him & for his wife; the greatest of which was a genuine autograph letter of Abraham Lincoln. Soon afterward she received a most courteous reply from His Lordship, written personally with his celebrated *quill,* & containing a pleasant enclosed note from Lady Dunsany! Of this letter from so great an author, Miss H. is justly proud in the extreme; & she will doubtless retain it as a treasure of priceless worth. I will here present a verbatim transcription!

"My dear Miss Hamlet:—

Thank you very much for your kind letter & present, & for the charming little presents to my wife. I had not seen the Lincoln Letter before, & I am very glad to have it. It is a stately letter, & above all, it is full of human kindness; & I doubt if any of us by any means can achieve anything better than that.

With many thanks,

Yours very sincerely,
Dunsany

P. S. I'll write plenty more for you."

Yʳ most oblig'd obt Servt
Humphry Littlewit, Gent.

Notes

1. Both "Lothario Chimney" and the greeting ("Philandering and Nicotinal Sir") allude to the fact that RK was a ladies' man and fond of smoking a pipe.

2. Probably Harold Bateman Munroe, visiting his brother Chester in Asheville, NC.

3. "Miss H." is Alice M. Hamlet, the amateur journalist who introduced HPL to the work of Lord Dunsany. Hamlet identified "Lee" as one Ed Lee, otherwise unknown.

4. George Pierce Baker (1866–1935), professor of English at Harvard (1892–1924) and professor of the history and technique of drama at Yale (1925–33); author of *Technique of the Drama* (1915) and other works.

5. "Why the Milkman Shudders When He Perceives the Dawn," in *The Last Book of Wonder* (1916).

6. *Fame and the Poet, Atlantic Monthly* 124, No. 2 (August 1919): 175–84; included in *Plays of Near and Far* (1923).

7. HPL alludes to Philip D. Sherman (1881–1957), a Brown graduate (class of 1902) and a noted book collector who, in 1930, donated 5000 first editions and other rare books to the John Hay Library.

8. The AHT typist has typed xxxx.

9. HPL's 1910 visit was probably to see his cousin Phillips Gamwell, who lived in Cambridge, MA.

[59]   [AHT; Post[1]]

Twickenham,[2] 3[d] Decr., 1919

[My Dear Kleiner:—]

As you infer, "The White Ship" is in part influenced by my new Dunsanian studies. There are many highly effective points in Dunsany's style, & any writer of imaginative prose will be the better for having read him. I have filed recommendations for *all* his works at the local publick library, & have met with favourable responses. Today I go down to obtain the very latest Dunsany book—just published—"Unhappy Far-Off Things",[3] which I first saw advertised in the November *Atlantic*. Recently I read "Time & the Gods", which is not only highly interesting but richly philosophical. You surely must read Dunsany—in places his work is pure poetry despite the prose medium. If anyone can restore the old literary Kleiner it is this same Edward John Moreton Drax Plunkett! As to the charge of *modernism* against me because of my predilection for Poe & Dunsany, why, Sir, I refute it! Nor do I follow my own taste back to my own 18th century by any genealogy as tenuous as the analogy betwixt allegory & the pastoral. The line runs through the dark romancers, Mr. Lewis, Mrs. Radcliffe, &c., to Horace Walpole, Esqr., author of the "Castle of Otranto".

I am glad to say that during the past two months my mother's health has shewn a more decided improvement than at any other time since her breakdown in January. She will not, however, be strong enough to return home for a very long time. She is now better able to receive callers, & I have twice visited her; on the last occasion carrying my camera & taking some photographs—which I will enclose, subject to return. The blurred or indistinct face in these is due to the low altitude of the sun which prevented the formation of the shadows necessary to bring out the features. As you will notice, my mother's present surroundings certainly lack nothing in sylvan beauty—indeed, they are quite ideal for the gradual recovery of one nervously prostrated.

With sincere assurances of profound esteem & unvarying regard, I am Sir,

Ever y[r] most humble, most obedient Servt

Horace Walpole.

Notes

1. In Post the letter is misdated 27 September.

2. Twickenham, now a suburb of London, was where Alexander Pope moved in 1718, residing there the rest of his life.

3. An account of Dunsany's visit to World War I battlefields in France.

[60] [AHT]

The Mitre Tavern[1]
27th Decr, 1719

Esteem'd St. John:—

According to the precepts of the most genuine art, the form is a reflection of the sense. I sincerely recommend the piece to the attention of Kleicomolo readers without alterations of any kind. I am moved to inquire as to a possible admixture of fiction in the peculiarly dramatick denouement. The discovery of the clipping wrapped about a volume of *De Quincey* purchased in *Ann*-Street, seems notably coincidental; considering the contents of the volume. Did you add certain touches to heighten the effect, or is the account an actual transcript of fact? The whole affair is one of vast singularity & mystery, & in my hands the tale would have become a horror story with a very different sort of climax. I should have the lady display odd flashes of knowledge of the immemorial past, coupled with a certain mingled horror & contempt of old age. I should have had her shew, on the occasion of a trip through the Metropolitan Museum of Art, a curious fear when confronted with a particular inscription on an Egyptian stone. Then I should have a friend of yours from Paris—let us call him M. Duval—meet her, & start back in fright— never quite daring to explain his fear, but afterward muttering to you that she queerly resembled a miniature which his great-great grandfather had worn in a locket, & which was connected with a peculiar family legend not pleasant to describe. And then I should have had you notice one morning before your mirror, that you were *aging* alarmingly & inexplicably—that your face, a few months before that of a youth, was now as that of a man of forty. You spoke of this to her, & her laugh sent a chill down your spine—& you noticed that she seemed younger than when you had first known her. Then your friend from Paris noticed the change in you & in her—& would often become very thoughtful. He sent to his ancestral chateau in Vaucluse for some documents—relating to some family financial arrangement, he told you, when one day you surprised him in the midst of the yellowed papers. And then you began to suspect that he was in the habit of following you & the lady—you even feared he would try to trace her to her home. One day the lady disappeared, & shortly afterward your friend returned to France. Then, three months later, you bought a copy of "The Wandering Jew"[2] in Ann Street, & found on the newspaper wrapping the following item; three months old:

Mystery in East Side Lodging

Police baffled by events in room at 136 East 25th Street.

Police today are on the watch for a young woman, old woman, & young man, believed to have knowledge of a skeleton found last night in the young woman's apartment at 136 East 25th street. The young woman, known as Miriam Smith, engaged the room two years ago; & is believed to have been a clerk or saleswoman. She is described as dark, comely, & somewhat sad in appearance, usually dressed in black & wearing a silver crucifix. She suffered from some obscure ailment, evidently of the heart, but had recently appeared in strangely better health, & much younger in aspect than before. The old woman & young man are not known in the locality.

Last night at about 11 o'clock Miss Smith was seen to enter her apartment, a light immediately appearing at her window. Five minutes later a handsome & well-dressed young man followed her into the building. Tenants report loud voices in the Smith apartment, followed by a series of screams too shocking to describe; & Mr. Isidor Fitzpatrick, who lives across the street, claims to have seen at the window an aged woman with streaming white hair, waving her arms in a frantic manner. Immediately afterward the young man left the house in great haste & was seen to walk swiftly in the direction of Madison Square. Moans proceeding from the Smith room caused an investigation on the part of Patrick J. Cohen, the landlord, who after failing to obtain a response to his knocking, had the door broken down by Officer McGoldstein of the —th Precinct. At first the investigators were overpowered by the hideous stench that emanated from the room, but later they entered & discovered on the floor a skeleton, seemingly of great age, since the bones crumbled to powder at the touch of the patrolman's club. Of the young woman no trace was found, though she was not seen to leave the apartment. Of the old woman seen by Mr. Fitzpatrick, nothing further was seen or heard. The skeleton bore no distinguishing mark, but is thought to have been that of a woman. One hand, seemingly raised to the throat, held in its grasp a silver crucifix.

Pardon my flight of fancy—but mysteries always arouse my imagination. It seems too bad to let them pass without providing material for a tale of the grotesque or arabesque. I fear if I were to try to become a lady's man like you, I should offend all my charmers at the very outset by weaving them into weird & horrible tales! But fortunately horror-writers are not often ladies' men—notwithstanding Mr. Poe's fondness for the fair.

I have just finished a ghastly tale entitled "The Statement of Randolph Carter", based on an actual dream of mine, in which the amateur Samuel Loveman was the central figure. Loveman & I have been discussing literary horrors at length, & he has been kind enough to recommend to me several volumes of weird & bizarre prose & verse; so that it is hardly remarkable that I should dream of him in this way.

In the dream, Loveman & I were standing in a very ancient, unknown, & abandoned cemetery at night; spades in hand, beside a newly opened sepulchre. Down into those charnel depths led a flight of damp stone steps. Loveman was trying to dissuade me from accompanying him into the noisome vault, saying that my frail nerves could not possibly stand the things we should have to see & undergo. Of the object of our quest I knew nothing, save that it was related to some awful & forbidden thing which L. had found in a rare & antique volume. At length Loveman descended the steps, carrying a portable telephone outfit; whilst I remained above, at the other end of the wire. I seated myself on a damp, crumbling gravestone & listened at the receiver. For a long time nothing happened, & I began to grow anxious. Then came a clicking—& Loveman's excited whisper:

"God! Lovecraft! If you could see what I am seeing!"

Silence again—then more clicking & the voice of Loveman:

"This is horrible—incredible! I never dreamed of THIS!!"

At this point I began to inquire what was happening, but no reply came up from those Stygian depths. Then the voice of Loveman, more shaken with fear than before:

"Lovecraft—for God's sake get out of this if you can! Run for your life—it's too late for me!"

I protested, asking what the peril might be, but Loveman only replied:

"I can't tell you—no man could bear it & live! Nothing can be done now—but for God's sake beat it!!"

By this time I was paralysed with apprehension. I strove to go to Loveman's aid, but was powerless to move. The effect of his voice, coming up from those hideous mortuary caverns, was indescribably terrifying. *What* was he seeing? Then Loveman became yet more excited, calling frantically

"Beat it! Beat it! Beat it!"

Suddenly his voice ceased, & there was prolonged silence. I called down, over & over again, "Loveman! Are you there? What's the matter?" But for aeons no answer came.

And then occurred the horrible—almost unbelievable thing—the awesome & dreadful climax & summation of all horrors. After an agonising wait there was again a clicking in the telephone receiver, & a *voice* came over the wire. I cannot describe that voice—& hardly wish to do so. . . . . . . I may call it deep; hollow; gelatinous; remote; unearthly. I heard it come up from that detestable ossuary; heard it as I sat on a crumbling gravestone under a wan, waning moon in a terrible, deserted cemetery. What manner of *thing* uttered the words I cannot—dare not—conjecture. This is what *it* said:

"You Fool, Loveman is Dead!!"

And then I awaked, racked with a fiendish headache! Altogether, that was *some* dream, as it were. Later, when I make a good copy, I shall let you read the story I constructed around this nucleus. A shudder in every paragraph!

Accept, Sir, the usual assurances &c., from

Yr Obt hble Servt

H. Paget Lowe

Notes

1. Samuel Johnson, James Boswell, and their circle congregated at the Mitre Tavern in Fleet Street, London.

2. Probably Eugène Sue (1804–1857), *Le Juif errant* (1844–45), translated as *The Wandering Jew;* there are, however, other novels of this title.

[61]   [AHT]

Home—as usual

January 23, 1920

Noble Don Juan:—

I have been wondering lately if I could ever manage, under the pressure of poverty, to accept a position in an *evening* school. A day school, of course, would be out of the question—for I can rarely keep up that long for two successive days. If fairly frequent absences could be pardoned, I might manage to keep up with the evening hours—but fancy my trying to hold in check a roomful of incipient gangsters! It seems as though every avenue of remunerative activity is closed to a total nervous wreck!

Turning to your welcome epistle—I am glad you found my modification of your story interesting. I may use that plot—divested of any element connecting it with your tale—in supplying one of my amateur proteges with something to write about. It does not *quite* conform to the general idea of my own tales, so I shall not use it myself. I have lately—by the way—been collecting ideas & images for subsequent use in fiction. For the first time in my life, I am keeping a "commonplace-book"—if that term can be applied to a repository of gruesome & fantastick thoughts. It is very interesting to know that the remarkable climax of the "Miriam" account is not even slightly coloured by fictional art. Verily, it seems to me that few actual experiences conform so readily to the requirements of a spirited narrative. It is really quite extraordinary! Would it not be a good idea to let Cook or Pryor[1] publish your story after it has traversed the Kleicomolo circuit? So moving & vivid a piece should have a wider audience than the B. P. C.[2] & Kleicomoloes alone. I am sure 'twould be appreciated.

Your brief for the defence in the case of Κόσμος versus Ἔρως is admirably eloquent, but I am not to be moved by any such idealist as R. W. Emerson or his master Πλάτων! Eroticism belongs to a lower order of instincts, & is an animal rather than nobly human quality. For evolved man—the apex of organic progress on the earth—what branch of reflection is more fitting than that which occupies only his higher & exclusively human faculties? The primal savage or ape merely looks about his native forest to find a mate; the exalted Aryan should lift his eyes to the worlds of space & consider his relation to infinity!! So much for the high-sounding argument. Really, I suppose my opinion is determined by the much simpler fact that I chance to have vastly more imagination than emotion. About romance & affection I never have felt the slightest interest; whereas the sky, with its tale of eternities past & to come, & its gorgeous panoply of whirling universes, has always held me enthralled. And in truth, is this not the natural attitude of an analytical mind? What is a beauteous nymph? Carbon, hydrogen, oxygen, nitrogen, a dash or two of phosphorus & other elements—all to decay soon. But what is *the cosmos?* What is the secret of time, space, & the things that lie beyond time & space? What sinister forces hurl through the black incurious aether these titanic globes of living flame, & the insect-peopled worlds that hover about them? Here—here, at last, is something worthy of the interest of enlightened mankind!!! The veil hangs tantalisingly—what lies on the other side?

However—do not take my rhetorical outburst as a wholesale denunciation of all amatory verse. Everything has its place in literature, & affection can be prettily handled by such bards as Mr. Waller, Mr. Lovelace, &c.[3] Your own work in this line is of high merit, & I assure you that I did not intend my praise of "One Year Ago" to be faint. Whatever faintness you may have observed, was determined by the subject in a large sense rather than by any objection to the piece itself, or even to your choice of a theme in this particular instance. As I have always maintained, your art stands on a very high plain; & my commendation of it is never lessened by the fact that I wish you would try other fields. I deem amatory verse a good landing-stage for Pegasus, half way up the slopes of Parnassus. It is the natural produce of Byronic adolescence, & well becomes a bard in his early twenties. But in time its superficiality palls, & we expect the poet to resume his upward flight. Is it not significant that *all* your Laureate-Winning pieces have been non-amatory? "Evening Prayer", & "America, I May Not Sing" represent the apex of your genius so far. Why not follow them with still more exalted themes? I shall await with interest your "Creed"— which may perhaps fulfil the requirements I am enjoining! But who am I that I shou'd prate of poesy? Have I not put that pastime behind me forever? At any rate, you doubtless perceive my position, & realise that my general distaste for "soft stuff" does not obscure for a moment my admiration for your genius & literary workmanship. It is because of my full recognition of your genius that I make these sporadical exhortations for an enlargement of field on your part!

By the way—since all habits must be broken gradually, I am breaking the poesy habit that way. Here is a recent backsliding of mine—

ON READING Lᵈ DUNSANY'S BOOK OF WONDER

The hours of night unheeded fly,
    And in the grate the embers fade;
Vast shadows one by one pass by
    In silent daemon cavalcade.

But still the magic volume holds
    The raptur'd eye in realms apart,
And fulgent sorcery enfolds
    The willing mind and eager heart.

The lonely room no more is there—
    For to the sight in pomp appear
Temples and cities pois'd in air,
    And blazing glories—sphere on sphere.

Naturally my changed literary province tends to group around me a new set of proteges & clients—the budding story writers. One of the brightest of these, a very worthy kidlet named Frank Belknap Long, is a resident of your own Manhattan; & I suggest that you look him up in the near future. I fancy he is anywhere betwixt 18 & 20 in age—& I will enclose his latest letter to give an idea of his personality. We must encourage fiction in the United! I have suggested to Morton that young Long might make good B. P. C. material—what do you think? At any rate, I trust the New York amateurs will make him feel at home. He is Campbell's recruit; & was secured, I believe, through *The Boys' Magazine*.

I had a vivid dream a few nights ago—involving the possession of another distinct personality. The period was 1864, & the crux of the dream was a horror in a doctor's secret laboratory. I think the dream-doctor was going to shew me an artificial man like M. Frankenstein's uncomely creation, but premature waking robbed the dream of its climax. In this dream I was *Dr. Eben Spencer,* an army surgeon home on a furlough. The sinister experimenter was a colleague of mine, *Dr. Chester.* Some dream![4]

Yr most hble Obt Servt
Theobaldus Fantasticus

Notes

1. John Clinton Pryor, amateur journalist and editor of *Pine Cones,* in which HPL's "Beyond the Wall of Sleep" had recently appeared (October 1919).

2. The Blue Pencil Club, an amateur organization in Brooklyn, chiefly associated with the NAPA.

3. Edmund Waller (1606–1687) and Richard Lovelace (1618–1657/58), English poets who specialized in romantic or erotic verse.

4. See *SL* 1.100–102.

[62] [AHT]

Feby. 10, 1920

Hail Bolingbroke!

That commonplace-book of mine is, as you surmise, rather out of the ordinary. I will quote a few of the items:

A very ancient colossus in a very ancient desert. Face gone. No man hath seen it.

Man climbs mountain toward some horrible goal. Cloud passes over. Man seen no more.

Man makes appointment with old enemy for final settlement. Enemy dies meanwhile. *But appointment is not broken.*

Old house & gardens—take on a singular aspect as seen at twilight by narrator.[1]

But *the* event of the season was the burning of the large Chapman house last Wednesday night—the yellow house across two lawns to the north of #598 Angell.[2] At about 12:30 a.m. I was seated at my table writing when a curious & persistent popping or crackling outdoors arrested my attention. Lifting the dark curtain & peering out, I beheld a red world as light as day, with the falling snowflakes glittering weirdly. Seeking the source of the uncanny glare, I repaired to a north window. There, in full view, was the most impressive sight my eyes have ever beheld. Where that evening had stood the unoccupied Chapman house, recently sold & undergoing repairs, was now a titanic pillar of roaring, living flame amidst the deserted night—reaching into the illimitable heavens & lighting the country for miles around. The heat was intense—even here in the house—& the glare was stupendous. Awaking my aunt, who watched the rest of the spectacle from the window, I went out to view the disaster at close range. Lights had now appeared in all the windows around, & the engines had reached the scene. The house next us caught fire along the edge of the shingles, but was speedily saved by the first spouting of the hose. A high east wind was blowing, & the sparks flew freely, but ice-coated roofs saved the neighbourhood. At one time the chimney of the doomed house fell, carrying with it the south wall, & precipitating the roof & all the floors to the cellar. At last the blaze died down for want of further material. Smoke arose in torrents from the ruins but the "show was over". The crowd dispersed & went back to bed, & the firemen idly soaked down the glowing embers. Of that once stately house, only the charred east wall was left standing. Today the view from our northern windows resembles devastated France or Belgium! The cause of the blaze was an overheated stove—in which careless workmen had left a fire.

But I must desist, subscribing my self, with customary evidences of regard & protestations of esteem, as

Yr most obt hble Servt

Archibald Maynwaring[3]

Notes

1. The first, third, and fourth of these entries are (with some variations in wording) nos. 21, 8, and 13 of HPL's commonplace book. The second was erased and written over with entry 7.

2. HPL may have incorporated a version of this incident in his discussion of the destruction of the "old Chapman place beyond Meadow Hill" in "Herbert West—Reanimator" (1921–22).

3. A pseudonym HPL used in some of his amateur poetry, derived from the minor Augustan poet Arthur Mainwaring, who translated parts of "Garth's Ovid" (1717; *LL* 728).

[AHT][1]

Feby. 10, 1720

Anent H. Rider—McD. has just sent me a card calling my attention to an article on him in the Living Age.[2] Cook has also been kind, outlining a reading course in Haggard. I shall not tackle the gentleman in question till I am through with Algernon Blackwood, whose rather mediocre fantasies I am absorbing one after another. When I do read "She", I will report my critical impressions in detail.[3] I have just finished Stoker's "Jewel of Seven Stars", lent me by Cook. It has defects, but is on the whole splendid—much better than Blackwood.[4]

Really—what pleasure one can gain from puffing away at nauseating & stifling fumes is beyond me! I did it once—when 11 to 14 years old—for no boy in my vicinity was then considered manly unless he surreptitiously emulated the graceful smokestack either behind the stables or in the neighbouring sylvan retreats. I sampled cigars, cigarettes, pipe, & the like; & puffed like a veteran; but always detested the infernal stuff. Glad enough was I to fling away tobacco when long trousers & increased inches made my manliness an obvious fact which needed no nicotinical corroboration! Nor have I any literary need of tobacco. When I go in for drugs, I am no "tin-horn", but buckle right down to opium—vide "Dagon". Since it is not I, but my heroes, who indulge, I do not feel the ill effects. Incidentally—I think Alfredus has given up his cherished hasheesh!

Just now I am hibernating. I have not been out of the house for over a month, & seem to have little wish to go out. But with the buds & grasses of April, my pastoral instincts will awaken; & I will hie me to the green wildwood on many a sun-blest afternoon. How many times have I perused Mr. Thomson's "Seasons" amid the lanes & hollows of lovely Quinsnicket! Each spring I wish I were young again—so that I might be able to ride a bicycle without attracting attention & exciting ridicule. Adults do not ride any more here. I miss the intimate contact with the country which my wheel gave me. Ten years ago there was scarce a cloudless day from May to October that I did not at some hour behold agrestic scenes & spin along quiet meadow-bordered roads where care & complexity dwelt not. I love the ancient things of the town, but my real love is the realm of Pan—the dryad-peopled groves, the brooks, the fields, the fountains, & the flowery vales. Pert urban criticks laugh at my pastorals as "artificial"—yet how much of any real delight in the contemplation of Nature animates their composition!

Ever yr most obt hble Servt
Theobaldus

Notes

1. This letter bears the same date as the previous but does not have a greeting. The editors believe it is simply a continuation of the previous letter and not a separate document.

2. E. C. Rashleigh, "Romances of Rider Haggard," *Living Age* 304 (6 March 1920): 598–604.

3. HPL did not read the novel until 1926. He obtained his personal copy still later.

4. See HPL's discussion in "Supernatural Horror in Literature." HPL's initial response to the work of Algernon Blackwood (1869–1951) was unenthusiastic (see letters to the Gallomo, 73–74), but he reevaluated the work beginning in 1924.

[63]   [AHT]

March 7, 1920

Revered Bolingbroke:—

I am glad that you find merit in my fictional attempts, & wish I had not dropped fiction in the nine years between 1908 & 1917. Somehow or other, I conceived the idea that my stories were poorer even than my verse & essays; though I now fully believe the critics who declare the reverse to be true. I am at present full of various ideas, including a hideous novel to be entitled "The Club of the Seven Dreamers".[1] Of the really great workers in the field of the weird, I hardly think there is any reason to question the leadership of Mr. Poe. I cannot say that Hawthorne appeals so much to me, since he seems hampered to some extent by reality & tameness. However, it is long since I have perused anything of his. I must include a re-reading of him in my present programme of absorption of the bizarre. I must get hold of more of Hearn's fantastic effusions.[2]

Your recent bibliothecal additions prove the genuineness of your poetick impulse. When I come to review mine own excursions into the province of the Muse, I am conscious that my attitude was never that of the true poet. For lyrical compositions I had little or no use, & believe that most of my zeal lay in the mere love of rhythm, plus the facility which antique verse affords in re-creating the atmosphere of the *past*. Aside from rhythm & archaism, nearly every element which I sought in verse can be supplied equally well by prose. The flight of imagination, & the delineation of pastoral or natural beauty, can be accomplished as well in prose as in verse—often better. It is this lesson which the inimitable Dunsany hath taught me. Poetry to me meant merely the most effective way of asserting my archaic instincts. I could convey more actual archaism in my couplets than in any other avenue of equal brevity & simplicity. Were I to grow sober & introspective like you & the Galpin Kidlet, I should describe mine own nature as tripartite, my interests consisting of three parallel and dissociated groups—(a) Love of the strange & the fantastic. (b) Love of the abstract truth & of scientific logick. (c) Love of the ancient & the permanent. Sundry combinations of these three strains will probably account for all my odd tastes & eccentricities.

I trust that you succeeded in outlining your agnosticism to your pastor without shocking the good soul. How well I recall my tilts with Sunday-School teachers during my last period of compulsory attendance! I was 12 years of age, & the despair of the institution. None of the answers of my pious preceptors would satisfy me, & my demands that they cease taking things for granted quite upset them. Close reasoning was something new in their little world of Semitic mythology. At last I saw that they were hopelessly bound to unfounded dogmata & traditions, & thenceforward ceased to treat them seriously. Sunday-School became to me simply a place wherein to have a little harmless fun spoofing the pious mossbacks. My mother observed this, & no longer sought to enforce my attendance. Your parson no doubt deplored the lack of theological tomes in the Kleinerian library which he complimented so freely. If his own ran more to science & less to sanctity he might have to resign his living! Galpin likes my arguments in the current Kleicomolo very much, & says his father does also. I hope they will not give good Bro. Mocrates a severe shock! About Percy's Reliques—why not obtain the edition I have—"Everyman's Library"? These books were only 35¢ each befo' de war, & I hardly fancy they would bankrupt you even now. No doubt you recall my set—2 volumes.

About your stagnation & melancholy—I shall have to give you a lecture when I get hold of you next summer!! Galpin upbraids *me* for being listless & unambitious—so I have plenty of optimistic arguments to pass along to the severer case! I hope that your recent state is merely one of transition from the idealism of youth to the realism of middle life, when the thinker realises that there is no such thing as ideal happiness & justice, & ceases to strive after illusions so empty & unreal. Solid bourgeois contentment—with the settled conviction that wild pleasures are too rare, elusive, & transitory to be worth seeking—is the best state of mind to be in. One should come to realise that all life is merely a comedy of vain desire, wherein those who strive are the clowns, & those who calmly & dispassionately watch are the fortunate ones who can laugh at the antics of the strivers. The utter emptiness of all the recognised goals of human endeavour is to the detached spectator deliciously apparent—the tomb yawns & grins so ironically! Whatever bliss we can gain, is from watching the farce, removing ourselves from the strife by not expecting more than we receive, & revelling in that world of the unreal which our imagination creates for us. To enjoy tranquillity, & to promote tranquillity in others, is the most enduring of delights. Such was the doctrine of Epicurus, the leading ethical philosopher of the world. If one's interest in life wanes, let him turn to the succour of others in a like plight, & some grounds for interest will be observed to return. About the time I joined the United I was none too fond of existence. I was 23 years of age, & realised that my infirmities would withhold me from success in the world at large. Feeling like a cipher, I felt that I might well be erased. But later I realised that even success is empty. Failure though I be, I shall reach a level with the greatest—& the smallest—in the damp earth or on the final pyre. And I saw that in the interim trivialities are not to be despised. Success is a relative thing—& the victory of a boy at marbles is equal to the victory of an Octavius at Actium[3] when measured by the scale of cosmic infinity. So I turned to observe other mediocre & handicapped persons about me, & found pleasure in increasing the happiness of those who could be helped by such encouraging words or critical services as I am capable of furnishing. That I have been able to cheer here & there an aged man, an infirm old lady, a dull youth, or a person deprived by circumstances of education; affords to me a sense of being not altogether useless, which almost forms a substitute for the real success I shall never know. What matter if none hear of my labours, or if those labours touch only the afflicted & the mediocre? Surely it is well that the happiness of the unfortunate be made as great as possible; & he who is kind, helpful, & patient, with his fellow-sufferers, adds as truly to the world's combined fund of tranquillity as he who, with greater endowments, promotes the birth of empires, or advances the knowledge & civilisation of mankind. Thus no man of philosophical cast, however circumscribed by poverty or retarded by ailment, need feel himself superfluous so long as he holds the power to improve the spirits of others. My advice to you would be to re-enter active amateurdom & follow my example of accumulating a Johnsonian circle of literary dependents—worthy folk who suffer more than you, & whose pain cou'd be assuaged by the exercise of the critical gifts which you possess in so great an abundance. Or if you are especially qualified to promote contentment in any other way, choose that way. There is a vast satisfaction in alleviating the misfortunes of another. When I am able to bring a smile of gratitude to the vacuous face of a *Crowley*[4] or the childish visage of a *Tryout Smith,* I am impressed with my own ability to do such a thing; & have thereby the better opinion of myself. And I can feel some share of their pleasure, since as a fellow-struggler I am able to appreciate their limitations. The secret of true contentment, I am convinc'd, lies in the achievement of the *cosmical* point of view; whereby the most cruel distinctions betwixt great & small things are shewn to be merely apparent & unreal. The next philosophical step is to acquire the impersonal attitude—to divest oneself of egocentrick consciousness, & assume the role of a spectator at the comedy of man. Thus depersonalised, one may roam through all history & all legend with imagination as a guide; enjoying the pleasant things of life without experiencing the anguish of participation. If lonely in his own life, the dreamer may find company at the tables of Will's or Button's, or may join the embattled hosts of some shadowy monarch who defends with fabulous sword the gates of his gorgeous & unheard-of capital, which rises among the gold & diamond mountains beyond the Milky Way. To the impersonal dreamer belongs all infinity—he is lord of the universe & taster of all the beauties of the stars. As for the future—what is sweeter than *oblivion,* which the humblest of us may share with the Kings of all the ages, & even with the gods themselves?

Believe me, Sir, Yr most obt hble Servt

Epicurus Lackbrain, Gent.

Notes

1. This work was evidently never begun.

2. HPL would later read such works by Lafcadio Hearn (1850–1904) as *Kwaidan* (1904) and *Fantastics* (1914).

3. In the battle of Actium (31 B.C.E.), C. Octavius (later Caesar Augustus) defeated his rival, Mark Antony (Marcus Antonius), thereby effectively putting an end to the Roman republic. He was crowned emperor in 27 B.C.E.

4. James Lawrence Crowley (1885–1962), a poet (on whose name HPL based his pseudonym Ames Dorrance Rowley).

[64]   [AMs]

3/31/20

Aonian Bolingbroke:—

I owe 17 letters besides this one to you, some of them dating back to February. I am also under pressure to write an article for good old Smithy's *Tryout.*[1] And yet through my constitutional perversity I choose to do the pleasant rather than the dutiful thing—wherefore my prompt reply to yours of the 24th, with obvious disregard of the chronological system I usually maintain in my correspondence.

H: Poe Lovecraft, 1840

But when all things are consider'd, I fancy that my breach of schedule will be deem'd pardonable; for I am at such a nervous tension that none but voluntary & interesting correspondence could possibly be expected of me. Whence, you ask, the tension? Usual reply—*D. V. Bush!* He has been of late bombarding me most shamelessly albeit lucratively.

˘ — ˘ — ˘ — ˘ — ˘ —
My purse hath swollen whilst my head hath reel'd.

—pardon the involuntary heroick—but as you know, I used to be a versifier. Day before yesterday things came to a climax. I had been unusually wretched—two Bush orders on top of each other had reduced me to despair, & Sunday evening I had fallen asleep in my chair, not awaking till 4 a.m. When the postman came Monday, I was about ready to "lay me doon & dee"[2] for good—but what should I find but **another** Bush order—*the largest in history*. The poor devil was in a woeful quandary. He has acquired the name of poet in his home town but not shewing any save his *revised* verses; but at the same time he has been careful to let his friends know that he is the author of *real books* of poetry. You remember the blue-bound trash I shew'd you. Last week, on the strength of his reputation as a bard, Bush was invited to speak before some club

[*Balance missing.*]

Notes

1. One of the installments of "Looking Backward" (*Tryout*, February–June 1920; *CE* 1.239–53), HPL's account of amateur journalism of the period 1885–95.
2. From "Annie Laurie," an old Scottish song based on a poem said to have been written by William Douglas (1672?–1748).

[65] [AHT]

Castle Theobald
4/26/20

My dear Bolingbroke:—

Anent the smoke nuisance—you may be correct in theory about the reason for my aversion for the weed, but I would lay a heavy wager that it would take years of practice for me to *cultivate* a taste which after all is not worth cultivating! I am a conservative soul, & am not as radically different in tastes from the 14-year-old Theobaldus as one might fancy from a mere reading of the numerals which proclaim my proximity to thirty. All I know is that smoke is smoke, & just as choking when from a pipe as when from a leaky stove! Of course, connoisseurs make fine distinctions—but I prefer to breathe pure air than to inhale malodorous fumes. Some persons like "high game"—but I don't! To me the ultimate horror of earth is a smoking car. As a rule, I avoid taking drugs to stimulate literary endeavour; but when I try to describe hell—if ever I do—I fancy I shall take a ride in a smoker to work up atmosphere! Of course, the quality of the tobacco doubtless means *something*—but I find I acquire just as severe headaches when calling on a friend of mine who smokes quarter cigars. After all, the Lady

Nicotine of the perfect & the bedraggled nymph of the ceramic "T. D." are 'sisters under the skin' as your fellow *R. K.* would express it![1]

Y[r] most Obt hble Servt

Lewis Theobald Junr.

Notes

1. The reference is to Rudyard Kipling's misogynist poem "The Ladies" (1895), in which a noblewoman and a prostitute are referred to as "sisters under their skins" (l. 64).

[66]   [AHT]

Twickenham

5/21/20

R. St. John, Viscount Bolingbroke

My Lord:—

Last night I had a brief but typical dream. I was standing on the East Providence shore of the Seekonk River, about three quarters of a mile south of the foot of Angell Street, at some unearthly nocturnal hour. The tide was flowing out *horribly*—exposing parts of the river-bed never before exposed to human sight. Many persons lined the banks, looking at the receding waters & occasionally glancing at the sky. Suddenly a blinding flare—reddish in hue—appeared high in the southwestern sky; & *something* descended to earth in a cloud of smoke, striking the Providence shore near the Red Bridge—about an eighth of a mile south on Angell Street. The watchers on the banks screamed in horror—"*It* has come—*It* has come at last!"—& fled away into the deserted streets. But I ran toward the bridge instead of away; for I was more curious than afraid. When I reached it I saw hordes of terror-stricken people in hastily donned clothing fleeing across from the Providence side as from a city accursed by the gods. There were pedestrians, many of them falling by the way, & vehicles of all sorts. Electric cars—the old small cars unused in Providence for six years—were running in close procession—eastward away from the city on both of the double tracks. Their motormen were frantic, & small collisions were numerous. By this time the river-bed was fully exposed—only the deep channel filled with water like a serpentine stream of death flowing through a pestilential plain in Tartarus. Suddenly a glare appeared in the West, & I saw the dominant landmark of the Providence horizon—the dome of the Central Congregational Church, silhouetted weirdly against a background of red. And then, *silently,* that dome abruptly caved in & fell out of sight in a thousand fragments. And from the fleeing populace arose such a cry as only the damn'd utter—& I waked up, confound the luck, with the very deuce of a headache!

Did I tell you in my last letter about my dreams (1) of the ancient house in the marsh, & the staircase that had no end, (2) of the mediaeval castle with the sleeping men-at-arms, & the battle on the plain between the archers of England & the *things* with yellow tabards over their armour, who vanished when their leader was unhelmeted & found to have *no head inside the empty helm,* & (3) of the street car that went by night over a route that had been dismantled for six years, & that lost five hours in climbing College Hill, finally plunging off the earth into a star-strown abyss & ending up in the sand-heaped streets of a ruined city *which had been under the sea?* Those were *some* dreams, believe your Grandpa Theobald!! I tell all these to the Kidlet, & he thinks them rather unusual—as does Mo also, who receives carbon copies. Oh—& one other dream![1] I was in a museum somewhere down town in Providence, (there ain't no sech place!) trying to sell the curator a bas-relief which *I* had just fashioned from clay. He asked me if I were crazy, attempting to sell him something *modern* when the museum was devoted to antiquities? He seemed an old & very learned man, & smiled kindly. I replied to him in words which I remember *precisely.* "This," I said, "was fashioned in my dreams; & the dreams of man are older than brooding Egypt or the contemplative Sphinx or garden-girdled Babylon." The curator now bade me shew him my bas-relief, which I did gladly. Its design was that of a procession of Egyptian priests. As I shewed the sculpture, the old man's manner changed suddenly. His amusement gave way to vague *terror*—I can even now see his blue eyes bulging from beneath his snow-white brows—& he said slowly, softly, & distinctly— "WHO ARE YOU?" I can reproduce the awe & impressiveness of his low voice only in capitals. I replied very prosaically—"My name is Lovecraft— H. P. Lovecraft—grandson of Whipple V. Phillips." I fancied a man of his age could place my grandfather better than he could place me. But he answered impatiently, "No! No!—*before that!*" I answered that I recalled no other identity save in dreams. Then the aged curator offered me a high price for the Thing I had made from clay, but I refused it; for intuition told me that he meant to *destroy* it, whereas I wished it hung upon the wall of the museum. Then he asked me *how much* I would take for the bas-relief; & I jocularly replied, having now no mind to part with it, *"One million pounds sterling."* (Currency mixed!) To my amazement the old man did not laugh. He seemed perplexed, dazed, & frightened. Then he said in a quavering tone: "Call again in a week, please. I will consult with the directors of the corporation." This is the end—although I did not awake here. At this point the dream changed to one of drifting down a stagnant river betwixt high basalt cliffs, & wondering why I drifted; *since the water had no motion, & there was no breath of wind in the awful SILENCE.* This pair of dreams occurred in the middle of an afternoon when I paused in my work from nervous exhaustion & rested my head on my arm on the table before me. I am coming to a stage where I doze off like this very frequently—it helps me keep up & accomplish more than usual. As mere yarns, these jumbled fantasies would be hardly worth notice; but being bona fide dreams, they are rather picturesque. It gives one a sense of weird, fantastic, & unearthly *experience* to have *seen* these strange sights apparently with the visual eye. I have dreamed like this ever since I was old enough to remember dreams, & probably shall till I descend to Avernus. My dreams are just as vivid as in youth, but no more so. Among my best remembered visions are those of the awful cliffs, peaks, & abysses—hideous bleak rock & loathsome blackness—over which I was borne in the clutch of black winged daemons to which I gave the original name of "night-gaunts", at the age of six! Verily, I have travelled to strange places which are not upon the earth or any known planet. I have been a rider of comets, & a brother to the nebulae. Your own "midnight seizures" are—or were—indeed curious phaenomena. What could you have been seeing—what sight so unthinkable that it must needs be erased from your memory by a merciful oblivion? There be worlds beyond the rim of space which no man hath seen—black worlds which are not round, nor of any shape, but which are *alive*. From them no traveller in the universe of dreams hath ever brought away a recollection—save one traveller only, & he was quite mad, & could never be understood. Have these worlds indeed been visited by you at night? As to day-dreams & Rossie George—I am afraid that the wildest of his flights is rather tame compared with what I have seen in other universes whilst asleep. He can't even get off this one poor planet, or rise much above the animal instincts here. Carcass-worshippers like Rossie & Elsie[2] make me so infernally sick & tired that I lack patience with them. This reminds me—I never shewed you that putrid fellow's letter, which he wrote me last summer. I promised to do so, & will enclose it herewith. My personal comment is twofold: (a) Nobody home. (b) Throw it in the garbage pail behind the house & cover well with chloride of lime. Kindly return this bit of mental & moral aberration for preservation as a horrible example in my private museum of mental pathology. Of genuinely fantastic dreamers, I have discovered but one in amateurdom—this being Mrs. Jordan. I will enclose—subject to return—an account of a Jordanian dream which occurred in the early part of 1919, & which I am some time going to weave into a horror story, as I did "The Green Meadow" dream of earlier date, which I think I once shewed you. That earlier dream was exceptionally singular in that I had one exactly like it myself—save that mine did not extend so far. It was only when I had related my dream that Miss J. related the similar & more fully developed one. The opening paragraph of "The Green Meadow" was written for my own dream, but after hearing the other, I incorporated it into the tale which I developed therefrom. The more recent Jordan dream is very vivid, but peters out miserably. I shall use it only as far as the point where the narrator reaches the palm tree. The narrator will be a neurotic youth of the Roderick Usher type.[3] I do not see how you can fail to be sensitive to these unreal things. Surely the strange excrescences of the human fancy are as real—in the sense of real phaenomena—as the commonplace passions, thoughts, & instincts of everyday life. There is a giddy exhilaration in looking *beyond* the known world into unfathomable deeps, & a haunting thrill in thoughts of the cryptically horrible. Prof. Sturm ____ _____[4] but it occurs to me that I have already quoted his graphic passage in the critical introduction to Baudelaire![5] I must not fall into the dotard's habit of repeating things over & over. I had a visitor the other night, who gave me an idea for a good story. He was a furry, four-footed young visitor, with a black coat, white gloves & boots, & white around the tip of his nose & the tip of his tail. He sat in a chair near me, purring most inspiringly, when I permitted my fancy to consider his ancient race & heritage. I am intensely fond of his species, as I have doubtless told you more than once; & as I looked upon him my thoughts ran thus:

. . . . . The cat is the soul of antique Ægyptus, & bearer of tales from forgotten empires in Meroë & Ophir. He is the kin of the jungle's lords, & heir to the secrets of hoary & sinister Africa. The Sphinx is his cousin, & he speaks her language; but he is more ancient than the Sphinx, & remembers that which she hath forgotten. . . . .

As I mused, a plot took form in my mind. A simple, yet a ghastly plot. And that plot will some day reach the amateur publick in the form of a tale to be entitled "The Cats of Ulthar".[6] I have never read the tales of Eugene Field,[7] & was not aware that he dabbled in the bizarre. Modern authors, especially of the States, are not very well known to me. I am only beginning my delvings into the world of literary fantasy.

Yr obt Servt

Theobaldus

Notes

1. The substance of the following dream, recorded as entry 25 in HPL's commonplace book, was incorporated into "The Call of Cthulhu" (1926).

2. Roswell George Mills and Elsa A. Gidlow. See RK 35n4.

3. Jackson's two dreams were the basis of the collaborative tales "The Green Meadow" and "The Crawling Chaos."

4. The underscores are in AHT; evidently the typist could not read some words of HPL's letter at this point.

5. Frank Pearce Sturm, *The Poems of Charles Baudelaire*.

6. The preceding paragraph, entry 28 in HPL's commonplace book, was copied almost verbatim into the story.

7. American poet and essayist Eugene Field (1850–1895) wrote such weird tales as "The Holy Cross" (in *The Holy Cross and Other Stories*, 1893) and *The Temptation of Friar Gonsol* (1900).

[67]   [AHT]

Theobald Manor
6/11/20

Revered Bolingbroke:—

Your recent indifference to cosmical ideas is actually puzzling to me. Of course, we know that there is no life after death; for life & thought are peculiar to complex material organisms; but about us stretches an illimitable expanse of space filled with other worlds—an expanse wherein we are as nothing—& the titanic questions it suggests fairly beat upon the human mind in a desperate tattoo. What I cannot comprehend, is how your *imagination* can fail to react to these mysterious abysses; how you can escape the burning curiosity of a child at a nearly-closed door through whose crevice come sounds of strange & unearthly wonder, & fragments of sights that suggest unthinkable things. How, after these terrible glimpses, you can still remain indifferent to ultramundane hints; can still take tiny mankind & his affairs & desires seriously, I find actual difficulty in understanding. My only solution is that in you emotion replaces imagination; that the keenly sensitive development which in the philosopher affects the imaginative and speculatives functinos, I the poet affects those simple nervous-ganglial centres which give rise to the emotions of human relationship.

You & I undoubtedly represent cases of unusually *localised* & precisely opposite nervous development. I am objective enough to realise that my lack of interest in purely human matters is in its way as inexplicable to the humanocentrist, as his lack of interest in cosmic problems is to me. We both *see the same things,* but because of our dissimilar receptive or interpretative organisations these things assume with us a totally different order in our active consciousness. You are looking through a microscope, I through a telescope; you tend toward subjectivity, I toward objectivity. Your valuecentric standard is man, mine infinity & eternity. Perhaps a good illustration of our differences—or of my difference from the average person in this especial matter—would be the manner of receiving that gradual unfolding of reality from ideality which comes with years, & which is sometimes called *disillusionment.* When young, we believe in the existence of many virtues which our older eyes perceive to be unreal. That is, as we grow older we perceive more & more keenly that the motives for human acts are exclusively selfish, and that the average person is governed by no moral law save appearances & self-interest. To most, & probably to you, this disillusionment was markedly *painful.* The discovery of the unreality of "Sunday-School" motives gives to the average person something of an unwelcome shock. But to me, this process had merely a *scientific interest.* All motives being simply material phenomena, I was not at all crushed at finding that the idealistic system is false; if I was annoyed, it was only in the way that a scientist is annoyed when an old theory breaks down & he is forced to assimilate the details of a new theory. For human ideals never had any personal interest or application to me. I was ever an intellectual outsider—a spectator & not a participant. Disillusionment's only pang was a sense of mortification at a slight scientific error—an error whereby I had estimated too large a gap betwixt the species *homo sapiens* & *homo niger vel Africanus*. I now saw that these species, together with the extinct *pithecanthropus erectus*[1] of Java, represent less evolutional separation than I had before calculated. But as for emotional disturbance over "lost ideals"—bah! Theobaldus was a cosmic observer—

> "What's Hecuba to him, or he to Hecuba,
> That he shou'd weep for her?"[2]

And so years have not changed me very much. An outlook like mine never has many disturbances; for no matter what I may observe in man, it neither surprises nor impresses me. Of course, I have personal preferences & disgusts; but to me all personal things are philosophically trivial. My human reactions remain as in childhood because I deem them superficial. I have the same repulsions & respects, & disillusionment does not "mature" or "broaden" them, because they were always based on *pure taste, never faith*. Some persons shrink from a fellow like Rossie Mills when young because they deem him an unique & leprous abnormality; yet tolerate him in later years because they learn that most mortals share his foulness. I shrank from such in youth merely because *I disliked them & was not like them*. And in later life I still shrink from them, *for exactly the same reason*. I am the same & they are the same—& it does not matter to me that their qualities are more widely diffused than I had fancied.

Dear me! In explaining these things I fear I have bored you fully as much as I did in the uncongenial *Kleicomolo* instalment! As to dreams—the only trouble with fictionising them is plot-invention. In spite of all the value of imagery, the real Ζωὴ καὶ Ψυχή[3] of a story is the *plot*—a connected, climactic unit which must move along with relentless coherence & suspense to a thrill of horror & surprise which shall impress the reader more than all the fine speech & scenery combined. The plot must be stronger than the atmosphere, else the "story" will degenerate into a mere fantasy. It is far easier to write prose-poems than to create real stories, & I am determined to make my products *stories* in every sense of the word. In "Randolph Carter" I did my best. I cannot always reach that level, but I can at least avoid such vague junk as my "Memory" in the *Coöperative*. De Quincey is familiar to me, but impressed me more with his language & erudition than with his fancy. I never took opium, but if I can't beat him for *dreams* from the age of three or four up, I am a dashed liar! Space, strange cities, weird landscapes, unknown monsters, hideous ceremonies, Oriental & Egyptian gorgeousness, and indefinable mysteries of life, death, & torment, were daily—or rather nightly—commonplaces to me before I was six years old. Today it is the same, save for a slightly increased *objectivity*. Today the percentage of dreams in which I am an observer & not an actor has slightly risen. As to the Rubaiyat of Omar &

Fitzgerald, it is so long since I read the thing that I have forgotten its details. I did not especially like it—which is doubtless the reason I never perused it a second time. I am now perusing some of the pessimistical writings of S. L. Clemens, which I find much to my taste. "What is Man?" is a veritable masterpiece.[4]

Yr most obt humble Servt
H: Lovecraft

Notes

1. A species conjectured by Ernst Haeckel as the putative link between the lower primates and human beings.

2. Shakespeare, *Hamlet* 2.2.564–65.

3. Life and soul.

4. Mark Twain (Samuel Langhorne Clemens, 1835–1910), *What Is Man?* (1906), a philosophical dialogue expressing bleak cynicism as to human motives.

[68]   [AHT; Post]

Still at the Old Stand
6/25/20

Venerated Viscount:—

[Post:] Doubtless you received the joint card which Daas & I sent you Tuesday. His visit here was a total surprise—he telegraphed Monday, saying he would be here in the evening, & I met him in the Union Station at 9 p.m. He spent Monday evening—up to midnight—in my lair, talking over amateurdom & scanning amateur papers. Tuesday morning I met him downtown, & we visited various points of interest. At the station we sent the amateurs some cards which we had purchased, & at 2:20 Daas left for the Hub. I understand that he will be with you soon, & attend a Blue Pencil meeting. I was exceedingly glad to meet the benefactor who introduced me to amateur journalism; & like him very much, though our tastes are not especially similar. His favourite branch of literature is the dramatic, while, as you know, mine is the philosophical & the fantastic. However, in every-day matters he seems phenomenally congenial, & his interest in amateur journalism is commendable to behold. I trust I may have subsequent opportunities of meeting him.

[AHT:] As to philosophy—its effects on various individuals are different. I merely know that in my case the cosmos dwarfs my interest in the tiny insects called men. Their doings seem so absurd & trivial when one reflects upon their absolute insignificance. I wish the poor devils (including myself, of course) could all be mercifully blotted out by a whiff of cyanogen gas in some comet's tail! The immortality myth is too childish to talk about. Of course there can be no technically positive knowledge of anything of the sort, but we may safely say that a life snuffed out survives no more than an electric light smashed to pieces. Life & light—both are forms of energy manifest only through material media. Destroy the medium in either case, & the energy is irreclaimably lost in transformation to other forms.

I have just written an essay describing the natural origin of mythological delusion, & commenting upon their present influence. It was evoked by the idiotic & babyish whine of that poor simpleton Amend in the July *United Amateur,* which you will behold soon.[1]

Yr most Obt Servt
Theobaldus

Notes

1. "Idealism and Materialism—A Reflection," *National Amateur* 41, No. 6 ("July 1919"): 278–81. The issue appeared in the summer of 1921. J. Gordon Amend, a member of the Penn State Club of the UAPA, contributed the essay "A Resume and a Query" to the *United Amateur* 19, No. 6 (July 1920): 131–34. It was written in response to the article "Pacifists and Patriots" by Paul J. Campbell in the April 1920 issue of Campbell's journal *Invictus.* Among other statements, Campbell had called Jesus Christ "a social outcast," "something of an I. W. W.," and "a young rebel." Amend found Campbell's essay to be insulting to Amend himself, to his country, and to his God. In his conclusion, Amend asked, "Will the UNITED AMATEUR . . . stand for Paganism?—or Christianity?"

[69]   [Post; AHT]

Home
8/12/20

Scintillant St. John:—

[Post:] You may be surprised to learn that since visiting Boston with you, a month ago, I have been there again.[1] One venture begets another, if successful. Before long, I may actually reach your metropolis. The occasion for this recent excursion, which took place last Saturday, was the Hub Club picnic; to which Mrs. Miniter invited me, & at which I hoped to meet James F. Morton. As it turned out, I missed Morton—who had to go to New Hampshire ahead of his schedule—but I was much appeased by meeting his brother, Nelson G. Morton,[2] whom I like immensely & shall try to recruit for the United. He was the host of the gathering, & proved a most delightful & capable one.

[. . .]

[AHT:] I had been miserable all the week—headaches & allied phenomena—& had fainted on the street only the day before; but having slept well Friday night, found myself able to be about Saturday. The day was hot—a good thing for me—& I left the house at 11 a.m., taking a train car for Boston via the little used Wrentham line. I hate the monotonous scenery of the Prov.–Boston main line, so thought I would try this more northerly, rambling route. I was well repaid, for all along the slow journey I obtained beautiful glimpses of New England hills, farms, woods, & villages. I had never been this way before, but shall go again some day just for the scenery. Practically no one uses this line for through travel, since it takes double the normal time; but as a picturesque ride it is pleasant indeed. The train was late, & I missed the 1:59 train for Melrose Highlands on which the Hub folk went; but was delayed only 11 minutes, since another train leaves at 2:10. This is a Haverhill train, & I felt tempted to keep on & pay *Tryout* a visit![3] In reaching the North Station, whence Melrose trains start, I had an excellent ride on the Atlantic Avenue elevated—over the street we traversed when you went to secure your steamship reservations. Reaching Melrose Highlands, I found the Morton home with very little trouble—I wonder if you could have found it so soon?

There were present—counting later arrivals—fourteen persons. Mrs. Dennis is a famous old-timer often referred to by C. W. Smith.[4] As Harriet C. Cox she won four story laureateships in the National, in the 'eighties. She was entirely out of touch with amateurdom, except for Mrs. Miniter, but seems rather interested again. Miss Outwater[5] had been to the Cleveland convention of the National, and I was interested to hear her description of Samuel Loveman—whose picture I saw also, in some group photographs. I had never before met anyone who had seen Loveman, & was surprised to learn that he does not look or act in the least poetical. One picture shews him with his hat on one side, & Miss Outwater said he was "feeling pretty 'kippy' that day".

During the afternoon there was a thunder shower, so lunch was eaten on the Morton piazza instead of in the beautiful Middlesex Fells Reservation, as planned. However, later on it cleared, so that Cook, Mrs. Miniter, Mrs. Dennis, Morton, & I took a stroll in the woodland. The Fells district reminds me of Quinsnicket Park, but it is even more beautiful in places. During the walk, Mrs. Miniter plucked some bays, & as the party rested on a rocky bluff overlooking a beautiful lake & valley, she formed them into a genuine Parnassian wreath—which she insisted on my wearing all the evening, even at the "convention banquet", in honour of my triple laureateship.[6] Which reminds me—I have not told you before that I won in the story competition as well as in the essay & editorial classes. It was "The White Ship" which gained the prize, though I really consider "Dagon" superior. I told Mrs. Miniter that I did not deserve the chaplet of bays—that no brow less noble than that of our poet-laureate, Samples, was worthy of such adornment—& when the evening was over, I folded it carefully in a cigarette box which someone produced, & sent it to John Milton.

At about eleven the gathering departed for the station. At Boston, I bade farewell to the Hubites, refusing overnight invitations & hastening to the South Station. I trod my native heath at 1:30 a.m. I reached home half an hour later, & removing only my collar & tie, slept like a mummy until the following noon.

   Yr most obt hble Servt
     Theobaldus

Notes

1. HPL traveled to Boston in early July with RK for a meeting of the Hub Club. He visited Boston again on August 7 for another Hub Club meeting.
2. Nelson Glazier Morton (1881–1941), brother of James F. Morton, Jr.
3. "Tryout" Smith lived in Haverhill, MA.
4. Harriet C. (Cox) Dennis (1868?–1936), Official Editor of the NAPA (1890–91).
5. Marjorie Outwater, amateur journalist and Official Editor of the NAPA (1920–21).
6. For the 1919–20 UAPA term, HPL won the laureateships for "The White Ship" (*United Amateur*, November 1919) (story), "The Pseudo-United" (*United Amateur*, May 1920) (editorial), and an unknown item for the essay laureateship.

[70] [Post; AHT]

           Identical Address
            Septr. 10, 1920

St. John Honeycomb, Esq.
Brooklyn, N. Y.

Revered Lothario:—

    [Post:] I now have a third trip to Boston to chronicle—probably a final trip for this year, since winter is a season of drear blankness & indisposition. This latest trip was in response to an invitation to deliver an address on amateurdom's future before the Hub Club Conference on Sept. 5th, at which I was told Cook, Morton, & the veteran Tilden[1] would be present.

    I was fairly well on the appointed day, & took the 9:31 train for the Hub, arriving only half an hour late—marvellous feat for the N.Y.N.H. & H. in these times! Thence I proceeded to Allston according to the route we traversed in July, reaching 20 Wilhelmstrasse[2] exactly at noon.

    Fancy my surprise when I encountered, as I crossed the portal, none other than George Julian Houtain, your genial & exuberant fellow-Brooklynite, whose presence I had not even remotely anticipated. I was really much pleased, for I cannot help liking the rascal! He is such a battery of animal spirits that he electrifies all the atmosphere about him, shedding & diffusing a goodly share of the overflowing vitality with which Nature has endowed him. Whilst I was looking at some interesting photographs of oldtime amateurs & conventions, a heavy step sounded on the piazza, & at last I succeeded in shaking hands with the elusive person I have wished so long to meet—James Ferdinand Morton, Jr.! Never have I met so thoroughly erudite a conversationalist before, & I was quite surprised by the geniality & friendliness which overlay his unusual attainments. I could but regret the limited opportunities which I have of meeting him, for Morton is one who commands my most unreserved liking.

Mrs. Harriet Cox Dennis was also present, with a valise filled with amateur relics of a generation ago. Some of the amateur books of the 'eighties were quite impressive, & Mrs. Dennis' volume of the *National Amateur* (1890–91) reflects great credit on her powers as official editor. Mrs. Dennis read a paper comparing the old & new amateurdom, much to the disadvantage of the latter; but won my gratitude by saying that my work reminded her of Edkins & Emery—the latter of whom she knew personally.[3] The Massachusetts amateurs, indeed, have reduced flattery to a fine art.

Soon other delegates began to arrive, one by one or two by two. Nelson Morton came, bringing his wife & their infant prodigy, Dorothy Louise, aetat about eleven. Leonard Tilden proved very interesting. He opined that the salvation of amateurdom lies in pound postage for amateur papers, & pleased me by saying that he likes my weird tales.

Mrs. McMullen[4] was present, & prepared to argue over a criticism I had recently applied to one of her verses; but I quickly ended the argument by calling in as my ally the omniscient James Ferdinand, from whose decisions there is no appeal. (The question had to do with the use of "mirror" as an intransitive verb. Such usage is incorrect.)

Cook was absent much of the time, & was feeling rather ill. Lynch had a beastly toothache which spoilt the occasion for him. Wagner is a poet of some inspiration—rather a serious man, who I think will join the United through me.[5]

The literary programme was rendered in the late afternoon, the irrepressible Julianus acting as chairman. The best feature was Mrs. McMullen's pathetic poem "Desiree Logier", which is to appear in the July *United Amateur*.[6] (I tried to get that poem on the front page, but Mrs. Renshaw overruled me.)

My address—long & tedious—was received with admirable courtesy.[7] I read from my ms. in a dull, monotonous fashion, & I suppose the pompous style moved everyone to inward laughter; but the patience & restraint of the audience were unfailing. The principal reply was given by James Ferdinand—of whose power & grace as an extemporaneous orator I need not speak to one who knows him far better than I do.

About 6 p.m. refreshments appeared, doubtless saving the lives of many who depend upon material fuel. After that there was more discussion, some cacophony about the parlour melodeon, & finally a series of leave-takings. Lynch & I were the last to go. His toothache excited my sympathy, but sympathy could not cure it. He left the car at the Boylston Street subway station, & thereafter I was alone. As I boarded the Providence train I beheld a somewhat amusing incident—three young fellows about to leave were serenaded by an odd-looking group on the platform outside the window. The would-be musicians—several vocalists & one quavering cornetist—had a repertoire of gospel hymns exclusively!

[Post]

Sept. 13

Again I take my pen in hand after an enforced relinquishment.

Saturday I went out for the first time since my journey, visiting the library & picking up an addition to mine own library at a bookstall on the way home. My new possession is entitled "Men & Manners of the Eighteenth Century," & is by one Susan Hale—who seems to me to have more of industry than of genius.

[AHT:] Just two weeks ago I made a pilgrimage to Quinsnicket Park, which you will recall we *almost* visited last July. I was accompanied by my two aunts, neither of whom had ever been there before; & both declare that the region is a revelation of scenic loveliness. We went on the same car which you & I took, & had the same walk through Saylesville. After viewing the Eleazer Arnold tavern—the limit of the expedition of July 4, we pushed on up the road & entered the reservation, following a special route devised by myself, & calculated to shew the beauties of the place in climactic fashion. Each scene attain'd was lovelier than the last—grassy lanes, spreading trees, towering rocks, woodland aisles, gentle hills, pleasing prospects, shady vales, sunny glades, & paths meandering along the edges of delectable ravines. Finally there was the famed glen & its appurtenances, & one scenic surprise which I will not describe to you, since I hope to lead you in person over that course next June or July. After the surprise—which delighted my aunts—we walked further westward through wood & farming land, finally emerging on the high-speed Woonsocket–Providence interurban car line & being whizzed back into the city without delay. I am sure that such a walk could not help making you a lover of sylvan solitude, & believe you would begin writing pastorals after taking it! Such slopes & forests are the natural domain of Damon & Strephon, to say naught of Pan, the Fauns, & the Dryades! My aunts plucked berries & flowers, whilst I absorbed material for Georgian couplets—although I shall trouble no one with the sight of them.

Ever y^r L^{d}ship's most oblig'd, most Obt Servt
Humphry Littlewit, Armiger.

Notes

1. Leonard E. Tilden (1861–1937), amateur journalist living in New Hampshire and later in Washington, DC.
2. HPL refers to 20 Webster Street in Allston, joint home of Edith Miniter and Charles and Laurie A. Sawyer.
3. Brainerd Prescott Emery (1865–1917), Official Editor of the NAPA (1885–86 and

1892–93) and publisher of *Athenia*.

4. S[usan] Lilian McMullen (1886–1981?), amateur journalist living in Newton Centre, MA, who generally wrote under the pseudonym "Lilian Middleton."

5. Wagner is unidentified. He evidently did not join the UAPA.

6. See HPL's "The Poetry of Lilian Middleton" (1922): "'Desirée Logier' is a masterpiece—extremely simple in plot, relating only an idyllic courtship in war-torn France which ended in the weeping of Desirée by the poppied grave of the young Fusilier Dennis O'Toole, it derives from its skilfully breathed atmosphere and inherent music a charm and brooding sadness which scores of more hectic and apparently intense emotional outbursts fail to exhibit" (*CE* 2.53–54).

7. "Amateur Journalism: Its Possible Needs and Betterment."

[71] [AHT]

598 Angell—12/14/20[1]

Venerated Viscount:—

[. . .]

"Nyarlathotep" is a nightmare—an actual phantasm of my own, with the first paragraph written *before I fully awaked*.[2] I have been feeling execrably of late—whole weeks have passed without relief from headache & dizziness, & for a long time three hours was my utmost limit for continuous work. (I seem better now.) Added to my steady ills was an unaccustomed ocular trouble which prevented me from reading fine print—a curious tugging of nerves & muscles which rather startled me during the weeks it persisted. Amidst this gloom came the nightmare of nightmares—the most realistic & horrible I have experienced since the age of ten—whose stark hideousness & ghastly oppressiveness I could but feebly mirror in my written phantasy. It occurred after midnight as I lay on the couch exhausted after a tussle with the "poetry" of that damned fool Bush. The first phase was a general sense of undefined apprehension— vague terror which appeared universal. I seemed to be seated in my chair clad in my old grey dressing-gown, reading a letter from Samuel Loveman. The letter was unbelievably realistic—thin, $8\frac{1}{2} \times 13$ paper, violet ink signature, & all—& its contents seemed portentous. The dream-Loveman wrote:

> "Don't fail to see Nyarlathotep if he comes to Providence. He is horrible— horrible beyond anything you can imagine—but wonderful. He haunts one for hours afterward. I am still shuddering at what he showed."

I had never heard the name NYARLATHOTEP before, but seemed to understand the allusion. Nyarlathotep was a kind of itinerant showman or lecturer who held forth in publick halls & aroused widespread fear & discussion with his exhibitions. These exhibitions consisted of two parts—first, a horrible—possibly prophetic—cinema reel; & later some extraordinary experiments with scientific & electrical apparatus. As I received the letter, I seemed to recall that Nyarlathotep was already in Providence; & that he was the cause of the shocking fear which brooded over all the people. I seemed to remember that persons had whispered to me in awe of his horrors, & warned me not to go near him. But Loveman's dream-letter decided me, & I began to dress for a trip down town to see Nyarlathotep. The details are quite vivid—I had trouble tying my cravat—but the indescribable terror overshadowed all else. As I left the house I saw throngs of men plodding through the night, all whispering affrightedly & bound in one direction. I fell in with them, afraid yet eager to see & hear the great, the obscure, the unutterable Nyarlathotep. After that the dream followed the course of the enclosed story almost exactly, save that it did not go quite so far. It ended a moment after I was drawn into the black yawning abyss between the snows, & whirled tempestuously about in a vortex with shadows that once were men! I added the macabre conclusion for the sake of climactic effect & literary finish. As I was drawn into the abyss I emitted a resounding shriek (I thought it must have been audible, but my aunt says it was not) & the picture ceased. I was in great pain—forehead pounding & ears ringing—but I had only one automatic impulse—to *write*, & preserve the atmosphere of unparalleled fright; & before I knew it I had pulled on the light & was scribbling desperately. Of what I was writing I had very little idea, & after a time I desisted & bathed my head. When fully awake I remembered all the incidents but had lost the exquisite thrill of fear—the actual sensation of the presence of the hideous unknown. Looking at what I had written I was astonished by its coherence. It comprises the first paragraph of the enclosed manuscript, only three words having been changed. I wish I could have continued in the same subconscious state, for although I went on immediately, the primal thrill was lost, & the terror had become a matter of conscious artistic creation. Still, the tale ought to hold a shiver or two for sensitive readers, & Loveman (the real waking Loveman!) was effusively laudatory when he beheld it. Altogether, that nightmare was *some* dream, believe me!

The other piece—"Celephaïs"—weaves together a large number of my recent dreams on a thread of pathos. It is the first non-horror story I have written since "The White Ship". The remaining three are not of the fantastic but of the realistically gruesome type—the last, which I finished day before yesterday, being rather unique. I am wondering what Loveman will think of it. The title is "The Picture in the House",[3] & it hinges on a very old engraving by the brothers DeBry—Plate XII of Pigafetta's "Regnum Congo", printed in Frankfort in 1598.[4] Please be sure to return the enclosed manuscripts—they are the original typed copies which will go to the publisher if I can find such a person. I suppose it is absurd for me to try to write, since there is no demand for my work, yet the pleasure is in the creation of the images, & I could not help scribbling if I wished.

Yr most obt Servt

L: Theobald Junr.

Notes

1. AHT incorrectly dates the letter "Dec 14—21." The recent completion of "The Picture in the House" indicates the letter should be dated to 1920.

2. HPL wrote the prose poem "Nyarlathotep" in early December.

3. *National Amateur* 41, No. 6 ("July 1919"): 246–49. For the date of the issue, see RK 68n1.

4. HPL refers to the woodcuts by the brothers De Bry in Filippo Pigafetta's *Regnum Congo* (1591). For HPL's numerous errors in citing this book (which HPL learned about from an essay in Thomas Henry Huxley's *Man's Place in Nature and Other Anthropological Essays* [1894]), see S. T. Joshi, "Lovecraft and the *Regnum Congo*," in *Lovecraft and a World in Transition* (New York: Hippocampus Press, 2014), 362–66.

[72]   [AHT]

Home as Usual

4/23/21

Honour'd Bolingbroke:—

About that tale "Celephaïs"—breathe easy. It was not to you I lent it after all. 'Twas W. P. Cook, & he hath duly return'd it. I must keep better track of the things I lend. I am picking up a new style lately—running to pathos as well as horror. The best thing I have yet done is "The Quest of Iranon", whose English Loveman calls the most musical & flowing I have yet written, & whose sad plot made one prominent poet actually weep—not at the crudity of the story, but at the sadness. Then I have written another hair-raiser, "The Moon-Bog". This was concocted half to order for the Hub Club. They invited me to their meeting of March 10, which was supposed to be in honour of the not unknown Sanctus Patricius—the Scotsman who drave from Hibernia all the snakes save the Sinn Fein. For this meeting they wished me to read some contribution pertaining to Hibernia, & not having any ready made, I perpetrated "The Moon-Bog". I read it aloud, inserting all the shivers I could, & hope two or three of the auditors understood it in part. Incidentally, I stayed all night at 20 Webster, occupying the Royal Chamber which housed St. Julian[1] last July. The next day was spent in exhaustive & (to my listeners, no doubt) exhausting conversation with Tat & the guardian spirits of Epgephi, & I did not depart till the hour of the 11:45 train approached.

I can in a measure sympathise with your indifference to new books. I have not much interest in anything nowadays unless it is wild & weird. I am so beastly tired of mankind & the world that nothing can interest me unless it contains a couple of murders on each page or deals with horrors unnamable & unaccountable that leer down from the external universes. And yet I am wading through some new books in an effort to keep up with my boy & the philosophical studies in which I am endeavouring to follow him. It is odd that an old man should be so much influenced by a kid so vastly his junior, but it remains a fact that no other one human creature has moulded my thought & opinions as extensively as has that Alfredus child. The secret is this: that he is intellectually *exactly like me* save in degree. In degree he is immensely my superior—he is what I should like to be but have not brains enough to be. Our minds are cast in precisely the same mould, save that his is finer. He alone can grasp the direction of my thoughts & amplify them. And so we go down the dark ways of knowledge; the poor plodding old man, & ahead of him the alert little link-boy holding the light & pointing out the path. The Gallomo is busted. Mo finds that the increasing convergence of Galpinio–Theobaldian thought is creating too solid an array of adverse opinion for him, & so has withdrawn from the triangle, taking with him his Christian piety. Thus both of the leading correspondence rings have ceased to exist!

I have never perused the works of Georgius Moore, Esq.,[2] though I may in the course of my Galpin-led explorations. In considering the origin of my opinions I have recently wondered whether or not my anti-erotic views are too hasty; formed from mere subjective prejudice rather than accurate & impersonal observation. I have opposed eroticism for several reasons, (a) because of the acknowledged repulsiveness of direct erotic manifestations, as felt by all races & cultures & expressed in reticence to a greater or less degree, (b) because of the obvious kinship of erotic instincts to the crudest & earliest neural phenomena of organic nature, rather than to the phenomena resulting from complex & advanced development (i.e., purely intellectual phenomena), (c) because of the apparent connexion betwixt ages of erotic interest & national decadence, & (d) because so far as I could judge erotic interests are overrated; being in truth mere trifles which engross crude minds when more worthy interests are lacking. It was my theory that eroticism would diminish if thinkers would awake & turn to really important phenomena. Such, in brief, were the bases of my opinions; but perusal of representative realistic works without prejudice leads me to attempt a revaluation; a revaluation possible because of my increased impersonalism. When I dissociate myself altogether from humanity, & view the world as through a telescope, I can consider more justly phenomena which at close range disgust me. Thus I am coming to be convinced that the erotic instinct is in the majority of mankind far stronger than I could ever imagine without wide reading & observation; that it relentlessly clutches the average person—even of the thinking classes—to a degree which makes its overthrow by higher interests impossible. Probably my recommendation of dismissing it by displacement by purely imaginative & cosmic interests is an absurdity based on ignorance of its extent & intensity. Furthermore, detached observation makes it evident that all ethical systems based on erotic repression have been futile & hypocritical. Beneath the surface of Anglo-Saxonism is apparently as much eroticism as existed openly amongst the Greeks; & even more repellent in form because furtive & little modified by aesthetic considerations. Mankind, in short, is less evolved than I had thought; his seeming improvement being a mask rather than an alteration. Lastly, the force of anti-erotic arguments is weakened by consideration of the origin of ideals of decency. These ideals are probably gained from very early race-experience, when martial & nomadic existence demanded a concentration of energy in the sternest channels, & when the emotional excitement of killing replaced the softer excitement of amorousness. Now the old joys of slaughter are suppressed, & the healthy blood-thirst becomes languishing romance. To sum up, the reality of erotic dominance is impressed upon the most reluctant observer by the sheer extent & pervasiveness of amatory phenomena. What has survived every attempt at modification must be important, & to criticise or try to correct is futile. Much as a delicate mind may grow nauseated at the bestiality of mankind, that same mind cannot deny what it discovers to exist—& surely romance is no more crude than the analogous phenomenon of hunger. All, then, that we must ask, is a more refined & artistic treatment of the erotic motive. From what I have heard, the fount of Saxon eroticism is its morbidness, which no doubt results from a social system which seeks to banish it, & which therefore only makes it the more obnoxious when it breaks out. I suppose that this is the trouble with George Moore. The only remedy would seem to lie in the gradual evolution of society out of the puritan phase, & the sanctioning of some looser morality or hetairism.[3] This seems to be the idea adumbrated by Nietzsche & other realists—to remove morbid erotic interest by removing the prejudices & inhibitions which make it doubly strong. It is quite possible that the net amount of vulgarism would thus be decreased rather than increased; surely, the decrease in hypocrisy would make for a gain in wholesomeness. Of course, the loss would be vast to the more delicate class; yet if observation teaches correctly this class is surprisingly small—much smaller than any person of conventional 19th century education could possibly suspect. And this class might be more than compensated by its new dignity—for its virtues would no longer be aped by coarser beings, or taken for granted as common qualities of mankind. The refined & imaginative anti-erotic person would under such a system be credited in full for his superior evolution, since none of his virtue could be imputed to the pressure of society or fear of censure. Thus I have changed my views on what I formerly censured. What is inherent in the majority cannot be extirpated—man cannot be moulded to an ideal society & literature; society & literature must conform to man as he is. Censure & moral prejudice are absurd—man is a rotten mess—let him roll in his own ordure. No more shall I chide vice *more Juvenalis,*[4] since Nature shews that vice is not vice. If men have the instincts of dogs, let them write it out & be done with it—I will not criticise, but merely leave them unread. A chapter is closed—Theobald the Moralist is dead. I expect nothing of man, & disown the race. The only folly is in expecting what is never attained; man is most contemptible when compared with his own pretensions. It is better to laugh at man from outside the universe, than to weep for him within. He is a joke & a blemish—I spit upon him.

Yr most humble & obt Servt,

L. Theobald, Junr

Notes

1. I.e., George Julian Houtain.
2. George Moore (1852–1933), Anglo-Irish novelist and essayist. Several of his works—including the novel *A Modern Lover* (1883) and the memoir *Confessions of a Young Man* (1886)—contain frank discussions of love and sex.
3. I.e., legalized prostitution (from *hetaira,* the Greek word for prostitute).
4. "In the manner of Juvenal," the censorious Roman satirist.

[73]   [AHT]

St. Angell's Priory, Friday the 13th
May 1921

Sir Wilful Wildrake, Bt.[1]
Brooklyn, in New-York

Distinguish'd Sir:

I observe with interest your present system of killing Time, which no doubt has much to be said for it. No doubt any scheme is deserving of commendation, which can keep a mortal reasonably contented throughout the length of time he is compell'd to exist; & each must discover those pursuits which are best suited to his humour. For mine own part, I presume that the animating principle of my weary days is much the same as your own; details differing only because my tastes differ. To me, the element of *conflict* is essential—I must always have something to hate & fight, & will never quit the field of controversy & satire. *Speculation* is also indispensable, for my mind is distractingly curious & sensitive as to the unknown phaenomena & abysses of space that press upon it from the world & the aether beyond. Anything savouring of quiet & tameness is maddeningly abhorrent to me—not in actual life, for that I wish as placid as possible; but in thought, which is my more vivid life. The strange, the unnatural, the terrible—all these things are necessary to me, & I revel in the shrieks of ghouls & the phantasmagoria of nightmare. Then, as a contrast, I like sometimes to gaze upon the immemorially ancient countryside as it sleeps under a lazy sun or magical moon, & mark the roofs of distant cottages or the spire of some distant hamlet amongst the hills. To me life is a picture, of which I have never been & never will be a part. I shall never be very merry or very sad, for I am more prone to analyse than to feel. What merriment I have is always derived from the satirical principle, & what sadness I have, is not so much personal, as a vast & terrible melancholy at the pain & futility of all existence in a blind & purposeless cosmos. My melancholy would be less if I had more power of endurance—it arises largely from my easy fatigue, & consequent inability to write & exert myself for long continuous periods. Give me an inexhaustible faculty of creating literary images, & I would be as happy as a prince; as it is, I shall probably die of my own hand some day, from the sheer desolating monotony of grey days which I am not strong enough to fill & diversify. In one matter we are alike—our scepticism regarding cosmic purpose, & our consequent contempt for owlish earnestness & hectic activity. Serious ethical effort, I become increasingly convinced, is hideously bourgeois, futile, & unsophisticated. Determinism— which you call Destiny—rules inexorably; though not exactly in the personal way you seem to fancy. We have no specific destiny against which we can fight—for the fighting would be as much a part of the destiny as the final end. The real fact is simply that every event in the cosmos is caused by the action of antecedent & circumjacent forces, so that whatever we do is consciously the inevitable product of Nature rather than of our own volition. If an act correspond with our wish, it is Nature that made the wish, & ensured its fulfilment. When we see an apparent chain of circumstances leading toward some striking denouement, we say it is "Fate". That is not true in the sense meant, for all of these circumstances might have been deceptive, so that a hidden & unexpected cause would have turned matters to an utterly opposite conclusion. The chain of appearances are as much a part of fate as the result, whichever the latter may be—& more; there is no such thing as a final result, since all cosmic existence is but an endless & purposeless chain beginning & leading nowhere. You are, for instance, following your "destiny" no more now than when you were pious. Inexorable circumstance made you pious once, & makes you sceptical now—perhaps it will make you pious again when the nymphs no longer divert you. No one state is any more natural to you than the other, since it is natural that you should pass through any stage which you do pass through. No life has any meaning or central principle—a man is merely an infinitesimal fragment of that cosmic mess of matter which is the playground of capricious, kaleidoscopic natural forces. We are what we are at the moment, merely because we are. Sometimes we may guess from our present state how we are likely to turn out, but all the real causes are in the hands of forces we can never fathom. All that one can say in the matter of "finding one's destiny" is that after a certain number of changes a person is likely to acquire an unchanging type. In the case of a pious youth turned a rake, we may not say that his nature is through destiny essentially rakish; we may simply say that he was designed to be first pious, then rakish. The piety was just as basic & natural as the rakishness. Of course, this is not to say that we cannot sometimes analyse early attitudes & predict from them & their surrounding conditions the future attitudes into which they are likely to develop. Natural processes have a certain degree of uniformity, & experience reveals much of the characteristic machinery of human mutation. But pardon me if I have by chance dropt into my Galpinian style. To a man of the world, these pedantick periods savour of an atmosphere too musty for enjoyment.

Yr most humble, most obedient Servt,

L: Theobald Junr.

Notes

1. The name of the central character of HPL's poem "The Pathetick History of Sir Wilful Wildrake," concerning the sad fate of a rake who contracts venereal disease. The poem, found in a letter to Frank Belknap Long dating to 7 February 1924 (*SL* 1.306–9), is dedicated to RK, and HPL states in the letter that it was written three years before; so it was probably included in a letter to RK of around this time.

[74]   [AHT]

June 12, 1921

My dear Klei:—

Psychologically I am conscious of a vastly increased aimlessness & inability to be interested in events; a phenomenon due partly to the fact that much of my former interest in things lay in discussing them with my mother & securing her views & approval.[1] This bereavement decentralises existence—my sphere no longer possesses a nucleus, since there is now no one person especially interested in what I do or whether I be alive or dead. However, the inevitability of such disasters renders tears & clamorous lamentation not only futile but puerile & vulgar as well. My mother has secured exactly what she most desired—complete oblivion & non-existence,—so that grief must needs be for oneself rather than for her. I am as active as possible—quite so in amateurdom—& externally appear as usual; since I never display emotion, but prefer to be calm or slightly satirical. For some time I was unable to dress or be about—the shock affected my throat & motor nerves so that I could not eat much, or stand & walk with ease; but even then I was free from all emotional displays. As I continued to stagnate in dressing-gown & slippers—increasingly active with the pen, but inert physically—my aunts endeavoured to arouse me to some variation of the indoor monotony, & insisted that I respond to an invitation which I had received a month before, to visit an exceedingly learned & brilliant new United member—Miss M. A. Little, A. B., A. M., a former college professor now starting as a professional author—in Hampstead, N. H., near Haverhill, Mass.[2] This I finally did, as you already know from the postcard mailed at the latter place.

On Thursday came the Smith call.[3] I had intended to stop there alone on my return trip, but Miss Little was so much interested in the genial Groveland-ite as revealed in his paper that she wished to go also. We found him in his little *Tryout* office behind the house, cordial & hospitable, & eagerly awaiting the visit which my card had heralded. He has, I am sure, been utterly misrepresented in the matter of hospitality; for never have I received a more hearty, genuine, & spontaneous welcome. He was sorry we could not stay longer, & made both Miss L. & me promise to visit him sometime when we could stay all day & eat a dinner of his cooking—he prides himself on his skill as an amateur chef. Smith is a lean, wiry man of medium stature & good features, with a short iron-grey full beard, a good head of iron-grey hair, & a bronzed weather-beaten complexion gained by his outdoor programme. He wears old clothes—which sit neatly & quaintly on his active frame—& has a pleasant voice with a somewhat rural accent. His deafness is no obstacle to conversation if one speaks incisively & near his ear. He confesses to *69* years, but does not look a day over 50. In person he bears out every impression which one gains from the *Tryout*—I like him immeasurably, for he is the most unspoiled, simple, contented, artless, & altogether delightful small boy of his age that I have ever beheld. He never grew up, but lives on without any of the dull complexities of adulthood—active, busy with his little press, stamp album, cat, & woodland excursions—in short, a perfect old Damaetas whom Theocritus would have loved to delineate. Let none tell me hereafter that my Georgian pastorals are not true to life; for I have with mine own eyes seen happy Tityrus in his beechen shade. Smith says he wants to leave me all his old amateur papers,[4] but I tell him he must live on for ever, like the kindly, gracious old faun that he is!

Tom, the cat, was inexcusably rude, being apparently afraid of both his visitors! After all the verse I have dedicated to him, this is a positive insult! We also saw Smith's tiny grandchild—"The Mascot"—who was less impolite, but withal of few words. *Tryout* office is a veritable curiosity shop, with all the odds & ends of forty years hung or strewn about. There are buttons, stamps, chromos, & dingy photographs on the walls, & in various corners sundry odd iron objects—a miniature anvil, for instance—washed in by the tides of the neighbouring Merrimack. My own personality was very much in evidence, since Smith was setting up my story "The Terrible Old Man", & had Theobaldian proofs & Mss. all around. He gave me a vast pile of old *Tryouts* for recruiting work, & gave Miss Little as complete a file of back numbers as he could. She is going to bake him a loaf of gingerbread as a reward—he dilated at length upon the excellencies of one which good Mrs. K. Leyson Brown baked & sent him recently. Altogether, there is scarce anyone alive as deliciously wholesome & pastoral as the Haverhill swain. We remained two hours, & wished the sojourn might have been longer. 408 Groveland Street is a dilapidated old cottage, but the locality is very beautiful; with woods extending up to the edge of *Tryout's* little yard & flower garden. I believe he is really a faun, just dwelling for a while on the rim of the sylvan shades that gave him birth! As his guests departed, he presented each with some of his cherished pansies, plucked with his own hands. He told me to wear mine as a boutouniere, which I did—till out of sight of the house. I shall preserve them pressed in my *Tryout* file! On the whole, I like few persons more than honest *Tryout*. I am a rustic at heart, & he is a character escaped from one of my heroic pastorals!

Yr most obt Servt

L. Theobald Junr.

Notes

1. HPL refers to the death of his mother, Sarah Susan Phillips Lovecraft, on 24 May.
2. Myrta Alice (Little) Davies (1888–1967), Historian of the UAPA for 1921–22, resided in Westville, NH.
3. HPL wrote about the visit to "Tryout" Smith's home at 408 Groveland Street, Haverhill, in "The Haverhill Convention."
4. In fact, Smith's collection forms the core of the New York Public Library's collection of amateur journals.

[75]   [AHT]

The Palace

7/30/21

O Sainted Prophet Iokanaan, Hail![1]

I heard from Mrs. Greene some time ago, & she is joining the United—as all philosophers should do. (Have you paid your own dues yet?) She spoke of reading "Nyarlathotep" & "Polaris", but confessed that both were incomprehensible to her mind—Teutonic mysticism is too subtle for Slavs. I furnished the necessary diagrams, sent some fictional specimens of more easy comprehension, & appended some philosophical remarks which ought to be more convincing than my oral arguments because they will have to be read quietly, without opportunities for interrupting the speaker & securing the approval of the Boeotian bystanders.[2] (In one case M. Oscar White, & in another, Charles W. Heins.)[3] Mrs. G. has an acute, receptive, & well-stored mind; but has yet to learn that impersonal point of view which weighs evidence irrespective of its palatability. She forms a welcome addition to the United's philosophical arena, & ought to find such metal giants as A. Galpinius Secundus highly interesting.

Vathek!![4] Boy, thou hast given new life unto thy Grandfather Theobald! I have wanted to read that thing for generations, but have never been able to secure a copy, since our small-town library is unprovided with it. I was discussing it at the convention with Jacobus Ferdinandus Secundus, & telling him that it was originally written in French—a thing which, mirabile dictu, he did not know before! I was indeed elated at finding I knew something that so great a personage did not—& now my joy is to be completed by a perusal of the thing itself! I will promise its safe return at or before the next convention. I understand that "Vathek" is in a richly exotic style—one of the first specimens of its kind in our literature. Since I am making a study of this style, I shall take particular interest in studying the Beckfordian masterpiece. Just now I am digesting some stuff by Theophile Gautier, translated by Lafcadio Hearn, which certainly bears all the polished ornamentation prose could possibly bear.[5] Loveman seems to have drawn some of his tendencies (cf. "The Faun")[6] from Gautier—a not unworthy source, though some might deem the style a trifle overladen with gems.

Yr most obedient humble Servt.,
H. von Liebkraft

Notes

1. In Oscar Wilde's *Salome,* Salome requests the head of Jokanaan (John the Baptist) on a silver platter as a reward for dancing the dance of the seven veils.
2. HPL alludes to the fact that he first met Sonia at the NAPA convention in Boston in early July.
3. Michael Oscar White was an amateur journalist living in Dorchester, MA; he and HPL tangled in 1922–23 over the merits of the poetry of Samuel Loveman, which White had censured as blasphemous and obscene. Charles W. Heins (1877–1967) was editor of the *National Critic* and forty-first president of the NAPA (1907–8).
4. William Beckford, *The History of the Caliph Vathek.* The novel manifestly influenced the fragment "Azathoth" (1922) and the novel *The Dream-Quest of Unknown Kadath* (1926–27).
5. Presumably Gautier's *One of Cleopatra's Nights and Other Fantastic Romances.*
6. Samuel Loveman, "The Faun" [a story], *Vagrant* No. 12 (December 1919): 4–12; rpt. *Out of the Immortal Night* 185–90.

[76]   [AHT]

Stonybroke Manor, Cypherwold
Nothingham-on-Zerowe, Blankshire
11th August, 1921

The Rt. Hon. Randolph St. John, Viscount Bolingbusted
Dear Fellow-Heartbreaker:—

[. . .]

However—as to these rhapsodic panegyrics of Mme. Greenevsky's—circumstances prompt us to return them with no feigned enthusiasm! Wherefore, you ask, this rhapsodical tendency on the part of a sober Saxon patriarch devoid of emotion? I reply—the most potent of all reasons—*gold!* For be it known that the lady in question has set an enduring example for all posterity in amateurdom, & put to shame all her piker contemporaries. *Some* liberality! Upon sending in her United application, & merely after having read a few stray papers & old official organs, Mme. Greenovna unsolicitedly & unexpectedly came across with a pledge of FIFTY (count 'em—50!) refulgent rubles—HALF A HUNDRED scintillant simoleons—for the Official Organ Fund. Ten of 'em cash down. Oh, boy! Is that the ideal amateur spirit? We'll notify the cosmos!! Believe Grandpa, La Belle Russe won't have no reason to complain of editorial coldness—we've given her two paragraphs in the July news notes, extolling her excellencies & holding up her philanthropy as an example to our revered tightwad veterans. If a *new* member plunks down fifty bucks, what ought the old ones to do? Viva Russia! God save Kerensky!

And even without the fifty, Mme. G. would be a notable addition to the United. Beneath the exterior of romantic spoofing & rhetorical extravagance she has a mind of singular scope & activity, & an exceptional background of Continental cultivation. My grandson (who is back at 536 College Avenue after a wonderful six weeks at the U. of Wis. summer school) has just asked me to loan her his new essay on Nietzsche[1]—after reading which I trust she will include him in her ecstatic encomiums; for gawd knows he *really* deserves such demonstrations, as his Grandpa Theobald most grotesquely does not! In a word, Mrs. Gr. seems to me likely to become a valuable & prominent amateur of the best *Gallomo* type—I have told her to write Campbell for a copy of *The Liberal,* which ought to interest her vastly & ensure her assimilation into that *intellectual* amateurdom which in N. Y. is represented only by yourself & Chief Oulokarenos. (Ουλωκάρηνος—Wollybean).[2] I hope Mrs. Campbell will not later blame me if the enterprising recruit captures P. J. C.'s mutable heart & replaces her as #IV! . . . . Fifty iron men from a new recruit who has not even received a certificate—& some of our loftiest old ex-Presidents will not even send in a two-spot for a renewal!!

Last Monday I had a pleasing & unusual experience—a trip of some fifteen years backward along the corridors of time; revisiting some scenes of youth, & recalling for the nonce the atmosphere of buoyant boyhood. I happened to be up in the morning—O condition most rare!—when the telephone brought to me the dulcet tones of my best childhood friend, Harold Bateman Munroe, who told me of his recent acquisition of a new camouflaged flivver & of his present desire to make an excursion to Taunton & Rehoboth, covering the territory through which we used carelessly & gaily to disport in those blessed days when the daemon Time had not brought us to a prosaic maturity. It is scarce needful to remark that I accepted the invitation, & that we were soon rattling over roads by us untrod for a decade & more—roads once very familiar to the oft-punctured tires of our cycles. As we reëntered these realms of our 'teens, the years imperceptibly dropt away from us; so that we were soon boys of 16 or 17 once more. Much had changed—saplings had grown to trees, red houses had been painted white, an old mill had tumbled down, & many verdant meads had become defaced by the sties & hovels of Italians & Portugese canaille—yet more was still unchanged; so that our quest of our lost youth was by no means without reward or realisation. The climax came when we sought the ruins of our old "country clubhouse" on Great Meadow

Hill, & to our delighted amazement found *the whole lowly & tar-papered edifice intact!!!* The locality was changed in aspect—a second growth of timber had sprung up, ensconcing the cabin in a cosy maple grove—but all the change was for the better, & the old place seemed as a gem in a fairer setting. Nothing was gone—not a stone displaced in the massive chimney which a good old Civil War Veteran (now dead)[3] helped us build with rock filched from neighbouring stone walls. Once more we stood at childhood's shrine, hardly realising that our locks were besprinkled with grey.

And then we decided upon a very ambitious plan to defeat the clawing monster Time, & to prove an avenue for occasional journeys back to youth. We have resolved to reorganise our old boys' club—whose prototype we formed in the Munroes' cellar in February 1902—when Grandpa Theobald was 11½, & which had its last reorganisation on April 11, 1906! We shall try to collect such of our old crowd as have enough imagination to discard grey adulthood at will—to repair the clubhouse & hold meetings in the old way, with every reference to the dire calamity of growing up strictly forbidden. We shall go back to 1906—using the boyish slang of 1906 & howling the old cheap popular songs of 1906. We shall roam the roads in the moonlight singing, & the good peasants in their cots will gape & whisper to one another of the ghosts of the boys they used to hear so many years ago. And we shall fight in the old way, & defy parliamentary law till Boss Munroe pounds on the pine table with his huge gavel (a carpenter's mallet) & shouts "Order! Order!"—or, "John Sherman, you sit down or you'll get put out of the clubhouse!!!"

Reminiscently & patriarchally yours,

Lothario Honeycomb, 13th Earl of Stonybroke

Notes

1. Alfred Galpin, "Nietzsche as a Practical Prophet," *Rainbow* No. 1 (October 1921): 4–7; in *Letters to Alfred Galpin and Others* 420–25.

2. The reference is to James F. Morton, so named because of his thick, curly hair.

3. HPL identifies this man elsewhere as James Kay (*SL* 1.146).

[77]   [AHT]

Still 598

8/30/21

Mon cher St. Jean Baptiste:—

Your voluble friend, the generous Mme. Greenevsky, announceth that she will be in Providence for two days at the end of the present week; & I can but hope that the lethal boredom of our archaic & provincial atmosphere may not asphyxiate her United activity altogether. It's a safe bet it won't, for just as I predicted, my boy Alfredus hath become her cherished idol; & will serve admirably as an anchor. He has told her the sad,

sad story of his whole life, & his mother will be lucky if she does not kidnap him some day. Also, she hath told him that I am egotistical from reading Nietzsche—which disturbeth me not in the least. Anybody can call me anything he damn pleases if he will give fifty sinkers to the organ fund & issue a United paper as good as the RAINBOW promises to be! It would take more than one siren to lure my chee-ild away from his own adopted Grandpa! And besides—so volatile a Slav means the censure no more than the taffy. Bless her heart, if she hasn't just sent Grandpa a beauteous gift, in the form of a copy of Shaw's new play, "Back to Methuselah"! I hope she didn't think I was hinting for the amateurs to keep my library supplied when I mentioned your "Vathek" gift! But one thing Mme. Greenevna says quite desolates me—she avers that her fair & frivolous offspring[1] is not to be captivated by the charms of any highbrow, not even the otherwise irresistible Bolingbroke! To think that the St. Johnly magic should fail, even in one case! Gad's blood, if any daughter of mine refused to pay homage to the graces of a Clynor, I'd disown the wench! Had I two daughters, I would have no sons-in-law but thou & Galpinius! Try being jazzy & lowbrow, my boy, & sport a flashier cane, & you may yet win the giddy fair! By the way—I have just returned proofs of my RAINBOW article, which is a melange of cynical aphorisms culled from two letters of mine.[2] Whoever was the printer knoweth his business, for errors were monstrous few. The R. will evidently be quite some paper—pictures 'n' everything. Surely Mrs. G. is the find of the present year amateurically, & I regret very much the recent indisposition to which you refer. But what the hell did you give away those CONSERVATIVES for? Bless you, my son, they are of no value to a philosophical newcomer. Much that is in them I have outgrown intellectually, & in any case their chief appeal is for the amateur who was active in the days they were issued. Don't be so beastly generous—though I am the last who should attach any value to the emanations of my own publishing office! Now I shan't send you any more CONSERVATIVES—until I publish some! Incidentally, I wish you were coming to Providence.

For an hermit, I have been seeing a great deal of the world lately. Two weeks ago tomorrow I went to Boston to call on Mrs. Renshaw, whom I had never before met in person, & who was visiting the sister of her inseparable companion Miss Crist in Newton Centre. She notified all the New England amateurs of her location in order to meet as many as possible, but local feuds of increasing magnitude made the meetings messy, fragmentary, & diffused. In the first place, Miss Hamlet hates all the other Massachusetts amateurs except her own recruits & proteges, & refused to attend any convocation, although wishing to see me to discuss the disposal of the Dunsany fund (reimbursing him for cable message.) I missed two trains—felt like hell that day—& arrived at Dorchester too late, finding Miss H. gone on a trip to see poor old Mrs. Bell, our invalid Quincy member.[3] It did not matter to me, but the super-hospitable family were so perturbed about it that they made me promise to repeat the visit in the near future. When I finally reached the School of Expression, where Mrs. Renshaw was holding forth, it was almost time to depart for Newton & the evening programme. Mrs. R. was duly on hand, & looks exactly like her pictures, stout & homely, but courteous, urbane, & intelligent in the extreme; as liberal an arguer as Chief Woollybean. With her was the inseparable Miss Crist, a colourless young woman who corrects the absent-mindedness of her divinity & tells the latter when she is forgetting her gloves or walking north when she wants to go south. Philosophical argument—Haeckel, Hegel, Kant, Schopenhauer, Nietzsche, cosmogony, relativity, &c. &c. held sway all the way to Newton Centre; no change of transportation media sufficing to stop the flow of argument—a flow that paused only when the trains puffed too loudly in the Trinity Place station. The more I talked with Mrs. R. the more she made me think of Morton—constant verbal warfare, but not a blow or a bitter word! At length the party reached the Wurtz mansion—home of Miss Crist's sister—& paused preparatory to a final descent on the McMullen Manor at Mortonstrasse 53. Mrs. R. & I went over to Morton Street very soon, having a dinner engagement there. Later the Crist–Wurzes joined the McMullenian gathering. At 53 Morton a quiet dinner was "et" by Mrs. A. Renshaw, Mrs. L. Middleton (our new United poet-laureate), Mrs. E. Miniter, & Grandpa Theobald. It amused me to see Mrs. Miniter at a McMullen gathering—probably because of Mrs. Renshaw's notification—because Mrs. McMullen & the Boston United folk are now far from partial to the Hub element. Still, everybody was wonderfully well-behaved. Such personalities sardonically amuse me, who am cosmic & unconcerned in the bitterness of mankind ever since I shook hands with wee Willie. Later the Aonian Nine sent their foremost representative W. V. J., who very civilly expressed surprise to Mrs. Miniter at the latter's presence—although it is said that later on Mrs. Miniter reported that W. V. J. did not speak to her for over an hour! And whilst the human cats aired their coolness, I held in my lap the prettiest actual kitten that I have seen for many a day—a grey furry double handful with a belled collar around his neck, who was brought in by a neighbour at the express suggestion of Mrs. McMullen, who knows of my predilection for the feline species. This neighbour also brought in two exactly similar collie dogs—rather a menagerie, all told. Subjects of discussion were varied & numerous, including some more or less practical Renshavian suggestions for a Theobaldian remunerative activity better than Bush work. One was that of publishing a text book of rhetoric![4] The other, less wild, was to correct English themes by mail for Research University, where Mrs. R. heads the English department. That would be tedious, but not nearly so bad as Bush. Songs were rendered—Mrs. McMullen gave her "Bumble Fairy", & Mrs. R. sang two songs of her own composition in an excellent contralto. I was asked to sing—but since there was no St. Julian to drown me out, I respectfully declined. Gawd, ain't I got the grand taste?

About 11:10 the riot was dispersed & the participants went their way. I caught the 11:45, & by 1:20 was safe at home after a drenching from a shower which came up just as I left the night car two blocks from my door. And the next day the whole thing had receded far into the distance—Theobald was his hermit self again.

  Pestiferously thine,
    Grandpa Theobald.

Notes

1. Florence Carol (Greene) Weld (1902–1979), who moved out of Sonia's Brooklyn apartment in 1923, shortly before Sonia's marriage to HPL. She later became a journalist.

2. "Nietscheism [*sic*] and Realism."

3. Clara L. Bell, amateur journalist living with Mrs. C. F. Lynch in Quincy, MA.

4. Many years later Renshaw asked HPL to revise a textbook of English usage, *Well Bred Speech* (1936).

[78] [AHT]

          Abode of Misery
          21 September 1921

Querido San Juan:—

     Another business opportunity recently appearing is that afforded by St. Julian's new magazine, *Home Brew*. He wants a series of six ghastly tales to order[1]—apparently unaware that art cannot be created to order. I doubt if any story from my pen could please the clientele of an essentially popular magazine, & have so informed the jovial publisher. However—if he will be satisfied with some frankly artificial hack-work, in no way related to my normal output, I will do my best for him. He offers five bucks per story—on publication. Rotten remuneration, but perhaps a better proposition than Bush work. Damn poverty!

  As to my social programme—you have doubtless heard part of it already from the Mme. Greenevsky, whose Providence visit formed half of it. This volatile & beneficent personage arrived in Providence's sylvan shades on the afternoon of Sunday, Sept. 4, obtaining Theobald Manor on the telephone & thus notifying Grandpa, who forthwith proceeded to the Crown Hotel—amateurdom's official headquarters in this village. I have been to the Crown only thrice—in 1914 to see W. B. Stoddard, in 1920 to see the incomparable St. John, & in 1921 to see Mme. G.—an amateur mission in each case. Arriving at the Crown about 3:15 p.m., I paused only to snap the fair with my V. P. Kodak, (the Brownie is still at 20 Webster!) & proceeded at once to show the quiet sights of Providence with the assurance born of practice on you & Daas. Though rather fearing that our tame & uneventful scenic pedestrianism would pall upon so effervescent a visitor, I repeated the familiar tour up the hill, to Prospect Terrace, & by the new Queen-Anne manor house where you & I snapped each other in the courtyard. This time the gate was closed, so I merely snapped the gable end as it stood majestic in the gold of afternoon's sunlight—a vivid bit of the old days re-created for the sight of a generation too stupid to appreciate it. Thence the route extended to Angell Street, & up the north side of that not unbeauteous thoroughfare to #598. Mme. G. appeared pleased with the aspect of this section with its detached residences, neat lawns, & abundant foliage, & even expressed admiration for the Colonial style of architecture—though not that intense admiration which can arise only from an unmixed Anglo-American heritage. She admired the classic beauty of the lines—I admire the whole atmosphere & spirit with the fervour which comes from a mind shaped by 1400 years of English heredity, & from a taste centreing primarily in the age of swords & periwigs. God Save King George the Third!

Finally #598 was reached, & the visitor was introduced to the present regent of these domains—my elder aunt. Both seemed delighted with each other, & my aunt has ever since been eloquent in her praise of Mme. G., whose ideas, speech, manner, aspect, & even attire impressed her with the greatest of favourableness. In truth, this visit has materially heightened my aunt's respect for amateurdom—an institution whose extreme democracy & occasional heterogeneity have at times made it necessary for me to apologise for it. During the session at #598, *Rainbow* proofs were the main topic. I read most of them, denatured a sketch which some might have taken as a caricature on myself, & set aside for revision a piece of verse entitled "Mors Omnibus Communis". I am told that you advised the inclusion of this piece in the R. If so, why the hell didn't you correct it? It could not stand as it was. The R. will be quite some paper—believe Grandpa! Since the visit I have let Mme. G. have Loveman's "Triumph in Eternity",[2] which will lend a finishing touch of exquisite classicism. It is one of the most splendid poems amateurdom has ever produced. At length the meeting adjourned, & Mme. G. generously invited both my aunt & myself to dinner at the Crown. Having had a noon meal, (we eat but twice daily) we were not ready for another; so my aunt had to decline, whilst I went along & consumed only a cup of coffee & portion of chocolate ice-cream. Mme. G., who is surely a full-fledged Hikawauka, again spurned the aid of the St. ry. co.,[3] & preferred to make the return trip another scenic walk. This time I showed her the southern & really antique residential district where I took you, though preceding the display with a glimpse of the neo-Colonial Orchard Avenue, where we photographed each other in 1919. Mme. G. seemed to like the antique & solemn hush of the venerable streets, & the Georgian dignity of the old mansions on Power Street—including the Brown residence where Gen. Washington was entertained in August 1790. She also liked the cloistral hush of the Brown University campus, especially the inner quadrangle; where in the deserted twilight there seemed to brood the spirit of the dead generations. Thereafter a descent of College Hill was made, & the visitor did not fail to grasp the sensation of anticlimax involved in the abrupt transition from the ancient to the garishly modern. The soul of Providence broods upon the antique hill—below there is only a third-rate copy of New York. The Crown Tavern regained, there followed a meal spiced with philosophy—the latter revolving round a letter to Mme. Gr. from my boy, which I was permitted to peruse. With her he adopts a vein slightly different from that he uses toward his Grandpas Mocrates & Tibaldus; being careful to show off his superior mind & varied erudition in a series of polished epigrams, curt cynicisms, & (I must admit despite a Grandparent's pride) modernistic affectations of prose style. He must, at all costs, be deem'd a young man of the world! The repast completed, I could think of no diversion more original than mine own hackneyed mode of killing a Sabbath Eve—the trite old band concert at Roger Williams Park. It was rather late for going thither, but some of the tunes were yet unplayed; so the trip was made. Mme. G., who does not care what she does with her spare cash, hired a horseless hackney-coach on the outbound voyage; though condescending to use the plebeian tramway on the return trip. After a brief final session of philosophical discussion in the lobby of the Crown—which recalled the Kleiner–Morton–Theobald session at the Brunswick on July 5–6—the meeting disbanded till the morrow; & Grandpa sought his domestick hearth once more.

Postero die the session re-convened at the Crown at 1 p.m. with three delegates present—Mme. G. having invited both my aunt & myself thither for a noon repast. Her generosity is, in sooth, quite unbounded; bespeaking a mind deserving of the highest commendation & respect. The repast being over, all adjourned to the R. I. School of Design; whose museum & Pendleton House (which we visited in 1919) were apparently of great interest to the distinguished visitor. Thereafter a return to #598 by tram-car was made, & the residue of the afternoon was spent in the examination of old amateur papers. As the hour of six approached, some haste was exercised in seeking the train scheduled to depart Manhattanward shortly after that hour. Finally it was seen that only extreme haste would enable Mme. G. to obtain the desiderate choo-choos, hence a hectic rush to the Crown, & an excited hackney-coach trip to the station, ensued. At last the line of railway-carriages was discovered in time, & a more than obliging brakeman assigned his important passenger a seat in a carriage devoid of fellow-travellers—which he announced to the world as "reserved for a special party!" Conversation held sway until the slow motion of the train indicated a start, whereupon Grandpa alighted & journeyed home. The event was assuredly a felicitous one, marred only by the absence of Randolph St. John, who was more than frequently alluded to. Mme. G. is certainly a person of the most admirable qualities, whose generous & kindly cast of mind is by no means feigned, & whose intelligence & devotion to art merit the sincerest approbation. The volatility incidental to a

Continental & non-Aryan heritage should not blind the analytical observer to the solid work & genuine cultivation which underlie it. This amiable & philanthropic personage is certainly due to make the greatest stir in amateurdom of any recent recruit; for unlike the majority, she takes the institution seriously enough to put real cash into it, & (so far) sees in its activities an actual branch of intellectual & aesthetic endeavour. Her latest idea is to have a sort of convention of freaks & exotics in New York during the holidays; inviting for two weeks such provincial sages as Loveman, The Chee-ild, & poor Grandpa Theobald![4] Only a sincere enthusiast could thus think of uprooting such outland fixtures from their respective native heaths! The practicability of such an enterprise may well be questioned—the fare from Appleton or Madison to N. Y. must be a young fortune—but if it could occur it would certainly be some convention! Damn me if I wouldn't give ten years of my declining life to see that little divvle Alfredus; to gaze one moment upon the flower-like face of my chee-ild, from whom the woild has crooly kep' me apart all these long y'ars! If the Kid should really come, I'd get to N. Y. if I had to go on foot & return in an ambulance! However—such titanic migrations are not likely to occur; & I fancy that the holidays will find the outland sages still chained to their hearthstones. N. Y. is rather an ambitious trip for an old gentleman whose limit is so far Hampstead, N. H., & whose sole immediate plan extends no farther than Athol, Mass. Still, the thing is by no means impossible—I have not utterly excluded a Brooklyn sojourn from my category of imaginings since 1918 or 1919, when your Providential advents suggested the idea of reciprocation.

One might well fancy that the Greenevitch visit would serve as the concluding event of my social season—but it wa'nt so! I have already told you of the revival of boyhood planned by my old school "gang" & centreing in the restoration of the Rehoboth clubhouse. On Wednesday, Sept 7, Harold Munroe called me up again; & some of us went out in his Ford to inspect & repair the place. It was *some* time! We shed every trace of adulthood, & returned altogether to the 1906–1910 period; singing the old songs with undiminished gusto & working about the clubhouse as in the old times. I fitted into the picture by wearing three articles of apparel which I had actually worn there before in my youth—an old fold collar which lingered about the attic (1908 or so period), a pair of flannel trousers purchased in 1910, & a pair of old low shoes obtained in 1909! Thus outfitted, Grandpa was a boy again! I took the V. P. Kodak & snapped my two best friends—Harold Munroe & Ronald Upham[5]—(we have known one another ever since we could talk!) & was later snapped with Harold—the best friend of all. When I have the reel developed I will shew you the views—only our elderly faces & figures will prevent them from passing as 1908 views! We are going to hold a grand banquet later in the fall, when Chester Munroe comes up from Asheville on one of his rare visits. Nothing shall be spared to give the event a boyhood atmosphere, & we shall fine any boy who sings a song later than 1911 or refers to the absurd myth of being grown up. We shall be as disorderly as possible, have a political fight, (with both tongues & fists, as of yore) & end up with an old-time group around the stone fireplace, murdering the popular airs of other days in reminiscent cacophony.

Refinedly & colourfully yours,
Squire Western

Notes

1. "Herbert West—Reanimator," published as "Grewsome Tales" (*Home Brew,* February–July 1922).
2. *Rainbow* No. 1 (October 1921): 13.
3. I.e., the Street Railway Company.
4. The gathering did take place on 6–12 April 1922 (see *SL* 1.175–83 and letter 83).
5. Ronald Kingsley Upham (1892–1968), boyhood friend of HPL.

[79]   [AHT]

The Rectory, 7th October, 1721

Revered St. John:—

I know not if Mr. Houtain hath told you, that I am become a Grub-Street hack for him; composing at his request a series of six daemoniack tales with the same hero, for his proposed new professional magazine. So far I have writ two, "From the Dark", & "The Plague-Daemone"; the whole set being intituled "Herbert West—Reanimator". In this enforced, laboured, & artificial sort of composition there is nothing of art or natural gracefulness; for of necessity there must be a superfluity of strainings & repetitions in order to make each history compleat. My sole inducement is the monetary reward, which is a guinea per tale—a lowness of price shewing that the breezy St. Julian can drive as hard a bargain as Osborn or Curll,[1] though with an infinitely greater deal of honour. I sent my fictions nearly a week ago, yet have heard nothing from them as yet. If they be unacceptable, I shall have laboured nearly in vain; for they are of insufficient merit for amateur use, though the last hath a plot which might be rewritten to some advantage in another hour & mood.

[. . .]

Believe me, yr most faithful & devoted Servt
L:Theobald Junr.

Notes

1. Thomas Osborne (d. 1767) was an English bookseller who published numerous reference works but was referred to by Samuel Johnson in *Lives of the English Poets* as "a man entirely destitute of shame, without sense of any disgrace but that of poverty."

James Boswell states that Johnson knocked Osborne down with a copy of his own *Dictionary.* Edmund Curll (1683–1747) was an English bookseller and pamphleteer whom Alexander Pope encouraged to publish an edition of his letters in 1735.

[80]　[AHT]

Jany. 15, 1922

Valued Bolingbroke:—

[. . .]

I yesterday receiv'd the first number of *Home Brew,* & am doing as well as can be expected. Misery loves company, & I have at least some sorry consolation in the companionship of yourself & Morton amidst the arid waste of ochreous commercialism. Like the painted punks in your dancing dactyls, the Muses have sold themselves for a golden guinea. However, pray refrain from transmitting my unceremonious opinion to the amiable St. Julian, who is no doubt dilated with pride at the appearance of so businesslike a publication. I am sure that my wishes for his success are second to no man's, nor would I do aught to hinder the success of his well-planned product among a publick more appreciative than myself.

[. . .]

Yr most hble, most obt Servt

L: Theobald, Junr.

[81]　[AHT]

Jany. 25, 1722

Revered St. John:—

I am grateful to Mrs. Greene for her editorial in support of my literary policies,[1] as indeed for many instances of a courtesy & generosity seldom found in this degenerate aera. You may be assur'd that I shall not diminish the frequency of the epistles I send her, tho' I am of opinion that S. Loveman & my grandchild Alfredus deserve much of the credit for her retention in the United. I regret that she hath suffer'd indignities from Mrs. Houtain; whose cast of mind, I suspect, is not exempt from the petty cruelty & fondness for gossip which blemish the humours of the most commonplace females.

Ever yr most devoted & Obt Servt

L: Theobald Junr.

Notes

1. See [Sonia H. Greene], "Amateurdom and the Editor: The Official Organ," *Rainbow* No. 2 (May 1922): 1–2. The editorial must have circulated in ms. before publication.

[82] [AHT]

Will's Coffee-House

March 12, 1722

Cherish'd Bolingbroke:—

Home Brew some time ago arrived, & I was vastly disconcerted by the stupid misprints in my graveyard tale, whereby some of the most carefully wrought sentences were chopt up till they look'd like the effusions of a schoolboy or the maunderings of some damn'd Whig pamphleteer. I had not perus'd the masterpiece of Dr. Grossman till you inform'd me of your share in it; but have now done so, & congratulate you on having made a Grossman less gross.[1] By deleting the indecency, you have made the article short; but had you been a censor of its dulness as well, nothing at all had been left! In truth, I fear that a court of judicature on dulness wou'd wreak more havock with *Home Brew* than wou'd any guardian of the publick morals. This periodical seems not only to attract to itself every Maevius & Bavius in Boeotia,[2] but to quench the genius of every man of parts who endeavours to write for it. Mine own fictions are miserably mechanical, whilst the Augustan Morton here sinks to flat & pitiable commonplaces. I might, however, make an exception of your own poetick offerings, as well as of the strange & powerful pictures of one Lawrence Johnson, Esq.,[3] who is unknown to me.

In the preceding paragraph I did not mean to class myself with those possess'd of genius, tho' the clumsy language, as read over, wou'd seem to convey falsely that egotistical design. I have lately completed the fourth of the West tales, entituled "The Scream of the Dead", & form'd a synopsis of the fifth, to be call'd "The Horror from the Shadows". I shall be glad when the burthen of this hack labour is removed from my back. I am now perusing a work in two volumes lent me by W: Cook, Esq., & intituled "Dealings With the Dead"—by an old Sexton.[4] It promises to be replete with an interest particularly cheerful to one having a partiality for churchyards.

Ever y^r l'dship's most devoted, most faithful Servt

L: Theobald Junr.

Notes

1. Dr. Maximilian P. E. Groszmann (1855–1922), "The Noted Educator": "Did You Want to be Born?" *Home Brew* 1, No. 2 (March 1922): 27–28; "Skirts That Flirt," 1, No. 3 (April 1922): 3–5; "Rouge et—Noir?"; "Verboten," 1, No. 4 (May 1922): 23–24; 1, No. 5 (June 1922): 37–39.

2. For Maevius and Bavius, see RK 6n5.

3. Lawrence Bradstreet Johnson (1893–1940) published poems in *Home Brew*. "Some Cubistic Touches" (comprising "Lunch in Trinity Graveyard," "Can This Be Love?," and "Thirty Days"), 1, No. 1 (February 1922): 46–47; "Cubist Pen Pictures" (comprising "The Gossip," "The Ghost," and "City Snow"), 1, No. 2 (March 1922): 25–26; "The Blind Tiger," 1, No. 5 (June 1922): 2; and "Calamity Howler," 1, No. 6 (July 1922): 18.

4. By Lucius M. Sargent.

[83]   [AHT]

Twickenham
Apr. 15, 1722

Benignant Bolingbroke:—

[. . .]

Your conjecture regarding my somnolent pursuits was form'd with equal shrewdness & accuracy. Having quit the metropolis Wednesday morning, on a coach leaving the Grand Central Tavern at half past eight, I was wholly wrapt in sleep till we reach'd the Union Tavern in Providence; tho' I have a few vague impressions of wayside inns, & of changing horses at Stamford, in the Connecticut-Colony. The remainder of Wednesday is hazy in my recollection, but at 11 p.m. I retir'd to bed, where I enjoy'd an unbroken sleep of 23 hours; arising at 10 p.m. Thursday. After that I attempted with indifferent success to cope with accumulated mail—22 letters, 5 packages, & 2 papers—& to read the file of the EVENING BULLETIN which had accumulated during my absence. At some hour to me unknown I laps'd gently into a slumber in my chair; later unconsciously transferring my bulk to the couch, where I slept till 1:30 p.m. Friday. Friday afternoon I sought to redeem some of my promises in letter-writing, but with ill success. Friday night I retir'd at 11 p.m., sleeping till 2 p.m. this afternoon. Now I am amongst the living once more, & much enlivened by your vivid & agreeable communication. Altogether, the journey was an event of the keenest pleasure & greatest singularity. Not for the wealth of Peru wou'd I have miss'd it, & when I consider the fatigue incident upon former travels, I am impress'd with my relative immunity from ill effects.

Concerning the personality of S: Loveman, Esq., I believe you are right in assuming that he seeks to cover his aesthetick predilections with a masque of the commonplace. In externals, it may be said that he succeeds to no mean extent; but the penetrating vision is not slow to discover the sensitive artist beneath his worldly robes. Perhaps I had a particular advantage in the making of such discoveries, since I had the honour of his company for a full day amidst the classical reliquiae of the Metropolitan Museum, where we cast aside the centuries & revell'd in antique visions that bore us through the tombs of Ægyptus, the Academes of Hellas, & the Forum & Temples of ROMA.CAPVT.MVNDI. In such an artistick paradise the need for protective colouring departs, & one may exhibit his appreciation of beauty without fear of the ridicule of the vulgar & stupid. The underlying sensitiveness of our colleague was many times display'd during our sojourn, largely in connexion with apprehensions regarding the impression he produced upon others. He was at great pains to inquire how well he fulfill'd my expectations of him, &

was a whole day miserable because of the seeming indifference of young Long; who in truth, however, entertain'd the most ardent regard & admiration for him. Loveman undoubtedly suffers very keenly from small things which scarce perturb the generality of mankind. He is not sufficiently a cynick, & is made timid by situations which have no effect at all upon me, who am contemptuous of all men & things. It is this sensitive desire to escape comment which impels him to adopt the disguise of commonplace demeanour—a disguise which I am myself adopting to an increasing degree, tho' I do it not from sensitiveness but from cynicism & contempt of pretence. Loveman himself remarks, in a note this morning receiv'd from him, "If you found me a little more human & a little less of the myth you had expected, impute it to no other desire than the one I have always had—to be perfectly natural & not too obviously the artist." His trip home, of course much longer & more tedious than mine, seems to have been a nervous ordeal; the coach fill'd with the vulgar & loquacious, many of whom ate sandwiches & otherwise subtracted from aesthetick tranquillity.

In recalling the journey just complete, no circumstance impresses me as more felicitous than the privilege of your guidance upon two golden occasions. I can but regret that unusual responsibilities prevented you from being more continuously with the exploring expedition; especially during its peregrinations in the Fordham region.[1] The evening jaunt through devious ways was delightful, & the only reason Loveman seemed fatigued was that he suffers from a slight affliction of the heart, which he is too stoical to mention save under pressure. He should not exert himself violently at any time, but the excitement of a visit leads all mortals to perform unwonted feats of endurance. For mine own part, I think I overdid not at all, from the point of view of safety, for my physical condition steadily improves from year to year.

Yr l'dship's most oblig'd,
Most obt Servt,
L: Theobald Jun

Notes

1. HPL refers to a visit to the Poe Cottage in Fordham (a district of the Bronx).

[84] [AHT]

Domus Theobaldi
May 13, 1722

Cherish'd Bolingbroke:—

As you see, I was right & you were wrong when, a few years ago, I said that I had but few real friends in the United & you maintained that I had many. You now perceive the unsubstantial quality of professed amity. The enemy approach, & none responds to the old man's call to arms. Thus is unbroken associational fidelity rewarded.[1]

Yr most obt Servt

L: Theobald Junr.

Notes

1. HPL refers to the upcoming UAPA elections in July, at which time HPL's entire "literary" party was voted out of office and another group of amateurs, led by Leo Fritter, was voted in. But they accomplished little during the 1922–23 term, leading to the eventual restoration of HPL's side in the spring of 1924.

[85]   [AHT]

Providence-Plantations
17th June 1722

Benevolent Bolingbroke:—

[. . .]

Your sorrow at the completion of my sinister stories, is balanc'd by mine own delight at the same event. The burden was frightful, the pay a myth after the second cheque,[1] & the results painfully wanting in authentick art. If I merit your encomium as a writer of tales, 'tis surely on less commercial products that you must have bas'd it. Hereafter *Home Brew* will reprint my older & better fables from the amateur press, obtaining without cost a much superior sort of writing—tho' a sort much less suited to the Mohocks & pretty fellows who no doubt form the readers of Sir George's rakish periodical.

[. . .]

Believe me, Sir, yr most hble obt Servt

L: Theobald Jun

Notes

1. In fact, HPL did eventually get paid for all six installments of "Herbert West— Reanimator." See HPL to Samuel Loveman, 17 November [1922]; *Letters to Maurice W. Moe* 487.

[86]   [AHT; Post]

Jany. 11, 1923

My Son:—

[Post:] I became sensible of the havoc made by increasing labours in the promptness I used to display. The National, with such official tangles as constantly appear for adjustment, is an unending burden; the more so as I perceive more fully the extent of the tasks I ought to perform.[1] I have this day written a long report for Martin's *National Amateur*, & design immediately to publish an appeal for official organ funds, in the form of an epistle to be mimeographed by Lynch. In my message, I am requesting volunteer critics & reviewers to communicate with Loveman;[2] in the hope that the National may gradually acquire that helpfulness to the novice which marked the United before its recent destruction.

[AHT:] As forecast in my former epistle, & confirm'd by subsequent cards, I went a second time to Boston & pass'd a pleasant season in the company of Mr. Cole. The meeting of the club on Decr. 14 was well-attended but orderly; & my remarks upon Ld Dunsany were allow'd to run to their close without interruption or audible snoring.[3] On the next day, I undertook an exploration of such parts of Boston as I had never before visited observantly, & was agreeably impressed with the antique atmosphere of the North-End, in whose narrow, crooked, & hilly streets so many edifices of my favourite age remain. There are, moreover, no less than three houses of the 17th century: the Goldsmith's shop of Mr. Revere (1676), Mr. Clough's house in Vernon-Court (1695), & Mr. Vernon's house in Charter-Street (1698). I beheld all of these, besides the North-Church (1723) & Copp's Hill Burying Ground. This latter spot hath for me a singular fascination, both because of its antient sepulchres, (including that of the Rev^d. Cotton Mather, whose "Magnalia" I possess) & because of the striking aspect of the whole scene, caus'd by the elevated locality & the horizon of sky, Colonial roofs, & venerable harbour; where the rebel frigate Constitution rides at anchor. As I beheld the black slate slabs rising ghoulishly above the snow, & cast my glance about at the adjacent chimney-pots, it was difficult to realise that full two centuries have pass'd since the heyday of my particular aera. Yet in truth the place is an Italian quarter of the most squalid sort; as insistently dinned into my ears & consciousness by a horde of ragged little ciceroni who surrounded me & blocked my feet whilst spouting history in lifeless, mechanical voices. It was worth a handful of farthings to be rid of these small highwaymen, whose desire to instruct the traveller is not unmixt with a craving after sweetmeats.

That afternoon my affable & learned host was at great pains to shew me the State-House, & the Georgian district of Beacon-Hill behind it. In the prospects of steep streets & centuried brick mansions I took the liveliest pleasure; deriving the utmost delight from Louisburg-Square, which hath scarce chang'd since that glorious victory of His Majesty over the French King, for which 'twas named. Cole is the most considerate of hosts, & his household is both pleasing & well-ordered. His wife is adorn'd with every domestic virtue, & both of his children are models of wit & precocity. Sherman I believe you know; Marion Elizabeth, generally called "sister", is the precise image of her erudite father; & talks, plays, & runs about with the greatest ease & animation though much below the age of two. Of such material are Galpinii & Belknaps made. We that night dined at the Myers', where I argued with interest & vigour with Mr. Myers, who is a Whig tho' a gentleman of fine parts.

[Post:] On Saturday, a trio composed of Cole, Mrs. Miniter, & myself conducted a minute exploration of several ancient sections. That evening, Mrs. Miniter dined at the Coles', & we sat till midnight discussing amateur journalism. Sunday was raining, so no outdoor trip was made; but the liveliness of the Cole establishment was agreeably enhanced by the colloquial presence of Albert Sandusky, a true & authentic "wise bozo" according to his own admission in the local dialect of Boston.

[AHT:] On Monday I departed, but so fired with the spirit of antient research that I went not home but to Salem, in the same province, for a solitary tour of observation & discovery. The result was an aesthetick & historicall orgy of delight such as I never before experienc'd; for truly, I had not dream'd so much of the *seventeenth* century still remain'd for the contemplation of the studious. Salem, as I may mention in case you have seen it not, retains whole streets & squares scarce alter'd since the reign of George the Third; with an impressive array of mansions built by the rich merchants whose ships traded in the Indies, China, & Japan. There is, besides, a surprising profusion of houses built as far back as Charles the First's time, the age of Cromwell's treason, the aera of the glorious Restoration, & King William the Third's reign; strange sinister edifices in whose queerly pitch'd roofs & diamond pan'd windows lurk a profusion of weird suggestions. I visited the *Old Witch House,* said to have been inhabited by Rev. Roger Williams before his coming to Providence-Plantations, & investigated the several scenes pertaining to the late ingenious Mr. Hawthorne, including his birthplace, & the house of Seven Gables, where I was shewn a secret staircase & permitted to ascend it. The Essex Institute is a Museum of universal celebrity, which I abundantly enjoy'd; & I did not quit the town without resolving to visit it repeatedly in various seasons, & to become saturated with that air of pleasing antiquity which is its particular property & chief pride. Salem, in truth, hath inherited from its past a dignity which for ever keeps it above the absurdity of a common rustick town.

But not even from Salem did I go directly home; for whilst conversing with natives there, I had learnt of the neighbouring fishing port of *Marblehead,* whose antique quaintness was particularly recommended to me. Taking a stage-coach thither, I was presently borne into the most marvellous region I had ever dream'd of, & furnish'd with the most powerful single aesthetic impression I have receiv'd in years.

Even now it is difficult for me to believe that Marblehead exists, save in some phantasticall dream. It is so contrary to everything usually observable in this age, & so exactly conformed to the habitual fabrick of my nocturnal visions, that my whole visit partook of the aethereal character scarce compatible with reality. This place was settled in King Charles the First's time, by fishermen of French & English blood from the channel islands. Its Town House, in the town-square, was finish'd in 1727, & by 1770 most of the land was well built up with plain but substantial houses. The ground is very hilly, & the streets were made crooked & narrow, so that when finish'd, the town had gain'd much of the eccentrick aspect of such antient Gothick towns as Nuremburg, in Bavaria, where the eye beholds small buildings heap'd about at all angles & all levels like an infant's blocks, & topp'd with a pleasing labyrinth of sharp gables, tall spires, & glittering vanes. Marblehead, indeed, was the scene of many romantick incidents; one of which concern'd Sir H: Frankland of Frankland-Hall, & was writ of by Dr. Holmes the poet.[4] Over all the rest of the scene tower'd a hill on which the rude forefathers of the hamlet were laid to rest; & which was in consequence nam'd Old Burying Hill. In subsequent years a newer part of the village rose across the bay, & became almost as great a watering-place as Bath or Brightelmstone. But the conservative temper of the old villagers excluded such invasions of their settled district, & produced the greatest modern miracle that hath ever met my gaze. That miracle is simply this: *that at the present moment the Georgian Marblehead of 1770 stands intact & unchanged!* I do not exaggerate. It is with calm assurance that I insist, that Gen. Washington could tomorrow ride horseback down the long street nam'd for him without the least sensation of strangeness. Wires are few & inconspicuous. Tramway rails look like deep ruts. Costumes are not marked in the twilight. And on every hand stretch the endless rows of houses built betwixt 1640 & 1780—some even with overhanging gables—whilst both to north & south loom hills cover'd with crazy streets & alleys that Hogarth might have known & portray'd, had he but crossed the ocean to discover them. It is a dream—a grotesque & unbelievable anachronism—an artist's or antiquarian's fancy stept out of his brain & fixt to earth for publick inspection. It *is* the 18th century. There are no modern shops or theatres, & no cinema show that I cou'd discover. The railway is so remote from the town-square, that its existence is forgotten. The shops have small windows, & the men are very old. Time passes softly & slowly there.

I came to Marblehead in the twilight, & gazed long upon its hoary magick. I threaded the tortuous, precipitous streets, some of which an horse can scarce climb, & in which two waggons cannot pass. I talked with old men & revell'd in old scenes, & climb'd pantingly over the crusted cliffs of snow to the windswept height where cold winds blew over desolate roofs & evil birds hovered over a bleak, deserted, frozen tarn. And atop all was the peak; Old Burying Hill, where the dark headstones clawed up thro' the virgin snow like the decay'd fingernails of some gigantick corpse.

Immemorial pinnacle of fabulous antiquity! As evening came I look'd down at the quiet village where the lights came out one by one; at the calm contemplative chimney-pots & antique gables silhouetted against the west; at the glimmering small-paned windows; at the silent & unillumined fort frowning formidably over the snug harbour where it hath frown'd since 1742, when 'twas put up for defence against the French King's frigates. Shades of the past! How compleatly, O Mater Novanglia, am I moulded of thy venerable flesh & as one with thy century'd soul! God Save His Majesty, George the Third, & preserve his Province of the Massachusetts-Bay!

My return to the Providence-Plantations was accomplisht without any events more untoward than a delay of three hours occasion'd by a railway wreck at Readville; but I can never again have any considerable part in the thoughts of this decaying aera. *I have look'd upon Marblehead, & have walk'd waking in the streets of the 18th century.* And he who hath done that, can never more be a modern.

Believe me, Sir, to be your most oblig'd, most obt Servant

L: Theobald, Jun.

Notes

1. HPL alludes to the fact that he was appointed interim president of the NAPA in November 1922 upon the resignation of William J. Dowdell. He served until July 1923. The Official Editor was Harry E. Martin.

2. Loveman was head of the Bureau of Critics of the NAPA for 1922–23.

3. "Lord Dunsany and His Work," a lecture delivered at the Hub Club.

4. Oliver Wendell Holmes (1809–1894), "Agnes," in *Songs in Many Keys* (1862). The poem tells of a woman who rescued Sir Harry Frankland from his burning mansion.

[87] [AHT]

Jany. 25, 1923

Blest St. John:——

I not long ago perus'd "The Hasheesh Eater", & am astonish'd & delighted at the range of phantasy there exprest. The poetick quality of Mr. Ludlow's visions is very high; & I might wish that he had employ'd them in verses or tales, rather than giving them a meer recital in the form of a catalogue. His temper appears to have been of a very nervous order, enhanc'd by a dogmatick belief in the myths & delusions of religion; & he has assuredly left a memorial which ought, so far as sheer richness & variety are concern'd, to rank above even Mr. De Quincey's immortal production. Aside from the pictures of terror, I think I was most imprest by those transformations of natural scenery which Mr. Ludlow so well records; especially those attendant upon his walk near his native Village of P———, when he saw the Great Wall of China, & a more magnificent Vale of Cashmere than any which Prospect-Park, in Brookland-Parish, can boast.[1] I am mov'd to wonder what Hudsonian town the anonymous P——— can have been; whether Peekskill, Poughkeepsie, or some lesser village of alliterative analogy.[2] Perchance your greater knowledge of the province of New-York will enable you to identify it. I am also curious to learn more of Mr. Ludlow, & of any other literary works he may have produc'd. I shall return the volume shortly, after having imbib'd more of the exotick splendour with which it so gorgeously abounds. In quitting these considerations of phantasy, I am mov'd to wonder why Mr. Ludlow found narcotick aid necessary to the perception of an ideal world of gorgeousness & sublimity. It seems to me, that a man of active imagination ought to be able to behold vividly before his closed eyes any vision whatever that his mind is capable of conceiving, independently of any external stimulation. I am sure that I have gazed on vistas as strange, as terrible, & as magnificent as most of Mr. Ludlow's; & all without having ever partaken of any drug or stimulant. It is my opinion, that most persons of ordinary cast depend too much upon the physical senses, to the neglect of those airier potentialities which are possesst by the unshackled fancy.

If you are in the least diverted by the terrible & the phantastical, I advise you to peruse as a rare treat a new volume which was recommended to me by both of my grandsons; "The House of Souls", by Arthur Machen, Esq., a living author of the Popish faith.[3] The first tale in the book is dull, but the remainder are of the greatest interest & merit; indeed, I have never seen a fiction more monstrously hideous than "The Great God Pan".

I am, Sir, yr most oblig'd & obt Servt
Theobaldus

Notes

1. A section of Prospect Park in Brooklyn was called the Vale of Cashmere. It became one of HPL's favorite haunts during his residence there in 1924–26.
2. Ludlow was a student at Princeton when he wrote *The Hasheesh Eater,* so the town of Princeton (NJ) may be the city in question.
3. Machen was an Anglo-Catholic.

[88]   [AHT][1]

Venerable 598
29 April, 1923

My Son:—

The Hoag book is now completed, & Mortonius hath sent me an unbound copy. It is pleasing to me, to behold mine own name upon the title-page of an actual volume, as writer of the biographical & critical preface.[2] You shall certainly have a copy of the finished product—as shall most of my other closest friends in amateurdom—since I have asked honest Jonathan for 20 copies; waiving all monetary remuneration for my share of the editing.

Antiquarian pilgrimages are now my leading diversion—what a realm of Colonial wonder I have found north of Boston! Nothing today can please me so much as a bit of Georgian skyline with gambrel roofs, Christopher Wren steeples, & old-world chimney-pots; or some shady bye-street with Colonial doorways, fanlights, iron railings, & small-paned windows looking out over ancient gardens or brick sidewalks. I am getting to be a mild sort of connoisseur of the various types of 18th century houses, telling their periods by their chimneys & decorations. Then, too, I love to glimpse the macabre survivals of the dark *17*th century—the age of Puritan diabolism & repression. On my trip this month I visited Danvers—the old "Salem-Village"—& saw the forbidding old farmhouse, built in 1636, whence poor Rebekah Nurse was dragged in 1692 to be hanged as a witch on Gallows Hill.[3] The place is restored to its original appearance, & stands sinister amidst its grove of crooked trees on the top of a low hill, with a terrible graveyard at the foot. Such a massive chimney—such a strange, nail-studded door—such a curious garden—such an odd vertical sundial on the front wall—such a depressing interior, with low barren rooms panelled in dark wood, & colossal beams almost touching one's head; scant, plain furniture, crooked staircases, small-paned lattice windows ...... & that eldritch, unmentionable attic! Yes—the 17th century has as much of terror as the 18th has of beauty!

Most of my sightseeing was of the 18th century. I attended the Hub meeting April 12, did Salem & Danvers the next day after stopping at the Parker–Miniter abode,[4] stopped at the same place the next night, & on Saturday went to the Merrimack region & joined forces with my new host—young Davis.[5] In Danvers, besides the old 1636 farmhouse, there are some magnificent Colonial mansions. I thoroughly explored the Fowler & Page houses—both owned by historical societies, & the latter the seat of a well-known tale—that of the lady who during the anti-Revolutionary tea boycott was forbidden by her husband to serve the beverage *under his roof*, but who evaded the regulation by holding a tea-party *on the roof*.

Saturday Davis & I did the Whittier region—Amesbury, & I stopped at his house. He's a marvellous kid—highest intelligence rating, by test, in Merrimac High School. He turned 15 a week ago Saturday, & is now wearing long trousers. His family are all intelligent—best stock in Merrimac—but his father is lamentably unsympathetic toward art & intellect. The boy will make an ideal amateur.

Sunday's Newburyport trip was delightful—the town is unbelievably quaint & Colonial, with a surviving 18th century business section, a wealth of old winding streets & Georgian alleys leading down to abandoned wharves, & a magnificent array of old mansions in High Street—including the home of the famous eccentric Timothy Dexter (1747–1806).[6] You should see it—with your taste for unusual streets, you shouldn't miss New England. I stayed at Davis' a second night, but returned home Monday via Haverhill. I tried to make *Tryout* join the expedition, but he pleaded nervous ill health. Haverhill is quite a place—note the bulletin from its pub. library.

With every good wish,

Yr. obt. Grandfather

L. Theobald Junr.

Notes

1. AHT misdates the letter to 1921.

2. *The Poetical Works of Jonathan E. Hoag.* HPL wrote the introduction (pp. iii–vii), edited the book, and, with James F. Morton and Samuel Loveman, revised the poems for publication. The book includes HPL's annual birthday poems to Hoag.

3. See *Letters to Alfred Galpin and Others* 247–48.

4. In 1922, Edith Miniter moved into a home in Maplewood (a district of Malden, MA), with Charles A. A. Parker.

5. Edgar J. Davis (1908–1949), amateur journalist living in Haverhill, MA. For another account of HPL's visit with Davis to Newburyport, see HPL to Samuel Loveman, 29 April [1923]; *Letters to Maurice W. Moe* 501–2.

6. Dexter was a partial source for the character Obed Marsh in "The Shadow over Innsmouth" (1931), resulting from HPL's visit to Newburyport in 1931. See *SL* 1.225 for a lengthy discussion of Dexter.

[89]   [AHT]

66 College St.,
Providence, R.I.
Feby. 6, 1936

Illustrious St. John:—

No—I didn't think Burroughs worth counting as a serious interplanetary author. His stuff is really almost juvenile—with all the cheap & unconvincing stock devices of commercial quantity-production.

Your most obt Servt
Theobaldus

[90]   [AHT]

April 25, 1936

Benevolent Bolingbroke:—

Yea, would that we still had the creative & reviewing energy of our youth! Your reviews in the United began in 1917, but you had previously done some infinitely valuable *private* criticism of manuscripts—a leading feature of the good old U. A. P. A. In looking over my U. A. file I stand aghast at the amount of junk I wrote—especially between 1914 & 1920. The columns of my criticism (pompous, dogmatic, & often ill-advised & immature) are well-nigh endless, though some of it lurks beneath a merciful anonymity. From '14 to '17 I appointed no assistants in the public department. Then you & Galpin & Cook begin to figure. Wish I had a *National Amateur* file containing your criticism, but I have only scattered numbers behind 1930. As we contemplate these copious products of our younger selves, we wonder what driving force ever enabled us to spout so much wordage without becoming weary. No doubt the secret is that we thought such work vastly more important than we can possibly think it now. Then again, it was relatively *new* to us (I was just evolving the critical stock phrases which today I take so much trouble to avoid), & novelty has an adventurous zest which familiarity lacks. Absurd though I was in 1914, I'd give a lot if I could recapture the same image of the external world which I possessed then!

Yr oblig'd obt Servt
Theobaldus

[91]   [AHT]

May 29, 1936

Thrice-Literate St. John:—

Age brings reminiscences. With all the drawbacks of 169 Clinton (including the purely theoretical nature of the steam heat, which forc'd me to depend on a Perfection oil heater—which I still retain!) that aera of 1925 is not without its idyllick glamour! The long informal sessions at various rendezvous—the complete disregard of the clock—the quaint familiar landmarks (Scotch Bakery—Chatham—78 Columbia Heights, &c)—the spirited weekly meetings (alternately with Leeds & Mac because of the celebrated feud[1])—the then burning issues & no less burning arguments—the bookshops & the tours of exploration—surely they glow with a golden light in the perspective of eleven long years. That age was the last of youth for our generation—the last years in which we could feel that curious sense of the importance of things, & that vague, heartening spur of adventurous expectancy, which distinguish the morning & noon from the afternoon of life. However—the world isn't quite barren yet, while Burton & Gibbon[2] & colonial houses & Dunsany & vernal landscapes & a few other redeeming influences yet remain! And the remnants of the old gang will have many a reunion yet, before the last survivors disintegrate into their constituent electrons!

I am ever yr most oblig'd, most obt. Servt—
Theobaldus

Notes

1. Arthur Leeds (1882–1952?) and Everett McNeil (1862–1929), members of the Kalem Club, were at odds in 1924–26 because Leeds was unable to repay a small amount of money that McNeil had lent him; as a result, separate "Leeds" and "McNeil" meetings were held, at which one or the other was not present.
2. Presumably referring to the English writers Robert Burton (1577–1640), author of *The Anatomy of Melancholy* (1621), and Edward Gibbon (1737–1794), author of *The Decline and Fall of the Roman Empire* (1776–88).

[92]   [AHT]

June 19, 1936

Venerated Bolingbroke:—

Descending from poetry to doggerel—our young friend Barlow is demanding from me all the verse that I am willing to see printed; having formed the design of issuing a volume of Theobald's complete metrical works.[1] When I came to survey the prosodical offences scattered through my files I was appalled by their limitless profusion—indeed, I can never hope to find all of them, since I lack indexes to the vast heap of old amateur papers in which many of them occur. However, the number I would be willing to see resurrected is very small indeed; so that the scattering is not to be regretted. The naivete & artificiality of virtually all my early stuff renders it entirely hopeless—so that only the weird verses, plus a few other specimens written since 1920, could possibly be considered. All my decently presentable verse makes a volume thinner than "The Goblin Tower".[2]

Sir, yr most oblig'd obt Servt—
Theobaldus

Notes

1. HPL's young friend R. H. Barlow was contemplating the publication of HPL's collected poetical works. The project came to nothing, but HPL did draw up a list of selected poems that he felt represented his poetic work at its best.
2. By Frank Belknap Long. The volume (25 pp.) was published by R. H. Barlow; some of the type was set up by HPL.

[93]   [AHT]

The Ancient Hill
July 11, 1936

Dear St. John:—

My kind of weather has arrived at last! After dragging along wearily & languidly since last September, I live again! 90° or so for three days—& the old man was on his feet once more! I've accomplished more in that brief period than in the whole fortnight preceding!

I am writing this in the grey dawn as I struggle with temptation. Shall I take advantage of the increased mental power brought by the hot weather & get some work done, or shall I take advantage of the glorious days & squander 10 hours—& 50¢—on a boat trip to Newport, with 6 hours allotted to the exploration of that ancient seaport? The absence of a postcard following this epistle will indicate that duty has conquered. A Newport card will attest the triumph of the siren pleasure!

Patriarchal blessings—
Theobaldus

[94]   [AHT]

The Ancient Hill
Aug. 16, 1936

Benign Bolingbroke:—

Yes—gawd forgive me—it was I who steered Old 'Dolph in your direction.[1] He desperately needs somebody to revise his junk on a speculative basis (reviser to get half the prices of anything that lands) & I thought you might like a chance to see whether any item of his could be made into something potentially profitable. Despite his charlatanry where history & anecdote are concern'd, the old boy really has abundant scholarship of a sort (he studied at Bonn), & many of his tomes might get by if in proper form. As you know, his Bierce biography (revised & prefaced by Belknap) got published by the Century Company in 1929. I couldn't undertake anything of old 'Dolph's at present—but you might be cleverer than I in hitting the right formula. If he tries to unload his philosophic catch-all "Letters to My Lady" on you, be prepared to take the historical & biological portions with a very ample saline seasoning. The author's imagination has in these cases gone off on rather a romantic spree! In the climactic chapter on the parentage & ancestry of Jesus there are more historic boners per square inch than in any other historic hoax I have ever encountered! But for all that Old 'Dolph is a good soul—& now & then an idea or synopsis of his might be well worth developing. He blew in here Aug. 6—on his way back from Boston, where he had been for the melancholy purpose of consigning his late wife's ashes to the open sea in accordance with her ante-mortem request. He stayed 5 days, so that I shew'd him quite a bit of the town & of its museums & libraries. On one occasion he, Barlow, & I sat on a tomb in the hidden hillside churchyard just north of here & composed rhymed acrostics on the name of *Edgar Allan Poe*—who 90 years ago used to wander in that selfsame churchyard when on visits to Providence. Naturally the results of such forced, mechanical, & overspeeded composition were nothing notable—but I'll let you see what they were like. Please return the enclosed at your convenience. Bob & Old 'Dolph worked extensively over their specimens after the contest (which R. H. B. proposed in the first place) was over, but I made only 2 later corrections, as indicated in the enclosed. I think de Castro's verse was better *before* he tinkered with it.[2] By the way—Old 'Dolph's statement that he *thinks* he has met you amuses me—for I told him all about our meeting of May 16, 1928 when he was here last week. I was over at Mac's that afternoon—in Fifth Street Brooklyn—& de Castro joined us there early in the evening. I then guided the two old duffers over to Bushwick on the elevated, & we all got together at 116 Harman. That is, some of us did—for I believe only Kirk showed up in addition to Mac & Old 'Dolph & Grandpa Theobald. If I remember rightly, Old 'Dolph contributed most of the discourse—unfolding impressive European reminiscences both authentic & apocryphal, & finding out casual allusions to the great men he had known—how he was really the man who made William H. Taft & Warren G. Harding president, & how he had been the chief behind-the-throne influence in shaping the recent history of Mexico. A great chap, Old 'Dolph—& curiously suggestive of the protagonist in a contemporary cartoon series called "Judge Puffle"[3] (do you ever see these amusing tho' sometimes overdone sketches?). Here's hoping that you & he can strike up some sort of mutually advantageous revisory pact!

      Sir, yr most obt

Grandpa Theobald.

Notes

1. HPL refers to former revision client Adolphe de Castro. De Castro had asked HPL to edit a book he had written: "The MS. is a full-length book of miscellaneous social, political, & historical essays rather vaguely entitled 'The New Way', & has very little internal coherence" (HPL to F. Lee Baldwin, 23 December 1934; *Letters to F. Lee Baldwin* 116).

2. The three acrostic poems, and others by M. W. Moe and Henry Kuttner, are reprinted in *Letters to Alfred Galpin and Others* 464–66.

3. Eugene Leslie Ahern (1895–1960) wrote and drew *Room & Board,* starring Judge Puffle, a cartoon strip created (not by Ahern) in 1936. Judge Puffle was a character very similar to Major Hoople in Ahern's own strip, *Our Boarding House.*

[95]   [AHT]

                                              Aug. 29, 1936

Benign Bolingbroke:—

            I feel distinctly guilty in having shoved Old 'Dolph on you—but when I advised him to consult you it was *not* about his hopeless fiction. I had told him to send the *stories* to someone else—young Bloch of Milwaukee,[1] who is an expert technician & might be able to salvage an idea & write a story around it to mutual advantage (although of course even this would be true in only a few cases). What I suggested that he submit to you was some of his historical & biographical & philosophical stuff, of which he has uncounted reams in the form of rough-hewn books. Despite the pervasive aura of charlatanry some of this undoubtedly has certain possibilities—for as you know, he *has* had work accepted by standard publishers, & that as late as 1929. His autobiography, for example, might well be whipped into shape & marketed as a sort of sensational-reminiscent item by any one with the time, energy, & knack. It was this kind of thing which I thought he would send—so that I was quite surprised when you spoke of *fiction.* You have my sympathy—& deepest apologies! All you can do is to repeat my own procedure & bow the job out with a maximum of tact for a poor old duffer soon to turn 77.

Sir, yr most contrite & obt Servt
Theobaldus

Notes

1. Robert Bloch (1917–1994), who had already published several stories in *WT*.

[96]   [AHT]

The Antient Hill
Nov. 20, 1936

Thrice-Gifted St. John:—
Well—the election was indeed satisfactory enough!
The general result was to be foreseen, but the *extent* of the landslide surely
was a pleasant surprise.[1] I did—for the second time in my life—what I did on
the night of Nov. 7–8, 1916, when the fortunes of Hughes & Wilson hung in
the balance[2] . . . . . went to a late cinema show where election returns were
announced. The national results were obvious from an early hour, but the
state figures (a clean Democratic sweep in the end) took longer to settle. By
the time the show closed—2:45 a.m.—there was no danger of any contrary
report next day as there was 20 years ago. On that occasion, as you may recall
from my vehement remarks in *The Kleicomolo*, I went to bed believing Hughes
was elected, but had my belief shattered by the ice man the next morning!
Yes, it was a glorious victory. The feeble arguments, obvious hokum, absurd
accusations, & occasionally underhanded tactics of the Republicans reacted
against them, while some obscure instinct of common sense seemed to keep
the extreme radicals from wasting their votes on obviously hopeless tickets. It
amuses me to see the woebegone state of the poor ostriches who constitute
Providence's reactionary clique, & away from whose past-drugged ideology it
is impossible to pull my aunt. Around election-time I came damn near having
a family feud on my hands! But even the white-moustached constitution-
savers of the Hope Club's easy-chairs must some day learn that the tide of
social evolution can't be checked forever. King Canute & the waves!
Yes—the Dec. *Weird Tales* contains a story of mine called "The Haunter
of the Dark", in which this house, & the westward view from my desk window, are quite accurately described. The tale in the preceding issue was a reprint of "Pickman's Model"—that story about the sinister North End of
Boston which first appeared in 1927. In the Jany. issue (unless it gets post-
poned) will be another tale of mine called "The Thing on the Doorstep".
Meanwhile my book-form "Shadow over Innsmouth" is ready at last, & can
be supplied—cloth-bound, 156 pp., & with 4 excellent illustrations by Frank
Utpatel—for the modest & reasonable sum of one dollar, postpaid, by the
publisher . . . William Crawford, 122 Water Street, Everett, Pa. There are 33
bad misprints, but a table of errata on an inserted slip helps to neutralise that.

Crawford also advertises a leather-bound edition—reg'lar de luxe stuff—for $2.50, but anybody who pays that much for such a lousily printed mess is a sucker! Fine bindings don't make good text![3]

> Sir, yr oblig'd & obt. Servt
> Theobaldus

Notes

1. HPL refers to the Democrat Franklin D. Roosevelt's defeat of the Republican Alf Landon and a third-party candidate, William Lemke, in the presidential election of 1936. FDR won 523 electoral votes to Landon's 8; he won the popular vote by more than 11 million.

2. HPL refers to the Democrat Woodrow Wilson's defeat of the Republican Charles Evans Hughes in the presidential election of 1916. It was initially believed that Hughes had won the election, but returns from the West, reported a day after the election, gave Wilson the victory.

3. An errata sheet was later issued, in which some (but not all) of the printer's errors were corrected. No leatherbound edition was published.

[97] [AHT]

Jany. 7, 1937

Noble Sinjin:—

So far as health goes, I'm feeling like hell-let-loose myself. I've just concluded that part of my malady is the prevailing grippe—or at least a slight suggestion of it. Those intestinal rumblings I spoke of now seem to be exchanged for a kind of diffused nausea & a sense of "a sleepiness" of extremities—coupled with a pervasive general weakness. This strongly resembles other spells of mine—especially one of just a year ago—whose synchronisation with reported grippe waves has led me to label them with that popular title. Yesterday & today I've been loafing around in a dressing-gown & dumping down on the couch every hour or two.

> Sir, yr most oblig'd & obt—
> Theobaldus

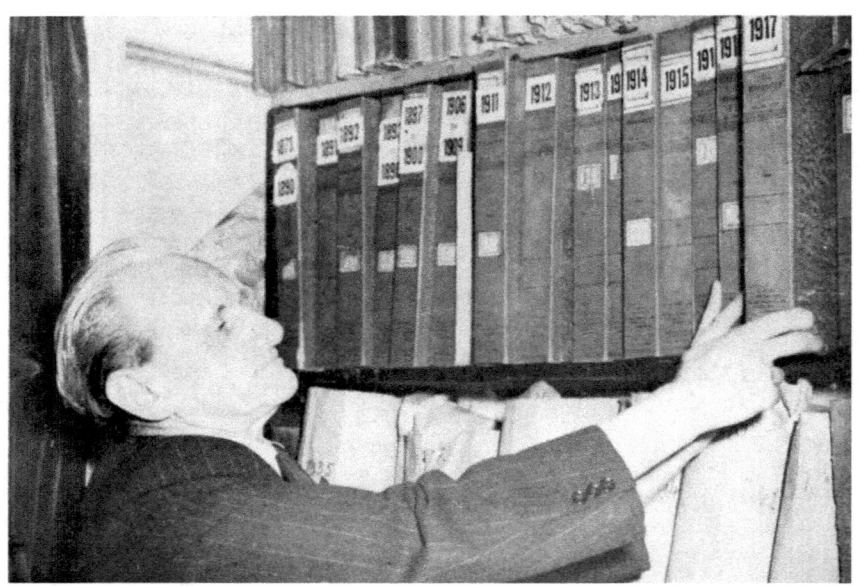

Arthur Harris and his collection.

Arthur and Irene Harris,
publishers of *Interesting Items* and
Irene's Items. *Fossil* (April 1958): 60.

Letters to Arthur Harris

[1]   [TLS]

598, Angell St., Providence, R.I.
June 20, 1915.

Arthur Harris, Esq.,
        Selwyn House, Llandudno,[1]
My dear Mr Harris:—

I yesterday received your welcome package, containing the letter and two issues of INTERESTING ITEMS. The magazine is a remarkably neat and attractive one, and doubly interesting from the fact that you do your own printing. Typography is an art which I have not myself mastered, and I am ever at the mercy of the local professional. Next issue, however, my CONSERVATIVE will be printed by a Cambridge amateur,[2] and will, I trust, impress you more favourably than the first. It will probably reach you by the middle of July.

I am delighted to behold my humble lines in print,[3] especially since there are no printers' errors; a type of evil from which I have suffered much in the past. Wherefore I am taking advantage of your offer to accept further work of mine, and am enclosing a poem of the nature suggested by you. Your letter was in a way an inspiration. I had wished to express in verse my horror at the Lusitania murders, yet had viewed the subject with so much awe that I scarce dared attempt to treat of it. But the sight of my printed piece, and the suggestion in your letter, gave me the necessary impetus, and the enclosed lines, entitled "The Crime of Crimes" were written by me last evening within the space of two hours.[4] Whatever its merit as poetry, it expresses at least a sincere and fervent indignation at a deed whose infamy is unparalleled in history. I trust that you may find it suitable for use in your pages, and shall await its appearance with interest.

If you have spare copies of the March number, containing my "1914", I would much appreciate your mailing one to Mr. John Russell,[5] General Delivery, West Tampa, Florida, U.S.A. Mr. Russell is a patriotic Scotchman, a native of Penicuik, near Edinburgh, and has two nephews in the army, one with the Gordon Highlanders and another with the Canadian Infantry. He has read the MS. of my poem, and has expressed the desire for a printed copy whenever it should appear. Russell is a United member, one of my own recruits, and I am anxious that he receive a warm welcome from the veteran amateurs.

I sent Mr. Stokes a few lines of mine not long ago, which he said that he would print in one of his magazines. The war, of course, disarranges all plans and alters all conditions, but you may yet see them in type.[6]

I only wish my health were such that it would permit me to take an active part in hostilities. As it is, I am a semi-invalid, having always been of very feeble constitution. I possess the most intense affection for Old England, the land of all my ancestors, and hope that the States will see fit to aid the mother country at no far distant period in the terrible struggle of civilisation against its outlawed ex-member.

In future I trust that I may receive INTERESTING ITEMS regularly; it is needless to say that I shall reciprocate with THE CONSERVATIVE. I believe in the development of more substantial ties between the British and American amateurs, and am casting my vote to cancel the words "of America" in the title of the United Amateur Press Association. I am a comparative newcomer to amateur journalism, having joined only a year ago last April. But the United members have been very kind in making me feel at home, and I am already Chairman of the Department of Public Criticism, with my reviews of amateur papers printed in every issue of THE UNITED AMATEUR,[7] and am now candidate for Vice-President. I believe that amateur journalism, ever improving, will some day become a serious and potent factor in literary education and development.

Thanking you once more for the letter and papers,

     I am

         Very sincerely yours,

           H. P. Lovecraft

Notes

1. Pronounced hlan'-did-no.

2. Albert A. Sandusky of the Lincoln Press, Cambridge, MA, printed four issues of the *Conservative*, starting with the July 1915 issue.

3. Presumably "1914."

4. The poem was about the sinking of the *RMS Lusitania,* a British ocean liner sunk by a German U-boat on 7 May 1915. A total of 1,198 out of the 1,962 passengers and crew lost their lives.

5. See RK 19.

6. George William Stokes of Newcastle-on-Tyne, England, published the amateur journal *Outward Bound.* No work by HPL is known to have appeared there.

7. HPL wrote the "Department of Public Criticism" column irregularly from November 1914 to May 1919.

[2] [ALS]

             598 Angell St.,

               Providence, R.I.

                 June 26, 1915

My dear Mr Harris:—

      I trust you may pardon this eleventh-hour revision, but

I have discovered a slight rhetorical imperfection in my poem, "The Crime of Crimes", which I now most ardently desire to correct.

Toward the beginning of the lines, the words "fearless" and "fear'd" occur too closely together, hence a synonym is required in one of these instances. I have decided to change "fearless" to "dauntless" in line 9, hence the couplet should now read:

"Upon the wave in dauntless grandeur rode,
Nor fear'd to bear its blameless, helpless load."[1]

Hoping that this emendation may reach you in time to have the change made without inconvenience,

I remain

Very Sincerely yours,

H. P. Lovecraft

Notes

1. Ll. 9–10. The suggested emendation, and that in the following letter, were not made for the appearance in *Interesting Items* or *The Crime of Crimes.*

[3] [ALS]

598 Angell St.,
Providence, R.I.
U.S.A.
July 14—1915

My dear Mr Harris:—

Can you pardon *still another* correction to my Lusitania verses? Careful re-reading brings trivial errors to light, & I am very anxious to have the poem accurate in metre. It seems that in line 46 I gave the word "bar-bar-ism" a *false* quantity of *four* syllables, making the line thus:

˘ ' ˘ ' ˘ ' ˘ ' ˘ '

"And | bar- | bar- | is- | m | rise | to | cov- | er | all"?

Now I could remedy this fault by substituting "arise" for "rise", thus:

˘ ' ˘ ' ˘ ' ˘ ' ˘ '

"And | bar- | bar- | ism | a- | rise | to | cov- | er | all"?

But this arrangement is not quite smooth enough to suit the ear. The passage is awkward.

Therefore I have boldly altered & improved the line to read as follows, this being the final & authentic form:

46—— And black barbarity engulf us all?

The couplet now reads:

"Shall man beneath the Prussian's madness fall,
And black barbarity engulf us all"?

I am sincerely sorry to have twice troubled you with corrections, but I take my amateur work very seriously. I hope you will be put to no inconvenience by my alterations, and that they may arrive in time to be printed in the text without difficulty. This poem was written, as it were, under a momentary inspiration, hence contained these technical flaws which a closer scrutiny detects.

I trust that you have received my latest *Conservative,* as well as *The Providence Amateur,* a club publication which I supervise.

With renewed apologies for the second disturbance of your peace of mind, and with the hope that the poem may appear satisfactorily in amended form,

I remain
Very sincerely yours,
H P Lovecraft

[4]   [ALS]

598 Angell St.,
Providence, R.I.
August 23, '15

My dear M*r* Harris:—

I should have replied to your interesting letter much sooner, had not my wretched health, coupled with unusually heavy duties in the U.A.P.A., left me without a moment of spare time. I can remain out of bed but three or four hours each day, and those three or four hours are generally burdened with an array of amateur work far beyond my capabilities. Besides the purely literary activity, there is always the more tedious routine of recruiting to deal with, and betwixt the two I am hopelessly overwhelmed.

I must thank you sincerely for the extra copies of my verses, and express, as before, my appreciation of your accuracy in setting up the work; for "The Crime of Crimes" is as free from typographical error as its predecessor. I am sorry I was so tardy in amending my crude original, but I am sure that the poem as published conveys a fair idea of my feelings concerning submarine murder.

I am rather anxious for you to read my comic satirical verse entitled "The Ballade of Patrick von Flynn". This ridicules the miserable anti-English Irishmen residing in the States, who are just now violently espousing the German cause. The piece will be published in M*r·* Winterbone's "Amateur Siftings", unless Dench's plans have gone awry.[1] The character of Patrick von Flynn is drawn from life, and represents a certain Irish-American member of the United. In my next *Conservative* I shall deal very severely with the passive attitude of the U.S., after the Lusitania, Arabic, and other calamities.[2] I believe with ex-President Roosevelt, that peace with Germany is no longer consistent with the honour of the American nation.

I shall indeed be pleased to have another piece of my verse in Interesting Items. "A Tale of Two Cities"[3] is a promising subject, & I wish that you would explain in detail just what sort of a piece you desire; whether you wish me to re-tell the story in metrical form (this would make the poem very long—1000 or more lines) or to compose a shorter piece, commenting on the characters & drawing a moral, or else complimenting Dickens on the plot & general excellence of the novel. I can certainly write as much as you can print, for I am an inveterate rhymester—have been rhyming ever since I was seven years old! I am interested in your design, & would like to hear from you in time to compose my verses before winter.

I am hoping soon to behold your name duly enrolled on the membership list of the United. As I mentioned once before, I am passionately fond of Old England, the land of my ancestors, and it gratifies me immeasurably to see any sign of resumed relations with America. Had I been alive in the trying times of the American war, I should certainly have staid by the mother country, and should have exerted every influence against the rebellion of the colonists. It is a favourite dream of mine that circumstances may some day rejoin America to the rest of the British Empire, giving a united Anglo-Saxon world, ready to resist invasion from any source. To quote myself—

> And when the mighty Empire shall become
> The World itself—the deathless heir of Rome.[4]

I hear with envy that Stokes has succeeded in joining the Durham Fortress Royal Engineers & is on his way to the front, whilst we must remain at home & scribble! But a good deal of my scribbling is going to be decidedly military in the near future. As you doubtless know, the latest form of German activity in America is the spread of "peace at any price" fanaticism. The Germans have purchased a controlling interest in all the cheap news syndicates, and we are veritably deluged with pro-German & pacifist matter. The *real Americans,* descended from English colonists, laugh at this crude stuff, but the less loyal Jews & other foreigners give it real attention. This mental poison creeps even into amateur journalism, and a recent paper, entitled "In a Minor Key", contains a slur on England, excuses for Germany, & a most effeminate plea for peace on America's part. You saw my first attack on this paper in The Conservative, but since my opponents are about to retaliate, I am planning further attacks; this time in satirical verse. One article contains this rather slurring passage: "mentally unpalatable, even as are the words of George Sylvester Viereck to the great (no kidding) English People." Viereck[5] is one of the most rascally German-American editors still working. This slur was made by a writer named Goodwin, and I am replying thus:

> *No kidding,* Goodwin, you with wisdom say
> That England likes not George Sylvester's way.
> The honest Truth poor Viereck ne'er could speak,
> And Britons hate a liar and a sneak!

Further on in the paper Isaacson the Jew refers to the Germans as a *persecuted* people!!! To this I say:

> Heav'n help the Prussian, tortur'd & oppress'd,
> Whose injur'd feelings lacerate his breast,
> O cruel World! This tender creature spare,
> That he may ravage land & sea & air!

Last of all, Isaacson says that the "truest bravery" and "greater courage" of the American people is to *submit to insult,* and *resolve never to enter battle.* He refers to Pres. Wilson's foolish phrase "Too proud to fight," and ends by saying "We will not fight!" "We will not go to war!" Observe my answer to this vile treason:

> Horatius at the bridge intrepid stands,
> A branch of olive in his gentle hands.
> Th' Etruscan host draws nearer; and with *pride*
> The manly hero bows and steps aside![6]

––––––––

I suppose that Dench will sooner or later send you application blanks for membership in the United. I am enclosing one, in case he should not have done so. Your little paper is so meritorious that I long to see it bearing the inscription "Affiliated with the U.A.P.A." I am afraid the war will make serious inroads on the B.A.P.A.,[7] hence the United, no longer an exclusively American body, will fill a real need in the United Kingdom.

As Vice-President, I have had the privilege of writing the United's recruiting circular this year, & in so doing I have tried to be unusually comprehensive.[8] This is now in press, & when issued I will send you several copies in case you wish to do some recruiting in England. Did you receive The Badger, issued in Wisconsin? This was edited partly by myself, & contains a long piece of my verse. If you have not seen it I will send an extra copy. One of the articles is by A. W. Ashby, a British member of the United.[9]

But I had better close ere I become too tedious. Hoping to hear from you very soon concerning the "Tale of Two Cities" poem, & trusting that you may see fit to join the United in the near future,

I remain

Very sincerely yours,
H. P. Lovecraft

Notes

1. Henry J. Winterbone (1885–1938) was a member of the British Amateur Press Association. Ernest A. Dench (1895–?) was a English-born amateur living in Brooklyn, author of *Advertising by Motion Pictures* (1916). It is not clear what role Dench had in the placing of the poem in Winterbone's journal. The poem did not in fact appear in *Amateur Siftings*.

2. "The Renaissance of Manhood." The *SS Arabic*, bound for the U.S., was sunk by a German U-boat on 19 August 1915, killing 44 passengers and crew. The *SS Sussex* was a cross–English Channel passenger ferry severely damaged by a torpedo from a German U-boat in 1916. In May 1916, Germany issued the so-called Sussex pledge, representing the suspension of its intensified U-boat campaign.

3. The novel (1859) by Charles Dickens.

4. "1914," ll. 67–68.

5. George Sylvester Viereck (1884–1962), a German-American poet, writer, supporter of the Germans in World War I, and, later, pro-Nazi propagandist.

6. The three quatrains are the entirety of "Gems from *In a Minor Key*." The "Goodwin" to whom the first quatrain is addressed is unidentified. For Isaacson, see RK 4n1.

7. I.e., the British Amateur Press Association.

8. *United Amateur Press Association: Exponent of Amateur Journalism.*

9. Arthur W. Ashby (1886–1953), professor of agricultural economics at the University College of Wales, Aberystwyth (1929–46) and Director of the Institute of Agrarian Affairs (1946–52). The article is "What May I Own?", *Badger* No. 2 (June 1915): 10–13. HPL remarked it was "an able sociological essay which displays considerable familiarity with the outward aspects of economic condition" ("Department of Public Criticism," *United Amateur* 15, No. 2 (September 1915); *CE* 1.62.

[5]   [ALS]

598 Angell St.,
Providence, R.I.
July 1, 1915 [i.e., 1916]

My dear Mʳ Harris:—

Permit me to thank you for your communication containing the September & December issues of *Interesting Items*. I appreciated them very much, and noticed with pleasure the artistic covers, particularly that of the Christmas Number. You are helping to keep amateur journalism alive in Great Britain through a very stormy period, and I rejoice to see that Mʳ McColl has come to your aid with *The Scot*. These two, together with the semi-professional *Poesy*, are all the amateur papers I am receiving from the Mother Country.[1] The present Mexican trouble[2] has commenced to affect amateur matters in the New World, for our capable Official Editor, Mr. Schilling, has just been called to the colours as a member of the Ohio National Guard.

I am endeavouring to reciprocate your recent favour by sending herewith under separate cover two publications of mine; *The Providence Amateur* and *The Conservative*. You will notice in the latter a very sharp attack on the treacherous Irish in America who attempt to arouse sentiment against England,[3] and to create sympathy for wretches like Roger Casement[4] and the "Sinn Fein" rioters. The lines bear the signature "Lewis Theobald, Jun.", but they are from my pen; "Theobald" being a *nom de plume* of mine.

I am devoting much time lately to the causes of England. In the July *Conservative* I shall have an essay in praise of England by Henry Clapham McGavack of Washington, D.C.[5] a deep student of history and diplomacy. In October I shall have another essay, this time one of my own, on the same plan.[6] I shall also republish my verses "An American to Mother England" which appeared last January in Herdman's *Poesy*.

I am sorry you did not receive the July, 1915, *Badger*. My long piece therein was later reprinted in the local newspaper,[7] and since I have several extra copies, I will enclose one to you. I have passed many delightful afternoons in the pleasing rural spot which I attempt to describe.

I also enclose a circular describing the United Amateur Press Association, which I wrote last fall, together with an application blank. It is my desire to obtain as many British members as possible, hence I sincerely hope you will think favourably of joining. You would receive regularly many papers which at present do not reach you. I have just secured McColl of Dundee as a member.

I am so busy of late, with professional as well as amateur duties, that I have not begun the metrical fusion of "A Tale of Two Cities". However, I may some day surprise you with a bulky mass of heroic couplets on the subject![8]

Excitement hereabouts is centreing mostly on Mexico. One troop of the R.I. National Guard has departed for the border, carrying with hit several of my acquaintances. Another very old friend of mine[9] is a Lieutenant in the regular army, already across the boundary, and now at Casas Grandes, in Mexico itself. I regret being so feeble that I cannot think of participating in activities, no matter what may develop. I half believe that there is German deviltry behind Carranza[10] and his insolence. But I will not bore you by a mere extended epistle.

With best wishes, and hoping to hear from you,
> I remain
>> Very sincerely yours,
>>> H P Lovecraft

P.S. I strongly hope you will see fit to join the U.A.P.A.

Notes

1. *Poesy*, which published several of HPL's poems, was edited by Edward F. Herdman (1859/60?–1935?). HPL described him as "a veteran amateur of Bishop-Auckland, Eng-

land" and his magazine as "a semi-professional medium through which the youthful bard may bring before the public his first efforts" (*CE* 1.85).

2. HPL refers to the Mexican Revolution of c. 1910–20.

3. HPL refers to his poem "Ye Ballade of Patrick von Flynn."

4. Roger David Casement (1864–1916), Irish-born civil servant who worked for the British Foreign Office as a diplomat, and later became a humanitarian activist, Irish nationalist, and poet. Known as Sir Roger Casement CMG from 1911 until he was executed for treason on 3 August 1916 for his participation in the events leading up to the Easter Rebellion in Dublin (24 April 1916). He was also stripped of his knighthood and other honors.

5. Henry Clapham McGavack (1888–1959), "The Genesis of the Revolutionary War," *Conservative* 3, No. 1 (July 1917): [1–3].

6. "Old England and the 'Hyphen.'"

7. "Quinsnicket Park," a poem of 112 lines.

8. HPL never wrote the piece.

9. Perhaps Manton Campbell Mitchell (1887–1929).

10. Venustiano Carranza Garza (1859–1920), one of the main leaders of the Mexican Revolution.

[6]   [ALS]

598, Angell St.,
Providence, R.I., U.S.,
Octr 23, 1916.

My dear M^r. Harris:—

I received and perused your letter of recent date with great interest, and shall await with eagerness the arrival of the next number of *Interesting Items*. I was surprised to hear of the new censorship regulation regarding printed matter, but do not imagine that permission will be very difficult to obtain, since McColl's *Scot* reached me the very day before your letter. He seems to have obtained mailing privileges quite easily. In general, the censorship seems rather variable. Only about half the letters & packages I receive from Great Britain have been examined or adorned with the familiar label "Opened by Censor".

I believe that censorship of American mail is very necessary on account of the Irish and German Anglophobes who unfortunately infest this country. These vermin are detestably noisy, though with the exception of a few wealthy Germans, they are almost entirely confined to the lower ranks of the community. The "International News Service," from which most of the anti-British idiots received their alleged "news" from England, has lately been debarred on account of its flagrant falsifications; but this will not affect the cheap Anglophobe press—most of its "news" was from the first "made in America". Luckily, this sort of thing has no standing whatsoever with the intelligent American public, as distinguished from the degenerate cosmopolitan masses. Our representative newspapers and periodicals are firmly on the side of England's welfare; in fact, the local "Providence Journal" is so staunch a supporter of the Mother Country that except for the date line, it might well pass for an English paper. I have heard that the British public is rather bitter against America for the extraordinary way in which our present administration has behaved, and I wish Britain could know how little that administration really expresses the sentiment of real Americans. The fact is, that real Americans are being almost submerged by foreign immigration. The slums of our cities are *entirely* foreign in thought and aspect, and since every citizen has a vote, the politicians have to cater to the whims and prejudices of this nondescript herd.

But the nicer residential parts of our towns are still as English as they were before the revolution, and contain no persons of other than pure English blood. If I should draw a circle with a radius of a mile and a half around my own house, the area thus formed would be just as English in population as any area of equal size in England itself. Thus you may see that although the humbler districts in America are frightfully contaminated with aliens, the real representatives of American ideals are of undiluted British origin. As a whole, America's race problem has not yet attained its crucial point. I am frankly horrified by the number of inferior immigrants and their descendants. I believe that in the city of New York there are more Jews than Americans, while there are villages here and there almost completely given over to aliens. What the result will eventually be, I dislike to picture. The foreigners multiply a hundred times more rapidly than the Americans, so that degeneracy of the worst sort may overtake the nation within a very few generations. All in all, I am inexpressibly sorry that the American Colonies ever parted company with the rest of the British Empire. The popular notion of cosmopolitanism, so widely diffused among the lower orders, will ruin the moral fabric of the country. What America is, England made it. Every American institution, laws, language, ideals, moral standards, virtues, and ethics, are the legacy of the parent land. When these things shall have ceased to be dominant, then America will have ceased to occupy a place in the first rank of civilised states. Through my paper, *The Conservative*, I am actively engaged in diffusing the truth concerning America's debt to England; a task in which I am ably aided by one of the most scholarly essayists in amateur journalism—Henry Clapham McGavack of Washington, D.C. I enclose the latest number in case you have not previously received it. I shall have an essay of my own in the next issue, and Mr. McGavack is preparing still another, exhibiting the British side of the American Revolution. Our efforts are already bearing fruits within the circle of amateur journalism, for the United has quite broken loose from that indeterminate "neutral" spirit which reigns within the National. Our society is now truly *Anglo*-American in every sense; in fact we are very anxious for recruits from your side of the Atlantic. I enclose our latest blank, in case you care to join, thus helping out the development of the United in Britain.

I am glad that in spite of poor health you have been enabled to assist England in a manner suited to your constitution. I wish there were something of the sort which I could do. I am a semi-invalid, and very impatient at my inability to help the land of my ancestors in the present crisis. The coming of the Hunnish sea-monster U-53 and the subsequent deviltry close to our coast made me feel the closeness of the war as never before. To think that a U-boat should come into the harbour of Newport, only a few miles south of Providence! I believe it should not have been allowed to depart on its nefarious mission; in fact, I believe that *all submarines* of Germany should be captured and sunk as international outlaws wherever discovered.[1] But nothing can be expected of Pres. Wilson and his Democratic cabinet. They are all hopeless cowards—afraid even of puny Mexico. Wilson is absolutely unfit to be chief executive of a nation. He has made the United States a jest throughout the world. But better things may be expected from Charles Evans Hughes, who will undoubtedly defeat him next month for the Presidency.[2] As a native of Wales, it must please you to know that America's next president will be also of Welsh stock. Hughes' father was a true-born Welshman—a Baptist minister.

I have not received Herdman's *Poesy* lately, and fancy it did not succeed. It seems that very few of our small papers prosper when they leave the purely amateur class. However, I sent in my contribution in time for publication. McColl is doing wonders with his *Scot;* in fact, it is the most regularly and frequently issued paper in the United. I liked Mr. Winskill's[3] sketch about Kent in the August number, since it appealed so much to my regard for the past, and for ancient things.

I have frequently thought about the proposed "Tale of Two Cities" poem, and how it might best be taken from the novel. I think the best and shortest way is to make a simple narrative ballad of it, using the time-honoured old "Chevy Chase" metre of 14 syllables, divisible into alternate lines of 8 and 6 syllables. This will demand *stanzas* of four lines each, making the whole rather long to print, but I will try to condense as much as possible. Yet even so, I fear you will be forced to publish it as a *serial!*

I enclose my latest monthly article on the heavens,[4] some details of which, however, will not suit the latitude of Great Britain. New England, as you know, is about 10° nearer the equator, though its climate is no milder than that of Old England. Providence is exactly in the latitude of Rome, so we see the sky as the Italians see it! I send under separate cover a copy of *The United Amateur,* which will come to you regularly if you join our association.

With best wishes, & hoping to hear from you at your convenience, I remain

Very sincerely yrs

H P Lovecraft

Notes

1. The German U-boat U-53 entered Newport harbor on 7 October 1916, and its commander, Hans Rose, paid courtesy visits to various American naval officers. The next morning, the U-53 stopped or torpedoed several steamers or passenger liners off of Nantucket, then evaded three British destroyers to return to Germany.

2. Charles Evans Hughes, Sr. (1862–1948), lawyer, 36th Governor of New York (1907–10), Associate Justice of the U.S. Supreme Court (1910–16), U.S. Secretary of State (1921–25), and 11th Chief Justice of the U.S. (1930–41). He lost narrowly to President Woodrow Wilson in the presidential election of 1916. See further RK 96n2.

3. Benjamin Winskill (1873–1948), English amateur journalist, and a contributor to the nonextant round-robin story "The Mystery of Murdon Grange." "Hoary Kent" appeared in *Scot* No. 12 (August 1916).

4. Evidently "October Skies," [Providence] *Evening News* 49, No. 104 (2 October 1916): 6.

[7]   [ALS]

598, Angell St.,
Providence, R.I., U.S.,
April 29, 1917.

Dear Mr. Harris:—

It was with great pleasure that I received your recent letter, as well as the file of *Interesting Items* from January to June of last year. Now that *The Scot* is suspended, your publication is the only genuine *amateur* magazine in the Mother Country; for Miss Trafford's *Merry Minutes*[1] is distinctly professional in object, as is Mr. Herdman's *Poesy*.

I fancy that the latest developments of America's policy have done much to remove the rancour which the British public must have felt during the days of Wilson's inexplicable lingering and note-writing. It is difficult to think that the man who wrote the admirable war message to the American Congress is the same President who a few months ago was vaguely talking about "peace without victory." So far as I can see, Wilson is trying to reflect the dominant sentiment of his nation, without much personal conviction. As long as the foreign element made the loudest noise, he favoured their side and was a pacifist; but now that the real American people have asserted their manhood and shewn their supremacy, he is with them and in favour of a righteous war. But vacillating as he has been, I cannot but feel that he is glad of the step he has taken. As a man of culture and undoubted intelligence—as a man of pure British blood—he must be relieved at abandoning an impossible position; a position which had in it neither justice nor logic; and coming at last to the decision which has really been inevitable since the commencement of the war.

I regard the entry of the States into the conflict as one of the most propitious events of recent American history. It furnishes indisputable evidence that despite the alien immigration of the past half century, the original British Colonial stock is still dominant in the republic. For never before was the line of cleavage between real Anglo-Americans and "hyphenated" newcomers so strikingly emphasised. The division leaped into prominence almost at the beginning of the war, when the native Americans espoused the Allied cause without so much as a conscious thought of dissent; whilst the foreign masses were equally ardent in their pro-Germanism or alleged neutrality. The reasons for the attitude of the alien populace are not difficult to discover. In the first place—most of the foreigners from Allied countries (mainly Italy) are from so low a peasant class that they have no opinion whatsoever, voting and acting at the dictation of (Irish) political "bosses". This makes self-evident the second reason—that the shrewdest and noisiest aliens are the Germans and Irish of the "Sinn Fein" type; who, by exploiting themselves as the typical "common people", are able to draw to their cause not only most of the other immigrants, but the more plebeian strata of the native stock. The Irish, by the way, are much more influential here than the Germans. They are born agitators, and make the most of their birthright! The third reason operating against America's entry into the war, was sordid materialism. What Europeans say about the "Great American Dollar" and its paramountcy, is undoubtedly true amongst the lower middle classes, and especially in that vast interior region loosely known as the "Middle West." Middle Westerners have been half asleep, and well content with the profits gleaned from war contracts—while the British fleet protected their own country. A fourth and not inconsiderable obstacle has been the "conscientious objector" or chronic pacifist. This idealistic element is never absent from society, and its well-meaning folly is always in evidence when questions of national policy are under consideration. The hysterical temperament of confirmed faddists, moreover, renders them acutely responsive to the suggestions of sly enemy propagandists, who seek to accentuate their pacifism in order to retard the military measures of the government. And this brings us to the fifth reason of my list—the actual German—not German-American—element of spies, dynamiters, propagandists, labour agitators, organisers, & diplomats, whose nefarious activities have been inspired directly from the Wilhelmstrasse, and financed directly with the gold of Berlin. The amount of evil perpetrated by these vermin is incredibly great, and it is to their efforts that much of the active pacifism & pro-Germanism of other elements may be traced. They were the leaven of all the seething disloyalty of the foreigners in general. They were the heart of that vast rabble of nondescripts who abused the name and institutions of democracy, and repudiated the Anglo-American traditions which have guided and glorified the United States throughout its history. And in the midst of this swinish herd dwelt the Americans of the ancient stock—the transplanted

Englishmen who were not dead to honour and principle, and who viewed with contempt the sordid peace-lovers about them. Thus it was from August, 1914 to April, 1917. In that interval the United States became a dual country. The genuine Americans, with Theodore Roosevelt as their spokesman, have consistently striven to assist the cause of England and of civilisation; whilst the rabble, whose noisy clamour swayed Pres. Wilson to their cause and leadership, sought the paths of cowardice and least resistance. The wondrous and glorious change, culminating in America's appearance as an actual belligerent, represents a triumph of intelligence and moral truth; a proof of the ascendancy of the Anglo-American ideal, and a vindication of the ultimate feasibility of democratic institutions. With the sentiment of the real Americans constantly before them, with the significant fact of the Russian revolution fresh in their ears, and with the glaring evidences of German perfidy accumulating with increasing rapidity before their eyes, the masses in the United States could no longer retain their anomalous position of neutrality without violating every tradition of the civilisation which they acknowledged as theirs. According to the most essential and fundamental definition of Americanism, it became impossible to be a friend and inhabitant of America without being a foe of Prussia & Prussianism. And so the inevitable occurred. Wilson, in deference to public sentiment and common reason, has seen the light at last, and America is assuming her rightful place by the side of the Mother Empire. It is with pride that I contemplate the visit of Mr. Balfour—a tangible link betwixt the old and the new English nations![2] As to the hitherto pro-German foreigners of the United States; I fancy that about seven-tenths of them are honestly converted, two-tenths reduced to a sort of conscientious harmlessness & inactivity, whilst the remaining tenth are under proper official surveillance—with restraint when necessary. A good case of actual conversion is afforded by one of the amateur journalists whose work you may have noticed—Rev. Eugene B. Kuntz, D.D., of Las Animas, Colorado. He is a native of Prussia, who was brought to America when two years old. His present age is about 53. During the early part of the war he was quite biased toward the land of his birth & ancestors; after the Lusitania atrocity he was rigidly neutral; but within the past few months he has come to appreciate the basic & incontrovertible justice of the Allied cause, and has gone so far in his atonement as to write patriotic poems, whose ardour & sincerity cannot be questioned. It is apparent that Germany has lost the support of her best descendants in other parts of the world—that she has become so completely an outlaw that even pan-Germanism is a vanished dream. In the last analysis, the Prussian bureaucracy is as much an enemy to Germany itself, as it is to the rest of the world!

Events on the battlefield are growing so encouraging that one is almost justified in believing the last stage of the conflict has commenced. I am sure that the combined efforts of England and America can check the disastrous effects of the submarine campaign till a decisive result shall have been attained on land. The greatest source of uncertainty is a separate peace on Russia's part, but that is balanced by the possibility, on the other side, of a separate peace for Austria. Meanwhile the neutrality of Spain hangs in the balance. But one thing is certain. Whatever be the duration & difficulties of the war, the world will not permit so monstrous a thing as Prussianism to survive. The Huns are doomed, and the sooner they realise it, the better for all concerned. Perhaps their next blow will come from within, for I cannot believe that the reports of strikes & labour troubles in and around Berlin are without great significance.

I will conclude by copying a piece of war verse which I wrote last January, and which will soon appear in one of the amateur magazines:

BRITANNIA VICTURA

by H. P. Lovecraft

———

When Justice from the vaulted skies
    Beheld the fall of Roman might,
She bade a nobler realm arise,
    To rule the world and guard the right:
She spake—and all the murm'ring main,
    Rejoicing, hail'd BRITANNIA'S reign!

The mind of Greece, the law of Rome,
    The strength of Northern climes remote,
On one fair Island made their home,
    And in one race their virtues wrote:
The blended glories of the past
    In ENGLAND evermore shall last!

Untrodden wilds beyond the sea,
    And savage hordes in lands unknown,
At ALBION'S touch rose great and free,
    And bless'd the pow'r of ENGLAND'S throne:
Discordant tribes, with strife o'er-run,
    Grew BRITONS, and join'd hands as one!

When Greed and Envy stand array'd,
    And madness threats a peaceful earth,
BRITANNIA'S sons with sacred blade
    Defend the soil that gave them birth:
Nor is their cause to that confin'd—
    They fight for Justice and Mankind!

> Though Fortune frown, and trials press,
>   Though toil and hardship weight the heart,
>   The dawn of Vict'ry soon will bless
>   Each BRITON who sustains his part:
>   For Heav'n's own pow'r is close ally'd
>   To Virtue's and BRITANNIA'S side!

With best wishes, & hoping to hear from you again,
            I remain
                Very sincerely yrs,
                    H P Lovecraft

P.S. I enclose my latest bit of verse—"April"—printed in the Providence Evening News. I fear its merit is but indifferent, for it was written quite hastily, and merely for my own pleasure.

Notes

1. Margaret Trafford also edited the *Little Budget of Knowledge and Nonsense,* in which she published several poems by HPL.
2. Arthur James Balfour, 1st Earl of Balfour (1848–1930), British Conservative politician, Prime Minister of the United Kingdom from July 1902 to December 1905. As Foreign Secretary he was notable for the Balfour Mission, an alliance-building visit to the U.S. in April 1917.

[8]   [ALS]

598, Angell St.,
Providence, R.I., U.S.A.,
Jany. 12, 1918.

My dear M^r· Harris:—

I was indeed pleased to receive your recent letter, & to learn that you have succeeded in entering something like military service. You will, in your present capacity, be just as important to the nation as you would be on the firing line. I am less fortunate than you, for my ill health is such that it condemns me to almost total inactivity. I am sorry to hear that you have been ill; & glad to know that you are now restored to usual, if not robust, health.

Regarding the interchange of magazines, I am a little puzzled as to the censorship regulations which are keeping some of the British amateur papers from America. I receive M'Keag's[1] *Spindrift* & Miss Trafford's *Little Budget* quite regularly; and lately two numbers of Herdman's *Poesy* arrived. Also— others in America have received Yaldren's *Mesopotamia Amateur.* Yet you find yourself unable to send *Interesting Items,* & McColl's *Scot* has ceased to reach me—though I hear it is still being issued. Censorship seems to be a complex & peculiar thing!

Under separate cover I am sending some of the magazines of the past year. The fact that you have not received them is probably due to your non-membership in the press associations. I enclose an application blank for the United, which I strongly hope you will use. I should much appreciate the honour of proposing your name, & trust you may decide to join.

The accompanying papers comprise all the duplicates I have, but I shall ask other publishers to remember you. Mr. Cook of Athol, Mass., is issuing a magnificent paper called *The Vagrant*, & will soon resume his older enterprise, *The Monadnock*. I think you must have received my *Conservative*, (I have issued none since July) but in case you did not, I am sending along another copy. I duly note your new address. The number of papers published lately has not been great; for the stress of war time has not only affected the purses of the amateurs, but has distracted much of their attention from the hobby.

News of the American amateur world is not very abundant, but a few items would doubtless interest you. We are not at all well represented in the war, though the number of soldier-members is increasing. Mr. Schilling, editor of the *Badger*, is now a photographer in the Aviation Corps of the Regular Army, in training at San Antonio, Texas. Mr. Moitoret, of the *Cleveland Sun*, is in the navy.[2] Mr. Kleiner, the poet, was drafted but exempted on account of defective vision—a trouble which now threatens to deprive him of all active occupations. Prof. McDonald, the critic, and myself, attempted to enlist; but were rejected. Many *former* amateurs whom you may remember, are in the service. Messrs. Darrow & Griffin of the old "Blarney Club" of Rocky Mount, N.C., are now 2nd Lieutenants.[3] Mr. Stewart of the same club is in the navy—as are the brothers of Mr. George Macauley.[4] The brother of Mrs. J. W. Renshaw is studying for a commission & will soon be a Lieutenant. William T. Harrington intends to enlist as soon as his affairs will allow him to do so. In his *Coyote* he calls himself a "Wilson conscript", but this is a mistaken use of the word. He has not been drafted, but is merely registered for the draft. Samuel J. Schilling, brother of George S., is a Lieutenant in the Veterinary Officers Reserve Corps, having studied veterinary surgery at college. Another Wisconsin member, Miss Merkel,[5] has a father now said to be in France as an officer in the so-called "Rainbow Division" of picked National Guard units; whilst Mr. Faville, also of Wisconsin, is with a National Guard regiment in Texas. Messrs. Thie and McKee[6] of Ohio are both in the service; the former in the Marine Corps and the latter with a Hospital Unit in France. It redounds to the credit of the United, that all our soldier-members are *volunteers*. None who was able to serve, waited for conscription. The only drafted man in amateur journalism is a Jew belonging to the National Association—the Jews are

not a very patriotic race.*[7] Of our Canadian members, both Messrs. Martin &
Kristjanson were wounded some time ago; but both are recovered. Messrs.
Spencer & Badke are in service and not reported injured. Many of the items I
have given are also in one of the papers I am sending you; but the mails are
so much less certain for printed matter, that I decided to include the news in
the letter. Probably some of the names are unfamiliar to you, but I made the
account complete lest something really interesting be omitted. A very interesting but less glorious thing, is the case of John T. Dunn, one of the Irishmen
of the Providence Club which I described to you a long time ago. As I then
said, I formerly endeavoured to help this humble society of would-be writers,
but was completely disgusted by their crude opinions and hatred of England.
Dunn was the brightest of all these Irishmen; not in any way cultured, of
course, but of keen intelligence and fair education for one of his class. He was
so bright in many ways, that I became quite interested in him; and conducted
a correspondence with him long after I had given up trying to civilise the others. I hoped to convert him from his pro-German & anti-British views, but
found him very obstinate & deaf to rational argument. When America entered the war, he became nearly as bitter against her as against England; and
vowed he should do nothing to help the cause. At that point I dropped the
correspondence altogether, for I saw the fellow was a hopeless case. The next
I heard of Dunn was in the papers—he had been arrested for failing to register for conscription! According to the news item, he maintained a defiant attitude and declared he would not fight under any circumstances. He was
forcibly registered. Then in July his name came up in the draft, and he was
again arrested—this time for refusing to report for military service. After
many legal steps, he was tried at Newport by court-martial and sentenced to
twenty years at hard labour in the Federal Prison at Atlanta, Georgia. He appealed from this sentence (which was for desertion) on the ground that the
military court had no jurisdiction over him; but the appeal was denied, & he is
now serving his long sentence. As reported in the press, his defence was conducted on "conscientious" and religious lines—which was absolutely menda-
cious, since Dunn is not at all opposed to warfare in general. It is strange to
think that this perverse slacker and traitor was once an amateur journalist. His
case received much publicity all over the United States, occupying heavy
headlines & receiving editorial comment. It is now frequently cited by anar-
chists & demagogues—who look upon Dunn as something of a "hero". He
has become the most famous—or notorious—amateur in existence, but few
will envy him his particular kind of "fame". He was fortunate not to be shot,
for an offence like his is a very grave thing. The war, before it is over, will
unmask many seditious persons of Dunn's type; and root out a great deal of

---

*I will make an exception of Lord Reading—whom I respect.

dangerous treachery. It may help in forming a definite homogeneity of thought which the States have hitherto lacked.

As for general amateur news—few very striking events present themselves for narration. I am now President of the United Association, & hope for a successful term. The National is headed by Mr. Henry E. Martin, editor of the excellent *Sprite,* a professor of English in Mt. Union College, Alliance, Ohio. His August *Sprite* was a paper of truly wonderful excellence. I advise you to write him for a copy. Mr. W. Paul Cook is returning to activity (as I said before) and is now the United's Official Publisher. He issued a splendid *United Amateur* for November, which I will send you if I can obtain an extra copy. Edward H. Cole has "come to life" with an issue of *The Olympian* and an issue of his smaller paper, *The Bema.* Rev. Graeme Davis of Vermillion, S.D. has returned, & is the National's Official Editor. The poet Samuel Loveman, after an absence of ten years, is once more on our membership lists; and is contributing some remarkable verse. He is a lover of antiquity, and writes largely in the Elizabethan style. Mr. Sargent of Ohio is issuing a remarkably meritorious paper—*The Adelphian,* whilst young James Mather Mosely continues his rather too commercialised *Phoenician.*[8] A remarkable new paper, *Eurus,* (the classical name of the eastern breeze) will soon appear from the pen of the poetess Mrs. Jordan, who is 2nd Vice-President of the United. This will be dedicated to amateurdom's oldest member—Mr. Jonathan E. Hoag, who is to reach his 87th birthday on Feb. 10. Mr. Hoag is a remarkable old gentleman—with faculties & poetic powers undimmed by the years. Going to the other extreme, amateurdom has discovered one of the most scintillantly brilliant youths alive—Alfred Galpin of Wisconsin, aged 16 years. This boy has all the culture & mental power of a grown man, and is a poet and philosophical thinker of the greatest depth and urbanity. He is 4th Vice-President of the United. The United has sought to increase its usefulness in many ways. Departments for keeping in touch with colleges & high-schools are being organised, whilst recruiting is being conducted among an excellent class of prospective members.

The *Brooklynite* I am sending, will inform you of the domestic events of many amateurs—especially the wedding of your former fellow-Briton, Mr. Ernest Dench. Mr. Dench is endeavouring to be so intensely American, that I find him even less of an Englishman than I—as I told him on the one occasion when I met him in person. Before the States entered the war, he strove to be "strictly neutral"—which I never was or could be. A more recent wedding of amateur interest is that of Paul J. Campbell, ex-President of the U.A.P.A., and Miss Eleanor Barnhart, our Treasurer,[9] which took place last November. Both appear to be satisfied with the step.

The secondary "United Association"—which consists of a faction which split off in 1912, & which insists on its right to use our name—is now almost extinct. Its leading local club is that in Montreal, and Mr. Cook believes he can persuade this club to transfer itself as a body to our Association.[10]

When I was elected to the Presidency, I resigned as chief critic, nominating Rheinhart Kleiner as my successor. He has done excellent work, but the recent failure of his sight forced him to abandon it for the present. Not finding any other critic available on short notice, I am doing the work myself again—though anonymously. I enclose one or two pieces of mine which appeared in the press lately. The "Winter Wish" was prompted by an extraordinarily cold spell which harassed New England just after Christmas. The thermometer descended to about -15° at one time. Our climate here is much more trying to endure than is yours. The extremes of winter cold & summer heat are very great. As one writer expressed it, "New England has the summers of Italy and the winters of Russia"—but that was really an exaggeration. I am a spasmodic & uneven worker, & am prone to make almost inexcusable delays—but I shall undoubtedly send you that "Tale of Two Cities" piece some day! As I said before, though, the result will give you many a trying hour over the type case; for the subject could not be handled with anything approaching brevity. A Christmas poem of 332 lines[11] is one of my recent efforts—and the "Two Cities" piece would undoubtedly exceed that compass.

As to the general situation today, I believe it is tense but not in any way hopeless. The collapse of Russia has increased the task immensely, as has the partial collapse of Italy, but I am sure no further disaster can occur till the American troops arrive; and these will eventually offset the loss of Russia and bring about victory. The enemy like to underestimate the ability of America to send a competent army; pointing out the pacifist & alien elements in the nation, which would apparently tend to decrease the fighting morale of the soldiers. But military science is more important than individual enthusiasm, and it is numbers that count; besides, the spirit of America has improved wonderfully within the last few months. Much of the seditious feeling formerly rampant, was of that ephemeral kind which comes from the perusal of inflammatory papers & articles. The publication of anti-government matter is now suppressed as far as possible, & the results have proved very gratifying. Without the usual incitements to discontent, the majority are behaving themselves very well—shewing that a great part of their agitation was not natural to them, but induced by a few disloyal workers. I think, indeed, that a partial censorship would not be out of place even in times of peace—it would mitigate restlessness & subdue anarchy. Another cause of improved American morale is the genuine awakening of the masses to the dangers of Prussianism. The common people are always selfish in a commercial nation. You could talk all day of outraged Belgium & menaced Europe to an audience of American workmen, without securing the slightest expression of sympathy—because they would not feel *themselves* concerned! But since the government hit upon the happy scheme of exposing the German plots discovered *in America* during recent years—especially the subtle villainy of von Bernstorff[12] & his system of hirelings—the people are beginning to believe & realise what they were too stupid to grasp before—that Germany actually is spreading her tentacles to the Western World, and seeking to undermine liberty, independence, & civilisation. We no longer have a legion of doubting, ignorant creatures who ask what they are fighting for. Our worst seditionist, Senator La Follette of Wisconsin, is losing his prestige, and will probably lose his seat in the Senate ere long.[13]

The longer the war progresses, the greater can we appreciate the *necessity* of an absolute victory. I am very glad that Wilson is awake at last, and delighted to see the harmony with which he works with Lloyd-George. A few years ago I admired neither of these men—I have always been a strong Conservative—but today I can honestly admire Lloyd-George, and at least feel no hostility toward Wilson—though I think he is infinitely less capable than his sturdy Welsh fellow-leader. Wilson, however, is valuable; for his rhetoric and *oratory* are peerless. Lloyd-George, the greater *man,* can enunciate the basic principles of polity; whilst Wilson, the greater *scholar,* can coin these principles into a form so captivating that they are quoted with admiration throughout the chancelleries of four continents. My old favourite, the Conservative party, is disappointing me—that is, if Lord Lansdowne represents it in any way.[14] Germany *absolutely must* be conquered; for now that Russia is no more, the influence of a victorious or even partially defeated Kaiser would be paramount throughout the Russian territories, creating a dangerous and well-nigh invincible empire stretching from Atlantic to Pacific. But I have no doubt that happily reunited Anglo-Saxondom can sooner or later end the menace!

Hoping to hear from you soon, I remain

Very sincerely yours,

H P Lovecraft

Notes

1. Ernest Lionel McKeag (1896–1974), English amateur journalist who began writing boys' fiction in 1921. Some of his novels are in the genre of science fiction.

2. Anthony F. Moitoret, Edwin D. Harkins, and William J. Dowdell were all editors of the *Cleveland Sun.*

3. Herbert Betts Darrow (1893–1989) and Wade Edward Griffin (1899–1980) were contributors to the *Blarney Stone.* The latter was the subject of HPL's satirical poems "On a Modern Lothario" and "Gryphus in Asinum Mutatus" (the latter unpublished in HPL's lifetime).

4. John Burr Stewart also contributed to the *Blarney Stone.* George W. Macauley (1885–1969) was coeditor with HPL of the *New Member* and an occasional correspondent of HPL. See "Extracts from H. P. Lovecraft's Letters to G. W. Macauley," *O-Wash-Ta-Nong* 3, No. 2 (Spring 1938): 1–4.

5. Gertrude L. Merkel of Appleton, WI. See HPL's brief discussion of a story she published in the *United Amateur* (*CF* 1.154), where he misspells her name as "Merkle."

6. HPL refers to John Faville of Appleton, WI; Harry C. Thie of Toledo; and Thomas McKee of Cleveland.

7. In the footnote HPL refers to Rufus Isaacs, 1st Marquess of Reading (1860–1935), at this time Lord Chief Justice of England (1913–21) and later Viceroy and Governor-General of India (1921–26).

8. Howard A. Sargent edited the *Adelphian*. HPL published the essay "The Truth about Mars" in Mather's *Phoenician* (Autumn 1917).

9. HPL wrote an essay on Eleanor J. Barnhart, "Little Journeys to the Homes of Prominent Amateurs" (*United Amateur*, July 1917; as by "El Imparcial").

10. The United Amateur Press Association of America, chiefly led by J. F. Roy Erford of Seattle, broke with the UAPA after the disputed election of 1912. HPL wrote two essays on the controversy, "The Pseudo-United" and "A Matter of Uniteds."

11. In fact, "Old Christmas" has only 322 lines.

12. Johann Heinrich, Graf von Bernstorff (1862–1939), ambassador to the U.S. (and Mexico), 1908–1917. While ambassador, he was involved in several intelligence and sabotage operations.

13. Robert Marion La Follette, Sr. (1855–1925), American Republican (and later Progressive) politician. He served as a member of the U.S. House of Representatives, was the governor of Wisconsin, and was a U.S. senator from Wisconsin from 1906 to 1925. He opposed the war and his statements about it were misquoted, and thus he was characterized as treasonous by speakers and editors across the nation. He ran for president of the United States as the nominee of his own Progressive Party in 1924.

14. Henry Charles Keith Petty-Fitzmaurice, 5th Marquess of Lansdowne (1845–1927), a distinguished English nobleman who reluctantly led the Unionists (the Conservative and Unionist peers) in passing the Parliament Act of 1911 that curtailed the House of Lords' veto power over legislation generated by the House of Commons. On 29 November 1917 he published the so-called Lansdowne letter, which advocated a negotiated peace with Germany.

[9]   [ALS]

598, Angell St.,

Providence, R.I., U.S.A.,

July 19, 1918.

My dear M^r. Harris:—

I was very glad to receive your recent letter and packet of *Interesting Items*. As a publisher you shew uncommon faithfulness through these stormy times, especially considering the military service you are rendering. Cannot Parks do your paper at fairly reasonable rates, now that he has a printing outfit?[1] Prices here are about as bad as in England, but W. Paul Cook's low prices have enabled me to issue a July *Conservative*, which you have doubtless received by this time. I trust you will like it. I suppose that by this time your postage has gone up to 1½d. In America, letter postage has been raised to this figure (3¢) since the first of last November. At first we thought it would interfere seriously with amateur journalism; but strangely enough, such has not proved the case. The mail is as bulky as ever, though I can certainly feel the added expense. I do not think any fears need be entertained concerning the survival of amateur journalism. The remarkable success of the Amateur Press Club even in these dark days is enough to prove the enduring vitality of the institution. I plan to enter quite thoroughly into the work of the A.P.C., & am preparing a MS. magazine called *Hesperia* for circulation in Great Britain.

I am sorry to hear of your afflicted hand, & am glad it is now so much better. I know what it is to be deprived of the use of the right hand, for I had a severe burn from phosphorus about eleven years ago—obtained in my chemical laboratory—which put the important member out of action for three months. My third finger yet bears the marks of this burn—at the time it was feared that I might lose it. I did most of my correspondence on the typewriter with my left hand, & even tried to scrawl with it, though the result was hardly ornamental. I am too nervous to do nothing. If unable to write, I am sure I do not know what would happen to me!

Cook's *Vagrant* is surely a wonderful publication. I do not think I exaggerate when I say it is the best & largest amateur magazine published today. I hope you received the large June issue. The July number is smaller, but I think the August number will be of good size. I doubt if Cook will, after all, revive *"The Monadnock"*. At least, he prefers not to do so unless he can have a 7 × 10 page, and follow the same plan he followed years ago in former issues. Just now he finds it best to issue the more informal *Vagrant*. He may increase the size of his page from 5 × 7 to 6 × 9. I wish I had some more duplicate papers to send you, but journals are scarce nowadays. Whenever I accumulate some, I shall send them along.

I trust the American soldiers you meet impress you favourably. I am not surprised that they express a desire to tour their great Motherland after the war. The only amateur from this side who has been in England is E. Bruce Chaplin, of the Canadian forces. He was down with mumps at an hospital in Essex, but is now—judging from a card I received—in France. Relatively few of the leaders of American amateurdom have been able to get into the service—we seem to be too feeble, too old, or something of the sort. W. Paul Cook has been twice rejected, as have I.

The United's high-school & college recruiting work has not progressed quite as well as we wished, owing to the inability of one of our officials to attend to the matter. We hope for better results next year. The Scouts have frequently been thought of, though many have claimed that they are not so literary, on the whole, as students. We are anxious to maintain a very high standard of scholarship. Attempts at re-uniting with the other "United Association" have proved unavailing. The two seem to have drifted apart rather widely in spirit, and exhibit little desire for reconciliation.

Before sealing this letter, I shall try to enclose a verse contribution of the length you desire. I shall also call the attention of others to your lack of copy, & fancy that you will not long be without enough to fill your paper. Over here the problem is to find space enough to print all the MSS. that flood the various bureaux.

I have received several British magazines lately—*Rosemary, Fairy,* & *Vanity Fair,* the latter for June. Miss Trafford has sold *The Little Budget* to Mr. J. Hull Goss, an old-time amateur, and I am led to believe it will appear this autumn in unusual splendour. I am trying to recruit Mr. Goss for the United. And this reminds me—would you not care to join? I enclose a blank, which I hope you may find yourself able to use in the near future.

I must ask you to pardon a most dry & unsatisfactory letter, since I am in a whirlwind of bustle, ending up the duties of my Presidential year. The annual election takes place on Monday next, and I am expecting to see Mr Kleiner made my successor. I had the pleasure of spending an entire day with this gifted poet three weeks ago. He is a most delightful person.

With best wishes, & hoping to hear from you whenever you find it convenient to write, I remain

Most sincerely yours,

H. P. Lovecraft

Notes

1. Joseph Parks of Saltburn-by-the-Sea, Yorkshire, editor of the amateur journal *Vanity Fair.*

[10] [ALS, 10 pp., not seen]

[1 December 1918]

[11] [ALS]

598, Angell St.,
Providence, R.I.,
Decr 13, 1918.

My dear Mr Harris:—

Since you stated your intention of joining the United upon the conclusion of the war, I shall open this letter with one of our new application blanks; for surely the armistice of last month leaves but little doubt of the thorough thrashing & elimination from belligerent existence of that inhuman nation which was so lately the powerful & common enemy of civilized mankind. It was hard to believe at first that the beast could succumb so suddenly—but a few days showed the facts which many had long suspected; namely, that Germany, like other bullies, is a coward at heart, and ready to cringe in submission as soon as the fortune of war turns adversely. So today the rampant, ravaging Hun is no more, & we have instead, a maudlin, whining, whimpering foe; abject in its utter defeat, and crawling cravenly at our feet—

begging for food and easier terms, as if we could forget its former atrocities & attempts to starve us with its submarines! The Kaiser & his precious Crown-Princeling[1] might have preserved at least a shadow of that dignity which is supposed to envelop even defeated & exiled royalty—but they failed to do so. Napoleon in just exile is a manly figure as compared with these Hohenzollern warlords who now babble babyishly to press correspondents about their innocence, & prattle of how they were forced by others into everything they did. And to crown it all—Little Friedrich-Willie's dominant thought is not about his crimes & fall at all—he is most anxious to eat sparingly and "preserve his slender sportsman's figure!" The tragedy of nations ends in a cheap farce—with Big and Little Willie as clowns! The future, however, has its difficulties. Armies must long be retained on the continent to restore order & check the rise of that insidious anarchy which took its rise in Russia. Then there are rival claims to be adjusted. Happily enough, the three major nations, Great Britain, France, & America, have no conflicting interests; but in the east the situation is less encouraging. The new Polish, Bohemian (Czecho-Slovak) and Ukrainian nations will create many disputes before their permanent boundaries are adjusted; whilst the differences of greater Serbia (Jugo-Slavia) & Italy furnish a still more delicate problem. On account of Italy's high civilisation & historic past, we are inclined to be pro-Italian in any question involving that country against a relatively unknown Eastern race; yet the Jugo-Slavs' claim must not be dismissed without investigation. Russia itself is a vast problem. I see no possible solution save a forcible Anglo-Franco-American military occupation & supervision for a long period of years, until the Bolsheviki shall have been subdued, & a responsible representative government placed in power. As for the German & Austrian empires—I confess I do not care much what becomes of them, so long as they cease to trouble the outside world. If they all turn Bolsheviki & kill one another off, so much the better! I am not like our fellow-amateur McKeag, who looks forward to a League of Nations whereof purified, reformed, & democratised Germany shall be a constituent part!

I appreciate very much the interesting bundle of *Interesting Items* which accompanied your letter. To combine military service with publishing activity is certainly unusual, & you are to be sincerely congratulated on your enterprise. I am glad *The Conservative* reached you safely, & am herewith enclosing the very latest amateur publication—*The United Coöperative*—of which I am serving as managing editor. I expect to be able to issue this regularly in future, with the assistance of other members of the United.

Hesperia, my MS. magazine, has probably reached you by this time. I fear it will prove rather a disappointment, for it seems somewhat lacking in interest. McKeag says that the younger members find it rather obscure. I shall try to do better in future issues, one of which I am now planning. Its leading feature will be an able reply by McKeag to the sociological article of Mr. Temple.

I hope for a general revival of MS. magazines, though very few are appearing on this side of the Atlantic.

Mr. Cook has *not* issued a *Vagrant* since the July number. In September his plans were totally disarranged by the wave of Spanish Influenza which swept the country, & he has been forced to defer the magazine till January. The same applies to Mr. Moloney's *Voice from the Mountains*.[2] Both journals, however, will seem very impressive & will receive a warm welcome when they do appear. Other journals will shortly spring into existence—all of which you will be certain of receiving if you join the United.

I trust the censorship on British mail may soon relax far enough to let all the amateur journals past. As it is, I have received none save the present assortment of I. I. since last spring. I must have missed a vast number, but Parks says he is saving up *Vanity Fair* for me. Do you receive C. W. Smith's *Tryout* regularly? In the December issue will appear one of my longest pieces of verse—"Old Christmas"—describing the good old feasts & ceremonies of a hearty Yuletide celebration on a prosperous country estate in Queen Anne's reign. It is in heroic couplets, like most of my verse, & contains 332 lines.

A plan has been set on foot by James F. Morton, Jr., (one of our most scholarly members—Harvard M.A.) to combine the United & National Associations on strictly equal terms in one entirely new "North American Amateur Press Association." Without a doubt the design is impracticable and impossible of adoption; but I favour an unrestricted discussion, since it will tend to promote a better mutual understanding & appreciation on the part of the two rival societies. Something is needed to counteract the rash & tactless utterances of Rev. Graeme Davis, present head of the National, who displays an arrogance savouring of Kaiserism.

But I must close, hoping to hear from you both by letter & by future issues of *Interesting Items*. Trusting you may like the enclosed *Co-operative*, & hoping you will now join the United, I remain

> Most sincerely yours,
>
> H. P. Lovecraft

Notes

1. Friedrich Wilhelm Victor August Ernst, German Crown Prince (1882–1951), who with his father, Kaiser Wilhelm II, signed the document of abdication on 9 November 1918 and left Germany. He was interned on the island of Wieringen, in the Netherlands. He was allowed to return to Germany in 1923.

2. James Joseph Moloney, W. Paul Cook's compositor at the *Athol Transcript* and editor of *Voice from the Mountains*. HPL published "On a Battlefield in Picardy" and "Ver Rusticum" in the paper.

[12]   [ALS]

[THE UNITED AMATEUR PRESS ASSOCIATION . . .]
598, Angell St.,
Providence, R.I.,
Septr 11, 1919.

Dear Mr Harris:—

I was very pleased to receive your recent letter with interesting enclosures, & have duly forwarded the membership application to the new Secretary—Mrs. Ida C. Haughton, 1526 Summit St., Columbus, Ohio.[1] I am glad to welcome you as a full-fledged member of the United, & hope that your affiliation may prove permanent. Regarding the National association, I have nothing to do with that society, but believe the Secretary is Miss Marjorie H. Outwater, Parker Hill Ave., Roxbury, Mass. She would doubtless be glad to furnish you with any information you might desire.

I can well imagine the relief you must have experienced on being released from hospital work. The scenes must have been depressing in the extreme, so that to a person of nervous temperament the life would be well-nigh impossible.

Your faithful publication of *Interesting Items* throughout your period of military service is indeed an achievement of which you may well be proud. Few, even amidst more favourable circumstances, have so long & regularly maintained a fixed schedule of publication. Amateurdom has reason to be grateful to you.

I trust you are now duly receiving most of the American amateur publications. Last July I sent you a *Conservative* & other papers; the *Conservative* being the only one I have issued since 1918. I am sorry to hear that *Tryout* comes so infrequently, & am sending you some sheets containing pieces of mine. You will note the long Christmas poem of which I spoke some time ago. The publishing programme for next year looks fairly bright, Cook planning many issues of his *Vagrant.*

Just now there is considerable hostility within the United, as a result of the activities of a group of commonplace & troublesome politicians in Cleveland, Ohio. This undesirable clique, which issues a paper called *The Cleveland Sun,* tried last July to elect one of their number—an ignorant fellow named Dowdell—to the Official Editorship.[2] I did my best, of course, to stop this disaster; & succeeded in securing Dowdell's defeat by a vote of 22 to 7 by exhibiting his bad past record in the association. The Cleveland clique is now furious at me, & is doing its worst to attack me; but so weak are its arguments, that I have little cause to worry.

Now that you are a United member, you will receive the official organ regularly; & I hope you may find it interesting. If you have not the issues for 1918–19, I can supply you.

With all best wishes, & again expressing my pleasure at your advent to the United, I remain

Sincerely yours,

H P Lovecraft

Notes

1. Ida C. Haughton (1860–1934), amateur journalist and foe of HPL, about whom HPL wrote the satiric poem "Medusa: A Portrait" (1921).
2. William J. Dowdell was the editor of the *Cleveland Sun* and *Dowdell's Bearcat.* For HPL's arguments against him, see "For Official Editor: Anne Tillery Renshaw."

[13]   [ALS]
[THE UNITED AMATEUR PRESS ASSOCIATION . . .]
598, Angell St.,
Providence, R.I.,
Jany 19, 1920.

Dear Mʳ· Harris:—

I am greatly indebted to you for the many copies of *Interesting Items,* & wish to express my unstinted thanks therefor. Your stories are very good—especially the Christmas tale, which has a genuinely original twist. I should advise you to print more of your own work, since you do so well in fictional composition. Of late I have been devoting most of my time to fiction also, though my stories are of a different kind—weird & imaginative. I am following the example of Lord Dunsany, whom I admire very much, & whom I heard lecture in Boston last October. Have you read anything of Dunsany's? I think you would enjoy his fantastic tales if you are in the least fond of imaginative literature.

Let me congratulate you on the merit of your paper. The Christmas number is delightful, whilst your typographical accuracy remains undiminished. There are no errors in my "Earth and Sky." The idea of giving the service record of all the British amateurs is a splendid one. I wish some one would perform a similar task for the American amateurs, although the result would be less impressive; since none of our leaders succeeded in getting into action.

Under separate cover I am sending the U.A. for Septʳ 1918; which is, unfortunately, the only issue for that year of which I have a duplicate. When I wrote you, I meant that I could supply papers for the *official year 1918–19*—beginning Septʳ 1918. I have none earlier. Since I wrote, I have evidently mislaid my extra Nov. '18 copy, for the Sept. copy is the only one available. I can supply May, July, Sept. & Nov. 1919 copies—but I presume you have these*. The policy of the official organ is a trifle changed under Mrs. Renshaw's editorship—it inclines more toward professionalism. I regret this alteration, but will not complain so long as a high standard is maintained. There will be suf-

*Sept. & Nov. were late. If they fail to come, notify Cook or myself.

ficient cause for gratitude if we can keep the U.A. out of the hands of Dowdell & his vulgar Cleveland clique, who wish to drag it down to their own
primitive standard.

I hope to hear encouraging news of the revived B.A.P.A. Reports up to
this winter have been deeply pessimistic, but a ray of hope seemed to be shed
by McKeag's mention of running for the official editorship. In America there
is much activity of a sort—many new members—but lamentably few publications. I hope to issue a *United Coöperative* in the near future, but cannot publish
a *Conservative* until next summer at least.

I am glad you enjoyed "Old Christmas" in last December's *Tryout*. It is
the longest—or next the longest—piece of verse I have ever written,[1] & sums
up fairly well my sensations & hereditary impressions of the festive Yuletide
season. It was this year reprinted in a professional magazine—*The National
Enquirer.*

With all good wishes, & hoping to receive *I. I.* regularly, I remain

Most sincerely yours,

H. P. Lovecraft

Notes

1. "Old Christmas" (322 lines) is in fact longer than the other long poems HPL had
written up to this time, "The Poe-et's Nightmare" (302 lines) and "Psychopompos: A
Tale in Rhyme" (312 lines).

[14]   [ALS]

[UNITED AMATEUR PRESS ASSOCIATION
Office of]
Asst.
[Official Editor . . .]

598 Angell St., Providence, R.I.,
May 16, 1920.

Dear M^r. Harris:—

I hope I am not too late in proffering remarks on *Interesting
Items,* to be printed in N°. 500. The following paragraph expresses my sentiments, & may possibly prove acceptable to you.

"I sincerely congratulate the Editor of *Interesting Items* on the issuance of
the 500th number of his attractive publication. Such fidelity to the cause of
amateur journalism is quite unique; & when we recall that the paper was issued regularly throughout the war despite its Editor's military service, we
cannot but think the case a truly marvellous one. To my knowledge, no other
amateur journal has ever reached its 500th number. It is my hope that the
magazine may extend to on many multiples of 500; increasing in size &
quality as it has in the past, & continuing to please its readers & to reflect

credit upon its Editor & amateurdom alike."

H. P. LOVECRAFT.[1]

Your Jany. & Feby. issues are excellent. I trust you will call upon our MS. Managers, Misses Hamlet & Zeeb, whenever you need copy.[2]

Before long I hope to issue a *United Coöperative,* but doubt if I can manage a *Conservative* this year. I am exceedingly busy of late with professional verse revision.

With best wishes & felicitations,

Believe me

Most sincerely yrs H. P. Lovecraft

Notes

1. It is not clear whether this letter was actually published in *Interesting Items.*
2. For Alice M. Hamlet, see 58n3. The other is Olga Zeeb of Milwaukee, WI.

[15]   [ALS]

598 Angell St.,

Providence, R.I.,

May 1, 1921.

Dear Mr Harris:—

Let me thank you for the recent copies of *Interesting Items,* including the fateful 500th issue, as well as for the interesting letter in which they were enclosed. I am glad to see your journal continuing on its prosperous way despite the scarcity of other publications. The photograph in No. 500 is very pleasing, & ought to prove highly prepossessing to your readers.

I am grateful for your kindly mention of my fictional efforts, & will be delighted to let I. I. have any specimen which is not too long for printing. But here is the difficulty—for very few fully developed stories are short enough for inclusion in one issue of your regular size, whilst serial publication mars a thing of this sort hopelessly. The only tale of mine to be published in sections is "Arthur Jermyn", & this was written with that form in mind. I have nothing like that on hand now. Still, in case you can think of some way to handle a long story, I am enclosing a fairly recent one entitled "From Beyond". If it is too long, or in any other way unsuited to your needs, do not hesitate to return it. I have more material on hand than the amateur press could ever find space to publish, & suppose the majority of my attempts will never see type. Some day I will try to write a short piece especially for publication in your journal. At present nearly all the amateurs have work of mine on hand, awaiting publication. Cook has a hideously gruesome thing—"The Picture in the House".

I am glad to observe the various improvements in *Interesting Items,* & hope that some time you may secure the leisure to enlarge it as you desire. Your unique fidelity to the amateur cause certainly deserves some distinguished reward! The greatest hope of British amateurdom at present would appear to be affiliation with the U.A.P.A. That is what I am advocating in *Hesperia,* & I am glad to see that McKeag is seconding me in *The Northumbrian.* As to *Hesperia,* I do not know exactly when I shall issue another number; but hope to put forth copies from time to time, even if at considerable intervals. There will soon appear a *United Coöperative* which I am editing, & I trust you are regularly receiving the *United Amateur*—that is, as regularly as it is published. The only issues this term have been September & November—that for January is now in the press. I regret deeply the conditions which have forced a drop from the quantitative standard of former years, but can hardly suggest any remedy.

I am vastly sorry to say that I have no duplicate copies of the *United Amateur* for March 1920. At present my only duplicates are for May 1920 (the worst misprinted issue in our history—too bad to use in recruiting) & March 1919—and the supply of the latter will soon be exhausted.

With all good wishes, & hoping you will find the enclosed tale of some interest, I remain

Sincerely yours,

H. P. Lovecraft

[16]   [ALS]

[THE UNITED AMATEUR PRESS ASSOCIATION . . .]

Novr 10, 1921

My dear Mr Harris:—

I am tardy in not having thanked you sooner for the letter & copies of I. I. which came last summer; but have been abysmally busy with both amateur & professional writing, & in miserable health.

Use "From Beyond" if convenient to do so in one issue, but do not over-exert yourself in issuing a specially large number on my account. Some time I may have something a bit shorter, & you can return the present tale if you like. I have not written as much as I should like lately—I have finished two of a series of six ghastly stories for a new professional publication;[1] but do not reckon these with my really artistic fiction, since made-to-order stuff is seldom of much literary value. I am trying to improve my work, & have laid aside two of my older stories for "repairs". Fortunately they were both unpublished. "From Beyond" I like as well as anything of mine except "Randolph Carter" & possibly "Dagon". Cook used both of these in his *Vagrant.*

About copy for I. I.—unfortunately the best things on hand here are too long for your purposes. I enclose some short things, & recommend that you seek more from our MS. Mgr, Miss Bromley.[2]

Enclosed is *The United Coöperative,* which I am issuing. Later I shall have a *Conservative* to send.

With all good wishes,

Most sincerely yours,

H P Lovecraft

Notes

1. "Herbert West—Reanimator," for *Home Brew* (published as "Grewsome Tales").
2. Grace M. Bromley of Washington, DC.

[17]   [ALS]

598 Angell St.,

Providence, R.I.,

March 15, 1922

My dear Mr Harris:—

Many thanks for the copies of *Interesting Items*. My own journal is delayed discouragingly, but I think I can bring forth two numbers of exceptional worth—June & July 1922—each by a different printer.[1] I shall mail them together. I trust the *United Amateur* continues to reach you—the latest is dated November. January copy is now in the press, & ought to prove fairly acceptable.

There is no hurry about "From Beyond"—do as you like with it. I write more junk than the whole amateur press could ever publish—it will never see print, but I am not vastly disturbed thereat. As I grow older I care less & less about publicity & print—such things do not amount to much in the end.

I am glad you like the *United Coöperative*, late as it is. The bulk of the edition is not mailed even yet—I plan to mail it with the two *Conservatives*. I see the British association is picking up—Lecoq sent me the new organ.[2] I wish it all possible good luck.

With thanks & good wishes, believe me

Most sincerely yours,

H P Lovecraft

Notes

1. In fact, the last two issues of the *Conservative* came out in March and July 1923.
2. Robert D. Roosma Le Cocq, of Worthing, Sussex, editor of *Le Cocq's Comment*.

[18]   [ALS]

[THE PROVIDENCE BILTMORE . . .]
598 Angell St.,
Providence, R.I.,
Jany 26, 1923

Dear Mr. Harris:—

Let me thank you for the papers received, which are all excellent. After all, I am having to postpone my amateur retirement; since when I was in New York I let Houtain, James F. Morton, & others persuade me into taking the presidency of the National to replace Dowdell. It is a trying & arduous job, & I doubt if I shall get any substantial results after the year's bad start; but I can at least do my best. The enclosed appeal is what I have been sending to all the members. We must surely manage to secure a revival somehow! I hope the B.A.L.A.[1] is prospering—I received its prosperous-looking official organ recently.

I hope you can travel in America some time. I, for my part, would like to see England & Europe generally; for *old* things—architecture & general antiquities—are what interest me. The other day I went to Marblehead, Mass., a town which has not changed much in 200 years. That is the only place of its kind in America, but I dare say England has scores of villages just as they were 200, 300, 400, or even 500 years ago.

Have you any *Roman* remains in your district? I was reading a story by Arthur Machen the other day,[2] & gained the idea that Wales is quite rich in these interesting antiquities.

Thanking you again for the papers, I remain
Sincerely yours,
H P Lovecraft

Notes

1. The British Amateur Literary Association, the successor to the B.A.P.A.
2. HPL had read Machen's *The House of Souls,* lent to him by Frank Belknap Long.

[19]   [ALS]

[THE Robt Morris HOTEL
17TH AND ARCH STREETS
Philadelphia, Pa.]

259 Parkside Ave.,
Brooklyn, N.Y.,[1]
July 22, 1924

Dear Mr. Harris:—

I should have replied sooner to your appreciated letter; but many events such as a little matrimony & much work have tended to delay my correspondence. Let me at this date thank you for the piquant numbers of *Interesting Items,* & wish for that periodical a long future & ever-increasing bulk.

I shall certainly be glad to see you if ever you strike America; & shall be interested in your impressions of the New World. The Providence mentioned in your book is indeed my native city—for although other towns of the name exist, there is none of even approximately equal prominence, & none in any way related to Roger Williams. Though now in New York, I hope to return to Providence some day; for it has a quiet dignity I have never elsewhere observed save in some of the Massachusetts coast towns. Some day I'll shew you a vast array of pictures of Old Providence—for much of the 18th century architecture is yet standing. I certainly envy you your sight of the Old English countryside. I know it only in pictures—which suggest just enough to tantalise one. Fancy being within reach of Roman remains! It makes my mouth water! Carnavon [*sic*][2] must be alluring. I hear also that Caerleon-on-Usk, the ancient *Isca Silurum,* is a veritable treasure-house of antiquity, although now only a small village.

New York has more old things—that is, 18th century things—than one would expect. I have found many districts savouring strongly of George II's & George III's time, whilst of individual buildings there are several fine specimens.

Did you receive the new *United Amateur?* We're trying to float the old U.A.P.A., though it's in a sad state.

With all good wishes, believe me,

> Most sincerely yours,
>
> H P Lovecraft

Notes

1. The address was that of the residence of HPL's new wife, Sonia H. Greene.

2. HPL's error for Carnarvon (now Caernarfon), a port in the province of Gwynedd in Wales.

[20]   [ALS]

> [Hotel Sinton / Cincinnati]
> 169 Clinton St.,
> Brooklyn, N.Y.,
> March 12, 1925

Dear Mr. Harris:—

You must pardon my tardy reply to your letter & the interesting envelope of *Items,* but many events have conspired to disrupt my correspondence. Amateurdom is in a bad way, & I expect to issue my final *United Amateur* this spring. After that, it will have to proceed from other hands if at all.

I was greatly interested in the remarks & cuttings anent Roman ruins, &

wish that I might some day be able to see these things for myself. I wish, also, that all the towns in this belt of antiquities might have suitable museums, as I understand is the case at Caerleon-on-Usk. You were lucky to get a chance at holding that Roman coin. I have several Roman coins, including two or three of Roman Britain; but the greatest fascination must come from seeing the thing fresh from its long burial—as Sir Thomas Browne saw the funerary urns dug up at Norfolk, & was thereby moved to write his "Hydriotaphia".[1]

As for me, I continue to console myself with such 18th—and sometimes 17th—century scenes as pass in this parvenu region for "antiquities". Most of the Georgian buildings of New York City are familiar to me, & my recent explorations have taken me through most of the old towns of Staten Island & the New Jersey coast. I enclose some things relating to these—as well as some matter about museums, which are especially rich in relics of a more colourful age.

Occasionally I extend my pilgrimages to farther regions. Last November I was in Philadelphia—metropolis of the colonial period—for several days, & obtained vast pleasure from the many surviving remnants of the 1700's. Soon I shall visit Washington D.C., spending much time in the colonial suburb of Alexandria, & at Gen. Washington's estate, Mt. Vernon.

I am now living in a fairly old neighbourhood—the oldest part of Brooklyn—built up about 1830 or 1840, where vistas of brick & brownstone crown the crest of a high bluff overlooking New York Harbour. My street is three squares inland, but our fellow-amateur Samuel Loveman dwells in a house on the crest itself, with a bow-window overlooking the bay & the fairylike skyline of Manhattan Island. The Blue Pencil Club enjoys your *I. I.* as much as you enjoy their Brooklynite, & is very keen in its appreciation of the vitality you are contributing to amateur journalism.

With every good wish,
     believe me,
          Most sincerely yours,
               H P Lovecraft

Notes

1. Sir Thomas Browne (1605–1682), English polymath and author of works in diverse fields including science and medicine, religion and the esoteric. *Hydriotaphia: Urn Burial, or a Brief Discourse of the Sepulchral Urns Lately Found in Norfolk* (1658) was inspired by the discovery of Bronze Age burials in earthenware vessels, resulting in a literary meditation upon death and the ephemerality of fame.

[21] [ALS]

[~~George W. Kirk~~
~~Bookseller~~
169 CLINTON STREET
BROOKLYN, N. Y.]

Decr. 6, 1925

Dear Mr. Harris:—

I was very glad to hear from you & to see the copies of *Interesting Items*. There's no need to worry because the paper can't be enlarged— its size gives it a very quaint aspect, & its faithful appearance year in & year out makes it something of an institution. Nowadays one does well if one can issue any paper at all!

As for American amateurdom—I can't say that I see much improvement, though the United means to make a desperate effort at recuperation. We elected a fine official board last July, but have lately been held up by the inexcusable delay of a printer & the illness of our Secretary—Howard R. Conover.[1] As soon as possible we shall get another printer & resume our progress—which reminds me that you might be interested in getting in touch with our present leader & Official Editor—Victor E. Bacon, 5932 Wells Ave., St. Louis, Mo. He was born on your side of the Atlantic, within sight of the old monastery ruins at Glastonbury.

Thanks enormously for the cuttings. I envy you folk in the Motherland who always have the alluring possibility of being able to dig up mediaeval abbeys & Roman baths in your gardens! This Cluniac priory must be a very important discovery, & I congratulate the man whose enterprise pushed through the excavation so successfully. Of Leptis Magna I've heard considerable. This is certainly a great day for archaeology—& North Africa is getting an unusual share of attention. I suppose you've read from time to time of the explorations of Count de Prorock [*sic*] in the Sahara & on the site of ancient Carthage.[2]

My own humble pursuit of the antique in America has continued steadily but not spectacularly. Lately I've touched a territory hitherto new to me—the towns on Long Island east of Brooklyn, some of which are being gradually engulfed by the spreading city, but others of which are still wholly or partly independent. Most of them have interesting Georgian churches, & in one— Flushing—there is a house built in 1661 & a Quaker meeting-house built in 1694. In this same village is a rock marking the spot where George Fox preached on June 7th, 1672. Flushing is still very free from the New York atmosphere & influence, but will probably become definitely suburbanised next year, when an extension of the city's elevated railway system will reach it. Jamaica—which has a fine old mansion built in 1750—has already succumbed. The place freest of all from urban atmosphere is Hempstead, (apparently a corruption of Hampstead) which lies 25 miles from New York. There one may still find the real village life, with little old white houses & a population descended from the original settlers. How long this idyllic spot will resist the onrush of the metropolis one can't say—it seems secure now, yet there are already proposed extensions of the city limits that would include it[.]

Yes—I fancy you might enjoy the Blue Pencil meetings. What I like even better are the weekly conclaves of a still smaller group—all men—whose interests are more literary than social. Of this group you will recognise the names of several as also connected with amateurdom—James F. Morton, Rheinhart Kleiner, Samuel Loveman, Frank B. Long Jr., &c. Long is about to issue a small bound book of his poetry, to be printed by our amateur friend W. Paul Cook of Athol, Mass.

Speaking of Cook—he is about to retire from organised amateurdom in order to engage in publishing enterprises of a little higher literary grade—books, & a quarterly magazine to be called *The Recluse*. But before he leaves he will discharge all obligations & accomplish a magnificent farewell gesture by issuing a monstrous *Vagrant* of **312 pages**—so far as I know the largest single publication ever produced in the history of amateur journalism. It will not, however, have a high literary quality; since it will embrace any & all MSS. he may happen to have on hand from the various members.

With all good holiday wishes, & trusting that *Interesting Items* may have as great & lasting a prosperity in the future as in the past, I remain

Most cordially & sincerely yrs—

H. P. Lovecraft

Notes

1. Howard R. Conover (1900–1980) was an amateur journalist from Ohio, part of the faction in the UAPA hostile to HPL's "literary" faction.
2. "Count" Byron Khun de Prorok (1896–1954), Polish-American amateur archaeologist, anthropologist, and author of four heroic travelogues. In the late 1920s and early 1930s, he undertook expeditions in Africa pursuing ancient legends and eventually claimed to have found evidence that Atlantis lay in North Africa and the location of the Biblical land of Ophir. HPL read his *Digging for Lost African Gods: The Record of Five Years Archaeological Excavation in North Africa,* with notes and translations by Edgar Fletcher Allen (New York: London: G. P. Putnam's Sons, 1926).

[22]   [ALS]

[GEORGE KIRK
Dealer in Rare Books and Modern First Editions
1894 Charles Road / Cleveland, O.]
169 Clinton St.,
Brooklyn, N.Y.,
Feby. 9, 1926.

Dear Mr. Harris:—

Many thanks for the lively little issues of *Interesting Items*. Long may the paper flourish—& may it live to see a day of generally renewed activity in amateurdom. American amateurdom is sadly languishing, though perhaps there is more hope of a revival than there was when I last wrote. A September *United Amateur* is out, & one for November–January will follow as soon as we can command the necessary finances. A new printer has been secured to replace the one whose tardiness so gravely hampered us, & in general we shew signs of achieving by next July the same all-around revival which we had hoped to establish last summer. The National, too, manages to get along; & has had somewhat better luck than ours with its official organ. Of the various local clubs only the Blue Pencil of Brooklyn seems to be holding its own. I attended its last meeting & found it very prosperous, & shall try to attend its annual dinner next Saturday evening. Let us hope that times of greater activity lie ahead for both British & American amateurdom—as perhaps they do, after all, since taste is as likely to swing one way as the other.

Yes—the destruction of old & historic edifices is certainly an evil greatly to be deplored, & I am glad that Great Britain has a society working to counteract this tendency. We have a very effective Society for the Preservation of New England Antiquities, & in certain cities & towns local organisations (like the Essex Institute in historic Salem) act capably in combating wanton change & safeguarding ancient buildings & traditions. New York's orgy of utilitarian destruction has twice been checked of late—the old Georgian town house of President James Monroe having been saved & restored, & the country-seat of Alexander Hamilton (long ago overtaken by the expansion of the city) likewise rescued from commercial vandalism.

Cook's large *Vagrant* is now all printed, but has not yet been bound & distributed. Meanwhile he is active as a book publisher, & has brought out an exquisite little edition of Frank B. Long's poems, which Long is selling at a dollar per copy. He will next issue in book form an edition of Samuel Loveman's long classic poem, "The Hermaphrodite", with a preface by the well known poet & critic Benjamin de Casseres. I read proof on the Long book, & shall do the same with Loveman's.

I'm sorry you lack a March 1920 United Amateur, & will ask editors to mention that fact in their columns, on the chance that some reader may be able to supply you. So far, despite diligent inquiries, I have not encountered an available copy; but a published notice might bring results.

But I must close, since I am this week fairly engulfed in a vortex of unperformed tasks. Best wishes to you & *Interesting Items,* & may both flourish valiantly till the rest of amateurdom catches up & justifies your lone vigil!

Hoping to see more of your vivacious & entertaining issues,

  I remain

    Most sincerely & cordially yours,

    H P Lovecraft

[23]   [ALS]

[~~GEORGE KIRK~~
~~*Dealer in Rare Books and Modern First Editions*~~
~~1894 Charles Road / Cleveland, O.~~]
note new   10 BARNES St.,
address   Providence, R.I.,
April 25, 1926

My dear Mr. Harris:—

I was exceedingly grateful for your letter with its generous enclosures, & can scarcely express how delighted I am to see the conjectural picture of Roman London. I had heard of the discovery of the forum, but did not understand the topography in detail as I now do with the aid of the artist. Certainly, all these Roman remains make one feel distressingly "parvenu" in the United States, where anything before 1800 is an "antiquity," & where a 17th century structure is hailed as well-nigh prehistoric! As to the threatened engulfment of Caerleon—I am infinitely distressed to think that this richly historic & wildly beautiful region, made famous in our generation by Arthur Machen, is menaced by the crawling octopus of commercial progress. The one consolation is that archaeologists will explore the choicest points before it is too late—& I shall be intensely curious to learn what the uncovering of the amphitheatre will bring to light.

I was glad, as usual, to receive the issues of *Interesting Items,* & congratulate you again upon your enterprise & perseverance. It was good of you to reprint the United appeal—an appeal as pertinent today as two years ago. Yes—I have noticed the recent evidences of activity in British amateurdom, & wish that some of its spirit might creep across the Atlantic. Our young editor Victor E. Bacon is doing his best, but he has a frightful burden of general apathy & impecuniousness to contend with. I shall still try to get you a March 1920 U.A., though copies seem almost impossible to discover.

As you will note by the present date-line, I have lately returned permanently to my own town after two years in the New York region. The more I saw of New York, the less I liked it. It is crude, overgrown, & so filled with heterogeneous & inferior foreigners that scarcely anything of the old Anglo-American spirit is left. Everything there seems vulgar in comparison with my native New England, so this spring I decided to go back for good. I have secured modest quarters in an excellent & ancient neighbourhood on the brow of Providence's great hill, from which, to the westward, I can see all of the lower town & the rural hills beyond. The adjacent houses are mostly of Georgian style & date—wood or brick, & set each in its own green & shady yard. One of these is a splendid modern reproduction of an English manor-house of Queen Anne's or King William III's time. Only a few squares away is the great domed Christian Science church—a pure Roman edifice which dominates the entire Providence skyline. It is delightful to be back home again, & most of the changes I have found have been for the better. Today marks the opening of the new art museum, which I shall attend. The building is an exquisite specimen of Georgian architecture.

Yes—I attended the Blue Pencil dinner & found it quite enjoyable. It was rather pleasant to meet the other amateurs whilst in N.Y., but this pleasure could not quite make up for my intense & constantly growing dislike of the town as a whole. I shall, of course, still keep in touch with the N.Y. members through correspondence.

But I must close, since I am still feverishly busy unpacking & settling. Most of the furniture is now arranged, but all my books & papers are yet to be classified—a most arduous & distressing job.

With every good wish, & trusting that *Interesting Items* may continue to enjoy its comfortable regularity, I remain

Sincerely yours,

H. P. Lovecraft

[24]   [ALS]

10 Barnes St.,
Providence, R.I.,
Jany. 27, 1927

My dear Mr. Harris:—

I am very grateful for the copies of *Interesting Items*, & found your boyhood reminiscences very charming. Your persistence in keeping the magazine alive is something I wish other amateur editors would share, for the state of amateurdom on this side of the Atlantic is deplorable indeed. I receive no papers regularly except *Tryout, The Brooklynite, The National Amateur,* & the newly founded *Driftwind* published by Walter J. Coates of Vermont; & the lassitude seems increasing rather than decreasing. A year ago I had high hopes for the United under the leadership of Victor E. Bacon, but he has had so little coöperation that even his great energy has not taken us far, & now his interests are centreing more & more in the National—for which I can't honestly blame him. Some day I hope there will be a general increase in prosperity in all amateur quarters—& that you can issue an *Interesting Items* of the size you desire.

Let me thank you most profoundly for the articles on Roman Britain. As you know, the subject is one of keen interest to me; & I find Weigall's handling of the subject unusually good for newspaper work. I am glad these subjects are coming into greater popular interest, & hope the phenomenon is not merely a temporary one. It interests me to note that Weigall believes the Roman legionaries left much of their blood in Britain, so that we may consider them as among our forefathers. This has not been the general impression in the past, but it is certainly tenable enough, & thoroughly consonant with the present trend of ethnological belief. Within the last half-century we have come to realise that the Saxon conquest of the island by no means involved a wholesale extirpation of the native Britons from England, but that victor & vanquished mingled in such a way as to give the modern Englishman as good a chance of being a Celt as a Teuton. By the same reasoning, it appears equally possible that the Romans mingled also, & that it was a mixed Britanno-Roman population instead of a wholly Celtic one which the followers of Hengist & Horsa found. I will confess that I rather relish the thought, for I have always admired Rome & its power tremendously, & would be glad to be able to think that there may be a little Roman blood in me!

Yes—it is certainly good to be back in Providence; for if one is such an inborn conservative as I, one cannot comfortably leave behind the scenes & associations of more than thirty years. I'm enclosing a newspaper view which will really give you a very fair idea of what Providence looks like. You will see at once that it resembles the quiet towns of the Mother Country rather than the garish & strident huddles of skyscrapers whose pictures you have doubtless seen. The old building in the square in the foreground is the Market House built in 1773, whilst the white steeple on the left is of the 1st Baptist church, (1775) & was designed by James Gibbs, a pupil of Wren, who also designed St. Martins-in-the-Fields in London. The dome that crowns the town as St. Paul's crowns London is a *new* one—of a church finished only a few years ago. I live on the crest of the hill just under the "x" in the margin.

With all good wishes,
Most cordially & sincerely yours,
H P Lovecraft

[25]   [ALS]

Home Address—
10 Barnes St.,
Providence, R.I.,
Aug. 22, 1927

Dear Mr. Harris:—

As you will see by the postmark of this letter, I am writing you whilst on a visit to our fellow-amateur W. Paul Cook of Athol; & I can assure you that I have seldom seen finer landscapes in all my life. I am writing this letter on the top of a high hill overlooking the town & all the countryside for miles around—a vista which I would give much to be able to draw or paint. Ancient farmhouses, village steeples, & lines of distant hills stretch out on every hand; & a bright sun reveals glimpses of a lake amidst foliage far to the southwest. I came up Friday, & have taken several side-trips since—notably to historic Deerfield, scene of the great French & Indian massacre of 1704. That is one of the quaintest old towns I have ever beheld, & I have bought many books & pictures of it. On another trip we went to Vermont & New Hampshire, stopping at Brattleboro to see the prominent amateur poet Arthur Goodenough. Goodenough lives in a house about 150 years old, amidst the finest & quaintest hill country imaginable. He is a splendid chap—a man about 55 years old, very old-fashioned in his speech, dress, & manners, & infinitely cordial & hospitable. I will enclose some postcard pictures of Athol & Brattleboro, since their amateur celebrity will doubtless make them interesting to you. Brattleboro is famous as the place where Rudyard Kipling lived when he was in the United States—his house being beside the road north of the town. By the way—with the exception of Cook, I am the first amateur journalist whom Goodenough has ever seen in person. He was very pleasant, & gave me a copy of his new book of poems, which Cook printed. This trip was my first visit to Vermont, & took me the farthest north I have ever been. We went as far as Lake Sunapee, N.H., a summer resort place of considerable popularity, though not so beautiful as the country around Athol.

Your letter, the copies of *Interesting Items,* & the cuttings on Roman Britain interested me greatly; & I thank you exceedingly for all. Your efforts in behalf of the United are sincerely appreciated, & I certainly hope that enough others will follow your example to start a revival of activity. It will be hard work, though; & the veterans find themselves more & more apt to conduct their work & correspondence independently, outside the formal limits of the organised associations.

Never mind the missing numbers of the Roman Britain series—I'm grateful enough for those which you did send! Some day I suppose Weigall will publish this matter in book form, & then I shall of course purchase the volume. I wish I could visit Britain & see some of these antiquities at first hand!

Your genealogical researches are very interesting. Welsh lines can of course trace themselves farther back than Saxon & Norman ones, for very little authentic English data antedates the Conquest. To all intents & purposes the Domesday Book is the real beginning of the very oldest English families.

Cook is engaged in an unusual number of publishing ventures just now, the fruits of some of which you will presently see. He has issued a monster number of the *Vagrant*—312 pages—as a formal farewell to organised amateurdom, & is about to commence a select literary magazine called *The Recluse,* which will not be formally connected with the amateur associations. He & I are also doing a professional job together—collecting & publishing in book form the poems of the late John Ravenor Bullen, whose work in amateurdom you may remember.

The picture of the view which I am enclosing is very much like what I am seeing at this moment. Truly exquisite—though I fancy you have finer & richer landscapes than this in Wales.

With every good wish,

Most sincerely yours,
H P Lovecraft

[26]   [ALS]

10 Barnes St.,
Providence, R.I.,
Jany. 12, 1928.

My dear Mr. Harris:—

I was very glad to receive your letter with its highly interesting enclosures, & must congratulate you as usual upon your steady maintenance of *Interesting Items.* Regular amateur papers are rare nowadays—at least in America, where *Tryout* & the *Brooklynite* seem to be the lone survivors of their kind!

Let me thank you exceedingly for the Llandudno views, which I have examined with the greatest pleasure. These wild hills & venerable castles far surpass anything which the Athol region can produce, & make one long for the opportunity to visit them in person. If these pictures were meant to be returned, please let me know. They are in any case safe—for I preserve choice scenic views in a collection now grown to quite formidable proportions. Your description of Llandudno & its headland vistas is very alluring, & convinces me that you are greatly to be envied your locale.

My trip of last summer was indeed a highly enjoyable one—& the parts which came after my writing you were even more picturesque & varied than those I described. From Athol I went by motor coach (now the principal means of interurban transportation in New England, & equivalent to what you call a "char-a-banc" in Great Britain) to Boston, & thence up the coast by the same means to Portland, Maine, a delightful city (the birthplace & boyhood home of the poet Longfellow) which I had never before seen. Stopping there several days, I visited all the antiquities of the place & its suburbs, taking a side-trip by railway to the White Mountains, where I beheld the most strikingly rugged scenery I had ever seen. I ascended Mt. Washington—tallest elevation in New England—by the cog-wheel railway; obtaining some of the most impressive views imaginable on the way up, though rain-clouds cut off the view at the bleak, wind-swept summit. Leaving Portland, I descended the coast again in easy stages, stopping at all the quaint old towns to study the antiquities. Of course, these are merely 18th century towns, with a few houses of the 17th century surviving; but they are what we are obliged to regard as archaic for want of really ancient reliques. I explored Portsmouth, N.H., & Newburyport, Mass.—from that point taking a short trip inland to Haverhill & having an interesting call on our good old friend C. W. Smith of the Tryout. Smith is now 75 years old, & totally deaf; but he is lean & vigorous physically, & has the delightful simplicity & keen interest in life of a small boy! He, like Goodenough, has been seen by very few amateurs; but I had called on him twice before—in 1921 & 1922. In the intervening five years he does not seem to have aged a jot! From Newburyport I went to Ipswich & thence crossed over to Gloucester, that quaintest of all American fishing ports, where I spend [*sic*] three days of exploration. After that I went to my favourite old towns of Salem & Marblehead, & finally returned home after a delightful saturation in the atmosphere of the past. Fortunately my own city is sufficiently archaic & beautiful not to break the spell. I think I have told you considerable about it, have I not?

Sorry you have not received the monster *Vagrant*.[1] I've just written Cook asking him if he has another to spare you; & if not, I'll send you a duplicate which I have. Its quality is nothing notable, but sheer size makes it impressive. Glad you have *The Recluse*—which is really a remarkable production both in size & in excellence. Cook will probably issue one number each year, striving to maintain as high a standard as he possibly can.

Lately Cook & I have been coöperating in the editing & publishing of a book of poems by the late Canadian amateur John Ravenor Bullen, who died last February. The enterprise was financed very liberally by a friend of the author's, so that we were able to turn out a volume of almost sumptuous beauty. Cook is taking charge of the sale, the price being $2.00 postpaid. It is 6 × 9, on art paper, 86 pp., bound in grey cloth, with genuine photographic frontispiece in sepia mounted on an impressed panel. I read the proofs, & believe it is absolutely free from errors in text.

Speaking of books—a story of mine has just found inclusion in an anthology on your side of the water, forming my first fictional appearance between cloth covers. If you come across a book called "You'll Need a Night Light", (Selwyn & Blount, London, 1927—price 2/-) look for the last tale in it, & you will see some of my work.[2]

I trust you haven't been wholly buried or drowned or both by the extreme snows & floods which the press reports in Britain. Last November there were some unprecedentedly severe floods in New England—not affecting Providence, but ravaging much of the territory covered by my summer pilgrimage.

Again thanking you for I. I. & the views, & trusting that 1928 may prove a keenly enjoyable year for you, I remain

Most cordially & sincerely yrs—

H P Lovecraft

Notes

1. The last issue—Spring 1927—had 312 pages.
2. The story in question is "The Horror at Red Hook."

[27]   [ALS]

10 Barnes St.,

Providence, R.I.,

July 26, 1928.

Dear Mr. Harris:—

I found your envelope of interesting material awaiting me at home after a trip of three months' duration, & was greatly pleased with all the contents. Thank you exceedingly for the photographic views, which increase my desire to see ancient Wales some time. The account of your trip to Conway is very tantalising to me. How delightful it must be to have such genuine antiquities at one's very door!

My trip this year occurred rather earlier than I had planned, on account of some special visiting opportunities. I had to be in New York in the early spring, but on the 8th of June went to visit a friend who is summering in Vermont not far from Arthur Goodenough's abode. I spent two weeks there, & rambled delightedly over the closely ranged green hills & brook-haunted ravines; after which I moved along to Athol, Mass., for another visit with W. Paul Cook. I then paid a visit farther south in Massachusetts, in the heart of the ancient countryside; & on the 7th of July commenced the more swiftly varied part of my travels. Crossing the Berkshire Hills of western Massachusetts by that marvellously scenic route known as the "Mohawk Trail", I arrived at Albany N.Y. & took a boat down the beautiful hill-fringed Hudson. At N.Y. City I took a train for Philadelphia, where I sought out my favourite antiquities & quaint corners. From there I went to Baltimore, which I had never before seen, & observed its many points of interest including the grave of Poe in a melancholy corner of Westminster Presbyterian Churchyard. I next went to the ancient town of Annapolis, (now seat of the U.S. Naval Academy) which has since 1694 been the capital of Maryland. This is one of the most archaic towns in America, preserving almost perfectly its 18th century appearance.

After Annapolis I went to Washington D.C., which I explored more fully than on my former visit. With Washington as a base, I took several side trips into the picturesque hills of northern Virginia; finding many historic old villages of the sort I like best. But the climax of the whole expedition was my excursion to the "Endless Caverns" in the Shenandoah Valley—a four-hour railway trip from Washington. This vast series of limestone grottoes, the first real caves I ever beheld, are among the finest in the country; & possess all those features—stalactites, stalagmites, &c—which lend picturesqueness & beauty to the underground world. It was easily the most impressive sight I have ever seen in my life, & I shall certainly keep it long in memory.

Yes indeed—C. W. Smith is surely a delightfully quaint character. He turned 75 on the 24th of last October, but is just as active as a young man, & as naively simple in his tastes as a boy. I suppose you have received his recent booklet of poems—which he calls the "Poetical Melange."[1] It is very odd that you have received no monster *Vagrant*, & I am now writing Cook to see that you are supplied. Cook, by the way, has just exchanged his house in Athol for a 100-acre farm in the wild countryside east of the village; so that he will shortly be duplicating the life of America's pioneer colonists.

Amateur journalism is at a very low ebb just now, & shows no signs of improvement ahead. The National association has elected Vincent B. Haggerty President & Damon S. Stanford Official Editor,[2] & has reduced the official organ from a bi-monthly to a quarterly. Individual papers are well-nigh extinct.

With best wishes, & hopes for the continued prosperity of *Interesting Items,* I remain

> Most cordially & sincerely yrs—
> H P Lovecraft

Notes

1. *Poetical Melange: Anthology.* Haverhill, MA: C. W. Smith, [c. 1928?]. The booklet contained HPL's "Ave atque Vale: to Jonathan E. Hoag, Esq. February 10, 1831–October 17th, 1927."

2. Vincent B[artholemew] Haggerty (1888–1943) amateur journalist associated with the NAPA in the 1920s and 1930s. Damon S. Stanford of Vermont felt unable to accept the official editorship, and so Edward J. Hollahan of Brooklyn was appointed in his place.

[28] [ALS]

> 10 Barnes St.,
> Providence, R.I.,
> Novr. 22, 1928

Dear Mr. Harris:—

Thanks exceedingly for your letter & the two issues of *Interesting Items.* You surely break all records for fidelity in amateur publishing!

That trip of mine doesn't really deserve to be called a three-month affair, because the first month & a half was a necessary sojourn in the New York region—which I detest. But the second half was an outing indeed, & one I shall long remember. I hope I can do something of the kind next year, even if not on so large a scale.

Your rambles around Conway excite my envy![1] I myself have been in the open considerably this autumn on account of the unusual mildness of the weather. Sometimes I have taken urban walks of architectural exploration, discovering many obscure regions of Providence which I never saw before, & sometimes I have taken my work out to the ancient fields & woodlands north of the town—sitting on a rock in some forest glen & attending to my revision, reading, writing, or whatever I had to do. This region is surely abundantly blessed in a scenic way—a circumstance for which I can never be sufficiently grateful.

Yes—our friend Tryout celebrated his 76th birthday on Oct. 25 [*sic*] last, but is as hale, hearty, & active as a boy. He takes long woodland walks & enjoys life keenly in every way—his only trouble being an almost total deafness. He is a tall, lean man, pleasant-faced & rather dark, with a closely-cropped full beard of iron-grey colour. He does not look more than 50 or 55 at the most. I am hoping he will turn out to be one of our centenarians. Our good amateur friend Mr. Hoag almost did—& I think he would have but for the accident which caused his death a year ago—at the age of 96¾. I'll ask Tryout to send you his "Poetical Melange." Glad Cook sent the *Vagrant* at last. Cook has just bought a farm in the country east of Athol, & meant to move in this autumn; but his inability to get a heating system installed before cold weather has forced him to take rooms in Athol for the winter. Our sensitiveness to *cold* in America is quite a biological puzzle. In the Mother Land you are usually quite comfortable with winter house temperatures of 60° Fahrenheit & under; but we, although of the same blood, could not endure anything so cool. 68° is as low as our hardiest specimens can stand, whilst most of us want our rooms well above 70°. I, personally, am an extreme case—so hyper-sensitive that I want a room about 74° to 76°, & can't control my finger muscles well enough to write legibly under 71° or 72°.

I wish I could say that amateurdom in America has improved, but in all truth I must admit that I haven't seen any signs of a revival as yet. The new official board, however, has ambitious plans; so that during the winter something may develop. The best symptom I have seen is the appearance of several postal-card papers—humble specimens, it is true, yet shewing at least some signs of continued interest. I hope conditions are somewhat better in the British Isles.

With thanks & best wishes,
Yrs most sincerely,
H P Lovecraft

Notes

1. More properly Conwy, a walled market town on the north coast of Wales, not far from Llandudno.

[29]   [ALS]

[H. P. LOVECRAFT
10 BARNES STREET
PROVIDENCE, R. I.]

Jany. 16, 1929

Dear Mr. Harris:—

I was glad to hear from you, & to receive the latest batch of *Interesting Items*. Your account of the eclipse which bad weather prevented you from seeing is very graphic, & reminds me of the one total eclipse which

I have witnessed during my lifetime.[1] This was the eclipse of Jany. 24, 1925, which I saw whilst in New York. The longest duration of totality was in the northern part of the city, so a party of us proceeded to Yonkers & took our station in an open field on the high ground above the village. Seeing conditions were absolutely perfect, & I shall not soon forget the grandeur of the corona & the general picturesqueness of the spectacle. The only drawback was the extreme cold, from which I suffered extensively.

I am glad you were able to take a trip lately, even if only a short one; & that you found an interesting ex-amateur at the place you visited. No doubt Llandudno itself still holds many new corners for you. It is interesting to study a map of one's own town & see how many places one has overlooked. Two weeks ago I was inspired to some sightseeing by the visit of our fellow-amateur Samuel Loveman, who was making a brief business tour of New England. His time was limited, so that I could shew him only a limited number of my favourite Providence antiquities; but I accompanied him when he went on to Boston, hence was able to point out some of the leading historic objects in that larger but equally venerable city. We also took a trip to Salem & Marblehead—those perfect survivals of the 18th century about which I have probably written you often before. These have a double charm & quaintness in winter, when free from crowds of summer tourists. One thing in Boston was new to me—the recently opened wing of decoration & architecture at the Museum of Fine Arts. This far surpasses the famed American Wing at the Metropolitan Museum of N.Y.—containing not only typical early American rooms with their panelling & furniture, but still earlier rooms from Britain & France, shewing the sources of New England architectural & decorative motifs. Among this very early source material is a painted window of 1435 from the private chapel of Hampton Court in Herefordshire, a complete Tudor room of 1490 from Somerset, panelled in black oak, a magnificently carved & wainscotted room of 1690 from Hamilton Palace in Lanarkshire, Scotland, & a fine drawing-room of 1750, in the Chippendale manner, from Woodcote Park, Epsom, Surrey. The New England specimens are of course numerous & varied; so that the whole really forms the best single exposition of domestic architecture & furniture I have ever seen.

I don't hear much from amateurdom lately, though I suppose it is never too late to hope for a revival. It is interesting to note the rise of Ireland as a centre of activity. In my amateur heyday there were relatively few amateurs there, & most of the papers were insignificant & schoolboyish. It doesn't take long to shift the centre of gravity in amateurdom!

With best of wishes, & hoping that the coming spring will enable you to get out more into the country & about Cambrian scenery & antiquities, I remain

   Most sincerely yrs—
    H P Lovecraft

Notes

1. But see AH 39.

[30]　[ALS]

> [~~Van Ross Hotel . . .~~
> ~~Kingston, N.Y.~~]
>> 10 Barnes St.,
>>> Providence, R.I.,
>>>> May 26, 1929.

Dear Mr. Harris:—

　　　　I found your welcome letter, with the piquant numbers of *Interesting Items* enclosed, upon my return from a month & a half's outing. It began with a two weeks' visit to a friend on the northern rim of N Y City, was prolonged by a week spent with Frank B. Long (the amateur) in that city itself, & then developed into one of my characteristic scenic & antiquarian tours. While in the N Y region I saw a good many of the local amateurs— especially Morton, Loveman, & my young host Long. You are right in re- marking how adhesive these amateur friendships tend to be—all of the par- ticular "gang" in question have hung together for ten years & more, & seem likely to do so indefinitely through the future. When I reached the independ- ent & migratory stage of my trip I began with the South, & decided to ex- plore that peninsular region of Virginia—between the York & James Rivers—where English civilisation first gained a foothold on this continent. Jamestown—founded in 1607 & since abandoned—proved a highly interest- ing & imaginatively provocative spot to visit. Of the ancient settlement only a ruined church tower, some crumbling house walls, & a few foundation-stones remain, but no one can visit the site without a certain amount of awe & inspi- ration. Williamsburg, the colonial capital of Virginia after the destruction of Jamestown, has more to offer the eye—indeed, it is now in process of restora- tion to its 18th century appearance. The college building there is the only struc- ture in America personally designed by Sir Christopher Wren. Richmond— scene of Poe's early days & famous in the Civil War of 1861–5—is an ex- tremely pleasant old town; whilst Fredericksburg, which has progressed less in a material way, is even quainter. From there I proceeded north to Washing- ton, where I explored galleries & museums & saw considerable of the ama- teur Edward Lloyd Sechrist. My next port of call was ancient Philadelphia; of which I am very fond, & where I this time visited the new art museum—an impressive Greek-temple structure perched on a hill at the end of a parkway like a veritable Acropolis, & reached by broad flights of steps flanked by arti- ficial waterfalls. I don't think I've ever seen another piece of contemporary architecture as thoroughly magnificent & inspiring as this. After Philadelphia

I crossed northward through N Y City again without pausing—being conveyed up the Hudson's shore in Long's motor. My next stop was the ancient town of Kingston, N.Y., where I visited a friend & absorbed the antiquities of the place. Kingston was founded by the Dutch in 1658, & still has a vast number of the old stone houses built between that date & 1720 or 1730. I also visited the quaint neighbouring villages of Hurley & New Paltz—the latter founded by French Huguenots. After exploring this region I ascended to Albany & crossed the Berkshires to my native New England, stopping first at Athol to see W. Paul Cook. During my few days there Cook took me up to Brattleboro in his car to see the poet Arthur Goodenough—whose exquisitely beautiful region I think I have described to you in the past. Finally, Cook brought me home last week, & I have since been busy settling down & reading up accumulated mail, magazines, & papers. It was a great trip; yet I am glad to be home again, for Providence is exquisite in the late spring. As usual, I do most of my writing outdoors on warm & pleasant days.

By all accounts, the European winter was a terrible one, though it was rather mild here. Our early spring, however, was chilly & wretched. Fortunately for my trip, a turn for the better came about May 1st., when I began the predominantly roving phase of my Odyssey.

As for amateurdom—it has little more than a technical existence hereabouts, though I suppose Morton will go through the motions of a National convention & election. Glad to hear that you have introduced the hobby to the public library officials at Llandudno—it surely would be beneficial if others would follow suit.

With best wishes, & thanking you for the set of I. I.'s which I read with pleasure & appreciation, I remain

Most cordially & sincerely yrs—
H P Lovecraft

[31]   [ALS]

10 Barnes St.,
Providence, R.I.,
Aug. 21, 1929

My dear Harris:—

Let me congratulate you on the delightful anniversary issue of *Interesting Items* which has just arrived. It is surely a memorable number, & your account of your visits to original subscribers gives it an added poignancy. Not many have the perseverance to keep an amateur paper going so faithfully—although I fancy our good old friend Tryout will do so if he lives long enough.

Glad you found the travel notes of interest. I have been too desperately busy since spring to take any extended trips, though a few short ones have occurred. Morton came here for a few days in June, & we visited several of the quaint old villages down the shores of Narragansett Bay—especially Wickford, which is off the railway & which has changed but little in a century & a half. Later the amateur Victor E. Bacon (who was born in Old England near the ruins of Glastonbury Abbey) stopped briefly in Providence, & we made a very pleasant trip to ancient Newport. Early this month I took a solitary trip to two places in Massachusetts which I had been wishing to see for a long time—the old Fairbanks house in Dedham & the celebrated "Wayside Inn" at Sudbury.[1] The Fairbanks homestead was built in 1636 & is the oldest edifice of any kind in New England—besides being the oldest dwelling-house (except for old Spanish houses in Florida & the southwest) in the United States. The only older buildings of English construction on this continent are two parish churches in Virginia dating from about 1632. I think, on the whole, that the Fairbanks house is the most picturesque structure I have ever seen—as you may perhaps realise from the enclosed view. It was built by the emigrant Jonathan Fayerbanke, who came from Sowerby, near Halifax, in Yorkshire; & has not been changed at all except for two wings added in 1641 & 1648. Erected in the same year that Providence was founded, & when Boston was a village only six years old! It is now a public museum conducted by a society of Fairbanks descendants. The beams are of old English oak taken from a dismantled ship, & the bricks of the chimney are also from England. The walls & roof are in places oddly sunken, & present a very picturesque silhouette from the road, but they are braced against collapse. The whole thing is fascinating in its colourful irregularity—steps up & down from room to room, vast hand-hewn beams blackened by time & smoke, great fireplaces, cobwebbed attics—in short, all the subtle earmarks of great age, bringing down to the present the strange, distant echoes of 1636, when New England was a frail infant colony clinging to the seacoast, & this house was a bold outpost on the edge of black unknown woods. The "Wayside Inn" or old Red Horse Tavern was scarcely less interesting in other ways. This was built in 1686, & from 1714 to the present has been a public hostelry—the present owner being Henry Ford. It is now restored to its ancient state.

My most recent trip was last week, when I spent four days on Cape Cod with Long & his parents. We saw a great deal of historic material, including the picturesque waterfront of the ancient whaling port, New Bedford; & at Onset (our headquarters) I took my first aëroplane ride—a highly exhilarating experience. Cape Cod also has some famous old windmills dating from the 18th century.

Yes—I'll recommend you as a correspondent to Long & Loveman, though they are both rather out of amateurdom nowadays. The National's existence is only nominal now—though a revival was promised at the Paterson convention of which you'll read in Tryout. With best wishes—

Sincerely yrs

H P L

P.S. I shall have stories reprinted in 2 anthologies this autumn—my "Call of Cthulhu" being in "Beware After Dark", edited by T. Everett Harré, & my "Pickman's Model" being scheduled for the 1929 volume of the British "Not at Night" series.

Notes

1. See HPL's essay "An Account of a Trip to the Antient Fairbanks House . . ."

[32]   [ALS]

10 Barnes St.,
Providence, R.I.,
Octr. 25, 1929.

Dear Mr. Harris:—

I was glad to receive the recent letter & copies of *Interesting Items*—surely it takes energy & devotion to carry an amateur publication along to its 573^d number! It seems to me that you must really hold the publishing record for all amateur journalism—in number of issues, at least. The National, as usual, is doing virtually nothing; although the first official organ of the new term has appeared. It is only quarterly now, as you are doubtless aware. The next convention will be in Boston—only 44 miles from here—so I shall probably attend it, although I don't anticipate that it will amount to much.

I trust you have been able to resume your explorations—& envy you the historic territory you have to explore. If my financial state ever improves, I want to visit Britain—spending a long time, & absorbing all the ancestral colour I have been starved for during the past forty years. As it is, my recent jaunts have been very limited—one-day or even one-afternoon affairs, to the idyllic countryside north & west of Providence. But even here I have secured some excellent landscape effects—many of them closely similar to old-world effects if pictures speak truly. There is one vista in the Quinsnicket region—6 miles N. of the city—which I never tire of seeing, & which I am sure must be almost a duplicate of many in England & Wales. It is from a rustic hillside, where the road winds down eastward into a valley with a glassy mere at the bottom—& where the distant roofs & steeple of a village can be seen through the foliage of the valley's opposite slope. On the right are rolling meadows & the edge of a deep wooded ravine, & on the left are uplands with granite outcroppings, orchards, ancient houses, & sheaves of harvested corn. With all the foliage autumnally resplendent, & with the golden glamour of late-afternoon sunlight on the distant spire across the valley, the picture is one to inspire an artist—& make a non-artist like myself bitterly resentful of his lack of skill.

Your speed-boating must be enjoyable. I have never ridden in a speed boat, but fancy the same sensation must have come when the seaplane in which I rode skimmed over the water in preparation for its ascent. That gave me almost the most vivid physical impression of speed I have ever experienced—though the impression vanished as soon as the machine rose in the air.

By the way—just now the champion traveller of amateurdom is James F. Morton, who is back from a long & vivid tour of the South. After covering the most historic spots of Virginia, he descended into North Carolina & Georgia—visiting amateurs & collecting mineralogical specimens for his museum. He also took many side-trips into the primeval wilderness, ascending Mt. Mitchell, the highest peak in the Eastern U.S. On his return trip he rode from Pittsburgh to N.Y. in an aëroplane, crossing the Alleghany Mountains at an altitude of 7200 feet.

I am enclosing my new bookplate—drawn for me by the amateur Wilfred B. Talman—which may be of some interest to you. The old Georgian doorway typifies both the reposeful & archaic atmosphere of Providence, & my own especial antiquarian tastes. I think it is marvellously well done, & am quite delighted with it. Talman is not a professional artist, but has an amateur mastery of drawing which I acutely envy.

This autumn I shall again be represented between cloth covers in Great Britain—my story, "Pickman's Model", being included in a weird anthology published by Hutchinson & Co., London.[1] I hope to see a copy soon.

> Best wishes—
> Sincerely yrs—
> H P L

Notes

1. *By Daylight Only* (actually published by Selwyn & Blount).

[33]   [ALS]

> 10 Barnes St.,
> Providence, R.I.,
> March 29, 1930

Dear Mr. Harris:—

Let me thank you exceedingly for your recent communication with its attractive enclosures. Your journalistic tenacity is worthy of wide emulation, & I hope that in time *Interesting Items* may again find itself surrounded by "live" contemporaries. But the outlook is far from bright. No—I did not get to the Paterson convention, though I shall doubtless be at the coming Boston one unless the lack of interest in that city causes a shift in the convention-seat.

It surprised me to see echoes of my last years' travels in print! This spring I am hoping I can take a trip of some sort—preferably in the southern states, where many objects of antiquarian interest can be found. If possible, I shall try to get down the coast as far as Charleston, S.C.—whose 250th anniversary occurs this spring. En route I shall no doubt see many amateurs, & on my return trip shall probably stop a week or two with Frank B. Long—incidentally seeing Morton, Loveman, & the other N.Y. members of the group.

Your ascent of Snowdon[1] was surely an absorbing & enviable experience—& I am infinitely grateful for the pictures which you so thoughtfully sent. You had good luck with weather—rather a contrast to my own experience with New England's highest peak—Mt. Washington—in 1927, when a mist sprang up some time before I reached the summit. Your account of the Snowdon trip in I. I. is very graceful & entertaining, & makes me hope I can get around to your part of the globe sometime!

But after all, your discovery of the old thatched cottage proves that much picturesqueness often lies unnoticed at one's very doorstep! I have no doubt but that many discoveries of the greatest interest & beauty still await me in Rhode Island—many regions of which are still unknown to me because of lack of convenient transportation facilities. However—I greatly doubt if R. I. ever yields any find quite the equal of that cottage scene with its ancient mill & stream & bridge. I hope you will photograph it some time before it succumbs to the encroachments of commerce—for I fear no part of the world is wholly free from the uglifying menace of the age of machinery. I have been told that the growth of Newport, in your own Wales, has seriously menaced the tranquil & historic beauty of Caerleon-on-Usk & the Arthur Machen country in general. Here in Providence I have been mourning the passing of some of the old brick warehouses along the waterfront, whose picturesque beauty has added so much to the city's charm. I wrote to the papers, both in prose & verse—but it was of no use. Still, we have a great deal of quaintness left. I enclose an illustrated article describing an old section of the town which lies only a few squares down the steep hill from where I reside. The steepness of the hill retards rapid change, & I fancy the region will remain quaint & old-fashioned as long as I live.

With best wishes, & hoping the coming spring will bring you many interesting trips,

I remain

Yrs most sincerely—

H P Lovecraft

Notes

1. Snowdon, in Gwynedd province, is the highest mountain in Wales (3560 feet above sea level).

[34]   [ALS]

10 Barnes St.,
Providence, R.I.,
Octr 30 1930

Dear Arthur:—

Thanks exceedingly for the new *Interesting Items*. The idea of amateur reminiscences seems to me admirable, & I am sure the majority of your readers will find the department of keen interest. In these decadent days, when there are more retrospective old-timers than youngsters in amateurdom, nothing could be more apt than a few piquant memories to bring back livelier times.

However—as you say, the recent National convention did much to revive interest, & I doubt if the coming year will be quite as completely dead as the few years just preceding. The attendance was something of a surprise, & I saw several old-time amateurs whom I had never before seen in person— such as E. H. Smith & L. C. Wills.[1] The young Official Editor, Helm C. Spink, was also there; & created an exceedingly favourable impression. I saw most of the Boston group for the first time since 1923, & it was amusing to note the changes—or in some cases lack of change—in each one. Cole has grown fat, I have grown thin, & Lynch looks exactly the same! The effect of seven years on a varied group is very curious. Naturally I took advantage of my presence in Boston to visit my favourite antiquarian haunts—Salem, Marblehead, &c—& found them quite as fascinating as usual.

Yes—I did indeed take that southern trip in the spring, & found Charleston the most archaic & fascinating spot in the United States. It is the most unchanged survival from 18th century times that I have ever seen, with whole districts composed of narrow old streets built up with quaint stucco-covered brick houses dating from 1720 or 1730 down to 1800 or so. The architecture is very different from that of ancient towns in the north; since many concessions were made to the subtropical climate, whilst a French influence was added by the presence of many Huguenots. There are steep tiled roofs, great tiers of verandahs covering whole sides of the houses, & curious porches reached by curving double flights of steps. Walled gardens are everywhere, & their street gates usually represent a marvellously high level of wrought-iron craftsmanship. The climate is idyllic, & I beheld for the first time a landscape & flora definitely different from that of the north-temperate belt I have always lived in. There are palmetto-trees everywhere, together with twisted-boughed live-oaks festooned with Spanish moss, & a profusion of strange flowers & vines unknown to northern latitudes. Negroes are abundant—one sees as many of them as white people in the streets—but they are very deferential & well-behaved, & do not intrude in the places where the regular population congregate. Foreigners are almost unknown—a strange & happy state of things as contrasted with the north, where Italians, Jews, Poles, & the like overrun half the countryside & city streets. Altogether, Charleston is the most perfect surviving example of the *old* American world—the elder agricultural America preceding the machine age & having quality rather than wealth & quantity as a standard. I am utterly charmed by the place, & shall certainly live there if ever I find myself wholly unable to bear the terrible winters of New England. On the return trip I stopped quite a while in Richmond, Virginia, another southern city of which I am very fond. This is not far south enough to be in the subtropical belt, hence its landscape & vegetation look much the same as those of Providence. Also, it is not nearly so old-fashioned as Charleston. But it is tremendously attractive & conservative for all that, & I enjoyed looking up scenes connected with the youth of my favourite author Poe. I likewise visited Williamsburg—the old colonial capital of Virginia which is being restored to its 18th century aspect—& found it even more fascinating than it was the year before. Fredericksburg, between Richmond & Washington D.C., is another exquisite remnant of the past. On the return trip north I repeated my programme of 1929; stopping in New York to visit Frank B. Long & see such amateurs as James F. Morton, Samuel Loveman, &c. Then I went up the Hudson by boat to ancient Kingston, spending a week there[2] & finally crossing over the magnificent Berkshire Hills to Athol, Mass., where I looked up W. Paul Cook. I found him in poor health, just pulling out of a nervous breakdown; & he has since left Athol, intending to settle later in Vermont & establish a publishing house in conjunction with a friend. Then returning home, I enjoyed a visit from James F. Morton in June & attended the convention in July. In August I spent a week around Cape Cod with Frank B. Long, renewing my acquaintance with the sights & antiquities I saw last year. Then early in September, as the last item of the season's programme, I reversed my compass-points & struck out for a farthest *north* to match my former farthest south; visiting for the first time the ancient fortress city of *Quebec*, 400 miles north of here, & the only *walled town* on the American continent. Nor was I disappointed in my expectations. On the contrary, Quebec proved the most utterly exquisite & fascinating city I have ever seen—so lovely & quaint that all my former standards of urban beauty become meaningless & obsolete in comparison. Vast castellated cliffs—forests of silver spires & pointed roofs shining in the sun—narrow, tangled, almost vertical streets full of brick & stucco houses of 200 years ago— Actually, it quite eclipses Charleston; though the winter climate is such that I could never live there. Despite nearly 175 years of British control it is still essentially a French city, though most of the population understand a good deal of English. It is as retentive of the past as Charleston, & probably does not look very differently from the way it looked when Wolfe captured it in a dying hour of triumph. I climbed the cliff where his army ascended, & followed his route along the now-built-up Plains of Abraham. I must visit Quebec again next summer, for I didn't see half what I wished to this time.

Best wishes—
Yrs most cordially—
H P L

Notes

1. Louis Charles Wills (1884–1975) of Brooklyn.
2. HPL was visiting his friend Bernard Austin Dwyer.

[35]   [ALS]

10 Barnes St.,
Providence, R.I.,
March 30, 1931.

Dear A. H.—

I was greatly pleased to receive yours of the 16th with the interesting cutting & copies of I. I. The soundness of your reminiscent policy seems to be proved by the similar policies of your contemporaries—you have doubtless noticed how the National Amateur has begun to recall past years in its alumni department. Glad to hear that you have formed a local library circle, & hope you can make it at least reasonably permanent. Very few seem to flourish now—at least, in America.

I shall be glad to report any meetings with amateurs, though my travelling schedule is rather uncertain this year. Wilfred B. Talman visited Providence last November—but I suppose he is merely an ex-amateur nowadays. Galpin—whom you probably remember—will travel in France during the coming summer, & I hope to see him in June before he sails. Cook's health is better, & he is contemplating a westward move to Oklahoma—although I hope he will remain in New England. I'll forward your good wishes. Paul J. Campbell mourns the death of his mother on March 11, after a year's illness with paralysis. His new address is 6119 Stewart Ave., Chicago—but he is planning a move to Oklahoma. It is he, indeed, who is luring Cook thither. C. W. Smith has been in poor health this winter, but is now rapidly improving. He will be 79 next October.

I haven't issued a *Conservative* since 1923, for the cost of printing is tremendous hereabouts. Some day I may try to get one out for old times' sake, though most of the present active generation of amateurs never heard of it or of me. As for that old story "From Beyond"—you can do as you like with it, either throwing it away or using it in serial form. It has never been published. If, incidentally, you would care for bits of verse instead, there are some I wrote a year ago which you might use. I'll copy one or two for you, & you can either print or discard them.[1] Most of the verse I have written lately has been of the same weird type as my stories.

Your visit to Deganwy Castle[2] must have been prodigiously interesting, & I keenly enjoyed the newspaper account of the place. I really ought to know more about Welsh antiquities, for one of my lines of ancestry comes from Wales—albeit from Glamorganshire, far to the south of you. Then, too, I am a confirmed devotee of Arthur Machen, & of his strange tales of the Gwent region around the Usk. I am preserving this Deganwy item for my files. Some day I hope I can get across the Atlantic & see some of these things for myself. Once I got in the midst of those old-world antiquities I'd probably never want to return! From time to time our young fellow-amateur Barr[3] sends me illustrated material concerning New Zealand—a region even younger than America. It is probably highly picturesque—with a type of vegetation & landscape quite unknown in the northern hemisphere—but I should miss the presence of historic background, just as I would in the western parts of the U.S.

Again thanking you for the enclosures, & congratulating you upon the faithfulness & piquancy of your journal, I remain

Yrs. most cordially & sincerely,

H P L

Notes

1. Ultimately AH published two of HPL's sonnets from *Fungi from Yuggoth* in *Interesting Items*: "Night-Gaunts" and "Background."
2. Deganwy Castle in Gwynedd province, a Dark Age fortress traditionally regarded as the headquarters of Maelgwyn Gwynedd, King of Gwynedd (fl. 520–47).
3. Robert G. Barr of Christchurch, New Zealand. "Harbour Whistles" from HPL's *Fungi from Yuggoth* made its first appearance in Barr's *Silver Fern*.

[36]   [ALS]

10 Barnes St.,

Providence, R.I.,

Octr. 27, 1931.

Dear Arthur:—

I am tremendously grateful for your generous envelope of the 12th, with varied picturesque enclosures. The views of the Menai region—& especially the unpronounceable church[1]—fill me with avidity to get over there, as indeed I hope to do some day. The only trouble would be that I probably never could persuade myself to return! As for tongue-twisting names—such as we have in America are generally of Indian origin, & the longest specimen I know is a lake "Chargogagogmanchangagogequngewang"—or something to that effect. It possesses variant forms.[2]

Interesting Items as usual lives up to its name, & I think your retrospective column is indeed a great asset. I am glad the local library group is flourishing, & believe the policy of dividing responsibility is an excellent one if all hands are active & interested enough to make it feasible. I hope, too, that the revival of the B.A.P.A. will be found practicable. The National really is receiving something of that new lease of life which the optimists predicted—the recent total of papers being quite astonishing as measured by present standards.

Galpin went from France to Germany & Austria, & is now for some reason or other planning a trip to Majorca. I surely envy him his travels—although I would proportion my time very differently if given a limited sojourn in Europe. I would devote most of the visit to Britain, & make one brief jaunt across the continent—seeing if possible something of France, the oldest cities of Germany, something of Spain, & the classic ground of Italy & Greece—with an Egyptian extension if possible.

Cook is now enormously better, & has business connexions in Boston. His present address is *7 Hancock St., Boston, Mass*—which is on the northern slope of quaint & Georgian Beacon Hill. He has lately visited Providence, & early this month I visited him in Boston—taking several side-trips to picturesque spots both north & south of that city. The enclosed cards show an especially quaint old church (though built in 1681 rather than 600) & a typical New England landscape of the sort which most captivates me. On one occasion we went to Haverhill & had an extremely pleasant afternoon with good old "Tryout" Smith—who looks just as young & vigorous as he did a decade ago. This was the first meeting, in the flesh, of Tryout & Vagrant.

A later expedition of mine was to a region very near at hand which, oddly enough, I had never before visited—the central Connecticut area between Providence & Hartford. I was obliged to go to the latter city for a conference about a book-revision undertaking,[3] & greatly enjoyed the unexpectedly fine scenery along the way. Hartford itself, however, is not nearly as quaint & attractive as Providence. On the return trip I chose an indirect route for variety's sake—through Norwich & Plainfield—& found the landscapes even lovelier than those along the direct route. Bold hills, picturesque valleys, crystal lakes, & occasional breath-taking vistas of outspread rolling countryside leading off to distant mystical horizons. Norwich—where I paused several hours for antiquarian exploration—is a fascinating old town built on the steep slopes that rise above a bend in the river Thames.

But it is growing too late in the season for very enjoyable outings now. Soon the splendour of autumn foliage will have given place to melancholy bare boughs. I may possibly have to make one short trip to Brattleboro Vt. before long—but I hope not. If I had my wish, I would be leaving for Florida very soon, for a sojourn of many months!

Best wishes & renewed thanks—

Yrs most cordially & sincerely—

H P L

Notes

1. HPL apparently refers to the Menai Strait, a body of water that divides the island of Anglesey from the Welsh mainland. There is also a town on Anglesey called Menai Bridge. The "unpronounceable church" is the Church of St. Tysilio, the name of which is nestled within the name Llanfairpwllgwyngyllgogerychwyrndrobwll*llantysilio*-gogogoch (italics added), a late 19th-century invention for the burgeoning tourist industry in the area. It is the longest place name in the United Kingdom.

2. Lake Chaubunagungamaug, also known as Webster Lake, is a lake in the town of Webster, MA, near the Connecticut border. Since 1921, the lake has also been known by a much longer name comprising fourteen syllables: Lake Char-gogg-a-gogg-man-chaugg-a-gogg-chau-bun-a-gung-a-maugg.

3. HPL's job was to edit Leon Burr Richardson's *History of Dartmouth College* for Vrest Orton of the Stephen Daye Press (Brattleboro, VT).

[37]   [ALS]

> 10 Barnes St.,
> Providence, R.I.,
> Feby. 4, 1932

Dear Arthur:—

Glad to see *Interesting Items* again, & to note that the Circle still exists in undiminished prosperity. Somehow or other, local clubs seem the most difficult of all features to reëstablish in American amateurdom. I think I mentioned before that none exists at the present time save the Blue Pencil Club—which has become too much of a purely social organisation to form a real representative of the amateur tradition.

The general prosperity of the National seems unabated, as you probably realise from papers which come your way. Much of this revival is undoubtedly due to the efforts of the returned old-timer Edwin Hadley Smith, who has put a tremendous amount of effort into reconstructive work. The President—Earl C. Kelley—appears to be a very bright & active youth. You have probably seen his quarterly paper *Ripples*.[1] It is unfortunate that you cannot secure early *National Amateurs*, but I imagine all such things must be very scarce. I have made no attempt to keep any extensive collection; but with your collection already so well developed, one regrets that any important department must be defective.

Cook's general health remains at a surprisingly high level—although he is just now faced with a dental siege. Did I give you his latest address—7 Hancock St., Boston? I visited him at the beginning of the year—taking advantage of the unusually warm weather—& we did a good deal of museum exploring. Some of the leading museums of the country—connected with Harvard University—are in Cambridge, just across the Charles River from Boston. By the way—here is a snapshot of Cook & me which the genial *Tryout* editor took in Haverhill. It is not a very good one, but you can keep it if you like. Sorry I have no duplicate of any shewing Tryout himself.

Glad you have had some rambles recently, even if only brief ones. It is surprising how many unvisited regions one can find comparatively near home. Sorry you failed to find Mr. Pearce in Manchester—I am sure his disappointment must be equal to your own.

I am not certain what travels I can take next spring, but hope to get southward at least a little way. Before the summer is over I want to see Quebec again—& Montreal also if possible. Morton has a very extensive travel programme mapped out, & expects to include New Brunswick, Nova Scotia, & Prince Edward Island in his itinerary.

With best wishes, & trusting that the Circle may continue to flourish, I remain

> Yrs most cordially & sincerely,
> H P L

Notes

1. Earl Clifford Kelley (1905–1932) of Burlington, VT, was president of the NAPA (1931–32), but died by his own hand while in office. He edited *Ripples from Lake Champlain* and accepted two sonnets of HPL's *Fungi from Yuggoth* for it: "The Pigeon-Flyers" and "A Memory." Only "The Pigeon-Flyers" was published.

[38] [ALS]

> 10 Barnes St.,
> Providence, R.I.,
> March 31, 1932

Dear A. H.:—

I am sorry to hear that your health has been below the average, & hope that an early spring may dispel all the residual chills. The winter here has been phenomenally mild, but spring warmth is rather tardy in coming. I always feel more or less run down at the end of a winter, & long for the arrival of warmth & open-air possibilities. I fear my travels this spring will be sadly hampered by an impending siege at the dentist's.

Thanks exceedingly for the two attractive issues of I.I. I see that the dateline is getting more & more contemporary! Glad to know that the Circle still prospers, & hope you will be able to preserve something of its literary flavour. I'm sorry the assembling of a Nat. Am. file presents so many difficulties. Thomson[1] is doing very well with the present volume, & I hope you will miss no issues of it.

Cook is still in Boston & in better health. I hope to see him shortly, though the chilly March weather has hampered travelling on his part, as it has on mine. Glad you found the snapshot of interest—though its size & quality make it somewhat doubtful as a physiognomical revelation. No—I've never seen a picture of you, but would very much like to do so.

    With every good wish,

        Yrs most sincerely,

              H P L

Notes

1. George A. Thomson, Official Editor of NAPA (1931–32).

[39]   [ALS]

                           10 Barnes St.,

                           Providence, R.I.,

                           Octr 1932.

Dear Arthur:—

    Thanks for your note & *Interesting Items*. Glad to see that the Literary Circle is still functioning prosperously, & to hear that you have a congenial walking club. With so much fine scenery close at hand, the latter surely has every reason to expect a prosperous career. I wish I could see some of those landscapes—as well as the bafflingly old-looking church which you describe so entertainingly.

    From your letter I judge that you did not receive any of the cards I mailed from my summer trip. That is very odd, since I very distinctly recall mailing at least one or two. Possibly, though, I did not add sufficient postage. Anyway, the trip did occur, & was a decided success—although the ending was attended with sadness. As I was paying Samuel Loveman a final visit in Brooklyn, I was summoned home on account of the acute illness of my semi-invalid elder aunt—& her death occurred on July 3d. Since she was, in latter years, the presiding genius of the household at 10 Barnes St., the event was of a particularly desolating sort; leaving a sense of vacancy not easily to be dispelled.

    The southern trip—beginning in mid-May—took me through the exquisite Shenandoah Valley in western Virginia, where occur some of the finest low mountain vistas in the U.S. I then branched westward into Tennessee—another fine scenic region—passing through Knoxville & descending to Chattanooga, on the Tennessee River. Chattanooga is only a century old, but has one of the most interesting settings imaginable; being built on & around the steep bluffs at a very circuitous bending of the wide, sluggish stream. It was the scene of some very sharp fighting during the Civil War of 1861–5, & is full of monuments & tablets connected with that event. Of the surrounding hills, Lookout Mountain is the highest—the view from this eminence being of singular breadth & beauty. Inside this mountain is a vast cave system where limestone strata were dissolved out by the action of water. An endless labyrinth of passages exists—culminating in a tremendous chamber 150 feet high, from near whose roof a waterfall bursts forth from the wall, dropping 145 feet to the surface of a black pool. I explored both the outside & inside of Lookout Mountain—this being the second cave system I have visited. (The first was that of the Endless Caverns in Virginia in 1928) Leaving Chattanooga, I travelled westward along the splendid line of Tennessee River bluffs—later skirting the southern border of Tennessee. Finally I reached Memphis, on the Mississippi River—my first sight of that lordly & famous stream. Memphis is very much modernised, & of no great antiquarian interest, so I headed at once down the river. (All this travelling—the entire trip, in fact—was performed by motor coach) The Mississippi is not as impressive to the eye as one might anticipate, although it is quite broad. It is bordered sometimes by bluffs of varying height, & sometimes by flat, muddy plains. In general it is rather inclined to curve & wind, & its constant changes of channel often destroy land areas as they occur. South of Memphis—in the state of Mississippi—there are vast alluvial plains covered with cotton-fields & inhabited only by negroes—an ugly, depressing region. Then, about where the Yazoo River empties into the Mississippi, the terrain rises into a series of very high bluffs, & the old city of Vicksburg (famous for its siege during the Civil War) is encountered. This is a very attractive & picturesque town, with quaint hill streets; but there are not many houses antedating 1840. Just south of Vicksburg the vegetation begins to assume its typical southern form—with gnarled live-oaks & festoons of Spanish moss. A little farther on one encounters the sleepy old city of Natchez, set in one of the finest subtropical landscapes in the world. This region was not part of the thirteen original colonies, but lay within the vast French domain of Louisiana—first visited by the Spaniard De Soto in 1539, explored & annexed to France by La Salle in 1682, & settled early in the 18th century. The French possessions then embraced virtually all the Mississippi Valley as well as Canada. After the treaty of 1763, (which followed Wolfe's victory of 1759 at Quebec, when the power of France in America was broken) the bulk of Louisiana was ceded by France to Spain; but those parts east of the Mississippi (except the city of New Orleans, which remained joined to the western part & was passed to Spain) were ceded to Great Britain for union with the thirteen colonies. Spain at this same time ceded Florida to Great Britain, & the southern part of the Louisiana region was joined to the western half of Florida as the British Province of West-Florida. During the American war of 1775–83 the Spaniards then ruling in New Orleans took advantage of the strife to seize & occupy West Florida. At the peace of 1783 Florida proper was ceded back to Spain, while the regions north of it were allotted to the new republic of the United States. Unfortunately Spain & the U.S. disagreed concerning the northern boundary of West Florida, so that a large area (including the region of Natchez & Vicksburg) was claimed by both nations. The Spaniards were occupying it, & did not finally leave till 1798, when it became definitely U.S. soil. Later, of course, the U.S. bought Louisiana in 1803,

& Florida in 1819. Thus you may see that the history of the lower Mississippi Valley is a highly complex one. Counting in the four years of secession from the U.S., (1861–5) when the short-lived Confederate States of America existed, this region has known *five* different governments—France, England, Spain, the U.S., & the Confederacy. Natchez was founded by the French in 1716 (two years before New Orleans) as a fort & Indian trading post. In 1729 all the garrison & inhabitants were massacred by the Indians, but it was quickly re-settled. Its name was then Ft. Rosalie. In 1763 a British garrison moved in, & it became Ft. Panmure. In 1779 it was captured by the Spaniards under Don Bernardo de Galvez, Governor of Louisiana, & became an important Spanish settlement. Houses of this Spanish period (when it received its present name from the Natchez tribe of Indians) remain to this day. When the U.S. took it over in 1798 it at once became a great port for the shipment of cotton, & enterprising people flocked to it from all over the United States. Its prosperity grew overnight, & the wealth of the people began to appear in the architecture of the new houses—a vast number of which, built from 1810 onward, still survive. This was the period of classic-revival architecture in America, & most of the great houses of Natchez followed the Greek temple pattern. They tended to be on a vaster scale than the houses of the East, so that residences look like public buildings. When American architecture suffered its spectacular decadence after 1830, the Mississippi Valley did not fully share in the lapse; so that very good classic specimens were built until 1860 or 1861. The Civil War ruined Natchez by destroying the slave-owning plantation system on which its prosperity was founded, so that after 1861 no new houses of any importance were built. But the town still keeps alive by means of a few industries & some small-scale agriculture—& a little cotton is still shipped down the river from the half-deserted wharves. For the antiquarian the place is a virtual paradise, since there is almost nothing new there. Some of the old mansions have fallen to ruin, but others manage to keep in a state of preservation. The population still consists largely of the descendants of Americans who came from the Eastern States between 1798 & 1820. The streets are sleepy & shady—overarched by great live-oaks from which Spanish moss hangs in profuse festoons—& the white columns of the many Greek porticoes gleam fascinatingly through this perpetual green twilight. The town proper—like the Upper Town in Quebec—is perched above a high precipice descending to the river; while along the shore there is a narrow strip of land containing wharves, factories, & poor negro residences. This latter is called Natchez-under-the-Hill, & was formerly a riotous resort of river boatmen. The roads in the country around Natchez have a peculiar aspect because of the friable nature of the soil—which causes constant traffic to wear them deeply below the general surface. The older roads (especially the "Natchez Trace", an ancient Indian, French, & Spanish highway leading up into Tennessee) are like gorges or cañons, with vertical walls 10 to 30 feet high &

overgrown with subtropical vegetation. They are not as well paved as those in the north & east, & their one drawback is that they afford a pervasive yellow dust which covers the traveller & all his belongings. The forests in this vicinity—live-oak & cypress, heavy with Spanish moss—are of ineffable picturesqueness, & probably formed a model for those described in the famous novel "Atala" by Chateaubriand (who visited considerably in Natchez during his exile from France.).[1] The ground is varied in contour, hills & valleys giving the scenery a pleasing variety. South of Natchez—across the line in the modern State of Louisiana (only a microscopic fraction of the old French Louisiana colony)—the topography is flatter & less picturesque. We here begin to find palm-like vegetation, which is absent in Natchez save for carefully nurtured palmettos in a few of the gardens. Baton Rouge, the modern capital of Louisiana, has lost most of its antiquities & does not long detain the traveller. South of there the land drops to a flat plain *below* the flood-time level of the Mississippi, & we see the beginning of the famous system of embankments or "levees", equivalent to the dykes of Holland. Now & then a rather shabby village appears—the cottages shewing distinct signs of French architecture, as anyone who has been to Quebec (or, I suppose, France itself) can at once recognise. Sometimes an old plantation manor-house (usually in disrepair) can be spied amidst a grove of trees. The American plantation-houses are of classic design like those of Natchez. The older French ones have steep slant roofs, plain verandahs, & high arcaded basements. At last the populous metropolis of New Orleans is reached. This was the capital of old French Louisiana, & was founded in 1718 by the Canadian explorer Jean-Baptist le Moyne, Sieur de Bienville as the only practicable seaport of the Louisiana colony. It is not really on the sea, but 125 miles from the delta & mouth of the Mississippi—since no more seaward spot had the right kind of ground for the building of a town. It grew quite rapidly, & was an important place when the Spaniards took over the colony in 1763. Spain never planted her civilisation there, since the French had settled it too thickly to make a change possible. The only Spaniards in the colony were soldiers, priests, & officials & their families; & the Spanish language was used only in the law courts. The city was much troubled by river inundations, & soon had an elaborate system of levees & drainage canals. The same system is in use today, improved & extended—& with the canals covered over to form streets. Even now the underground water is so near the surface that cellars are few, while burials are generally in vaults above ground. Tropical fevers greatly [?] troubled the city till the present generation, when science has helped to stamp out such diseases. The ground—all on a flat level—was originally given over to cypress swamps, live oaks, & scrub palmettos. The swamps have been drained, the ground cleared, & many fine varieties of palm introduced. Under the French New Orleans became a centre of much gayety & cultivation—a state of things which has never disappeared. There were many disastrous fires in the old days, that of 1788 being the worst. At this time the Spaniards controlled Louisiana, & the government helped the citizens to rebuild in an especially solid way—with brick & stucco—lending the aid of military engineers & architects. As a result, the rebuilt town of 1795 or 1800 showed a strong Spanish influence in its architecture despite the predominantly French nature of the population. Old New Orleans architecture, thus joining the traditions of France & Spain, is like nothing else in the world. The roofs & casement windows are French—like those of Quebec & old France—but the arcaded first storeys, iron-barred transoms & lunettes, inner courts or patios, & elaborate systems of balconies all attest the influence of Spain. The patios—laid out as gardens with foundations & huge water-jars—are almost infinite in their tasteful variety, & are certainly among the most distinctive features of old New Orleans. The old Franco-Hispanic town lay on the river in what is about the centre of the modern city—occupying a rectangle 4000 feet long & 1500 ft deep. This area is today called the "Vieux Carré" or "old French Quarter", & has miraculously preserved almost all its ancient buildings—including the great cathedral (1795) & the Ursuline Nunnery (1727). In 1803 the U.S. bought Louisiana, & Anglo-Saxons descended in droves on New Orleans. The new American quarter took form along the river to the south of the ancient city, & developed its own commercial district. Today it is the principal part of modern New Orleans—the main business thoroughfare being the street (Canal St.—a very wide filled-in canal) which separates it from the "Vieux Carré". The French have overflowed their old quarter on the northern side. After the American "invasion" there was some mixing of English & French elements, but the fusion has never been complete. The descendants of the French (& of what few Spanish there were) are known as "Creoles", & continued to retain the French language till 25 or 30 years ago. Now, however, the influence of American education & periodicals has Anglicised the entire population; so that there are no more newspapers, magazines, or signs in French. Much, however, of the Gallic spirit remains; as manifest in the elaborate Mardi Gras carnival held each year, & in the general attention paid to elaborate cooking & other Epicurean amenities. Under American rule New Orleans grew to be a mighty cotton-port, but like other Southern towns it suffered ruin in the Civil War. Since then it has recovered because of its strategic commercial & geographic position, so that it is today a great city (abt. 500,000) & the second seaport in America. The wide palm-shaded streets & fine estates of the American section make it one of the most beautiful cities in the world, & the old French quarter is a potent attraction for the lover of architecture or history. This "Vieux Carré" at one time sank to the condition of a slum, but it has been largely reclaimed by sympathetic housebuyers & developers; & is now to some extent a region of antique shops & artists' studios. Its focal point on the river-bank—the old Place d'Armes, with a park in the centre, & the Cathedral & ancient government house on the inner side—is a very fascinating spot, now called Jackson Square. Besides the native Americans & Creoles, New Orleans has a large foreign population, mostly Italians living in the northern part of the Vieux Carré. Negroes also exit in great numbers. The climate of New Orleans is mildly subtropical, though there are unpleasantly cold days in midwinter. It is in N. Latitude 30°—about the same as that of St. Augustine, Florida, & corresponding with North Africa (Morocco, Tripoli, Cairo) in the Old World. The climate exactly suits me, for I am prostrated by cold weather, & at my best in the subtropics. I was in New Orleans more than a fortnight, & came to know & like it very well. A friend of mine—the weird writer E. Hoffmann Price[2]—lives there, but I would prefer a quieter place like Natchez for permanent residence. On my return trip I paused at Mobile, Alabama, a quaint old port founded by the French in 1711, & having a few old houses reminiscent of New Orleans. I then struck northeast through quiet Montgomery (capital of Alabama), the modern metropolis of Atlanta, Georgia, the western part of the Carolinas, & good old Richmond, Virginia, (full of Poe associations) of which I am always extremely fond. After that I touched at many of my usual antiquarian points—Fredericksburg, Va., Washington, Annapolis, Md., & Philadelphia— & finally paused in New York to visit Loveman.

My second long trip of the year was in exactly the opposite direction— northward to Boston, Montreal, & Quebec. It began with an expedition with W. Paul Cook to see the solar eclipse of Aug. 31 from the belt of totality, & continued as a solitary Canadian jaunt. The eclipse was a success, though many places in the total zone were clouded. We chose the ancient town of Newburyport as a post of observation—proceeding via Haverhill & calling on our good old friend "Tryout" Smith, who will be 80 on the 24th of this month. We could not persuade him to go along with us, but in the end he had an excellent view of the eclipse at home. It was total in Haverhill, though not for so long a time as at Newburyport. We reached Newburyport long before the eclipse started, & enjoyed the striking antiquities of the venerable town—about which I must have written you in the past. As our observatory we chose a hilltop meadow with a wide view—near the northern part of the town. Floating clouds in the sky made us anxious; but the sun was out part of the time, & gave us glimpses of all stages of the phenomenon. The landscape did not change in tone until the solar crescent was rather small, & then a kind of sunset vividness became apparent. When the crescent waned to extreme thinness, the scene grew strange & spectral—an almost deathlike quality inhering in the sickly yellowish light. Just about that time the sun went under a cloud, & Cook & I were apprehensive of failure at the crucial moment. At last, though, the thin thread of pre-totality glitter emerged into a large patch of absolutely clear sky. The outspread valleys faded into unnatural night— Jupiter came out in the deep-violet heavens—ghoulish shadow-bands raced along the winding white roads—the last beaded strip of glitter vanished—&

the pale corona flickered into aureolar radiance around the black disc of the obscuring moon. The climax had arrived! The earth was darkened more deeply than in the eclipse of 1925 (which, as you may recall, I witnessed from Yonkers, N.Y. in a half-frozen condition!), though the corona was not so bright. There was a suggestion of a streamer extending above & to the left of the disc, with a shorter corresponding streamer below & to the right. Finally—after a surprisingly long totality—the hooded crescent reëmerged, the valleys glowed again in faint, eerie light, & the various partial phases were repeated in reverse order. The marvel was over, & accustomed things resumed their wonted sway. We had viewed the whole phenomenon with the utmost impressedness & appreciation, & shall certainly remember it vividly. I may never see another—but it is not everyone who has, like me, witnessed two total solar eclipses.

The Montreal–Quebec trip was also a decided success. Both of these ancient cities lie in the Province of Quebec, corresponding to the more settled parts of old French Canada. This province, since its French population was of a more stubbornly nationalistic, self-assertive, & piously conservative calibre than the French of New Orleans, has always kept the French language & institutions alive; & is today officially bi-lingual. When Canada was conquered in 1759—& confirmed to the Empire by treaty in 1763—there were many who wished to extirpate the French character & make the English language & institutions dominant. The best minds in England, however, aided by the observations & reports of such competent & sympathetic administrators as Genl. James Murray, Gen. Sir Guy Carleton (afterward Lord Dorchester), & Genl. Sir Frederick Haldimand, decided that the region was too overwhelmingly French in character to admit of Anglicisation without great hardship & inevitable resentment; hence adopted Parliamentary measures tolerating the French language & legal code, & the Roman Catholic religion. English was introduced merely as an alternative legal language. Since that time there have been influences potent in spreading English through part of Quebec Province, but French has never been seriously threatened as the dominant speech—especially in the easterly regions including Quebec City. The greatest accession of English-speakers to Canada came at the close of the American war, when the successfully revolted colonies expelled all citizens who refused to repudiate allegiance to the Crown. About a third of all the people of America were at that time driven from their homes; those of the South settling in the West Indies, while loyal Northerners flocked by the thousand to Canada. This vast migration was the real origin of Ontario, Nova Scotia & New Brunswick as populous English-speaking provinces, & it likewise gave Quebec Province a substantial English element—especially on the southern border & around Montreal. At one time even Quebec City had a large English population. With the years, however, the highly prolific French have been regaining ground. Emigrants from Great Britain prefer to settle in the more westerly parts of Canada where no large French majority exists, whilst the English in Quebec do not multiply as rapidly as the French. As a result, the

French have become overwhelmingly preponderant in most of their ancient domains, & are gradually filtering into many regions originally settled by the English. Indeed, they have drifted down into New England—especially the factory districts—so that there are towns in Rhode Island almost as solidly Gallic as Quebec City. Since Quebec Province is bi-lingual, all official notices are printed in both languages. Thus at railway crossings the warning sign reads both "Railway Crossing" & "Traverse du Chemin de Fer." Montreal—which on this occasion I saw for the first time—is more British than Quebec City, & does not seem at all foreign except in the French section east of St. Lawrence Blvd. There is one suburb—Westmount—with a wholly English population, & with street signs in English only—though the *legal* signs have to be bi-lingual. Indeed, in the best sections of Montreal all the shop signs are in English. The city is highly attractive, & is well set off by the towering slope of Mt. Royal, which rises in its midst. The ancient parts are those along the southern waterfront—containing the Cathedral, the 1705 Governors' House, the sailors' chapel of 1771, the old market, & other vestiges of the past. Montreal was founded in 1642 by the Frenchman Maisonneuve, & later became a centre of the fur trade—finally surpassing Old Quebec in size. Today it would seem, in the main, like any high-grade American city but for the profusion of horse-drawn vehicles. I saw the town fully, & also visited the nearby Lachine Rapids in the St. Lawrence. However, Montreal is too much modernised to have the charm of Old Quebec, hence I was glad to get along to the latter place. There is absolutely nothing else like Quebec in the Western Hemisphere—a perfect bit of Old Europe! I must have told you about it in 1930. As then, I revelled in the atmosphere of massed antiquity—the vertical cliff, the frowning citadel, the silver steeples & red tiled roofs, the narrow, winding hill streets, the centuried facades, & the massive city walls—& also took a trip around the neighbouring Isle of Orleans, where the old French countryside remains in a primitive state—just as when Wolfe's troops landed in 1759. There were endless brick farmhouses with curved eaves, wind & water mills, wayside shrines, & quaint white villages clustering around ancient, silver-steepled white churches. Nothing but French is spoken here, & descendants of the original settlers still live on their hereditary acres. After Quebec I returned to Boston—taking one brief afternoon trip to old Marblehead as a finale to the whole excursion. ¶ With all good wishes—

     Yrs most cordially — H P L

P.S. The dental trouble was all disposed of by the middle of last May, thank Heaven!

Notes

1. François-René, vicomte de Chateaubriand (1768–1848), *Atala* (1801), a romance

based in large part upon a visit that Chateaubriand had taken to wild and uninhabited regions of the American continent.

2. E. Hoffmann Price (1898–1988), pulp writer and correspondent of HPL.

[40]   [ALS]

10 Barnes St.,

Providence, R.I.,

Jany. 14, 1933

Dear Arthur:—

Many thanks for the new I. I., which well sustain your unbroken tradition. Glad to hear that you have had some pleasant trips in new territory, though sorry the hiking club has suffered disruption. These pedestrian organisations seem rather difficult to keep together, since individual opinion plays so great a part in determining itineraries, distances, & the like. Morton's Paterson Ramblers have suffered a sort of schism, with the advocates of long & arduous hikes arrayed against the upholders of short, easy routes. But I'm glad the literary circle still remains unimpaired.

What you say of that ancient & deserted house by the churchyard fascinates me extremely, & I surely envy you the glimpse of it. A few years ago I wrote a tale called "The Unnamable", in which something very much of this sort figured—a very old house abutting on a centuried burying-ground in a venerable New England town. My idea really came from a house in Salem, Massachusetts, whose rear adjoins the ancient cemetery where burials have occurred since 1650 or thereabouts. Hawthorne also used this house & cemetery in his macabre "Dr. Grimshawe's Secret."

Congratulations, by the way, on your approaching wedding—which I trust may be productive of permanent happiness & contentment.

Though this is my season of hibernation, I lately took advantage of the mild weather to visit Frank Belknap Long, Jun., in New York—also seeing a number of other old friends such as Loveman, Kirk, Talman, &c. Unfortunately Morton was out of town, & I could not get in touch with Kleiner. I explored most of the museums, as usual, seeing among other things the remarkable archaic Greek Apollo recently acquired by the Metropolitan Museum of Art. I saw the old year out at Loveman's new apartment at 17 Middagh St., Brooklyn—not far from his old place in Columbia Heights. It has three rooms, & gives his many art treasures a more appropriate setting than they have ever had before.

Amateurdom seems to be prospering almost unprecedently, the number of amateur papers I have lately received being quite surprising. I trust the condition may prove permanent. The amateur William J. Clemence,[1] by the way, has moved from East Providence into Providence proper; so that I have seen him a number of times recently. He may issue a paper before the year is over.

With every good wish for 1933,

I remain

Yrs most cordially & sincerely,

H P L

Notes

1. William J. Clemence (1871–1938), amateur journalist and lyric poet from Rhode Island, most active in the 1890s and 1900s, who co-edited the *Rapier* with Louis B. Gardner. W. Paul Cook related how HPL gave Clemence a suit when he was down on his luck during the Depression.

[41]   [ALS]

10 Barnes St.,

Providence, R.I.,

March 18, 1933

Dear Arthur:—

Congratulations on your new venture—may it prove happy & permanent! I shall look for the story in the next I. I. Thanks, by the way, for the current issues—& for the prominent place accorded to my metrical effort in the Sept. number.[1] I also note with interest the item concerning the Cook-Lovecraft eclipse expedition.

Yes—the New-Year trip was very pleasant. Since then I have had occasion to go to Hartford, Connecticut (87 miles west of here) to assist on a research job, & found the ancient suburbs of that city (which is itself not especially interesting) extremely fascinating. Farmington is a quaint village 9 miles from the town, situated amidst beautiful scenery & having a wealth of splendid elm trees. Most of the houses are old—the inn where I stopped was built in 1638—& there is a fine steepled church built in 1771. Wethersfield is also attractive—with vast elms, a broad village green, a steepled church built in 1763, & a large number of ancient houses. This whole region must be magnificent in summer.

I envy you your sight of London—had you ever been there before? I have read so much about it, & have seen so many maps & pictures of it, that I really believe I could find my way to the principal points of interest without a guide. It would take weeks, though, to absorb it properly—to study the atmosphere of all its parts, & to seek out all its quaint & glamourous vistas. Certain of the northern streets all unknown to tourist fame have attracted me ever since I read of them in the rambling reminiscences of Arthur Machen. (Who came from your own Wales, & whose fantastic descriptions of Caerleon I have often mentioned to you.)

The prosperity of the N.A.P.A. seems to continue, & a still further rise is forecast by the recent appointment of Edwin Hadley Smith as Secy. of Publicity[.] He is planning a particularly energetic recruiting campaign.

New England's winter has been a very mild one, but I am nevertheless glad to hail the advent of spring. I fear, though, that financial considerations will keep me from making a spring tour of the sort I have been accustomed to make during recent years.

With every good wish, & with renewed congratulations on your marriage, I remain

Yrs most cordially & sincerely,

H P L

Notes

1. "Background" appeared on the first page.

[42] [ALS]

[H. P. LOVECRAFT

~~10 BARNES STREET~~ 66, College St.,

PROVIDENCE, R. I.]

[May 1933]

Dear Arthur:—

Thanks exceedingly for the new I. I.'s—especially the de luxe wedding issue with your piquant account of the great event & of the London trip. You have certainly produced a number worthy of the occasion, & I am sure all your readers will appreciate it. I envy you the sight of London—& hope that some day I can manage to get across the ocean & absorb some of the ancestral atmosphere.

Incidentally—please note & record my changed address. I think I said in my former letter that financial pressure was forcing me to seek more inexpensive quarters—but as matters turned out, I am really much better housed than before; having taken the upper part of a delightful old Georgian dwelling in conjunction with my surviving aunt. Despite my fondness for old houses, I had never actually *lived* in one before; but now I really inhabit one at last! The edifice—yellow & wooden—is of a kind frequently built in New England about 1800, though I am not sure whether many similar houses were built in Great Britain. It is situate on the crest of Providence's great hill in a quaint grassy court just off College St.—behind & next to the John Hay Library of Brown University (which contains the famous *Harris* Collection of American Poetry), & about half a mile south of my former Barnes St. residence. The fine

Georgian doorway is very much like that depicted on my bookplate—which I think I shewed you. In the rear is a picturesque, village-like garden at a higher level than the front of the house. The upper half taken by my aunt & me contains five rooms plus attic storerooms. My own quarters—a large study & a small adjoining bedroom—are on the southern side, with my working desk under a west window affording a splendid view of the lower town's outspread roofs & of the mystical sunsets that flame behind them. The interior is as fascinating as the exterior—with Georgian fireplaces & mantels, chimney cupboards, curving staircase, wide floor-boards, old-fashioned latches, small-paned windows, six-panel doors, rear wing with floor at a different level (3 steps down), quaint attic stairs, &c.—just like the old houses open as museums. Moving in was a frightful job (I had 2000 books to sort & arrange), but now that I am settled I find it tremendously homelike. It is hard to realise from externals that this move is an *economy* measure—yet it is just that. The house is owned by the university.

Amateurdom continues to prosper unprecedentedly, & I fancy that E. Hadley indeed deserves much of the credit. Hope an analogous condition prevails in the mother land.

All good wishes—

Yrs most cordially & sincerely—

H P L

[43]   [ALS]

66, College St.,
Providence, R.I.,
July 29, 1933.

Dear Arthur:—

Many thanks for the new I. I.'s—which surely live up to their name. I was especially interested in the "Caynton" article,[1] & envy you your pilgrimage amongst ancestral scenes. It must be fascinating to be in contact with the tangible reliques of a continuously bequeathed past—not only early-modern & mediaeval things, but occasional Roman fragments linking one with the vast fabric of the ancient world. Of course we have houses as early as 1640 over here—but they are very scarce & generally small. And yet we are really quite amply backgrounded as compared with the people of very new regions like the American West or Australia. In those localities a house much more than a century old is an unknown marvel.

My new Georgian abode is surely fascinating—though the process of settlement was marred by an accident which has spoiled the entire summer. On June 14 my aunt fractured her ankle on the stairs, & she has since been confined to bed with the injured member in a heavy plaster cast—at an hospital for three weeks, & since then at home with a nurse. Her incapacitation has put a number of rather confining burdens upon me—so that I have been unable to take any really extensive trips this year. The cast will be removed before long, & then will come a period on crutches—of a character still undetermined. My aunt's mishap occurred before the house was fully settled (except for my quarters), but even so, things are now somewhat straightened out.

Naturally, I could not attend the N.A.P.A. convention—which I am told was an extremely successful event. Attendance was large, & included many notable old-timers. W. Paul Cook stopped here briefly on his way to the festivities. The new board of officers seems to have the endorsement of all, & looks to me quite adequate. I have been appointed chairman of the critical bureau—& fear I shall have a rather hard time completing the board.

Such outings as I have had, have been exceedingly brief—& usually in connexion with visitors. At the end of June I had a visit from the weird writer & Orientalist E. Hoffmann Price, who came in his car & did considerable exploring around the ancient & picturesque Rhode Island countryside. Next week I expect James F. Morton—whose advent is always an occasion for delight. Last Monday, Tuesday & Wednesday I visited Frank B. Long & his parents in the Cape Cod (Massachusetts) region, where they were staying for a short time. The weather was poor, but we managed to enjoy ourselves—spending most of the time in literary & philosophical discussion. We had one motor trip along the ancient roads & through the quaint villages of the Cape. My favourite place there is Sandwich, whose centuried houses & slender white steeple are in an excellent state of preservation. Enclosed is a card shewing the typical scenery of the region—not vastly different from that of Britain, I fancy. Indeed, I believe that New England reproduces the scenery & vegetation of the Mother Land more closely than any other part of the globe.

Enclosed is a circular of a brochure issued by one of the old United members—the gifted weird artist, poet, & fiction-writer Clark Ashton Smith.[2] These stories are exceedingly powerful, & I can conscientiously advise you to order the book if your tastes run at all toward the bizarre.

Some very decent weather since my return from Cape Cod, so that a good deal of my writing has been done in the open air—largely on the wooded river-bank which I have probably described to you. Took one trip to Newport by boat—revelling as usual in the numerous antiquities of the ancient seaport.

With best wishes, & again congratulating you upon the excellence of your recent issues, I remain

Yrs most cordially & sincerely,
H P L

Notes

1. Perhaps a reference to the Caynton Caves, manmade underground chambers in the grounds of Caynton Hall, near Beckbury, Shropshire, England.

2. Clark Ashton Smith (1893–1961), prolific California poet and writer of fantasy tales. He received a "fan" letter from HPL in 1922 and corresponded with him until HPL's death.

[44]   [ANS][1]

[Postmarked Quebec, Canada,
3 September 1933]

In the old ancestral Empire for an all too brief 4-day sojourn—my only real outing of 1933. Quebec is without question the most beautiful & fascinating city I have ever seen—a fantastic dream—a picture into which one can walk bodily & actually touch the wonders of time & space delineated! I hate to think of leaving. Am now sitting on the Ramparts looking out on a scene absolutely unparallelled in North America—dizzily cliff-climbing streets, outspread river & countryside, distant mountains, huddled red roofs & silver spires—I don't wonder that Sir Michael Sadler of Oxford calls Quebec the loveliest city in the Western Hemisphere & one of the 20 loveliest in the world. I stopped in Boston to see W. Paul Cook & look up a 1637 house in the suburbs. Hope to see Salem & Marblehead on my way back. Have had fine hot weather so far. Home again Thursday. It takes only a single night to get up here.

Best wishes—
H P L

Notes

1. *Front:* View from Parliament Buildings, Quebec, Canada.

[45]   [ALS]

66 College St.,
Providence, R.I.,
Dec. 24, 1933

Dear Arthur:—

Thanks infinitely for your envelope of interesting material, so opportunely received at Yuletide. I. I. continues in its pleasing course—the special Christmas issue being unusually tasteful.

Your recent trip excites my profoundest envy, & makes me wish anew that I could find some way to visit the ancestral soil. I cannot say how grateful I am for the views of Chester—of whose quaintness & beauty I have long known, since a friend of my late elder aunt's was born & grew up there. The Cathedral must be magnificently impressive—& it is highly interesting to know that Wolfe's battle-flag is there. That is certainly one of the first things I would look for. I think I told you that I found the exact route of Wolfe's ascent of the cliff last September. The French inhabitants, not being over-anxious to perpetuate the details of their conquest, leave it unmarked & are vague about directing one to it; but this time I secured authentic information from non-French sources. The precise spot is little changed since Wolfe's time, though there is a park at the top & some sort of industrial development—with a railway & steamship terminal—at the bottom. Chester's "Rows" & Tudor houses would fascinate me ineffably. We have plenty of *imitation* Tudor houses in New England, but the real thing would undoubtedly present unmistakable differences. I believe I mentioned that we have no houses older than 1636. The oldest houses I have ever seen are the Spanish buildings in St. Augustine—some going back to 1571.

Uriconium,[1] naturally, is still further beyond all hope of New World competition—save for the Aztec & Maya ruins in Central America. I have absorbed your well-told article with extreme interest, & shall file it for permanent reference. Classical antiquity will never cease to fascinate me—& at this moment I am exulting in a Christmas gift of an archaic Greek mortuary vase. Nesscliffe Cave sounds enormously attractive, too.[2]

I am glad to say that my aunt is now vastly better—out everywhere with a single cane, & all around the house with no cane at all. Since she has assumed charge of domestic matters, the house begins to look infinitely more home-like—curtains hung, more old family furniture brought out of storage, & so on. It really makes me think—despite its smaller extent—of my birthplace. I am enclosing a picture of the exterior which you can keep if you like. The window over the door is that of my bedroom, whilst the other two at its left are the south windows of my study—which also has 2 west windows. My desk is at the northernmost of these west windows, with a highly pleasing view of old roofs & boughs, steeples & belfries, & a bit of distant horizon. In the picture note the Georgian doorway with fan carving above. My aunt is shewn standing in it.

My period of relative hibernation has now begun; though I kept up my rural & woodland rambles throughout October, & even made a few such trips in November. As late as Nov. 30 I visited Plymouth—founded in 1620—the oldest town in New England. It is still very picturesque, with houses as early as 1664, though 18th century material predominates.

At the present moment—after a home observance of Yule—I am going to visit Frank B. Long in New York & enjoy a duplicate Christmas as I did last year. Naturally I shall see some of the local amateurs—though unfortunately Morton will be absent during most or perhaps all of my sojourn. The July convention was, from all accounts, by far the best in recent years. Some of the comparative lack of activity since then is due to unexpected trouble (now probably solved) in financing the mailing bureau. As for the critical department—it will really be much as before, though the addition of Cole as prose reviewer is a great asset.

All good wishes for the holidays & for the coming year.

Yrs most cordially & sincerely—

H P L

Notes

1. Uriconium (more properly Viroconium Cornoviorum) is the Roman name for the village of Wroxeter, in Shropshire. It was first established in 55 C.E.
2. Nesscliffe Rock Cave, better known as Kynaston's Cave, in the town of Nesscliffe, in Shropshire.

[46] [ALS]

66 College St.,
Providence, R.I.,
April 13, 1934.

Dear Arthur:—

       I regret infinitely that I cannot be of direct help in supplying the missing *National Amateurs*. The sad fact is, that I have no duplicates of *any* number, & lack most of the issues mentioned myself! In the old days, as you know, I was wholly a *United* man, & kept only such numbers of the N.A. as contained some special topic of interest. Then when the United (i.e., the main branch) lapsed, I stopped saving any amateur papers except those of personal concern. In fact, I was virtually out of amateurdom. My interest returned when the National braced up at the 1930 convention, & I have a personal file of the N.A. complete since then—but unfortunately there are no duplicates. My *United Amateur* file extends unbroken from March 1914, when I entered amateurdom, to the finish in 1927. I did have earlier copies, but gave them to Paul J. Campbell in 1926 when fire destroyed his own collection. Well—I'll mention the dates you need to other amateurs, & see if anyone else has any extras. There surely ought to be some somewhere.

       I read the recent I I's with usual interest & appreciation, & certainly envy you your trip to London. I'll have to get over sometime—though only the gods know how I can manage it. The trouble is that no brief trip would do more than tantalise me. Once I landed on British soil I'd want months to poke about the country, visit the unspoiled, old time villages, quaint seaports, & Roman remains, & in general absorb everything from Cornwall up to the Firth of Forth & beyond. The expense of such a venture, even under the most primitive conditions, can well be imagined!

       I hope you can soon revisit the ancient Roman town of Deva![1] Last January I picked up the late Arthur Weigall's "Wanderings in Roman Britain", some of which consists of the newspaper articles you sent me several years ago. It is the most fascinating work I have encountered in ages, & I was really surprised at the extent of surviving Roman material—much of which has been excavated during the present century. It appears that the amphitheatre at Caerleon-on-Usk has been found virtually intact beneath the grassy mound that covered it, so that today it forms one of the finest specimens of its kind in the world. I was interested likewise in the full presentation of Weigall's evidence that the Britons were thoroughly Romanised & Latin-speaking, that they were widely intermarried with the imperial legions, & that the resulting Britanno-Roman population was absorbed rather than expelled or exterminated by the Saxon invaders. It gives one a pleasant sense of connexion with classical antiquity to realise that, in all probability, a good proportion of one's own blood-ancestors spoke Latin, wore togas, served under the imperial eagles, bore names like M. Julius Civilis or P. Valerius Gallus, & gloried in the title of *civis Romanus*. The chapter on Uriconium interested me doubly because of your own recent account of that place.

The old-time amateur Ernest A. Edkins (active 1883–1910; editor of *The Stylus*) intends to visit England this summer, & is reading my Weigall book in preparation. I certainly envy him his itinerary. Most of his time, I think, will be spent in the minute exploration of London. He was born in England, but was brought to America in infancy, & has no recollection of the ancient land.

Yes—I met a goodly number of the amateurs on my N.Y. visit last December–January. Morton, Loveman, Kleiner, &c. I saw the old year out at Loveman's, & he quite overwhelmed me by presenting me with some antiquities from his notable collection—an impressive looking Egyptian tomb-statuette (ushabti) almost a foot high, & perhaps 4000 years old, a small Mayan image of stone, &c. I didn't see anything of the Blue Pencil group except for Morton & Kleiner.

This reminds me—you have probably seen in the *Tryout* & *Brooklynite* that Morton was married last month to Miss Merritt of the B.P.C. So far, judging from his letters, he is bearing up well under his new responsibilities.

I have hopes of getting down to Florida later this month to visit my young friend & amateur recruit Robert H. Barlow—this year's N.A.P.A. story laureate. I shall certainly welcome the warmth of the subtropics, for this past winter has been the worst in New England within the memory of the living. As you probably know, our climate is more given to extremes than that of the British Isles. On February 9 the thermometer sank to -17° F. at Providence—the lowest temperature by a wide margin ever recorded by the weather bureau here. The only comparable winter I can recall was the terrible one of 1917–18. For anything worse, one has to go back to the frightful two of 1778–9, & 1779–80. I hope this present one isn't the first of a pair! On my way south I expect to stop a week with Long—also seeing Loveman, Morton, & Kleiner, of course.

W. Paul Cook spent the winter in the subarctic milieu of northern Vermont, but has an idea of returning to Boston later. He has issued two brochures of ironic sociological material (from Walter J. Coates's Driftwind Press, in N. Montpelier, where he is staying) during the past few months, but these have not had a general amateur circulation.

I was interested in your Southern contributor's article on house names in America. What he says is generally true of the "new South"—the piedmont

region away from the coast—but in the old tidewater South virtually all the gentlemen-adventurers & planters named their estates as their forefathers had in Great Britain. Thus the seat of the Byrds was *Westover,* that of the Washingtons *Wakefield,* that of the Lees *Stratford,* & so on. In New England house & estate names (that is, of the original colonial period) are relatively uncommon, though a considerable number can be cited—such as *Careswell,* the Winslow seat in the Plymouth Colony, & the Rhode Island country houses called *Vaucluse, Whitehall, Redwood, Elm Grove,* & so on. In the 19th and 20th centuries many houses have been named in a whimsical or antiquarian spirit. Most old houses, though, are known mainly by the names of the principal families who have occupied them—as the Pierce–Nichols House, the Whipple–Moffett– Ladd House, the Sargent–Murray–Gilman House, &c. Some of the finest country-seats in New England never bore an individual name. My present abode is by some people called *The Garden House.* All good wishes—
   Yrs most sincerely— H P L

Notes

1. Deva Victrix, the Roman town built on the site of Chester, in Cheshire.

[47] [ANS][1]

          [Postmarked Charleston, S.C.,
                30 April 1934]

Greetings from my favourite town! Had a pleasant week in N Y with Long, Morton, Loveman, Kirk, Kleiner, &c.—& left for the South at midnight April 22–3. Spent the next morning in Washington—exploring the ancient Georgetown section, which was there before the capital was laid out. Richmond, Va. in afternoon; Raleigh, N.C. in evening. Reached Charleston at dawn April 24. Stopping at the Y M C A & absorbing the atmosphere of the old town as usual. Marvellous place—perfect survival of the 18th century! It is full summer down here—rich green vegetation, hot days, &c. In Washington it is merely springlike—with delicate young foliage. And when I left N Y it was still wintry there—chill winds & bare boughs. There is a peculiar charm in passing from winter to summer in a few hours. On to Savannah tomorrow, & the next day I shall be in De Land, Florida, visiting R. H. Barlow. This card shews one of the principal landmarks of Charleston. The churchyard contains the grave of the eminent statesman John C. Calhoun.
Best wishes—
H P L

Notes

1. *Front:* St. Philip's Church, Charleston, S. C.—19.

[48] [ANS][1]

[Postmarked Saint Augustine, Fla.,
8 May 1934]

Greetings from the oldest city in the United States—founded by the Spanish in 1565, ceded to Britain 1763, ceded back to Spain 1783, sold to U.S. 1821. Many of the old Spanish houses—dating back to the 1580's & 1590's—still remain in good condition; these being the oldest houses I have ever seen. The subtropical climate braces me up like a tonic—I shall hate to return north! Have a splendid balconied room overlooking the Matanzas River. Exploring the town by gradual degrees. Much of the quaint atmosphere is still there, though of course there is no such solid continuity with the past as Charleston has. My favourite haunt is the ancient fort—begun in 1676—on whose parapet I do most of my writing. I am also fond of the old public squares & parks with their perpetual green twilight of palm foliage. Stopped in Charleston on the way down, & hope to again on the way back. Shall also see Long, Morton, Kleiner, Loveman, &c. in New York. Best wishes—
H P Lovecraft

Notes

1. *Front:* Entrance to St. Augustine, Fla.

[49] [ANS][1]

[Postmarked De Land, Fla.,
4 June 1934]

Still having a tremendously enjoyable time down here in De Land. My host is a brilliant young fellow—present N.A.P.A. story laureate, & a painter, sculptor, pianist, landscape gardner, [*sic*] & book collector besides. The Barlow place is 14 miles from the town—in a wild country, on a lake. Splendid subtropical scenery. Hopes of reaching Havana very slight, but shall pause a week in ancient St. Augustine & return north by easy stages—stopping in Charleston, Richmond, & Washington. Florida suits me physically better than any other climate I've ever sampled.
    Regards—
H P L

Notes

1. *Front:* 196 A Cocoanut Tree, Florida.

[50]   [ANS][1]

[Postmarked Saint Augustine, Fla.,
23 June 1934]

Amongst my favourite antiquities! Staying in St. Augustine a week, & absorbing ancient atmosphere to the full. It is interesting to note that this town has
houses of Elizabethan dates—not only older than any others in the U.S., but
older than any *private dwelling* (as distinguished from churches & public buildings like the Tower &c) in London. The oldest private houses in London are
some gabled structures in Holborn, dating from James I. ¶ North again—
alas—by the middle of July. ¶ Regards & best wishes—
H P L

Notes

1. *Front:* Oldest House, Aviles Street, St. Augustine, Fla. *Back:* This is said to be one of
the first houses built after the city was destroyed by Sir Francis Drake, in 1586. —
Built entirely of Couquina. [The strikeouts in the printed text are HPL's.]

[51]   [ALS]

Nantucket Island
—Sept[r] 1, 1934

Dear Arthur:—

Yours of the 14th reached me at the central stage of my final
outing of the 1934 season. I spent a few days in Boston last week as the guest
of Edward H. Cole—W. Paul Cook coming down from Vermont & participating in the sessions. We went to Haverhill to see good old Tryout Smith—
who does not seem to age at all, though he will be 82 in October—& had
glimpses of Salem & Marblehead. Also had dinner at the Myers home in
Cambridge. Young Peter—whom I hadn't seen since he was 6, in 1923, has
grown up to be a splendidly brilliant youth; a thorough aesthete & discriminating antiquarian. The Coles brought me home in their car Sunday, & the
next day I set out on the second half of my outing—taking a coach for New
Bedford & the Nantucket boat.

Nantucket Island, the scene of my present week of antiquarianising, lies
30 miles off the Cape Cod coast—54 miles from New Bedford & 90 from
Providence. It is, I truly believe, the most marvellously preserved bit of the
elder America in existence—& it is curious that I had never seen it before,
since it is only a 6-hours' trip from my own doorstep. It was settled around
1660 by Massachusetts men who had been persecuted for giving harbourage
to Quakers—thus having something in common with the liberal heritage of
Rhode Island. In a short time it acquired a good-sized population—including
many Quakers—& the settlers were always very honourable & scrupulous in
dealing with its Indian aborigines (who became extinct a century ago). Until

1692 it formed part of the Province of New-York, but since then it has belonged to Massachusetts. Agriculture & fishing were its first pursuits, & in the 18th century *whaling* became dominant. At first whales were killed just off the shore from land or small boats; but when they became extinct in these waters the Nantucketers began to fit out great whaling brigs & pursue long voyages—even to the Pacific. They became exceedingly prosperous, & the chief town of the island (called *Sherburne* until 1795, but thereafter *Nantucket* after the island itself) grew to be a place of considerable size & beauty, with handsome houses, churches, mansions, & public buildings in the Georgian style. It resembles Salem & Newport, though not so large. And it has kept to its original colonial appearance better than any other town in the United States. In time the whaling industry declined, leaving the town greatly impoverished. On this account no new buildings were erected—so that to this day we have here a perfect surviving specimen of the Yankee whaling port of a century or more ago. Later summer visitors began to invade & dominate the island—& their fortunate appreciativeness has aided in the preservation of everything just as it was. The original families, however, still survive—as is attested by the constant presence of such historic names as Macy, Folger, Coffin, & Starbuck on the old-fashioned silver doorplates. Nantucket town is of a rare beauty, with great elms & other fine trees. The rest of the island—low, rolling country—has been denuded of its forests, though laborious attempts are constantly made to reintroduce them. Agriculture has badly declined owing to the exhaustion of the soil. The only considerable settlement besides Nantucket town is Siasconset (locally pronounced "Sconset") on the southeastern shore. This consists of some highly quaint fishermen's cottages ranged along rambling, flowering lanes—now restored & occupied by the omnipresent summer visitors. The island averages only 15 miles long & 7 miles wide. Fresh water is so pure & abundant that it is thought some curious subterranean or submarine reservoir must underlie the terrain. The climate is very equable, though too cool for my comfort just now. Because of their isolation, the islanders have a few traditions, customs, & idioms of a distinctive sort; though the standard of education has always been to[o] high to foster grotesque peculiarities. During the Revolution Nantucket was neutral ground, & many of her sons remained loyal to our rightful Sovereign. Admiral Sir Isaac Coffin, Bart., who founded a school on the island in 1826, was descended from an old Nantucket line.

A folder which I lately mailed to you—together with the enclosed postcard views—will give you some idea of the charm of this marvellous old town. There is nothing else like it—whole networks of cobblestoned streets lined with colonial cottages & Georgian mansions—narrow, garden-bordered lanes—ancient belfries & steeples—picturesque waterfront—*everything* that the antiquarian could ask! I am quartered in an hotel formed from an old Georgian house—with small-paned windows, six-panel doors, wide floor-boards, & other signs of venerable age. My room is on the top floor, with a splendid view of town, harbour, & sea. In the 5 days now elapsed I have explored old houses, the 1746 windmill, the Historical Society & Whaling Museums, the ancient churches, & the Maria Mitchell Observatory—at which latter place I had an excellent view of Saturn through the 5-inch telescope. This observatory adjoins the birthplace of the celebrated female astronomer Maria Mitchell, who became a professor at Vassar College. I have minutely explored all the centuried streets & alleys on foot, & am strongly tempted to rent a cycle for wider excursions. At the outset I took a motor sightseeing trip around the entire island—which allowed a quarter-hour stop at Siasconset for pedestrian exploration. Shall be home again Sept. 4.

Edkins intensely enjoyed his visit to the Mother Land, though his crowded schedule did not permit of any personal contacts. I had suggested his looking up amateurs. During the course of his wanderings he generously sent me a veritable wealth of literary & pictorial travel material—including a splendid London book with Pennell plates.[1] His trip ended with a dash to Paris & Switzerland.

And now let me thank you most abundantly for the interesting material enclosed in your letter—the postcards & the illustrated article on Roman Britain. This latter is veritably a godsend, since the pictures admirably illustrate the Weigall book I read last winter. I shall treasure all these things permanently. The text of the article mentions several important steps in British archaeology since the date (1926) of "Wanderings in Roman Britain". Needless to say, I prodigiously envy you your proximity to these ancient sites—& your chances for visiting a goodly number of them. You are fortunate in having one of the Roman coins of the Llandudno find.

The Shrewsbury & Meeting-house cards are of extreme interest. Friends' Meeting-Houses surely look the same, the world over! The sect is almost extinct in New England, though it once flourished in Rhode Island & on Nantucket. The Dyer line in my ancestry was Quaker. The Quaker meeting-house in Nantucket dates from 1838 & is preserved as an annexe to the historical museum. A Newport meeting-house of 1698 is still standing & in use as a "community centre" for children. The Providence meeting-house (1845) is still used by the remaining handful of Quakers; but it is for sale & may soon disappear. Oddly enough, its predecessor (1740) is likely to outlive it—for it was removed to another site & is now a dwelling in a region little touched by change.

Your recent journeys seem to have been very pleasant, & the trip to ancestral scenes must have evoked all sorts of memories. It is five years since I have visited the western Rhode Island country whence sprang so many of my lines, & where some of the old homesteads yet remain. I wish I had that collection of warming-pans—I encounter such things frequently in the old houses & museums I visit.

Thanks, as usual, for I. I.—which always lives up to its name. I read it with the utmost pleasure, & found the meeting-house article a valuable companion to the postcard.

James F. Morton visited me early in August, & we took the usual trips to points of interest in Rhode Island—including ancient Newport. He later travelled in Massachusetts, New Hampshire, & Maine, being joined by his wife.

Again thanking you for everything—

Yrs most sincerely—

H P L

Notes

1. Joseph Pennell (1857–1928), American graphic artist and illustrator, noted for landscapes and architectural scenes. The volume in question may be *Haunts of Old London* (London: T. N. Foulis, 1914), consisting of 25 of Pennell's etchings. Sidney Dark's *London* (London: Macmillan, 1924; *LL* 234) also had illustrations by Pennell.

[52]   [ALS]

66 College St.,

Providence, R.I.,

Dec. 29, 1934.

Dear Arthur:—

Delighted to receive yours of the 13th with the two recent issues of I.I. & the card of the spider-web painting in Chester Cathedral. This painting must be a tremendously remarkable thing—& I can imagine the effect when it is viewed as a transparency with the light behind it. I notice with pleasure your account of the August journeyings—& it veritably makes my mouth water to think of the regions through which you passed. That church at Great Ness with Saxon foundations must have been fascinating.[1] Have you ever seen the *complete* Saxon church at Bradford-on-Avon?[2] Edkins visited it last summer, & sent me a generous array of postals depicting its exterior, interior, & notable details. I read with great interest your wife's article on Windsor Castle, & hope that you can arrange to see it for yourself during your January visit to the London region. By the way—not long ago I acquired a set of booklets with illustrations covering the whole range of Britain's history, in which is a view of the Jordan Meeting House in Buckinghamshire. This exterior view finely supplements the interior view you so kindly sent. The booklets I refer to are of great attractiveness, interest, & educational value—to adults as well as to school children, though I fancy they are designed largely for the latter. They consist almost entirely of simple line drawings covering every phase of British life from prehistoric times to the present—houses, costumes, utensils, art forms, weapons, transportational devices, historic events, industrial processes, &c.—& forming an admirable supplement to any standard written history. For a writer attempting to visualise the past, many of these illustrations are supremely valuable; for they include diagrams of old towns & types of buildings, typical scenes of former ages, & any number of pictures of common objects of all periods, drawn from originals in the British Museum. The series, compiled by C. W. Airne, consists of seven booklets—one briefly covering the whole ground, the next five taking up various periods in detail, & the last covering the Empire outside Britain. I have all except this last-named one—& am endeavouring to get hold of that.[3] They are published by Sankey, Hudson, & Co. of Manchester, & sold at Woolworth Stores on both sides of the Atlantic. Each one costs only 10 cents in America—so I imagine it would be 5d. in Britain. I strongly advise you to get a set of these if you are at all interested in the visual aspect of the past. Don't despise them as "children's picture books"—for they really make plain a great many things about which the average adult has only the haziest ideas.

The autumn in New England was not especially pleasant, so that I took fewer trips than last year. In October, when the turning foliage was at its greatest splendour, I visited Edward H. Cole for a few days, & was taken in his car to an exquisite scenic region in northern Massachusetts. Later he came to Providence & I shewed him the lovely Narragansett country in southern Rhode Island—where, amidst a landscape but little changed since the 18th century, there broods beside the Narrow River the ancient snuff-mill in which the eminent painter Gilbert Stuart was born in 1755. In this region also is the quaint seaport of Wickford, virtually unaltered in aspect for the last 150 years. In November I briefly visited Boston & saw W. Paul Cook, who was down from New Hampshire for a week. We discussed the memorial booklet to be issued for the late Mrs. Miniter,[4] & examined many old documents connected with her family. Also saw Cole & Lynch. Weather was too cold for much exploration, but we did visit the fine old Royall mansion (1737) in Medford—now a museum. This is one of the finest early Georgian houses in New England.

Christmas was highly enjoyable hereabouts—my aunt & I had a *tree* for the first time in years. In the morning we listened to the remarkable British Empire broadcast, which included conversations over the ether between London & all the Dominions—India, Canada, Australia, South Africa, &c—besides messages from various points in the home land, & a graceful concluding address by the King. I don't know when I've ever encountered a more impressive phenomenon. One message was from Wales—partly in the aboriginal Cymric speech.

Every good wish for a prosperous New Year—
Yrs most sincerely—
H P L

P.S. Enclosed is a little magazine which may be of some interest. I have many duplicates. ¶ Glad to see my "Night-Gaunts" in I. I. ¶ Am going to N.Y. tomorrow to visit Long. Shall also see other amateurs—& will give them your regards. Barlow—my Florida host of last spring—is also in N Y. I shall be glad to see him again.

Notes

1. Great Ness is a parish in Shropshire. It is the site of St. Andrew's Church, which originated as a church in Saxon times.

2. Bradford-upon-Avon is a town in Wiltshire. It is the site of St. Lawrence's church, built c. 705.

3. See Bibliography for the books HPL owned. Apparently the one he sought was *Our Empire's Story Told in Pictures* (Manchester: Sankey, Hudson & Co., 1934).

4. The booklet did not materialize. Material intended for it was instead published in the Memorial issue of the *Californian* for Miniter, which did not appear until Spring 1938. R. H. Barlow published her story "Dead Houses" in *Leaves*.

[53]   [ALS]

66 College St.,
Providence, R.I.
May 31, 1935.

Dear Arthur:—

I certainly envy you the recent travels so graphically described in I. I., & so tantalisingly suggested by the two delightful cards. Thanks exceedingly for all these things. I wish I could see Canterbury—the ancient Durovernum, & later the objective of so many memorable pilgrimages. The cathedral must be magnificent, while streets like Mercury Lane seem to harbour all the lingering charm of the Middle Ages. I think I have mentioned to you that, although the very first houses in New England towns (from 1630 to 1690 or 1700) were often of the many-gabled overhanging type so common in mediaeval Europe, such buildings have today very largely disappeared. Only a few specimens—mostly in Salem & other Massachusetts towns north of Boston—remain to suggest the peaked-roofed old-world aspect of our towns in the 17th century. In the 18th century most of these houses were extensively altered—roofs being made over to the common New England gambrel type, & no more of the ancient pattern being built. Even so, however, there must have been many more remaining in the 18th & early 19th century than today. Providence has *none* of these gabled dwellings left—although of course modern antiquarianism has produced many *imitation* Tudor specimens which look as if they had been moved bodily from Canterbury or Ipswich or Stratford-on-Avon.

By the way—College St. is about to lose some of the quaint & ancient buildings near its foot (far below #66). The R.I. School of Design, which owns the property, plans to erect a new main building on the site very soon.

Included in the demolition is the home of Brown University's first president—built in 1771—& also one of those rare old archways leading under parts of a building to inner courtyards . . . of which the only perfect survivors in America are those on Providence's ancient hill. (There is a bricked-up specimen in Richmond, Virginia, & a boarded-up specimen in Philadelphia) Amidst this melancholy destruction of landmarks two palliating & consoling factors exist—(a) the preservation, restoration, & inclusion in the new building of the bottom (& only brick) house of the ancient row—the old Franklin Inn, with its quaint inn-yard archway. Thus the survival of *one* of the archways is assured. And (b) the choice of a very appropriate Providence-Georgian type of architecture for the new edifice. The structure's lower units will harmonise with the surviving Franklin Inn, whilst the upper units will harmonise with the residential buildings higher on the hill. One part will even have a so-called "monitor roof" like 66 College St.—a form especially typical of Providence in  the 1790–1810 period. The change is regrettable, yet it is fortunate that the character of the new building will be the same as that of the displaced structures. Obviously, Providence is remaining dominantly true to its traditional Georgian heritage, & avoiding the "modernistic" or "functional" epidemic from which so many cities both in America & Europe are suffering.

Glad you obtained the illustrated brochures at Woolworth's. I find them fascinating & valuable—a delightful supplement to any written history. Certainly, they vividly visualise many things which one tends to know only imperfectly through written descriptions.

The present spring has been wretchedly tardy, so that I have had very few outings of my favourite sort. There is a possibility that I may get down to Florida in June to pay Barlow another visit. He himself will return home from Washington on June 3d. My two best outings so far have been in connexion with visits from a very interesting member of amateurdom's second generation—young Robert Ellis Moe, elder son of our old colleague Maurice Winter Moe. The youth graduated from the University of Wisconsin in 1933, & is now an electrical engineer connected with the General Electric Co. This year he has been stationed in Bridgeport, Conn.—60 miles from N.Y. & 130 miles from Providence—so that he is more or less in touch with his father's old friends in the northeast. His visits to me have been made in his car—& I have guided him to a number of historic places within easy cruising distance of here. The principal trips were made during a visit covering April 27 & 28—& in this brief time we surely saw a surprising variety of interesting antiquities.

The welcome guest arrived on the morning of Saturday the 27th, & we almost immediately set out to visit ancient Newport—which I suppose I have described to you many times. On the way down we saw some very idyllic rustic scenes—especially after we crossed the bridge to the island of Aquidneck or Rhode Island (which gave its name to the entire colony), at whose southern extremity Newport is situate. Here (as elsewhere along the southern New England coast) the terrain is very flat & devoid of rushing brooks—hence an abundance of ancient windmills suggesting landscapes in Holland. I am enclosing a photograph which includes one of these—& which also shews some old farm building, a flock of sheep, & a venerable stone wall. Pastoral scenes of this sort—many features of which must be closely akin to scenes in Britain—fascinate me immeasurably. The present age of machinery seems very far away in such an environment. Approaching Newport, we visited "Whitehall" (built 1729), the country-seat of Dean (later Bishop) Berkeley when he visited America (1729–31) in a vain attempt to found a college for the Indians. We also glanced at Berkeley's favourite outdoor haunt—the Hanging Rocks—& at a curiously impressive rock cleft on the coast called "Purgatory", where the sea pounds thunderously in. Arrived at the ancient town itself, we went on the usual round of sights—beholding the 1698 Quaker meeting house, the 1726 Anglican church, the 1739 colony-house, the 1749 Redwood Library, the 1760 market-house, the 1763 Jews' synagogue, & numerous private dwellings as old as 1675. On our return trip we stopped to inspect another of the ancient windmills.

Sunday the 28ᵗʰ we went to ancient New Bedford—Nantucket's successor as the world's greatest whaling centre, whose last lone exemplar of the industry put to sea only 11 or 12 years ago. The marine museum was closed, but after a tour of the centuried waterfront we set off for something still better. This was the Round Hills estate of Col. E. H. R. Green in S. Dartmouth, where the old whaling barque *Charles W. Morgan* (built 1841) is preserved at a realistic-looking wharf—but solidly embedded in concrete as a permanent exhibit. We went all over the vessel—which is tremendously fascinating—& snapped some pictures of it. I enclose one in case it may be of interest. On the Green estate is also an ancient windmill moved from R.I. We then explored a region—where southern Mass. adjoins southeastern R.I.—which I had never seen before in my life. Splendid unspoiled countryside with rambling stone walls & idyllic white-steepled villages of the old New England type. Of the latter the two best specimens—Adamsville & Little Compton Commons—are both in Rhode Island. Adamsville contains the world's only known monument to a *hen*—perpetuating the fame of the "Rhode Island Red", a breed developed in that village from East Indian & Chinese gallinaceous forbears. At Little Compton Commons can be found the home & grave of Elizabeth Alden Pabodie—daughter of the famed John Alden & Priscilla Mullins of Plymouth, & first white woman born in New England. This region was once the seat of the Sakonnet Indians—whose squaw-sachem Awashonks was persuaded by the noted old warrior Capt. Benjamin Church not to join King Philip's conspiracy of 1675. It was settled from Plymouth about 1673, & (like Barrington, Warren, & Bristol, to the north) came into Massachusetts in 1696 & into Rhode Island (when a boundary dispute was settled by George II) in 1747. At last we turned north through Tiverton, where on our left we had some marvellous vistas of low-lying fields & blue water. Here we passed the home of Capt. Robert Gray, who in 1792 discovered the Columbia River in the far-off Oregon country on the Pacific Coast—naming it after his stout Rhode Island brig. Then back home via Fall River (an ugly mill city across the line in Mass.) & ancient Warren—after which I regretfully guided the guest toward toward [*sic*] the Bridgeport road & bade him adieu. The next week-end—May 3–4–5—I visited Cole in the Boston zone (Wollaston), but cold weather seriously hampered our sightseeing. We explored old Marblehead, however—which is attractive under any conceivable conditions. I also saw the amateurs Mr. & Mrs. Myers.

Cook is vaguely considering a printing venture in St. Louis—on a paper in which the old-timer Paul J. Campbell is interested. This is by no means certain, however.

I was shocked indeed to hear of the tragic end of Mr. Herdman—with whom I had some pleasant correspondence 20 years ago. Curiously—as you will probably recall—this is the *second* time an amateur journalist has suffered such a fate; the American amateur George A. Kilpatrick having been murdered in precisely the same way about a decade ago in some southern city (I forget what one).[1] Kilpatrick was an editor & publisher, & his murder was probably the work of some criminal ring whose activities he had attacked in his paper. The case was never solved.

Amateurdom seems to be fairly active this year. Attempts are being made to improve the quality of the current writings, & a larger critical bureau is a possibility for next year.

     All good wishes—

              Yrs most sincerely,

                H P L

Notes

1. Edward F. Herdman had been beaten to death on 31 December 1934 by an intruder in his house. George A. Kilpatrick (1888–1928), Official Editor of the NAPA (1912–13); owner and editor of the *Brunswick Gazette* in Lawrenceville, VA. He was supposedly shot to death by a disgruntled former employee.

[54]   [ALS]

              66 College St.,

              Providence, R.I.,

              Septr. 19, 1935

Dear Arthur:—

        Your welcome letter, with the delightful enclosed issues of I. I., was awaiting me last Saturday when I returned from an absence of 3 months

& 9 days. Repeating last year's history, I visited young Barlow in De Land, Florida—remaining until Aug. 18, & thereafter edging homeward in a very gradual way. I had a week in ancient St. Augustine & several days in Charleston—as well as a day each in Richmond, Washington, & Philadelphia. All of these places are familiar to you from previous descriptions. In New York city I paused for a fortnight as the guest of Donald Wandrei[1] (a writer of weird & other fiction)—seeing all the old group including Long, Loveman, Morton, Kleiner, Talman, Leeds, & so on. Reached home on the 13th, & have since been struggling desperately with accumulated tasks of every sort—to say nothing of reading up 3½ months of old papers! It will be weeks before my programme is straightened out. Just now I am on the brink of another very brief trip—a week-end with Cole in the Boston zone, during which we expect to get out to Wilbraham & restore the ashes of the late Mrs. Dowe (Mrs. Miniter's mother)[2] to her native soil in accordance with her lifelong wish. I feel the chill of the north acutely after my summer in the subtropics, but manage to get along with an oil heater pending the turning-on of the steam. The Barlows urged me to stay in Florida all winter, but I could not remain away from my books & files for as long a time as that. Even this 3½ months of absence has produced a bothersome degree of chaos!

The College St. buildings are all down now, & the new edifice will doubtless arise very soon. As I think I said, the bottom house of the row was preserved & will be incorporated (together with its ancient archway) into the new building. I surely lament these changes, though it would be worse if something "modernistic" were to be inflicted on us. This new & grotesque fashion is somewhat evident in the west & in N.Y. City, but has made little headway so far in either New England or the South. Our only specimens are certain shops in the commercial district—sorry to hear that Llandudno is more numerously afflicted.

Yes—my expedition of last April was surely enjoyable. Like you, I prefer to vary a return route when I can; although this is not always possible. It could not, for example, be done very advantageously in the case of a Florida trip.

Glad to hear that you have had some interesting excursions. The crossing to Boulogne must have formed a piquantly exotic note—albeit a tantalisation in the direction of further continental explorations. I can in some measure visualise your experience through my trips to ancient Quebec—which is in many ways still a typical French provincial town, though it of course lacks the 1417 tower. Too bad your sojourn had to be so brief & crowded, but you can doubtless make up for that on another occasion. In point of sheer beauty, I fancy that your second trip—along the Dee—may have surpassed the first. Mention of that 1417 tower & 1345 bridge surely makes my mouth water! The oldest structures I have ever seen are, of course, the Spanish houses of St. Augustine—whose antiquity does not exceed the late 16th century. 1571 is the earliest authenticated date.

I enjoyed the new I. I.'s, & congratulate you on the appealing cover of the Jubilee Issue. The faithfulness with which your piquant publication carries on is surely a matter for emulation! Which reminds me that amateurdom is trying to effect a sort of qualitative renaissance this year. The erudite old-timer Truman J. Spencer has accepted chairmanship of the critical bureau, & others like Edkins, Moe, Kleiner, &c. are offering their services in a less formal way. Papers also promise to shew much improvement. Have you seen the Summer & Fall issues of *The Californian?* Barlow has acquired a printing & binding outfit with the intention of issuing privately printed books, & one of his projects is the publication of an amateur paper of the highest grade, to be called *The Dragon-Fly*.

All good wishes—

Yrs most cordially,

H P L

Notes

1. Donald Wandrei (1908–1987), of St. Paul, MN, poet and author of weird fiction, science fiction, and detective tales. He corresponded with HPL from 1926 to 1937.
2. Jennie E. T. Dowe (1840–1919), amateur journalist and mother of Edith Dowe Miniter.

[55]   [ALS]

66 College St.,

Providence, R.I.,

Feby. 26,[?] 1936

Dear Arthur:—

Yours of Dec. 26—with welcome issues of I. I. enclosed— would have been sooner acknowledged but for my desperately congested programme & a recent attack of grippe which has greatly sapped my energies. Thanks exceedingly for the issues of your ever-faithful journal. The Christmas cover represents the kind of scene into which I wish I could stroll! Hope your London trip materialised last month. My own autumnal travels did not end with the conclusion of the long trip in September. Later in the same month I visited the amateur E. H. Cole in the Boston zone, & made several motor excursions with him—to ancient Marblehead, around Cape Cod, & to the wild hills of the Wilbraham region. The latter journey was for the purpose of restoring the ashes of the late Mrs. Dowe (Mrs. Miniter's mother, who died in 1919) to her native soil in accordance with her lifelong wish.

Early in October I had a day's visit in New Haven, Connecticut—about 100 miles S.W. of Providence, or half-way from here to N.Y. City. The day was ideally sunny, & the ride through autumnal Connecticut scenery delightful. New Haven is not as rich in antiquities as Providence, but has a peculiar charm of its own. Streets are broad & well-kept, & in the residential sections (some of which involve hills & fine views) there are endless stately mansions a century old, with generous grounds & gardens, & an almost continuous overarching canopy of great elms. I visited ancient Connecticut Hall (1752—oldest Yale College building), old Centre Church on the enormous green; the historical, art, & natural history museums, & other points of interest.

Most impressive of all the sights, perhaps, were the great *new* quadrangles of Yale University—each an absolutely faithful reproduction of old-time architecture & atmosphere, & forming a self-contained little world in itself. The Gothic courtyards transport one in fancy to mediaeval Oxford or Cambridge—spires, oriels, pointed arches, mullioned windows, arcades with groined roofs, climbing ivy, sundials, lawns, gardens, vine-clad walls & flag-stoned walks—everything to give the young occupants that massed impression of their accumulated cultural heritage which they might obtain in Old England itself. Nor are the Georgian quadrangles less glamourous—each being a magical summoning-up of the world of two centuries ago. Many distinct phases of Georgian architecture are represented, & the buildings & landscaping alike reflect the finest taste which European civilisation has yet developed. I must visit New Haven again, since many of its treasures would require weeks for proper inspection & appreciation.

Late in October I had a visit from Samuel Loveman, & we did considerable exploring of bookstalls, museums, & general antiquities both here & in Boston. Loveman's book of poems is now out, & I enclose a circular containing a description of it. I hope it will be well treated by reviewers. The autumn in general was phenomenally mild, & I took outdoor trips quite often until the very verge of November. Yuletide was pleasant—with no sign of the severer weather ahead.

Around New Year's I visited Long in N.Y., & saw many of the amateur & weird-fiction group there—Morton, Loveman, Kleiner, Kirk, Talman, the Wandreis,[1] &c. We had several gatherings, & I attended a dinner of the American Fiction Guild. On two occasions I visited the new Hayden Planetarium of the American Museum of Natural History, & found it a highly impressive device. It consists of a round, domed building of 2 storeys, joined at one point to the museum edifice. On the lower floor is a circular hall whose ceiling is a gigantic orrery—shewing the planets revolving around the sun at their proper relative speeds. Above it is another circular hall whose roof is the great dome, & whose edge is made to represent the horizon of N.Y. City as seen from Central Park. In the middle of this upper hall is a projector (that looks like a fictional "space ship", or like one of the armoured Martians in H. G. Wells's "War of the Worlds") which casts on the whitened concave surface of the dome a perfect image of the sky—capable of duplicating the natural apparent motions of the celestial vault, & of depicting the heavens as seen at any hour, in any season, from any latitude, & at any period of history. Other parts of the projector can cast suitably movable images of the sun, moon, & planets, & diagrammatic arrows & circles for explanatory purposes.

The effect is infinitely lifelike—as if one were outdoors beneath the sky. Lectures—different each month (I heard both Dec. & Jan. ones)—are given in connexion with this apparatus. In the annular corridors on each floor are niches containing typical astronomical instruments of all ages—telescopes, transits, celestial globes, armillary spheres, &c.—& cases to display books, meteorites, & other miscellany. Astronomical pictures line the walls, & at the desk may be obtained useful pamphlets, books, planispheres, &c. The institution holds classes in elementary astronomy, & sponsors clubs of amateur observers. Altogether, it forms the most complete & active popular astronomical centre imaginable. It seems to be crowded at all hours—attesting a public interest in astronomy which did not exist when I was young.

Since my return home I have been inundated with work & rather laid up with grippe. The winter has turned out very severe, with much snow & continuous low temperatures. I have scarcely been out of the house since mid-January.

Amateur activity was slow in starting this year, & has been much retarded by puerile political dissensions; but in spite of all these obstacles some good results are likely. The *Dragon Fly* & *Californian* are notable papers, & the criticism in the official organ by Spencer, Kleiner, & Cole reaches a high level. A very welcome event will be the publication of a paper—called *Causerie*—by the old-timer Ernest A. Edkins, who has issued no individual journal since 1897 or 1898. Edkins represents the highest level of literary achievement yet reached by amateur journalism, & his return to activity is a great asset for the cause.

The passing of the king last month gave me a sense of very genuine melancholy. No one ever symbolised more perfectly the most cherished virtues & aspirations of the English race, or won a wider & more spontaneous affection. The vanishing of an era seems accentuated by the loss of one who formed so typical a landmark.

With every good wish, & hoping that Llandudno's winter has not been as severe as Providence's, I remain

Yrs most sincerely,

H P L

Notes

1. Donald Wandrei and his younger brother Howard (1909–1956), weird artist and prolific author of weird fiction, science fiction, and detective stories.

[56]   [ALS]

66 College St.,
Providence, R.I.,
April 20, 1936.

Dear Arthur:—

Very glad to receive yours of March 30, together with the

copies of *Interesting Items.* Your visit to Windsor must have been a vastly interesting event, even if it did not include the interior of the castle. The chapel is, I have long realised, an object of extreme beauty & historic significance, & I envy you your trip through it. It is just as well, perhaps, that you were there before the spot became associated with recent sorrow. On some later occasion I trust you may be able to inspect the things you had to forego—the castle, & the interior of the Staple Inn. By the way—I hope your London visit included a farewell glimpse of Adelphi Terrace—that Georgian masterpiece of the brothers Adam[1] which I hear is now in process of demolition. Nothing in recent years has more enraged me than the news of this wanton destruction. Some accounts hold it necessary in connexion with the rebuilding of Waterloo Bridge, but it seems to me some alternative course could have been devised. Few structures of the last two centuries have a greater architectural importance—all apart from the historic interest imparted by those who have dwelt there. It was the Adams who took Georgian architecture into its third & finest phase—the phase marked by purely classical design & proportions, & inspired by the progress of excavation at Pompeii. Yes—I certainly believe that the Georgian age marks the summit of beauty in dress, furniture, & architecture alike—at least, since the times of Greece & Rome. I rejoice that the period has left so strong an impress upon Providence, & mourn whenever any specimen of its art is destroyed. However, as I believe I have said, most of the *new* buildings here are now designed in the Georgian manner— especially in the ancient hill neighbourhood where I now reside. To replace the demolished structures in lower College St. there will be an impressive edifice of many units—following the best traditions of 18th & early 19th century Providence architecture, & joining on to the one ancient building which was left standing in that row. By the way—one of the stateliest of the old Georgian mansions of Providence, the Carrington house in Williams St., built in 1809, has just been presented to the Rhode Island School of Design for use as a public museum. It will retain all its original furniture & decorations intact, & will afford future generations a striking picture of the more lavish life of the great Rhode Island maritime era. Although late in date, this house retains many characteristics of middle-18th-century architecture—a typical illustration of the habitual conservatism of Providence designers. New influences did not cross the Atlantic quickly, & the severely classical Adam styles were not common in America till 1800 & after. The South took the new fashions quicker than the north—the earliest Adam designs I have seen (1765) being in the old Brewton house in Charleston, S.C.

So your winter was as bad as ours! We had a phenomenally mild March— which brought the grass & buds out prematurely—but April so far has proved unprecedentedly cold. You have doubtless read in the press of America's extensive *floods,* of which I enclose a typical view. The business section of Haverhill was under 6 to 10 feet of water, & if the Merrimack River had risen another foot our good old friend Tryout would have been inundated. In Pittsburgh young Babcock saw everything around him flooded. His college remained above water, but much inconvenience was occasioned by the breakdown of usual facilities.

Yes—the amateur year has been somewhat disappointing; unforeseen obstacles & political dissensions having interfered with the ambitious plans of last summer. However, there have been many redeeming features. The return of the old-timer Edkins to activity, & the publication of his splendid paper *Causerie,* is an extremely auspicious event (By the way—if you haven't received *Causerie,* I can let you have a copy.); whilst the appearance of *The Dragon Fly,* the excellent volume of *The National Amateur,* & the record-breaking *Californian,* all form reasons for congratulation. Indeed, the year would not seem at all bad if we had not rashly expected so much more.

1936, however, has been a bad year for me. A touch of grippe in late January & early February badly disrupted my programme—& immediately after that the severe illness of my aunt imposed still further obstacles. I have had to transfer many duties & responsibilities, & doubt if I can ever straighten out my schedule except through neglect & repudiation! My aunt was at an hospital for a month, & is now at a convalescent home. Tomorrow she will return to 66 College.

With every good wish, & renewed thanks for I. I.

—Yours most sincerely—

H P L

Notes

1. The buildings in Adelphi Terrace were built in 1768–72 by John, Robert, James, and William Adam.

[57]   [ALS]

66 College St.,
Providence, R.I.,
Aug. 27, 1936.

Dear Arthur:—

Very glad to receive your letter & enclosures of Aug. 11. Thanks as usual for I. I., with its pleasing amplitude of material. The account of your motor-coach trip interested me vastly, & I envy you all the sights encountered along the way. I can imagine each scene in Stratford, since my files contain a great variety of pictures of that spot. Holy Trinity beside the river forms one of the finest landscape-&-architecture combinations I have ever seen depicted. The Harvard house would have interested me profoundly, for I have often rambled through the grounds of the university which bears that name.[1] The oldest surviving building of the college—Massachusetts Hall—

dates from around 1720. Warwick Castle & Long Compton must take one quite back to the feudal age.[2] We have a *Little Compton* in Rhode Island, about which the atmosphere of the 18th century still lingers. I'd give much to see the spires of Oxford—but fear I'd have a hard time tearing myself away. Another thing I'd like to see is Amersham—of which I've heard repeated descriptions.[3] A combination of motor-coach & pedestrianism is about the best way to accomplish a long round of sightseeing—the former for jumps from one centre to another, the latter for the intensive exploration of each centre. Then there are remoter byways which can scarcely be reached except through private transportation. I certainly wish, as you do, that I might own a Georgian house appropriately furnished. Providence has the finest collection of Georgian furniture in America, in a museum (made to represent a typical mansion of about 1790) only a square down the hill from 66 College.

Abundant thanks for the cutting about the Roman industrial centre at Prestatyn.[4] How I envy you your proximity to the reliques of genuine antiquity! Have you seen any of the excavations, coins, or artifacts?

Commiserations on your cold & rainy summer! Rhode Island also had a rather cold summer until recent weeks, but now warm days are frequent. I was nearly worn out by the cold until some good 90° days began to appear in mid-July. The East has not experienced the extreme & continuous heat (which I'd enjoy!) reported in the middle West.

Glad you have been well. My aunt's recovery is now well advanced, & I am feeling somewhat better now that the weather is warmer. Circumstances have prevented me from taking any long trips this year, but I keep outdoors quite a bit & have had some enjoyable single-day excursions—to Newport & elsewhere. Just now I am enjoying a long-term visit from young Barlow, my host in Florida last year & the year before that. He is stopping at the boarding-house just across the garden, & forms a most congenial neighbour . . . . absorbing local sights one by one, raiding all the bookstalls, & occasional[l]y looking up genealogical data at the libraries. We find, incidentally, that we are *6th cousins* by virtue of a common descent from one John Rathbone of Block Island, R.I., who was born in 1658. Another recent guest was old Adolphe de Castro, once a friend of the author Ambrose Bierce, & later a revision client of mine. On one occasion he, Barlow, & I sat on a tomb in the hidden hillside churchyard just north of here & wrote rhymed acrostics on the name of Edgar Allan Poe—who 90 years ago used to haunt this selfsame necropolis when on visits to Providence.[5]

In July I had an interesting visit from Maurice W. Moe & his elder son, which included considerable local sightseeing. Moe hasn't changed much in the 13 years since I last saw him—& I was sorry he couldn't stay longer.

The Grand Rapids Convention was very much of a success, & resulted in the election of the complete "Michigan Ticket". Mrs. Martin is President, & Bradofsky[6] was elected Official Editor—although he later resigned & was replaced by ex-Pres. Clyde G. Townsend. Spencer is again critical chairman, & Kleiner will probably continue to do some of the most important reviewing. The year will probably be a distinctly average one—the loss of *Causerie* (unless Edkins' health improves) & *The Dragon Fly* (owing to Barlow's probable removal from De Land & his best printing facilities) being a marked handicap. Edkins is severely ill with a kidney trouble of long standing, & is now in the hospital for the second of two serious operations.

Sorry you haven't had *Causerie* before—but I sent the two issues as soon as I received your letter. I believe you'll find it about the best amateur product of recent years—the most mature, balanced, & scholarly writing the association has seen in a generation or more. Edkins is a true survivor of the Golden Age of the '80's. By the way—Barlow seems not to have sent you *The Dragon Fly*, so I'll forward the two issues out of my small supply of extras.

Barlow & I had an interesting trip to ancient Salem & Marblehead Aug. 20. These old places never lose their charm—& Salem is the one spot in America where one may see in appreciable numbers the mediaeval-like gabled houses (vide enc.) which preceded our Georgian architecture. ¶ All good wishes—
Yrs most sincerely— H P L

Notes

1. HPL refers to Holy Trinity Church (often referred to as Shakespeare's Church, as Shakespeare is buried there; its earliest portions date to the 13th century) and Harvard House (26 High Street; built 1596 by Thomas Rogers, grandfather of John Harvard, the benefactor of Harvard University) in Stratford-upon-Avon, in Warwickshire.

2. Warwick Castle (built in the 12th century) and Long Compton (a village) are both in Warwickshire.

3. Amersham is a town in Buckinghamshire. Arthur Machen lived there from 1929 until his death in 1947.

4. Prestatyn is a seaside resort in the province of Denbighshire in northern Wales. It is the site of a Roman bathhouse, but most of its Roman remains are now destroyed.

5. See RK 94n2.

6. HPL refers to Margaret Nickerson Martin and Hyman Bradofsky (1906–2002), the latter a late correspondent of HPL and editor of the *Californian*.

[58]   [ALS]
66 College St.,
Providence, R.I.,
Jany. 21, 1937.

Dear Arthur:—

Very glad to see I. I. again—though sorry it is obliged to bring news of amateur losses. I had heard often of both Du Soir & Ventura,[1] though was never in direct correspondence with either. 1936 surely took heavy toll in amateurdom—a recent death of which you may or may not have heard being that of the poet Arthur Goodenough on Sept. 13. Our papers—especially *Tryout*—will scarcely seem the same without his contributions; & to Cook & me, who (alone of all the amateurs) had met him in person & visited him at his picturesquely situated rural home, the loss is doubly acute. Goodenough's wife died last year, but he is survived by a son & three grandchildren. He was 64 years of age.

You have my sympathy concerning the ordeal of moving—a process which I have undergone five times in the course of my life, & which always leaves me exhausted & debilitated. Glad, however, that you didn't have to migrate far. I am duly noting the new address on my records.

Hope you'll soon have a chance to see the Roman excavations—& am glad you are likely to know Amersham better in the future. According to all accounts, it is one of the best-preserved of all the surviving fragments of the older England. London, I fear (& am confirmed in my fear by Mr. Winskill's article in your Christmas number), is rapidly losing its atmosphere of antiquity, even though certain landmarks will always remain. I surely hope that your wife's arm may recover soon enough to make the contemplated visit possible.

Glad you safely received *Causerie*. Edkins is now in Florida, & recovering well from his August operation although somewhat set back by a bronchial cold. The year in amateurdom is not turning out very brilliant, although many solid accomplishments may go on record. *The Californian* is allotting the critical bureau a generous amount of space for overflow reports; & if the critics can arrange to take full advantage of it, the result will be extremely helpful. At present, Kleiner is proving himself the most useful of the critics.

Recently Edwin Hadley Smith presented me with a large number of old issues of *The National Amateur*, raising my file from an almost negligible to a fairly substantial status. I am surely grateful for this generosity—a generosity likewise exercised toward Morton & Kleiner.

I surely enjoyed Barlow's visit—which reminds me (in case I haven't mentioned it before) that his present address is *810 W. 57th St. Terrace, Kansas City, Missouri*. Morton was here Sept. 11, 12, & 13—participating in some very enjoyable sessions. The autumn was not as severe as I had feared it would be, & I continued my outdoor rambles until early November. Curiously enough, I discovered two very fascinating woodland regions within a three-mile radius of this house which I had never seen before in my life! One is a region of slopes & valleys on the high plateau west of the city, & the other an extremely picturesque dell down the eastern shore of Narragansett Bay.

I trust your Yuletide was suitably festive. Ours here was commendably cheerful—including a gaily-decked Christmas-tree surrounded with gifts. The first half of the winter, like the autumn, has not lived up to early prophecies of severity—indeed, 1936–7 will probably go on record as one of Rhode Island's warmest winters. I have, however, been in rather indifferent health—

an old winter malady of mine (involving swollen feet & ankles) being aggravated by a mixture of indigestion & general weakness perhaps vaguely allied to the prevailing grippe.

Have heard several interesting lectures recently—on subjects as varied as Peruvian antiquities, Italian Romanesque architecture, & the relation of biology to modern philosophy.

In December my first cloth-bound book was published—a short novel called "The Shadow Over Innsmouth", issued with four illustrations by the Visionary Pub. Co. of Everett, Pa. It is a rather poorly printed & bound job, & I think the quoted price of $1.00 is rather high for it.

All good wishes—
    Yrs most sincerely—
            H P L

Notes

1. Arthur Du Soir (1866–1936), amateur journalist and song writer. John O. Ventura (1863?–1936) is otherwise unidentified.

James Larkin Pearson

Letters to James Larkin Pearson

[1]   [ANS]¹

598 Angell St.,
Providence
5/3/15

Dear Mʳ Pearson:

Please accept my thanks for the recent copy of "Pearson's Pet".² I admire your easy dialect verse & fluent prose immensely, & am giving your paper a very favourable review in the May United Amateur.

Sincerely,
H P Lovecraft

Notes

1. *Front:* Blank.

2. Pearson's amateur magazine. See "Department of Public Criticism" (May 1915): "*Pearson's Pet* for April is a bright and attractive little paper throughout. 'Burnin' Off' is a delightful specimen of dialect verse which conveys a graphic image. We have never witnessed such an agricultural function as Mr. Pearson describes, but can gain from his clever lines a vivid idea of its weird impressiveness. 'How I Met Elbert Hubbard' is narrated in commendably easy prose, which same may be said of the sketch or editorial entitled 'Broke Loose Again'. Mr. Pearson is assuredly a competent exponent of amateur journalism's lighter and less formal side." (*CE* 1.41)

[2]   [ALS]

598 Angell St.,
Providence, R.I.,
Dec. 31, 1916.

Jas. Larkin Pearson, Esq.,
Moravian Falls, N.C.,

My dear Mʳ· Pearson:—

Having perused your remarkably excellent book of verse,¹ loaned me by Pres. Campbell of the United Amateur Press Association,² I am impelled to inquire whether you would care to become reinstated the the [*sic*] ranks of that society. We are seeking to build up as ideal a list of members as possible, and feel that we could gain no better material than those whose worth & literary ability have already been proved in amateurdom. While it is probably true that the press associations now offer less to their adherents than they were once able to offer, I am sure that you would have no occasion to regret a renewal of membership. It is only by such action on the part of experienced amateurs that amateurdom can hope to revive its former glories. We should indeed welcome the reappearance of *Pearson's Pet.*

Hoping that you may care to render a favourable decision, I am

Very truly yours,

H P Lovecraft

Notes

1. Unknown, but probably *Castle Gates* (1908).
2. In 1916, Paul J. Campbell was elected president of UAPA; in 1917 HPL, who had been elected Vice-President, was elected president.

[3]   [ALS]

598 Angell St.,

Providence, R.I.,

April 6, 1918.

James Larkin Pearson, Esq.,
    Boomer, N.C.,

My dear Mr Pearson:—

I have for some time been intending to write you my thanks for the issues of *Good News* which you have been kind enough to send me. While I must, like our mutual friend Paul J. Campbell, be counted amongst the ranks of the agnostics, I can nevertheless appreciate the clearness with which you handle your subject, and expose the fallacies & paradoxes of orthodox theology. If, as I am forced to doubt for want of evidence, the Hebrew scriptures are in truth "inspired" to a greater degree than the similar writings of other ancient races; then your deductions are without a doubt vastly more logical and likely to be true than those of the conventional clergy.

Your publication is of a nature which appeals strongly to many minds, & I believe it is destined for success. Both in prose & verse you have a certain personality & literary style which create a very favourable impression. I have read with much admiration a volume of your poetry which Mr. Campbell loaned me some time ago. The astronomical remarks anent "periodicity" which you make on page 4 of the March *Good News* interested me very much. I have been an ardent amateur astronomer for sixteen years, and for twelve years have been writing regular monthly articles on astronomy for local dailies.[1] Regarding the revolution of the visible universe around a "central sun" in the Pleiades cluster—I must beg to protest that this theory, originally promulgated by Mädler in 1845, has for some time been abandoned. About 1904 the Dutch astronomer Kapteyn made extensive researches concerning "star-drifts", and arrived at the conclusion that stellar motions are rectilinear;

but that certain stars have a curious connexion with one another—moving together in parallel lines though otherwise apparently unrelated. Recently—I think about two or three years ago,—Mr. O. R. Walkley endeavoured to revive the "central sun" theory; though he places Canopus (in Argo Navis) as the central body, rather than Alcyone or any other of the Pleiades. Personally—through analogy—I think the idea of a central sun a very probable one; though it cannot be said that Mr. Walkley has established his hypothesis. Kapteyn's rectilinear theory of star-drift is the favoured belief today.[2] At any rate—the centralism of the Pleiades has been definitely disproved. I have given much time to speculations on infinity & eternity; and if the philosophical doctrines of a confessed atheist are not repugnant to you, should be glad to unfold some of them at a later date.

In the hope that you may care to reaffiliate with the United Amateur Press Association, I enclose an application blank. Our standards are higher than ever this year, & we are having the best official organ ever published by any press association. I should feel honoured in securing your reinstatement during my term as president. Your exquisitely tuneful little poem in *The Silver Clarion* leads me to believe that you may be considering a return to the congenial realms of amateurdom. I have some poetical ambitions myself; but lacking real gifts in this direction, have been forced to content myself with turning out mediocre verse by the yard. I am fond of the heroic couplet, & the metre & manner of the XVIIIth century. And before I forget it, I should like to express my delight at "Israel" in your February number. That attractively phrased & well-executed piece almost makes me forget my deeply-seated prejudice against the Jewish race. In the north, where there are so many undesirable Russian-Jewish immigrants, we cannot look so favourably & academically upon the merits & historical glory of the Hebrew! I hope, as you do, that the Jews can be rehabilitated as a nation in Palestine. I doubt their capacity for full self-government, for their physical courage & national (as distinct from religio-cultural) sense has been broken by long dispersal & Aryan contempt; but I fancy they will do very well under British protectorate. I am passionately anxious for the destruction of the Germanic power, & the continued world-domination of Great Britain. England and her glorious Anglo-Saxon civilisation is the greatest force for good in the world today; and no effort is too great, no suffering too dire, to be endured patiently in the hope of preserving the paramountcy of that nation & that civilisation. The military situation is very grave this month, but nothing should deter the Allied powers from standing resolutely till the menace of the Hun is definitely & permanently dispelled. Here, for once, the religious enthusiast and the prosaic rationalist are in complete agreement!

I enclose the latest of my astronomical articles, together with an attempt at a "spring poem"—which I trust you will view with a charitable eye![3]

Thanking you again for *Good News,* & hoping that you may decide to participate once more in amateur affairs—even to the extent of a renascent *Pear-*

son's Pet, I remain

               Most cordially & sincerely yours,

                              H. P. Lovecraft

Notes

1. In fact, HPL published no astronomical columns between June 1908 and January 1914.

2. HPL refers to Johann Heinrich von Mädler (1794–1874), German astronomer; Jacobus Cornelius Kapteyn (1851–1922), Dutch astronomer whose major contributions were in the field of stellar astronomy; and O. R. Walkley, English astronomer. The discussion in this letter closely follows a passage in "August Skies" ([Providence] *Evening News,* 1 August 1916; *CE* 3.193–94).

3. "April Skies," [Providence] *Evening News* 52, No. 92 (1 April 1918): 4; "Ver Rusticum."

[4]   [ALS]

                              598 Angell St.,

                              Providence, R.I.,

                              Aug. 3, 1919

My dear Mʳ Pearson:—

               I was very glad to receive your letter of recent date, & to hear of your desire to rejoin the U.A.P.A. For the latter purpose I am enclosing herewith a home-made application blank—the only kind I can obtain until the regular supply for the new official year is printed. Under separate cover I am forwarding the complete file of the *United Amateur* for the past year, with the exception of the July issue, which is not yet out. I think you will agree that our literary standard has reached a height unequalled before. At the convention Mrs. Renshaw was elected Official Editor by a vote of 22 to 7, & she is now preparing to enter on her duties. The enemy are badly disappointed, & are planning to contest the election on the false & flimsy ground that the ballots were late; but I fancy their disturbance will amount to nothing more than a dose or two of crude slander & abuse in the *Bearcat* or *Cleveland Sun.* The administration has decided to pay no further attention either to Dowdell or to Moitoret, since both are undesirable amateurs bent on creating a disturbance for its own sake. Under Mrs. Renshaw the *United Amateur* will certainly maintain the highest standard, & we have reason to look forward to an excellent year. I enclose a slip showing the new official board.

               I am exceedingly sorry to hear of the many trials which have beset you, & certainly hope that before long you will have established your present business as firmly as that which you lost. With your aptitude & spirit of enterprise I am sure it could not be otherwise. I can sympathise very keenly with anyone who has known adversity, for my own life has been little more than a series of disasters and illnesses. Owing to my nervous afflictions, lifelong in duration but especially prostrating since a breakdown in 1908, I am debarred from most forms of professional activity; and from those pinnacles of educational thoroughness to which I have always aspired. My health prevented me from attending the university, hence whatever I have acquired beyond high-school studies has been the result of general reading & research at home. Still, I am grateful for the advantages which I have been able to enjoy; for I realise that I am fortunate as compared with many.

What you say of your early rhyming is very interesting. Truly, like Mr. Pope, you

> "—lisp'd in numbers, for the numbers came."[1]

I *recited* verses before I could write, but did not compose any till able to set them down. It is curious that I could write fair verses before I could compose smooth & coherent prose. While my 7 & 8 year old verses are quite readable, I wrote prose rather awkwardly till I was 9 or 10. The rules of rhyme & metre, I fancy, served as guides. My tendency toward old-fashioned forms is curious, because it is so spontaneous & early in origin. I seemed naturally to gravitate to the classics & the 18th century. In art as well as literature I am partial to Graeco-Romanism.

Concerning theological matters, my mental evolution was rather swift. I began life as a Baptist—your own original denomination—but doubt if I ever believed *much* in the supernatural. I used to shock everyone at Sunday school by my questions when only five or six, and about this time was prone to in-quire why the Christian religion had any more right to supremacy than any other. When seven, I formally announced my rejection of Christianity & adoption of Greek paganism; & for a while was a comically assiduous wor-shipper of Jupiter, Mars, Minerva, & all the classical pantheon. I built altars in the back yard, & sacrificed daily to the Gods. But really, I think I half knew how foolish it was, & did it mainly for fun. Later on I was persuaded again to attend Sunday School, but being older & more inclined to question, I was even more disturbing than before. When I would question, my teachers would generally tell me that I must stop trying to reason, & voluntarily have "faith." But, I replied, if one is to reject reason, why may he not just as well have "faith" in Buddhism, Mohammedanism, or any other religion? Theologians say that when one tries to believe, the so-called "truth" will become manifest to him—yet almost anyone knows that such a "revelation of truth" is merely an emotional, subjective, or auto-hypnotic phenomenon without value. As I said to my teachers, one can just as easily fool himself into belief in *any* reli-gion; in fact, if anyone is looking for the "truth" in this way, it behooves him to try them all! Accordingly, I became a Mohammedan for a time, and dab-bled in Buddhism; finding it just as easy (or as hard) to accept any of these as to accept Christianity. But meanwhile I had been studying science; & by the time I was twelve I saw very clearly that all religious belief is essentially primi-tive & vestigial—merely a remnant of early man's attempts to explain the un-known. In the light of facts I reëxamined the various doctrines I had experimented with, & found all more or less alike in basis, though different in ethical value. After becoming an agnostic, I came to respect Christianity as a moral agent more highly than I had respected it when weighing it as a theist with other faiths. Viewing it purely objectively, as a beneficent system of natural mythology, I came to see its value as a regulator & comforter of the majority; & its many advantages over most of its rivals & predecessors.

Naturally I cannot share your belief in the Hebrew Bible, since to me it is only one of many similar collections of Oriental maxims, history, laws, poetry, & legends. There is nothing in the least distinctive about it. Many parts are genuine history, but other parts are obviously pure mythology. Half of the supernatural legends can be traced back to anterior sources. All Asiatic cultures had collections like this, & only chance throws the Jewish collection into prominence. Most of the so-called "prophecies" are vague & ambiguous, & can be made to fit almost any event by the use of a little imagination & artful symbolism. The one about 1914 to which you refer must, *if widely discussed before 1914*, have been rather an interesting coincidence; though in fact it would hardly prove anything. Incidentally, what was it? You are no doubt aware that chronology has many errors. How was the year (actually *1,918* years after the birth of Jesus) computed? Also, are there not many *other* "prophecies" of various upheavals at *other times*, just as emphatic as this one? It does not pay to found one's whole faith upon a single coincidence. As to later "interpretations" applied to the several events of the war—it is easy to find "prophecies" of events which have already happened. Ambiguousness is the keynote of all oracles & divinations.

Your theory that Anglo-Saxons are lost Israelites can be punctured in an instant by the facts of ethnology. Semitic races like the Jews & their kindred have distinctive ethnic traits, none of which appear in the Englishman. The English, on the other hand, are most obviously and positively related to the Aryan Teutonic races of Northern Europe. The anthropological gulf between Jew & Saxon is so great as to be utterly impassable. No common ancestry this side of the Quaternary age is conceivable. They are as different as two white races can possibly be.

All this, however, is of minor importance in the ultimate matter of theism. The great outstanding absurdity of all religions, is the assumption that the entire governing force of eternal & infinite creation concentrates all its attention upon the affairs of *mankind*—an insignificant race of vermin crawling over a puny atom called the "earth". This race & the earth are as *nothing*—not so much as a grain of sand on the shore—in the unbounded cosmos. Read Munro's translation (or any other good translation) of the Roman philosopher Lucretius.

Apologising for my obdurate belligerency, & hoping to hear from you again & often, I remain

Most sincerely yours,

H P Lovecraft

N.B. I appreciate *Good News*, & always read it with keen interest.

P.S. I enclose Kleiner's *Piper*, one of the best individual papers of the year.

Notes

1. Alexander Pope, *Epistle to Dr. Arbuthnot* (1735), l. 128.

[5]   [ALS]

598 Angell St.,
Providence, R.I.,
Aug. 22, 1919

My dear M^r. Pearson:—

I was pleased to receive your letter of the 12th, & to hear that your reinstatement in the United is now an accomplished fact. If you do not receive the May *United Amateur* soon, let me know, & I will supply a copy. And incidentally, if I did not include the *March* issue in the bundle I sent, kindly advise me—& I will atone for the deficiency.

I have never seen the Russell books to which you refer, & have never heard of them alluded to in any discussion of theology. In fact, I never saw a reference to them in any academic work. However, I have often seen allusions to Russell in the press, & believe he was quite popular with many. Yet you must admit that the utter failure of cultivated thinkers as a class to recognise him—and no one has ever thought it worth while to write *against* his work from the standpoint of scientific naturalism—argues against the weight of his pronouncements. The public libraries do not contain his writings, but if I ever happen upon them I will look them over to see what you mean by his prophecies.[1] Still, you can hardly expect me to become a convert; since over against all the arguments of sophistry & theistic philosophy stands the one great pair of essentials—the absolute limitations of human knowledge, & the utter *improbability* of the supernatural.

Please labour under no belief that your writings fail to measure up to the United's standards. What I have seen of your verse makes me confident that you can compete with the best; & if ever you wish criticism or revision of any sort, you can obtain it freely either from the Department of Private Criticism or from me personally. The hostile Cleveland element has laid aside its political designs on account of pressure exerted by W. P. Cook on its ringleader, Anthony F. Moitoret. It will, however, continue to persecute me as an individual; because my *Conservative* editorial played a substantial part in Dowdell's defeat.[2] I am told that the next issue of the *Cleveland Sun* will be grossly libellous, with a cartoon designed to ridicule me.

Your collection of old amateur papers must be a cherished & interesting possession. My own collection is not large, but I keep the most notable issues of all papers, & complete files of many. I hope you will have time to contribute to our publishing activity by at least one issue of *Pearson's Pet*—or more, if possible. Cook will try to issue his *Vagrant* every month, & other veterans are planning to increase their activity.

  With all best wishes, I remain
    Sincerely & fraternally yours,
      H. P. Lovecraft

Notes

1. HPL apparently refers to Charles Taze Russell (1852–1916), founder of the Watch Tower Society (an organ of the Jehovah's Witnesses), who predicted that the end of the world would occur in October 1914.
2. "For Official Editor—Anne Tillery Renshaw."

[6] [ALS]

           598 Angell St.,
           Providence, R.I.,
           Septr 19, 1919

My dear Pearson:—

    I will snatch a moment & reply immediately to your inquiry. Let me assure you that your renewal has been duly received & entered on the books, & that your name will be published in the July *United Amateur*. Your failure to hear from the association officially is due to the negligence of the new Secretary, a rather eccentric elderly woman who was given the post merely because she happens to live in the next convention city.[1] You might speak about it to the President—Miss Mary F. Durr, 526 Third St., Marietta, Ohio.

  I will try to straighten out the Kilpatrick–Smith matter.[2] Smith is not a member of the United, & I fear he does not know that Mrs. Haughton is our Secretary; but I will tell him, also writing Kilpatrick. I wish Mrs. H. would get some blanks printed—I have typed them till I hate the sound of a machine! We shall be very glad to welcome Kilpatrick again, for he is remembered as an active & desirable amateur.

  With all best wishes,
    Cordially & fraternally yours,
      H P Lovecraft

Notes

1. Ida C. Haughton of Columbus, Ohio.
2. HPL apparently refers to George A. Kilpatrick (see AH 53n1). "Smith" could either be Edwin Hadley Smith or Charles W. Smith. The nature of the dispute is unknown.

[7]   [ANS]

March 19 [1926]

My dear Mr Pearson:—

Desperate as is my pressure of business at this particular moment, I cannot refrain from expressing my appreciation of the volume which you so kindly sent me, & which has just arrived. I had the pleasure, thro' Mr. Morton, of looking over this book some months ago; & can truthfully say that much of the contents is poetry in the truest & most exquisite sense.[1] I am looking forward very eagerly to the volume of selected verse[2] which you are contemplating, & am certain it will command some very respectful attention from critics who may have undervalued the larger book because of the inclusion of immaturer work.

Thanking you again, & extending every good wish, I am

Most sincerely yrs
H P Lovecraft

Notes

1. Presumably *Pearson's Poems* (1924), (*LL* 745).

2. Pearson's *Selected Poems* did not appear until 1960, though he published other volumes of poetry in the interim. HPL aided Pearson in selecting poems for his *Fifty Acres and Other Selected Poems* (1937).

[8]   [ALS]

169 Clinton St.,
Brooklyn, N.Y.,
March 21, 1926

My dear Mr Pearson:—

Your note arrived in the late Friday mail, & since then I have been in bed with grippe. Today, however, I am bestirring myself; & thinking of taking the first nourishment in some 36 hours. The only thing to do for the beastly thing is to stay horizontal & eschew all burdens for the stomach.

I hope you will like the results of our collective appraisal of your book.[1] In order to secure perfect fairness & objectivity, the various members of our group are not comparing notes, but arriving at all opinions independently. Morton will collate all these opinions with his own, & by the use of his trained critical faculty formulate as nearly as possible an absolutely impersonal & unbiassed series of decisions. It would gratify you very much to hear the favourable opinions expressed on every hand regarding your best work, & I think you can depend on a warm reception for a book with selective contents. We all agree that few indeed of the amateur poets rise to the level you attain in your "high spots".

I'm sorry that you are suffering from a lack of financial prosperity—& must admit that I am myself rather hard pressed just now. So, in fact, are most of our local circle; since the particular sort of literary material we create is not of a highly marketable character. Morton—with his providential appointment as museum curator a year ago[2]—is the only one of us who may really be said to have "landed" as yet.

As to amateurdom—you may have at least the slender gratification of knowing that you haven't missed much. The institution is now at its very lowest ebb; with little activity anywhere manifest, & both associations virtually fighting for their lives. The United, under the leadership of a very energetic young man named Victor E. Bacon of St. Louis, is attempting a renaissance of somewhat ambitious scope; but has been sadly hampered by lack of cash, & by difficulties with printers. I will enclose the latest copy of the official organ we have been able to issue——together with an application blank in case you should feel able to rejoin at any time. Also, I'll send a Tryout of which I happen to have a duplicate. If you would drop a line to Smith, I believe he would be glad to put you on his mailing list whether or not you formally belong to either of the associations.

Well—again let me congratulate you on the excellence of your book, & in particular of certain of the later poems which shew a very high development of the lyrical & image-making faculties. The symposium of opinions in the circular ought to be very heartening—I know many people who know Clement Wood,[3] (tho' I have not myself been introduced to him) & can assure you that his judgment is highly to be valued.

With every good wish,
  Most sincerely yours,
   H P Lovecraft

Notes

1. HPL's comments to JLP are cordial, but his comments to others were considerably less so. See HPL to Lillian D. Clark, 9 October 1925: "Morton [imposed] upon us the task of reading a dull book of poems by the amateur James Larkin Pearson, who wants help in selecting the best ones for a smaller volume. He asked Morton's aid, & Jacobus Ferdinandus wants us all to submit a symposium of verdicts. Anything to please—but I do dread wading through those 400-odd pages!" (*Letters to Family and Family Friends,* 439) See also HPL to James F. Morton, [November 1925]; *Letters to James F. Morton* 85–86.

2. Morton was appointed curator of the Paterson (NJ) Museum.

3. Clement Wood (1888–1950), American poet, biographer, and activist. HPL often recommended his *Hints on Writing Poetry* (1924) to aspiring poets.

[9]   [ALS]

note new   10 BARNES St.,
address   Providence, R.I.,
                             April 25, 1926.

My dear Mr. Pearson:—

Well, it seems as if all my correspondence were fated to be conducted under handicaps this spring! First it was the grippe, & now it is long-distance *moving*—so that I have a mile-high stack of unanswered mail on my desk at this moment. But this move is worth all the trouble it has caused, for it has brought me home to my own town of Providence, R.I., where I was born & lived for 34 years, & where I now hope to live the remainder of my days & die. There is no use in trying to transplant a real New Englander to modern New York. The Manhattan milieu is alien & oppressive, & suggests—after the first glamour of the fairylike skyline has worn off—nothing but cancerous squalor & decay. For over a year I have hated the place like poison, & was merely awaiting a favourable opportunity to transfer my household back to Providence. Now that chance has come, & I am home again for good—in a modest establishment on the crest of the ancient hill above the river, whence I can look out over the lower town & see the rural hills beyond. The streets near me are old, quiet, & shady, with pleasing & reposeful colonial doorways on both sides, & with piquant little winding alleys threading their way down the precipitous slope toward the business section. It is a locality I have known & loved all my life, & the strongest possible contrast to the dreary New York & Brooklyn desert of brick & brownstone which I have just left. Nevermore shall I dwell in any other sort of place if I can help it!

I hope that our "gang" may complete their work on your book before long. Just now I understand that the delay is due to Loveman's extra work at his bookshop, which exhausts him so completely that he has no energy left after the day's toil is done. His verdict, however, is eminently worth waiting for; & will be all the better for being deferred till such a time as the mind behind it may be fresh & unworried. Morton will be very prompt in his task of digesting, comparing, & selecting when he receives all returns from the others; & I think he will give a very intelligent & valuable series of decisions. His taste is exceedingly keen & phenomenally impartial—in fact, he seems to me the most open-minded & balanced of all our crowd.

Yes—it is certainly too bad that amateurdom is so decadent, but I really don't see a single thing to be done about it. Several causes, separate in themselves but operating through malign coincidence toward a common end, seem to have laid a blight upon our activities—the principal troubles being the high cost of printing & the engrossment of the younger generation with other & easier forms of recreation. Still—the institution is far from dead yet, & I hope to see several bursts of Indian-summer energy before the flame finally flickers out. Young Bacon is doing his best to reclaim the United, &

similar efforts seem to be going on in the National as well. Meanwhile *Tryout* & *Brooklynite* combine to be our only regular papers.

Did young Long send you a copy of his new book of poems—"A Man from Genoa & Other Poems"? I think it forms a delightfully auspicious beginning for a youthful bard, & hope to see many more like it from the same pen. It has received exceedingly favourable mention from several papers of importance, including the *London Times*.

Well—I must close for the present, but hope to write less uninterestingly when the work of settling is done. Just now, although my furniture is all in place, my *books* are not yet arranged on their shelves; & this task will occupy a disconcertingly long time. Still, it is better to have books & bother with them, than not to have any books to bother with!

With all good wishes, & looking forward expectantly to your new selective volume of verse, I remain

Cordially & sincerely yours,
H P Lovecraft

[10]   [ALS]

10 Barnes St.,
Providence, R.I.,
July 21, 1926

My dear Pearson:—

I was glad to hear from you, & to learn that you have landed material with the N.Y. Times.[1] There is a comfortable sense of acknowledged achievement about a sale, even if its effect on one's total finances be only that of a drop in the bucket!

Yes—I'm certainly ecstatically glad to be back in Providence, & shall never live anywhere else if I can help it! New York is merely a spectacular show, which has enough of the colossal about it to interest one for a few months, but which then becomes successively a bore & a nightmare. It has no mellowness or background, & absolutely no sense of continuity with its own or any past. The only really beautiful thing about it is its skyline of tall buildings as seen from a distance, & the only real food for the mind it offers is its array of bookshops & museum faculties—& of course, its plays & concerts for those with a special interest in drama and music, which I don't happen to have. Aside from these things, it is merely a mess of spreading squalor, with bits of parvenu garishness stuck in here & there. It has been absolutely ruined by immigration, so that one can hardly find an honest American face on the streets—nothing but dense, vulgar crowds of swarthy, squint-eyed, undersized foreigners. Even the parks look ill-nourished & moth-eaten—as though a subtle blight extended over the whole miserable place.

If you've seen Washington, you've seen one of the most charming places in existence; & one where I wouldn't mind living myself. When I visited there—from New York—I felt that I had emerged from an unclean cesspool into a crystal & purifying fountain. The memorial amphitheatre at Arlington is one of the most beautiful & impressive objects I have ever beheld, & Alexandria is a delightful survival of eighteenth-century quaintness. Baltimore I have never seen—only ridden through it on the train. I'd like to explore it some time, though. Philadelphia is a favourite of mine among large cities—it retains a surprising amount of its colonial architecture, & preserves a very satisfying sense of history. But my chief delight is in exploring the smaller & quainter old seaport towns of the New England coast. In most of these the shipping has vanished, but an incomparable atmosphere of antique charm remains. Since coming home I've visited Bristol & Newport in my own state, & Plymouth, New Bedford, Boston, Lexington, (not a seaport, but a quaint inland town) Salem, & Marblehead. At Salem I saw the town's tercentenary celebration. I wish I had more postcards left to give you an idea of these places, but will enclose what I have for your collection. Some time I'd like to explore your part of the country, for I know that many of the Southern towns retain delightful traces of former years. I'd like especially to see Richmond, Charleston, St. Augustine, & New Orleans. I've never been farther south than the vicinity of Washington. However—Providence satisfies me so well that my travel-urge isn't all that insistent. Enough of the old village atmosphere remains here, especially on the ancient hill where I live, to give the requisite background & sense of repose.

Yes—Loveman hates N.Y. as much as I do, & it is exceedingly unfortunate that he can't find financial connexions in his native Cleveland. I spent three weeks there in 1922, & can understand the charm it has for him, although of course there is not much of antiquarian significance in so modern a town. His long classic poem, "The Hermaphrodite", will appear very soon now in book form—published, as Long's was, by W. Paul Cook of Athol. He will undoubtedly send you a copy, & I think you will find it a very mature & remarkable performance—no mere beginning, but a well-rounded & substantial addition to American poetry. I only hope that the reviewers will treat it well—for it is so remote from any dominant modern mood, that one is a bit apprehensive about their understanding or appreciating it. Long, however, has had a very good reception from those qualified to speak with authority.

Morton is prodigiously busy, but I'm sure he'll get around before long to the task of collating & digesting the various selections of your poems which members of our "gang" have made. I have great confidence in his judgment—he is really the only thoroughly balanced critic of us all—& I know that you will make no mistake in following his suggestions. The resultant book will undoubtedly be very fine, & I feel sure that it will bring you a gratifyingly favourable recognition.

With every good wish, & hoping in time to see a gorgeous new volume from your press, I remain

Most cordially & sincerely yours,

H P Lovecraft

Notes

1. No signed article by JLP can be found in the *New York Times* for this period.

[11]   [ALS]

10 Barnes St.,
Providence, R.I.,
Septr. 28, 1926

My dear Pearson:—

I found your interesting letter upon my return from a two weeks' trip whose ultimate point was Philadelphia. The centennial there is very mediocre, but for me was redeemed by the marvellous reproduction of a colonial street. However, most of my time was spent in exploring the old town itself—both the compact part, & the picturesque suburbs—& I certainly found enough to repay my journey. The nearby valley of the Wissahickon Creek, now partly within the city limits, is another major attraction; & forms probably the finest bit of natural scenery I have ever beheld—deep gorge with precipitous wooded slopes, & scores of tributary brooks & cataracts. Going & coming I was detained several days in New York by members of "the gang", & attended two of the weekly meetings. While there I heard your work very highly spoken of, & Morton expressed the opinion that your new volume of selections will meet with gratifying success.

The fact that your own choice of poems coincided so well with that independently made by many others—& especially by Morton, whose taste is especially reliable—ought to gratify you very highly, proving as it does your sound critical ability. This selective sense will undoubtedly influence your future creative work, so that it seems likely that your output will continue to average higher & higher in steady literary quality. I hope you will be able to find a good publisher for the new book—one who will not only produce an attractive volume, but will see that it is properly marketed & advertised as well. You are to be congratulated on your sale of verse to Munsey's,[1] & I hope you may eventually find a steady demand for your work among magazines of the better grade. Recognition is slow, but would be greatly accelerated by the appearance & favourable reception of such a book as you are now planning. Long has had very gratifying responses to the volume he issued last winter, & Loveman expects considerable from the one he is about to have. I am told that Arthur Goodenough also plans a book.[2]

Your remarks on the contemporary south proved highly interesting, & I certainly hope I shall be able to visit it sometime. In my opinion, much of the future of American civilisation lies in the south, for the population there is less contaminated with foreign blood & customs than in any other section. The Civil War gave it a tremendous blow, & set back its culture fully half or three-quarters of a century; but in spite of this apparent backwardness (as manifested in such things as the anti-evolution craze) it has the greatest of all advantages over its neighbours—which makes it the legitimate heir of the original colonies & early American nation. Fifty years from now I believe the cities of the south will exert a quiet cultural dominance hardly imaginable to-day—while the north will possess a more or less hybrid culture akin to that of the decadent Roman Empire, with spectacular luxury & imposing architecture rather than a profound refinement of the spirit.

In coming home from N.Y. I had a delightful motor coach ride through rural Connecticut—a section of my native New England with which I was not very familiar. I found it unutterably delightful—leagues of rock-ribbed hill pastures, vistas of stream & forest, & hills beyond hills, & scores of white ancient villages dreaming under their elms. The coach stopped 40 minutes for lunch in New London, but I eschewed the meal & spent the time exploring. New London is very quaint, with old houses & narrow streets, & I must find an opportunity to revisit it when I have more time to spend. The enclosed card shews one of its most typical buildings.

Speaking of enclosures—I'll send along the latest copy of the United Amateur, which may remind you pleasantly of old times. It's too bad amateurdom can't flourish as of yore, but something or other seems to divert the energies of the younger generation in other directions. The National is getting sadly unliterary, & the United—though still literary—is having a hard fight to exist at all.

With every good wish, & trusting that your new book may encounter a heartening degree of success, I remain

Most cordially & sincerely yrs—
H P Lovecraft

Notes

1. Presumably "Journey's End," published in *Argosy All-Story Weekly* (2 October 1926), a magazine published by the Frank A. Munsey Co.
2. *Songs of Four Decades* (1927).

Winifred Virginia Jackson

Letters to Winifred V. Jackson

[1]   [Draft ALS]
[Mrs. E. Berkely (*sic*)][1]

[c. 25 December 1920]

Dear Madam:—

I am sensible of the honour conferred upon me by the gift of a portraiture as artistic, elaborate, & faithful as that which through your kindness cheered my recent Christmastide. A picture of so great beauty one is undecided whether to place in a gallery of art or a pantheon of celebrities; but since it represents a union of such aesthetick perfection & such extraordinary genius, a solution may be found in its enthronement above both classes, companion'd only by the immortals of Parnassus & Olympus.

Since any ordinary prose expression of gratitude were inadequate to the occasion, I have sought imperfectly to convey my appreciation in the enclosed lines.[2] Pray impute their many & glaring deficiencies to the author's dulness & want of skill alone, since the intentions which animate them are so unaffectedly encomiastick.

But amidst these remarks let me not overlook the merits of the artist responsible for so striking & excellent a likeness. The production is a phenomenal one, & the creator hath as much occasion as his subject to rejoice in a genuine triumph.

From your amended, or restored, signature, I assume that your court case hath come to a successful termination; a circumstance which will cause universal rejoicing because of the inevitable suspense & tension from which it doubtless relieves you. At the same time, amateurdom's 300 adherents cannot but heave a passing sigh at the disappearance of a name which hath come to signify that which is loftiest, most ethereal, & most versatile in poetick accomplishments. "Winifred Virginia Jordan" hath become almost more than a name; achieving the distinction of a symbol. But since the genius which made it great still survives in full splendour, it will not be long ere the honours are suitably transferred to another name so fortunately similar in initial and in prosodick quantity. "Winifred Virginia Jackson" forms a pleasing successor to the signature so long & favourably known; & to a few, such as Mrs. Renshaw, it will mark the agreeable return of a name formerly familiar.

I trust that "The Crawling Chaos"[3] safely reached you, & that it did not prove too inferior for consideration. The many defects of my version are as regretted as they are numerous, & I can but lament my want of constructive genius.

Reiterating my thanks for a gift which in excellence & delightfulness could not have been surpassed, & extending sincerest good wishes for the New Year,
Believe me,
Yr most oblig'd,
most obt Servt.
L. Theobald

Notes

1. Note added by R. H. Barlow.
2. HPL wrote "On Receiving a Portraiture of Mrs. Berkeley . . ." on 25 December.
3. "The Crawling Chaos" is a short story written jointly by Jordan and HPL, probably in December 1920. First published (as by "Elizabeth Berkeley and Lewis Theobald, Jun.") in the *United Co-operative* (April 1921), a cooperative amateur journal edited by HPL, Jackson, and others.

[2]   [Transcription by R H. Barlow]
598 Angell St.,
Providence, R.I.
June 7, 1921.

My dear Miss Jackson:—
It may indeed be said with justice that you have lost a friend in my mother,[1] for although you never heard directly from her, she may be reckoned among the earliest and most enthusiastic admirers of your work. As I recall her especial appreciation of your poems, from the very first she saw, I regret the more that you did not know her personally, either by letter or meeting. Of amateurdom in general her opinion was not high, for she had a certain aesthetic hypersensitiveness which made its crudenesses very obvious and very annoying to her—in fact, she was rather ashamed of my complete absorption in an institution having so many mediocre phases. But from the mass of amateur writings she singled your poetry out at once for the highest praise and keenest liking, and never ceased to read every scrap of your work which she could secure. Moreover, she regarded it not merely as amateur writing, but as literature to be enjoyed apart from its setting. Many of your poems she knew by heart, and frequently repeated; especially "A Merchant from Arcady" and the didactic piece "If You Think You are Beaten, Well, Why?"—this latter as an antidote to my own frequent and unavoidable depression. . . . . . . Considering her literary taste as manifested in other fields, I believe you have a right to feel very substantially complimented by the extreme liking she displayed—a liking which I have here set forth without exaggeration in any particular, no matter how odd it may seem when related of one who never met you, or wrote you directly. In case it would interest you to know my mother's appearance during these latter days, I enclose a snap-

shot—inadequate enough, I regret to say—which I took a year ago last autumn. Her appearance was as handsome as mine is homely, and her youthful pictures would form close rivals to your own in a contest for aesthetic supremacy. Her beauty was of the opposite type—a very fair complexion, but dark eyes and dark brown hair before it became grey. Some of her portraits have, in truth, been mistaken for art studies. Of the amateurs my mother met only Cook and Kleiner. Cook she did not like especially, since his limitations in appearance and mannerisms were just sufficient to grate on a nervous person of keen sensitiveness. (In fact, she regarded me as rather a barbarian on account of my lack of social graces.) Kleiner she liked very much, his quiet voice appealing to her taste. I can but wish that she had met you, as she hoped to do when your trip was discussed some years ago. . . . . Moe has deserted us—I fear he is becoming a religious fanatic like Ira Cole. Galpin and I never hear from him, and it would seem that his formal severance from the GALLOMO was but a mask for completely disowning both of his wicked atheistical correspondents. We only hear of him as a stranger through a new and enthusiastic (but discouragingly dull) recruit named Lehmkuhl[2]—Hun, of course—who appropriately holds forth in the city of Milwaukee. But I ramble in senility. If I do not catch TRYOUT on the outward trip, I may try again Thursday as I return—unless my former failure be accompanied by plain marks of hasty flight and negative welcome. I am ambitious to see a celebrity whom so few human beings have ever seen—to prove once for all that Tryout is a real mortal and not the centre of a mere mythological cult like the cults of Atys, Ishtar, Osiris, Dionysus, Aesculapius, and (as Drews[3] and other searching critics maintain) Christus. If I do succeed in catching this beloved old faun, I shall indeed have a tale of interest to tell the assembled Hubites!

Yr most oblig'd & Obt Servt:
H P Lovecraft

Notes

1. HPL's mother, Sarah Susan (Phillips) Lovecraft (1857–1921), died on 24 May.
2. Harry N. Lehmkuhl (1890–1973).
3. Arthur Drews (1865–1935), a German writer, historian, and philosopher who rose to international prominence with his book *Die Christusmythe* (*The Christ Myth,* 1909).

[3]   [Transcription by R H. Barlow]

August 7, 1921.

My dear Miss Jackson:—

[. . .] The official organ fund[1] has received rather an impetus through that learned but eccentric human phonograph Mrs. Greene, who was at the National convention. After receiving United papers she instantly became an ardent United partisan—began to correspond with Galpin and subscribed *fifty dollars* to the fund! This is the largest subscription since the days of McGeoch–Cook philanthropy—and ought to serve as an example to many veteran members of ample means, whose good wishes seldom extend beyond the domain of rhetoric.

Yr most humble, most Obt Servt,

L. Theobald, Jun.

Notes

1. The Official Organ Fund was devoted to collecting donations from members for the publication of the official organ, the *United Amateur*. See also RK 76.

[4]   [Transcription by R H. Barlow]

Castle Theobald, 9/3/21

My dear Miss Jackson:—

I am exceedingly tardy in acknowledging yours of the 25th, with "Deafness" and "Hoofin' It", but of late my entire programme of writing has suffered through my decreasing store of energy. It is grimly amusing that whilst I appear outwardly better than I have since youth, and emerge into the world more frequently than at any time later than 1908, I am actually far less able to cope with a varied array of duties, and am almost totally swamped with the drivel of that indescribable monstrosity Bush.

[5]   [Transcription by R H. Barlow]

Conservative Office
Sept. 11, 1921.

Dear Miss Jackson:—

Speaking of my fiction, and the probable order of merit amongst the stories which are exclusively mine, I believe that "The Statement of Randolph Carter" heads the list, although Laureate Judges would probably disagree with me—they prefer exotic fantasy, giving the award to "The White Ship" in 1920 and to "The Doom that Came to Sarnath" in 1921. I will wager that if I secure a laureateship in 1922 it will be for "The Quest of Iranon", which is the best English I have ever written. What "Iranon" lacks is novelty of theme—it is the old, dismal allegory of the ghastly jest called life, hence contains nothing but the bleak, barren truth. In this piece I have probably escaped farthest from my natural pompousness of style—the language and tone-colour satisfy me more than in any other of my attempts. But as a story, "R. Carter" seems to me to hold the most genuine shudders. Next to it I would place "Dagon" and "The Picture in the House", with "Sarnath" and "The Temple" trailing closely at their heels. I think you already have "Randolph Carter" in the May 1920 VAGRANT. If not I will send you a copy soon. I have none at present, but so many have asked to see it that I am about to conquer my hatred of typistic copying enough to do a new version with many carbons from the printed copy in my files. Personally, I am fond of "The Beast in the Cave", but everyone else laughs at it as soon as I reveal the fact that it was written at the age of fourteen! I am flattered that you should deem an attempt of mine worthy of preservation. Galpin tells me that my style is decadent—that I am copying Dunsany and losing originality. Perhaps he is right—for I am feeling miserably this year. Whether I shall ever have a renaissance and write something worth reading, I know not. Surely I have a multiplicity of gruesome ideas, but they look inadequate on paper. I was prodigiously elated over my "Nameless City", but Galpin tells me that it is stilted, clumsy, and obvious—that I gave away the cataclysmic secret by implication early in the story, so that the climax is spoilt. I am getting old and feeble; probably my prose is just as bad as my verse, if I but realised it!

> Yr most humble & Obt Servt.,
> L. Theobald, Jun.

[6]   [Transcription by R H. Barlow]

> 598, Angell St., Providence, R.I.
> October 7, 1921.

Dear Miſs Jackson:—

I regret infinitely the ill-health from which you have been suffering, and can assure you that experience affords ample ground for intelligent sympathy. In one respect, however, you are the most fortunate; for you have the certain consciousness of artistic merit to sustain you, whilst I am contemptuous of myself for continuing to live without the least valid excuse for prolonging so dismal a farce. I seldom awake without disgust at the necessity of remaining conscious another 16 or 17 hours before I can find oblivion again; and shall sooner or later be sensible enough to take steps toward a sleep of more merciful permanence. Meanwhile, one must laugh—and surely the baseness and stupidity of mankind furnish an ample field for satirical merriment.

Cook can do the United no conceivable harm by helping at this juncture as a publisher, though naturally his utterances will be scrutinised more or less closely. He is an excellent person, but hopelessly vain and given to a certain quasi-important subtlety. Just now I am vastly in his debt for the favour of lending me a copy of the rather rare Episodes, designed by W. Beckford, Esq. for insertion in "Vathek" but never published during the author's lifetime. These bizarre fictions have revived in me that Orientalism which first appeared when I perused the Arabian Nights at the age of five, and I have a design of writing a weird Eastern tale in the 18th century manner; a tale perhaps too long for publication in amateurdom, but whose writing may help to make endurable the declining days of a harmless old ex-critic.

I am indeed grateful for the Anthology notices, both of which should go in the Septr. U.A.[1] with which I am now struggling amidst the whining and opposition of the Columbus Won'tbes.[2] This news will surely electrify amateurdom—the first really classical recognition an amateur journalist has ever achieved, and captured by a purely *United* poet! I am glad also of the descriptive Braithwaite leaflet—William Stanley is certainly at the head of American criticks of poetry, as indeed I realised before from the *Transcript* reviews. When a tiny coal-black kitten came to visit me in 1918 I called him "William Stanley Braithwaite"[3] and used to let him chew even important papers and feather dusters with the natural destructiveness of a literary reviewer. But this William Stanley deserted me after 1919—he must have found my "poems" unpalatable. I wish I knew what became of him!

My labours—trivial but exhausting in view of my limited energy—now include professional fiction at starvation prices for no less a "boss" than the celebrated George Julian Houtain! The enclosed epistle (which please return) is self-explanatory—a steady "job" if the ambitious magazine should by any miracle survive and prosper! Weird fiction of artistic quality cannot be written to order, nor can plots or characters be artistically dragged through tale after tale—yet I have sought to turn an honest penny by grinding out some of the most blood-curdling morbidness ever beheld of mankind. It is crude and machine-made, of course—but it is not good stuff to read after dark. The name of the series is "Herbert West—Reanimator"—Herbert being a likely young medical student with original ideas on raising the dead. He gets his specimens in the dark of the moon, with spade and lantern. The opening tale is called "From the Dark"; the next is "The Plague-Daemon". I have written no more as yet—I will wait and see what becomes of the magazine. Houtain has not yet acknowledged the two tales I concocted for him. If he rejects them I shall extinguish his laugh in boiling oil. The stories would be wasted—not good enough for the United.

Temperamentally I give St. Julian and the Hub Gang up. I can't solve 'em, and I doubt if any human being is really worth solving. Some philosophers try to "understand" mankind, but after some observation of the species I am content to divide it into the empirical classes of wolves, hyaenas, swine, fools, and madmen and let it go to Phlegethon without any further delay or analysis on my part. The disposition of the majority to harass and injure their fellows is psychologically ineradicable, arising from a primitive wish to gain a factitious self-exaltation by depressing everyone else. It is part of the beast— and is seldom absent save amongst those whose vanity gives them sufficient gratification without injuring others, or those who despise the whole louse-litter of humanity too much to add any condemnation to that contained in mere membership in the human species. "Human being" is the worst thing one can be called—the true cynick hath no time for nugatory supererogation. Let puny scoundrels detract one another—if, being human, I must therefore be a scoundrel; I am determin'd to be a scoundrel in the grand manner, and spit upon the entire accursed race of man, including myself. . . . How bright the birds shine and how sweet the sun twitters in the treetops! I have not heard from the Hubites—save the mimeographed Sept. meeting card—for a month or so; not since I sent Mrs. Sawyer[4] those anti-National verses I quoted you. I wish my camera were rescued!

[Enclosure:]

206 Broadway, New York
September 16, (1921)

Dear Howard:

Litsen (*sic*) to this:

HOME BREW
Full of Moonshine
A THIRST QUENCHER FOR LOVERS
OF PERSONAL LIBERTY
A SPARKLING EFFERVESCING STIMULANT OF
WIT AND HUMOR
EDITED BY MISSUS AND MISTER G. J. HOUTAIN
25¢ a copy $2.50 for 12 numbers
To be published monthly. 64 pages and two color cover.
To be professional.

Litsen once more:

You are engaged as a contributor—and you are to get $5 for each one—on publication. We are too poor otherwise. You are to write a series of Grewsome Tales—they are to be spine shiverers and blood curdlers—you cannot make them too morbid—preferably 1,500 words—not more than 2,000 words. You can go your limit as to subjects. Want a series of at least six. Need two right away. Must appear under the name of Howard Phillips Lovecraft—no alias of any kind. Articles to be property—full rights—of Home Brew. If we can make it a success—I'll show you how we put HPL on the map. Will consider anything else of yours under nom—must be in the lightest of veins—preferably saucy and spicy. Important; have your titles especially alluring—with a punch— a wee bit—well, making one feel a wee bit devilish y' know.

You notice, I hope, the editorial style of this letter. You are directed to proceed forthwith to send on your first two (or should I say two firsts or neither) anyhow we want one for the issue going to press and the other on hand for announcement for next issue. If possible keep the same characters throughout the series. If HB goes—Lapoint[5] will write a play using the characters therein—called Home Brew.

Have we your endorsement—do you approve—may we get your help—when will the two articles be forthcoming.

Sincerely,

George

[Other enclosures (with which letters?):]

["Ars Gratia Artis (For THE CONSERVATIVE)"]
["To a Youth (Dedicated to Master Alfred Galpin, Jun." Notes following poem:] [*next to pseudonym "Richard Raleigh":*] How is this for an Elizabethan pseudonym?

During a recent relapse of my antient poetick malady, I tried—purely for fun—an experiment in the Elizabethan–Jacobean style of Herrick, Suckling, &c. &c.—choosing as my subject the incomparable Alfredus. This is it! Rotten, but of course only a first attempt. Possibly I shall let Mr. Raleigh live, and perpetrate other Elizabethan atrocities. He is Mr. Theobald's great-grandfather, on the maternal side.

N.B.—Please do not let *any* other amateur see this—not even the Hub circle. I should like to hear what is said of it (if aught!) before its authorship is known. I doubt if anyone could recognise my fine Italian hand in this—it savours of 1620, a century behind *my* day.

Notes

1. "News Notes" in the September *United Amateur* (written by HPL) states that Jackson's poems "Fallen Fences," "Miss Doane," "The Farewell," and "Cross-Currents" were selected for Braithwaite's *Anthology of Massachusetts Poets* (1921). HPL also announces that Braithwaite selected poems by Jackson for his annual anthology of magazine verse. The anthology "reprints" seven poems that supposedly had first been printed in HPL's *Conservative*. They were not (HPL published no issue of the *Conservative* in 1921). See Appendix.

2. HPL refers sarcastically to the amateur group The Woodbees of Columbus, OH, who bitterly opposed HPL when he served as president of the UAPA.

3. So named because a few months previous, HPL learned that Braithwaite was African American. See RK 35.

4. Laurie A. Sawyer, amateur journalist and president of the Interstate Amateur Press Association (1909). She issued the *Tryout* supplement, *In Memory Edith May Miniter: A Coworker in Amateur Journalism 1884–1934* (Haverhill, MA: C. W. Smith, [1934]).

5. William W. Lapoint (1870–1933), a minor playwright.

Arthur Leeds

Letters to Arthur Leeds

[1]   [ANS, JHL][1]

[Postmarked New Orleans, La.,
14 June 1932]

Have just had that *sunrise* view of the cathedral & adjacent roofs—in connexion with an all-night session with the Weird Tales writer & orientalist E. Hoffmann Price—whose "Peacock's Shadow" & "Stranger from Kurdistan"[2] you'll remember. He's a great guy—West Point graduate, World War Veteran & ex-Captain, Arabic scholar, amateur fencing-master, Persian rug connoisseur, &c. &c. I've never corresponded with him, so wasn't going to look him up; but Robert E. Howard gave him my N.O. address & he got in touch. I spent *25½ hours*—from 9:30 Sunday night to 11 Monday night—discussing the cosmos & all its subdivisions with him. He lives in the Vieux Carré (although he's soon going to move out), & at dawn we went down to the French Market for coffee & doughnuts—hence the view. I'm staying till Thursday—hence will see the Quarter under decidedly gibbous moonlight. Hope all is going well up your way. Will see you soon—regards
Grandpa Theobald

Notes

1. *Front:* Interior, French Market, New Orleans, LA.
2. "The Peacock's Shadow," *WT* 8, No. 5 (November 1926): 580–96. "A Stranger from Kurdistan," *WT* 6, No. 1 (July 1925): 95–98; rpt. *WT* 14, No. 6 (December 1929): 848–51.

[2]   [ANS][1]

[Postmarked Brooklyn, N.Y.,
28 June 1932]

Ave, Arturo! Back north at last, via Mobile, Montgomery, Richmond, Fredericksburg, Washington, Annapolis, & Philad[a]. Staying a week on Columbia Hts. as guest of Saml Loveman, Esq. He bids me second him in urging your presence at a Kalem meeting to be held at 130 Columbia Hts. at 8 p.m., FRIDAY, JULY 1, 1932. Hope you can make it—Mortonius has promised to be on deck. I'll tell you all about my N.O. impressions—we'll see who got the most of the old town!
Regards—HPL

Samuel Loveman

Notes

1. *Front:* Fraunce's [*sic*] Tavern, New York City.

[3]   [ALS, not seen]

66 College Street
Providence, R.I.
[11 January 1934]

Dear Arturo

[. . .] the Dorset ghost story [. . .] gave me the strongest kick.[1]

[. . .] He [A. Merritt] turned out to be a tremendously likable chap of about 50—stout, sandy, & affable. [. . .]

HPL.

Notes

1. Leeds sent three stories. The other two were "Conscience" and "The Revolt of the Gods," weird tales set in Egypt. All apparently were unpublished.

[4]   [AHT 31.1]

De Land—
June 4, 1934

Ave, Arturo!

[. . .]

As for "The Black Cat"[1]—I guess Edgar Allan might very well have written the cinema version so far as any resemblance to the work of our friend Eddie Poe is concerned!

Yr obt hble Servt
H P L

Notes

1. *The Black Cat* (Universal, 1934), directed by Edgar G. Ulmer; starring Boris Karloff, Béla Lugosi, and David Manners. The screenplay was in fact written by Peter Ruric.

[5]   [ANS, Owings][1]

[Postmarked Charleston, S.C.,
29 June 1934]

[Ave, fro]m old CHARLESTON! Nearly flat [broke. I'm] down to a food quota of 20¢ per day. [Here fo]r 2 days only—got in at 3 a.m. & the [night] clerk at the Y let me have a room [for the] first half-night for nothing! I would _____ have stayed up & awaited the dawn. [Grea]t to be among Georgian doorways & _____ again after 2 months on old Spanish [soil?]. This is the most home-like place in the [country] except Providence. Hate to move north! [Here? be]yond Sunday, then Washn., Phila. & NY. ___ I'm afraid I can't stop in NY more than [a nigh]t or two—for Belknap's maid has left, [& he] can't act as host. It all depends on how [broke] I am, & whether I can get a cheap [some]room. I may have to shoot straight [back] to Providence without see-ing anyone. [I'll] let you know how it turns out. Had a [great?] week in St. Au-gustine—every day [was] sunny. Am getting the foundation of quite a coat of tan. ¶ Hoping for the [best?]. [Yr ob]t Servt [HP]L

Notes

1. Dealer's catalogue does not identify picture on card, and text on left of card is cut off.

[6]   [ALS, not seen]

[De Land—
June 1934]

[. . .] For quantity-producing hacks like Price & Wandrei & (nowadays) Belknap, it[1] ought to be a veritable godsend.

Notes

1. A device for writers to use to develop story plots.

[7]   [ALS, JHL]

De Land—
June 19, 1934.

Arturo, Hail!

Thanks prodigiously & effusively for the Bailey[1] sketch—which will go into my permanent files when I get home. While passing through N.Y. I'll try to look up Ardlea Court[2]—undoubtedly a fascinating backwater. I surely wish I had the whole lot of Bailey pictures. If he ever issues a book of them at a decently reasonable figure I shall surely be among the customers. They make me think of Laswell's "Corners & Characters of Providence",[3] which appeared in our local paper a decade ago.

Speaking of Baileys—I'm in touch with one of them . . . . James Osler Bailey, Box 414, Chapel Hill, N.C. . . . who is preparing a history of science fiction [on which he's just secured a Ph.D. from the U. of N.C.] & would like to get in contact with anyone who might have suggestions to contribute. In its present form it is 835 typed pages long—which will give you some idea of its exhaustiveness. It includes popular material—Merritt, G. A. England, Victor Rousseau, &c.—& extends down to recent times. If you think you could help or be helped by this guy in any literary way, drop him a line.[4]

I think I will send for that plot stuff—the free information, that is—if you'll let me have the address. I've forgotten the place I sent for the Plot Robot.[5] I also sent somewhere else in California for something called a "plot graph"—which wasn't so hot, either. Hope I get as generous a response to my enquiry as you did! The Hartrampf[6] advertisement is highly interesting—guess I'll send & see what the free stuff is. I think I've heard of this before. Doubt, though, whether I'll ever try to use anything beyond good old Roget.

Hope the new Poe mangling didn't disappoint you too badly—I've seen neither it nor the so-called "Black Cat." Just what the cinema would do to the "Tell Tale Heart" is more than I can imagine at the moment! I'll look for "Rome Express"—though I saw neither "The Man Who Laughs" nor "Caligari" in their respective days. What I *did* see last week was "The Double Door"[7]—in which the grim Miss Morris looked & sounded exactly the same as in the stage production. Wasn't the timid sister Caroline also of the original stage cast? She seemed exceedingly familiar in her role. The "twist" at the end was typically cinematic—but detracted from the lifelike quality possessed by the play. Barlow liked the thing extremely, & I was glad to have seen it.

Well—I certainly didn't expect to be in De Land so long, but the hospitality of the Barlow household is of an almost unprecedentedly cordial & insistent sort . . . . so that every suggestion of breaking away is sunk in some plan for another week's activities. This week, however, I simply must be getting in motion. I shall pause in ancient St. Augustine a bit, & thereafter drag myself north by easy stages—seeing you, I trust, when I pass through the metropolitan zone. A fortnight ago I visited a most impressive place—Silver Springs, some 60 miles N.W. of De Land. Here is found a series of placid lagoons whose floor is riddled with vast pits 30 to 80 feet deep, & covered with curious marine vegetation. In many places divers have exhumed the huge bones of prehistoric animals, & there is an old sunken, moss-encrusted ship's boat which the local folk try to connect with the early Spanish explorers. I saw these varied wonders from a glass-bottomed boat. Out of the lagoons flows the Silver River—as typical a tropic stream as the Congo or Amazon, with tall palms, trailing vines & moss, & bending cypresses along the swampy banks. Alligators, turtles, & snakes abound, & on either side the jungle stretches away uninterruptedly for miles. It is here that the cinema of "Tarzan" was photographed.[8] I took a 10-mile launch trip on the river, & could easily have imagined myself in the heart of Africa. It was the first time I ever saw an alligator in his actual setting—outside zoos & alligator farms.

And so it goes. See you within a month!

Blessings—Grandpa H P

Notes

1. Vernon Howe Bailey (1874–1953), American artist, staff member at the *Philadelphia Times* and the *Boston Herald,* and contributor to *Scribner's* and *Harper's,* noted for his views of New York City.

2. Between Third Avenue and East Fifty-first Street, where antique shops were located.

3. "Corners and Characters of Rhode Island" was a long-running column in the [Providence] *Evening Bulletin* written mostly by George D. Laswell. Laswell also published a book of that title (Providence: The Oxford Press, 1924).

4. James Osler Bailey (1903–1979) eventually published *Pilgrims through Space and Time: Trends and Patterns in Scientific and Utopian Fiction.* New York: Argus Books, 1947.

5. HPL had purchased "Robo: The Game that writes a Million Story Plots," devised by Wycliffe Hall, but ultimately found no use for it.

6. Gustavus Hartrampf (1875–1934) wrote several books on vocabulary building. It is not certain what "free stuff" HPL considered obtaining.

7. *Bucket of Blood* (Fox Film Co., 1934), directed by Brian Desmond Hurst; starring Norman Dryden, John Kelt, and Yolande Terrell; based on the story "The Tell-Tale Heart" by Edgar Allan Poe. *Rome Express* (Gaumont British, 1932), directed by Walter Forde; starring Muriel Aked, Joan Barry, and Donald Calthrop. *The Man Who Laughs* (Universal, 1928), directed by Paul Leni, starring Mary Philbin, Conrad Veidt, and Julius Molnar; based on the story by Victor Hugo (Veidt's role as Gwynplaine later inspired The Joker of the *Batman* comics). *The Cabinet of Dr. Caligari* [*Das Kabinett des Doktor Caligari*] (Germany, 1919), directed by Robert Wiene; starring Werner Kraus, Conrad Veidt and Friedrich Feher; distributed in the U.S. (1921f.) by MGM. *Double Door* (Paramount, 1934), directed by Charles Vidor; starring Evelyn Venable, Mary Morris (as Victoria Van Brett), and Anne Revere (as Caroline Van Brett); based on the play by Elizabeth McFadden.

8. Six of the original Tarzan movies, starring Johnny Weissmuller, were filmed on location at Silver Springs between 1932 and 1942, including *Tarzan the Ape Man* (1932) and *Tarzan and His Mate* (1934).

[8]   [ANS, JHL][1]

[Postmarked St. Augustine, Fla.,
23 June 1934]

Ave, Arturo! Back amongst my favourite antiquities at last! It's like a homecoming to see ancient roofs & city gates after 7 continuous weeks of modernity! The Barlows brought me up here in the car last Thurs., & I secured a room at the same place I stopped in 1931—the Rio Vista, 120 Bay St. Fine tower room with running water—& a magnificent view—for only $4.00 per week. Am staying a week. ¶ Doing the old buildings as usual. Several more are open as museums than in 1931. Also picking up a coat of tan—writing on the terreplein of the old fort, & on the deserted beach of Anastasia Island. ¶ Nearly broke so will have to cut out some of the intended stops on the way north. Hope to see you in a little over a fortnight.

Blessings—
Grandpa

Notes

1. *Front:* Old City Gates, St. Augustine, Fla.

[9]   [ANS, JHL][1]

[Postmarked Providence, R.I.,
15 August 1934]

You lose, brother . . . for I *did* hear it! And did it bring back good old 1904? I could hear the clatter of cabs in the street, & see the little red & green trolley cars as they h[urri?]ed past the Providence Opera House! Thirty years! . . . & the cabmen were whistling "Bedelia",[2] while the newsboys hummed "Good Bye, Eliza Jane" & "Meet me at St. Louis, Louis".[3] Time . . . time . . . time . . . . ! Shall be on hand for Pinafore[4] next week. ¶ Yes—bought T. T.[5] & read it through, but it's no good at all. Cheapest kind of junk. ¶ New W. T. is so-so. ¶ Had a good visit from James Ferdinand—we went to Newport on the final day & saw the ancient town, the rugged cliffs, & the same fleet that you saw in N.Y. last spring. ¶ On Aug. 23 I'm going to visit a chap near Boston & shall see W. Paul Cook . . . whom you know about, even if you haven't met him. He may come to N.Y. to seek his fortune if he can't land anything in Boston. If so, he'll make a good addition for the gang. ¶ Hope you are flourishing. I hear indirectly that Loveman is in poor health—hope he'll be on his feet soon. ¶ And thanks for the P of P tip!
—H P L

[P.S. on front:] Do you know the weird work of William Hope Hodgson? I've just read his "Boats of the Glen Carrig", & it's really great!

Notes

1. *Front:* The Public Library, New York City.
2. A popular song from 1903 (words by William Jerome, music by Jean Schwartz). See HPL's extensive discussion of it in a letter to J. Vernon Shea (4 February 1934); *Letters to J. Vernon Shea, Carl F. Strauch, and Lee McBride White* (New York: Hippocampus Press, 2016), 229–30.
3. "Good Bye, Eliza Jane" (1903), words by Andrew B. Sterling (1874–1955), music by Harry Von Tilzer (1872–1946). "Meet Me in St. Louis, Louis" (1904) celebrated the Louisiana Purchase Exposition (i.e., the St. Louis World's Fair); words by Andrew B. Sterling, music by Kerry Mills (1869–1948).
4. *H.M.S. Pinafore; or, The Lass That Loved a Sailor* (1878), a comic opera in two acts, with music by Arthur Sullivan and a libretto by W. S. Gilbert. "P & P" below refers to

their *The Pirates of Penzance; or, The Slave of Duty* (1879).

5. *Terror Tales* (1934–41), a "weird menace" pulp magazine published by Popular Publications and edited by Rogers Terrill. HPL presumably read the first issue, dated September 1934 but on the stands at least a month before the cover date.

[10]   [ANS][1]

[Postmarked Nantucket, Mass.,
30 August 1934]

Hail, Arturo! See where the Old Gentleman is! On my last outing of the season. Visited a friend in Boston as a start, & am now revelling amidst the concentrated antiquity of the quaintest old place in North America! And to think I never saw it before—a place only 90 miles from Providence! ¶ Nantucket has whole networks of cobblestoned streets with nothing but colonial mansions & cottages on either side—narrow lanes—ancient belfries—picturesque waterfront—*everything* that the antiquarian could ask. Am seeing the whole thing in a week's sojourn. Have a 3d story room with a titanic view of town & harbour & sea. Have explored old houses, windmill, whaling museum, historical society, Maria Mitchell Observatory, &c. Also took rubberneck-wagon trip of entire island—seeing quaint Siasconset, &c. I hate to think of going home! ¶ Got Pinafore last week on the radio—an aftermath of your original tip. ¶ Trust that all prospers along Surf Ave. & vicinity.
Blessings—
Grandpa

Notes

1. *Front:* Colonial Mansions, Nantucket, Mass.

[11]   [ANS][1]

[Postmarked St. Augustine, Fla.,
20[?] August 1935]

Ave, Arturo! On the way north after a record-breaking visit with Barlow & his parents—2 months & 9 days! Certainly had a great time. Barlow has built a cabin across the lake from his place—in a picturesque oak grove—& has installed complete printing & binding apparatus, so that he can produce books from idea to dust jacket! The Barlows have now gone to Daytona for a fortnight. ¶ St. Augustine, with its ancient houses and cathedral chimes, looks pretty good after my long dose of rural modernity. I'm here for a week—got a basement (but above ground) room *with bath & kitchen added* at the old Rio Vista for only *$3.50*. May be too broke for a sizeable stay in Charleston, & probably can't stop at all in N.Y. Trust all goes well in the book business. Did I tell you that

Barlow [grab]bed up "Faust & the Demon" in Washington for a *dime* . . . & that right after getting "Wagner the Wehr-Wolf" in N.Y.[2] for 15¢. Just a sheer coincidental stroke of luck. ¶ Regards—& with a slender hope of being able to see you—
H P L

Notes

1. *Front:* Watch Tower, Fort Marion, St. Augustine, Fla.
2. Both by George W. M. Reynolds.

Paul J. Campbell

Letters to Paul J. Campbell

[1]   [ANS][1]

[Postmarked Boston, Mass.,
6 July 1920]

Greetings from the private convention at Allston![2]
Rheinhart Kleiner
E. Miniter
Mrs. Dooley | Winifred V. Jordan
H. P. Lovecraft
Alice Marion Hamlet
M. E. Jackson
Best regards from Houtain
E. Dorothy MacLaughlin
Wish you could have been here. Cole.
S. Lilian McMullen
[illegible name written vertically]

Notes

1. *Front:* Birdseye View State House and Common from The Little Building, Boston, Mass. Addressed to Mr. & Mrs. P. J. Campbell.
2. A neighborhood in Boston. HPL paid a visit on 4 July to Winifred Virginia Jordan, Laurie A. Sawyer, and Edith Miniter at 20 Webster Street. "Mrs. Dooley" is in fact Sawyer. See, e.g., "Mrs. Dooley Attends the Convention" (1930) in which she gives her report in "Irish" dialect: "Mr. Lovecraft came up from Providence, the same foine lad as iver. Wan thing he did that no wan else has iver done at the Dooley house—he tamed the wild baste we have there that answers fer a cat" [p. 1].

[2]   [AHT]

[25 January 1924]

My dear Campbell:—
                    [. . .]
    Had an interesting amateur visitor a week ago Wednesday—the Washingtonian Edward L. Sechrist. We recognised each other at once from pictures, & proceeded to spend an enjoyable afternoon in that antiquarian exploration which has become my favourite pursuit. Seldom have I guided a more appreciative observer through our local wealth of Colonial architecture & 18th century atmosphere—he had never seen New England before, so the surviving monuments of antiquity rather staggered him! He is an agricultural expert employed by the government, & came to address some sort of beekeepers' meeting. As

a cosmopolite, he holds the amateur record, having lived in Hayti, Africa, & Polynesia. He comes from Maryland, & his chief interest is Polynesian folklore.

Yes—your W.T. opinion appeared in good company![1] You'll find another tale of mine, "The Hound", in the Feby. issue; marred by several misprints. I've just received a flattering letter from Baird,[2] which swells my egotism considerably—he calls me one of his two star writers, Seabury Quinn being the other.

Here's hoping your novel progresses well,[3] & that your business worries will clarify enough to give you some artistic repose. The practical world certainly is a most infernal nuisance, as I'm finding this winter![4]

With all good wishes, most sincerely yours,

HPL

Notes

1. "The Eyrie," *WT* 3, No 1 (December 1923–January 1924): 86: "P. J. Campbell of Ridgefarm, Illinois, declares 'the same story [HPL's "Dagon"] is a little masterpiece of its kind.'" Others with letters (or brief comments) published in "The Eyrie" included HPL himself, Seabury Quinn, James F. Morton, Jr., Henry S. Whitehead, and Clement Wood.

2. Edwin Baird (1886–1957), the first editor of *WT* (March 1923–April 1924).

3. PJC was still working on *The Pursuit of Happiness* in March 1927, but it was destroyed the following month in a fire at his home.

4. At the time, HPL was ghostwriting "Under the Pyramids" for Harry Houdini.

[3]   [ANS][1]

[Postmarked Philadelphia, Pa.,
21 November 1924]

Meant to write sooner, but have been in a turmoil of business & worry. Wife ill—in hospital from Oct 21 to 31—& now on a farm near Somerville, N.J. recuperating. Since the latter place is so far toward [?] Philadelphia, & since I'd gone there to ensconce my wife in her rustication, I decided to come the rest of the way & give the old Quaker burg the thorough exploration I've long wanted to give it. Made a good beginning last night. I ought to know it by a day or two! I find much of my favourite colonial material.
Yr obt servt HPL

P.S. Will probably have to break up 259 Parkside & board soon.[2] Alas!

Notes

1. *Front:* Hotel Wister House, Germantown, Philadelphia, P.A.

2. By 31 December 1924, HPL was dwelling at 169 Clinton St. in Brooklyn, where he remained until April 1926 and then returned to Providence. Sonia went to work at a department store in Cincinnati. HPL never lived with his wife again.

[4]   [AHT]

10 Barnes St.,
Providence, R.I.,
Feby. 2, 1927

My dear Campbell:—

Well, I'll be damned! So that poor Bush is still alive! I've often wondered whatever became of him—the last I saw of him was in New York in 1924,[1] when he tried to persuade Morton & me to undertake some magazine work which looked so bad that we passed it up. I thought he was provoked at me for my refusal—but I guess he practiced that large Christian forgiveness which his former Methodist & Congregational pastorship insidiously instilled into his subconscious being. . . .

Well—if Bush has any junk to be tinkered up, he'll find me still doing business in the old way if not precisely at the old stand. I could use his cash very conveniently just now, for revision has been slack since last fall. At that time I was doing a tremendous amount for the conjuror Houdini, with a prospect of handling an enormous amount in future—a whole series of exposés of the different branches of occultism. Then some bally idiot had to give him a ventral punch which sent him back to Abraham's bosom in a week, & all demand for anti-occult revision naturally evaporated.[2] It was really quite too bad, for that work was genuinely interesting & involved no blah or fakery. Houdini was after real facts & nothing else, & had to have his work absolutely proof against all rebuttals & flaw-pickings from his opponents. . . . .

I've been trying slightly longer things recently—finished an 110-page fantasy the other day, & am now working on a novelette with antiquarian background which will probably come to 50 or 75 pages. . . .[3]

Thanking you for mentioning the Bush matter, & thanking you in advance for mailing Davy the enclosed, I remain

Most cordially & sincerely yrs—
HPL

Notes

1. See Kenneth W. Faig, Jr., "Lovecraft's Third Meeting with David V. Bush." *Lovecraft Annual* No. 8 (2014): 162–77.

2. HPL ghostwrote the story "Under the Pyramids" (1924; published as "Imprisoned with the Pharaohs") for Harry Houdini (stage name of Ehrich Weiss, 1874–1926), celebrated escape artist and opponent of spiritualism, at the behest of *WT*. HPL was engaged in other work in 1926, including *The Cancer of Superstition,* which seems to have been written primarily by C. M. Eddy, from HPL's outline. Houdini died of peritonitis, secondary to a ruptured appendix on 31 October, from punches to the stomach delivered by someone attempting to test his endurance.

3. *The Dream-Quest of Unknown Kadath* and *The Case of Charles Dexter Ward.* The latter was much longer than prognosticated, longer than the first novel.

[5]   [AHT]

10 Barnes St.,

Providence, R.I.,

March 2, 1927

My dear Campbell:—

Thanks tremendously for sending the card to Bush. What he wanted this time was something for nothing—a lecture (subject unspecified) from me, to be delivered at his summer camp of fakers & lunatics—"New-Thoughters", "Vibrationists" & all that sort of cattle—at Meshoppen, Pa. No pay, but an opportunity to talk things over. My declination was unexceptionable in its cordial urbanity. But anyhow, he has my address now, & if he ever wants any real work for real pay again, he knows where to write!

Your newly-discovered Oasis group seems to be rather vivid & colourful, & probably resembles many in the Greenwich Village section of New York. My observation of such phenomena has not been extensive, since I am pretty much of a conservative & antiquarian by nature, & more prone to talk about McIntire[1] carving, fluted pilasters, bolection moulding,[2] & other appurtenances of Colonial houses than about communism, Nietzsche, democracy, & other fashions of contemporary Bohemia; but I have looked in superficially on one or two assemblages of advanced souls, & have been impressed by the manner in which they seem to enjoy themselves. . . . . I'm afraid they would find me a very recalcitrant old reactionary, for I never did see much use in intellectual panaceas. Very little in life ever can be the product of cerebral deliberation, & society shapes itself as a general thing very blindly, with instinct & emotion as the really determinant forces. When changes come, it is largely an automatic & fortuitously matter—the conscious theories generally being more post-facto rationalisations of movements already under way than actual originators & agents of the transformation. Every age has a characteristic fetish which, although meaning absolutely nothing in a purposeless & unmoral cosmos, comes to fill men's minds & emotions to the exclusion of everything else, & to serve as an artificial criterion & standard of values. Once it was *beauty*, (& it still is with me, for I find this illusion to be the only one worthy of the respect of a civilised & cynical soul) & we had the art of Greece. Once it was *power*, & we had the majesty of Rome. Once it was *sanctity*, & we had St. Simeon Stylites[3] & the Pope. Once it was *reason*, & we had the Encyclopaedists & the Evolutionists. Now it happens to be *social justice*, & we have the bolsheviki, Scott Nearing,[4] & assorted eloquence of various brands. But all the time the world is going on by instinct & linked circumstance just the same, & each of the new doctrines is just as much a chance mechanical thing as the conditions it dislikes & the conditions which will follow—whether it wishes them or not. Personally I'm not interested in the future except speculatively, because it represents a very steady decadence according to all the standards (artificial & fortuitous, of course) which happen to be mine. What I respect is a brilliant & powerful culture which creates beautiful things in all the arts, develops a highly organised mental life among a certain percentage (I'm not particular how great a percentage) of its members, attains a clear & vigorous vision in its plumbing of the cosmos, & has enough potentialities of permanence & enough unbroken linkages with the past to form a real historic entity with claims on one's loyalty & dramatic imagination. That's all I give a damn about in the world, & when I don't see a prospect for the maintenance of such a thing I'm frankly uninterested. The "justice & equality" stuff doesn't catch my fancy at all, & I can say with sincerity that Mussolini's fascist Italy is about the only nation today which commands my whole-hearted respect—as apart from my natural loyalty & affection as an Anglo-Saxon toward England & America. If you want a clear light on the disintegrating conditions of today, read the greatest philosophico-historical work of this generation—of which the first volume has just been translated from the German: "The Decline of the West", by Oswald Spengler. This was written (though not published) before the war, & shews the most remarkable insight & fearlessness I have seen in any recent work. Spengler's main contention, of course, is the almost universally recognised truth that all cultures have a life of birth, growth, culmination, decay, & death as definite & inescapable as the life of an individual organism. Egypt, Babylon, Persia, Greece, Rome—where are they? He then shews that the only decent criterion of a culture is its art life—the creative expression of its collective brain as distinguished from the mechanical addition & subtraction of facts as practiced by its pedants & scientists. A young culture has a naive, healthy & imperatively powerful art life at the same time that it has an unbroken will, ambition, & military ardour. When these inseparable impulses are at their zenith, we have the very height of culture—an Augustan or Elizabethan age. Such an age cannot be democratic, because the individual must be lost in a blind & impulsive service of the common vision & common ambition. His egotism must still be in that unsophisticated stage of evolution in which its perfect gratification cannot be attained apart from the concept of the state—his relation to the state, & the state's relation to the world. Nationalism in its narrowest sense is the sine qua non of vigorous culture. The social scene is more rural than urban, & of a landlord-&-tenant sort which fosters that leisure class necessary to a well-rounded & well-mannered life. Commerce must not dominate agriculture, for the idea of *money* in the abstract as divorced from the entities it represents is a distinctly decadent symptom. The country gentleman is the highest type & symbol of a culture's health—a man of healthy surroundings, civilised leisure, & a set of emotions attuned to patriotism & beauty. But of course this sort of thing can't last. Trading & haggling succeed direct exchange, & commercial & industrial life are born. Naive enthusiasms become exhausted with age & racial experience, & languid ideals succeed the old virile ones. Along with this, of course, the authentic vigour of the arts begins to die, until at last we have only the artificial & over-sophisticated perversions & imitations—widely deviating from the essential national standard—of which cubism, futurism, imagism, & such bedlam aesthetics are current samples. At the same time rural life gives place to an unhealthy, artificial, & over-excited urban life; & scientific progress invents machines which disorganise the social system & remove life so far from the hereditary types to which our emotions respond, that its normal expression in art becomes no longer possible. Sentimentality and pacifism set in, & the nation becomes defenseless [*sic*] before less over-ripe foes. The impoverished imagination turns to realism, & a dull unfruitful reign of matter-of-factness & dryasdust pedantry ensues. Spengler becomes an innovator in his distinction betwixt "culture" & "civilisation". The former term he applies to a young & healthy national condition, the latter to a mechanical, prosaic, commercial, democratic age of decadence. He is also unique in differentiating radically betwixt Greek & modern art. The former excluded time & space, he points out, & dealt in plastic harmonies; (to my mind the only true art) whilst the latter (which he calls "Faustian") dealt with dramatic change & development, & therefore played itself out through trying to keep pace with the aging culture. Spengler considers modern art as dead as ancient art, since he considers our true *culture* dead. What we have is only a *civilisation* sterile of the true art impulse. The last real manifestation of art was that of XIX century France, with the Symbolists in literature & the impressionists in painting. This is the one place where I do not wholly agree with Spengler, for I believe that a *reminiscent* art based on more or less tangible legacies from the past will be possible for several generations among limited conservative groups. Spengler says that *no* art can be produced; & advises first-rate men to turn away from it & put their energies in something more vitally identified with our dying civilisation—engineering, politics, or tangible activity of some sort. Here the first volume ends—but my own views are so much like Spengler's that I can predict pretty well what the rest will be. Everything is running down, & it would take a catalogue longer than Homer's catalogue of the ships[5] to enumerate all the instances. In the first place, as men like Lathrop Stoddard & Madison Grant[6] shew, our most important fundamental element of all—*race-stock*—is going absolutely to hell. The way that competent & desirable Nordics of unbroken spirit & healthy emotions restrict birth whilst cringing mongrel Jews & Slavs & South Italians (bearing all the stigmata of physical & emotional degeneracy, as any unprejudiced biologist can shew) multiply like accursed rabbits is enough to seal our fate if nothing else were lurking ahead to harm us. God! The stinking crowd of Asiatic hybrids & bastards & vermin that swarm the streets of N.Y.! Then machinery with its consequent industrialism is doing the devil's own work. Easy transportation, factory social problems, & the diffusion of uniform, standardised products (even in the realm of literature & the arts) are taking all the variety, individualism, picturesqueness, & local spirit out of life; & making aesthetic craftsmanship & originality virtually impossible. Artistic & balanced life demands a definite relation to race, traditions, climate, & landscape—& what are we getting with one widespread uniform output of articles & ideas all over the world, & a constant shifting of peoples which permits relatively few families to remain properly merged with the locale that moulded them? In place of local & original thought & feeling we have a mongrelised cosmopolitan taste & an ovine herd-psychology that follows the loudest demagogue. Government is going to the deuce because irresponsible idealists are asking more of it than any government run by human beings can possibly give, whilst industry is evolving a class of men who think in isolated parts—owing to modern mass-production methods—rather than integrated wholes in which they can take a creator's pride. And this transformation of life to a complicated, inter-related system of blind piece construction & specialised assembling is rendering every phase of existence so helpless in itself, & so utterly dependent on an increasingly complex tangle of administrative details, that there is a very real danger of the whole thing's breaking down from sheer exhaustion, through the ultimate inability of any set of mortal minds to correlate all the bewildering & labyrinthine data necessary to make anything move at all. And behind it all is the slow advance of biological senility. Our minds are growing old, till like the little Chinese boys described by De Quincey, the sense of youth in the individual is lost in the sense of antiquity of the race.[7] It is not that we are losing *brain-power*—we think & calculate as well or even better than before—but that we are losing *will-power*. In our increasingly wide grasp of scientific facts we are learning the true nature, dimensions, & futility of the eternal, infinite, & cyclic cosmos; & are realising our own utter insignificance & transiency as scaled against its boundlessness & endlessness. We are learning that it doesn't matter a damn what we do or how we do it or whether we do it at all or whether we're alive or dead—& with this inescapable conclusion beating in, (subconsciously even when not consciously, & strongly affecting even those who violently deny the circumstance) it is natural that everything in life aside from the most primitive processes seems less & less worth doing. The world has nothing to give us in any way worth the trouble of striving for it—apart from mere physical comfort—& we are refusing more & more to strive for something which we know can never bring us the pleasure & excitement & sense of significance that results used to have. For in pulling down our false idols, we have pulled down all that we ever possessed! Everything which gave us real & lasting pleasure was a naive illusion, & we have been well-meaningly & industriously destroying all our illusions! Knowing too much of philosophy for our own good, we can no longer harbour the pleasing mirage of free-will; so that life becomes a mere helpless game of pawns in the hands of a blind cosmos; where it used to look like a stirring contest of conscious forces, any one of which might of its own volition alter the course of things. The loss of that delusion has been a great blow, for there is not much fun in being merely one of a set of loaded dice. We realise too keenly nowadays that nothing can be altered—that everything which happens is the inevitable resultant of all the circumjacent & antecedent forces; & that all which is or ever will be, has been conclusively predetermined through all the gulf of eternity behind. And man—what the hell is that poor louse? The most merciful thing would be to wipe him altogether off the earth—if he deserved the trouble it would take.

So, as I say, I can't get excited about the New Social Order & all that sort of thing. I don't see much for a gentleman to do—provided he hasn't the guts to shoot himself—but to live up as best he can to the tradition that bred him. That is as near to any kind of harmony or beauty as he'll ever get in a world where no absolute values exist, & where morals, aesthetics, & interests are alike a local matter of period, race, & geography. Some people can get enough fun out of this to make continued existence worth while in a mild way,—I probably do myself—but doubtless others can't, & for them it's a very hard world indeed unless they can feed themselves on new illusions of a 'better world coming' after they are dead. It's a weary business—but in dreaming & fantasy-weaving & exploration of ancient things one may find a sort of haven & a sort of substitute for the aspirations & allurements which more ingenuous ages used to provide. Meanwhile the man of sense sits amusedly by & lets the world & the human race go to hell in their own way. Liberalism—ochlocracy—collapse—Mongolian conquest—Mongolian collapse—hybridism—new civilisation—new culture—new decay—new collapse— Anatole France had the right idea in that delicious last paragraph of "Penguin Island".[8] And some day the sun will cool, & there will be no human race or organic life of any kind on the earth, nor any record to hint to the blind ultimate outer gods that there have ever been such things.

I trust that all your oleaginous enterprises may develop favourably, & hope you have had a pleasant trip. Odd that Galpin didn't reply, but I suppose he's rushed to death betwixt teaching & music—I haven't heard from him myself since Christmas. If you want to look up a very pleasant chap & good talker, (though not a philosopher) get in touch with Arthur Leeds at the Marion Hotel, wherever that is. A cheap joint, I'll wager, for Leeds is always broke & in debt. He was a very congenial member of our old gang in New York, & went to Chicago about the time I came home to Providence. Let him talk—but don't let him borrow any cash of you. He *means* to pay back—in fact, he never ceases to mean! You might also like to meet Farnsworth Wright, the editor of Weird Tales, whose letters seem to bespeak a very agreeable personality.

I have just finished my second short novelette of the year—"The Case of Charles Dexter Ward". I don't know when or where it will ever be published, & I certainly hate to face the typing of its 147 pages. Soon I must type my 60-page history of weird fiction, which Cook wants in a hurry for his paper.[9] Cook also talks of bringing out one of my longer short stories as a thin book uniform with Long's & Loveman's blue cloth volumes—though I've warned him it would probably form a financial flop.[10] My first novelette—begun last fall & finished in January—is in the vein of extreme oneiroscopic fantasy, & is called "The Dream-Quest of Unknown Kadath". It runs to 110 pages—& I haven't typed that either! I hope your own novel is getting in shape. It's full-length, I assume, & you have my heartiest commiserations in the matter of the typing.

That Oasis programme seems to have an interesting spot or two. I assume that the "Jesus Myth" review touches on the late Georg Brandes' recent book[11]—a thing I mean to read some day. I'm frankly undecided about the possible historicity of any one character corresponding to the crucified saint of tradition. He may be only a cultus-figure like Atys or Adonis, as some contend; but the East is so full of preaching ascetics & mildly touched Gandhis & such messiahs that I almost fancy it's easier to assume that the Christ tradition was built up around some actual one of the thousand itinerant exhorters of the period. The whole affair was really as insignificant to the civilised world as a local squabble among the Moros in the Philippines would be to us today, & on account of its obscurity—an obscurity overridden by some very amusing post-facto developments—we are never likely to get any conclusive data. Brandes can really prove little or nothing either way—but it will be interesting to see what he says.

With best wishes—

Most cordially & sincerely yrs—

H P L

Notes

1. Samuel McIntire (1757–1811), American architect, craftsman, and sculptor best known for the Chestnut Street District, a classic example of Federal style architecture.

2. A decorative molding, usually convex, that separates two planes or surfaces, especially around a wooden panel.

3. St. Simeon Stylites (390?–459), a Syriac ascetic who lived 37 years on a small platform atop a pillar near Aleppo, Syria.

4. Scott Nearing (1883–1983), American economist and public speaker who opposed American entry into World War I and was indicted under the Espionage Act, but found not guilty. By the mid-1920s he had evolved from socialism to communism.

5. The Catalogue of Ships is an epic listing in Book 2 of Homer's *Iliad* (2.494–759) of the contingents of the Achaean army that sailed to Troy.

6. Theodore Lothrop Stoddard (1883–1950) was an American historian, journalist, eugenicist, and political theorist. Madison Grant (1865–1937) was an American lawyer known primarily for his work as a eugenicist and conservationist. He wrote one of the most famous works of scientific racism, *Passing of the Great Race; or, The Racial Basis of European History* (1916).

7. See Thomas De Quincey (1785–1859), *Confessions of an English Opium-Eater* (1821), under the date May 1818: "The mere antiquity of Asiatic things, of their institutions, histories, modes of faith, etc., is so impressive, that to me the vast age of the race and

name overpowers the sense of youth in the individual. A young Chinese seems to me an antediluvian man renewed."

8. See Anatole France (1844–1924), *Penguin Island* (*L'Île des pingouins*, 1908), tr. A. W. Evans (1909): "It grew very rich and large beyond measure. The houses were never high enough to satisfy the people; they kept on making them still higher and built them of thirty or forty storeys, with offices, shops, banks, societies one above another; they dug cellars and tunnels ever deeper downwards. Fifteen millions of men laboured in the giant town."

9. Cook published "Supernatural Horror in Literature" in the *Recluse*.

10. Cook typeset and printed HPL's story "The Shunned House" in 1928 but never bound or sold the book. Arkham House obtained and bound the printed sheets and sold the book more than 30 years later. HPL never typed either novelette.

11. Georg Morris Cohen Brandes (1842–1927), Danish critic and scholar who influenced Scandinavian and European literature from the 1870s to the turn of the 20th century. HPL refers to his book *Sagnet om Jesus* (1925; *Jesus, a Myth*).

[6]   [ANS][1]

[Postmarked Providence, R.I.,
30 April 1927]

Just got a card from Smithy[2] telling of your fire & the loss of your amateur collection. Please accept my sincerest sympathy—& let me hope that the general loss is not great. If I can help—in conjunction with other amateurs—in partly replacing your loss, I shall be glad to send some old-time items which I still retain. I have about three issues of *The Scotchman*,[3] which you really ought to have if your own file is gone, & can give you two or three United Year-Books & many *United Amateurs* from to [sic?] my own ____. Let me know what you especially desire. What burnt—the cottage you built with your own hands? That would really be a pity. Again, let me express my profound & sincerest sympathy,
HPL

Notes

1. *Front:* Hotel Empire, New York City.

2. Charles W. "Tryout" Smith, long-time amateur journalist and printer.

3. An early amateur journal by PJC, following *The Ideal Politician, Scottish Highlanders,* and *Prairie State Journal* and succeeded by *Corona, Invictus,* and *The Liberal.*

[7]   [ALS, JHL]

10 Barnes St.,
Providence, R.I.,
Octr. 30, 1927.

Dear P J C:—

Thanks exceedingly for the Vincennes view—I envy you the

trip, for Vincennes has seemed doubly fascinating to me since studying the guidebook you so kindly sent me some time ago. I certainly must see the place eventually.

Late in the summer an unexpected bit of cash enabled me to take a New England scenic tour which afforded two weeks of concentrated feasting on historic antiquities. First I spent five days with Cook in Athol—a delightful town embosomed in picturesque vistas of hills beyond hills—& was taken by him to innumerable points of interest, including famous old Deerfield, & many regions in Vermont & New Hampshire. At West Brattleboro—an exquisite rural region—we stopped to see Arthur Goodenough; whom I am the only amateur, except Cook, to behold in person throughout his 40 years as an amateur. He is a delightful old-school Yankee who wears a rusty black Prince Albert for Sunday best—I'll show you the picture Cook took of him when he sends me duplicates. After leaving Athol I proceeded from Boston up the coast to Portland—a magnificently early-American place which I explored in great detail, & from which I took a side-trip to the White Mountains—seeing real mountains for the first time & ascending to the summit of Mt Washington. Then I slowly descended the coast, stopping at all the quaint colonial towns en route—Portsmouth, Newburyport, Ipswich, Gloucester, Salem, & Marblehead—& absorbing antiquarian colour. From Newburyport I took a side trip to Haverhill to see good old Tryout Smithy—who has'nt [*sic*] aged a jot in the 5 years since I saw him last, though he turned 75 last Monday. I'll send you some printed matter touching on points along my route. By stopping cheaply at Y M C A's, I made a slender fund go a long way. Since getting back I've been too deliriously busy with accursed revision to take any but one-day trips, but even these brief hikes have given me some marvellous autumn scenery—for Providence is exceptionally happy in its scenic setting.

Glad oil matters continue to prosper. By the way—I got the rest of my amateur papers out of storage last week, hence have some more additions for your depleted collection. Not knowing what others may have supplied, I'll merely send a list of available titles. Check off the ones you want, return the list, & I'll be glad to shoot on the desiderate items.

With regards to all—
  Sincerely yrs—
   H P L

[8] [ALS, JHL]

        10 Barnes St.,
         Providence, R.I.,
           Novr. 10, 1927.

Dear P J C:—
  Well—the papers are all wrapped for sending, & I shall get

them off the first time I go downtown. I was glad to uncover such an unexpected batch—about which I had very largely forgotten. I'm really surprised that more of the old-timers haven't come across with various items, & feel sure that sooner or later you'll stumble on a windfall—as, for instance, when some veteran definitely abandons his collection & looks about for some recipient who will ensure it against dispersal. That's the kind of thing which will build up your file for the more vital years of the institution—the years preceding the relatively decadent period covered by most of my duplicates.

I trust that your present venture in drilling may not only come out successfully but form a really brilliant "strike". I presume that almost any well has the *possibility* of proving fabulously profitable, even though such results are not often secured. Meanwhile the work no doubt has rewards of its own, in the form of varied gradations of excitement & constant changes of scene. Thanks for the pictures—I didn't realise how big Donald James was getting to be! Kentucky looks quite mystic & alluring in the trans-fluvial distance.

Speaking of rivers & travel—a good many points along my route of last summer are now either under water or perilously near it—a condition very unusual for New England, & one which we had come to regard as typically mid-western. Goodenough is out of it—both his farm & the city of Brattleboro being on very high ground—but Walter J. Coates, the amateur of North Montpelier, must have seen some exciting things.[1] Athol is not far from the flooded area, & I've just dropped Cook a line asking whether he's afoot or afloat. He was to have come down here this week, but hasn't sent any word. In R.I. some of the northern & western districts have been considerably flooded, though Providence has not felt the disturbance at all. Up in Haverhill honest Smithy reports water in the street between his house & the centre of the city, & says that the great piers of the Groveland Bridge across the Merrimack—only a block or two from Tryout office—are entirely submerged.

I've heard considerable of this new book—"Grandmothers"[2]—but haven't read it . . . . . any more than I've read any other of the newer books. I'm getting too old to keep up with the times, & find a great deal more pleasure in reading the works of other—& to me vastly more interesting—periods. My degree of contemporaneousness may be gauged by the fact that my current reading is a translation of the Æneid—a version in pentameter blank verse by James Rhoades which I'd never gone through before, but which I find infinitely superior to both Dryden & Conington in its fidelity to the Vergilian language & spirit.

By the way—has Cook sent you his new monster *Vagrant* & his still newer *Recluse?* If not, get after him relentlessly until he does! They are the most notable—if not the *only* notable—products of the present amateur season!

With best wishes—

Sincerely & cordially yrs—

H P L

Notes

1. HPL mentions the Vermont floods in "The Whisperer in Darkness."
2. By Glenway Wescott. It is a partly autobiographical novel about the members of a family whose lives were strongly affected by the Civil War.

[9]   [AHT]

> 10 Barnes St.,
> Providence, R.I.,
> August 8, 1928

My dear Campbell—

[. . .] I surely wish that I could visit the Mammoth Cave with you—I presume I wrote you that I was about to visit the Endless Caverns, which turned out to be no disappointment. I had never been in an actual cave before, & this magnificent specimen nearly took my breath away. Many consider these caves the best of all in point of elaborate stalactitic formations, but of course they cannot compete with the Mammoth where vast spaces & imposing dimensions are concerned. I must see the latter before I die—you may recall that one of my early tales is based upon it, the details being the result of a very careful study which I made in advance. . . . .

My trip, on the whole, was surely a great event; & one that I shall long remember. I would have added some leisurely Connecticut wanderings on the homeward stretch, but received word of the illness of my aunt—with a very painful kind of lumbago—which made me decide on an immediate return. She has a nurse, but also needs someone about for various errands & sundry kinds of supplementary assistance. As I look back on my voyage—already receding into the pleasant background of half-legendary things—three points stand out as especially notable & distinctive: the wild, closely ranged hills & deep, brook-haunted ravines of Vermont, the graceful & archaic charm of colonial Annapolis, & the strange spell & macabre mystery of the Endless Caverns.

Have just finished a new 38-page tale[1] which I like pretty well myself. Financially I can't classify its degree of success until I have sunk my shaft into the editorial clay. Then we'll see how much oil—if any—it brings its hopeful driller!

With best wishes for all your concernments oleaginous & otherwise,

> Most sincerely yrs—
> H P L

Notes

1. "The Dunwich Horror." See RK 10.

[10]   [AHT]

10 Barnes St.,
Providence, R.I.,
Novr. 12, 1928

My dear Campbell:—

[. . .] I myself have been too crowded with revision to do much original work of late, but I did get one long short story (or short novelette) written last summer, which sold to *Weird Tales* for $240.00. I was also greatly pleased to find myself on Edward J. O'Brien's annual short story list in the *Boston Transcript* for Octr. 20. He gave me his highest three-star or Roll of Honour rating for my "Colour Out of Space", so that I am feeling almost like a literary guy these days! Also, a man wants to reprint my "Call of Cthulhu" in a new anthology of unusual tales[1]—a matter which depends somewhat on whether or not the editor of *Weird Tales* has further plans for it.

This has been a great autumn around here—really quite the warmest & finest I ever remember. Until late in October I took my work & reading out to the woods & fields every day, so that I miss the excursions now that colder weather has come at last. [. . .]

With best wishes & hopes for good luck—
Most cordially & sincerely yrs—
H P L

Notes

1. T. Everett Harré published the story in *Beware After Dark!*

[11]   [AHT]

10 Barnes St.,
Providence, R.I.,
Septr. 17, 1930

My dear Campbell:—

I was very glad to hear from you again, though sorry that the news involved financial loss & hardship on your part. Most of all is such a condition tantalizing [*sic*] & provoking when, as in the present case, it holds up some likely recuperative measure for lack of an ironically small amount.

I certainly wish—apart from all probable profits—that I could be of aid in this matter as indicated; but must ruefully confess that my own fiscal position just now is so alarming that even the most trivial daily expenses involve a strain of the tensest sort. This autumn is a season of unprecedented down-&-outness with me because of the admittedly unwise amount of travelling I have done since spring. Last winter (like all winters, damn 'em, only more so!) was particularly hard on my health, so that I had to spend most of the warm weather recuperating & getting braced to stand the next cursed winter; & as a result I became more reckless than usual with expenditures. To counteract my continuous indoor-ness of the cold months I branched out geographically; making a spring trip to Charleston, S.C. & Richmond, Va. in my usual quest of early-historic atmosphere; & only two weeks ago I took a last fling of summer by visiting the ancient fortress-town of *Quebec* for the first time in my life. The sequel is that I am financially in the zero or minus class at present— even conducting personal experiments in shirt-washing to save laundry fees!

[. . .]

As for myself—I haven't as much in *Weird Tales* as I'd like to have, since the pressure of revisory work has left me with all too little energy for original composition. . . . This coming winter I intend to rebel against the tyranny of revision—which I have endured because of the certainty of remuneration as opposed to the element of chance in original placement—& grind out a batch of tales.[1] It might conceivably pay more than revision—for each tale that lands brings 5 or 6 times more than I could get for a job of revision involving the same amount of time, & a great deal more patience & energy. Last winter all I did was a batch of verse.[2] My general programme is much the same as usual during recent years—the only novelty since our last exchange of news in 1928 being my return to the proud & independent estate of celibacy. Without the least trace of bitterness or blame, it became apparent that the tastes & aspirations & environmental needs of Mrs. Lovecraft & myself were more basically unlike & divergent than we had thought—one wishing the metropolitan milieu & influences, while the other remained an immutable small-townsman to whom the historic & antiquarian conservatism of a Providence setting was absolutely essential. Accordingly, at Mrs. L's wish, the dawn of 1929 saw the joint venture peacefully dissolved by the R.I. Superior Court[3]— since which time I have lapsed back completely into that bookish hermitage so characteristic of me prior to 1924. My prime pleasure is in antiquarian travel, taken in such snatches as a lean purse permits; & the enclosed cards give a rough idea of the sort of objectives I make for. In 1929 I went to Philadelphia, Washington, Richmond, Williamsburg, Yorktown, & Jamestown; viewing in the latter place that earliest of all American settlements which I had so long wished to see. On the return trip I also tapped new antiquarian soil by exploring the rural Dutch & Huguenot region up the Hudson— around Kingston & Hurley & New Paltz, in the shadow of the Catskills & Shawangunks—finally ending my trip by crossing the Berkshires to Athol, Mass., & looking in on W. Paul Cook before going home. Later in the year I spent a week in the Cape Cod region with your star United recruit, Frank B. Long,[4] & his parents—my first opportunity to become acquainted with that terrain despite its proximity to Providence. This spring, as I said, I took a trip to Charleston—going by motor-coach & spending 11 days in the most fascinating & completely colonial city which the U.S. can boast. Charleston's ancient houses & general 18th century atmosphere captivated me completely, so that it is even possible for me to endure the thought of moving there in case the severity of northern winters becomes absolutely impossible for me to bear. I explored the city very minutely, & absorbed its spirit & scenery to such an extent that I am sometimes almost homesick for it! Never before had a city outside Providence so instantly appealed to me. On the way back I stopped 8 days in Richmond, looking up all the sites & surviving buildings connected with Poe's life there. Later I repeated my Hudson valley & Athol itinerary of the preceding year after a visit to Long in N.Y. In Athol I was sorry to find Cook's health very poor. He had suffered a nervous breakdown in January, when his wife died after a long & trying illness; & now a recurrence of his chronic appendicitis was bothering him. He has since been treated at an hospital, though he refuses to hazard the operation which he really needs. In July I attended the N.A.P.A. convention in Boston, & was surprised to see how much vitality was left in the old society. A large array of old-timers was there—Tilden, Morton, Edwin Hadley Smith, Wylie, W. R. Murphy, L. C. Wills, Haggerty, Suhre,[5] &c. &c., & the local members—Lynch, Cole, Mrs. Sawyer, &c.—turned out in force despite their virtual retirement from amateurdom years ago. Lynch really engineered the success of the thing, while Morton was (as always) the leader in the conducting of the programme. The young official editor, Helm Spink, was also there, & produced the best sort of an impression. A semi-invalid,[6] but exceedingly brilliant & capable. He stopped off for a couple of days in Providence on his return trip to Indiana. I saw some of the Boston amateurs for the first time in several years, & was amused to note that Edward H. Cole has begun to grow stout. A number of plans for reviving & promoting amateurdom were broached; & if they are lived up to, there ought to be quite a revival of activity within the next few months. As a measure of enhancing amateur unity, a number of prominent Nationalites are joining the Erford association[7]—including Morton, Bacon, & (wonder of wonders!) Tryout Smith, who always refused to join our United in the old days! What a pity our United couldn't have carried on! Altogether, I rather enjoyed the convention. My next outing was a week around Cape Cod—a repetition of the 1929 trip—with Long & his parents—but the grand climax of my travelling season came early this month; when I took advantage of a cheap excursion to the oldest & quaintest city in North America, a city I had been wishing to see for years . . . . the ancient fortress town of *Quebec.*

I doubt if I can ever get Quebec out of my head long enough to think about anything else. Never had I seen anything like it, & never do I expect to. It leaves one inarticulate.[8] All my former standards of urban beauty are superseded & obsolete. If it weren't in so subarctic a zone I'd move there tomorrow! Really, I can hardly believe that such a place exists! A mighty headland rising out of a mile-broad river & topped by a mediaeval fortress—*city walls* of cyclopean masonry scaling vertical cliffs or towering above green tablelands—great arching *city gates* & frowning bastions—huddles of pointed red-tiled roofs & silver belfries & steeples—archaic lanes winding uphill or lurking in the dark shadow of beetling precipices—horse-drawn vehicles, & all the vestiges of a mature, leisurely, older civilisation—these things are only a fraction of the marvellous totality that is Quebec. The place is really a part of Bourbon France—a Norman hill town of 1700 or thereabouts.

[. . .] But at last my travels are over, & I am taking my last breaths before settling down to frost-bound hibernation. Again let me say how sorry I am that I must be so useless in the present oil-seeking business, & express the hope that other sources may turn your luck & lead the way toward fortune.

Regards to Mrs. Campbell—

Best wishes—

Most cordially & sincerely—

H P L

Notes

1. In the end, he wrote only *At the Mountains of Madness,* which, per his comment on the risk of original composition, was rejected. HPL was so crushed by the rejection of what he considered to be his finest work that he virtually gave up fiction writing at all.

2. The sonnet sequence *Fungi from Yuggoth,* and a few other poems.

3. In fact, HPL did not sign the divorce papers, so technically he remained married for the rest of his life. He told very few correspondents of this.

4. Long began publishing in the *United Amateur* in March 1920.

5. Willard Otis Wylie (1862–1944) of Boston, noted philatelic editor and writer, editor of *Our Compliments,* and member of both the NAPA and UAPA. William R. Murphy, fortieth president of the NAPA (1906–07), won all the NAPA laureateships: poetry, essay, story, history, and editorial (twice); he was editor of the *Pioneer* and a member of the editorial staff of the *Philadelphia Evening Ledger,* specializing in dramatic and musical criticism. Vincent B[artholemew] Haggerty (1888–1943), amateur journalist associated with the NAPA in the 1920s and 1930s. Edward F. Suhre (1879–1939), editor of the *Missourian* and *Occasional Press,* and forty-fourth president of the NAPA (1910–11). See Glossary for the others.

6. Spink was diabetic.

7. See AH 8n10.

8. Quite the opposite. Over the next few months, HPL wrote "A Description of the Town of Quebeck," his longest composition.

[12]   [ALS, JHL]

10 Barnes St.,

Providence, R.I.,

Septr. 27, 1930

My dear Campbell:—

Yours of the 21st coincided with an inquiry from good

old Tryout Smith about your address. He has been sending his paper to the old Ridgefarm headquarters for the past two years, yet infers from something in your recent letters to him that you have not received it. I repeated your present Chicago address, & hope he will duly place it on his mailing list. Rare old Tryout! There wouldn't be much amateurdom today without him. As if aware of his important post in a rejuvenating process, he shaved off his whiskers a few weeks ago—the first time he has used a razor in about 50 years! I'll wager he doesn't look over 55 or 60 this minute, though actually he will turn 78 on the 24th of next month. I last saw him in 1927.

You have certainly missed something if you have not seen Charleston—but I, for my part, have not seen Savannah. I thought of a side-trip thither when in Charleston, but lean finances made it inadvisable. I had 4 hours in Columbia en route, & was quite delighted with it—although it cannot compare with Charleston. But all the S.C. lowlands are a paradise to encounter after one has been riding through the incredibly ugly pine-&-sand terrain of the piedmont region. The stretch between Charlotte N.C. & Camden S.C. is about the most accursedly ugly piece of ground I know, except for the New Jersey coastal area.

Your anecdotal old soldier reminds me of my very fortunate experience at the battlefield of Petersburg, Va., on my way back from Charleston. In the first place, the battlefield guide was a delightful Confederate veteran who had taken part in this very battle at the age of 14. But to make things complete, one of my fellow-visitors turned out to be a Union veteran from Massachusetts, also in this battle, & eager to identify the various topographical features he had noticed in 1864. When the two got to discussing, history certainly lived itself over again; & the various hearers carried away a closer impression of the conflict than they had ever had before. Actually, the battlefield is very little changed. The old Union tunnel has been cleared out & is now open for inspection, & the place where the "crater" was formed by the exploding mine is still a vast hollow. What the old Massachusetts soldier chiefly missed was a spring—now dried up—where he & his comrades used to crawl out under fire to get water. His inquiry brought a flood of memory to the Confederate guide, for both sides had used the spring. That Charleston anecdote is highly interesting. Charleston did not receive as savage treatment from the invaders as Atlanta & the open countryside did, in consequence of which there is less residual bitterness there than there is farther inland. I'll wager your old soldier found Charleston much as he remembered it in the war time—& for that matter, so would Lord Rawdon, who occupied it in 1780! In both wars the respective occupying forces used the same house—the ancient Brewton mansion in lower King St.—as headquarters; & today it is just the same as it was. The majority of the Charleston houses were built between 1720 & 1800, & to see long unbroken rows of them, with brick & stucco facades & red-tiled roofs, is to realise exactly what an 18th century Southern seaport was like. In all my experience, only Quebec surpasses it. I must, of course, see New Orle-

ans some day—as well as St. Augustine, Fla., which Morton saw for the first
time last month, & which especially excites his enthusiasm. But I doubt if either of these could best Quebec. Too bad you missed seeing it long ago—but
I can assure you that it can't look any different today, except for the lone sky-
scraper which one can exclude from one's line of sight through the exercise
of a little skill. I must see it again some time, & at greater leisure.

I am sorry that so much upheaval has marked your recent days—one of
the inescapably unfortunate things about life is that goals & objects are always
conflicting, so that one thing has to be curtailed in the interest of another.
With some this reciprocal annulling of rewards becomes so complete that the
net return is very slight—& it would be hard to determine the respective
shares of luck & judgment & boldness in shaping the course of the few who
manage to salvage a consoling residue from the whole ordeal of consciousness. In my opinion a kind of even tranquillity is about the best thing to cultivate—with major interests sunk in permanent & inanimate & abstract things
rather than in fellow-humans with their inevitable mutability & complex reactions. The active pleasures one misses are more than compensated for by the
active pains one avoids—but then, individual temperaments differ, & no one
person can prescribe for another.

I surely hope that you can get business affairs reorganised as you wish, &
fancy the prospects will be very bright after the present difficulty is past. Too
bad it's so hard to get privacy for concentration, but in time you may work
out a system whereby an utterly inviolate den can be reserved for your exclusive use somewhere around the house. Such a thing really is a necessity, & I
always wonder how anyone can get along without it.

Moe's address is 2303 Highland Ave., Milwaukee. I wish you could get
him to rejoin amateurdom, but just now he is holding off because of remaining bitterness over the Whitaker feud of 1925—when the Warren group then
controlling the National took sides against him for intricate political reasons.[1]
I think such grudge-harbouring rather childish—indeed, I think the original
feud rather silly on both sides—but one has to forgive the touch of naive
self-esteem which gives a certain type of person that easily ruffled & amusing-
ly humourless sort of austere dignity. Whitaker himself is out of amateurdom—but what a comic figure he was in his heyday!

Long's present address is 230 West 97th St., N. Y. City. He is wholly out
of amateurdom, but still entirely a devotee of literature. Had you chanced to
pick up the Spring, 1930 *Science Wonder Quarterly*[2] you would have seen his picture—published in connexion with a story in the issue. He is constantly having both prose & verse in Weird Tales.

I was greatly interested to hear about Schilling & Lockhart. The other day
I saw a flamboyant magazine cover on a news stand marked *Chain Lightning*,
& idly wondered whether the reformer of Milbank had taken up his old pursuits again. My curiosity did not, however, extend far enough to prompt a

further investigation. Hope he is doing well—though the relinquishment of a good position is sometimes unwise. That's what Loveman found out when he left Dauber & Pine's excellent bookstore three years ago. Last week, I rejoice to say, he went back there at a good salary. The returned prodigal! Hope the lesson sticks. His address, by the way, is 130 Columbia Heights, Brooklyn. I haven't seen or heard from Stoddard in 15 years—except through Daas, who never gets quite out of touch with me. And I don't believe I've seen Adams[3] since I left Brooklyn 4½ years ago. I hear now & then from our naive Baptist friend John Milton Samples, who continues to have a rather hard & struggling time supporting his prodigious brood. He is now in Atlanta, (852 White St.) economic opportunities having apparently dwindled to nothingness in his beloved Macon.

Thanks for the glimpse of the photograph—which I am herewith returning, safely, I trust. The enclosed (which kindly return at your leisure) shows what I look like these days—it was taken in the idyllic countryside near Kingston, N.Y., by Bernard A. Dwyer, my genial host in that ancient town.

Amateurdom surely seems to be looking up. A journalistic bundle recently came from Haggerty, & I hear that the veteran Edwin Hadley Smith has just issued another paper. Naturally, we cannot expect a return of the palmy days—even the dwindling though tolerable days that I can recall—but it is not too much to hope for something better than the virtually total stagnation of the period just closed.

With every good wish—both for your business fortunes & for your general tranquillity—I remain

Yrs most cordially & sincerely—

H P L

Notes

1. See HPL to Hyman Bradofsky, 12 January 1936 (ms., JHL): "Human psychology is such that one who complains against an offender is always placed in an oddly disadvantageous light—as M. W. Moe discovered a decade ago when he asked for official redress after the undeniably insulting attacks of one Noah F. Whitaker. Whitaker was inexcusable—but Moe ought to have fought him independently instead of requesting his expulsion. If he had done so, all sympathy would have been with him. Instead, he made an appeal & succeeded in having Whitaker voted out at the next convention—but his victory proved a hollow one. As soon as the official screws were put on Whitaker, popular sympathy turned in his favour; & at the next convention the expulsion & punishment were rescinded. This displeased Moe so much that he was amateurically inactive for years." See also *Letters to Maurice W. Moe.*
2. "The Thought-Materializer," *Science Wonder Quarterly* 1, No. 3 (Spring 1930): 414–17.
3. A[lbertus] M. Adams (1878–1952), husband of Hazel Pratt Adams.

[13] [ALS, JHL]

10 Barnes St.,

Providence, R.I.,

Octr. 31, 1930

My dear Campbell:—

Yours of the 28th contained some highly interesting & memory-evoking items—& I am exceedingly glad to hear that E. H. Smith proved more than a mere reminiscer! He is a tremendously pleasant person to meet—I saw him face to face for the first time at the recent Boston convention. You seem to have solved that Nat. Am. problem which was so deeply agitating him—as well as other old-timers—at the convention. Possibly the missing volume is just as well off in the museum as it would be anywhere else, for the amateurdom of today isn't a very stable or substantial affair. But at any rate the association ought to know where it is.

My old friend in Asheville—from whom I haven't heard in long years—is named Chester P. Munroe. His old address was % Grove Park Inn, Asheville, N.C., but I think he left that position long ago. It seems to me he became secretary to some banker elsewhere in North Carolina, but I cannot be certain. If you want to take a chance on ultimate forwarding from the Grove Park address, I suppose the possibilities are about even regarding successful delivery. At worst, it could cost you only some labour & stationery, plus one postage-stamp. Spoerri's[1] old Washington address, according to my U.A. file, was 304 House Office Bldg.—do you suppose it would do any good to send a letter there? E. L. Sechrist can still be reached at the old stand—423 Dorset Ave., Chevy Chase, Washington, D.C. Mrs. Renshaw, whose School of Expression is a great success, is at 1739 Connecticut Ave., N.W. Samples is 852 White St., Atlanta, Ga.—but he's more broke—if possible—than I am, so he wouldn't be of any commercial use. Old Dr. Kuntz—the Presbyterian preacher-poet—is Box 943, Clovis, N.M. And Frank B. Long, Jr. is 230 West 97th St., New York City.[2]

Poor old W. Paul Cook has been having a frightful time—with financial failure piled on top of his nervous breakdown & physical illness. For months I had been vainly trying to get at him—especially because of the imperative proddings & threats of legal action on the part of some people to whom he had failed to deliver a promised & paid-for order—but only last week he wrote of his own accord, without having received any of my insistent appeals! What he had done was to flee irresponsibly from all obligations, lest his overstrained mind actually collapse under the intolerable burden. He had left Athol for good, & without giving the P.O. any forwarding address—so that everything sent to his old address since July remains unclaimed & without any likelihood of ever being claimed! He is now staying at his sister's in Lake Sunapee, N.H., but will very shortly settle in Clarendon, Vermont, joining with a brilliant young man in the establishment of a private publishing venture to be called (since it will be housed in a former parsonage) "The Parsonage Press."[3]

I am indeed glad to hear that the oil matters seem to be shaping themselves favourably, & hope you will be able to take advantage of all the opportunities offered. By the way—I've at last encountered the novel "Cimarron",[4] (through its being published as a serial in the local daily) & appreciate it all the more from having had a glimpse of the oil background from another angle. It's not a bad piece of work. Its conventionally-mannered start didn't promise well, but it perked up as it went along—despite an inartistic coincidence or two. It seems to get the epic feel of frontier expansion, & to capture something of the psychology of the elements involved. Another angle on oil is furnished by the young one-time amateur Wilfred B. Talman, (is he your recruit?) who is editing a group of four trade magazines for the Texas Oil Co. I think he is looking for good material for these sheets—especially *The Texaco Star*, which is the choicest of the lot. If you have any brief descriptive or even oil-angled fictional items to contribute, you might write him. His address is 2215 Newkirk Ave., Brooklyn, N.Y. Yes—& another oil-country glimpse comes through one of my fellow contributors to *Weird Tales*—Robert E. Howard of Cross Plains, Texas.[5] He is a most interesting Old Texas character, as picturesque in some ways as our old plainsman Ira A. Cole, & with a far more balanced (though self-acquired) education & disciplined literary faculty. He has seen the coming & going of the derrick in many a locality, & has had a chance to observe its social, political, & aesthetic effects, & correlate it with the whole long stream of Texas life. Naturally, it hasn't much appeal to one who thinks in terms of the heroic age—of barbaric gun-fighters & the lost miles of open plains stretching into the sunset.

Sorry to hear that Moe is under the weather—my last from him was over a month ago, & he didn't mention the trouble then. Glad his book was accepted.[6] I read it in MS., made some suggestions, & contributed some specimen verses & exercises. The whole thing seems to me great stuff—the best, & practically the only, attempt I've seen to get at the real differences between authentic poetry & Eddieguest[7] hokum & make them so plain that any kid or layman can see them. I'm really tremendously enthusiastic about it, & am giving it advance recommendations among all the amateurs & among the various pseudo-poetic attempters for whom I do revision.

With best wishes & hopes for success—

Yrs most sincerely—

H P L

Notes

1. J[ames] Fuller Spoerri (1899–1969), an amateur living in Washington, DC.
2. PJC had requested that HPL invest $200 in a project. HPL declined but recommended others to PJC, though they, likely, were equally impecunious.

3. The proposed venture of Vrest Orton and W. Paul Cook came to nothing.

4. A novel about the Oklahoma Land Rush by Edna Ferber.

5. "The Ghost of Camp Colorado" appeared in the *Texaco Star* in April 1931.

6. HPL refers to Moe's *Doorways to Poetry,* which in fact never was published. The publisher alluded to is unknown. Macmillan initially had been interested in the book, and upon rejection, Moe also tried the book on the American Book Company.

7. Referring to Edgar A. Guest (1881–1959), English-born American poet who published verse prolifically in newspapers and collected them in many books, but who was scorned by critics for superficiality and conventionality of thought and expression.

[14]   [TLS, JHL]

10 Barnes St., Providence, R.I.
March 31, 1931.

Dear P.J.C.—

I was tremendously sorry to hear of the recent misfortunes besetting you, and must extend my sincerest sympathy regarding the recent death of your mother.[1] Such an event is a melancholy and almost bewildering one under any circumstances, and the fact that you could not reach the scene yourself must have made it doubly sad. However, it is consoling to reflect how closely you kept in touch by letter, and what recent word you had before the shock of the final bad news came. And more—the immediate worries surrounding your mother in latter days must always have been tempered by a knowledge of your own resourcefulness, and an ultimate assurance that the varied anxieties would be weathered through somehow.

Paul Marion's malady, I trust, is now receding safely into the past; so that the quarantine is now only an irritating memory. It was indeed disastrous for this thing to develop just when it did—especially after the exhausting ordeal of moving. Still, the recovery of the patient is a source of gratitude which neutralises much. I trust that before long the accumulation of your funds and the consequent exploitation of the Atoka[2] well will usher in a fresh period of brighter days.

I was tremendously interested to hear of your meetings with various old-time amateurs, many of whom belong to my day, while others represent illustrious names of which I have always heard. I always liked Macauley, and corresponded with him frequently in the 1915–16 period.[3] Fritter, too, had his likeable side despite some prim and peculiar idiosyncrasies, and I am sorry his serious mind still broods so heavily over the trifles of yesterday. Spink is a great kid, and I was highly pleased to meet him at the Boston convention and later to show him a bit of Rhode Island. He is surely making a marvellously brave fight against his illness, and I hope that before many years some new discovery of medical science will be able to give him really permanent help. Davis always was a man of extreme ability and cultivation. I admired his Lingerer tremendously even when disagreeing with some of its aesthetic tenets—

disagreeing, by the way, rather more widely than I would today. Glad to hear that he is flourishing still, and enjoying himself according to his own lights. Another of your recent encounters which interested me intensely is that with Edkins. His amateur day was long before mine, but I have always regarded his literary work with sentiments akin to idolatry. He was, as you probably recall, about the most Poesque character even connected with amateur journalism. I read loaned copies of his "Amenophra" years ago, and would give a good deal to get hold of a copy for myself. I likewise admired his weird short story "Phantasus",[4] which was in one of the bound books you so generously lent me back in 1916. I am told that he has completely repudiated all his literary interests—even looking back to writing days with something of contempt—but that can never annul the solid merit of what he wrote. Hope you had an interesting chat with Galpin—who is all for music nowadays. I hope to see him myself when he passes through the east en route for Europe in June. I was surprised to hear that Lockhart has started Chain Lightning again, and hope he will try to keep it within bounds this time.[5] Too bad he is still in the difficulties of which he wrote in 1928, when last I heard from him. Moe will form another welcome breath of old times. He is getting ahead gratifyingly in the pedagogical world, and ought to have some highly valuable books to his credit before many years are over. I owe him a letter right now, but have had my correspondence all balled up lately through pressure of work and a spell of poor eyesight which may force my return to the full-time use of glasses.

I shall watch the Texaco Star—which Talman sends me regularly—for your article; and imagine that you will have many other things to contribute in future. Talman is a bright kid, and goes with tremendous thoroughness into anything he undertakes. I fancy he will become a very important factor some day in the Texaco publications.

Cook seems to look very favourably on the prospect of an Oklahoma migration, and is immensely grateful for the influence you propose to lend him.[6] In New England, though, we look very ruefully at his threatened exit from our midst; and keep wishing something would turn up to preserve his linkage with the old-time soil. It is hard to think of such a veteran Yankee fixture as dissociated from his rock-ribbed hills, stone walls, and white village gables, and transplanted to the flat red barrens and spidery derrick-forests of the Cimarron country. I have a half-hope of seeing him this spring, though he may not be able to get down.

I have been in hibernation all winter, but hope to break out into the open fields and woods before long. My long-planned southern jaunt depends utterly upon what financial returns the next two or three weeks bring in. I shall need a little over sixty bucks for coach fare, and can get it if everybody who owes me something will pay up—but alas, in these days payments are doubly slow. Which reminds me—have you ever heard of a goddam pompous crook in your town named Lee Alexander Stone, M.D.? From his talk, he must have been quite a visible Chicago fixture at one time or another; but what he means to me is a $7.50 revision bill which he has owed for aeons—part from Feb. 1929 and part from Sept. 1929. He ignored all my polite statements and reminders, until finally I wrote him the choicest insult I could think up and let him slide—telling him to keep the change, and hoping that my small financial contribution might be of service to him![7]

The other day my egotism was a bit inflated by a letter from the publishing house of G. P. Putnam's Sons, asking to see some of my fiction with a view to collected publication in book form. Further inquiries revealed continued receptiveness, so today I am biting to the extent of shipping about 30 stories for inspection. I dare say nothing will come of it, but it costs no more than the express fee to take a chance. And if a miracle did happen, I would feel quite mildly elated as the author of a real, cloth-bound book with the solid old Putnam imprint.

And so it goes. By this time you are doubtless preparing to jump off for Oklahoma, but I imagine the Chicago address is the authentic one still. Again let me express my most genuine sympathy, and the hope that good times ahead may do much to neutralise the strain of past misfortunes and anxieties.

  With every good wish,
    Yours most sincerely,
      H P L

Notes

1. Mary J. Campbell (b. c. 1853).
2. An oil drilling site in OK.
3. See AH 8n4.
4. See RK 23n5.
5. Lockhart spent time in Leavenworth for printing obscene material in his pro-temperance paper *Chain Lightning*.
6. Ultimately, Cook did not take up PJC's offer.
7. Lee Alexander Stone (1879–1955) had an international reputation as a pioneer in the field of social hygiene. See *Letters to James F. Morton* 233–34. Not long after, HPL learned that Stone was ailing at the time, and he regretted sending his letter.

[15] [AHT]

         10 Barnes St.,
         Providence, R.I.,
         Septr. 11, 1931

Dear P J. C.:—

  [. . .] I certainly had a great trip last spring, & did not get home till the 20th of July. I stayed in Dunedin with Whitehead till the 8th of June, & then started on some southerly exploration.[1] Crossing the state & skirting Lake

Okeechobee, I went through Miami to the glamorous tropical Keys—finally reaching Key West, the most southerly point in the U.S. All this travel, of course, by motor coach—the cheap medium which has made such extensive wanderings possible for me. K.W. is only 90 miles from Havana, & I was furious because my slender funds did not permit me to complete the journey to that colourful, old-world capital. [. . .]

From Miami I returned to ancient St. Augustine—most fascinating & historic spot of all—& spent another week there; finally beginning the long & gradual return to the north. [. . .]

Then came New York, & a series of get-togethers with the good old gang—Morton, (who soon, however, left for a geological & genealogical trip to Nova Scotia) Long, Kleiner, Leeds, Talman, Loveman, Kirk, & so on. I stayed with Long a week & a half, & just as long again with Talman; so that our various conferences did not need to be hasty. . . .

I am out in the open each warm day; taking my work to the woods & fields in an old black bag. The last 3 days have been delectably hot—just my sort—so I am now enjoying a golden sunset on the banks of the Seekonk. . . .

Well—twilight steals on the ancient river-bank, so I fancy I'd better start moving. Best wishes—& keep up the literary work.

Regards—

Yrs most sincerely—

H P L

Notes

1. HPL visited the writer Henry S. Whitehead (1882–1932) in Dunedin, FL, on a trip that took him to St. Augustine, Key West, and Savannah.

[16]   [postcard, not found]

[18 March 1932]

[17]   [ANS][1]

[Postmarked Nantucket, Mass.,
31 August 1934]

Greetings from the absolutely quaintest & most ancient place of all in Nantucket. Odd that I haven't been here before—only 90 m. from Providence. A completely preserved Yankee whaling port of a century or more ago—cobblestoned streets, colonial houses, ancient belfries, windmill, picturesque wharves, winding, garden-bordered lanes—nothing lacking! Here for a week—in a 3d story room with a splendid view of town, harbour, & sea. Exploring streets intensively on foot, & took a motor trip around entire island! ¶

Didn't meet Thrift at the Myers either![2] Indeed, Cook had a sort of nervous collapse & had to hustle back to Vermont. The Coles brought me home in their car Sunday, & Monday morning I had the ticket for New Bedford & the Nantucket boat. ¶ Trust things are picking up in your vicinity. Best wishes —H P L

Notes

1. *Front:* Colonial Mansions, Nantucket, Mass.
2. Timothy Burr Thrift (1883–1947), editor of *Lucky Dog, Tim Talks,* the *Aonian, The Mailbag,* and *Tim Thoughts,* and thirty-ninth president of the NAPA. Mr. and Mrs. Denys P. Myers were old-time amateurs.

"My second well at Dupo."

Books to borrow
or to buy,
Nowadays are
ever nigh;
Borrowed, once,
they're apt to roam,
Let's be sure they
all come home.

EX ~
LIBRIS

Rheinhart Kleiner ~
Chester, N.J.

❖ ❖ ❖

R.K. 1941

Appendix

Poems by Rheinhart Kleiner

Alas!

Oh, twist and turn it how I may,
    I but repeat
What bards have said and yet will say—
    That you are sweet!

And oh, what dreary commonplace,
    When I declare—
Enraptured to behold your face!—
    That you are fair!

Alas, alack, that other tones,
    More full and clear,
Forestall your poet when he owns
    That you are dear!

Dream Days; or, Metrical Musings

III. "As Howard P. Lovecraft Might Have Given It Eighteenth Century Garb, in His Favorite Metre"

Descend soft-shaded night! Remove our cares,
Soothe us with slumber, lull with Lydian airs!
Banish the hurts that harass'd human kind,
And may we now in thee sweet solace find!
Bring to our senses, bound in Lethe's pow'r,
Visions of childhood and a kinder hour,
When we in busy street, or shady lane,
Our simple sports prolong'd, a merry train!
Where "London Bridge" might fall on lad and lass,
And each must pay some penalty to pass;
Where "Mulberry Bush," besides, and "Ding Dong Bell,"
For childish mirth and laughter served as well.
Ah, never have we join'd in sport as rare
As innocence has frisk'd and gambol'd there!
So, kindly sleep, come down—but stay! the blush
Of dewy morn, wakes sparrow, now, and thrush;

And though we fain in dreaming would engage,
For bread we choose the turmoil of the age!

Another Endless Day

Another endless day;
 A night that flies too soon;
Unwilling toil, half-hearted play,
 From new to waning moon!
No joy, nor heart to laugh;
 No hope where once 'twas high;
The cup I've but begun to quaff
 Is stale—the fountain dry!
Oh, for a cause to fight;
 A passion or a pang;
A love to thrill with new delight;
 A grief I never sang!
Something to stir my soul
 As not in life before;
To make the weary spirit whole,
 And bless the day once more!

Motes

This world is so full of such dullards and drones
And folks in glass houses who live to throw stones;
So many whose egos are hopelessly blind;
Who've chips on their shoulders or axes to grind;
Who carry cracked pitchers to wells every day
And padlock the stall after Dobbin's astray;
Who count every chicken before it is hatched
Or otherwise show that their brains are half-thatched;
In short—how my memory wanders and plays!—
This wobbling old earth is so crowded with jays,
And, could we but peer through the chimneys and roofs,
So close-packed with bozos, with boobs, saps and goofs,
We'd find very soon that we're far from alone
In fanning the ether, or pulling a bone;
And neither above or below all the rest
Whom crazes or whimsies have burdened or blest;
If some have a mote or a beam in the eye
To baffle or queer them—my friends, so have I!

At Providence in 1918

I left my own Manhattan, seeking pleasure,
 And having journeyed hence
A hundred miles, I found it in full measure
 In teeming Providence!
I sought her hidden ways and quaint old places
 That nestled ev'rywhere,
And found that Time had left benignant traces
 On alley, street, and square!
I thought of one for whom these ways had beauty
 And splendour all their own:
My friend, whose path of pleasure and of duty
 These scenes had only known.
And over all the cloud of war hung drearly;
 The summons to the strife
Was soon to come; and one whom I held dearly
 Was near the close of life!
But with unclouded brow and heart uplifted,
 All unaware, among
These scenes and sights, by golden summer gifted,
 I mov'd—for I was young.

Brooklyn, My Brooklyn

Though other scenes might lure me far
 From happiness and home,
No peace would they procure me, far
 Away across the foam.
To Brooklyn should I turn again
 From fairest towns and shires,
And all my bosom burn again
 To know her streets and spires!

I'd turn from Glory's very house—
 And were it sacrilege?
To see the Fulton Ferry house,
 Beside the Brooklyn Bridge;
To hear the passing roar above
 Of elevated trains,
That thrill me as they soar above
 Unnumbered marts and fanes.

I'd miss the book so pleasingly
    Displayed on Fulton Street;
The other wares that teasingly
    Remind of things to eat.
I'd weary for that restful place,
    Where benches, warm and wide,
In Montague's most zestful place
    Look down upon the tide.

'Tis there when Spring were flowering,
    I'd yearn to watch the bay,
And old Manhattan towering
    Beyond the river's play;
'Tis there I'd light my pipe at eve,
    And watch the sun go down,
For random thoughts are ripe at eve,
    When dusk is on the town.

Oh, Brooklyn offers graciously
    The gifts she has to give;
Her sons, who speak veraciously,
    Say, "Here's the place to live!"
When Fate, no longer lenient,
    Gives cause to sink and sigh,
There's hardly so convenient
    A place in which to die!

Epistle to Mr. and Mrs. Lovecraft

(Imitated from Mr. Pope)

My Friends, though Phoebus held the lyre,
And play'd with true, celestial fire,
While, close around, the Heav'nly Nine,
Applauded ev'ry strain divine,—
Yet could not he, whom Loves imbue,
Contrive a fitting song for you!

Alone, did each of you possess
More Worth, than Bard might well express;
Together, your Desert is such,
That none could sound your Praise too much!
No Panegyric, then, shall be
The Motive of these lines from me!

But I shall hope that wedded years
May strengthen all that now endears;
That Venus, with as kind an air,
May guard your Love from Doubt and Care;
And Hymen ever linger nigh
To trim the Torch still burning high!

May Truth and Beauty walk beside,
To warn, to counsel, and to guide;
And Faith and Hope, as well, to keep
Your footsteps t'ward the tow'ring steep,
Upon whose Summit rests the Crown
Of endless Honour and Renown!

The Four of Us!

(Rondeau)

The four of us forsake the street
For this aloof and calm retreat,
And rest us from the cares of day
That fly, while fresher fancies play
Around us where the hours are fleet!
How sad that Time's unwearied feet
Should hurry most when life is sweet
And we have much to do and say,
                    The four of us!

How often, brothers, shall we meet
With hearts that still serenely beat?
How many years are ours to stay
With minds as cloudless and as gay?
May days to come but kindly greet
                    The four of us!

The Double "R" Coffee House,
Feb. 15, 1925

PRESENT:
    H. P. Lovecraft
    S. Loveman
    G. Kirk

After a Decade

Dear George, I stood dreaming a moment today,
Where once your old bookshop enlivened the way.
The house of decrepit and shabby red brick,
Whose stoop was all cracked, and whose locks would not click,
Has added a decade of dust and despair
To decades already deposited there.

What matter? I thought of the room where the boys
Once came to partake of your fireside joys;
Where lyrics and laughter were frequently heard,
And poets to prosers were greatly preferred;
Where you, genial George, watched the glass or the cup,
Ever prompt in presenting or filling it up.

I thought of the boys—for as boys they appeared,
Though some by old Time had already been sheared;
Of Sam and of Howard, of Arthur and Vrest—
And some who have wandered to East or to West;
Of "Tal" and young Belknap, of James and old "Mac"—
And some whom no summons can ever call back.

But mostly I thought of the one in whose mirth
The brightest and best of our moments found birth:
The skeptic, who beamed with the kindliest cheer;
The cynic, who wanted his friends ever near;
The host, always ready to serve and to do—
In other words, George, I was thinking of you.

H. P. L.

You sit among us when we pour the wine
And read the lyric or intone the song,
When melody and mirth the hours prolong,
And talk is fervent, and our faces shine;
Shedding a glory or a spell benign
Among the fancies that about us throng,
Your presence seems as certain and as strong
As if your voice had called, or you had made a sign!
We speak of you and what you felt or thought;
We quote you as we might some friend away,
And chuckle at some foible all your own;
So vividly and variously you wrought
Your magic in our pliant hearts, that they
Hold warm a name now chiseled on a stone.

Essays by Rheinhart Kleiner

A Note on Howard P. Lovecraft's Verse

Comment occasioned by the verse of Mr. Howard P. Lovecraft, who is a more or less frequent contributor to the amateur press, has not consisted of unmixed praise.

Certain critics have regarded his efforts as too obviously imitative of a style that has long been discredited. Others have accepted his work with admiration and have even gone so far as to imitate the couplets which he produces with such apparent ease.

Between these two opinions there is a critical neutral ground, the holders of which realize how large an element of conscious parody enters into many of Mr. Lovecraft's longer and more serious productions, and who are capable of appreciating the cleverness and literary charm of these pastoral echoes without being dominated by them to the extent of indiscriminate praise and second-hand imitation.

Those who would beguile Mr. Lovecraft from his chosen path are probably unaware of the attitude which he consistently maintains toward hostile criticism. Mr. Lovecraft contends that it gives him pleasure to write as the Augustans did, and that those who do not relish his excursions into classic fields need not follow him. He tries to conciliate no one, and is content to be his sole reader! What critic, with these facts before him, will think it worthwhile to break a lance with the poet?

But even Mr. Lovecraft is willing to be original at times. He has written verse of a distinctly modern atmosphere, and where his imagery is not too obtrusively artificial—according to the modern idea—many of his quatrains possess genuine poetic value.

Many who cannot read his longer and more ambitious productions find Mr. Lovecraft's light or humorous verse decidedly refreshing. As a satirist along familiar lines, particularly those laid down by Butler, Swift and Pope, he is most himself—paradoxical though it seems. In reading his satires one cannot help but feel the zest with which the author has composed them. They are admirable for the way in which they reveal the depth and intensity of Mr. Lovecraft's convictions, while the wit, irony, sarcasm and humour to be found in them serve as an indication of his powers as a controversialist. The almost relentless ferocity of his satires is constantly relieved by an attendant broad humour which has the merit of causing the readers to chuckle more than once in the perusal of some attack leveled against the particular person or policy which may have incurred Mr. Lovecraft's displeasure.

The Kleicomolo

While amateur journalism's prime function is to provide an incentive for the beginner in literary effort through the medium of print, it provides opportunity for correspondence of such high order as is rarely to be found elsewhere in this age. For the most part the letters of today rise so seldom above the level of concise news bulletins that we merit the charge that the art of real letter-writing is practically extinct. The experiences of the trenches, combined with periods of enforced idleness, have spurred our boys to unusual efforts in their letters; but as a rule we lack either the time or the inclination—or both—to make our letters a long, leisurely narrative or discussion, with plenty of attention given to the choice of the exact word, the well-turned phrase, and the cadenced sentence. If the average amateur realised what a wonderful school of self-expression a correspondence of this kind may become, he would straightway seek him out an amateur of kindred tastes and start his epistolary education.

What promises to be one of the most noted correspondence groups fostered by amateur journalism, is indicated by the cryptic title of this article, composed of the first few letters from the surnames of the four writers: Rheinhart Kleiner, of Brooklyn; Ira A. Cole, of Bazine, Kansas; Maurice W. Moe, of Madison, Wisconsin; and Howard P. Lovecraft, of Providence, Rhode Island.

Added spice is afforded by the fact that the four not only have some tastes in common, but differ so radically on certain points that each letter is a keen contest of words in which every effort is used to prove the point and silence the opponent. A glance at the members of the group reveals interesting possibilities, both in similarity and difference in taste.

Our honoured president is so well known for his melodious poetry and his keen critical ability, which sometimes gets him into hot water, that he needs no introduction to present-day amateurs.

Co, a cowboy poet, is a unique personality who furnishes an extremely interesting and unusual element to the letter. Though born on the prairies and brought up a wild, free range-man, then a ranchman, with little opportunity for the usual bookish education, he has carved an education out of life for himself, reading, communing with nature, and confiding his groping thoughts to a faithful typewriter until he has risen to high levels of poetic and spiritual beauty, and achieved such habitual grace of phrase and figure that his prose is pure poetry. There is a strain of mysticism in his makeup which further distinguishes him, and his views on dreams, visions, and manifestations of the supernatural, real or alleged, have given play to vigorous discussions.

Mo, the teacher of English and originator of the Kleicomolo idea, is by the unanimous verdict of his three colleagues acclaimed as leader of the quartette. Though better known as an active amateur to a former generation, he is today recognised as our deepest and most thorough scholar and litterateur. A graduate of the University of Wisconsin, he has also distinguished himself in post-graduate work; and is an authority on a multitude of subjects unknown to the lay reader, including the Assyrian language as recorded in the cunei-form inscriptions unearthed by archæologists.

His wide experience in life combines with his deep learning to make him an ideal preceptor, and his work at Appleton High School has brought him no little prominence in educational circles. The cause of education lost much, when, in accordance with his strongly religious bent, he resigned his school activities to become Extension Secretary of the Biblical Alliance.

As might be expected in one of his former profession, Mo is apt to make a fetich of accuracy, which leads him into long Macauleyesque sentences. He has a mind, however, which is eagerly open to all currents of modern thought, and all his utterances are distinguished by phenomenal interest and cogency. Mo is a man of strong likes and dislikes; a rider of hobbies. He is a determined, if mistaken, champion of deformed spelling in its less repellent aspects; and likewise espouses with keen vigour Esperanto, osteopathy, and orthodoxy in poetry and religion. An argument levelled at any one of these is certain to arouse warm controversy.

Lo, lover of profundity and erudition, has made himself more widely known to the fraternity in the years of his membership than probably any other amateur. Like good wine he needs no bush, for he is a most prolific writer, and his copious productions have given quality to every issue of recent official organs and to many other journals beside.

His dominant characteristics are scholarship and dogmatism. As he has acquired most of his contact with life between the covers of books, his views of life are not always those of one who has rubbed shoulders with the world and learned that a thing may seem inconsistent with pure reason and still re-main practical. As he is intensely rational, it is natural that he should be de-cidedly liberal in his religious views, tending to nearer kinship in this regard, according to his own admission, with the ancient Greeks than with any mod-ern sect. He venerates the heroic couplet as the supreme poetic medium, the Georgian Age as the apex of English literary history, and the Teutonic branch of the Aryan race, especially the Anglo-Saxon sub-division of that branch, as the predominant combination of intellect, physique, and racial stamina that this world has produced. With an almost uncanny skill at versifying, he makes the pages of his letters ring with the martial clank of couplets whose fidelity to the heroic tradition is so exact that one is tempted to declare that Pope in his heroic epistles never did anything better and frequently fell below. For solid interest and versatility Lo easily takes the lead in the group.

During the last year Alfred Galpin, Jr., of Appleton, a pupil of Mo's, was admitted to the charmed circle by unanimous consent; although it was voted at this time to retain the charter name of the letter, whatever changes might occur in the personnel of the group. Gal is by far the youngest of the writers, but he runs with the swiftest. With all the fire of adolescence, and a precocious ability for coining new words, he overleaps the barriers of the English language and cavorts in the untrodden fields of etymology, usually to the great amusement of his readers. But when the occasion or the subject demands serious treatment, he displays a maturity of thought and expression that is a perennial surprise.

Such a combination of ability and varied charm of personality guarantees a correspondence of unique interest and excellence, and one which may well be held up as a model for those who would assist in rescuing the art of letter-writing and restoring it to the high plane it once occupied.

And now a word as to the method of circulating the letters. Klei writes to Co, who adds his instalment and sends the whole to Mo. Mo does the same and sends it to Lo, and Lo completes the articles and sends it back to Klei, who takes out his letter, writes another, and starts the packet around again. With the admission of Gal and the gradual warming up of the writers to the opportunity, the time required for a whole circuit has gradually increased until now it takes from six to ten months, although prompt attention to the letter upon its arrival would cut that down to two or three months. One of the members was desirous of keeping a complete copy of the correspondence, and began by copying the letters as they went through his hands. This task soon became so great as to be impracticable, and the rest elected him librarian and promised to send him carbon copies of their instalments. It is not at all unlikely that the future may see the best parts of the *Kleicomolo* given to the public as a book.

There is nothing new under the sun, but here, amateurs, is a new twist to an old idea that will bring you more real pleasure than any other correspondence you ever indulged in, and that will give you the equivalent of a course of training in English composition. Get two or three congenial partners and try it.

After a Decade and the Kalem Club

The Kalem Club flourished in New York City a decade ago. It was an extremely informal organization, and never definitely allied with amateur journalism. Nevertheless, among its members were a few amateur journalists of sufficient note to justify this brief chronicle of past glory by a self-appointed historian.

James F. Morton, Howard P. Lovecraft, Samuel Loveman, and Belknap Long, were among those who found the club a congenial place for the completest and most untrammeled expression of opinion. Personal convictions, as well as the merest whimseys of thought, were here openly paraded and insisted upon, and there was no one too diffident to wage battle for the most astonishing paradox, if it happened to be his own.

James Morton had long been prominent as a writer and lecturer on controversial subjects, while amateur journalists knew him as a Moses who dispensed the law from Mt. Sinai. To Kalemites he appeared as the arbiter of literary taste, ready to quote chapter and verse from the most recondite classics, and prepared at any time to enter the lists in support of the Elizabethan dramatists.

Howard Lovecraft possessed a scholarly equipment of formidable thoroughness, aided by a memory quite incapable of losing anything which had ever been entrusted to it. He was regarded as the chief defender of Eighteenth century literature, architecture, and manners, but his versatility led him in many other directions, among which his ability in the art of writing weird stories deserved, and still deserves, conspicuous mention.

Samuel Loveman had just arrived from Cleveland with George Kirk, and the singing robes he wore about him seemed to trail clouds of glory as he came. His burst of lyrical power as a young poet in the National Amateur Press Association, followed by a long and inexplicable silence, had made him somewhat of a legendary figure. There was some uncertainty as to whether he should be regarded as a Chaucer or a Chatterton, but critical opinion agreed in considering him one of the few real poets to appear in amateur journalism. "The Hermaphrodite", which has recently found handsome second publication at a western press, was then shortly to make its first appearance, in tasteful format, from the press of W. Paul Cook, in Athol, Mass.

Belknap Long, most youthful of the group, brought Shelleyan fire to his poetry and to his opinions. Rather more under the influence of extreme modernism—or what was such ten years ago—than the rest, he uttered convictions of a psycho-analytical cast which not infrequently non-plussed the representatives of the Elizabethan, Augustan, and Victorian ages. His inspiration as a poet was drawn from the true Pierian spring, as readers of "The Man from Genoa and Other Poems" (W. Paul Cook, Athol, Mass.) have discovered for themselves.

Among other members of note, was Everett McNeil, then at the height of his fame as an author for boys. His tales of adventure, published by E. P. Dutton & Co., filled an entire library shelf, and librarians reported that worn out copies of his books could not be replaced fast enough to meet the demand. His most popular story was "Tonty of the Iron Hand", published in 1925, which went into several editions. Some of his other titles were "The Totem of Black Hawk", "In Texas With Davy Crockett", and "Fighting With Fremont". He was easily the patriarch of the club, and, with his silvery hair and somewhat quizzical expression of face, presented a striking appearance. He was kindly of heart, and often entertained the club in his bachelor apartment on the west side. The complexities of modern life at times awakened a suggestion of the querulous in him, which none understood. He died just when it seemed likely that the delayed rewards of a life of industrious authorship were about to be his.

Vrest Orton, another member, was the personification of the "Man about town"—that idealized character of whom one so seldom hears today—

and it was hardly surmised that a genuine bibliographer lay concealed beneath his air of dilettantism. He has since achieved fame as the bibliographer of Theodore Dreiser, and as the one who has been given credit by Bennett Cerf, and others, for the organization of The Colophon Club, whose publications are prized by scholars and bibliophiles the world over.

Wilfred B. Talman was one of the "dependables" of the club. At the time, he was a reporter on a Brooklyn daily, with an amateur career as poet and publisher behind him. He had once conceived the idea of printing a book of his own verses on a hand press, and had set up two pages, facing, which fitted into one form. After printing many sheets, he discovered the omission of a word in the set-up, and forthwith scrapped the entire project. More fortunate in his professional ventures, he succeeded in selling stories and poems to magazines of national circulation.

Arthur Leeds, actor, story writer, and authority on cinematic affairs of the day, contributed the accumulated experience of much travel and observation, as well as the knowledge gained from extensive literary browsing, to the deliberations of the group.

Most of the meetings of the Kalem Club, during the period of its greatest efflorescence, took place after business hours at George Kirk's Chelsea Bookshop, on West 15th Street, near Ninth Avenue, New York City. George dealt in bibliographic rarities and fine press books, and his magnificently stocked shelves reached from the floor to the ceiling, entirely around the room. He, himself, possessed a finely discriminating taste in literature, and his equal as an amiable and generous host would have been difficult to find. In such an environment, and with such a host, it is not surprising that hearts were lightened and spirits soared.

George's ability and perseverance in brewing coffee, and his liberality with buns and sandwiches, left nothing to be desired. Nor need it cause wonder if certain individuals became so attached to proprietor and shop as to appear every evening, often with the expectation—which was never disappointed—of sleeping there. A host, whose bed in the rear room could accommodate five guests, if they did not toss much, was never at a loss when visitors declined to go home.

What was said and done at home of these hilarious gatherings could never effectively be retold or reenacted. Our discussions and diversions were nothing if not spontaneous—and they were undoubtedly spontaneous. From some of our more serious sessions, the mind recalls a comprehensive appraisal of Walt Whitman's poetry, by James; a bit of amusing cynicism regarding Jane Austen's novels, from George; and a stout pronouncement that no woman over forty ever wrote a true lyric, on the part of Belknap. On one occasion, Sam read T. S. Eliot's poem, "The Waste Land", aloud, and those who did not succumb to torpor were aroused to torridity in the expression of opinion.

Recollection comes of a solemn evening when George announced that

Otto, the house-cat—large, plump, and royally bewhiskered—had been killed in front of the door by a passing motor. Otto!—singularly gifted feline, with a genius from impromptu acrobatics in the hall stairway, and a benign imperturbability of demeanor in the face of false lures that were vainly designed to torment him! Lamentations and panegyrics became the order of the evening, and all poets present set to work upon suitable expressions of Kalemite grief. So far as can be ascertained, none of these notable productions was preserved, but the poems produced by Howard and Sam were regarded as masterpieces, that evening. Had these been spared from the maw of Time, it is not unlikely that so long established a favorite in this kind of poetry as Gray's "On the Death of a Favorite Cat, Drowned in a Tub of Gold Fishes", would have had its supremacy challenged.

* * *

Of a preliminary phase in the Kalem Club's history, involving Brooklyn, when George, Sam and Howard had rooms very near one another, on the Heights, much might be said, but who will say it?

Suffice it to conclude this incomplete and rambling record with the explanation—perhaps undesired—that "Kalem" was based upon the letters K, L, and M, which happened to be the initial letters in the names of the original group—McNeil, Long, and the writer—and those who joined during the first six months of the club.

Howard Phillips Lovecraft

News of the death of Howard Lovecraft on March 15, 1937, at the age of 46, was disseminated so quickly throughout amateur journalism, that this attempt at commemoration is not likely to come as a shock to any member of the National or United Association. Lovecraft's actual passing, however, came as a blow to many friends who had heard from him but shortly before, in letters which gave no clue to the fact that the writer of them was a man mortally stricken.

Lovecraft, as the recruit of Edward F. Daas, joined the United Amateur Press Association—Helene Hoffman-Cole faction—in April, 1914. As a boy, not yet nine years old, he had published *The Scientific Gazette,* a weekly periodical devoted to chemistry, which was written in pencil and issued in editions of four carbon copies. This appeared from March, 1899, to February, 1904. A second venture, *The Rhode Island Journal of Astronomy,* began as a weekly in 1903 and ended as a monthly in 1907. It was printed in hand-lettering, duplicated on the hectograph and issued in lots of twenty-five copies. These details, first given by Andrew F. Lockhart, in *The United Amateur,* so long ago as September, 1915, show Lovecraft to have followed a course similar to that of many youngsters of literary imagination, some of whom eventually find their way into amateur journalism.

The first number of his amateur journal *The Conservative* appeared in

March, 1915, and many were immediately aware that a brilliant new talent had made itself known. The entire contents of the issue, both prose and verse, were the work of the editor, who obviously knew exactly what he wished to say, and no less exactly how to say it. *The Conservative* took a unique place among the valuable publications of its time, and held that place with ease through the period of seven or eight years during which it made occasional appearances. Its critical pronouncements were relished by some and resented by others, but there was no doubt of the respect in which they were held by all. That the publication was sometimes the center of rather heated literary controversies cannot be denied, but Lovecraft's ability to parry and thrust was such as to confound all beholders by its mere brilliance of technique. Those of his opponents who were able to withdraw from such encounters with dignity and prestige unimpaired were somewhat few. Yet Lovecraft was never averse to acknowledging the prowess of a foeman even while pinning him to the wall. Mellowing considerably in after years, he all but abandoned those keen-edged tools of invective and satire in whose use he had once delighted. Amateurs who recall the old literary affrays with William B. Stoddard, Charles D. Isaacson, Ida Haughton, Elsa Gidlow, Roswell George Mills, and Noah F. Whittaker—not at one time, but in succession—will think of them as diverting occasions, and perhaps regret that nothing quite like them has occurred in a long while. It even came to pass that Lovecraft changed his mind about certain former adversaries and their literary creeds. An interesting instance was that of *Les Mouches Fantastiques,* a paper published by Elsa Gidlow and Roswell George Mills. Upon first encountering this organ of an asthetic [*sic*] conviction which bore no recognizable traces of having been influenced by that of Dryden or Pope, Lovecraft attacked it with his customary vigor. The publication, never of frequent issue, finally vanished completely, as did the editors, but a day came when its severest critic recalled *Les Mouches Fantastiques* with something like regret and an admission that there may have been something, after all, in its approach, even if not in its accomplishment.

Howard Lovecraft was opposed to politics in the amateur associations, but circumstances more than once drew him prominently into the political arena. His first love was the United Amateur Press Association, and when, in 1917, it was urged by influential members that the literary standards of the association could be raised only by the example of a truly literary president, Lovecraft consented to run for the office. He was elected, and literary standards were indubitably given first consideration in the United from that time on. Lovecraft, in fact, became so potent a force in the life of his faction of the United that he was able to sway later elections for a number of years, although not a candidate himself. That influence was invariably used on the side of the literary element, and the result was a group of poets and prose writers who performed notably while the association held together. Acute commentators have since pointed out that more varied elements of interest and activity are essential to the maintenance of a successful amateur club, but the question has been asked whether history offers any example of a cultural center which was not finally overwhelmed by barbarians.

Anyone acquainted with Lovecraft's amateur predilections up to the year 1922, would have considered him irrevocably bound to the United, and just as irrevocably opposed to the National. Nevertheless, in that year, when William J. Dowdell, the elected president of the National, resigned his office, Howard Lovecraft accepted the appointment of the National Executive Judges to fill out the term. The occasion of his capitulation, in the home of Mr. and Mrs. George Julian Houtain, on Bedford Avenue, Brooklyn, was a mèmorable one. It is true that he had begun to waver in his first resolution not to accept, but a final plea from Mrs. Houtain—a plea most irresistibly offered—completely shattered his last defences. The amateur world rocked with the sensation when Lovecraft's name was announced as that of the new president.

Little has thus far been said of his intellectual equipment for a career of literary activity, but to say that it was phenomenal is to characterize it briefly and adequately. There seemed few remote corners of human knowledge into which he had not, at some time, ventured with lasting profit to himself. Upon his first entry into amateur journalism, the style of his essays and the verse-forms he habitually employed, indicated the extent to which he had been influenced by the literature of the reign of Queen Anne. In after years, his literary output revealed other, and more modern tendencies, but those qualities of grace, urbanity and precision, which had marked his best work from the beginning, were always to be found there. It was in the field of the short-story that he ventured farthest from the severely classical ideals of the Augustan Age, and it was as a master of the "grotesque and the arabesque" that he achieved distinction in the professional world. His earlier stories have been reprinted, from time to time, in *Weird Tales,* and similar publications, as classics of their kind, and this practice of editors is likely to continue for some years to come. "Dagon," "The Rats in the Walls," "The Shunned House," and "The Cats of Ulthar," are only a few of the stories of this type written by Lovecraft during the past twenty years.

Many amateurs will remember him as a prolific letter-writer. The exact number of his correspondents may never be known, but, from the evidence already at hand, it would seem that no one is yet justified in regarding his own collection of Lovecraftian epistles as exceptional either for quality or for bulk. There are at least four or five such treasuries in Greater New York, and the existence of others in various parts of the country is known or surmised. The present writer has a collection dating from 1915, which, in addition to letters of staggering length, includes humorous, satirical and serious poetry in large quantities, as well as carefully drawn caricatures and portraits of well-known amateurs, to say nothing of documents, booklets and folders, all patiently printed and colored by hand. More valuable collections may contain the manuscripts of stories not yet printed, for Lovecraft cast his largess abroad with a prodigality quite unsurpassed in modern amateur history.

The habit of the confirmed recluse had begun falling from Lovecraft at the time of his emergence into amateur celebrity. Sometimes a temarious [*sic*] pilgrim from another city would lift the knocker of the modest door at 598 Angell St., Providence, R. I., and receive a most cordial welcome from the lonely scholar within. Rumors of his ascetic life among ancient tomes began to be supplemented by reports of his humor and companionability. A band of Blue Pencil members, changing from boat to train at Providence, on the way to Boston for the 1916 convention, found him waiting at the station with complimentary greetings. Only a few years later, he attended all the sessions of still another National convention at Boston, and established social relations of friendly intimacy with several local amateurs. In 1924, he came to New York, and made his home in the Borough of Brooklyn for several years. He became an active participant in the monthly literary programs of The Blue Pencil Club, as well as one of the mainstays of that unusual and informal organization, The Kalem Club.

It may be that he appeared at his very best, socially, at the sessions of the Kalemites. Here, where no parliamentary rules obstructed the easy flow of spontaneous talk, he seemed to expand. The strongly marked lineaments of a countenance which, at times, seemed expressive of naught but austerity, became animated with a conviviality of emotion directly traceable to an intense satisfaction with his surroundings. He relished the wit of others, and indulged in sallies of his own which usually topped the best efforts of the rest. He was capable of singing a song, in a high, clear tenor, which would evoke appreciative applause, and his knowledge of the operettas that had won popularity at the turn of the century was nothing less than astonishing. Lovecraft never made any secret of the esteem in which he held his friends, and every member of that group felt himself regarded as a rare being in his own right.

Eventually, the call of the "Providence Plantations"—as he fondly termed his native locale—proved too strong for him, and he returned to New England. To some extent, he resumed his old life of semi-seclusion, but now there were seasonal visits to South Carolina and Florida, with brief stop-overs in New York. His work as official critic—a phase of his amateur activity almost from the beginning—was continued, as were his characteristic epistolary diversions. Regret has been expressed that he did not concentrate more fully upon his production of short-stories, but an examination of his papers may prove him to have been much more persistent in these labors than some suppose.

A fairly intimate friend of a man like Howard Phillips Lovecraft may not be the most impartial of judges as to his character or achievements. It would be much too soon, in any event, to express an opinion as to the place he may yet be granted in a special department of the short-story, but it is natural to hope and expect that this will be high. In expressing an appreciation of his character and personality, however, there is no longer any need for reticence.

Lovecraft impressed himself indelibly upon his own generation of amateur journalists, and whatever unfriendly reactions may at first have been apparent in certain localities and among special groups, are long since forgotten. As the years passed, it was found that he never hesitated to assume a responsibility, at whatever expense of time and drudgery, if the cause demanded it. By his letters he encouraged the newer members who showed promise, and by the same means he reclaimed others who had once been active, but whom more pressing concerns had temporarily drawn away. To those who stood in the relation of old friends, he was unfailing in acts of kindness and consideration. Old loyalties died hard with him, and the friend who once won his approval was unlikely ever to find that approval withdrawn. He will be remembered by many as the wit, and the scholar, or the gifted writer, but a small group of his one-time intimates will ever cherish his memory as that of a peerless friend.

Lovecraft in Brooklyn

Something should be said about Howard P. Lovecraft, the man, and the impression he made upon me, aside from the strong and favorable effect of everything he had written and published up to the time of my meeting him.

I was aware of a touch of the unusual in his appearance from the very start, but there was nothing particularly strange or striking in this. All of his features were good, but the chin was a trifle long. Yet this was not an especially singular characteristic in him nor one peculiar to himself. I have met other men, at various times, whose chins, in shape and length, were much like Lovecraft's. I admit that my first thought was that these men looked something like him—even moved their lips and smiled as he did.

Not everyone may agree with me, but I used to think there had originally been a slight obliquity in Lovecraft's vision which his glasses helped to correct. I think I was unduly aware of it in him for the reason that I once met his mother, on an early visit to Providence, and was immediately struck by the strong resemblance, in the upper part of the face, between them. There was not only the suggestion of an obliquity in her vision, but there seemed to be a slight difference, at least in the depth or shade of color, between the eyes. This may possibly have been my reason for thinking I detected the obliquity mentioned. In the case of Lovecraft, it was never more than a momentary impression and after I had begun seeing him frequently I never noticed it again.

He was really a tall man and broad in the shoulders. His physique was not by any means that of an invalid, and if the studious habit of years had not given his posture a forward inclination, he might well have been admired as a good physical specimen of manhood. In fact, during the first World War, Lovecraft, under the compulsion of his pro-Allied militarism, tried to enlist in the Rhode Island National Guard and was forthwith accepted. His mother and family physician got him out again, after a few days.

His method of shaking hands was certainly not the usual one. He generally extended a few fingers, which were cold and claw-like, and withdrew them as quickly as possible. The open, friendly and hearty American handclasp was something he never made any attempt to acquire. As I have said, his hand was usually cold and, for that matter, so was he. He detested the winter season, and in his furnished room in Brooklyn, after he had left his wife, could never get enough heat. Writing to me, in reminiscential mood, after his return to Providence, he referred to the "Theatrical nature of the steam heat," which he had been obliged to augment with a portable oil stove.

This is no more than a surmise, based on scanty information, but it does not seem to me that Lovecraft ever bought a suit of clothes in all the time I knew him. I may be mistaken in this point, too, but I never saw him wear anything but black in that time. He was extremely careful of his wearing apparel, the various items of which may have been survivals, preserved and cherished, of an earlier and possibly more prosperous period. He might occasionally, when among intimates, indicate the suit he was wearing, and tell us it was seven or eight years old.

He was always an abstemious eater, with the exception of the brief period of his married life. Mrs. Lovecraft was accomplished in the household arts, and the preparation of a good meal offered no difficulties to her. Lovecraft ate and drank (but only tea, coffee and milk) with a regularity, a heartiness and a lack of squeamishness—always excepting sea-food—which amazed his friends. During that period he put on weight to an astonishing degree. Looking up after him, as he was ascending the steps of an "el" station, I suddenly realized that this was a stout Lovecraft—almost but not quite a Dr. Johnson in bulk!—and his jowls, his neck and his waist had all become much heavier and more noticeable. He and his wife may have parted shortly after this. At any rate, once he had returned to the cafeterias and coffee-houses, he soon shrank to his former and more becoming dimensions. In fact, there came a sad day when his daily fare—when he paid for it himself—consisted mainly of coffee and doughnuts, because doughnuts were cheap and filling. But it was not long after this final period when thru the good offices of his young and devoted friend, Belknap Long, he returned to Providence for good.

Some Lovecraft Memories

The other day I bundled up the letters I had received from Lovecraft in years long past and sent them to August Derleth, to use as he pleased. But one thing remained, and that was to put down such recollections as might occur to me of the days and hours when I had held personal communion with H. P. Lovecraft.

This was not easy to do. It is possible that I met him a little sooner—in 1916, to be exact—than some who, making his acquaintance later, did more to improve the resultant opportunities for correspondence and personal friendship. But a few details remain in memory of those early years and, as best I can, Ishall try to recapture them.

My meeting with him in 1916 was not due to any planning of my own, although I had already been receiving his letters for more than a year. I happened to be one of a party of Blue Pencillers on their way to Boston for the NAPA convention, and Providence was where we changed from the boat to the train. One of our group phoned him, and he appeared to greet us at the station. He was still somewhat young in looks then, and as I thought, of a very prepossessing appearance. What struck me was his extreme formality of manner, and the highly complimentary style of his approach to those with whom he had had previous epistolary contact.

The following year, however, I went to Providence for the purpose of spending a day or two with him. I was greeted at the door of 598 Angell Street by his mother, who was a woman just a little below medium height, with graying hair, and eyes that seemed to be the chief point of resemblance between herself and her son. She was very cordial and even vivacious, and in another moment had ushered me into Lovecraft's room. I was impressed anew by his conversational powers, which were rapid and precise and showed him to be unusually well informed. In those days, he had not yet overcome a certain tenseness of manner, which a stranger might have taken, in some of its manifestations, as a desire for argument. If it became at all obtrusive—and I do not say it did—it showed itself in an insistence upon facts which his hearer did not question, and sometimes even in an "asperous" contradiction! Lovecraft, however, was much too carefully self-schooled in the correct 18th century code of conduct to be guilty of any crudities of this sort, and we shortly got along very well together.

I noticed that at every hour, or so, his mother appeared in the doorway with a glass of milk and he forthwith drank it. Something was said about a cup of tea for me, but I had become aware of the heat of the room and suggested it might be a good idea to take a short walk.

I digress sufficiently to say that the room in which I sat was fairly small and lined around three sides with books, mostly old ones. On the wall near his desk were small pictures of Robert E. Lee, Jefferson Davis and one or two others. An almanac hung against the wall directly over his desk, and I think he said it was the *Farmers' Almanac* with which he had been familiar for many years.

Just before broaching the subject of an outdoor stroll, I absent-mindedly took my pipe out of my pocket. I don't know why, but I suddenly felt that pipe-smoking in that house might not be quite the thing. At that very moment his mother appeared in the doorway and espied the pipe sliding back into my pocket. To my surprise, she gave an exclamation of pleasure and wished that I could persuade Howard to smoke a pipe, as it would be so soothing for him. This may have been New England courtesy to cover a guest's embarrassment, but I know that I never even made the slightest attempt to convert Lovecraft to pipe-smoking!

We found ourselves outside very shortly. Lovecraft suggested certain favorite buildings and localities which I might care to see. They were survivals of that more spacious century in which his mental home seemed to be, but I should have difficulty in finding them today! On our way back to his home, and while we were still downtown, I suggested stopping in at a cafeteria for a cup of coffee. He agreed, but took milk himself, and watched me dispose of coffee and cake, or possibly pie, with some curiosity. It occurred to me later that he may have regarded this visit to a public eating house—a most unpretentious one, by the way—as a distinct departure from his own usual habits.

I may be pardoned for explaining that Lovecraft, the friend and companion of all genial and well-intentioned literary men, was still in embryo in 1917! In his New York period of the early 1920s, he ate and drank like other men, and coffee never came amiss to him. He never touched liquor or tobacco, but he had company in our own group who shared this abstinence with him. He could sit with friends who drank beer or whiskey, and who smoked cigars, cigarettes or pipes, without batting an eyelash!

The following day, Lovecraft came to my hotel, and we set out on a tour of second-hand bookshops. I wish I could recall some cogent observation or shrewd quip in this instance, if he made any, but we were too dignified at that time to unbend and be quite natural with each other. It was on later visits that I met his aunts, Mrs. Clark and Mrs. Gamwell. I thought them very gracious ladies, but other details of those trips have quite left my memory.

It has always seemed that Lovecraft's fundamental instincts were normal. Removed from the repressive sickroom atmosphere of his house, and the attendance of his mother or aunts, he blossomed out astonishingly. Furthermore, he had a real knack for making himself liked. W. Paul Cook attributes Lovecraft's development to his sojourn among the amateur journalists of the metropolis, and I am willing to believe it—albeit even Cook is aware that the progress of that development was not entirely painless.

Winfield T. Scott in his excellent article in *Marginalia* says that Lovecraft did not sleep away from his home until after his 30th birthday, and he is probably quite right. But it was certainly very early in the course of my friendship with him that Lovecraft came to the Broadway Central hotel in New York for the NAPA convention, and that he and I occupied the same bed for one night. I know that neither he nor I paid for the room, and so I have a suspicion that we must have used one of the rooms in George Julian Houtain's suite—especially rented by him for the use of convention guests. The point I wish to make has to do with Lovecraft's sleeping gear, which was a long nightshirt, reaching almost to his ankles. I believe this article of apparel had long been relegated by modern folk to the attic, even at that time, but its use by Lovecraft certainly indicated his love of the old and the orthodox. Lovecraft had already grown considerably on me by that time and his frequent letters were received more gladly and read more carefully than the daily newspaper that was left at my door.

At a Boston NAPA convention in the very early 1920s, on the deck of a harbor boat which was to take us to some neighboring beach, I introduced him to his future wife, Mrs. Sonia Greene. She, somewhat in the spirit of George Moore's "Euphorion in Texas," decided to fall in love with him, marry him, and give a child of his to the world—the child to be a literary genius, of course. On our return to Brooklyn, she sought out all those who were friends of Lovecraft—myself among them—and spent most of the time talking about him. I have no intention of dwelling unduly on this matter, but I do remember very well that it was while riding in a taxi with Mr. and Mrs. Houtain that the startling news of the Lovecraft–Greene marriage was imparted to me. At once, I had a feeling of faintness at the pit of my stomach and became very pale. Houtain laughed uproariously at the effect of his announcement, but agreed that he felt much as I did.

Sonia Greene, very attractive and of Junoesque proportions, was an excellent woman in every way. All the women of the Boston circle pronounced her a bore, but morally she was an absolute puritan. As Winifred Harper Cooley—noted figure among members of the "dining out" clubs of the period—once expressed to me, "Where does she get it? If I were Sonia, I'd be the Russian widow!" No doubt, some of Mrs. Greene's standards of conduct, at least for men, were a bit naïve. I do remember her once remarking with finality, to a circle of Lovecraft's companions, gathered at her home, "No gentleman ever carries a pocketknife!" Forthwith, Lovecraft, Long, Kirk, Loveman and I produced ours.

As an example of the favorable impression Lovecraft could make upon strangers, I recall that he had one of his stories to type at this time, but his machine was still in Providence. Passing a printer's shop on Flatbush Avenue, he saw an unused typewriter on a table inside, and entered to ask whether he could use it. The printer not only gave him permission but told him to come whenever he wished.

Lovecraft's generosity with books was well-known. He would lend any volume to almost anybody. The special feeling for a book as an entity, a thing of beautiful type, artistic illustrations, and appropriate binding, did not seem to be a part of him. He probably admired all these details, but the printed word that was sumptuously presented was the main consideration with him. Even in the case of favorite authors, he showed much the same lack of interest in the book as a book. After all, a book could always be replaced!

One of his acquaintances in the Flatbush period of his life was a light versifier of some local note named La Touche Hancock. He appeared regularly in magazines of the *Puck* and *Judge* variety. To this individual, whose home address was not known even clearly at the time, Lovecraft entrusted certain volumes to be read and returned. Hancock died suddenly, and the return of the books remained doubtful for some time. If they were ever restored to Lovecraft, I do not know.

In those days, Lovecraft and [Frank B.] Long spent much time together and they frequently browsed among the outside stalls of second-hand bookshops. Sometimes Lovecraft thought of a friend in connection with some particular book which came to his hand on a stall, and if it cost no more than 15 cents or a quarter he would buy it for presentation purposes. He was kind enough to think of me in that way, when, on an outside stall, he found a dilapidated copy of Margaret of Navarre's "Heptameron." It was minus the covers and about 30 pages at the end. The price was only 15 cents. What could be more appropriate to the known proclivities of a certain Brooklyn rhymester—myself—than a copy of this very book? It was purchased and duly presented to me, with a delightful 18th century inscription on the flyleaf in Lovecraft's own hand. That may have been almost 25 years ago, and the library I possessed in those days has long vanished, but I am prepared to show that shabby "Heptameron" to anyone interested in seeing it.

Lovecraft and I sometimes would walk across the Manhattan Bridge, the view of the skyscrapers from various parts of the footwalk being part of artistic efforts in the letters I had written him. To me, these views were scenes in a drama which only awaited the right author to find proper appreciation. To Lovecraft, what he beheld here had secret links with a number of dreams of mysterious horror of which I had no inkling at the time. One night he relapsed into a benign 18th century mood, as we were taking this walk, and suggested that we compose impromptu couplets about what we saw. I remember that his own efforts reflected the influence of the "decent-church-that-topped-the-neighboring-hill" school, while my own were probably feeble imitations of the same thing.

I wonder if Long or [Samuel E.] Loveman recalls that extensive treatise on the "Cat" which Lovecraft wrote at about this time on the subject assigned to the Blue Pencil members by the literary director. The subject grew under his hand, historic and literary allusions beyond number suggested themselves, and it was not finished in time for the meeting at which it was supposed to have been read. It was in James F. Morton's possession for a time, and I had little more than just a glance at it. In bulk alone, the manuscript alone was sufficient to make a book, and it seems to me that if it could be found and published at this late date, it would be a notable and valuable addition to our store of Lovecraftiana.

Speaking of cats, I am reminded of Lovecraft's acute appreciation of humor in others, whether that humor was intentional or not. I don't know how it came about, but he and I were sitting in George Kirk's Chelsea Book Shop one night, after hours, and we were discussing the word *parallelopipedon*. Lovecraft, as usual, was primed with information, but what I could have had to say on the subject quite baffles me, as I certainly could not say anything on it today! At any rate, it suddenly occurred to me that *parallelopipedon* would be quite a name for a cat, a pleasing supposition which I mentioned to him. Then, beholding the usual kitten playing around his chair, I stooped, and soothingly murmuring, "Here, my little parallelopipedon," began to pet it. Looking up at Lovecraft, I beheld him in a state of helpless mirth. His face was contorted and he shook all over. He was so completely convulsed that it took him some time to return to normal!

This may be as good a place as any for a little incident showing his very real interest in the welfare of his friends. Loveman had been looking for a new room on Columbia Heights, but in a rather more expensive part of that thoroughfare. He finally located quite a desirable room with the magnificent view of the downtown Manhattan skyscrapers on the other side of the river. The landlady, however, became unexpectedly capricious and did not seem able to make up her mind to part with the room. Loveman mentioned this at the Kalem Club one night and awakened Lovecraft's active interest. His aunt, Mrs. Gamwell, came to town at that time, and the two of them found opportunity to call upon this recalcitrant landlady. They were a formidable guarantee of anyone's desirability as a tenant! Loveman received such a high rating that the room became his without further ado.

Prowls and long walks were always a part of Lovecraft's scheme of life and the hours of darkness were probably his preferred time for such ramblings. It is well known that Thomas de Quincey and Charles Dickens were notable night-prowlers, and I would place Lovecraft's name well near the top of such a list of kindred spirits!

In Greenwich Village—for whose eccentric denizens he had little use—he was fond of poking about in back alleys where his companions preferred not to go. In the prohibition years, with murderous affrays among bootleggers and rumrunners likely to erupt anywhere, this was a particularly dangerous business. Every other house in the neighborhood was open to suspicion as a speakeasy. I recall that at least once, while stumbling around among old barrels and crates in some dark corner of this area, Lovecraft found a doorway suddenly illuminated and an excited foreigner wearing an apron, an almost infallible sign of a speakeasy bartender, inquiring hotly what he wanted. Loveman and Kirk went in after Lovecraft and got him safely out. None of us, surely, was under any illusions as to what might very well happen in such an obscure corner.

There were many other trips to all parts of the city and its boroughs, in not too many of which I was able to participate. At least once, Lovecraft and Kirk offered to walk me home from Columbia Heights. Since I lived in Bushwick, this was quite a jaunt for a nocturnal hour, along block after block for mile after mile, until flashes and thunders of the Broadway "el" became evident, and half a mile remained to be covered after that! Lovecraft was undoubtedly a persistent and tireless pedestrian but I think this walk proved a little too much even for him. We finally reached Bushwick Avenue, which was near my destination, but here Lovecraft's physical powers suddenly waned. He became dizzy and weak and had to sit down on a nearby stoop. He was probably much more of a sick man, even in those days, than some of us realized. Three more blocks remained to be walked, but here I made my farewells and being hopeful that Lovecraft had merely yielded to a passing weak spell, left him with Kirk. There were transit systems within easy reach, and I know they did not walk home.

Rheinhart Kleiner vs. H. P. Lovecraft

To Mary of the Movies

You palpitate upon the screen,
    A shadowy delusion,
And live your crowded hour between
    Beginning and conclusion.
But sometimes I forget that you
    Are just a passing flicker,
And wonder if your eyes are blue
    That make my heart beat quicker!

I've seen you as a haughty dame,
    Aloof, aristocratic;
Or one who turned, when evening came,
    From factory to attic.
I've found that you are just as sweet
    A princess as a peasant—
Whatever ways your little feet
    Traversed to me were pleasant!

Shy maid, may all the winsome grace,
    As pictured on the screen there,
Forever shine upon your face,
    And never frown be seen there!
May every ill that mars the day,
    Or care that looms above you,

Prove fleeting as a phantom play
      At thought of all who love you!

And tho' we'll never meet, I know,
      Yet when you're most beguiling
I wish 'twere you that thrill me so,
      Not just your shadow, smiling.
And still for each remembered time
      Your art had power to cheer me,
I sing to you this little rhyme,
      Tho' you may never hear me!
                 Rheinhart Kleiner

To Charlie of the Comics

(With profuse Apologies to Rheinhart Kleiner, Esq.,
Poet-Laureate and Author of "To Mary of the Movies".)

You trip and tumble o'er the sheet
That holds your life-like image.
You shuffle your prodigious feet
Thro' love-scene, chase, or scrimmage.
As gazing on each comic act
I stare at your perfection,
I find it hard to face the fact
That you're a mere projection.

I've seen you as an artist rare,
With brush and paint-smear'd palette;
I've seen you fan the empty air
With ill-intention'd mallet.
I've watch'd you woo a winsome fay
(You must a dream to her be),
But ne'er have caught you in a play
Without that cane and derby!

Dear lad, I trust your happiness
May be like that you give us,
And since ripe years the mirthful bless,
That you may long outlive us.
May you the smiles of Fortune see,
Nor know what want of cash is;
And may your times of trouble be
As short as your moustaches!

I'd like to meet you, Charles, old chap,
Tho' vast the space dividing;
Yet I must merely sit and clap
At your fantastic gliding.
But tho' you're far away, we know,
You still have pow'r to rouse us:
Your films can pack a picture-show
That's roomy as your trousers!
                    H. P. Lovecraft

To a Movie Star

We see you as you love or hate;
    And dry our tears or hush our laughter,
While trembling at relentless Fate
    That where you go must follow after!

Yet joy and pain seem strangely sweet
    When shown by charm so captivating;
And twenty reels were all too fleet
    In which you moved, our hearts elating!

Now please take care—from yonder cliff
    The "heavy's" very apt to throw you;
We shudder when we wonder if—
    But, ah, the hero's there below you!

And though, perhaps, you love in vain
    Today, and sicken with your sorrow;
We'll dry our eyes; forget our pain;
    And hope for better luck tomorrow!
                    Rheinhart Kleiner

To Mistress Sophia Simple, Queen of the Cinema

Before our sight your mobile face
    Depicts your joys or woes distracting;
We marvel at your winsome grace—
    And wish you'd learn the art of acting!

Your eyes, we vow, surpass the stars;
    Your mouth is like the bow of Cupid;
Your rose-ting'd cheeks no wrinkle mars—
    Yet why are you so sweetly stupid?

The hero views you with delight,
    To win your hand forever working;
We pity him—the witless wight—
    To fall a victim to your smirking!

And yet, why should we wail in rhyme
    Because so crudely you dissemble?
We can't expect, for one small dime,
    To see a Woffington or Kemble!
                    H. P. Lovecraft

Ruth

Oh, it was you, whom I had always held
So cold and weary and so passionless,
Long disillusioned, with all hopes dispelled
That once might please or trouble or distress.

Sweet, very sweet that moment of surprise
With which I glimpsed your spirit's hidden deep,
And came to know that you were not too wise
Nor yet too weary or too worn to weep.
                    Rheinhart Kleiner

Grace

With Unstinted Apologies to the Author of "Ruth"

In the dim light of the unrustled grove,
    Amidst the silence of approaching night,
I saw thee standing, as thro' boughs above
    Filter'd the pencils of the dying light.

Grace! I had thought thou wert by far too proud,
    Too harden'd to the world and all its pain,
To pause so wistfully, with fair head bow'd,
    Forgetting all thy coldness and disdain.

But in that instant all my doubts and fears
    Were swept away as on the evening breeze,
When I beheld thee, not indeed in tears,
    But rack'd and shaken with a mighty *sneeze!*
                    H. P. Lovecraft

John Oldham: 1653–1683

Written after a perusal of his poems, the same having been presented to the writer by a friend.

Neglected Oldham! Who will heed
The rhymes that Dorset lov'd to read?
Moderns, I fear, would call him dunce,
Tho' he was prais'd by Dryden once!
His long-admir'd satiric vein
Seems strangely stupid and inane;
His wit has pall'd; his rhymes are flat;
No two opinions as to that!
But if we seek a fitting cause
For some slight measure of applause,
Be it in this: he made it pay,
In that old Restoration day!

Rheinhart Kleiner

John Oldham: A Defence

Written with every conceivable apology to Rheinhart Kleiner, Esquire.

Whilst modern wits with scorn may rage
O'er honest Oldham's rugged page;
May vow his Muse was weak and pale,
His rhyming harsh, his humour stale;
May censure with a knowing leer
The failings of a pioneer,
And dulness ev'ry bard must own
In Oldham damn, in self condone;
I sometimes think, had he not dy'd,
Old John might shew another side:
For what could not the poet say
Of things these witlings scrawl today?

H. P. Lovecraft

Ethel: Cashier in a Broad Street Buffet

Beautiful and calm and proud,
Only Ethel's soul seems bowed;
Throngs may pass her, kind or curt,
They can neither heal nor hurt;
There she sits with manner strange,
Taking checks and making change!

Eyes are dark, but something fled
Leaves them heavy as the dead;
Brow is white, but something there
Lingers like an old despair;
Lips are sweet, but coldly curled—
Oh, so weary of the world!

Ethel's always dressed in black;
Parting thus may leave its track.
Ethel's always wan and pale;
Pining is not known to fail.
Though a life or love you rue,
Ethel, how I pity you!
                    Rheinhart Kleiner

Cindy: Scrub-Lady in a State Street Skyscraper

Black of face and white of tooth,
Cindy's soul has lost its youth.
Strangely heedless of the crowd,
O'er her mop forever bow'd:
Eyes may roll and lips may grin,
But there's something dead within!

Brow serene—resign'd to Fate—
Some three hundred pounds in weight—
Cindy wields a cynic's broom,
Thinking not of hope or doom.
For the world she cares no more—
She has seen it all before!

Cindy's always dress'd in red,
With a kerchief round her head.
What may blight the damsel so?
Watermelon, work, or woe?
Tho' her days may placid be,
Glad I am, that I'm not she!
                    H. P. Lovecraft

On Collaboration

[Poems written by H. P. Lovecraft.]

1.

When two bright bards in friendly conf'rence sit,
To pool their genius and to join their wit,
Well may the world expect them to indite
A nobler lay than each alone could write;
Yet in their lines th' impartial mind must trace
A double labour, and but half the grace!

2.

In solemn truce behold the twain
    Who seek to draw three diff'rent ways;
Tho' serving sep'rate clubs, 'tis plain,
    We're both *UNITED* in thy praise!

3.

'Tis fitting that when poets meet,
    Their talents they should try;
In friendly odes and songs compete,
    And make the pencil fly.
But now, in spite of all our art,
    No lustrous lines appear;
For, tho' we play the poets' part,
    The Muses are not here!

4.

Two aged bards conferr'd one night,
    To test their letter'd skill;
Each vaunted his Aonian might,
    And felt a poet's thrill.

But when they sought to prove their pow'r,
    Their might they seem'd to miss;
And tho' they labour'd for an hour,
    They fashion'd only—THIS.

5.

Within these walls my fathers pray'd,
    With warm pragmatick zeal,
Tho' I, of coarser fabrick made,
    A lesser flame must feel.

But whilst I scorn a childish creed,
  A true respect I know,
When pond'ring o'er each Christian screed
  Of Kleiner, Cole, and Moe.

6.
The classic East in vain must seek
  (Tho' two exponents join their wits)
In purest melody to speak,
  When KUNTZ in loftiest ether flits.

7.
Whilst thou, McDONALD, with hot modern rage
Contemnst the ling'rers from a Georgian age;
Two tott'ring relics of the ancient time
Forgive thy scorn, and wish thee well in rhyme.

8.
In praise of a superior band
  Two lowly pens industrious join;
Yet tho' we labour long and hard
  We cannot rise to verse like thine!

9.
If unaffected warmth atones
  For want of genius and of art,
Pray take our greetings, blest PINE CONES,
  Penn'd, tho' unskilful, from the heart!

10.
Thrice rev'rend sir, behold in each dull line
The wicked atheist with the Christian join;
KLEI hails thy soul in sanctify'd address,
Whilst pagan THEOBALD greets with warmth no less.

11. *To the Editor of the United Amateur*
As when two sober statesmen meet
  To mould a mighty nation,
See KLEINER and TIBALDUS sit
  In solemn convocation.

Here presidential minds unbend
  To light poetic passion,
And warm congratulations send
  In our poor halting fashion.

12.

Two scribblers of the presidential line
Their humble names in admiration sign,
And hail a brother, chieftain in his day,
Whose wits proclaim him greater far than they!

13.

Behold two bards of lesser fame
    Their bright superior jointly greet,
And in admiring tones proclaim
    The graces of a Muse complete.

14.

Leader, on whom unnumber'd hopes depend,
    Mayst thou the foe with wonted valour quell;
Let ev'ry force the hostile cohorts bend,
    Till we may write at last, here *lies Dowdell.*

15.

SCRIBA, accept the wishes kind
Of scribblers who with eager mind
Are here assembled, to behold
DUNSANY, Lord of Lands Untold!

16.

O wondrous stripling, to rehearse thy praise
Two timid bards their trembling voices raise;
But tho' ev'n Boston lend its Brahmin tone,
Our work must sink inferior to thine own!

17.

Bright bard, accept a hasty line
From two whose gifts are less than thine;
If wanting in the words be aught,
Pray deem it present in the thought.

18.

Madam, behold with startled eyes
A source of wonder and surprise;
Your humble serfs are two of many
Who will this night hear Ld DUNSANY!

19.

Accept, inspir'd and tender bard,
Two dull Dunsanians' joint regard;

Nor scorn the spirit, tho' each line
Fall far below the worst of thine!

20.
Grave Sir, accept in weak uncertain lays
The atheist's and the pious Christian's praise;
Nor think the first, for all his wickedness,
Indiff'rent writes, or venerates thee less!

21.
Behold two bards with eager ear
When great DUNSANY lectures here.
Such art as his no peer can own
Save thine and GALPIN'S art alone!

22.
Great Sage of Athol, lend an ear
To wise DUNSANIANS gather'd here;
Soon shall we list to one whose grace
To CROSSMAN'S only must give place!

23.
Dear Madam, here in thine own cultur'd city
Behold the sessions of a grave committee;
This eve we hear with wondrous delectation
DUNSANY, Monarch of Imagination;
But tho' for prose he wear the laurel wreath,
JORDAN, with matchless verse, falls not beneath!

24.
Out of the vortices of cosmic space,
See KLEI appear with Heliconian grace;
A little while his roving soul remains
To join with THEOBALD in Parnassian strains.
Intent they strive, yet naught can they indite
Meet for AL FRIHDO, Peerless Prince of Light.

25.
The struggling bards, in rhythmic toil combin'd,
Strive to salute thee with composite mind;
Yet their lean verse, tho' from two sources grown,
Shines not so far as that thou mak'st alone!

[Poems written by Lovecraft in collaboration with Kleiner; bracketed lines are Kleiner's.]

1.
Two heads, they say, a paltry one excel;
Hence these smooth couplets should be written well;
[And yet; in vain, one giddy poet strives
To reach the goal at which the first arrives.]

2.
[Hail Poet! From the city by the sea,
    Two fellow-bards by sportive fancy mov'd,]
In friendship send these halting lines to thee,
    Content with dulness, if by thee approv'd.

3.
From Eastern shores their joint esteem
    Two lab'ring rhymesters strive to send;
[And may you relish if the theme
    Sustain you to the bitter end.]

Poems by H. P. Lovecraft Addressed to Rheinhart Kleiner

The Bookstall

An Epistle to Rheinhart Kleiner, Esq., Poet-Laureate

Congenial KLEINER, whose broad brow sustains
The bays that prove the sweetness of thy strains:
To rougher rhymes than thine an audience lend,
And take th' admiring tribute of a friend.
What shall I say? Must I in pain rehearse
The deadly dulness of a modern verse,
Or prate of Whitman, whose Boeotian bawl
Can scarce be justly labell'd verse at all?
Alas! such themes no charms for me afford,
Nor can I scan them happy and unbor'd.
Pox on the rogues that writ these lifeless lays!
My fancy beckons me to nobler days!
Say, waking Muse, where ages best unfold,
And tales of times forgotten most are told;
Where weary pedants, dryer than the dust,

Like some lov'd incense scent their letter'd must;
Where crumbling tomes upon the groaning shelves
Cast their lost centuries about ourselves.
Mine be the pleasure of the grimy stand
Where age-old volumes sleep on ev'ry hand.
Mine be the joy to live in Thought's demesne
The bygone hours of volumes thick and lean;
With Wittie's aid to count the Zodiac host,
Or hunt with Johnson for the Cock-Lane Ghost.
O'er Mather's prosy page, half dreaming, pore,
Or follow Hawkesworth to the distant shore.
Ye old familiar friends whom ages bless,
How oft ye greet me in a diff'rent dress!
Watch shining Maro, who on ev'ry side
Adorns the dingy walls with Roman pride.
Untouch'd or English'd; French or Leipzig made,
The lustrous lines of Virgil pierce the shade.
O Mantuan Lamp! what bard before or since
Can such a wealth of polish'd force evince?
Thus the quick question, but the answer lies
Where yonder rotting Homer meets our eyes.
The blind, the bearded bard before us burns,
And thrills our temples with his tragic turns.
Of Ilion's siege each time as new we hear,
While shrewd Ulysses charms the eager ear.
These share we all, yet what affection twines
About obscurer, less remember'd lines!
Each knows his fav'rites, and in fancy claims
For boon companions those forgotten names.
Would ye read Lucan? Start ye then and go
Where Lucan gains Britannic garb from Rowe.
Full many a Grecian lyrist smiles or grieves
To English tunes thro' Elton's quarto leaves.
Or if our own originals you'd see,
Go smell the drugs in Garth's Dispensary!
What shades scholastic thro' the twilight flit
Where Knapton's sagging folios loosely sit!
The skull-capp'd dealer, crouching on his stool,
O'er the vague past can claim a wizard's rule:
On his seam'd face the myriad wrinkles play,
And subtly link him to the yesterday.
Rise, Stanhope, rise! Thy macaroni train
Dance in the beams that pierce the dusty plain.

Hail! sportive Rochester, bestir thy feet,
And mince in fancy o'er the cobbled street!
House after house appear in gabled rows,
And the dim room Old London's spirit shews!
Upon the floor, in Sol's enfeebled blaze,
The coal-black puss with youthful ardour plays;
Yet what more ancient symbol may we scan
Than puss, the age-long satellite of Man?
Egyptian days a feline worship knew,
And Roman consuls heard the plaintive mew:
The glossy mite can win a scholar's glance,
Whilst sages pause to watch a kitten prance.
Outside the creaking door a nation boils,
And Progress crushes Learning in its coils.
The blessed Past in mad confusion fades,
And Commerce blasts Retirement's quiet shades.
Unnumber'd noises, in demoniac choir,
Wake the curs'd Pit, and stir the seething fire.
A million passengers, in hast'ning heat,
Jostle their fellows, and disturb the street.
From their coarse lips barbaric tones diffuse,
To shock the sense, and affront the Muse.
Decadent day! that Culture must return
To cloister'd cell, and Men, secluded, learn.
O! for the days when I would idly dream
In grassy meads by Seekonk's swelling stream;
When leafy groves adorn'd the rising hill,
And in the copse the feather'd train would trill.
When fragrant zephyrs fann'd the summer green,
And stars, undimm'd, lit winter's snowy scene.
Then flow'd the verse spontaneous from the heart,
That now demands the student's labour'd art.
Then pour'd Creation's blessings on us all,
Which now we strain from books in dingy stall.
Yet let us bless the bookstall whilst it stays;
That, too, may soon be part of other days!

Content

An Epistle to RHEINHART KLEINER, Esq., Poet-Laureate, and
Author of "Another Endless Day".

> Beatus ille qui procul negotiis,
>> Ut prisca gens mortalium,
> Paterna rura bubus exercet suis.
>>> —HORACE.

KLEINER! in whose quick pulses wildly beat
The youth's ambition, and the lyrist's heat,
Whose questing spirit scorns our lowly flights,
And dares the heavens for sublimer heights:
If passion's force will grant an hour's relief,
Attend a calmer song, nor nurse thy grief.
What is true bliss? Must mortals ever yearn
For stars beyond their reach, and vainly burn;
Must suff'ring man, impatient, seek to scale
Forbidden steeps, where sharper pangs prevail?
Alas for him who chafes at soothing ease,
And cries for fever'd joys and pains to please:
They please a moment, but the pleasure flies,
And the rack'd soul, a prey to passion, dies.
Away, false lures! and let my spirit roam
O'er sweet Arcadia, and the rural home;
Let my sad heart with no new sorrow bleed,
But rest content in Morven's mossy mead.
Wild thoughts and vain ambitions circle near,
Whilst I, at peace, the abbey chimings hear.
Loud shakes the surge of Life's unquiet sea,
Yet smooth the stream that laves the rustic lea.
Let others feel the world's destroying thrill,
As 'midst the kine I haunt the verdant hill.
Rise, radiant sun! to light the grassy glades,
Whose charms I view from grateful beechen shades;
O'er spire and peak diffuse th' expanding gleam
That gilds the grove, and sparkles on the stream.
Awake! ye sylphs of Flora's gorgeous train,
To scent the fields, and deck the rising main.
Soar, feather'd flock, and carol o'er the scene,
To cheer the lonely watcher on the green.
Sweet is the song the morning meadow bears,

And with the darkness fade ambitious cares:
Above the abbey tow'r the rays ascend,
As light and peace in matchless beauty blend.
Why should I sigh for realms of toil and stress,
When now I bask in Nature's loveliness?
What thoughts so great, that they must needs expand
Beyond the hills that bound this fragrant land?
These friendly hills my infant vision knew,
And in the shelt'ring vale from birth I grew.
Yon distant spires Ambition's limit shew,
For who, here born, could farther wish to go?
When sky-blest evening soothes the world and me,
Are moon and stars more distant from my lea?
No urban glare my sight of heav'n obscures,
And orbs undimm'd rise o'er the neighb'ring moors.
What priceless boon may spreading Fame impart,
When village dignity hath cheer'd the heart?
The little group that hug the tavern fire
To air their wisdom, and salute their squire,
Far kinder are, than all the courtly throng
That flatter Kings, and shield their faults in song!
And in the end; what if no man adore
My senseless ashes 'neath Westminster's floor?
May not my weary frame, at Life's dim night,
Sleep where my childhood first enjoy'd the light?
Rest were the sweeter in the sacred shade
Of that dear fane where all my fathers pray'd;
Ancestral spirits bless the air around,
And hallow'd mem'ries fill the gentle ground.
So stay, belov'd Content! nor let my soul
In fretful passion seek a farther goal.
Apollo, chasing Daphne, gain'd his prize,
But lo! she turn'd to wood before his eyes!
Our earthly prizes, tho' as hotly sought,
Prove just as fleeting, and decay to naught.
Enduring bliss a man may only find
In virtuous living, and contented mind.

To Mr. Kleiner, on Receiving from Him the Poetical Works of Addison, Gay, and Somerville

Since the cold Muses, heedless of my mood,
Deny me pow'r to sing my gratitude;
These limping lines, in grace and genius slight,
Must feebly hint the warmth I yearn to write!
KLEINER! whose gift, and greeting nobly penn'd,
Reveal the brilliant bard and gen'rous friend;
Whose taste and judgment so acutely find
The very book to suit a Georgian mind;
Condemn me not, if dull thanks I deliver,
Or poring o'er the gift, neglect the giver!
Happy the day that prompted you to dare
The dingy bookstall's subterraneous air;
The shadowy cave, within whose depths are mass'd
The ling'ring relics of a lustrous past:
Where drowse the ancients, free from modern strife,
That crusty pedants fain would wake to life!
As kindly souls an orphan'd waif remove
From publick refuge to paternal love,
So have you now a lonely volume sent
Where, warmly welcom'd, it will find content:
Midst kindred tomes in new importance rest,
With studious care and constant reading blest.
What mem'ries haunt the retrospective brain
That views once more the bright Augustan train!
See peerless ADDISON, whose virtuous quill
Refin'd the town, and purg'd the times of ill.
Whilst clumsy Puritans, with heavy rage,
But injur'd when they meant to help the age,
Our bland SPECTATOR ply'd a lighter art,
And with his humour cleans'd the gen'ral heart.
Vice thrives on preaching; feeds on melancholy—
He who would cure, must laugh it off as folly!
Turn now to Gay, whose sprightly thoughts embrace
A fund of fancy and a world of grace;
In whom simplicity and art, combin'd,
Shap'd the bright virtues of an active mind.
With him we tread the town, or roam the lawn;
Or are with beasts in fabled converse drawn;
At Lincoln's Inn Fields clap his tuneful play
Till Nicolini flings his mask away.

The Dean we fear; the Guardian we approve;
Pope we admire—but simple Gay we love!
Attend, ye rural groves, and hear the praise
Of honest Somerville's Arcadian lays.
Scorn not his theme, nor slight his rustic fires,
But hail the laureate of our country 'squires:
Honour to them, whose deeds our pride provoke;
Who form Britannia's dauntless heart of oak!
Thrice blessed books, whose fav'ring pow'r permits
Our stupid age to scan the ancient wits;
From crystal springs a purer nectar draw,
And led by sages, learn each time-try'd law;
Keep from the past a few remaining gleams
Of Will's and Button's Heliconian beams,
Nor sink too deeply in the quicksand snares
Of modern manners and affected airs!
KLEINER, to your kind thoughtfulness I owe
This bright addition to the genial glow;
This golden guide to pastures rare and new,
Where classick beauties greet the grateful view.
Can I my pen with decent ardour lift
To sing in fitting strains so choice a gift?
Pleasure more keen one thing could bring alone—
A new-imprinted book of *Kleiner's* own!

R. Kleiner, Laureatus, in Heliconem

Blest by Apollo and th' admiring Nine,
On Helicon see tuneful KLEINER shine.
Euterpe close his piping lay attends,
And with his notes her own in concord blends.
Fleet Pegasus th' enchanting music hears,
And beats his pinions, and pricks up his ears;
Whilst the skill'd Erato, with sacred lyre,
Joins in the strain, and feels the noble fire.
Melpomene forgets her dark alarms,
And Polyhymnia lays aside her psalms:
The fair Thalia smiles with brighter grace,
And gay Terpsichore suspends her pace:
Calliope and Clio rest their quills,
As wise Urania at the chorus thrills.
The mighty Phoebus trembles on his throne,
For KLEINER'S chords are sweeter than his own!

To Rheinhart Kleiner, Esq.,
Upon His Town Fables and Elegies

'Tis hard, I vow, that Fashion's crowded pit
Should clap a player for his want of wit,
Yet such we find whene'er our glance surveys
Our modern critics, and the bards they praise.
Zoilus declares no verses to be good
Which by the public can be understood,
Whilst babbling Macer puffs with pomp profound
Him who least shews the world we see around.
Oh, for a tongue to speak in calm defence
Of just perspective and untwisted sense!
Oh, for a hand to fit the laurel bough
On the sane slopes of some well-balanc'd brow!
Oh, for a time when art may have its due
For painting what it sees, unwarp'd and true!
Perchance some future age, with clearer sight,
May dawn to set our addled judgment right;
To melt the clouds, and shed a fav'ring glow
On quills that scintillate, whate'er they shew:
Then may we spy the solid worth that gleams
In easy numbers and familiar themes;
Worth that our biass'd eyes have vainly sought
Beyond the tumid realms of inward thought.
'Tis then, when sense may guide our growing taste,
And prove our depths but emptiness and waste,
That decent wreaths and proper fame shall crown
The bard of wit, and singer of the town.

Your stanzas, KLEINER, shine with flawless grace,
And a light world with fluent lightness trace;
For you no stupid groves, remote and drear,
Without the play's and coffee-house's cheer;
No idle pastures of the languid Muse,
Where not a fop his powder'd course pursues;
Bright as the lamps that gild your well-lov'd streets,
Your verse parades, adorning all it treats!
Who shall contend that rural themes surpass
The talk of towns, and Fashion's bevell'd glass?
What nymph or faun could wake a nobler strain
Than the pert belles and beaux of Drury-Lane;
What sylvan bow'r excite a warmer spark
Than the trim windings of St. James's Park?

And what fam'd castle furnish more delight
Than any theatre we haunt at night?
Yours, then, skill'd KLEINER, to record in song
The godlike pleasures of the polish'd throng;
The little stratagems, shifts, hates, and greeds
In which the buck and idol find their needs;
Ombre and basset, and the puppet-show,
The opera's tinsel, and the tie-wig's snow;
Lap-dog and link-boy, journeyman and jade;
Mob, Mohock, madness, and the masquerade.
What fields are here, where epic pens may range
Round Vauxhall-Gardens, and the New-Exchange!
What more could Homer (but for blindness) ask,
Than yonder party-patch or vizard-masque?
Swords, canes, and buckles; curls and flounces vie
To prompt an Iliad or an Odyssey!
And you, blest bard, have kept in crystal rhyme
These gay memorials of the town and time;
In your brisk line see Chartres rise again,
And with its revels shock the sober train;
See Nash, at Bath and Tunbridge, wield his sway,
And on our careless joys an order lay;
See each smooth trifle—in the cosmic plan
As grave and weighty as the fate of man!
For you have learnt the hollowness of all,
And match an Adam's with a tucker's fall!
Let none maintain, that truer life is found
In some Arcadia's dreary distant ground:
Chaos rules all, and no distinction keeps
Betwixt the place which stirs, and that which sleeps.
'Tis yours to draw that living, flowing Styx
Where chairs and coaches, lords and beggars mix;
Where in one seething, glitt'ring, pois'nous tide
Our mortal vermin wriggle side by side;
Life here prevails, as thro' the surface breaks
That tawdry force, which man's chief nature makes.
KLEINER, we hail you! Laureate of the town;
First of your order, ripe for high renown;
May purer taste increasing honours give,
And crown you Cham whilst yet you write and live.
Your tuneful lines the greater value prove
Of routs in town, o'er vigils in the grove;
And subtly change, with wizard's art divine,
A slough of folly to a sea of wine!

[On Rheinhart Kleiner Being Hit by an Automobile]

Mechanick Force the gentle Poet feels,
And Genius sinks beneath insensate Wheels;
Unfeeling Matter, careless of its Way,
Rides down the Light that sheds PIERIA'S Ray.
But lo! from ev'ry Grove and Fountain run
Consoling Nymphs with healing Orison.
So whilst the dull Destroyer hides in Shame,
The Bard triumphant shines with brighter Flame!

Arthur Harris

The Birth of British Amateur Journalism

There is no doubt that there had been quite a number of attempts to organize amateur journalism in Great Britain ever since 1884 when it is recorded "an effort was made to join the scattered units of amateurdom and fuse them into one harmonious whole" and through this and subsequent attempts proved more or less failures, it is fairly safe to say they lead up to the inception of the British Amateur Press Association which took effect in August, 1891. The honour of being the founder seemed for some little time to be somewhat of a mystery but the late R. D. Bird, who was the first official editor, in 1899 spent considerable time unravelling the tangled skein of which this honour seemed to be entwined and at length clearly demonstrated that the honour of founding it was evenly balanced between two brothers—Robert and James Goss. A pro tem. number of officials were gathered together, the first issue of "The Amateur Journalist" the official organ, was brought out in May, 1891 and with numerous amateur magazines being printed all headed for the most historic first convention of the British Amateur Press Association. This was held in London in August, 1891 and Thomas Adams was there elected its first president. But, however enthusiastic the first year had been, the second year, beginning with the second convention, which was held in Manchester on August 1st, 1892, under the presidency of Fred A. Whitehead, certainly seemed to wane. To combat this it was decided to publish the official organ every month. For three months this was done—September, October and. November, then blank—for, it was discovered this was leading them in heavy debt and the official organ appeared no more during the session. The third year saw the convention again in London being held August 7th, 1893 and Arthur Du Soir was appointed president. The town of Hull captured the fourth convention which was held in August, 1894, and under the presidency of Alfred H. Pearce saw renewed activity and closed with a large-sized official organ.

The fifth convention was held at Manchester in August, 1895 and Alfred H. Pearce was re-elected president. This Edwin Hadley Smith attended as an American associate, and as a result interest in the two countries was beginning to be manifest and exchanges of magazines began to arrive fairly frequent. The sixth convention was held at Blackport in August, 1896 but of this I have no details. Thus I hope I have given some little insight into the early days of the British Amateur Press Association.

Charles Dickens

Of all the novelists Charles Dickens certainly is my favourite, and the place he holds in literature today, though so many years after his death, is a tribute not only to his stories but to the touching messages he has conveyed through them.

Born in Portsmouth under poor circumstances, Dickens felt the keenest feelings of the pathos of childhood at an early age and those scenes left an indelible picture on his mind as is seen in many of his writings for he reverts time after time to scenes of his early days, fitting it to one or another of his characters.

When two years of age, his parents moved to London, and though the city always had a fascination for him, as he grew older he became very fond of Rochester not far away. There was a quaint house at Gad's Hill near that always attracted him right from boyhood days. This, he hoped against hope, that one day would be his—an ambition he was able to realize when he was forty-five years of age, and the love he had for this place went through his whole life.

Leaving school at the age of fifteen, he obtained employment at a solicitor's office, but disliking the drudgery did not remain long in this occupation. He began to study shorthand with a view to becoming a reporter, and so well did he succeed that at the age of eighteen he was employed in that capacity in the Courts of Doctors' Commons.

During this time he became acquainted with Maria Beadwell, but as she was of a respectable banker's family Dickens had no status as a newspaper reporter, and the meetings of these two could only be clandestine ones and though nothing came of the affair, it was, no doubt, this meeting with Maria that lead him, as he told her in one of his letters, "to fight his way out of poverty and obscurity."

At the age of twenty-two he obtained a position on the staff of the *Morning Chronicle* and his start on the ladder of fame began. In the midst of his reporting activities he wrote his first story, "Mr. Minns and His Cousin," which appeared in a paper called the *Monthly Magazine*. After that, these sketches were published regularly during 1834, and when the *Morning Chronicle* started an evening paper in 1835, Dickens was engaged to write similar sketches for that paper also. In 1836, his first volume, "Sketches by Boz," appeared and the name of Dickens became a household word.

By April "The Posthumous Papers of the Pickwick Club" appeared in monthly parts and, success achieved, he married Kate Hogarth, whose father was also engaged on the *Morning Chronicle*. By his twenty-fifth birthday, he had indeed become famous. The Pickwick Papers had been running for nearly a year and almost everyone by now was familiar with the green coloured cover that appeared each month and were more than captivated with the adventures of Pickwick. Then he followed with "Oliver Twist" which, while a contrast to the other, deals mostly with the seamy side of life, yet containing nothing vulgar or repellent—it is certainly a triumph of literary art.

He visited America in 1842 and his reception in Boston was overwhelming. People crowded in and out of the hotel to catch a glimpse of the creator of Pickwick. "If I turn into the street," he wrote, "I am followed by a multitude. If I stay at home the house becomes, with callers, like a fair." He received invitations to visit almost every important city, a tribute due to the cordial and human nature of his genius.

In 1846, Dickens started the *Daily News* of which he was editor, but finding the work uncongenial, a friend of his by the name of John Forster succeeded him after only three weeks.

Not only was Dickens a novelist, but he had a passion for the stage and became quite talented as an amateur actor. He also became a reader of his own works and in this achieved immense success all over England which resulted in financial gain both for charity and himself.

The number of stories he wrote up to 1860 was considerable, for he wrote many shorter ones than those most popularly known. Of them all, my favourite is the "Tale of Two Cities": its passages from the old stage coach at the opening to the supreme sacrifice of Sydney Carton being so well written.

Now he had taken permanent residence at Gad's Hill and at a farewell reading in London hinted that he was starting another novel. This proved to be "The Mystery of Edwin Drood," only six parts of which, however, were published, for within a few weeks of that farewell reading he had himself taken the longest farewell of all, and the mystery was left unsolved, for the pen of its creator was laid aside forever.

Such is the story of Charles Dickens, the man who overcame adversity to be acclaimed the most popular novelist of the century.

James Larkin Pearson

You Jes' as Well Laugh as to Cry

Yes, honey, I know it's a tough old world—
    I've tried it a right smart whet;
Been joggin' along the best I could
    An' I ain't got nowhere yet.
But say! I've studied me out a plan
    That I sorter wish you'd try:
Let in an' smile for a little while—
    You jes' as well laugh as to cry.

Yes, honey, I know how bad it hurts
    To be on the losing side;
To trudge your honest way on foot,
    While thieves and rascals ride.
There's always something to hold you back,
    An' you can't tell hardly why;
But a great long face won't win the race—
    You jes' as well laugh as to cry.

Yes, honey, I know that you an' me,
    If we could have our way,
Would like to reform the human race
    An' hasten a better day.
But jes' because the job's too big,
    An' the victory nowhere nigh,
There ain't no call to sit and bawl—
    You jes' as well laugh as to cry.

Fifty Acres

I've never been to London,
I've never been to Rome;
But on my Fifty Acres
I travel here at home.

The hill that looks upon me
Right here where I was born
Shall be my mighty Jungfrau,
My Alp, my Matterhorn.

A little land of Egypt
My meadow plot shall be,

With pyramids of hay stacks
Along its sheltered lee.

My hundred yards of brooklet
Shall fancy's faith beguile,
And be my Rhine, my Avon,
My Amazon, my Nile.

My humble bed of roses,
My honeysuckle hedge,
Will do for all the gardens
At all the far world's edge.

In June I find the Tropics
Camped all about the place;
Then white December shows me
The Arctic's frozen face.

My wood-lot grows an Arden,
My pond a Caspian Sea;
And so my Fifty Acres
Is all the world to me.

Here on my Fifty Acres
I safe at home remain,
And have my own Bermuda,
My Sicily, my Spain.

Contemplations

Oh, give to me the quiet evening hour,
    When all the lazy village has retired,
And let the silence charm me with its power,
    And let my soul with poetry be fired.

Then through the sacred watches of the night
    With my own swelling thoughts I will commune,
Nor mark the moments in their speedy flight,
    Until the morning breaketh, all too soon.

Men, with their gossip, loafing in the street,
    May beckon me with dirty hands and lips;
But on I hasten to my safe retreat,
    Where, from its fount, the heavenly nectar drips.

And, oh, the richness of a life so spent
　　In silent contemplation soon and late,
Where care is drowned in oceans of content,
　　And sweet dreams at my elbow stand and wait.

So when my nightly musings have an end,
　　And slumber folds me 'neath her dreamy wings,
I, with a million fairies to attend,
　　Shall find the source of all mysterious things.

When Inspiration Fails

If I could write a poem every day,
　　And sell it to a magazine for cash;
If naught of mine were ever turned away,
　　And spoken of as doggerel and trash;

Why, then, I'd court the Muses right along,
　　And never let 'em leave me any more;
My sleep would be a sort of slumber-song;
There'd even be a rhythm in my snore.

Because, in that event, you understand,
　　The thing would pay in dollars and in cents;
I'd have a dozen servants at command,
　　And, oh, the way I'd live would be immense!

But when a fellow has to scoot around
　　And scare up grub to last him over night;
When aged butter's thirty cents a pound,
　　And meat and flour simply out of sight;

Yes, when he has to stand up to the rack
　　And write for daily bread instead of fame;
When all his verses keep a-coming back,
　　And he ain't got a dollar to his name;

Well, say it ain't much wonder that a bard
　　Is sorter slow to get his soul in tune;
For living on the wind is mighty hard,
　　And one would perish at it pretty soon.

The Poetry fer Me

I wish the poets wouldn't write
So much about the nasty fight;
I wish they'd sorter change their style
An' let the war-stuff rest awhile.

I want some poetry 'at's got
The speckled hen 'at laid an' sot,
An' hatched some little biddies out
To run an' foller her about.

The kind o' poetry fer me
Has got to have an apple-tree,
All blossomed out with white an' pink,
With nectar for the bees to drink.

I never could see no excuse
Fer all the poets breakin' loose
An' praisin' war at sich a rate
A thing that all good people hate.

Some cows must wander through the scene,
A-grazin' where the grass is green,
An' they must also stand an' wait
At milkin' time beside the gate.

A poem never is complete
Without some fields o' waving wheat,
Some men at work in overalls,
Some rivers an' some waterfalls.

Put in some blue an' tender sky,
An' then some clouds a-sailin' high,
An' then, to finish up your lines,
Put in a patch of old-field pines.

All sich as that is what it takes
To build the kind o' verse 'at makes
The reader clear his throat an' cry,
An' he can't tell exactly why.

The River and the Sea

Adown the patient stream of Time
    In Life's impatient little boat
Through scenes both awful and sublime
    My lonely spirit is afloat.
And on this river's moving crest
There is no place to stop and rest;
    From empty night to hungry dawn
    I must go on and on and on.

There is no one to take my place
    When I am fainting at the wheel,
To steer the boat along its race,
    And fend the dangers from its keel.
The light that leads me through the dark
Has faded to a tiny spark,
    And just to keep that spark alive
    I have to strive and strive and strive.

But every river has an end,
    And every struggle has to cease,
And somewhere, I shall find a friend,
    And somewhere I shall be at peace.
When I shall reach the broad and free
Still waters of Death's silent sea,
    With folded hands across my breast,
    I then shall rest and rest and rest.

The Lives of Men

The lives of men are little sailing ships
    That sail for ever under unknown skies,
The question of all questions at their lips,
    The wonder of all wonders in their eyes .

The winds of Time are blowing toward the west,
    The sails are set, and every ship must go
Forever onward on its unknown quest—
    Into what storms and terrors none may know.

They cannot turn, as turn the traffic fleets,
    And come again with treasures from afar,
Nor meet out-going vessels as one meets
    Familiar faces at the harbor bar.

Howbeit they are many that embark,
> They shall not be companions on the way;
But each alone shall stumble, through the dark,
And each alone shall hurry through the day.

The lives of men are tragic little flocks
> Of silent little ships that onward wend;
The lonesome lost winds drive them on the rocks,
> And Death receives them at the journey's end.

The Grave-Tree

A row of white and silent stones
> Is very nice to see,
When standing guard above the bones
> Of folks that used to be.

But as I watch them there in line,
> So straight and white and still,
There seems to pass along my spine
> A sort of deadly chill.

The chisel'd words are stiff and cold,
> And sting like Arctic air;
The love that never can be told—
> How could they write it there?

I don't want any stone for me
> When I am lying dead;
I'd rather have a great big Oak
> A-standing at my head.

O white-oak tree with spreading top,
> Wherein the birds may sing;
A tree that bears a brand-new crop
> Of green leaves every spring.

I think that I could somehow sense
> Its shelter o'er my head,
Like some good angel of defense
> At watch above the dead.

A strong, warm-hearted living tree
> Could spread its roots around

And telegraph its love to me
    Beneath the grassy mound.

Just plant me on some sunny slope
    Where such a tree has grown,
And do not fear and do not hope,
    But leave me there alone.

Israel

A song, O Israel, for thee,
    Thou wonder of the ages,
Whose fadeless blood all men may see
    On history's red pages.

Thy destiny was written large
    In God's first dream of nations,
And there He gave His angels charge
    Concerning all thy stations.

From being led of God secure
    Through all the unknown dangers,
Ye listened to ambition's lure,
    And served the gods of strangers.

And then upon thy truant eyes
    There fell an awful blindness,
So that ye failed to recognize
    God's greatest deed of kindness.

Because of Judah's slaughtered Lamb
    Thy highest hopes were shattered,
And thou, the seed of Abraham,
    Through all creation scattered.

Oh, sadder than all tragic tales
    That touch our hearts to pity,
Arose thy never-ending wails
    For thy lost Holy City.

For every land hath been to thee
    Gethsemane's sad garden,
And many a red Golgotha tree
    Hath pleaded for thy pardon.

But now, forgetting all the past,
    Its age-long tragic story,
Thou shalt be gathered home at last
    In all thy former glory.

For Judah's sun is in the east,
    And Israel's dawn is breaking;
The night of wandering has ceased,
    And Zion's hope is waking.

When broke is the oppressor's rod,
    And all thy wrongs adjusted,
Thou wilt not doubt the Living God
    In whom thy fathers trusted.

Thou who hast borne the exile's brand
    Through ages of oppression,
Behold to-day thy Promised Land—
    Thy dearly-bought possession.

Now let thy hand reach out and take
    Thy harp from off the willow;
No more the thorn thy bed shall make,
    No more the stone thy pillow.

But pleasant paths in valleys sweet,
    By Zion's living waters,
Shall bless at last the bleeding feet
    Of Israel's wandering daughters.

Say not thy hopes are burned away
    To silent dying embers;
Lift up thy smiling face and say:
    "God lives, and still remembers!"

The Secret of Attainment

When the clouds are all around you, and you get to feeling blue,
And you come to the conclusion that nobody cares for you,
That's the time that you should rally all the courage that you can
And determine, with God's helping, that you mean to be a man.

Take an interest in living—champion a worthy cause,
And content yourself with little in the way of man's applause.

Then you won't be long a-learning that the riches of reward,
Is the promise of perfection in the Kingdom of the Lord.

Always look upon your failures with an optimistic eye;
If you'll only keep a-going you will get there by and by,
And at last when you are standing on attainment's sunny brow,
You will feel like smiling—smiling at the things that grieve you now.

There has never been a voyage but a little gale has blown,
And there is no path of roses that will lead you to a throne.
So, my worthy friend, believe me, it is much the wiser plan,
Just to pull yourself together and move onward like a man.

Winifred Virginia Jackson

Song of the North Wind

From whence I come or where I dwell
    Is never for you to know,
Be it height of heaven, depth of hell,
    I hold you in my throe;
But before I come men signal me—
    Red rag and rocket flare—
And I send my calm from over sea
    To say I will be there.

Sired was I ere the world was born,
    Old when the world was young,
An alien I from space outworn,
    My shriek the first song sung:
Old was I ere thought was hurl'd
    As fire by whirling pow'rs;
My cold breath iced a molten world
    As play in dead-year'd hours.

When life, a weakling, writh'd in earth,
    I held my chilling breath,
And mountains, rivers, men had birth
    In the breast of unconscious death;
And I gave to earth, from out my side,
    My children, changelings three:
The bacchic blood of my amorous bride
    Flows in them measureless, free.

My beacon light is the setless star,
    I roar in the Arctic track,
My breath, as a cyclone, rages afar,
    I sing,—and mountains crack;
I smile, and the lure is deathless fame
    And the sail of the iron ship;
I frown, and naked is stripp'd its frame,
    And crunch'd in my crushing grip.

I lay in waste the fertile land,
    I strike the flower's heart;
I barren the yield wherever plann'd
    As I blight the bud at start;
I strip the tree of leaf and bough,
    However my fancies stray,
I fling disaster into the Now
    From a thousand miles away.

I lust the sea with hellish roar,
    I storm its portals round,
I strew with wrecks its rock-sunk shore
    From Open to the Sound;
I whirl and rip on the steamer's deck
    Till they hammer the hatches down,
I mock and flaunt ere I taste the wreck—
    Before they sink to drown.

From whence I come or where I dwell
    Is never for you to know,
Be it height of heaven, depth of hell,
    I hold you in my throe;
But before I come men signal me—
    Red rag and rocket flare—
And I send my calm from over sea
    To say I will be there.

Galileo and Swammerdam

One look'd into celestial light,
Saw moon and stars in th' infinite;
    Their beauty stirr'd his heart.
The telescope came to his eyes,
And harmonies, set in the skies,
    Became of life a part.

The other lov'd the creeping things,
The atoms small, the world of wings,
    The puny stir of breath.
The microscope show'd earth at war;
Devouring Nature's doling law;
    And his love brought him death.

April

    Winter's sway
    Pass'd away
'Neath a blue sky's leaven;
    In its place
    Out of space
Dropp'd a golden heaven!

    Soft and low,
    Sweet and slow,
Singing in the hollow;
    Sun and rain
    Back again,
Blithesome blooms a-follow!

    Robins preen
    'Mid the green
Draping Nature's altar;
    In the mead
    Happy reed
Lifts from dream-bound psalter.

    Hopes and fears,
    Smiles and tears,
In each gleam or shower;
    Laugh and weep,
    Sow and reap,
April's in her bower!

In Morven's Mead

In Morven's Mead I heard a cry
And sound of glad wings passing by;

And searching softly o'er the ground,
A smiling, star-fac'd flower found!

The Night Wind Bared My Heart

The Night Wind bared my heart;
I felt the old, keen smart
Of grief: cold Mem'ry's eyes
Her subtle misery plies
      With art!

The Day Wind heal'd the smart
That fasten'd on my heart;
But, Oh, from grief was prest
The joys that from my breast
      Depart!

Insomnia

The Thing, am I, that rides the Night,
    That clips the wings of Sleep;
The Thing, am I, in sunshine bright
    That goads, with hag-mind, deep;
The Thing, am I, with forked knife
    That prods the weary brain,
And snarls when Pleasure strives for life
    Within my haunts of Pain.

I laugh: Ha! Ha! Ho! Ho! Hoo! Hoo!
    When all the house is still;
I quaff: Ha! Ha! Ho! Ho! Hoo! Hoo!
    When ghost-sheep run up hill!
My slaves count hundreds—fives and tens,
    Till shadows stab their eyes!
They jump ten thousand sheep in pens
    Until their counting lies!

Their music is a fun'ral march;
    They see the wreath'd flow'rs fair;
They see their robes, as white as starch,
    They feel the Eyes that stare.
They tramp the path of Fear and Flame
    That narrows to four walls,
With minds red-hot with Curse and Shame,
    Above the Pray'r that falls.

And then, I stage anew the trick
    That brought me hell-curs'd gold;
I spread the reek of hunger thick
    Upon a white-fac'd fold!
And Mem'ry, loath to serve my ends,
    I heckle at the throat,
Till she her Province far extends
    Beyond her hate-black moat.

And then—my Slaves will laugh, "Ha! Ha!"
    And count sheep white and grey,
And moan in numbers mumblings mar,
    Through night, through dawn, through day;
While lips that quiver pray for rest,
    And dear hearts crucify,
Till those that dare, 'neath Pity's breast,
    In frenzy beg to die!

THE THING, AM I, THAT RIDES THE NIGHT,
    THAT CLIPS THE WINGS OF SLEEP;
THE THING, AM I, IN SUNSHINE BRIGHT
    THAT GOADS, WITH HAG-MIND DEEP;
THE THING, AM I, WITH FORKED KNIFE
    THAT PRODS THE WEARY BRAIN,
AND SNARLS WHEN PLEASURE STRIVES FOR LIFE
    WITHIN MY HAUNTS OF PAIN.

The Pool

Above my head a leaf-lock'd sky,
    A brown bowl set beneath my feet;
About my face pale ferns grow high,
    And over all is silence sweet.

But Oh! sometimes in dreams I hear
    A whisper, then a torrent's roar;
The shriek of wind, the belch of fear,
    That I have known somewhere before!

The Vagrant

A Wind walk'd in the West
    At edge of night,
While from a white star's crest
    It elbow'd light.

It to a garden sprang
    And gaily blew
Warm kisses, while it sang
    And filch'd the dew.

It tapp'd, with pretty blow,
    On nest-noos'd tree,
Then rapp'd, first swift, then slow
    And tenderly.

It leapt to black-brow'd hill;
    Tweak'd glow-worm's ear,
So damp and small and chill,
    With elfin leer!

It rac'd, on dancing feet,
    Into a dell
Where dreams creep in to meet
    And cast their spell;

And there, with merry cry
    And noisy shout,
It fleck'd them hasting by
    And chas'd them out!

Then on and on, with turn
    And lisping trill,
It came to golden fern
    Beside a rill.

It whisper'd low and long,
    On toes a-sway,
Then burst into a song
    And sped away.

And fast and far it went,
    For when the Dawn
Her soft-shod graylings sent—
    The Wind had gone!

On Shore

The trees are wailing,
And grim night—a grayling—
Swoops hawk-like down on
    The gale-gall'd day.

The sea, 'neath thunder
And wolf-winds' plunder,
On wreck-wound shore whacks
    The writhing spray.

And Oh, my soul's nearest,
My heart's own dearest,
Is out there tonight in
    A water-logg'd shell!

I can but be praying,
'Neath wind and sea's flaying,
And shut from my ears
    The Pollock's Rip bell!

April Shadows

I shall hide from April shadows;
    I shall lightly tread the grass;
I shall leave no sign behind me
    To betray where I must pass!

For my Love waits in the Junetime,
    Beautiful and sweet to see;
Only sunshine shall enfold her,
    Only joy her portion be!

Who Will Fare With Me?

Oh, who will fare afar with me?
    Oh, who will fare with me?
We'll tread the green and happy land,
    We'll sail the salt blue sea!
And east and west and north and south
    We'll take the trail away,
And always with Tomorrow hold
    The joys of Yesterday!

We'll take the Trail of Dreamers out
　　Across the leagues of dew;
We'll pass where grand green willows lean
　　In bonnets silv'ry blue.
We'll play with young white violets
　　In velvet pinafores,
Just taken, sweetly scented, from
　　A May-elf's woodland drawers.

We'll take the Trail of Dreamers, that
　　Is gay with bloom begun;
And as we're faring onward we
　　Will sail a sea of sun;
We'll find our way to shaded wood
　　Where pools lie, still and deep,
And tease from them the secrets that
　　We know they cannot keep.

We'll take the Trail of Dreamers to
　　The minstrel folk of dream;
We'll beg their charm that we may hear
　　The fairy singing stream;
We'll hear the jolly river wind
　　Sing songs it learn'd at sea,
A-rollicking with fantasies
　　As sweet as sweet can be.

We'll take the Trail of Dreamers on
　　An hour that's all our own,
When hope's glad thrilling kisses are
　　Upon the skyways blown;
And love will fare on with us, and
　　Will shield from stress and strife,
And grant the gift of happiness
　　To bless us into life!

Oh, who will fare afar with me?
　　Oh, who will fare with me?
We'll tread the green and happy land,
　　We'll sail the salt blue sea!
And east and west and north and south
　　Well take the trail away,
And always will Tomorrow hold
　　The joys of Yesterday!

The Cobbler in the Moon

I

Cobbler, cease your stitching!
   Put down your awl!
I've long been waiting
   Before your stall.

Cobbler, cease your pegging!
   Who pays your wage?
And whose the ugly,
   Dry shoes of Age?

I have shoes for mending;
   A patch or two
Will make them nearly
   As good as new.

Mine too worn for patching?
   It cannot be
The shoes just finished
   Were made for me?

II

Time went dancing down the road
   Yesterday;
It was sweet to watch Time dance
   On her way.

Not one sigh was in my heart!
   How could I
Know that when to-morrow came
   I should cry?

III

Joy came winging down to me,
   A brown, song-throated bird,
But on a honeyed tree's dark branch
   A scarlet note was heard.

Joy was singing, soft and low,
   A tender little lay,
But, oh, my ears were deafened by
   The scarlet note that day!

IV

Once I cried a little cry,
　　Nor wiped the tears away;
And bitter was the taste of them
　　The long, long day.

Oh, but that was long ago!
　　To-day I sit apart
And smile and watch young laughter run
　　About my heart!

V

I cannot bear to hear the grasses sing!
　　Their tiny fingers press the notes of grief
Where apple blossoms pinkly sway and swing
　　And nod to each uncurling, greening leaf.

I cannot bear to hear the grasses sing!
　　Nor watch them tiptoe on the sun-sweet ground,
For, oh, I know how their small hands will cling
　　Upon the earth that is my body's mound!

VI

If I am quiet, when the twilight comes,
　　My dead love I will see;
Like breathless whisper in a lilac bloom
　　My love will come to me.

If I am quiet, all the lapis night,
　　My love will be my guest;
But, oh, that she may never touch my hand
　　Nor lean against my breast!

VII

My feet are shod in golden shoes,
　　That glimmer in the sun,
With lacings made of sweet delight
　　And laughter's fun.

The soles so studded are with nails
　　That press up, prick and pry,
I can but sit still in a chair
　　And softly cry!

Finality

The farm was lonely, set so far
    Back from the town;
If neighbors came, he'd rant and rave
    If they sat down.

And when they went he forced upon
    Her hateful thought,
And nagged; made ugly use of words
    With meaning fraught.

Her back was bent with work she'd done
    Beyond her strength;
For he planned more than she could do
    In each day's length.

The days seemed all alike to her
    Until, one day,
She found a blue bird, maimed in wing,
    So bright and gay.

She loved it, cared for it, and soon
    The bird loved her;
When he came, she would hide it and
    It would not stir.

One noon he came and caught her with
    The bird in play;
He killed it right before her in
    A fearful way.

A neighbor came, to ask about
    A plough, that night;
He never could forget that strange
    And awful sight.

She'd used the kitchen knife on him
    And he was dead;
She sat, a bruised and battered thing
    From feet to head,

And hummed a little song, or spoke
    A tender word,
*An*d *tried to make blue feathers stay*
    Upon a bird!

The Tricksy Tune

The Hired Man Speaks:

"He never spoke a civil word
 To her; it was his rule
To snarl or shout; his best for her
 Was 'Mooncalf, dolt an' fool!'"

The Story:

The house was built back from the Road;
 It stood there grim and gray
And silent, 'mid great aspen trees
 That quivered night and day.

The Road was narrow; old stone walls
 Arose on either side
Begrudging from the farm the land
 The roadbed had to gride.

And she had lived with him and drudged
 For over twenty years;
He drove her on, from harrowing
 To breaking in the steers.

At first when she was called a fool,
 A hurt look dulled her eyes,
And she would slip off by herself
 And have her little cries.

But once he caught her; after that
 She never dared to cry;
The days seemed all alike to her
 That wearily went by.

And often, when he snarled and cursed,
 She played a little game;
She tried to make believe that he
 Had called her some sweet name.

Then one day came a tricksy tune
 That hummed within her head;
In spite of all that she could do
 It held the words be said.

She heard the song and shuddered at
    Its "Fool, dolt, fool, dolt, fool!"
The while she gripped her hard, worn hands
    And drabber looked and cool.

And this kept up for weeks; she worked
    With hope to still the song
By weariness; it sometimes went away
    But would not stay for long.

When evening came, he sat about
    The kitchen while she rid
The sink of dishes, nagging her
    Through everything she did.

And then he'd go to sleep and snore,
    Sprawled in the rocking chair;
The light shone on his long, gray beard
    And bristling, grizzly hair.

And so he lolled; she mended, darned,
    The while she scarce could see;
The song beat time within her head
    That ached unceasingly.

A day came harder than the rest;
    He snarled at her and raved,
And of the nagging words he knew
    There was no word he saved.

And night came with the supper; wash
    Of dishes in the sink;
And afterwards his snores; her song;
    She ceased to try to think.

The Hired Man Speaks:

"I found him crooked upon the floor;
    The ax was sharp, for he
Had sharpened it that day an' whet
    It sharp as it could be.

She didn't notice me; she sat
    As white's a sheet, but cool,
An' hummed a song: the words wan't much,
    Jest, 'Mooncalf, dolt an' fool!'"

Eyes

When life is very lonely
    I close my eyes and go
Across a field and up a hill,
    A way I know;

And there I find a garden
    With a little house in it,
And both are wistful whispering,
    "Come in and sit!"

Then you come, always singing,
    On down the garden's walk,
And we, in white front doorway, stand
    And softly talk.

I often light a candle,
    In my small sitting-room,
To show you some new picture or
    A bit of bloom.

And all our time together
    You love as much as I:
But, oh, my open eyes that watch
    You passing by!

Deafness

Wall-mountain rimmed around the sky
    And bellied down, a bowl
With chipped and crackled edge; the farm
    Dropped in like leaf-lopped cole.

Scrub trees crouched low on mountainside,
    Their fingers locked and bared
Upon black rocks; at base great spruce
    Stood close and leaned and stared.

The house, with up-curled shingles, hugged
    The ground, a silent thing,
Like a gray bird squatting on its perch
    In a cage, and cannot sing.

When she went up to bake for him,
    To tend the house and such,
His deafness was a sorry chafe
    She pitied overmuch.

A day came when he ceased to speak;
    She did not care, for he
Was far more ugly in his speech
    Than there was need to be.

But when the long days dragged on by
    Without a word from him,
The crumbs of peace fell from her mind
    As leaves drop from a limb.

At first she zigzagged in her mind
    'Twixt old Hen Levy's Place
And his: she knew Four Corners brooked
    No showing of her face.

And then she planned shrill words to shriek
    To stab his deafness through;
And he would watch, with cunning eye,
    Her stirred mind's boil and brew.

Then slyly he would egg her on:
    He'd cup his ear with hand,
The while her throat rasped hoarse with words
    She hoped he's [*sic*] understand.

In summer loneliness was lulled
    By birds that came to sing;
An old black creaker, by the door,
    Was always a friendly thing.

Slim poplars grew close to the barn
    And whispered all day long;
The Plymouth Rocks scratched in their shade
    And cackled or made song.

But in the winter when the jays
    Sat shrieking, limb to limb,
It seemed somehow that he must hear;—
    That she *must* talk with him.

And when a lone, lean crow would light
    Upon a fire-stubbed pine,

It seemed a black thought from her heart,
    That blurred her brain like wine.

One day a storm drove down; the wind
    Banked snow in drifts on farm,
Encircling, with one deep drift,
    The house like a gripping arm.

She shoveled a path from house to barn;
    The cattle must be fed:
He let them go a day and night—
    At her plea shook his head.

The crow came to the barn that night;
    She took care of the cat;
The crow, on top-loft ladder's round,
    In brooding silence sat.

When Sunday came the storm had cleared.
    Some city folks snow-shoed
Through Toby's Gap to Brimmer's Place,
    And one of them, a dude,

Was cold, and knocked upon the door;
    When no one answered, he
Just turned the knob and went on in—
    To see what he could see.

Old Aaron sat, bound in a chair;
    His face was snarled with fear;
His hair cut off'n him quite close;
    His throat cut, ear to ear.

She sat in a rocker, muttering,
    A-waggling of her head;
But when she saw the dude, she rose:—
    "He heard! He spoke!" she said.

Hoofin' It

Pork an'
Beans an'
    Apple pie!
Doughnuts,
Swagen,

> *By Gor-ri!*
> *We'll hit*
> *Great Pond*
> *By an' by!*

I am but a river hog,
  River hog, river hog!
I am but a river hog
  Hoofin' it to Great Pond!

Ellsworth is a meachin' town,
  Sick 'em town, lick'em town,
Ellsworth is a meachin' town,
  Ring-a-round-a-rosy!

Ellsworth has a pretty pound,
  Pretty pound, pretty pound,
Ellsworth has a pretty pound—
  Pin on me a posy!

Waltham has no use for us,
  Use for us, use for us;
Waltham has no use for us
  When our heads are groggy!

They wun't give us feather beds,
  Feather beds, feather beds;
They wun't give us feather beds—
  No, we bunk with hoggy!

K-J he don't give a damn,
  Give a damn, give a damn;
K-J he don't give a damn
  If in hell we're seated!

Great Pond's miles an' miles away,
  Miles away, miles away;
Great Pond's miles an' miles away
  But the soup is heated!

K-J's waitin' there for us,
  There for us, there for us;
K-J's waitin' there for us—
  He's a damn good-fellow!

K-J makes us pick our shirts,
    Pick our shirts, pick our shirts,
K-J makes us pick our shirts—
    Makes us work O hell-o!

I am but a river hog,
    River hog, river hog,
I am but a river hog
    Hoofin' it to Great Pond!

      Pork an'
      Beans an'
         Apple pie!
      Doughnuts,
      Swagen,
         By Gor-ri!
      We'll hit
      Great Pond
         By an' by!

The Purchase

Once, on a gold May morning,
    As I walked through a town,
I met a Merchant crying,
    "One white, one purple gown!"

He stopped me, swift demanding,
    "Which will you have of me?
This white—is yours for nothing!
    This purple—thalers three!"

"I'll take from you, Old Merchant,
    The gown for which I pay!"
I gayly donned the garment
    And went my careless way!

The skies grew dark and darker;
    A fog brought mystery;
Beside me stalked black shadows
    That pecked the heart of me!

I sought the wary Merchant;
    He gave me but one look:

"Hope's robe was yours for nothing!
    Despair's was what you took!"

Have You Met My Buddy?

(DEDICATED TO PRIVATE NORMAN MACPHEE)

Have you met my Buddy? Good old grub-stake Buddy?
He's the man to keep the boche from getting gay!
He's a Yankee Doodle Dandy, and with guns is mighty handy;
He can whip his weight in wild-cats any day!

> Buddy, Buddy, Buddy,
> He's my rough and ready Buddy!
> He's the man to finish what he has to do.
> He will send K. Bill to hell,
> And he'll do the job up well,
> And, I say, old pup-tent Buddy—here's to YOU!

Have you met my Buddy? Good old husky Buddy!
Gee! the way that he can fight is sure a sin!
He's a white man hale and hearty, and he's joined up with the party
That is set to can the Kaiser in Berlin!

CHORUS

That I Might Be in the Cool Blue Wind

O, dear my dear, that I might be
    The soft gray mists, at twilight free,
Then I would run across the land
    To clasp your hand!
Oh, dear my dear, that I might be
    The cool blue wind, sweet-swept from sea,
That I might whisper, Sweet, to you
    My love so true!
Oh, dear my dear, that I might be
    The starbeams from immensity,
That I might place before your feet,
    My heart, my Sweet!

Winifred Virginia Jackson

Arthur Leeds

The Man Who Shunned the Light

I recognized Langhorne's handwriting the moment I glanced at the envelope; and to say that I was surprised at hearing from him, after so long a silence, was putting it mildly. But my astonishment and curiosity were tripled at the message which the envelope contained.

"Do not be alarmed, my dear Marden," it read, "at the contents of this letter, my first to you in so long a time. But above all, I beg of you, if ever friendship bound us together, do not fail in doing just what I am about to ask of you. If you do this for me you will see me once more; but you will never talk with me again. Yet, I have another and a very important message for you. There is something that you, if not the whole world, should know, and which will be communicated to you when next you see me. I have been living for the past two years and a half at number 108 West 57th Street—the old Partington residence—and for the past six or seven months I have been entirely alone. Now, Marden, I want you to come to me at this address, any time this afternoon after two o'clock. The experiment upon which I am now engaged will have been fully completed by that time; and I do not wish to have anyone—not even you—disturb me before I have quite finished. You will find the front door unlocked. Admit yourself, and come straight into my workroom, the door of which faces the front entrance. Do not fail me, old friend; there is much that you should learn concerning me and my work."

In spite of Langhorne's admonition not to be alarmed, there were two things in his note which puzzled and even startled me considerably. What did he mean by saying that if I complied with his wishes I might see him *once* more? And above all, what did he mean by saying that though I should *see* him again, I might never *talk* with him thereafter? Surely my old friend had not, in some strange way, been stricken dumb? Yet, what else could prevent him from conversing with me?

It was then eleven in the forenoon, and I spent the best part of the time until two o'clock making wild guesses as to what Langhorne could possibly mean, and what it was that he so earnestly desired to communicate to me. The taxicab which I engaged took me to the address mentioned in the note in less than half-an-hour; and as I dismissed the driver and mounted the steps, I remembered thinking that, in this great city of New York, a man might very easily become as far removed from his former associates, if he so desired, as if he were to journey to St. Petersburg or Yokohama.

As I opened the door and stepped into the hallway, I noticed that the accumulated dust of many months covered everything. I suppose I am somewhat of a crank on that subject, for on discovering nothing anywhere that resembled a hat-rack or hall-tree, I continued to hold my hat in my hand in preference to laying it on the heavily coated chair standing against the wall on my left. It did not need my old friend's letter to convince me that he had been living alone for a long time. And what in the name of common sense was the man doing with the whole house—as it seemed to me, if one could judge by the heaviness of the air—sealed up on a stifling August afternoon? The place was as musty and close-smelling as a department store on a Monday morning; I held the street-door open for a moment or two, allowing the bright sunlight and what little breeze was stirring to enter, before I advanced farther into the hall.

At the end of this hallway, and facing the front entrance, was another door covered with a heavy damask curtain. I closed the street-door quietly, and advancing toward the rear door, laid my hand on the knob. I cannot explain what it was that made me hesitate to turn it. I can only compare the sensation to that which one experiences when, having laid a hand on one side of an electric knife-switch, he hesitates to complete the circuit by touching the other side, not knowing the severity of the shock which he may receive.

A moment's pause, and then the curiosity to know all that my old friend's letter had meant, urged me on. I swung open the door and advanced into the room.

The stuffiness of the hallway was nothing compared with the odorsome closeness of this apartment. I glanced about, wondering if it were possible that the room was without a window. As my eyes turned to the left, however, I saw that a window was there; but it, like the door by which I had entered, was heavily curtained. Observing this, I seemed to become conscious, for the first time, of the fact that the room was lighted solely by the electrolier that blazed down from the center of the ceiling—at half past two on a bright autumn afternoon! If Langhorne had recently been at work or reading in this room, why did he choose the electric light instead of the illumination provided by nature?

The intense curiosity, mingled with a vague alarm, that had filled my mind since reading his note, was growing momentarily greater. Where was he now? Why was he not here to receive me?

A second glance around the room showed me almost exactly what I had expected to find there. In the corner to the right of the curtained window, stood a roll-top desk, before which was placed a three-fold, tapestry-covered screen, in such a way as to hide the greater part of the desk from my view. Shelves, reaching to the ceiling, lined that side of the room opposite the window; these were partly filled with books, portfolios and scientific magazines.

There were, however, several things in the room from which I deduced the fact that Langhorne had been living, practically, in this one large apartment, for some time, at least. In one corner stood a rather short Davenport-bed. Not far from it, and connected by a rubber tube with an iron pipe rising a few inches from the floor, was a small gas-stove standing on a little table. It was evident that Langhorne had not only been sleeping in this room of late, but had also prepared his own meals there. I remembered having noticed a first-class restaurant only a block down the street, and my surprise increased accordingly. My friend's epicurean tastes in the past had more than once caused me to warn him against dire results of eating and drinking too well.

Everywhere about were distributed the tools, so to speak, of his trade—a professor of chemistry. Langhorne, wild as he had been in his student days, was always an enthusiast, loving his work as a part of himself. His lapses into dissipation served only to emphasize more strongly the true nature of the man—his determination, his originality of thought and ideas, his firmness in the face of argument, even of ridicule, when he put forward a theory too startlingly original to be passed over in mere controversy, and his absolute devotion to his life work.

I was aware of the fact that up to the time when I had completely lost track of him, about three years before, he had contributed regularly to various medical and scientific journals; of late, however, I had not seen his name mentioned in any of the reviews, nor, so far as I was aware, had any of his articles been published. But I knew Langhorne was the kind of a man who, having his work to carry on, could readily adapt himself to any part of the world; and for some time it had been my belief that he had gone abroad, without advising any of his old friends, and was now, probably, conducting his experiments and researches in one of the European capitals.

It suddenly occurred to me that the professor might have stepped out to make a purchase at one of the nearby stores; that that was his reason for telling me in his note to admit myself upon my arrival. Concluding that this must be the case, I prepared to sit down and await his return. No chair was to be seen, however; the only seat was the Davenport in the corner. But a glance in the direction of the screen caused me to conclude that there would naturally be an office-chair before the desk which, as I have said, the screen almost hid from view.

Advancing, I took hold of it by both sides and drew the folds together, preparatory to putting it to one side. As it closed up, it almost fell from my hands as I stepped back in startled bewilderment.

A chair was there, as I had expected. But in it sat Randall Langhorne, head and shoulders bent over the desk, his face the color of the cigar ash that lay on a little tray at his side. The left arm hung straight down over the side of the chair; the hand was tightly clenched. His right arm was sprawling across the desk, and the hand, which gripped a graduate-glass, was resting against the drawers at the back. There still remained on the inside of the glass perhaps a teaspoonful of dark, purplish liquid, and the fingers which grasped it, as well as the white blotter beneath, were stained a deep brown, recalling the discoloration left by a solution of potassium permanganate.

After the first shock, I had involuntarily reached out to grasp Langhorne's shoulder. But even as I did so, I paused and drew back my arm.

His face was turned to the right; his eyes, wide open, seemed fixed with staring fascination at the glass in his hand. And in the corner, close to the hand, an envelope stood upright against the drawer. On it I read the one word—"Marden." In front of this, flat on the desk, lay a sheet of typewriter bond paper, upon which, in large letters, had been written the startling request:

"Do not touch me, Marden! Do not lay a finger upon me until you have read this letter!"

In spite of myself, I shuddered as I read the admonition. There was something terrifying, some sinister suggestion in the words. Not that it was necessary to touch the man to tell that he was dead. The ashen face, the wide, staring eyes, the blackened lips, stained with the same brown color which disfigured the hand—from all these signs I judged that at least an hour must have passed since life had fled from this pitiable heap before me. It was the note that I dreaded; some unknown horror seemed to be lurking in its message. In spite of myself, I felt that I would give almost anything if I could only avoid opening it at all.

But Langhorne's last wish, his dying request, in fact, had been that I read this message and share his secret, whatever it was, with him. With a trembling hand I picked up the envelope and tore it open, and read:

"My dear old friend, in this, my last hour, I can turn only to you. Not for pity, though, Marden; pity and sympathy are not for such as I. I seek only your assistance in what will be my final experiment. I have met with considerable success in the past, as you know. I have proved my theories correct, as a rule; only once or twice have my experiments failed. My heartfelt prayer to God, now is, that this last test of my knowledge will be successful also. First, however, I must tell you my miserable story.

"You will remember the night when, just after you had returned from the Pacific coast, we met at the bar of the Cadillac. Kenyon was with me when you came in, and so was young Ludlow—the fellow some of the boys used to call 'the Lucios diamond kid.' You will remember, also, that while you were with us, Ludlow behaved himself extremely well—for Ludlow.

"About ten o'clock, you left us, saying that you were going home. After you had gone, we drifted over to Churchill's; and it was shortly after one o'clock when Ludlow and I (Kenyon went off about midnight) were requested to leave the back room of a saloon in the neighborhood of Columbus Circle. I can remember passing the monument as we started home. I hadn't told you where I was living, Marden—in fact, I hadn't told anyone. Knowing me as you did in the old days, you know why. When I worked, I worked with all there was in me to labor with. I didn't want to be disturbed; I didn't want to be tempted away when my work called me. I knew my weakness; so I cut myself off from everyone. I met you three fellows that night by the merest chance.

"But it was the devil in the form of Ludlow who walked with me that night, Marden. As we staggered along, he kept up a running fire of sneering remarks. First I was a 'would-be-famous scientist.' Then I was 'the greatest bluff that ever graduated.' Finally he declared that I was a 'hermit, a recluse merely for the sake of being called eccentric, but clever.'

"The liquor, I suppose, must have made me good-natured, rather than otherwise, for I simply laughed at his insults; and we went on together. Then, two blocks away from here, I said good-night and tried to leave him; but it was of no avail. Again and again, he asked me to take him to where I was living. At last he dared me to take him home with me. Mad, drunken fool that I must have been, I did.

"What followed, I must write down quickly. Even now my hand trembles, and I need all my strength for what is to come.

"Ludlow threw himself into this very chair where I now sit, one leg over the arm, swinging himself in a half-circle. At once he recommenced his drunken abuses, and I, as before, laughed at him. Suddenly, he took from his pocket a flask of brandy—I had no idea that he had any liquor upon him—and, after swallowing nearly half of it, he tossed it over to me. With drunken recklessness, I drained the flask; and just then Ludlow swung around and faced the desk.

"Marden, you remember the woman in my case? The *one* woman? I know you do; so I won't disgrace her fair name by putting it into this horrible confession. But *her* photograph was there, on top of the desk; and as Ludlow saw it he snatched it down. With a laugh that seemed to me like the cry of a beast, he swung around and faced me again.

"I won't—I could not repeat his words, old friend; they were unuttera-bly vile. And he meant *that* of *her,* Marden, the woman upon whose grave, every Sunday since God took her from me, I had placed the white roses. I heard only his first sentence or two; from that moment, as God is soon to judge me, I forgot what really happened. I can dimly remember that Ludlow, very suddenly, became silent. Then, like one under the influence of an anes-thetic, I lost consciousness of everything.

"And, now, Marden, the end, but briefly. It must have been the morning sun, falling across my face as it entered this window which you see now darkly curtained, which at last awakened me. The moment I sat up I saw Ludlow; and in that moment I knew that he was dead. Then, in a flash, all came back to me, dimly—all, that is, up to the time he spoke those words. Weakly, I got up and went to him. As I leaned over the body, I saw, with horror, the deep cut in his left temple, and then the empty flask lying on the rug at his feet. That flask had been in my hand as he started to speak of her—the last words he had ever spoken! But he had driven me to it—he, the beast, the loose-tongued idler! Then the greatest horror of all came home to me. No one had seen Ludlow entering the house with me. I could easily tell Kenyon that he had left me and started for his home. I could just as easily dispose of Ludlow's body—which, Marden, I finally did—in such a way that it would never be found. But could I, could I ever again be happy, care-free, unhampered by the guilty chain that I had bound myself with on that accurs-ed night of folly and dissipation? Would not the accusing sunlight, God's sunlight, which now flooded the room, forever cry out and mock me? Would I not hear forever in my ears the words, 'At the setting of one sun you were an innocent man. Life was yours to make what you would of; Fame was yours to win; Honor was yours, and Happiness—the memory of Love, sweeter, often, than the realization, belonged to you. But the night came in between; and at the rising of another sun you were a murderer, a useless thing, an outcast until life shall be over for you. Only then will come peace!'

"Marden, from that day to this, I have never seen the light—God's light. I could not; the horror of the past would only have been intensified. Up to about six months ago, I kept one servant, a combined valet and assistant. He was a good fellow and faithful, but I let him go. Since then I have been quite alone. The telephone brought to me all that I required; but everything was left in the hallway; I never saw the front door open. I have contributed to the scientific journals frequently—you may have read something by 'Franklin Mathison.'

"But, now, Marden, it must end. 'Only then will come peace!' Now, I ask your aid—it will be easily given. For two months I have been working continuously on something which, had I lived an innocent man, might have brought me fame. Years ago, I conceived the idea of a liquid which, when in-jected into a dead body as we now inject embalming fluid, would have a di-rectly opposite effect to that produced by the latter preparation. In other words, instead of preserving the body, it would destroy it utterly, bone and tissue alike. My theory was that the liquid would be entirely absorbed by every portion of the body, so that, having finished its subtle work of destruction, it would leave the corpse literally a mass of clay in the form of a man or woman—clay that could be almost instantly converted into an unrecognizable heap of dust. The idea was originally suggested by the remarks of a cousin of mine, who had a horror of being buried alive, and who, nevertheless, dreaded the idea of cremation. Again, I thought would not this be the easiest and most practical way of disposing of the bodies of executed criminals? There would also be a dozen different uses to which it could be successfully put in surgical work of different kinds.

"Well, old friend, I have at last completed my work. I believe I have succeeded; but it will be for you to prove that. The failure or success of this, my last experiment, will never be known to me. But, I pray, you know not, Marden, how earnestly I pray, that it may be as I have hoped.

"By the addition of one other ingredient I have prepared a special fluid which, when I drink it, as I shall do after signing this, will, I believe produce in my body the changes of which I have spoken. Thus will I efface myself from the world of men—and of sunlight. Thus, in this death-chair, will I give my life to atone for the taking of *his* life, unworthy though he was. You will keep my secret, I know. God grant that the keeping of it may not weigh too heavily upon you! And now for the final test, and may God have mercy upon me! May happiness and peace be yours, Marden. Farewell!"

Tears filled my eyes as I concluded this terrible letter, the laying bare of a man's innermost soul. I knew Langhorne's sensitive nature; I realized how the constant brooding upon his crime had so preyed upon him, that the poor, broken, prematurely gray-haired wreck of a man that now sprawled in the office-chair was the result. As for his "experiment"—poor Langhorne. I understood, now, that toward the end, his mind had given away, and that the swallowing of the draught in the graduate-glass had produced no other result than he might have brought about with a well-aimed revolver bullet.

Something seemed to bedim the brightness of the electrolier, and a gloom which penetrated to the depths of my soul filled me as I laid the letter back on the desk and looked around. The Davenport caught my eye; I would lay the remains of my poor friend there, while I went out to notify the proper authorities. That part of the letter referring to his crime, I would destroy; and his secret, as he had said, would be safe with me. The other parts of his note would make plain the manner in which he had ended his own life. I could, of course, have made use of the telephone to get in communication with those who must now be called in, but I longed to get a breath of fresh air, and to escape into the very sunlight that poor Langhorne had apparently dreaded so deeply.

I had laid my hat down on the Davenport; now I picked it up and put it on the table. Then, crossing again to the chair—truly as he had said, a death chair—I stopped and placed my left hand upon the man's shoulder—while at the same time I grasped his right hand in an attempt to detach the glass from the cramped fingers.

As I did so, that part of what sat there in the chair, crumpled under my touch and fell away, like the sand falling through an hour-glass, and as I reeled back in unutterable dismay and horror, I saw the right sleeve flatten out limply upon the desk, while in place of the hand which held the graduate was a small heap of gray-black dust!

I closed my eyes. As I opened them again, I saw in the chair only a disordered pile of clothing, with a great deal more of the gray-black dust on the floor and the arms of the chair. Scattered about were little bunches of prematurely gray hair, and I knew, as I gazed, *that Randall Langhorne's last experiment had been crowned with success!*

Paul J. Campbell

Ideals of the Amateur

The prosperity of Amateur Journalism is dependent upon the enthusiasm of youth, and this in most cases is a transient afflatus that has its rise in the dawn of maturity, when aspiration is the dominant note of life and valiant Youth sallies forth to conquer the world.

Youth, at the dawn of maturity, is the happiest human estate. It is the blossoming stage of humanity when whatever there is of beauty and sweetness in the individual, flowers forth upon the waiting world. Flowers have their day and fade, having served their purpose. Some of them last longer than others, but all blossoms are transient, their tinted petals fall and mingle with the dust, their subtle fragrance is swallowed by the vagrant winds.

Amateur Journalism is a department in the Garden of Youth. Within its pleasant precincts aspiring youth finds the congenial atmosphere of inspiration, and flaunts his (or her) intellectual plumage for the admiration of all. From the late 'teens to the early twenties is the promenade of the average amateur. But soon or late the sterner duties of life summons each joyous reveler, and paged by business or matrimony they drop out of the enchanted circle and are gone.

Efforts to enlarge and perpetuate Amateur Journalism, which do not take into consideration the brevity of the average amateur career, are futile and useless. The realm of the amateur is well defined. Those who would build for Amateur Journalism must erect their edifice within its borders.

Amateur Journalism offers opportunity for self-development, congenial companionship, and the inspiration of an appreciative audience. The hospitality of the organization, however, is rather crude. The aspirant is merely invited to step in and help himself to a self served intellectual banquet. The self reliant recruit who acts without hesitancy upon the invitation never goes away hungry, nor says "there is nothing in it," but the less assertive individual who hesitates upon the threshold is lost.

The most practical means of popularizing Amateur Journalism would be to place its benefits within more convenient reach of the average young person, and make its pleasures more accessible. This could be done by increasing the size and scope of the UNITED AMATEUR and making it something more than an Official Organ. An amateur journal of 40 or 50 pages containing the best literary efforts of members of the association, with ample and up-to-date critical and review departments, issued monthly in attractive form could be placed in every high school and public library in the land, and could not fail to attract hundreds of bright young people to our ranks, for the subscription price (and membership fee) for such a journal would need no delicate and ingenious explanations. The increased size of the UNITED AMATEUR would afford greater opportunity for the average amateur to get his work published, which is one of the staple desires of the recruit, and by its wider appeal and increased field the membership would be sufficiently increased to make it self sustaining.

The boy with a press needs little assistance to get into the midst of things amateur—he naturally gravitates there. But for the less fortunate individual, who would like to indulge in an amateur paper if it were not so much trouble, there could be arranged a department of publication and mailing established by the Official Printer of the United Amateur Press Association where amateur papers could be printed at the cost of material and workmanship, at, say $3 for 4 pages 5 × 7 or $5 for 4 pages 7 × 10 and these could be mailed as supplements to the UNITED AMATEUR at small cost.

Under such a regime amateur activity would be wide-spread and the membership would be enumerated in thousands, in fact the field is too large for a single organization to cover.

There are now about half a dozen amateurs in each state. These people are not essentially different from a hundred others in their respective states except that they have heard about Amateur Journalism and the others have not. It would not be very hard to remove this difference and with its removal Amateur Journalism would become the popular institution it deserves to be instead of being as it is today the isolated Prince of Hobbies known to the extremely few.

A Representative Official Organ

The beginnings of Amateur Journalism lie far back of the inception of the oldest amateur press association. Organized Amateur Journalists came, like most other things, in response to "a long felt want," for we live in a materialistic fairyland where intelligent wishes energetically wished eventually become established realities. The lone amateur literary aspirant oppressed by unfriendly isolation instinctively sought to affiliate himself with his kindred in spirit and his brethren in the flesh. "We like the people who like the things we like," because we feel within ourselves the assurance of their good taste.

Amateur Journalism flourished and grew strong under the stimulus of the amateur press associations. The banding together of youths of similar tastes, hopes, talents, ambitions and aspirations, pooled their enthusiasm, and a sufficient amount of enthusiasm (so long as it remains alive) has always constituted "an irresistible force."

The Gardens of Eden are always situated in the golden mist of memory's romantic past, as the Elysium Fields always beckon to us from the farther reaches of the future's faintest dawn. The essence of romance is unsatisfied longing, so romance in her sublime form dwells not with the present, but ever haunts the past, and in dreams is the hand-maiden of the future. So the Halcyon days of Amateur Journalism are reckoned with the past, but as yet there is nothing mythical about them. Except perhaps, to the extremely few, there is nothing blasphemous about the statement that the Halcyon Days of Amateur Journalism were contemporaneous with the advent and popularization of the small printing press. Until the novelty had been worn thread-bare, ten boys out of every thousand had to have their smell of printer's ink, or their parents or guardians could know no rest. Amateur printing was a vogue of the juvenile world.

But the Procession of Progress is perpetual. The amateur printing press has many competitors for [a] boy's time and attention, now, and the fickle (or versatile) heart of youth, has in great measure forsaken the typographical hobby of the fathers. There is no way in which we could change this—even if we would. The clock of time will not turn back. We must conform to conditions as they are, and keep on making revisions to meet the requirements of future developments. "He who stands still is left behind," as he who leans too heavily upon an absolute truth awakens sometime to find his foundations have shifted.

The success of Amateur Journalism in its best days was due to its conformity to current conditions. It fitted the situation then and fitted it well. Times have changed somewhat in the interlude and the infant has outgrown its swaddling clothes. To bring back an[d] eclipse the success of former days we must study the needs of the time and make our Association supply them as nearly as is practical.

The passing of the popularity of the hand press has been the "most unkindest cut of all" to Amateur Journalism. The present high price of commercial printing is another. The difficulty of getting out an amateur paper to those unfamiliar with the task, has deterred many a brilliant aspirant from breaking into print. The detail work and drudgery sometimes galls a poetic temperament to such an extent that it leads to literary suicide.

To cure, or at least alleviate this list of ills (both imaginary and real), I suggest that we make the *United Amateur* a more representative Official Organ by the admission of Staff Contributors, who shall pay five dollars annually into the treasure, and who shall be allotted space in the *United Amateur* costing that amount, for the publication of such of their own writings as are found acceptable by the Official Editor, the names of these Staff Contributors to appear in the editorial head, and any active member of the United Amateur Press Association in good standing, to be eligible, subject to the approval of the Official Editor.

An amendment incorporating this idea is being submitted for the approval of the membership.

Going to a Funeral

Do you remember the wealth of gloom a funeral brought to the community, when you were a boy? How the neighbors around about donned their somber suits of Sunday black, and pulled down their faces to a religious length. How the womenfolks got together in the spare bedroom of the house that had been visited by the "rider of the pale horse," and whispered near-scandal about the deceased, while the menfolks trampled out the grass in the front-yard, spit tobacco-juice on the flower-bed bordered by a fringe of assorted bottles set on end, whittled the paling-fence, and regaled each other with comments on the condition of the crops and stories of horse trades.

In the stuffy front-parlor, which hadn't been opened to fresh air and the public since Miranda was married, lay the necessary part of the funeral, nicely encased in a coffin covered with black cloth, upon which every now and then, the unctuous undertaker from the village bestowed a caressing glance as he mentally calculated his profit on the "outfit" that now held the "remains" of a well-to-do farmer, whose family would be scandalized if he should charge them less than a hundred dollars for it. Here, too, were the heavy-eyed watchers who sat up with the "corpse" last night and were still forced to forego sleep in order to attend the funeral.

The children moved about the house with white, drawn faces. This funeral was a terrible reality to them. While the adult members of the community had been expecting old man Jones to die for a year or more, the murk of funeral gloom had fallen upon the children like a clap of thunder from a clear sky. Games and frolic had ceased with the dread announcement of a funeral. The solemnity of their elders was transferred to the children increased tenfold, for childhood is the age of sincerity. Children have not yet learned to enjoy their miseries, as their elders do.

You wondered why all the joy went out of life for the whole community for the space of a day or two, because old man Jones had died, just as everybody expected he would, as his heirs hoped he would, and as undoubtedly he should, after some eighty years of life. Nobody cared so much about old man Jones when he was alive, but old man Jones dead was a potent factor. It was Saturday morning when the dread news came that old man Jones had "died last night."

Old Mrs. Morgan ran over to give your mother the gruesome details. Of course, you couldn't hear all they said, for you were cording wood in the wood-shed while the conference took place in the kitchen, and when something especially awful was related, old Mrs. Morgan dropped her rasping voice to a kind of sizzling whisper—you could still hear the tortured air escaping from her thin lips, and could imagine the horrors she was recounting, but you couldn't catch her exact words, though you strained your ears to the bursting point.

You had things pretty much to yourself that day. Your mother could not long resist the temptation to run over to Jones's, leaving you few chores to do. Somebody had given you "Hero Tales from American History," and you tried to read that because you had no heart to play, and a haunting feeling of fear kept you within doors, but you couldn't get interested in George Rogers Clarke and the Conquest of the Northwest. You sat for long intervals and looked out at the November day, and toward night you began to wonder why you had ever been born. It caused so many people so much trouble for one to get out of the world, that you were sorry you had ever started the job of life, at all.

That evening the cold chills ran down your back whenever a door creaked, and you stole fearful glances over your shoulder, half expecting to see ghostly figures outlined in the darkness. At the supper-table you remarked longingly that you'd like to find somebody who was cheerful and your mother answered you that it had been a sad day for a good many. At last you gave up in despair, and went up to your attic room and to bed, to dream of ghosts and spirits and deathbeds and coffins and mourners and undertakers!

The funeral, proper, came off next day. It was one day early, but old man Jones was hurried off just that much ahead of time, because Sunday is such a propitious day for a funeral it seemed a pity to miss it. You could always count on a larger crowd and a bigger send-off from the preacher. "A Sunday funeral was worth waiting for," as old Mother Gordon remarked, and Aunt Julia Smith admitted that she was always sorry for anyone who died "the fore part of the week!"

Despite the fact that you scrubbed your physiognomy with exceptional vigor that Sunday morning, you failed to pass your mother's inspection, and she retouched your toilet with an energy that brought forth your earnest and deep-felt protests. You wore your highest and stiffest collar, and your "Sunday Go To Meetin'" clothes seemed blacker and gloomier than ever before. About nine o'clock your father said it was time to "go over to the house." At Jones's all was quiet confusion and silent hubbub. Everybody talked and nobody listened—perhaps that was because there was so much to say, and so little worth listening to.

After nearly an hour's delay, during which much sweating and fuming was done by those who take charge of such affairs "by natural right," and some prancing and fretting had been indulged in by the undertaker's span of blacks, the pall-bearers issued forth from the front door, some of them awkwardly putting their hats on backwards with their left hands, one stumbled on a loose brick in the walk, and a corpulent member hubbed [*sic*] the gate-post and said something under his breath that made little Johnnie Patterson giggle—altogether it was with winded sighs, and faces relaxed in relief, that the dead-weight of old man Jones was deposited in the hearse.

The preacher, the pall-bearers and the hearse soon got under way, but confusion and consternation reigned in the rest of the procession. The adjustment of mourning veils and other feminine paraphernalia delayed the loading of the mourners; then Parker's team of plow-horses were specialists in procrastination, and Parker, placidly oblivious of the fact that he was blocking the procession, spraddled his fat legs and settled back comfortably against his buggy seat, letting the reins rest on the dash-board while he leisurely contemplated the landscape and made speculative comments, to his wife, on the hazelnut crop. When Parker had caused an eighth of a mile to yawn between his rig and the next one in front of him, some one behind yelled that he'd lose the procession entirely if he didn't drive up. Parker heard what was said well enough, but he asked his wife, and when that meek little woman, from her compressed third of the buggy seat, replied diplomatically that Bill Cameron had asked him to please drive a little faster, he flapped the lines over the backs of the lazy bays, and grumbled at the swiftness with which a man is hurried off now-a-days. "They've even got to trot you to the grave-yard," ruminated Parker. "Now when I wuz a boy they wuz more respectful to the dead." By the time the procession arrived at the church, Parker wasn't more than a hundred yards behind the team in front of him.

A good many people had already congregated at the church when you got there, and the increasing number of long faces added to the depths of your depression. It was with some relief that you settled down in the uncomfortable, high-backed pew, that had either been designed and executed by one ignorant of human anatomy or by one who believed that bodily comfort, in church, was bad for the soul. When the congregation joined the combined efforts of their lungs with the wheeze of the organ in a characteristic rural rendition of "In the Sweet By and By," you began to cheer up a little, for the song seemed to suggest that the thing would soon be done and over with. But when they sang "Where Congregations Ne'er Break Up and Sabbaths Have No End," your spirits sank into the depths of gloom again.

The preacher arose, and after a perfunctory prayer for guidance and inspiration, laid his manuscript on the pulpit desk, and launched forth with a text on "Everlasting Life." He explained the plan of salvation from Adam down to date. He told of the atonement, the resurrection, and the promise. He explained the Holy Trinity, the mysteries of baptism, confirmation, and sanctification, and for reasons best known to himself he made assurance doubly sure by placing old man Jones in the sanctified class. That was the only piece of news the sermon contained. But you noticed that he stroked the tails of his shiny Prince Albert when he sat down, with a wistful, wishful look that wandered until it rested upon the bald pate of Solomon, eldest son and chief heir of the deceased, and lingered there with caressing hopefulness until it was time to "view the remains."

How you did shrink from the ordeal of looking upon the dead and when at last it came your turn to march past the coffin of old man Jones to the accompaniment of "Rock of Ages," your imagination was fired by the phraseology of the hymn and mentally you had visions of "the water and the blood," so that you were afraid to take more than the swiftest glimpse of old man Jones's face, as you crowded past, but in that one swift glance, you were surprised. Old man Jones didn't look so bad. It seemed to agree with him to be dead. As you thought about it on your way out of the church, you concluded that he looked better than he did in life. That new undertaker was something of an artist in his line, anyway.

The fresh air made you feel better, and the final planting of old man Jones, in the grave-yard close at hand, was accompanied by a general relief of tension that could be felt in all quartets—a clearing of the atmosphere. People talked more freely, and the children even dared, now and then, to laugh modestly.

As you rode home with an appetite that made the anticipation of dinner pleasant, your mother chatted about the number of people whom she had met that day, that she had not seen for ever so long, and your father seemed to have hatched a scheme for a horse trade over which he could hardly keep from chuckling.

Old man Jones was dead and buried. It had been a hard pull at the glooms for you, but you were glad it was over with. He had shed a good deal of gloom, had old man Jones, in his time and with his off taking. He used to cane the boys out of his orchard so that the hogs got full benefit of the fallen fruit, and he took a sinister pleasure in breaking up marble games on Sunday and in bringing the participants to grief, if not to repentance. Old man Jones was dead and planted, and you heaved a sigh of relief. It was a disagreeable job done and over with, and in the natural paganism of your boyish heart, you didn't care whether his wings sprouted or not. Old man Jones was dead and done for; he'd had his day and his funeral had been by far the most important and impressive part of his career; he had served his purpose and now a charitable oblivion would swallow him up. Old man Jones was dead and the funeral was over; you could be happy now, or reasonably so, until another festival of gloom occurred, when, of course, you would have to participate. But by and by you either began to develop the relish of your elders for funerals as social functions, or else you wandered away from the rural districts and became sufficiently cosmopolitan to look back with sympathetic tolerance upon the uncultivated taste of childhood which revolts at gloom and grief in their artificial social aspect.

Adventures in Amateur Journalism

I discovered amateur journalism through the National Amateur Press Association in June 1902, when as a farm boy with a yen to write, at the age of 17, I had succeeded in getting a story published in the "Stub-Pen," a semi-professional magazine brought out by a literary club in Minneapolis, Minn. Like Edgar Lee Masters, I had found the stories in the Chicago "Weekly Inter-Ocean" inspired me to try my hand at writing, but unlike Masters I did not go to Chicago and ask the Inter-Ocean editor for a job. I got to Chicago years later to find Masters busy in his State street law office, deep in writing "Mitch Miller," so busy, in fact, that I did not ask him to act as judge of a Laureate Contest, but proceeded to the Cunard building on Dearborn street and persuaded Clarence Darrow to be the judge. He came down to the Atlantic hotel a month later when our convention was in session, and made his report in an excellent talk. That was in July 1917.

When Louis M. Starring of Grand View, Tenn., saw my story in the Stub-Pen, sent me a copy of the National Amateur and his own paper, the Reflector, and invited me to join the National Amateur Press Association, I lost no time in sending in my dollar and my manuscript, as a credential. An applicant for membership is required to have "an original composition published in an amateur paper." Starring published my doggerel about "Seventeen Year Locusts" in his 4-page 7×10 paper the Reflector, and invited me to become co-editor, an invitation I also accepted. He was a kindly young man of considerable culture, who lived in East Tennessee. He was nearly blind and had little money, but had enjoyed the Nashville convention of the N.A.P.A. in 1901, and found in amateur journalism an escape from the drabness of his life.

By way of preparation for amateur journalism, I had worked at publishing lead pencil papers for family circulation, before I went to school, and by the time I was in the fifth grade I was turning out pen and ink copies of the "Mississippi Steamboat News" dedicated to Sharon school's most ambitious play project, a ditch across the school yard which served to float what we fondly thought were effigies of the steamboats we read about in "Tom Sawyer" and about which my great uncle, who lived at our house, liked to spin yarns.

One of my readers, I recall, requested that my pen and ink journal "tell how to run the boats without getting your feet wet," a request I was never able to satisfy, as I was not yet aware of the sage advice: "Hang your clothes on a hickory limb, but don't go near the water!"

The News closed its career by the teacher's request, which I took as a flattering compliment. Much was being said at that time about the farm pest, English sparrows, so I conceived the idea of running a serial story entitled "Snatchen-corn," wherein I described the counter revolt of the sparrows against the efforts of the farmers to exterminate them. Some of my readers became so much more interested in the weird flights of my imagination, than they were in studying their lessons, that the teacher did away with the competition.

The Ridgefarm Republican, our local weekly, published my report of a trip to the Pan-American Exposition held in Buffalo, N.Y. in 1901; the Orange Judd Farmer and Farm Life, both published in Chicago, had printed brief contributions from my typewriter; the Home Journal of Lafayette, Ind., and the Bohemian of Ft. Worth, Tex., had published stories of mine before I discovered amateur journalism, and I had about a bushel basket full of manuscripts that had been accumulating rejection slips from all over, so I was ripe for the N.A.P.A. and its hundred amateur papers.

The Prince of Hobbies

The National Amateur Press Association, and the United Amateur Press Association which I also joined a little later, were made up of boys and girls with a desire to write, many of whom published small papers or magazines which were circulated among the members and their personal friends. The associations held annual conventions, conducted stories, poems, essays, sketches, and histories. They each had a department of criticism which gave helpful advice, and a Manuscript Manager whose duty it was to get members' literary effusions published. The social side of these conventions was an attraction, and there was keen rivalry for the various elective offices each year.

After being in the N.A.P.A. for a year, I took a hand in the campaign of 1903, and got myself properly jumped upon from Boston to San Francisco. But some prominent amateurs came to my defense, and for the next three years amateur journalism was the most important thing in the world to me. There was hardly a day passed but what my mail had one amateur paper in it, and sometimes there were half a dozen, and the desire to see my name in print was amply gratified. There was caustic criticism of my crude ideas and inelegant expressions, and there was fulsome praise and ample appreciation for my successful sallies.

"Amateur journalism," I used to say, while serving on the recruit committee, "is a department of the University of Hard Knocks, wherein we temper the caustic teachings of experience with the kindly friendship of youth, while we learn to write by writing. Within this enchanted realm, greed and monetary gain are banned. We pursue the literary art for its own sake, for the joy of self-expression, and self-development. It is a democratic school where we hold high ideals and help each other. The realm of the amateur journalist is one of the pleasantest byways in the golden land of youth. In it those who have the urge to write will find Helicon days."

Fellowship in the School of Experience

Outsiders never quite understood the devotion of an amateur journalist to his hobby, they asked what he got out of it? Why he spent money to print papers and to circulate them all over the country to other amateur journalists, when he got no financial return? Some of the uninitiate set this down to vanity, but that was not the answer. I had had the vanity very effectively taken out of me that second year when I published my first amateur paper, a typographical atrocity produced by the local print shop, and which I called "The Ideal Politician," an impossible name as I soon learned, and the Politician died with the second issue.

Having stirred up a hornet's nest, I brought out the "Scottish Highlanders," to avenge the literary and political insults that had been heaped upon the upstart editor of the Ideal Politician. A dead-louse printer in Milwaukee took my money and delayed getting out the paper for four months, and when I finally received the 16-page 5x7 it was so full of errors that I could not send it out, but had 12 pages (which was as far as my money went) reprinted by E. L. Fantus, a professional printer in Chicago. Most of the critics were kindly boys and girls, who when they saw what a fight I could put up, when stepped upon, gave me credit for being sincere, at least.

The liking people have for having their better qualities understood and appreciated by those of their own kind, was, and is, perhaps the chief charm of amateur journalism. Having found out what a crude ignoramus I was in the eyes of my fellows, with the publication of my first amateur paper, I was fired with a great ambition to cure as many of those defects as humanly possible. This consumed my time and energy for years—in fact, when you polish off one rough corner, the vantage ground you gain enables you to see another rough spot. Amateur journalism is a powerful stimulant for a writer who wants to know what is the matter with him!

The "Prairie State Journal" was my next amateur paper, printed by a former amateur journalist in Palos Park, Ill., who used 6-point type on a double column 6x8 page, and I published many stories, poems and articles in the several 20-page issues that I got out, quarterly. By the autumn of 1904 I was ready to launch "The Scotchman," my most ambitious amateur paper, a 7x10 8-point page that ran 12 issues, totalling 312 pages in all. By this time I could write editorial comments without all of them being controversial.

Around Amateurdom

I met my first amateur journalist, Russell L. Joseph, on a visit to Indianapolis, with my mother in the fall of 1902, and my second, Otto A. Kamber, an old-timer, in Terre Haute, Ind., a few days later on the same trip. I could not persuade my mother to allow me to attend the Chicago convention in July 1903, and there was some grounds for her hesitancy, for when I did get to a meeting of the Chicago Amateur Press Club, later in the summer, riding a cheap excursion to the city and was the guest of Carl Hegart, one of the Chicago members, I added to the merriment of the boarding house table at dinner when asked by the waitress, "How will you have your steak?" not knowing there was "rare, medium and well done," I answered after painful hesitation: "On a plate!"

A mild scandal had been raised by a Brooklyn recruit who submitted as a credential, a selection from McGuffy's Fifth Reader. This plagiarism inspired me to propose a little group of the Chicago Amateur Press Club, that we start a fund to buy a set of Encyclopedia Britannica for this new member, as a sort of literary bone-yard from which he could draw perhaps more impressively than from McGuffy's Fifth Reader, but Hegart spoke for the group and "declined to lend his name to any such clever folly."

On this trip I met Amanda E. Frees, Jennie Irene Maloney, and Masie A. McLaughlin, Chicago's girl amateurs, as well as Walter Mellinger, Hal T. Bixby and J. P. Calloway, the two latter being lodge brothers of mine in the boys order called Coming Men of America. Among the younger boys was Charley Zekind, who later visited me at Prairie Queen Grange.

The same summer I made an impromptu trip east with my grandfather who was tempted by an Elk excursion rate to Baltimore. Uncle Joe Cannon was then Speaker of the House of Representatives, and my grandfather and he had been boys together in the little Quaker village of Annapolis, Ind., so we did Washington to our satisfaction, and passed on to Baltimore where I made an attempt to contact an amateur by the name of Walsh.

Grandfather readily agreed that we should see Philadelphia and New York, and in the former I met Will Murphy, then a student at the University of Pennsylvania, and later to be employed by the Ledger as music and dramatic critic. Will Murphy, despite the handicap of a crippled back, was active for many years and was one of the finest examples of the amateur journalist that I have ever known.

One of my first and last correspondents in amateur journalism is Edwin Hadley Smith (he just persuaded me to renew my membership in the N.A.P.A. the other day). At that time Smith and I had been arguing about vegetarianism, and since I couldn't find him on such short notice through his post office box address in New York, I decided to steer my grandfather to the vegetarian restaurant in Brooklyn that Smith talked about. We found the place easily enough but when grandfather saw a dead cat in the gutter in front of the vegetarian restaurant he insisted on going some place else for lunch.

Amateur Journalists' Day at the St. Louis Fair

July 2nd, 1904 was Amateur Journalists' Day at the Louisiana Purchase Exposition in St. Louis, and there and then I met a score or more of amateur journalists, the Chicago delegation most of whom I already knew; Seymour, Thalman, Brown, Block and Coble of Kansas City; Boud of Philadelphia; Anson Lindbeck of Sarento, Ill., who came in on the same "Clover Leaf" train with me; and Homer Pickrell of Wichita, Kan., who was later to share a bachelor apartment with me in Chicago while he was on the Record-Herald, and I was on the Board of Trade.

I had met Henry Wehking of the St. Louis Club on a previous trip to the Fair with my grandfather; now I met the rest of the club, A. M. Adams, Will Stoddard, Tommy Thomas and a dozen others. But the meeting I remember most on Amateur Journalists' Day was meeting E. H. Whitaker, part negro, from LaSalle, Ill., The N.A.P.A. had been in controversy about admitting negroes to membership, and I had supported the proposition to exclude them. Now some of the amateurs who had lectured me about "the curse of race prejudice" slipped away and I had to step into the breach and ask Whitaker and his family to sit at table with me, at lunch time, as I did not want his feelings hurt, although I thought him out of place in our association.

Over against the Whitaker incident was the membership of Rosalee Selfridge, daughter of H. Gordon Selfridge, foster son of Marshall Field, the great Chicago merchant. Selfridge had in his youth been an amateur journalist and insisted that his daughter join the N.A.P.A. and publish a paper. She called it, "Will o' the Wisp," and its contents were mostly junior social notes from Lake Shore Drive, Chicago, where the Selfridges lived prior to the opening of the London store. After that Rosalee Selfridge issued her paper from England, and I remember an interesting article on the November celebration of Guy Fawkes Day. Later, Rosalee Selfridge married a prince and amateurdom knew her no more.

Cleveland Convention Trip

I attended my first convention of the National Amateur Press Association at Cleveland, Ohio in July, 1905. Determined to get my money's worth in travel, I bought an Elk excursion ticket to Buffalo, N.Y. (where the Elks were conventioning that year), and leaving several days early, I visited Niagara Falls, journeyed on to Amherst, Mass., for a brief stop at the Massachusetts Agricultural College from which I had had a correspondence course in agriculture, and on to Boston to meet Charley Parker, Nelson Morton, Edith Miniter, Ethel May Johnston and Laurie Sawyer of the Hub Amateur Journalist's Club, and incidentally to visit Old South Church of Paul Revere fame and climb Bunker Hill Monument and get lost in the mazes of Milk street.

I arrived in New York on the Fall River boat to be met by my friend, A. M. Adams, who had left his Wabash railroad job in St. Louis to work on the New York Tribune, and was later to go to the Hotel World. We had breakfast and while Adams put in an appearance at the office I sought a Lexington avenue composer who had, for a consideration, written music for a song of mine. I found him in due course and was assured that the song was being considered by a publisher—maybe it still is, I've never heard any more from it. At noon, Adams steered me along Broadway and we met half a dozen amateur journalists on their way to lunch, and added most of them to our gang, we ate together and they saw me off on the Mary Powell for the afternoon trip up the Hudson.

Somebody suggested we have a drink in a water front saloon before I left, and agreeable therewith I "split a bottle of Black Bass" with C. Fred: Crosby who edited a trade paper called "Tobacco." Adams took a white soda, while Charley Heins and Clifford Gregory drank beer. I have only a hazy notion of who the other amateur was or what he drank, but I was to hear a lot about that Black Bass, later on, in a newspaper war between Heins and myself that raged for three years.

From the deck of the Mary Powell I waved to my friends on the dock and remarked to a passenger at my elbow, in what I thought was a cosmopolitan manner, that New York was really a small place after all for I knew only a dozen people in the city and I had met half of them by accident at the noon hour on Broadway. He missed the point, and started to explain to me how extensive the metropolis was.

At Kingston, where the Mary Powell turned back, I disembarked and took a West Shore train to Albany, stopped over at the Ten Eck hotel, and rode the "Empire State Express" to Buffalo the next afternoon, where I bought a lake boat ticket to Cleveland and delayed my dinner by ordering a sherry cobbler, which could not be served until the boat cleared the Buffalo harbor and the bar opened. When it was at last served I looked at it in some surprise, sipped a little of the iced wine and left it to the appreciative waiter. I had learned what a sherry cobbler was.

Elected Official Editor

I thoroughly enjoyed the Cleveland convention. I knew many of the amateurs and all the others through their papers or through correspondence. There was Warren Brodie, dean of the Cleveland amateurs, who had published a splendid volume of the National Amateur; there was Tim Thrift whose magazine, the "Lucky Dog," was the artistic publication produced by the fraternity; there was Feather and Fingulin and Ziegler, and there was "Bill" Nye, a Cleveland (girl) who evaded me when I made a trip back to Cleveland to following winter to see what she was really like.

There was Bertie Klump, a New Jersey girl, whom I sat next to during the election, and who ribbed me about my mispronunciation of the name of her paper, "Caprice." When the election of the Official Editor was announced, the bored Bertie turned to me and asked, "Who was it?" Then she stared incredulously while I got to my feet and made an halting speech of acceptance, for I had just been chosen for that coveted honor, when the two announced candidates were deadlocked.

John T. Nixon, of Crowley, La., an old timer and author of a History of the N.A.P.A., then a professional newspaper publisher, had placed me in nomination, and friends from all over had voted me into the Editorship. It was one of the proudest moments of my life.

That evening at a summer garden performance of The Mikado, Edwin Hadley Smith had primed the "Lord High Executioner" so when he read the names of the "High Officials" they included President Thrift and Official Editor Campbell, for Tim Thrift was to be my chief, and we got on famously throughout the ensuing year. The Chicago amateurs were there in force and I met and liked Vida Combs, one of the new members.

A Plunge in Printer's Ink

Returning to Danville, Illinois, I set about finding a shop in which I could get the National Amateur printed. The official organ was a 9x11 page paper in those days, and there were only two shops in town that could handle it, and fate decreed that I pick the weak sister. W. R. Jewell, the publisher of the Danville Daily News, was Joe Cannon's campaign manager, whom I had met with my grandfather many times. He had printed some of my stuff in the paper and he now passed me on to his job printing department which he had just sold to three printers, Bridges, Park and Stuebe. They had two rather large rooms behind the newspaper presses, in the basement and under the clattering linotypes on the floor above, with an entrance down the alley. But the smell of printers' ink fascinated me.

When Bridges was elected Fire Chief, I bought his third of the shop for $1,500. The September number of the National Amateur appeared only a few days late, but there was hardly a page that wasn't marred by typographical errors. The proof reading was wished off on me and I couldn't read proof. After it was printed I dreaded to look at it, some fresh error bobbed up to stare at me each time. A critic in New England remarked that "Campbell's printer ought to be shot." He also said Paul Cook and I were "Literary Blacksmiths."

Our linotyping was done by the newspaper operators after hours, and nearly every time you corrected one error two would show up when the slug was reset, and we were always running late. The customers had to have their work on time, I was just a partner and could wait. I had begun the year hoping to make a record with my six issues of the National Amateur. I made a record in two ways, I did publish a volume of 120 pages which placed me in the upper brackets for quantity, and I perpetuated more typographical errors in my volume, perhaps, than had ever been perpetrated in the official organ in the previous years of its existence.

Youthful enthusiasm is a wonderful thing, for I liked that shop of "the printer who ought to be shot," so well that I put ten thousand dollars of my inheritance into it for a new building with north skylights, and into first payments on new equipment for which it had but little use. Park, the managing partner, thought you got business by virtue of being well equipped for it. After writing my personal check for our payroll of 26 union employees for a while, I suspected that he was wrong and bought him out. Stuebe, the remaining partner, was unhappy and grouchy without his pal, so I bought him out, and had the white elephant to myself for two years, during which time with Adams and Wehking I launched the "Passing Show," a professional news review, an idea which has since been quite successful, but we did not go at in a large enough way, and when the Teddy Roosevelt gold panic came along, I sold out my equity in the printing and binding plant to the thrifty German language newspaper, the Herald, taking a thirty thousand dollar loss. Even so, that white elephant I had concocted in my youthful enthusiasm for printer's ink, broke the Herald's publisher and sent him into bankruptcy.

I Start Out to Conquer the World

The 1906 convention of the National Amateur Press Association was held in Philadelphia, and I ran into several snags in my pre-convention plans. Having inherited some land and money from my grandfather, I planned to round out my education and bring my literary career into blossom by a trip around the world. In those days I had no doubt but that I would, sooner or later, write the great American novel. An around-the-world tour should, I reasoned, make this occur sooner. I was just 21 and romantically inclined and seeking a sympathetic help-mate to share my dream of life and the literary distinction which I meant to win.

My attempt to attain story-book love with a Quaker girl with whom I had grown up, had failed. My dreams were not real to her. Tommy Thomas, of the St. Louis amateurs, had gone to New York and married while I admired from afar. "Freezette" [Amanda Frees—ED.] of the Chicago amateur press club had given me council in the Tommy Thomas matter, and when Tommy had flown I turned to Freezette and tried to persuade her to join forces with me, get married in Washington after the convention and start immediately on a honeymoon trip around the world.

My mother was actively opposed to my plan; Dad was neutral and rather amused by the family rumpus I had stirred up. But telling the Quaker girl about my plans and one-way ticket to Philadelphia was a hard job, and that night I got home very late and quite hungry. It was late June and Dad had been fishing in the Wabash, and there were slabs of cold fried catfish on the kitchen table. I ate heartily. I awoke late next morning with a revolt in my stomach. I could eat no breakfast. This was the day of my planned departure. I walked a mile across corn fields in the broiling sun for a last conference with my farm foreman, Bert Hughes. When I started back toward the house a black blankness engulfed me; for the first time in my life I had a sun stroke. Hughes carried me to the shade of a cottonwood and revived me with the contents of his water jug, and I managed to get back to my room on my own power. I stayed in bed for 24 hours, missing the afternoon train for Chicago that I had planned to take.

Next day Dad took me to an Indianapolis train that connected with the Pennsylvania Express for Philadelphia. The convention was in full swing when I arrived for the second session. Politics were seething, I had just made an activity record of 354 separate articles published in the amateur press during the year. It was a tradition that the retiring Official Editor be elected President. I was side-stepping the Presidency for the honeymoon trip around the world, throwing my support to Will Murphy, who I thought deserved the honor more. But it took a lot of side-stepping at the convention and I hardly had any time I could call my own. Freezette was very popular, a talented writer, amateurs from all over crowded to see her. I got only a brief word with her during the convention in a Belleview-Stratford hotel corridor. "I'll wait at the Roycroft Inn till I hear from you," I said, and she nodded as a group of friends whisked her away, and the proxy committee claimed me. She was going to the banquet with Tim Thrift, the retiring President, so I took M. Beulah Ferguson, of Baltimore, one of my recruits.

Losing a Girl and Winning a Cup

Considering the circumstances, I still think my toast at the banquet was a good one. I ran across it the other day, scribbled in a youthful hand on small sheets of Belleview-Stratford's social stationery. In it I paid my last formal tribute to "The National Amateur." It was scoffed at as a "painful pause" by a disciple of broad wit, but in that toast I paid tribute to Amateur Journalism (as I am endeavoring to do in this article) for what it had done for me, and I like to think that the sentiments I voiced then had been shared by many amateurs before me, and would be held by many more yet to come.

Finding that old bit of manuscript, which I carried in my cuff to the banquet, is perhaps the reason for my writing this. I have long wanted to picture Amateur Journalism as I knew it. Though this attempt seems inadequate some of the high-lights may register and be passed on to a new generation. The National Amateur Press Association is still going strong though most of the members of my day are gone. The young writer, the young in heart, the keenly alert to life with the literary urge will find there fellowship and fun and fulfillment within its ranks. The editor [i.e., Campbell—ED.] will be glad to supply information to those who wish to join.

Friends who wanted to elect me president of the National Amateur Press Association at the Philadelphia convention, when I declined, elected to present me with a sterling silver loving cup, which rests on my desk as I write. It is inscribed: "Philadelphia 1906, to Paul J. Campbell for distinguished services to the National Amateur Press Association."

After the convention closed I spent a day at Atlantic City and then went to East Aurora, N.Y., to wait at the Roycroft Inn. I got better acquainted with Elbert Hubbard, I wrote an essay on "The Prince of Pessimists" for Edward Cole's paper, and was in a fair way of becoming a pessimist myself, while waiting for a message that did not arrive. At the end of two weeks I went to

Chicago and learned that the honeymoon trip around the world was off. Freezette was going to marry Tim Thrift.

I was very much at loose ends for a while. The desire to visit foreign lands vanished. The high ambitions were unhorsed for a while and I felt small enough to consider oblivion had not the water of Lake Michigan, along Chicago's filled-in shore line, been muddy enough to repel me. I bought an Oldsmobile and started down state, stopping at Pontiac to see a visiting amateur who had sent me a post card. I spent a day at the print shop in Danville reading a basketful of mail, then on to St. Louis where I stopped for six weeks palling around with Stoddard and Wehking. In the autumn I went to Wichita, Kan., and in November married Ada Parkhurst, the amateur journalist I stopped to visit in Pontiac.

Once An Amateur Always An Amateur

The years rolled on, some issues of the Scotchman appeared, I attended two Milwaukee conventions, my marriage failed, so did my printing business, I took an automobile agency which was a success but hurt a lame knee in 1912 that put me to bed for three years. Amateur journalist visitors, Edward F. Daas and George S. Schilling, and correspondence with Dora Hepner [later Mrs. Anthony F. Moitoret—ED.], a Columbus, O., amateur did much to keep up my interest in life.

Just before I lost the lame leg by amputation in 1915, I began another amateur paper, "Invictus." In 1916 I was again at a Cleveland convention where I was elected president of the United Amateur Press Association, and where I met Eleanor J. Barnhart, a talented Minneapolis amateur, whom I married the following year. Together we entertained the Chicago convention in 1917.

Back on the farm after the World War I printed with my own hands my last amateur paper, "The Liberal," on a hand press acquired from Eddie Daas. Dissatisfied with the first results I called in my old pressroom foreman from Danville, and watched his fruitless efforts through all of a Sunday afternoon. Finally I hit on the scheme of putting glue on the loose adjustment screws at the back of the platen and made them stay put. I averaged a page a day on a 40-page issue in the winter of 1922, and decided that I had learned the printing business from the top down.

Eleanor and I had played at being gasoline gypsies in Florida in the winter of 1921, had been joined by Eddie Daas and Eugene Deitzler, who were en route to Cuba, and we all visited Verna McGeoch in St. Petersburg. There was the Columbus convention of 1922 to which Eleanor and I motored, taking with us her sister, Elizabeth Barnhart, and Eddie Daas.

We built a house on the farm next year in which there was a den for the amateur papers and press, but with the advent of our first son in 1923, the press was moved out to make room for the baby's crib, and that marked the close of my career as an active amateur journalist.

There was a long and interesting correspondence with Howard Lovecraft, brilliant amateur and writer of weird tales; there were literary contributions to Hyman Bradofsky's peerless amateur magazine, the "Californian"; there was a visit to George Macauley in Grand Rapids, Mich., and with Helm Spink and his father in Washington, Ind., and an all night session with Graeme Davis and a luncheon with Ernest Edkins at the Electric Club in Chicago. There was a wildcat oil trip to East Texas with Herbert P. McGinnis of West Virginia (another of my recruits), on which Sam Schilling and his charming wife were visited in Kansas City, and in 1935 Paul Cook, who shared with me the distinction of being called "a literary blacksmith," came out to East St. Louis and helped me publish the Canteen News for a year.

Now my 18-year-old son, Paul, Jr., stands on the threshold of a writing career. I could hold no better wish for him than that amateur journalism should give him as much as it has given to me.

When oldtimers came back on the membership list, as I have just done, we used to say, "Once an amateur always an amateur." The old love of writing for its own sake, the friends we made in our youth, the wonderful dreams we dreamed in the enchanted realm of the amateur recall many of us back to sit on the side lines and revel in memories, no matter how busy we are in the professional world.

In the Benjamin Franklin Memorial building in Philadelphia there is a Library of Amateur Journalism, collected by my friend Edwin Hadley Smith, comprising 36,500 amateur papers, 1,100 amateur books, 2,500 clippings from magazines and newspapers, 2,500 photos of amateurs, 3,500 printed relics, and 16,500 catalogue cards. It is a magnificent monument to the Prince of Hobbies.

The Alumni and the United Amateur Press Association

I have mentioned my "Adventures in Amateur Journalism" in these columns, and dwelt at some length on the cultural and fraternal aspects of amateur journalism. To me the time spent with "the Prince of Hobbies" in my younger years is filled with many happy recollections.

Some months ago Charles W. Heins, one of the founders of the United Amateur Press Association, in 1895, also with a print shop at his disposal sought to preserve old and cherished memories and set about the organization of the United Amateur Press Alumni Association, through his publication *The Phoenix*. With painstaking care and many letters to old time amateur journalists and the help of a few friends, he succeeded in bringing the Alumni Association membership up to 115.

It was a commendable piece of work; a labor of love, for old time's sake. It warmed the cockles of my heart to see the names I had known, some of them back 41 years in 1902 when I first entered amateur journalism. And Heins published many reminiscences of old times it was pleasant to read.

T. G. Mauritzen, of Thor's Book Service, Los Angeles, Calif., was chosen president of the Alumni Association. Mauritzen, who edits *Welcome News,* a professional publication, got out an issue of *Chips,* his amateur paper, with his associates Walter Pannell and Edith Ericson, which took some interest in last year's election in the United, and displeased J. F. Roy Erford.

This J. F. Roy Erford, a Seattle lawyer, is an old timer who must be 60 years old, at least. He was quite active in the old days not in a literary way but as a politician and wire puller. He liked to play with the "short pants boys" as the United was playfully called by the Shillalah man, and guide them in the way they should go. He was a hard loser in politics and by hook or crook he managed always to win. At the Le Grand, Oregon Convention in 1912 where the proxies elected a rival candidate not of his picking, he had them thrown out and retired with his minority loudly shouting that they were the whole show.

1912 was a year of splits, witnessing the branch of the Republican party called "Progressives" or "Bull Moosers." As the candidate elected by the proxies was the first girl president of an amateur press association, Erford's quibble about why he had the proxies thrown out, seemed immaterial, inconsequent and irrelevant (he threw them out so he could elect his candidate). And it seemed, to me at the time, a particularly ungentlemanly and soreheaded thing to do. The literary element and at least 60 per cent of the membership stayed with Miss Helene Hoffman and the eastern faction. But that crooked work at the Le Grand Convention married Roy Erford to his mistake and he has lived with it as a cherished ball and chain for the past 31 years, keeping it alive by personal effort whenever its momentum lagged.

The eastern United had two girl presidents and I headed the association for a year in 1916 when we used to publish the winning entries in the poetry, essay, story and history contests in the official organ. In 1922 I attended my last United convention at Columbus, Ohio. With Eddie Daas of Milwaukee I was interested in seeing Howard Lovecraft elected president. Lovecraft was one of the most brilliant amateur journalists ever to join the United and I do not doubt that the eastern United would be alive today if he had been elected. However, Daas and I were not willing to stoop to political trickery to win. We wanted to win fair and square, and one of my recruits, a nice boy but not to be compared with Lovecraft, was the rival candidate, and the Columbus Woodbee Club took him up and elected him in spite of our best efforts.

So Daas and I, believing in democracy rather than ward boss rule, sat back and let the majority rule. The United had a mail election, then no election and disappeared from the scene. The more literary members joined the National Amateur Press Association.

I have a copy of the Erford United Amateur before me. It is edited on rather a sorry note. A leading article denies the authenticity of the Alumni Association, and accuses it of attempting to steal the Erford United's thunder (as though anybody would want it!) It indulges in yellow journalism innuendo and tries to foment discord between Heins and Mauritzen, and prints a proposed amendment that would bar members of any other similar organization from joining Erford's. That might be a good idea—make it an exclusive Erford club, and have every member swear to be true to their own J. F. Roy! This issue looks like an understudy to a Hearst newspaper; there is nothing of the literary aspirant about it.

So far as repudiating the Alumni Association is concerned this Erford United has nothing to do with it. It stems from a stolen election in 1912. It would be like Mussolini repudiating the Roman Empire!

The Alumni Association stands for the achievements of the past, for writers and poets and journalists and people of charm and manner who have passed through its portals, and have played a while in the mead of the amateur journalist in the days of their youth. There are exceedingly few members of the Erford United who are eligible to membership in the Alumni anyway. Let J. F. Roy have the bad ending of a stormy juvenile association. It will die with him unless something happens to it which hasn't yet occurred.

I'll wager that nobody will take the trouble to organize an alumni association for the Erford United.

The Joke Was On the White Man

Crazy Snake, Whose Liking for "Tintop" Proved His Undoing

Crazy Snake, a Creek Indian, by means of his oratory had lashed a dozen braves to fury over the land allotments to his tribe in 1900, when the 'Frisco Railroad was being built from Sapulpa, Oklahoma, to Denison, Texas. George Danver, construction engineer of the Red River division of the railroad, and his brother were in charge of a train load of construction supplies one night when they were attacked by Crazy Snake and his Indians. They survived the attack, and Mr. Danver was later the only civilian member of a scouting party that captured the Indians. He is now traveling engineer for the Illinois Central Railroad.

We were lunching on the thirty-ninth floor of the new Civic Opera Building in Chicago. An impressive panorama of skyscrapers could be seen through the window, stretching away to Lake Michigan, where our host had pointed out the island location of the 1933 World's Fair, which is to celebrate Chicago's first century of progress.

The engineer, George Danver, wanted to know if Chicago's lakeward expansion would continue until the Michigan shore hove in sight, and I recalled a time, 24 years ago, when the lake waves lapped upon an artificial beach just behind the Art Institute. Our host told us that 50 years ago fishing boats tied up at the Michigan Boulevard curb, and pointed with pride to the man-made land reaching a mile out into the lake at the Adler Planetarium.

A graceful, silver ship of the sky sped across out view and I hailed it as the true symbol of the modern age—a triumph of steel and oil—the two most potent factors in modern progress.

"They do seem to go together," remarked our host, "but progress sometimes gets in its own way, doesn't it?"

"Even from the very first," smiled George Danver, "when the white man pushed the Indian off on the supposedly worthless red flint hills of Indian Territory, and awoke some years later to find he had forced upon his red brother the most valuable land on the continent! That was the best joke that white men ever played on themselves and evens up the score made by the Dutch who bought Manhattan Island for 24 dollars!"

"Many a shrewd trader has been trapped by his own schemes," remarked our host. "There's a kind of poetic justice about it in the case of the Indians. I wonder if they appreciate the joke."

"They didn't at the time of the land allotments," said Danver. "They objected very strenuously to being given those lands and it took a lot of soldiers and gunpowder and diplomacy to ram those millions down the red man's throat. We were building the Red River Division of the 'Frisco Railroad from Sapulpa, Oklahoma to Denison, Texas, in the spring of 1900 and I saw a good deal of the trouble."

We wanted to know about that, and lighting a fresh cigar and settling himself comfortably in his chair, the engineer continued:

"It was purely accidental that the Creeks, who migrated from the southeastern states back in Thomas Jefferson's administration, should have established themselves in the western foot-hills of the Ozarks, but the Government brought in the remnants of the Osages, Kickapoos and a lot of other tribes, just after the Civil War, and deposited them in Indian Territory.

"The Indian Agent at Sapulpa had had a lot of trouble getting the Creeks to settle on their land allotments before the 'Frisco road was built through. By shutting off commissary supplies of flour and bacon and tobacco, he had forced most of the reluctant Creeks to settle on their land. He nipped in the bud one rebellion by taking with him on a trip to Washington the young

Creek prophet obsessed with the mission of 'killing off the whites.' He was a reservation Indian, and the white population of Kansas City, the first stop, made quite an impression on him, but after passing through St. Louis, Chicago, Cleveland, and New York, the young man's mathematical faculties were swamped and by the time he reached Washington his dream was exploded.

"But building the railroad through Indian lands raised another rumpus and a lot of Indians left their land and began wandering around living on the country and the white settlers. Chief Crazy Snake took the stump against land allotments—'All the land Indian land' was his text—and he orated against the railroad and everything else that smacked of the white man's civilization. He stirred up considerable commotion among the Indians with his tongue, for he was a fiery orator, and those settlers whom he was unable to lash into action with his tongue were stirred from their lethargy by his young men, who dragged these traitors to their tribe from their cabins at night and lashed them with rawhide until they agreed to abandon their land allotments.

"About the middle of March I took a supply train out of Sapulpa loaded with steel rails and ties for the construction front below Ada. It was just after dark when we stopped for water at Mounds. I was oiling the drivers on the right side when the shooting started. Our brass bell seemed to be the target. When I came around the pilot of the engine with my torch held high I could see a bunch of squatting Indians on the opposite bank of the cut. I thought every gun was pointing at me and hastily retired, keeping the engine between me and the Indians. In the cab I found my brother, who was firing for me, crouching behind the boiler. The Indians had shot at him when he started to lower the water spout.

"We lost no time in pulling out of Mounds. Some miles farther we found a bridge burned out, and it took all hands most of the night to make a temporary replacement. It was a nervous job, too, working there in the glare of the headlight, expecting any minute to be shot in the back by an Indian, but nothing happened and we learned afterward that Crazy Snake and his band had confiscated a 'tintop' joint and got drunk.

"Just before daylight we started again and running cautiously, looking out for burned bridges or track tampering, we got to Holdensville about noon. There I received orders to set out the train and wait for two companies of soldiers from Fort Sill.

"By sundown we had a company of infantry and a company of cavalry on hoard and were headed back for Crazy Snake's country, the Okmulgee Hills. Twenty-five miles north of Henryetta the soldiers disembarked. The cavalry officer and his scouts set out at once, and on the officer's invitation, I accompanied them. It was a fine Spring, moonlit night and it looked to me as though we had a poor chance of catching up with any Indians, but along about two o'clock in the morning we came upon some Indian ponies grazing in a little valley. We dismounted and explored the vicinity very cautiously on foot, and there under a sheltering ledge of limestone, wrapped in drunken slumber, were a dozen Indians. The 'tintop' had so effectively done its work that we had a gun against the ribs of every one of them before they awakened; it was Crazy Snake and his braves. They were speedily disarmed, handcuffed and taken back to the train.

"Crazy Snake and his band were destined for the Federal Prison at McAlester, and as I could speak the Creek tongue, I went along as interpreter—anyway, I was interested in seeing Crazy Snake safely locked up. He took his arrest philosophically, however, and along in the morning, asked for coffee and tobacco. After I had supplied these wants he took me into his good graces, and invited me to go to prison with him and be his right hand man!

"The following year oil was discovered in Texas, but at that time nobody had any idea that we were forcing wealth upon the reluctant Creeks. I passed up my chance at Indian oil money and came back to Illinois to become Traveling Engineer for the Illinois Central."

"What I want to know," remarked our host, "is what this particularly potent 'tintop' may be?"

"Tintop was a beverage, supposedly non-intoxicating, which was permitted to be sold in Indian Territory, but it was effective if you got enough of it," Danver answered. "I remember once my fireman and I tried to find sleeping quarters in Ada. The only available room was over a 'tintop' bar. The floor was of rough, unmatched boards and the smoke and fumes of the bar came up through the cracks and nearly stifled us. Finally my fireman dropped off into a heavy sleep and emitted a fog-horn snore, which seemed to disturb the patrons of the bar. They began shooting up through the floor with the demand that the snoring cease. We flattened ourselves in the corners until they had emptied their guns, then ran down the stairs, which were outside, and finished the night in the roundhouse."

PAUL J. CAMPBELL, who wrote "The Joke Was on the White Man" for this issue of *The Texaco Star,* is a journalist, oil drilling contractor, and wildcatter. He has been active in the oil fields of Illinois, Indiana, Kentucky, and Michigan, and is now drilling some wildcat tests in Atoka County, Oklahoma.

His interest alternates between oil exploration and literary work. His first novel, three years' work, was burned with his ancestral home, and he says he is trying to reconstruct the story "to the accompaniment of the mocking bird's song on balmy Oklahoma nights." Mr. Campbell lives in Chicago, is 46 years old, married, and has two sons.

The Good Will of a Dog

He was a brown bulldog of common type, with the usual white spots about the head, and I made his acquaintance on a muddy street in a dismal, half-deserted mining town in the Ozarks. His master was the driver of a ramshackle poultry wagon that groaned its protesting way along the rutted road. It was March, and the plastic pavements of that rural borough were in their most impressionable state. As I paused on the cinder sidewalk to appreciate this bit of local color, the protesting poultry wagon made good its oft-squeaked threat to break down. The left hind wheel descended with too much enthusiasm into a deep chuck-hole and collapsed, standing the chicken-coop on end and demolishing a corner of it. One red rooster of Leghorn lineage hailed with glad acclaim this providentially provided avenue of escape, and while the more docile fowls flopped about in futile excitement in the up-ended coop, he took advantage of a broken slat and made a bold break for liberty.

The driver slid off his feet with an appropriate ejaculation, and promptly mired in the mud. The brown bulldog, who had been following a few yards behind, now looked on, an interested and puzzled spectator. Evidently he could not make up his mind whether intervention on his part would be welcomed or resented by his master. After making a few fumbling efforts to apprehend the escaped cockerel, without success, his master called lustily for the dog's assistance.

The dog responded with alacrity, and after a series of strenuous exertions, half running, half swimming, he laid hold on the red rooster's yellow legs, and that discomfited bird opened wide his mouth and emitted a squall of angry protest that had all of his roostership's lung capacity behind it.

The poultryman, fearing that the dog's zeal might make the chicken unsalable, yelled "Brindle!!!" in such a stormy tone, as he reached for the rooster, that the dog in dismay relaxed his hold a moment too soon—and the agile rooster again busied himself with life, liberty and the pursuit of happiness. The angry poultryman bestowed a vicious kick upon the bewildered dog, and then "sicced" him on the escaped chicken once more.

The dog entered with less enthusiasm upon this second chicken chase, but the wearied rooster proved a less expert dodger than before, and was soon caught. Then the same misunderstanding between the dog and his master was reenacted. The rooster squalled "bloody murder." The excitable poultryman stormed at the dog, who released the chicken just as his master reached for it, and in consequence was rewarded with another kick, and again admonished to pursue the elusive chicken. But this time the disgusted dog refused, and retired beneath the broken wagon, where his master assailed him with a whip, while the rooster disappeared down a convenient alley.

It was at this point that I interfered in behalf of the dog. My mild suggestion brought down a shower of profanity upon my head, and would probably have afforded the dog but temporary security had not a passing wagon halted at that moment, and the enraged poultryman's attention was turned to negotiations for the transfer of his load. While his master was thus engaged, the brown bulldog crawled from beneath the wagon and came over to where I was standing. I stooped and patted his head. He licked my hand, and when he looked up at me there shone in his great yellow eyes the dumb appreciation of having found a friend.

Some hours later I again encountered the brown bulldog and his master on the principal street of the town. The poultryman was turning into one of the numerous saloons, and the dog followed. I had hardly passed the ill-smelling entrance when out came the brown bulldog in a manner betokening forcible ejection. He hesitated on the curb and looked forlornly up and down the dingy street. I spoke kindly to him as I passed; a look of recognition shone in his eyes, and he followed me to the hotel where I was stopping. The frowsy clerk, deep in a game of checkers with a fat friend, did not look up as we passed through the front office and up the rickety stairs to the floor above. The dog was close at my heels as I went down the dark hall, and when I stooped to fit the key in my door he laid his cold muzzle in my hand. I patted his head and invited him in. He wagged his stubby tail in acceptance of the invitation, and once inside my room, we became very good friends. It was nearly midnight when I finally crawled into bed and "Brindle" laid down on my overcoat in the corner.

Some two or three hours later I was awakened by a great commotion. Somebody seemed to be exceedingly anxious to depart through the open window, and "Brindle" seemed equally determined that he should not, or at least if he did go, he should leave a considerable portion of his raiment behind. I sprang out of bed, lit the gas, and was going to "Brindle's" assistance when the wild struggles of the intruder to free himself from the dog's retarding influence knocked the prop from beneath the heavy window-sash, and it came down with a loud crash, securely imprisoning the scant ten inches of trousers-seat that the dog was stretching across the sill with all his might, while the agitated occupant of the trousers dangled helpless in the air outside, with all his limbs in futile action.

When the town marshal relieved my burglar from his suspended position, he proved to be none other than "Brindle's" former master, the discomfited poultryman.

This Ain't Love

There were several couples in Maul's Bar when I went across the street for a drink at eleven o'clock, when my helpers left. Maul throws a party on Thursday night. He gave me some fresh shrimp and I listened to the jazz orchestra a few minutes while I drank a glass of beer and ate the shrimp. There were five couples dancing, and something about one of the dancing pairs attracted my attention. I think it was the girl's bright-eyed eagerness. She was young and blonde and much excited. I remember thinking it must be the first time she had been to Maul's—for Maul's is nothing to get excited about.

I went back to the print shop when I had finished the beer and went on making-up Friday's paper.

It must have been about one o'clock when I heard running feet on the cinder street outside the open windows, a scuffle, panting breath and then a high chiding voice, "You leave me be!"

More sounds of struggle and panting breaths.

"You can't run out on me like that," growled a gruff masculine voice.

"What are you goin' to do to me?" apprehensively.

"You're just puttin' on—what did you come for, if you're so scared?"

"Don't you s'pose I git tired o' stayin' home—I want to git out and see the world!"

More scuffling in the cinder street, and an angry "Oh!" from the girl, followed by a soft thud indicating she had been lifted into the car and dropped on the cushion.

The car springs squeaked as the struggle continued.

"Oh!" gasped the girl at breathless intervals. There was anger in her voice. She sobbed, probably at the futility of her efforts to free herself from the embrace of her companion.

There was a quiet spell; some armed truce, while each regained breath. The only sound was my type clicking rhythmically into place in the composing stick. Some of the column heads had to be rewritten. There were only 15 places in a line of 24-point Gothic Condensed, and now and then words had to be changed to fit the space at the head of the newspaper column.

Low masculine murmurs were coming from the coupe outside. The September air was balmy, and the autumn moon was full. Then the girl's strident voice rose above his persuasive murmur.

"This ain't love!" she shrieked.

"Don't—Oh! don't," she pleaded.

Despair had mellowed the strident voice. I forgot the brash gutter-snipe maid drinking in the cheap finery of Maul's night club, and picked up the heavy wooden mallet lying on the composing stone and strolled toward the door—wondering how Don Quixote felt when he went forth to fight wind-mills!

Before I reached the door there was a burst of sobbing punctuated by little groans, "Oh! Oh! Oh!" Then the boy's voice, raw with disgust: "Shut-up! You cry-baby—I'm taking you home."

The automobile starter whirred, and the car dashed away as I stood in the print shop doorway and looked out into the September night. The moonlight was reminiscent of other days and other scenes, of a sand dune overlooking Lake Michigan at the end of a summer holiday of holding hands with a blue-eyed girl, the touch of whose hand made my heart sing. When she ran her fingers through my hair and gently pulled my head down to her breast I was transported to the seventh heaven, and when we knew each other on that last night of the first real summer either of us had ever lived to the full, it seemed (even after twenty years) that we melted together, blended so completely that neither knew quite what the limits of one body were, but only that the "twain were ecstatically one flesh!"

Founding the Fraternity of the Wooden Leg

When I began wearing a wooden leg twenty-five years ago, I began to notice others who were using artificial walking equipment. I had never done this before. Doubtless I had passed by many wearers of artificial limbs without being aware of the fact, in the days before I wore one myself. But having a wooden leg sharpened my perception.

After I began walking on a wooden leg I greeted and talked to many of these people. Most of them were especially approachable to another wooden-legged person. There seemed to be a freemasonry between us. We swapped experience, and passed good cheer and parted with good wishes, and I always went on my way feeling better for having fraternized with one of my tribe. I would explain to my family these visits with strangers by saying that we both belonged to the "Fraternity of the Wooden Leg."

My mother used to repeat the phrase, "Fraternity of the Wooden Leg," as though she liked it—as though it was a distinction of which one might be proud. And the more I think about it, the more I am convinced that it is a distinction that justifies greater pride than wearing false teeth or horn-rimmed glasses or carrying a cane.

The initiation you have gone through in acquiring your wooden leg has been, (or should have been), a refining process. You went down into the Valley of the Shadow and you came back, but you are never quite the same person you were before. The fellow who came back is wiser, kinder, gentler, more sympathetic with his fellow men. He has acquired new values. Having almost renounced life, he is more determined to live fully; he is ready to settle down to the true business of living on a live and let live basis.

It is the obstructed current that produces incandescence.

Overcoming a handicap adds to the mental stature. In my own case, the loss of a leg gave me time to develop a sense of proportion for which I had been in too big a hurry before. I took stock of life and evaluated it, and I developed tolerance and a sense of humor.

I had often wished that I could bring together the many interesting people I had met along the way—met because they had wooden legs and had stopped to talk to me because I had a wooden leg—but I never did anything about it.

When my friend Augusta "A. B." Weaver lost a foot last year, I wrote her a hospital letter with wooden-legged philosophy and welcoming her to the

"Fraternity of the Wooden Leg." She immediately proposed that we organize such a fraternity and we sent out 12,000 circulars announcing the Fraternity of the Wooden Leg and offering an invitation to join. Many people responded. A magazine to serve as a medium of exchange between these people was the next step planned, and after considering many names Miss Weaver and I chose *Courage* (Courage is the first essential for people like us).

We want to make *Courage* your magazine, truly representative of the Fraternity of the Wooden Leg. This first issue has been long delayed, as I have been too deep in the Illinois Oil Field to do more than dream and plan very briefly what I would like to do in the making of this magazine, if there were only more than 24 hours in a day.

With the launching of *Courage* goes the invitation to join the Fraternity of the Wooden Leg—let us unite, we have nothing but our loneliness to lose. Together we can be of mutual assistance.

W. Paul Cook

The United Amateur Press Association— An Historical Survey: 1895–1912

In the early part of the 1890's there sprang into prominence a portion of the professional press of the country devoted to the publication of stories and articles designed to appeal to the youth of the land, and to the boyish youth in particular. There were a large number of these periodicals, but of these. two attained an especially wide circulation and influence. These were known as *Golden Hours* and *Golden Jays*. The matter contained in these papers was of a distinctly unliterary grade, bordering frequently upon the actually sensational, and, indeed, being in many respects but a slight degree better than dime novel "literature." However, it was a decidedly cleaner character than most o(the dime novels of the period, was much better written, and dealt largely with sports instead of with outlaw or detective heroes. Prominent authors contributed to these papers under noms-de-plume, and many of their serials have since enjoyed success in book form. But the distinctive success of *Golden Hours* and *Golden Days* was due to the kindly personal interest which they took in their thousands of boy and girl readers. Correspondents' columns were maintained. and letters and exchange notices were published from the readers. Prize contests for literary contributions were conducted, portraits of the winners were published, and the papers generally endeavoured to keep in close touch with their bright juvenile readers.

Among the immense clientele of these two papers it was natural that acquaintanceships should be formed, like those which we have already noted in the case of *Oliver Optic's Magazine*. Gradually there came into being correspondence circles, and then by an easy transition "clubs" were formed. known as "Golden Hours Club No. 100," or "Golden Days Club No. 99," as the case might be. Every "club" had officers and an official organ, and soon there were literally hundreds of small papers published. The contents of these club papers seldom ran to a higher level than "club notes," which were short items concerning the club members, and personalities dealing with the editor's pet enemy among his contemporaries. Several clubs were frequently merged into one, thus allowing a larger and more impressive club paper which could print longer literary contributions. Thus was born an idea in the mind of a boy of Philadelphia, a boy named William H. Greenfield.

In 1895 there came to William Greenfield a vision of the union of all these scattered club papers and club editors and authors into one large and all-embracing organization. At this time Greenfield was fourteen years of age, but was already earning money from the products of his pen—had, in fact. already adopted the literary career by which he earned his living and no inconsiderable fame during the rest of his life. Greenfield at once boldly organized and proclaimed the "United Amateur Press Association." He appointed himself president and selected and appointed to their posts the rest of the board of officers. He promulgated such laws as were needed, and paid what bills had to be paid. In short. for a few months, William H. Greenfield and the United Amateur Press Association were one and the same.

The growth of the association was not as rapid as had been anticipated, since Greenfield had proclaimed the organization as a literary one, and all club editors and members were not in haste to join. Also, many of the membership were anything hut "literary."

As the association increased in numbers. the necessity of an election of officers became apparent, and accordingly an election board was appointed and an election by mail conducted. Just how out of sympathy the membership was with Greenfield's "literary" views, may be shown by the fact that the founder of the association was defeated for even the minor office for which he was a candidate—the Secretaryship. Greenfield, now deceased, never afterward appeared as an officer of the United Amateur Press Association.

For several years attempt to have the association publish its own official organ were failures, as the money for such an undertaking was not forthcoming, and accordingly papers published by individual members were elected to serve as the official organ. The irregularity and frequent suspension of papers so elected seriously hampered the association for many years.

Fortunately, the first elected president of the association, Edward H. Weigel, of Harrisburg. Pennsylvania, was not only an energetic and able executive, but was in sympathy with the literary side of the work to such an extent that he used his influence toward the suppression oi the "club note" in favour of longer and more ambitious attempts at writing. Only the lack of a regularly published and adequate official organ prevented his administration from being noteworthy, as the secretary. Harris Reed, Jr., of Philadelphia, was likewise an able and efficient officer, and left his books complete and in excellent condition.

The second election and the first convention was held in Philadelphia in 1897. This was a largely attended convention, was addressed by Col. A. K. McClure of the *Times*, and was fully reported and illustrated in all the city papers. J. Frederick Crosson was elected president, and the bright spot of his administration was the official organ *Bits und Chips*, published by Frank E. Merritt of Utica, New York, which by its regularity kept the membership in touch. and which by Mr. Merritt's lofty ideals of journalistic endeavour aided still further in discouraging note writing.

Real progress was made at the Milwaukee convention of 1898. James C. Bresnahan was elected president, and the final blow was dealt to note writing by the inauguration of the Laureateships. The literary standard was likewise raised by the act of the association in taking a definite stand toward the elimination of the *Golden Hours* and *Golden Days* class of literature and the striving for something higher and better. Mr. Bresnahan's administration was hampered only by the lack of an official organ. Many large and worthy papers appeared, and a decided advance was made in the tone of literary effort.

At the 1899 convention in New York the first Laureateships were awarded. William H. Greenfield was awarded the Story, Essay, and Editorial Laureateships; while Dwight Anderson gained the Poetry Laureateship with a poem, "The Bachelor's Shrine," which set a high standard for future Poet Laureates to attain. The year's work was marred by the lack of a good official organ and by political turmoils and troubles in administration which necessitated the removal one by one of practically all the elected officers. Yet much good work was accomplished. the salient feature of the year being the sudden leap to prominence of William R. Murphy, who contributed literary material of a high quality in both verse and prose to all the best papers, and who in various papers started the first real criticism known to the association.

At the Jersey City convention of. 1900, James C. Bresnahan was a second time elected president, and William R. Murphy was awarded the Essay and Editorial Laureateships. While Mr. Bresnahan's health compelled his resignation early in the year, yet the association was fortunate in having a good official organ in the *Dewey*, published by Charles E. Wing. The *Dewey* was by far the best paper connected with the association. and would he a credit to the organization at any period of its history. Too much credit cannot be given Mr. Wing for his determined efforts to raise the standard of our literature. Mr. Murphy in an unofficial capacity continued his criticisms and his other contributions to the amateur press.

At the Minneapolis convention of 1901, the long delayed move was made of voting that the association publish its own official organ. Up to this time the project had been often advocated, but the finances of the association had never warranted the step. Even in 1901, financial reasons could easily have been urged against such a move, but the sanguine ones forced the motion through. It was the greatest single step ever taken by the association, and to Guy N. Phillips, who was elected president, and James M. Reilly, Jr., belongs much of the credit. As a matter of fact, the association could not then or at any time since finance an adequate official organ from the treasury. Donations for the purpose have always been necessary. But from the time of its first issuance, in August 1901, the *United Amateur* nevertheless had a continuous existence till the abeyance of one of the two branches in 1926–7/ Not every volume consisted of six issues, but the exceptions to the constitutional rule were rare. The issue for August, 1901, was the only one sent out by Mr. Cull, the elected official editor, and. as was very fitting, James M. Reilly, Jr., was selected to complete the volume. No attempt was made at official criticism, and Mr. Reilly's volume was strictly business-like. But it was newsy, and splendidly upheld its purpose of keeping the membership in touch with one another. The only criticism of worth continued to be that of William R. Murphy, who was now an editor oi the *American Gem,* published by Charles A. Wendemuth of St. Louis. In the columns of this paper appeared Mr. Murphy's best critical work, as well as the best work of practically all amateur writers. It may be mentioned here that at the 1901 convention Mr. Murphy was awarded the Poetry and Story Laureateship.

The year 1902–1903 marked a great advance in all the activities of the association. At the 1902 convention held in Philadelphia, one of the ablest executives the United ever had, James A. Clerkin was elected to the presidency. Erwin B Ault was elected official editor, and issued a splendid first number of the *United Amateur.* Mr. Cull was compelled to resign, however, and Albert E. Cull was again placed in the editorial chair. Mr. Cull completed the year as official editor in splendid manner. In this year the membership of the association approached the three hundred mark. while about 115 different papers were published by members. The Eastern Manuscript Manager handled over eighty manuscripts, and the western manager over one hundred, nearly all of which were placed for publication. Several papers equalling the *American Gem* put in an appearance, perhaps the feature of the year being the rise to distinction of the *Pioneer,* these published by Arthur R. Stanton of Philadelphia. The *Pioneer* had a long and active existence, being at different times in the hands of Arthur R. Stanton, William R. Murphy and Joseph E. Cohen, alone or in partnership, and being especially noteworthy for its criticism and its literary standard. Mr. Cohen was as able a writer of fiction as the United has ever seen. He was awarded the Story Laureateship in both 1902 and 1903.

At the Minneapolis convention in 1903, Ira Eugene Seymour was elected president because of his remarkable recruiting record of the previous year. Charles H. Russell of Philadelphia was given the official organ, and he responded with the largest volume of the *United Amateur* published up to that time, making a record which endured until 1907–1908. Mr. Russell's volume consisted of six issues aggregating 104 pages, and was a well balanced, progressive yet conservative organ. In December, 1903, the Western Manuscript Manager of the United had by arousing intense interest in his office, actually handled 128 manuscripts, one hundred of which were placed with publishers. The writer has no record to show how many manuscripts this official, Charles K. Cullom, handled during the entire year. 1902–1903 witnessed the springing into amateur prominence of Paul J. Campbell, his paper being the *Prairie State Journal.* In 1903, Morgan D. Hite issued from New Orleans, Louisiana, a unique duplicated and hand ornamented paper, the *Moon,* issuing also a booklet containing the laureate poems of the association to that year. This was a forerunner of the Year Books, which were later a valuable feature of the association. The year 1903–1904 witnessed the flowering as an authoress of Flora Stewart Emory, who in the ensuing years was awarded two Story Laureate- ships, two Poetry Laureateships, an Essay Laureateship and several honorable mentions in the different classes. There continued to be no systematic official criticism. but publications were so numerous that much good criticism was produced. The work in criticism of O. Byron Copper in his own *Copper's Critique* and in John C. Burchmore's *Initial* deserves special mention. In the June, 1904 *United Amateur* the Laureate Recorder reported 271 Laureate entries.

At the convention in Baltimore, Maryland, in 1904, John W. Smith was elected official editor of the association. Mr. Smith issued only two number of the *United Amateur* before resigning, but the change he made in the policy of the official organ is one of the two bright spots in what was otherwise a very unsuccessful year. Mr. Smith instituted the first literary department to appear in the *United Amateur,* and also added a "Department of Instructive Criticism." In this critical department the different laureate winners handed the subjects in which they were supposed to be proficient, and signed their criticisms. The other feature of the year, was the issuance of the first Year Book of the association, containing the laureateship-winning articles, historian's report, statistical tables, and other important matter. This Year Book was issued unofficially through the well-directed energy of Hal C. Chase of Philadelphia, and was financed by voluntary subscriptions of a number of amateurs. Mr. Chase urged the immediate passage by the association of an amendment to the Constitution making the Year Book an official publication.

The Kansas City convention of 1905 ushered in a year of political turmoil, during which almost every elected officer of the association either resigned or was removed. But the official organ was notable in a year when although there were a great number of papers, Very few were devoted to the literary side of amateur journalism. Homer P. Pickrell, the elected official editor, retained his office long enough to issue two numbers of the *United Amateur.* The "Department of Instruction and Criticism" was made official, and

Henry J. Wehking was made its chairman. Criticism was handled under the different heads of "Stories," "Essays," "Editorials," etc., and each was handled by a supposed expert who signed his work. Too much praise cannot be given Mr. Wehking for his constructive work in placing the United official criticism on a firm and accepted basis, and making it so sound and authoritative that it became recognized as the most important feature of the official organ and of the work of the association. Mr. Wehking himself wrote in almost all of the popular literary forms. All of his work in stories, essays, poetry or editorials was well above the average, and he seldom allowed his personal point of view to influence his criticism. Upon Mr. Pickrell's resignation as official editor, Louis C. Brechler was appointed to the position, and completed the year by issuing three numbers of the official organ, continuing Mr. Pickrell's policy as to contents.

The Milwaukee convention of 1906 ushered in a new and a brilliant period for the United Amateur Press Association . It may be mentioned that at this convention the late Arthur H. Goodenough was awarded the first of his many Poetry laureateships in the United. William C. Ahlhauser, one of the most solid amateurs in the country, was chosen to lead the association into the promised land, and was given Louis G. Brechler as official editor. The Milwaukee convention also made the publication of the year hook an official matter. Mr. Brechler published the greatest volume of the *United Amateur* issued to that time. It consisted of six numbers and 112 pages with covers. Mr. Wehking continued as chairman of the Critical Bureau, and a change of policy was made: whereby the criticism was anonymous. During this year Mr. Maurice Winter Moe, later a prominent figure in the literary life of the association, and an important to the critical work, became affiliated with the United. A Year Book of 48 pages was issued in the name of the association. For the first time the Critical Department: was allowed practically unlimited space: in the official organ, and gained a recognized and influential place as one of the most important factors in the association's work. To Messrs. Brechler and Wehking must be given credit for the final result in forcing recognization [*sic*] of official criticism as an essential part of the associational work.

Edward F. Daas was elected to the executive office in Seattle in 1907. The year was very successful, the official editor, Homer P. Pickrell, strengthening all the departments of the *United Amateur* and issuing a volume of 142 pages. An attempt was made to double the membership of the association, which at the beginning of the year was barely 150. In spite of the unprecedented recruiting effort of J. F. Roy Erford, the attempt was not successful, but nearly one hundred names were added to the membership list. Mr. Wehking continued as Chief of the Critical Bureau. A Year Book of 52 pages was issued by the official committee.

At the Milwaukee convention in 1908, Mr. Brechler was given the presidency because of his work as official editor, and as secretary in the two preceding year. Alter issuing an inadequate initial number of the *United Amateur,* the elected official editor resigned, and John D. Christiansen completed the year in an excellent manner. Mr. Christiansen featured the news department of his official organ, but allowed some space to the critical department. Miss Litta Voelchert served efficiently as Chief of the Critical Bureau, and Maurice W. Moe appeared as a member of her staff. A summary of the work of this year gives: Total number of papers, 110; stories, 58; poems, 73; essays, 71; editorials, 111; miscellaneous, 115. The actual preponderance of other branches of literature over poetry is especially to be noted in this report. The Year Book for 1908 was a really remarkable achievement by Vincent B. Haggerty. It consisted of 84 pages. and besides the essential matter, included a vast amount of valuable historical material, statistics, portraits, etc.

At the Seattle convention in 1909, S. Parker Rowell was elected president and James R. Dolin, official editor. Mr. Dolin issued two excellent numbers of the official organ, but was compelled to resign, and Vincent B. Haggerty completed a truly splendid volume of the *United Amateur.* J. F. Roy Erford served as Chief of the Critical Bureau, and Mr. Haggerty allowed the Bureau liberal space in the organ. The "'Department of Instruction and Criticism'" contained not only criticism of amateur publications, but also formal articles on the different forms of literary work. No Year Book was issued, but Mr. Haggerty carried all the Year Book matter in the *United Amateur,* thus preserving it for future reference and use. This feature of his volume is especially to be noted.

Mr. Haggerty was elected to the presidency at the convention in Chattanooga, in 1910. F. Roy Davidson was selected as official editor. and Mr. Erford was again placed in charge of the "Department of Instruction and Criticism." The work of this department continued along the lines of the preceding year, and was exceedingly valuable. An attempt was made to remove the constitutional requirement for a Year Book, but the move was not successful. In spite of this fact, no Year Book appeared, and while Mr. Davidson devoted a great deal of pace to the critical department, he did not publish the Year Book matter in his volume. In March of this year the United membership total reached 277, the largest in the history of the association since 1905. Perhaps one of the features of the work during 1909–1910 was the activity of George H. Couger of Bridgeport, Conn., who published two or three papers at monthly or even shorter intervals and was exceedingly democratic in selecting his material, his papers containing work varying from the polished product of the experienced author to the crude credentials of the new comer.

Messrs. John D. Christiansen and C. O. A. Kramer were named respectively president and official editor at Bridgeport in 1911. Mr. Kramer issued an adequate *United Amateur,* devoting a fair amount of space to "Instruction and Criticism," and featuring "News Notes" to a greater extent. A departure was made in the "'Department of Instruction and Criticism," by placing a professional English teacher at its head in the person of George D. Knight, professor of English in the University of Redlands, California. Much of the work of the "department" for the year consisted of authoritative articles by professional writers. Through the energetic efforts of Edward F. Daas a Year Book was issued in this year, thus preserving this important historical matter. While no especially noteworthy or epoch-making event occurred to signalize this year, yet the association was in a healthy condition. The membership list was large and contributed liberally to special funds so that the Treasurer was able to pay the official editor more than the constitutional allowance for the official organ.

An Historical Survey: 1915

Continuance by Paul J. Campbell of History begun by W. Paul Cook.

Unfortunately, this era of quiet prosperity did not long continue, and the administration of Helene E. Hoffman, the first woman president of the United, began under trying circumstances. For the third time in its history the association was shaken by the purgative action of the elements of political unrest, which periodically disrupt such organizations as ours. The conduct of the election by the La Grande, Oregon, 1912 convention, created a dangerous division of opinion which threatened to turn the chief activities of the membership &om literature to political sharp practice, with discouraging results.

The closeness of the vote caused each set of candidates to consider itself elected, and to this day dispute regarding the legality of the rival claims exists. The outcome of the contest was a schism creating two separate associations with the same name and the same assumption of descent from the parent United. Of these, one is still active; while the other, which attained the most favourable literary development at the outset, became abeyant in 1926–7. It is with the latter that the present history is concerned.*

Miss Hoffman proved an able leader with unusual ability as an organizer of local clubs. With twelve such centres of enthusiasm supporting the association in as many cities and towns throughout the country, the losses sustained by the membership list through partisan differences were fairly well made up. It was a feminine year in literary activity, all four Laureateships being awarded to girls. An able department of criticism was conducted by Maurice W. Moe, and a hundred-page volume of the official organ was issued containing the Laureate literature. The elected official editor, Paul H. Hilt, having resigned, Edward F. Daas was appointed his successor and edited the last two numbers of this volume.

The second administration of Helene E. Hoffman began more auspiciously. The Milwaukee 1913 convention at which she was re-elected, had a

---

*It appears that is the clarifying paragraph that HPL said he wrote.

representative attendance, and much enthusiasm and interest were awakened . Fourteen amendments to the constitution, which it was hoped would prevent a repetition of the unpleasantness of the previous year, were adopted. Ill health compelled the resignation of Roscoe W. Goens as official editor almost immediately after election, and Edward F. Daas, the able prime minister of the administration, was appointed to the editorship and published an excellent volume of the *United Amateur* of over one hundred pages, much space being devoted to literature and to dub news. The local clubs had now grown to seventeen in number. Among the new clubs, perhaps the foremost was the "Blarneys" of Rocky Mount, North Carolina, who were later to play an important part in the history of the United and were to entertain the 1915 convention . Mr. Moe again served in the capacity of official critic, and the number of papers published was slightly increased over that of the preceding year. The Year Book material was again published in the official organ and *the* literary element was paramount throughout the volume.

The association having prospered during the two administrations of its first woman president, a second woman president was elected at the Columbus, Ohio, 1914 convention, in the person of Dora M. Hepner, who, in the main, carried out the policies of her predecessor. M. Weddell Hart of the "Blarneys" was elected official editor and published two issues of the official organ. after which the mechanical difficulties of publication from Rocky Mount, N. C. caused a long delay. The office of publication was then changed to Georgetown, Illinois, where the remaining three numbers of the volume were printed; first under the supervision of Paul J. Campbell, and later under that of George S. Schilling. The fifth and last issue of the year was edited by Mr. Hart. The department of criticism \Vas this year vigorously conducted by Howard P. Lovecraft, the news feature of the official organ was given a good deal of prominence, and the literary department contained the Laureate winning entries, and several contributions of note. A Year Book was issued by Paul J. Campbell and Edward F. Daas, 114 members were admitted and the membership list climbed to 227. The association could again rightfully boast of being in a healthy condition.

Glossary of Frequently Mentioned Names

Bacon, Victor E. (1905–1997), amateur journalist and editor of *Bacon's Essays*, which published work by HPL and Clark Ashton Smith, and Official Editor of the UAPA (1925–26).

Barlow, R[obert] H[ayward] (1918–1951), author and collector. As a teenager he corresponded with HPL and acted as his host during two long visits in the summers of 1934 and 1935. In the 1930s he wrote several works of weird and fantasy fiction, some in collaboration with HPL. HPL appointed him his literary executor. He assisted August Derleth and Donald Wandrei in preparing the early HPL volumes for Arkham House. In the 1940s he went to Mexico and became a distinguished anthropologist. For HPL's letters to him, see *O Fortunate Floridian*.

Bush, David Van (1882–1959), prolific author of inspirational verse and popular psychology books, many of them revised by Lovecraft.

Coates, Walter J[ohn] (1880–1941), poet, printer, bibliographer, Universalist minister, and storekeeper in Vermont. He published *Driftwind*, a poetry magazine, for fifteen years starting in 1925. His Driftwind Press specialized in Vermont literature and small edition vanity books of poetry. He published ten sonnets from HPL's *Fungi from Yuggoth*.

Cole, Edward H[arold] (1892–1966), longtime amateur associate (chiefly in NAPA) living in the Boston area who established contact with HPL in late 1914; editor of the *Olympian* and *Bema*.

Cole, Ira A. (1883–1973) of Bazine, KS. Historian of the UAPA and member of the Kleicomolo. He edited the *Plainsman*, which published HPL's poem "On the Cowboys of the West" (December 1915). He was no relation to Edward H. Cole.

Cook, W. Paul (1880–1948) of Athol, MA, publisher of the *Monadnock Monthly*, *Vagrant*, *Recluse*, and other amateur journals; a longtime amateur journalist, printer, and lifelong friend of HPL. He first visited HPL in 1917, and it was he who urged HPL to resume writing fiction after a hiatus of nine years. In 1927 Cook published the *Recluse*, containing HPL's "Supernatural Horror in Literature." Author of *In Memoriam: Howard Phillips Lovecraft* (1941).

Daas, Edward F[rancis] (1879–1962) of Milwaukee, amateur journalist who joined the UAPA within a year of its founding in 1895. He was elected President in 1907 and served as Official Editor in 1913–14 and 1915–16. He recruited HPL to the UAPA in 1914. At the time of his death, he was serving as UAPA Secretary.

Davis, Graeme (1881–1938), of Vermillion, SD, a "self-proclaimed Buddhist," fifty-third president of the NAPA, and editor of *The Lingerer*. He wrote harshly of the UAPA in there, leading to HPL's "A Reply to *The Lingerer*," (June 1917): [9–12].

de Castro, Adolphe [Danziger] (1859–1959), author, co-translator with Ambrose Bierce of Richard Voss's *The Monk and the Hangman's Daughter*, and correspondent of HPL. HPL revised his "The Last Test" and "The Electric Executioner." For HPL's letters to him, see *Letters to Alfred Galpin and Others*.

Dowdell, William J. (1898–1953), amateur journalist who abruptly resigned as president of the NAPA in late 1922, leading the executive judges to appoint HPL as interim president.

Dunn, John T[homas] (1889–1983), Irish-American living in Providence who came in touch with HPL in late 1914 in the Providence Amateur Press Club. He assisted HPL in editing two issues of the *Providence Amateur* (June 1915, February 1916). Dunn was briefly imprisoned for refusing to register for the draft. After the war he became a Catholic priest. He was interviewed late in life by L. Sprague de Camp (see "Young Man Lovecraft," *Xenophile*, October 1975; rpt. *Ave atque Vale*). *Letters to Alfred Galpin and Others*.

Dwyer, Bernard Austin (1897–1943), weird fiction fan living in West Shokan, NY, and correspondent of HPL. For HPL's letters to him, see *Letters to Maurice W. Moe and Others*.

Edkins, Ernest A[rthur] (1867–1946), longtime amateur journalist with whom HPL began corresponding in 1932. HPL persuaded him to rejoin the amateur journalism movement, and Edkins subsequently edited several issues of the journal *Causerie*.

Galpin, Alfred (1901–1983) of Appleton, WI, amateur journalist, French scholar, composer, and protégé, then longtime friend, of HPL. See *Letters to Alfred Galpin and Others*.

Goodenough, Arthur H[enry] (1871–1936), amateur poet who resided in West Brattleboro, VT. HPL visited him there in 1927 and 1928. He wrote a poem about HPL, "Lovecraft—an Appreciation," to which HPL responded with "To Arthur Goodenough, Esq."

Greene, Sonia H[aft] (1883–1972), HPL's wife (1924–29). Born Sonia Haft Shafirkin in Ichnya (near Kiev), in the Ukraine. Settling in the United States, she eventually joined the amateur journalism movement, publishing two lavish issues of the *Rainbow* and becoming president of the UAPA (1924–25). After her divorce from HPL, she moved to California and married Dr. Nathaniel Davis. *The Private Life of H. P. Lovecraft* (1985; rev. 1992) is her memoir of HPL.

Hoag, Jonathan E. (1831–1927), amateur poet living in Greenwich, NY, and dedicatee of numerous birthday poems by HPL from 1918 until his death. HPL co-edited and published *The Poetical Works of Jonathan E. Hoag* (1923).

Houtain, George Julian (1884–1945), amateur journalist and editor of the *Zenith;* later editor of the professional humor magazine *Home Brew,* for which HPL would write "Herbert West—Reanimator" (1921–22) and "The Lurking Fear" (1922).

Kirk, George W[illard] (1898–1962), member of the Kalem Club. He published *Twenty-one Letters of Ambrose Bierce* (1922), ran the Chelsea Bookshop in New York, and was a member of the Kalem Club.

Kuntz, Eugene B. (1865–1944), Prussian-born poet, Presbyterian minister, and amateur journalist. HPL edited Kuntz's slim collection of poems, *Thoughts and Pictures* (Haverhill, MA: "Cooperatively published by H. P. Loveracft [*sic*] and C. W. Smith," 1932), probably revising the poems in the process.

Lockhart, Andrew Francis (1890–1964), of Milbank, SD, amateur journalist, editor of the temperance journal *Chain Lightning.*

Long, Frank Belknap (1901–1994), amateur journalist, fiction writer, poet, member of the Kalem Club, and one of HPL's closest friends and correspondents.

Loveman, Samuel E. (1887–1976), poet, translator, and longtime friend of HPL and Hart Crane, and associate of Ambrose Bierce, Hart Crane, George Sterling, and Clark Ashton Smith. He wrote *The Hermaphrodite* (1926), *The Sphinx* (1944), and other works. See *Out of the Immortal Night: Selected Works of Samuel Loveman* (Hippocampus Press, 2004). For HPL's letters to him, see *Letters to Maurice W. Moe and Others.*

Lynch, Joseph Bernard (1879–1952), amateur journalist and member of the Hub Club.

Macauley, George W. (1885–1969), of Grand Rapids, MI., editor of the *Trail* (with Dora M. Hepner), *Pep, Red Letter Days,* and *O-Wash-Ta-Nong,* in which he published extracts of his letters from HPL. He conceived a plan to plant a grove of trees in Michigan, each dedicated to a president of the NAPA.

McColl, Gavin T. of Dundee, Scotland, edited the amateur journal the *Scot,* which published HPL's "The Doom That Came to Sarnath" (June 1920).

Miniter, Edith (Dowe) (1869–1934), amateur journalist chiefly associated with the NAPA and its forty-third president (1909–10). See HPL's "Mrs. Miniter— Estimates and Recollections" (*Californian,* Spring 1938; *CE* 1.378–86).

Moe, Maurice W[inter] (1882–1940), amateur journalist, English teacher, and longtime friend and correspondent of HPL. He lived successively in Appleton and Milwaukee, WI. For HPL's letters to him, see *Letters to Maurice W. Moe and Others.*

Moitoret, Anthony F. (1892–1979), editor of the *Boys' Sun, San Francisco Sun, Cincinnati Sun, Cleveland Sun,* and the *Meteor.*

Morton, James Ferdinand (1870–1941), amateur journalist, author of many tracts on race prejudice, free thought, and taxation; longtime friend of HPL and member of the Kalem Club. He married the amateur journalist Pearl K. Merritt in 1934. For HPL's letters to him, see *Letters to James F. Morton and Others.*

Myers, Denys P. (1884–1972), and **Ethel May Johnston Myers** (1882–1971), whom HPL described as "old-time amateurs."

Parker, Charles A. A. (1878–1965), amateur journalist, publisher, and editor of the little magazine *L'Alouette,* chiefly devoted to poetry, *Bavardage,* and *The Literary Gem* (with Nelson Glazier Morton). HPL published an advertisement for his revisory services in issues of *L'Alouette* for 1933–34.

Renshaw, Anne Tillery (1890–c. 1945), prolific amateur journalist and professor. She met HPL during the latter's visit to Washington, D.C., in April 1925. In 1936 she commissioned HPL to revise a textbook of English usage, *Well-Bred Speech* (1936), although much of the work HPL did for it was excised and remains unpublished. For HPL's letters to her, see *Letters to Elizabeth Toldridge and Anne Tillery Renshaw.*

Samples, John Milton (1887–?) of Macon, GA (later Atlanta), editor of the *Silver Clarion.*

Sandusky, Albert A[ugust] (1896–1934), , member of the Hub Club and amateur journalist whose use of slang amused HPL. He printed several early issues of HPL's amateur journal, the *Conservative.* HPL met him frequently during trips to the Boston area.

Schilling, George S., replaced Edward F. Daas as Official Editor of the UAPA for the 1914–15 term. He was the editor of the *Badger,* for which HPL was an assistant editor of the June 1915 issue.

Sechrist, Edward Lloyd (1873–1953), amateur journalist and beekeeper. HPL met him on several occasions, especially during visits to Washington, DC.

Smith, Charles W. ("Tryout") (1852–1948), longtime amateur journalist, editor of the *Tryout,* and friend and correspondent of HPL.

Smith, Edwin Hadley (1869–1944), a leading amateur journalist of the period, chiefly associated with the NAPA; editor of the *Boys Herald.* The Library of Amateur Journalism (also known as The Edwin Hadley Smith Collection and The Fossil Collection), initially housed at the Franklin Institute in Philadelphia, is now at the University of Wisconsin–Madison. HPL directed that, upon his death, his amateur journals be turned over to Smith.

Spink, Helm C. (1909–1970), printer and Official Editor of the NAPA in 1930 and again in 1935 (with O. W. Hinrichs). He printed and published HPL's *Further Criticism of Poetry* (1932).

Talman, Wilfred Blanch (1904–1986), correspondent of HPL and late member of the Kalem Club. HPL assisted Talman on his story "Two Black

Bottles" (1926) and wrote "Some Dutch Footprints in New England" for Talman to publish in *De Halve Maen*, the journal of the Holland Society of New York. Late in life he wrote the memoir *The Normal Lovecraft* (1973). For HPL's letters to him, see *Letters to Wilfred B. Talman and Helen V. and Genevieve Sully*.

Whitehead, Henry S[t. Clair] (1882–1932), author of weird and adventure tales, many of them set in the Virgin Islands. HPL corresponded with him and visited him in Florida in 1931. HPL wrote a brief eulogy of Whitehead for WT.

Bibliography

A. H. P. Lovecraft

Books

The Ancient Track: Complete Poetical Works. Edited by S. T. Joshi. 2nd ed. New York: Hippocampus Press, 2013.

The Annotated Supernatural Horror in Literature. Edited by S. T. Joshi. 2nd ed. New York: Hippocampus Press, 2012.

Collected Essays. Edited by S. T. Joshi. New York: Hippocampus Press, 2004–06. 5 vols.

Collected Fiction: A Variorum Edition. Edited by S. T. Joshi. New York: Hippocampus Press, 2015–17. 4 vols.

The Crime of Crimes. Llandudno, Wales: A[rthur] Harris, [1915].

H. P. Lovecraft in the Argosy: *Collected Correspondence from the Munsey Magazines.* Edited by S. T. Joshi. West Warwick, RI: Necronomicon Press, 1994.

Letters to Alfred Galpin and Others. Edited by S. T. Joshi and David E. Schultz. New York: Hippocampus Press, 2020.

Letters to Elizabeth Toldridge and Anne Tillery Renshaw. Edited by David E. Schultz and S. T. Joshi. New York: Hippocampus Press, 2014.

Letters to F. Lee Baldwin, Duane W. Rimel, and Nils Frome. Edited by David E. Schultz and S. T. Joshi. New York: Hippocampus Press, 2016.

Letters to James F. Morton. Edited by David E. Schultz and S. T. Joshi. New York: Hippocampus Press, 2011.

Letters to Maurice W. Moe and Others. Edited by David E. Schultz and S. T. Joshi. New York: Hippocampus Press, 2018.

Letters to Wilfred B. Talman and Helen V. and Genevieve Sully. Edited by David E. Schultz and S. T. Joshi. New York: Hippocampus Press, 2019.

O Fortunate Floridian: H. P. Lovecraft's Letters to R. H. Barlow. Edited by S. T. Joshi and David E. Schultz. Tampa: University of Tampa Press, 2007.

The Shadow over Innsmouth. Everett, PA: Visionary Publishing Co., 1936. (*LL* 591)

United Amateur Press Association: Exponent of Amateur Journalism. [Columbus, OH: Leo Fritter, 1915?]. In *CE* 1.

Fiction

"The Alchemist." *United Amateur* 16, No. 4 (November 1916): 53–57. In *CF* 1.

"The Beast in the Cave." *Vagrant* No. 7 (June 1918): 113–20. In *CF* 1.

"The Call of Cthulhu." *WT* 11, No. 2 (February 1928): 159–78, 287. In T. Everett Harré, ed. *Beware After Dark! The World's Most Stupendous Tales of Mystery, Horror, Thrills and Terror.* New York: Macaulay, 1929. 223–59. In *CF* 2.

The Case of Charles Dexter Ward. In *CF* 2.

"The Cats of Ulthar." *Tryout* 6, No. 11 (November 1920): [6–11]. *WT* 7, No. 2 (February 1926): 252–54. In *CF* 1.

"Celephaïs." *Rainbow* No. 2 (May 1922): 10–12. *Marvel Tales* 1, No. 1 (May 1934): 26, 28–32. In *CF* 1.

"The Colour out of Space." *Amazing Stories* 2, No. 6 (September 1927): 557–67. In *CF* 2.

"Dagon." *Vagrant* No. 11 (November 1919): 23–29. *WT* 2, No. 3 (October 1923): 23–25. *WT* 27, No. 1 (January 1936): 118–23. In *CF* 1.

"The Doom That Came to Sarnath." *Scot* No. 44 (June 1920): 90–98. *Marvel Tales of Science and Fantasy* 1, No. 4 (March–April 1935): 157–63. In *CF* 1.

The Dream-Quest of Unknown Kadath. In *CF* 2.

"The Dunwich Horror." *WT* 13, No. 4 (April 1929): 481–508. In *CF* 2.

"Facts concerning the Late Arthur Jermyn and His Family." *Wolverine* No. 9 (March 1921): 3–11; No. 10 (June 1921): 6–11. *WT* 3, No. 4 (April 1924): 15–18 (as "The White Ape"). *WT* 25, No. 5 (May 1935): 642–48 (as "Arthur Jermyn"). In *CF* 1.

"From Beyond." *Fantasy Fan* 1, No. 10 (June 1934): 147–51, 160. In *CF* 1.

"The Haunter of the Dark." *WT* 28, No. 5 (December 1936): 538–53. In *CF* 3.

"Herbert West—Reanimator." *Home Brew* (as "Grewsome Tales") 1, No. 1 (February 1922): 84–88 ("From the Dark"); 1, No. 2 (March 1922): 45–50 ("The Plague Demon"); 1, No. 3 (April 1922): 21–26 ("Six Shots by Moonlight"); 1, No. 4 (May 1922): 53–58 ("The Scream of the Dead"); 1, No. 5 (June 1922): 45–50 ("The Horror from the Shadows,"); 1, No. 6 (July 1922): 57–62 ("The Tomb-Legions"). In *CF* 1.

"The Horror at Red Hook." *WT* 9, No. 1 (January 1927): 59–73. In Christine Campbell Thomson, ed. *You'll Need a Night Light.* London: Selwyn & Blount, 1927. In *CF* 1.

"The Hound." *WT* 3, No. 2 (February 1924): 50–52, 78. *WT* 14, No. 3 (September 1929): 421–25, 432. In *CF* 1.

"The Little Glass Bottle." In *CF* 3.

"Memory." *United Co-operative* 1, No. 2 (June 1919): 8. In *CF* 1.

"The Moon-Bog." *WT* 7, No. 6 (June 1926): 805–10. In *CF* 1.

"The Nameless City." *Wolverine* No. 11 (Nov. 1921): 3–15. *Fanciful Tales* 1, No. 1 (Fall 1936): 5–18. In *CF* 1.

"Nyarlathotep" (prose poem). *United Amateur* 20, No. 2 (November 1920): 19–21 (the issue appeared in early 1921). In *CF* 1.

"Pickman's Model." *WT* 10, No. 4 (October 1927): 505–14. In Christine Campbell Thomson, ed. *By Daylight Only.* London: Selwyn & Blount, 1929. 37–52. *WT* 28, No. 4 (November 1936): 495–505. In Christine Campbell Thomson, ed. *The "Not at Night" Omnibus.* London: Selwyn & Blount, 1937. 119–31. In *CF* 2.

"The Picture in the House." *National Amateur* 41, No. 6 ("July 1919"): 246–49 (the issue appeared in the summer of 1921). In *CF* 1.

"Polaris." *Philosopher* 1, No. 1 (December 1920): 3–5. *National Amateur* 48, No. 5 (May 1926): 48–49. *Fantasy Fan* 1, No. 6 (February 1934): 83–85. In *CF* 1.

"The Quest of Iranon." *Galleon* 1, No. 5 (July–August 1935): 12–20. In *CF* 1.

"The Secret Cave." In *CF* 3.

"The Statement of Randolph Carter." *Vagrant* No. 13 (May 1920): 41–48. *WT* 5, No. 2 (February 1925): 149–53. In *CF* 1.

"The Temple." *WT* 6, No. 3 (September 1925): 329–36, 429, 431. *WT* 27, No. 2 (February 1936): 239–44, 246–49. In *CF* 1.

"The Terrible Old Man." *Tryout* 7, No. 4 (July 1921): [10–14]. In *CF* 1.

"The Thing on the Doorstep." *WT* 29, No. 1 (January 1937): 52–70. In *CF* 3.

"The Tomb." *Vagrant* No. 14 (March 1922): 50–64. In *CF* 1.

"The Tree." *Tryout* 7, No. 7 (October 1921): [3–10]. In *CF* 1.

"The Unnamable." *WT* 6, No. 1 (July 1925): 78–82. In *CF* 1.

"The White Ship." *United Amateur* 19, No. 2 (November 1919): 30–33. *WT* 9, No. 3 (March 1927): 386–89. In *CF* 1.

Poetry [all poems are in *AT*]

"Ad Britannos—1918." *Tryout* 4, No. 4 (April 1918): [3–6]. *National Enquirer* 6, No. 4 (25 April 1918): 10. [No appearance in *Little Budget of Knowledge and Nonsense* has been found.]

"An American to Mother England." *Poesy* 1, No. 7 (January 1916): 62. *Dowdell's Bearcat* No. 16 (November 1916): [12–14].

"An American to the British Flag." *Little Budget of Knowledge and Nonsense* 1, No. 9 (November 1917): 110.

"April." [Providence] *Evening News* 50, No. 121 (24 April 1917): 6. *Tryout* 4, No. 3 (March 1918): [3–5].

"April Dawn." *National Enquirer* 8, No. 2 (10 April 1919): 3. *Silver Clarion* 4, No. 1 (April 1920): 1.

"Astrophobos." *United Amateur* 17, No. 3 (January 1918): 38 (as by "Ward Phillips").

"Autumn." *Tryout* 3, No. 12 (November 1917): [3–5]. [Providence] *Evening News* 51, No. 125 (5 November 1917): 3. *National Enquirer* 9, No. 4 (23 October 1919): 7.

"Ave atque Vale: to Jonathan E. Hoag, Esq. February 10, 1831–October 17th, 1927." *Tryout* 11, No. 10 (December 1927): [3–4]. In [C. W. Smith, ed.] *Poetical Melange:* [*sic*] *Anthology.* Haverhill, MA: C. W. Smith, [c. 1928?]: 32–33.

"Background" (*Fungi from Yuggoth* XXX). *Providence Journal* 102, No. 91 (16 April 1930): 13. *Interesting Items* No. 592 (September 1932): [1].

"Ye Ballade of Patrick von Flynn." *Conservative* 2, No. 1 (April 1916): 3–4 (as by "Lewis Theobald, Jun.").

"The Bay-Stater's Policy." *Bay-Stater* 4, No. 3 (June 1915): [3].

"The Beauties of Peace." [Providence] *Evening News* 49, No. 123 (27 June 1916): 6.

"The Bookstall." *United Official Quarterly* 2, No. 2 (January 1916): [9–11].

"Britannia Victura." *Inspiration,* Tribute number (April 1917): 3–4. *Little Budget of Knowledge and Nonsense* 1, No. 2 (May 1917): 27–28. *National Enquirer* 6, No. 8 (23 May 1918): 10.

"Brotherhood." *Tryout* 3, No. 1 (December 1916): [7]. *National Magazine* 45, No. 3 (December 1916): 415.

"Brumalia." *Tryout* 3, No. 1 (December 1916): [1]. [Providence] *Evening News* 51, No. 152 (7 December 1917): Sec. 2, p. 2.

"C. S. A. 1861–1865: To the Starry Cross of the SOUTH."

"Content." *United Amateur* 15, No. 11 (June 1916): 150.

"The Critics' Farewell." See "The End of the Jackson War."

"The Crime of Crimes." *Interesting Items* No. 459 (July 1915): 8–10.

"A Cycle of Verse." *National Enquirer* 7, No. 25 (20 March 1919): 3 ("Oceanus" and "Clouds"); 7, No. 26 (27 March 1919): 3 ("Mother Earth"). *Tryout* 5, No. 7 (July 1919): [19–22] (as by "Ward Phillips").

"Damon and Delia; A Pastoral." *Tryout* 4, No. 8 (August): [23–26] (as by "Edward Softly").

"Despair." *Pine Cones* 1, No. 4 (June 1919): 13 (as by "Ward Phillips").

"Earth and Sky." *Little Budget of Knowledge and Nonsense* 1, No. 4 (July 1917): 43. *Pine Cones* 1, No. 1 (December 1918): 1. *Interesting Items* No. 494 (September 1919): [2–3].

"An Elegy on Franklin Chase Clark, M.D." [Providence] *Evening News* 46, No. 137 (29 April 1915): 6.

"An Elegy on Phillips Gamwell, Esq." [Providence] *Evening News* 50, No. 129 (5 January 1917): 8.

"The End of the Jackson War." *Argosy* 77, No. 3 (October 1914): 718 (under heading "The Critics' Farewell").

"Fact and Fancy." *Tryout* 3, No. 3 (February 1917): [7].

["Fragment on Whitman."] Contained in "In a Major Key." *Conservative* 1, No. 2 (July 1915): 9–11.

"Futurist Art." *Conservative* 2, No. 4 (January 1917): [2].

"A Garden." *Vagrant* (Spring 1927): 60.

"Gems from *In a Minor Key.*" *Conservative* 1, No. 3 (October 1915): 8 (unsigned).

"Gryphus in Asinum Mutatus."

"Harbour Whistles" (*Fungi from Yuggoth* XXXIII). *Silver Fern* 1, No. 5 (May 1930): [1]. *L'Alouette* 3, No. 6 (September–October 1930): 161.

"Helene Hoffman Cole: 1893–1919: The Club's Tribute." *Bonnet* 1, No. 1 (June 1919): 8–9 (unsigned).

"The House." *National Enquirer* 9, No. 11 (11 December 1919): 3. *Philosopher* 1, No. 1 (December 1920): 6 (as by "Ward Phillips").

"In a Sequester'd Providence Churchyard Where Once Poe Walk'd." In *Four Acrostic Sonnets on Edgar Allan Poe.* [Milwaukee, WI: Maurice W. Moe, 1936.] *Science-Fantasy Correspondent* 1, No. 3 (March–April 1937): 16–17 (as

"In a Sequestered Churchyard Where Once Poe Walked"). *WT* 31, No. 5 (May 1938): 578 (as "Where Poe Once Walked: An Acrostic Sonnet").

"Inspiration." *Conservative* 2, No. 3 (October 1916): [12] (as by "Lewis Theobald, Jun."). *National Magazine* 45, No. 2 (November 1916): 287.

"Iterum Conjunctae." *Tryout* 3, No. 6 (May 1917): [3]. [Providence] *Evening News* 51, No. 8 (12 June 1917): 6. *Little Budget of Knowledge and Nonsense* 1, Nos. 5/6 (August–September 1917): 77. *National Enquirer* 6, No. 5 (2 May 1918): 10. *Tryout* 19, No. 3 (May 1938): [16] (as "Intrum Donjunctae").

"The Introduction." *O-Wash-Ta-Nong* 2, No. 3 (December 1937): [10] (as by "Humphry Littlewit, Esq., of Grubstreet Manor").

"The Isaacsonio-Mortoniad."

"John Oldham: A Defence." *United Co-operative* 1, No. 2 (June 1919): 7.

"Laeta; A Lament." *Tryout* 4, No. 2 (February 1918): [15–16] (as by "Ames Dorrance Rowley").

"Lines on Gen. Robert Edward Lee." *Coyote* 3, No. 1 (January 1917): 1–2.

"Lines on Graduation from the R.I. Hospital's School of Nurses." *Tryout* 3, No. 3 (February 1917): [15–17] (attributed to John T. Dunn).

"Lines on the 25th. Anniversary of the *Providence Evening News*, 1892–1917." *Tryout* 4, No. 1 (December 1917): [3–5]. [Providence] *Evening News* 51, No. 154 (10 December 1917): 7 (as "Our 25th Anniversary, 1892–1917").

"The Magazine Poet." *United Amateur* 15, No. 3 (October 1915): 51.

"March." *United Amateur* 14, No. 4 (March 1915): 68. [Providence] *Evening News* 52, No. 66 (1 March 1918): 7.

"A Mississippi Autumn." *Ole Miss'* No. 2 (December 1915): 5–6 (as by "Howard Phillips Lovecraft, Metrical Mechanic").

"Mors Omnibus Communis: (Written in a Hospital)" (with Sonia H. Greene). *Rainbow* No. 1 (October 1921): 8.

"Mother Earth." See "A Cycle of Verse."

"Nemesis." *Vagrant* No. 7 (June 1918): 41–43. *Weird Tales* 3, No. 4 (April 1924): 78.

"New England Fallen." *Here and There* 1, No. 1 (October 1914): 1–8.

"Night-Gaunts" (*Fungi from Yuggoth* XX). *Providence Journal* 102, No. 73 (26 March 1930): 15. *Interesting Items* No. 605 (November 1934): [6] (as "Night Gaunts").

"1914." *Interesting Items* No. 457 (March 1915): 3–5.

"The Nymph's Reply to the Modern Business Man." *Tryout* 3, No, 3 (February 1917): [2] (as by "Lewis Theobald, Jr.").

"Ode for July Fourth, 1917." *United Amateur* 16, No. 9 (July 1917): 121. *National Magazine* 45, No. 10 (July 1917): 616 (as "Ode to July 4th: 1917"). [Providence] *Evening News* 51, No. 26 (3 July 1917): 3.

"Old Christmas." *Tryout* 4, No. 12 (December 1918): [1–11]. *National Enquirer* 9, No. 13 (25 December 1919): 3.

"On a Battlefield in Picardy." *National Enquirer* 6, No. 9 (30 May 1918): 10.

Voice from the Mountains (July 1918): 11 (as "On a Battlefield in France").

"On a Modern Lothario." *Blarney Stone* 2, No. 4 (July–August 1914): 7–8.

"On a New-England Village Seen by Moonlight." *Trail* No. 2 (Summer 1915): 8–9.

"On Reading Lord Dunsany's *Book of Wonder*." *Silver Clarion* 3, No. 12 (March 1920): 4.

"On Receiving a Picture of Swans." *Conservative* 1, No. 4 (January 1916) 2–3.

"On Receiving a Picture of the Marshes at Ipswich." *National Magazine* 45, No. 4 (January 1917): 588. *Merry Minutes* 3, No. 12 (March 1917): 3.

"On Receiving a Picture of yᵉ Towne of Templeton, in the Colonie of Massachusetts-Bay, with Mount Monadnock, in New-Hampshire, Shewn in the Distance." *Vagrant* No. 5 (June 1917): 5 (as "To Templeton and Mount Monadnock").

"On Receiving a Portraiture of Mrs. Berkeley, yᵉ Poetess." Attributed in the AMs. to "L. Theobald Junr."

"[On Slang]." *Conservative* 1, No. 1 (April 1915): [6].

"On the Cowboys of the West." *Plainsman* 1, No. 4 (December 1915): 1–2.

"On the Death of a Rhyming Critic." *Toledo Amateur* (July 1917): 11–12.

"Pacifist War Song—1917." *Tryout* 3, No. 4 (March 1917): [10] (as by "Lewis Theobald, Jun.").

"The Pathetick History of Sir Wilful Wildrake."

"Percival Lowell." *Excelsior* 1, No. 1 (March 1917): 3.

"The Pigeon-Flyers" (*Fungi from Yuggoth* X). *Ripples from Lake Champlain* 2, No. 4 (Spring 1932): 31.

"The Poe-et's Nightmare." *Vagrant* No. 8 (July 1918): [13–23]. *WT* 44, No. 5 (July 1952): 43–46 ("Aletheia Phrikodes" section only).

"The Poem of Ulysses."

Poemata Minora, Volume II:

"Ode to Selene or Diana." *Tryout* 5, No. 4 (April 1919): [8] (as "To Selene"; as by "Edward Softly").

"To the Old Pagan Religion." *Tryout* 5, No. 4 (April 1919): [17] (as "The Last Pagan Speaks"; as by "Ames Dorrance Rowley").

"On the Ruin of Rome."

"To Pan." *Tryout* 5, No. 4 (April 1919): [16] (as "Pan"; as by "Michael Ormonde O'Reilly"). *Tryout* 13, No. 2 (September 1929): [15] (as "Pan"; as by "M. O. O.").

"On the Vanity of Human Ambition."

"The Poet of Passion." *Tryout* 3, No. 7 (June 1917): [25] (as by "Louis [*sic*] Theobald, Jun.").

"The Power of Wine." [Providence] *Evening News* (13 January 1915): 8. *Tryout* 2, No. 5 (April 1916): [5–7].

"A Prayer for Universal Peace." Revision of a poem by Robert L. Selle, D.D. that appeared in *Apples of Gold in Pictures of Silver* (Louisville, KY: Pentecostal Publishing Company, 1917), 50–53.

"Prologue" to "Fragments from an Hour of Inspiration" by Jonathan E. Hoag. *Tryout* 3, No. 8 (July 1917): [17]. *Troy Times* (October 11, 1917): 10 (as "Prologue" to "Amid Inspiring Scenes (Near Greenwich, N.Y.)"). In *The Poetical Works of Jonathan E. Hoag.* [Ed. H. P. Lovecraft.] New York: [Privately printed,] 1923. 41 (as "Prologue" to "Amid Inspiring Scenes").

"Providence in 2000 A.D." [Providence] *Evening Bulletin* (4 March 1912): Sec. 2, p. 6.

"Psychopompos: A Tale in Rhyme." *Vagrant* No. 10 (October 1919): 13–22. *WT* 30, No. 3 (September 1937): 341–48.

"Quinsnicket Park." *Badger* No. 2 (June 1915): 7–10. [Providence] *Evening News* (8 February 1916): 8.

"R. Kleiner, Laureatus, in Heliconem." *Conservative* 2, No. 1 (April 1916): 2.

"Respite." *Conservative* 2, No. 3 (October 1916): [6–7]. *National Magazine* 45, No. 6 (March 1917): 826.

"The Rose of England." *Scot* No. 14 (October 1916): 7.

"A Rural Summer Eve." *Trail* 1, No. 2 (January 1916): 12–13.

"The Rutted Road." *Tryout* 3, No. 2 (January 1917): [17] (as by "Lewis Theobald, Jun."). *Tryout* 10, No. 8 (March 1926): [17].

"The Simple Speller's Tale." *Conservative* 1, No. 1 (April 1915): [1].

"Sir Thomas Tryout: Died November 15, 1921." *Tryout* 7, No. 9 (December 1921): [31–32] (as by "Ward Phillips"). *Tryout* 21, No. 1 (March 1941): [3–4].

"The Smile." *Symphony* No. 12 (July 1916): [3–4]. *Little Budget of Knowledge and Nonsense* 1, Nos. 5–6 (August–September 1917): 68.

"Sonnet on Myself." *Tryout* 4, No. 7 (July 1918): [2] (as by "Lewis Theobald, Jun.").

"The Spirit of Summer." *National Enquirer* 6, No. 13 (27 June 1918): 10. *Conservative* 4, No. 1 (July 1918): 1.

"The State of Poetry." *Conservative* 1, No. 3 (October 1915): 1–3.

"Sunset." *Tryout* 4, No. 1 (December 1917): [8]. *Presbyterian Advance* 7, No. 7 (18 April 1918): 6. *United Amateur* 17, No. 5 (May 1918): 90. *Californian* 5, No. 1 (Summer 1937): 24. *Tryout* 19, No. 3 (May 1938): [15].

"Temperance Song." *Dixie Booster* 4, No. 4 (Spring 1916): 9.

"The Teuton's Battle-Song." *United Amateur* 15, No. 7 (February 1916): 85.

"To a Youth." *Tryout* 7, No. I (February 1921): [18] (as by "Richard Raleigh").

"To Alan Seeger." *Tryout* 4, No. 7 (July 1918): [1–2]. *National Enquirer* 6, No. 20 (15 August 1918): 10. *United Amateur* 18, No. 2 (November 1918): 24.

"To Arthur Goodenough, Esq." *Tryout* 4, No. 9 (September 1918): [1–2]; In Arthur Goodenough. In "Further Recollections of Amateur Journalism." *Vagrant* [Spring 1927]: [28–29] (as "To Mr. Arthur Goodenough of New England, on His Most Meritorious Poetrie").

"To Charlie of the Comics." *Providence Amateur* 1, No. 2 (February 1916): 13–14.

"To Col. Linkaby Didd: Guardian of Democracy."

"To Gen. Villa." *Blarney Stone* 2, No. 6 (November–December 1914): 8.

"To Greece, 1917." *Vagrant* No. 6 (November 1917): 15–17.

"To Jonathan E. Hoag, Esq., on His 87th Birthday: February 10, 1918." *Eurus* 1, No. 1 (February 1918): 5–6. *Troy Times* (February 9, 1918): 6 (as "To Jonathan E. Hoag (of Greenwich)"). In *The Poetical Works of Jonathan E. Hoag.* [Ed. H. P. Lovecraft.] New York: [Privately printed,] 1923. 61–63.

"To M. W. M." *United Amateur* 16, No. 9 (July 1917): 134 (in column, "News Notes").

"To Mr. Lockhart, on His Poetry." *Tryout* 3, No. 4 (March 1917): [7–8]. *Little Budget of Knowledge and Nonsense* 1, No. 3 (June 1917): 35–36 (as "To Mr. Lockhart, of Milbank, South Dakota, U.S.A., on His Poetry"). Also published in a South Dakota newspaper (presumably in Lockhart's hometown of Milbank), but only a clipping of this has been seen.

"To Mistress Sophia Simple, Queen of the Cinema." *United Amateur* 19, No. 2 (November 1919): 34 (as by "L. Theobald, Jun.").

"To Samuel Loveman, Esquire, on His Poetry and Drama, Writ in the Elizabethan Style." *Dowdell's Bearcat* 4, No. 5 (December 1915): [7].

"To the Late John H. Fowler, Esq." *Scot* No. 7 (March 1916): 25–26.

"To the Members of the Pin-Feathers on the Merits of Their Organisation, and of Their New Publication, *The Pinfeather.*" *Pinfeather* 1, No. 1 (November 1914): 3–4.

"To the Members of the United Amateur Press Ass'n from the Providence Amateur Press Club." *Providence Amateur* 1, No. 1 (June 1915): [1–3].

"To the Nurses of the Red Cross." Attributed in the AMs. to "Lewis Theobald, Jun."

"To the Rev. James Pyke." *United Official Quarterly* 1, No. 1 (November 1914): 1.

"Unda, or the Bride of the Sea." *Providence Amateur* 1, No. 2 (February 1916): 14–16 (as "The Bride of the Sea"; as by "Lewis Theobald, Jr."). *O-Wash-Ta-Nong* 2, No. 3 (December 1937): [10–11] (as part of "Perverted Poesie or Modern Metre").

"The Unknown." *Conservative* 2, No. 3 (October 1916): [12] (as by "Elizabeth Berkeley" [i.e., Winifred Virginia Jackson]).

"Ver Rusticum." [Providence] *Evening News* 52, No. 92 (1 April 1918): 4. *National Enquirer* 6, No. 7 (16 May 1918): 2. *Voice from the Mountains* (July 1918): 27–29 (instead of *Vagrant* as HPL had stated).

"The Volunteer." [Providence] *Evening News* (1 February 1918): 7. *National Enquirer* 5, No. 19 (7 February 1918): 6. *Tryout* 4, No. 4 (April 1918): [11–13] (as by "Ames Dorrance Rowley").

"A Winter Wish: A Pseudo-Poetical Disaster Occasioned by the Recent Spell of Cold Weather." [Providence] *Evening News* 52, No. 19 (2 January 1918): 3. *Tryout* 4, No. 2 (February 1918): [3–5].

Nonfiction

"An Account of a Trip to the Antient Fairbanks House, in Dedham, and to the Red Horse Tavern in Sudbury, in the Province of the Massachusetts-Bay." In *CE* 4.

"A Description of the Town of Quebeck." In *CE* 4.

"The Allowable Rhyme." *Conservative* 1, No. 3 (October 1915): 3–6. In *CE* 2.

"Amateur Journalism: Its Possible Needs and Betterment." In *CE* 1.

"Ars Gratia Artis." In *CE* 2.

"Can the Moon Be Reached by Man?" *Pawtuxet Valley Gleaner* (12 October 1906): 2. *CE* 3.

"Commonplace Book." In *CE* 5.

"Department of Public Criticism." *United Amateur* 15, No. 9 (April 1916): 111–17. In *CE* 1.

"The Despised Pastoral." *Conservative* 4, No. 1 (July 1918): 2. In *CE* 1.

"Finale." *Badger* No. 2 (June 1915): 17–16 [i.e., 20]. In *CE* 1.

"For Official Editor—Anne Tillery Renshaw." *Conservative* 5, No. 1 (July 1919): 11–12 (unsigned). In *CE* 1.

"Greetings from the N.A.P.A. President Lovecraft." *Gothamite* No. 1 (April 1923): 5.

"The Haverhill Convention." *Tryout,* 7, No. 4 (July 1921): [21–25]. In *CE* 1.

"Introducing Mr. Chester Pierce Munroe." *Conservative* 1, No. 2 (April 1915): [2]. In *CE* 1.

"Lord Dunsany and His Work." In *CE* 2.

"A Matter of Uniteds." *Bacon's Essays* 1, No. 1 (Summer 1927): 1–3. In *CF* 1.

"Nietscheism [*sic*] and Realism." *Rainbow* No. 1 (October 1921): 9–11. In *CE* 5.

"No Transit of Mars." *Providence Sunday Journal* (3 June 1906): Sec. 2, p. 5. In *CE* 3.

"Old England and the 'Hyphen.'" *Conservative* 2, No. 3 (October 1916): [1–2]. In *CE* 5.

"The Poetry of Lilian Middleton." In *CE* 2.

"The Pseudo-United." *United Amateur* 19, No. 5 (May 1920): 106–8 (unsigned). In *CF* 1.

"The Renaissance of Manhood." *Conservative* 1, No. 3 (October 1915): 8–10. In *CE* 5.

"A Reply to *The Lingerer.*" *Tryout* 3, No. 7 (June 1917): [9–12]. In *CE* 1.

"Supernatural Horror in Literature." *Recluse* No. 1 (1927): 23–59. In *CE* 2.

"The Symphonick Ideal." *Conservative* 2, No. 3 (October 1916): [10–11]. In *CE* 5.

"Trimmings." *Bonnet* 1, No. 1 (June 1919): 10–12 (unsigned). In *CE* 1.

"The Vers Libre Epidemic." *Conservative* 2, No. 4 (January 1917): [2–3]. In *CE* 2.

"Winifred Virginia Jackson: A 'Different' Poetess." *United Amateur* 20, No. 4 (March 1921): 48–52. In *CE* 2.

"Winifred Virginia Jordan: Associate Editor." *Silver Clarion* 3, No. 1 (April 1919): 9–11 (as by "El Imparcial"). In *CE* 1.

B. Rheinhart Kleiner

Books

Ernest A. Edkins: A Memoir. Newtonville, MA: Published by Edward H. Cole at the Oakwood Press, 1947.

Lovecraft's New York Circle: The Kalem Club, 1924–1927. Ed. Mara Kirk Hart and S. T. Joshi. New York: Hippocampus Press, 2005. *Contains:* "At Providence in 1918"; "Epistle to Mr. and Mrs. Lovecraft"; "The Four of Us (Rondeau)"; "Brooklyn, My Brooklyn"; "Columbia Heights, Brooklyn"; "[Frisky]"; "On a Favorite Cat: Killed by an Automobile"; "To George W. Kirk, Upon His 26th Birthday"; "To His Peculiar Friend, G. Kirk, Esq."; "Your Street"; "Blue Pencil Anniversary Song"; "What My Ancestors Were Like"; "The Great Adventure"; "If I Had Lived a Hundred Years Ago"; and "[To H. P. L.]" (i.e., "H.P.L.").

Metrical Moments. Ysleta, TX: Edwin B. Hill, 1937.

Nine Sonnets. Ysleta, TX: Edwin B. Hill, 1940.

Old Mortality. Fairlawn, NJ: Haywood Press, 1949.

Pegasus in Pasture: Latter-Day Limpings of a Light Versifier, with Some Callow Cavortings from More Coltish Days. North Montpelier, VT: Driftwind Press, [1943]. A 100-copy edition of 14 poems reprinted from *Ghost* No. 1 (Spring 1943).

To Mistress Katherine Anna Talman, born July 7th, 1936. [n.p., 1936.] In H. P. Lovecraft. *Letters to Wilfred B. Talman and Helen V. and GenevieveSully.* Ed. David E. Schultz and S. T. Joshi. New York: Hippocampus Press, 2019. 540–41.

A Trilogy of Sonnets for Edwin B. Hill. Ysleta, TX: Edwin B. Hill, 1943.

Poetry

Items indicated with an asterisk were found referenced in various amateur publications, but the original appearances have not been found.

"After a Decade." *Californian* 4, No. 2 (Fall 1936): 44.

"Alas!" *Philosopher* 1, No. 1 (December 1920): 3.

"Adams–Pratt." *Brooklynite* new series No. 1 (October 1914): [77].

"America, I May Not Sing." *United Amateur* 17, No. 4 (March 1918): 64.

"Another Endless Day." *Conservative* 2, No. 1 (April 1916): 1.

"At Providence in 1918." *Conservative* 5, No. 1 (July 1919): 8.

"B. P. C. Hikers at Huntington." *Brooklynite* 14, No. 3 (July 1924): 2.

"Before and Behind the Scene." *Brooklynite* 23, No. 2 (September 1934): [1].

"The Blue Pencil Club." *Brooklynite* 7, No. 2 (January 1917): 11.

"Blue Pencil Club Anniversary Song." *Brooklynite* 13, No. 4 (October 1923): 3; 19, No. 5 (March 1930): 9.

"Books." *Ghost* No. 1 (Spring 1943): 23.

"The Books I Used to Read." *Piper* No. 2 (May 1915): 6.

"Books of My Youth." *Bay State Advocate* 2, No. 1 (September 1912): [1]–2, 4 (as by "Rheinhart Kaufmann").

"Broadway Elegies: I—A Light o' Love." *Home Brew* 3, No. 1 (February 1923): 2–3.

"Broadway Elegies: II—The Manicure Girl." *Home Brew* 3, No. 2 (March 1923): 20–21.

"Broadway Elegies: III—Cora: A Chorus Girl." *Home Brew* 3, No. 3 (April 1923): 32–33.

"Broadway Loves." *Home Brew* 1, No. 1 (February 1922): 2.

"Brooklyn As Distinguished from Manhattan." *Obo* 3, No. 1 (February 1916): 3.

"Brooklyn, My Brooklyn." *New York Evening Post* (date unknown). In Christopher Morley, ed. *The Bowling Green: An Anthology of Verse.* Garden City, NY: Doubleday, Page, 1924. 101–2.

"Bulgaria's Surrender." *Brooklyn Daily Times* (date unknown). *United Amateur* 18, No. 2 (November 1918): 24.

"A Carnation." *Piper* No. 1 (December 1914): [1].

"Caution Advised." *Ghost* No. 1 (Spring 1943): 21.

"The Christmas Spirit." *Brooklynite* 18, No. 3 (September 1928): [1].

"The Complete Hiker." *Brooklynite* 13, No. 1 (January 1923): 4.

"Consolation." *Conservative* 1, No. 4 (January 1916): 2.

"A Creed." *United Amateur* 19, No. 4 (March 1920): 69.

"Dangerous Ages." *Brooklynite* 12, No. 2 (April 1922): 2.

"Design For Living." *Brooklynite* 23, No. 2 (September 1933, 25th Anniversary Issue): 2.

"Dream Days; or, Metrical Musings." *Piper* No. 3 (September 1915): 9–10.

"Epistle to Mr. and Mrs. Lovecraft." *Brooklynite* 14, No. 2 (April 1924): 1.

"Ethel: Cashier in a Broad Street Buffet." *Tryout* 6, No. 6 (June 1920): 19 (as by "Randolph St. John").

"Evening Prayer." *Olympian* 6, No. 6 (September 1914): 118–19. *National Amateur* 41, No. 6 (July 1919): 240.

"Fads and Foibles." *Brooklynite* 27, No. 2 (September 1937): [2].

"Fond Recollections." *Brooklynite* 26, No. 4 (March 1937): [2].

"Forever." *Olympian* 6, No. 3 (June 1914): 54.

"The Four of Us!" In Mara Kirk Hart. "Walkers in the City: George Willard Kirk and Howard Phillips Lovecraft in New York City, 1924–1926." *Lovecraft Studies* No. 28 (Spring 1993): 9. In Peter Cannon, ed. *Lovecraft Remembered.* Sauk City, WI: Arkham House, 1998. 233.

"The Good Old Days." *Brooklynite* 18, No. 1 (February 1928): 2.

"Good Wishes."

"The Great Adventure." *Brooklynite* 17, No. 2 (May 1927): 4.

"H. P. L." *Olympian* No. 35 (Autumn 1940): facing p. 1.

"Heart, Do Not Wake." *Piper* No. 1 (December 1914): 4.

"Her Smile." *Brooklynite* 14, No. 4 (November 1924): 4.

"Hike It!" *Top-Notch Magazine* 54, No. 5 (1 July 1923): 60. *Californian* 4, No. 2 (Fall 1936): 59 (under heading "Contemporary Verse").

"Hiking at Plainfield." *Brooklynite* 13, No. 2 (May 1923): 3.

"I Tell My Love." *Brooklynite* 9, No. 3 (April 1918): 14.

"The Idealist." *Brooklynite* 18, No. 3 (September 1928): 8.

"Idyll, *circa* 1921." *Ghost* No. 1 (Spring 1943): 22.

"If I Had Lived A Hundred Years Ago." *Brooklynite* 19, No. 5 (March 1930): 2.

"The Inns of England." *Californian* 4, No. 2 (Fall 1936): 61 (under heading "Contemporary Verse").

"Invitation." *Ghost* No. 1 (Spring 1943): 21.

"Jazz!" *Brooklynite* 25, No. 3 (December 1935): [4].

"John Oldham: 1653–1683." *United Co-operative* 1, No. 2 (June 1919): 7.

"The June Meeting on the Palisades." *Brooklynite* 13, No. 3 (July 1923): 6.

"Light the Old Pipe." *New York Evening Post* [not found]. *Vagrant* [Spring 1927]: 167. In Robert Frothingham, ed. *Songs of Adventure.* Boston: Houghton Mifflin, 1926: 160–61.

"Love Again." *Inspiration* 1, No. 5 (November 1914): [1].

"Love, Come Again." *Olympian* 6, No. 4 (July 1914): 69.

"Love's Enigma." *Obo* 5, No. 1 (June 1919): 7.

"Lucille," *Vagrant* No. 6 (November 1917): 37.

"Maids of Broadway and Park Row." *Vagrant* No. 14 (March 1922): 84.

"A Man's Pipe." *Top-Notch Magazine* 49, No. 5 (1 April 1922): 40.

"Manhattan Streets." *Brooklynite* 20, No. 4 (March 1931): [1].

"Merry Christmas." *Home Brew* 2, No. 5 (December 1922): 24–25.

"A Midsummer Interlude." *Brooklynite* 19, No. 3 (September 1929): 11.

"Modern Adventures." *Brooklynite* 23, No. 4 (March 1934): 3.

"The Modern Muse." *Piper* No. 2 (May 1915): 5.

"Molly: A Moth." *Home Brew* 1, No. 2 (March 1922): 22.

"Motes." *Brooklynite* 19, No. 2 (June 1929): 6.

"A Mother's Song." *Brooklynite* 5, No. 2 (January 1916): 9. *National Amateur* 39, No. 3 (January 1917): 19, *National Amateur* 41, No. 6 (July 1919): 240.

"My Books." *Piper* No. 4 (April 1919): 16.

"My Dream." *Brooklynite* new series No. 10 (July 1914): 72.

"My Favorite Amateur." *Piper* No. 1 (December 1914): 3

"My Favorite Month." *Brooklynite* 23, No. 1 (June 1933): [1].

"My Favorite Newspaper." *Brooklynite* 23, No. 2 (July 1923): 7–8.

"My Friends in Rhyme." *Zenith* (March 1916): 1.

"Oh, if the Gods." *Rainbow* 1, No. 1 (October 1921): 14.

"On Collaboration." *AT* 353–58. Poems written in Boston just before seeing Lord Dunsany lecture at the Copley Plaza on 20 October 1919. No. 6 is written to Eugene B. Kuntz, an amateur poet; No. 7 to Prof. Philip B. McDonald; No. 9 to John Clinton Pryor, editor of *Pine Cones;* No. 11 to

Anne Tillery Renshaw; No. 14 to William J. Dowdell; No. 15 to Jonathan E. Hoag; No. 16 to "Galba" (i.e., Alfred Galpin, Jr.); No. 18 to Verna McGeoch; No. 19 to Rheinhart Kleiner; No. 20 to Maurice W. Moe; No. 21 to Muriel P. Kelly; No. 22 to W. Paul Cook; No. 23 to Winifred Virginia Jordan; No. 24 to Alfred Galpin.

"On Miss Mary Pickford's Recovery from a Serious Illness." *Piper* No. 4 (April 1919): 13.

"One Year Ago." *United Amateur* 19, No. 3 (January 1920): 50.

"Our Boys." *Brooklynite* 9, No. 4 (July 1918): [16].

"Our Friends." *Brooklynite* new series No. 8 (January 1914): 55. *National Amateur* 44, No. 1 (September 1921): [1].

"Over Here." *Brooklynite* 9, No. 4 (July 1918): [16].

"Pictures." *Ghost* No. 1 (Spring 1943): 22.

"Pills without Sugar." *Brooklynite* 27, No. 3 (December 1937): [2].

"The Power of Literature." *Brooklynite* 10, No. 3 (July 1920): 3.

"Prejudice." *Brooklynite* 25, No. 1 (June 1935): 2.

"Price Tags." *Brooklynite* 19, No. 5 (March 1930): 6.

"Quatrains." *Gothamite* No. 4 (January 1924): 3

"Ready though Uncalled." *Brooklynite* 10, No. 1 (November 1918): 1.

"The Reason." *Vagrant* No. 7 (June 1918): 28.

"The Reason Why." *Gothamite* new series No. 6 (January 1926): [1].

"The Reckoning." *People's Favorite Magazine* 34, No. 3 (March 1921): 57.

"The Rhyme of the Hapless Poet." *Piper* No. 1 (November 1914): 2.

"Round the Camp Fire." *Top-Notch Magazine* 59, No. 2 (15 August 1924): 72.

"Ruth." *Brooklynite* 9, No. 2 (February 1918): [1].

"Sheridan Square." *Piper* No. 4 (April 1919): 14.

"Soldier Song." *Amateur Arena* (March 1916): [4].

"Smoke Up!" *Ghost* No. 1 (Spring 1943): 26.

"Snackin' Around." *Brooklynite* 11, No. 2 (April 1921): [1].

"Spring." *Brooklynite* 4, No. 1 (April 1915): 10. *Piper* No. 2 (May 1915): 8.

"Still Another Inning." *Top-Notch Magazine* 62, No. 6 (15 July 1925): 51.

"Thank God for Dreams." *United Amateur* (1915).* Laureate Poem for 1915 reported in *United Amateur* 18, No. 3 (January 1919): 66.

"Thorns and Roses." *Brooklynite* 20, No. 3 ([December 1930]): 4. *Ghost* No. 1 (Spring 1943): 24.

"'A Timid Grace,' etc." *Ghost* No. 1 (Spring 1943): 25.

"To ———." *Rainbow* No. 1 (October 1921): 12.

"To a Book." *Amateur Arena* No. 13 (May 1913): [1] (as by "Rheinhart Kaufmann").

"To a Certain Bus." *Ghost* No. 1 (Spring 1943): 22.

"To a Flapper." *Home Brew* 1, No. 4 (May 1922): 34.

"To a Movie Star." *United Amateur* 19, No. 2 (November 1919): 34 (as by "Randolph St. John").

"To a Professional Secretary." *Ghost* No. 1 (Spring 1943): 26.

"To Alicia." *Californian* 4, No. 2 (Fall 1936): 58 (under "Contemporary Verse").

"To Celia." *Conservative* 1, No. 4 (January 1916): 4.

"To Charles LeRoy Adams." *Dope Sheet Junior* (June 1920): [1].

"To Chloe (An Echo of the Late Depression)." *Ghost* No. 1 (Spring 1943): 21.

"To Ernest Adams." *Brooklynite* 24, No. 3 (December 1934): [1].

"To Grace." *Piper* No. 5 (January 1922): 4.

"To Himself." *Californian* 4, No. 2 (Fall 1936): 58 (under heading "Contemporary Verse").

"To Iva." *Brooklynite* 11, No. 2 (April 1921): 5 (as by "Reinhart Kleiner"; with Otto P. Knack).

"To Julian Swain Houtain." *Zenith* (May 1916): 3.

"To Lalage [On Her Resignation as File Clerk]." In Christopher Morley, ed. *The Bowling Green: An Anthology of Verse.* Garden City, NY: Doubleday, Page, 1924. 99–100.

"To Madeleine (On Seeing A Portrait of Her at the Age of Eight)." *Piper* No. 5 (January 1922): [1].

"To Mary of the Movies." *Motion Picture Magazine* (May 1915): 121. *Piper* No. 3 (September 1915): 12.

"To Our Helene." *Brooklynite* 6, No. 2 (July 1916): 5.

"To Pyrrha in the Poconos." In Christopher Morley, ed. *The Bowling Green: An Anthology of Verse.* Garden City, NY: Doubleday, Page, 1924. 97–98.

"To Raymond Pratt Adams." *Hazel Nut* 4, No. 1 (May 1918): [1].

"To S. C." *Brooklynite* 17, No. 4 (November 1927): 4.

"To the Shade of Elia." *Californian* 4, No. 2 (Fall 1936): 60 (under heading "Contemporary Verse").

"Trail-Mate." *Californian* 4, No. 2 (Fall 1936): 59 (under heading "Contemporary Verse").

"Travelling by Reel." *The Photodramatist* (December 1921).

[Untitled quatrain: "The quality of mercy is not strained . . ."]. *Brooklynite* new series No. 11 (October 1914): 81.

"Vacation." *United Official Quarterly* (November 1914).*

"Virtue Admitted." *Ghost* No. 1 (Spring 1943): 25.

"Week-End Trips." *Brooklynite* 26, No. 2 (September 1936): [3].

"A Welcome." *Gothamite* No. 1 (April 1923): 10–11.

"What I Know about Me." *Brooklynite* 26, No. 1 (June 1936): [4].

"What My Ancestors Were Like." *Brooklynite* 11, No. 1 (January 1921): [1] (as by "Reinhardt Kleiner").

"What's the Matter" [*sic*]. *Brooklynite* new series No. 9 (April 1914): 64.

"A Whiff from the Past." *Brooklynite* new series No. 7 (October 1913): [45] (as by "Rheinhart Kauffman").

"Will You?" *Brooklynite* 16, No. 2 (May 1926): 4. *Californian* 4, No. 2 (Fall 1936): 60 (under heading "Contemporary Verse").

"Winter in the Hills." *Ghost* No. 1 (Spring 1943): 21.
"You!" *Ghost* No. 1 (Spring 1943): 23.
"Young Boswell." *Pine Needles* No. 8 (Christmas 1936): 6.

Essays and Miscellany
"After a Decade and the Kalem Club." *Californian* 4, No. 2 (Fall 1936): 45–47.
"At Random." *Piper* No. 5 (January 1922): [1]–4.
"Bards and Bibliophiles." *Aonian* 2, No. 4 (Winter 1944): 169–74. In Peter Cannon, ed. *Lovecraft Remembered.* Sauk City, WI: Arkham House, 1998. 188–94.
"Bards of Passion and of Mirth." *Aonian* 2, No. 1 (Spring 1944): 106–9.
"The Bed in the Corner." *Home Brew* 1, No. 3 (April 1922): 6.
"The Blue Pencil Club Past and Present." *Empire* 2, No. 3 (February 1937): [3]–4.
"Book-Borrowers." *Ghost* No. 1 (Spring 1943): 42–43.
"Bureau of Critics: A Criticism in the Poet's Corner." *National Amateur* 58, No. 2 (December 1935): 12–14.
"Bureau of Critics: Poetry." *National Amateur* 58, No. 3 (March 1936): 14–16.
"Bureau of Critics: The Amateur Parnassus." *National Amateur* 58, No. 4 (June 1936): [1], 15–16.
"Burrowings of an Old Bookworm." *Ghost* No. 4 (July 1946): 1–31.
"By Post from Providence" by H. P. Lovecraft. Comp. by Kleiner. *Californian* 5, No. 1 (Summer 1937): 10–23.
"Comment and Criticism." *Californian* 4, No. 4 (Spring 1937): 51–62.
"Concerning Consolidation." *Piper* No. 1 (December 1914): [1] (unsigned).
"Discourse on H. P. Lovecraft." *Amateur Scribe* No. 15 (June 1951): 12–19. In Peter Cannon, ed. *Lovecraft Remembered.* Sauk City, WI: Arkham House, 1998. 157–63.
"F. D. W. [Frank D. Woolen]: A Poet of 'The Golden Age.'" *Californian* 5, No. 1 (Summer 1936): 65–66.
["Fables for Flappers" I through IV: in *Home Brew* 2, No. 1 through 4?]<are these fables verse or prose?>
"Fables for Flappers: V—Two Little Country Girls." *Home Brew* 2, No. 5 (December 1922): 30–31.
"Fables for Flappers VI—Mary's Lovers." *Home Brew* 2, No. 6 (January 1923): 22–23.
"For President, Miss Von Der Heide." *Piper* No. 2 (May 1915): 5.
"Friendship." *Brooklynite* 21, No. 4 (March 1932): 2.
"Greetings from the President [of the Gotham Press Club]." *Gothamite* No. 1 (April 1923): 2.
"Halcyon Days with the Blue Pencil Club." *Amateur Scribe* 4, No. 14 (November 1950): [1]–37?.
"Helene Hoffman Cole as a Writer." *Brooklynite* 10, No. 3 (April 1919): 6.
"Historian's Report." *National Amateur* 46, No. 6 (July 1922): 1–2.
"Howard Phillips Lovecraft." *Californian* 5, No. 1 (Summer 1937): 5–8.

"Howard Phillips Lovecraft." *Phoenix* 3, No. 1 (September 1943): 73–74.

"James Morton." *Ghost* No. 5 (July 1947): 15–20. An introductory note states: "The following comprises Chapter IV of *Recreations of an Amateur Journalist*, a lengthy manuscript which is scheduled for publication in the far distant future if all concerned live long enough."

"John Masefield: A Living Leader of Literature." *Sea Gull* No. 48 (May 1934): 12–14.

"The Kleicomolo." *United Amateur* 18, No. 4 (March 1919): 74–76 (unsigned).

Letters to the Gallomo. In *Letters to Alfred Galpin*. Edited by S. T. Joshi and David E. Schultz. New York: Hippocampus Press, 2003.*

Letters to the Kleicomolo. In *Letters to Rheinhart Kleiner*. Edited by S. T. Joshi and David E. Schultz. New York: Hippocampus Press, 2005.*

"Lovecraft in Brooklyn." *Campane* No. 18 (September 1951): 1–3. *Lovecraft Studies* No. 34 (Spring 1996): 35–36.

"A Memoir of Lovecraft." *Arkham Sampler* 1, No. 2 (Spring 1948): 52–61. In H. P. Lovecraft. *Something about Cats and Other Pieces*. Sauk City, WI: Arkham House, 1949. 229–33. In Peter Cannon, ed. *Lovecraft Remembered*. Sauk City, WI: Arkham House, 1998. 195–203.

"My Hobby." *Brooklynite* 9, No. 4 (July 1918): [15].

"The National Convention." *Brooklynite* 4, No. 2 (July 1915): 14.

"The New Criticism." *Piper* No. 1 (December 1914): 2–4 (unsigned).

"A Note on Howard P. Lovecraft's Verse." *United Amateur* 18, No. 4 (March 1919): 76. In Peter Cannon, ed. *Lovecraft Remembered*. Sauk City, WI: Arkham House, 1998. 401–2.

"Our Meetings." *Brooklynite* new series No. 12 (January 1915): 92.

"The Power of Literature." *Brooklynite* 10, No. 3 (July 1920): 3.

"Pipings." *Piper* No. 4 (April 1919): [13]–16.

"The Power of Literature." *Brooklynite* 10, No. 3 [*sic*] (July 1920): 3.

"Praise for Miss Von Der Heide's Poetry." *National Amateur* 39, No. 4 (March 1917): 27–28.

"Presidential Message." *United Amateur* 18, No. 3 (January 1919): 59–60.

"Presidential Message." *United Amateur* 18, No. 6 (July 1919): 133–34.

"President's Message." *United Amateur* 18, No. 5 (May 1919): 104.

"The September Meeting." *Brooklynite* 11, No. 5 (October 1920): 2.

"Some Amateur Poets and Their Songs." *National Amateur* 39, No. 2 (November 1916): 12–13.

"Some Lovecraft Memories." *Campane* No. 145 (May 1990): 1–12.

"Some Recent Magazines." *Brooklynite* 5, No. 1 (October 1915): 2.

"Something I Should Never Miss." *Brooklynite* 22, No. 4 (March 1933): [4].

"Special Message." *United Amateur* 18, No: 5 (May 1919): 104–5.

"Stepping Out." *Brooklynite* 28, No. 1 (June 1938): 1.

---

*To be included in *H. P. Lovecraft: Miscellaneous Letters* (forthcoming).

"Three Poets of Amateur Journalism." *Brooklynite* 8, No. 2 (July 1917): 12–13.
"With the Boston Amateurs." *Brooklynite* 6, No. 2 (July 1916): 5–6.
"Why I Stick to the Blue Pencil Club." *Brooklynite* 22, No. 1 (June 1932): 1.

C. Arthur Harris

"The Birth of British Amateur Journalism." *O-Wash-Ta-Nong* 3, No. 1 (January 1938): 3.
"Charles Dickens." *Californian* 2, No. 4 (Spring 1935): 16–17.
"More Regrettable Passings." *Interesting Items* 42, No. 620, Coronation Number (May 1937): [6–7] (unsigned). In S. T. Joshi and David E. Schultz, ed. *Ave atque Vale: Reminiscences of H. P. Lovecraft.* West Warwick, RI: Necronomicon Press, 2018. 445.

D. James Larkin Pearson

Castle Gates: A Book of Poems through Which the Knowing Ones Are Admitted into Some of My Castles in Spain. Moravian Falls, NC: Pearson Printing Co., 1908.
Early Harvest: The First Experimental Poems of a Self-Taught Farm Boy. Guilford College, NC: Pearson Pub. Co., 1952.
Fifty Acres and Other Poems. Wilkesboro, NC: Pearson Publishing Co., 1933.
Fifty Acres and Other Selected Poems. Wilkesboro, NC: Pearson, 1937. Guilford College, NC: Pearson Pub. Co., 1960.
My Fingers and My Toes: Complete Poems of James Larkin Pearson. Nashville: Ingram Book Co., 1971.
Pearson's Poems. Boomer, NC: James Larkin Pearson, 1924. (*LL* 745)
Poet's Progress: Autobiography of James Larkin Pearson; or, The Life and Times of James Larkin Pearson 1879–1981. <1965> Wilkesboro, NC: Wilkes Community College, 2010.
Selected Poems. Charlotte, NC: McNally, 1960.
The Soul of Poetry. [Raleigh, NC?: State Literary and Historical Association?, 1934.]
Things That Come No More: A Collection of Poems by James Larkin Pearson. A recording. Taylorsville, NC: Masterpiece, 1973. Music by Janet Brookshire, Kay Miller, vocalist.

"Back at It Again." *Pearson's Pet* 8, No. 1 (March 1913): [1].
"Broke Loose Again." *Pearson's Pet* 9, No. 1 (April 1915): [2–3].
"Burnin' Off." *Pearson's Pet* 9, No. 1 (April 1915): [1].
"Contemplations." *Vagrant* No. 6 (November 1917): 19.
"Editorials." *Pearson's Pet* 9, No. 2 (July 1915): [3–4].
"For President." *Pearson's Pet* 6, No. 1 (June 1910): [2].
"The Grave-Tree." *Vagrant* No. 15 (Spring 1927): 237–38.
"How I Met Elbert Hubbard." *Pearson's Pet* 9, No. 1 (April 1915): [3–4].

"How It All Started." *Pearson's Pet* 8, No. 1 (March 1913): [2–4].

"Israel." *Good News* (1 February 1918): 1.

"It Do Beat All." *Pearson's Pet* 6, No. 1 (June 1910): [4].

"Journey's End." *Argosy All-Story Weekly* 180, No. 6 (2 October 1926): 910.

"The King Is Dead." *Pearson's Pet* 6, No. 1 (June 1910): [1].

"The Law of the Earth." *Pearson's Pet* 7, No. 1 (May 1911): [1].

"The Lives of Men." *Vagrant* No. 15 (Spring 1927): 236.

"Mammon Worship." *Pearson's Pet* 7, No. 1 (May 1911): [4].

"Pet-als." *Pearson's Pet* 8, No. 1 (March 1913): [4].

"The Poetry fer Me." *Vagrant* No. 10 (October 1919): 9.

"Preserve Your Papers." *Tarheel* 1, No. 2 (February 1910): [1].

"President's Message." *Southern Amateur Journalist* 6 (new series), No. 1 (September 1910): 2; *Southern Journalist* 6, No. 3 (March 1911): [1]; 6, No. 4 (June 1911): [1].

"President's Report." *Southern Journalist* 6 (new series), No. 2 (December 1910): [1].

"Report of Corresponding Secretary." *Southern Journalist* 5, No. 4 (June 1910): 3.

"The River and the Sea." *Vagrant* No. 15 (Spring 1927): 235.

"The Secret of Attainment." [Original appearance not found.] *National Amateur* 41, No. 6 (July 1919): 230.

"Singing on the Way." *Silver Clarion* 1, No. 12 (March 1918): [1].

"Unanswered Questions." *Pearson's Pet* 7, No. 1 (May 1911): [4].

Untitled editorial. *Pearson's Pet* 7, No. 1 (May 1911): [2].

"You Jes' as Well Laugh as to Cry." *Vagrant* No. 5 (June 1917): 20.

"What Constitutes a Man?" *Reflector* 10, No 1 (January 1911): [1].

"When Inspiration Fails." *Vagrant* No. 7 (June 1918): 25.

"When the Dollar Rules the Pulpit and the Devil Rules the Pew." *Pearson's Pet* 7, No. 1 (May 1911): [1].

"The Writing of Editorials." *United Amateur* 13, No. 3 (January 1914): 51–52.

E. Winifred Virginia Jackson

Backroads: A Book of Poems. Boston: B. J. Brimmer Co., 1922.

Backroads: Maine Narratives, with Lyrics. Introduction by William Stanley Braithwaite. Boston: B. J. Brimmer Co., 1927.

Selected Poems by Winifred Virginia Jackson and Ralph Temple Jackson. Compiled by Ralph Dighton Jackson. 1944.

Verse

Items in Braithwaite (1921) are all indicated there as having appeared in HPL's *Conservative*, but HPL never published the poems.

Items marked * appeared under the byline "Winifred Virginia Jordan."

"Absence." *Merry Minutes* (December 1916/January 1917).*

"Adoration." *Vagrant* No. 7 (June 1918): 88.

"Afar and Near." *Silver Clarion* (August 1918).*

"Alley." *Merry Minutes* (December 1916/January 1917).*

"And One Is Two." *Ellsworth* (Maine) *Weekly* (30 March 1925). In Braithwaite (1925), 169.

"April." *Conservative* 2, No. 1 (April 1916): 1–2. *National Magazine* 46, No. 1 (April 1916): 61.

"April Shadows." *Conservative* 5 No. 1 (July 1919): 7.

"Apples and Pears." See "Tales of Women."

"Atavism." *Argosy* 120 (17 April 1920): 24.*

"Baby Bluebird." *Brownies' Book* 2, No. 6 (June 1921): 179

"Be Not Afraid." *Silver Clarion* 3, No. 7 (October 1919): 3.*

"Bigby's Bar." See "Tales of Women."

"Black Aiken's Lot." *Broom.* In Braithwaite (1924): 133–34.

"The Bleak Road." *Silver Clarion* 3, No. 8 (November 1919): [1].*

"Blindness." *Silver Clarion* 2, No. 8 (November 1918): 2.*

"Bobby's Wishes." *Brownies' Book* 1, No. 12 (December 1920): 372.

"The Bonnet." *Linnet* (August 1920): [3].* *National Magazine* 49, No. 12 (March 1921): 499.

"Brandy Pond." *Maine Bulletin* (August 1924). In Braithwaite (1925), 176–79.

"Brown Leaves." *Crisis* 20, No. 3 (July 1920): 137.

"But There Is Love." *Vagrant* No. 15 (Spring 1927): 281.

"Captive Threads." *Gypsy* (Winter 1925).

"Chores." *Eurus* (February 1918).*

"Clem's Fool." *Maine Bulletin* (November 1925). See "Pitch o' Pine Sonnets."

"The Cobbler in the Moon." In Braithwaite (1921), 85–88.

"Contentment." *Dowdell's Bearcat* (December 1915).*

"Crooked Sticks." *North East Journal* (1927–28). In Braithwaite (1928), 184–85.

"Cross-Currents." In Braithwaite (1922a): 75.

"Days of Laughter." *United Co-operative* 1, No. 1 (December 1918): 6.

"Deafness." In Braithwaite (1921), 92–95.

"The Death-Watch." *Vagrant* No. 6 (November 1917): 51–55.

"Difference." *Tryout* 4, No. 6 (June 1918): 7.

"The Discontented Daisy." *Tryout* 2, No. 3 (February 1916): [22].

"Do You?" *Tryout* 4, No. 1 (December 1917): 2.

"Dora of Aurora." *Boston Post* (13 December 1920): 13. *United Amateur* 20, No. 5 (May 1921): 65.

"Driftwood and Fire." *National Magazine* 49, No. 11 (February 1921): 453.*

"Dust Song." *Emerson Quarterly* (June 1923). In *Fellowship Anthology of the New England Poetry Club.* Natick, MA: Suburban Press, 1922: n.p. In Braithwaite (1923), 179.

"Earth-Breaths." *Boston Transcript.* In Braithwaite (1924), 132.

"Ellsworth to Great Pond." *Broom* 5, No. 3 (October 1923): 150.

"The Enemy." *Muses* (February 1925).

"The Ewe." *Northern Farmer* (3 April 1925).

"Eyes." In Braithwaite (1921), 92.

"Faith." *Silver Clarion* (January 1917).*

"Fallen Fences." In Braithwaite (1922a), 71–74.

"The Farewell." In Braithwaite (1922a), 76.

"Fear Flame." *Ellsworth Journal* (September 1925). In Braithwaite (1926), 214.

"February Sings." *United Amateur* 19, No. 3 (January 1920): 50.

"Finality." In Braithwaite (1921), 88–89. In *Backroads*.

"Flesh-Pots." *Contemporary Verse* (December–January 1927).

"Fog." *Tryout* 4, No. 6 (June 1918): 11.

"Galileo and Swammerdam." *Conservative* 1, No. 4 (January 1916): 3.*

"Grace." *Maine Bulletin* (February 1929). In Braithwaite (1929), 167.

"Gray Man." *Gypsy* (March 1927). *Lariat* 10, No. 2 (August 1927): 358.

"Hands." *Broom*. In Braithwaite (1924), 134–35.

"Have You Met My Buddy?" *United Co-operative* 1, No. 1 (December 1918): 6.

"Heart and Will." *Silver Clarion* 3, No. 5 (August 1919): 2.*

"Heaven Lies Around Us." *Vagrant* No. 10 (October 1919): 10.

"Hedge-Rows and Sea-Weed." See "Tales of Women."

"Her First Party: A Poem." *The Brownies' Book* 1, No. 11 (November 1920): 336 (as by "Winifred Virgnia Jordan").

"Her Tongue Was Long." See "Tales of Women."

"Heritage." *Voices: A Journal of Verse*. In Braithwaite (1922), 100.

"Hoofin' It." In Braithwaite (1921), 95–97.

"A Hope" *Tryout* 4, No. 1 (December 1917): 3.

"How Fares the Garden Rose?." *Coyote* (July 1916?).*

"The Howl-Wind." *Brownies' Book* 1, No. 12 (December 1920): 365.

"I Have Tasted of the Waters." *Vagrant* No. 7 (June 1918): 27.

"I Would Out to April Weather." *United Co-operative* 1, No. 2 (June 1919): 2.

"In a Garden." *Scot* (August 1916) (as by "Winifred Virginia Jordan").

"In April." *Voices: A Journal of Verse*. In Braithwaite (1922), 98.

"In Moreh's Wood." *Broom*. In Braithwaite (1924), 133.

"In Morven's Mead." *Conservative* 2, No. 1 (April 1916): 2.*

"In the Shade." *United Co-operative* 1, No. 2 (June 1919): 3.

"Insomnia." *Conservative* 2, No. 3 (October 1916): [2–3].*

"The Jester, Fate." *Tryout* 4, No. 4 (April 1918): 7.

"Jimmy Joe John." *Maine Bulletin* (1927–28). In Braithwaite (1928), 183–84.

"John Worthington Speaks." *National Amateur* 41, No. 6 (July 1919): 269.

"John's Boy." *Ellsworth Weekly* (30 March 1925).

"John's Mary." *Maine Bulletin* (November 1925). See "Pitch o' Pine Sonnets."

"Joy." *Tryout* 4, No. 4 (April 1918): 12.

"A Lad o' Sixty-One." *Sunday Post Sunday Magazine* (27 February 1921): 2.

"Lady Summer." *National Magazine* 46, No. 2 (May 1917): 300. *United Amateur* 18, No. 6 (July 1919): 122.

"The Lament of March." *Tryout* 4, No. 3 (March 1918): 1.

"The Last Hour." *Sunday Post Magazine* (1920).

"Life's Sunshine and Shadows." *Dowdell's Bearcat* (December 1915).*

"List to the Sea." *United Amateur* (November 1915 .*

"The Little Stranger." *Silver Clarion* 4, No. 2 (May 1920): 2.*

"Loneliness." *Crisis* 21, No. 4 (February 1921): 172.*

"Longing." *Coyote* (January 1916).*

"Lord Love You, Lad." *Coyote* (October–1918–January 1919).*

"Love's Magic." *Vagrant* No. 6 (November 1917): 38.

"Maid April." *Spectator* (July 1918).*

"Makin' Rhymes." *Magnet* (November 1924). In Braithwaite (1925), 171–72.

"A Merchant from Arcady." *National Magazine* 45, No. 4 (January 1917): 574.

"Midnight at the Mill." *Magnet* (January 1925). In Braithwaite (1925), 169–71.

"Miss Doane." In Braithwaite (1922a), 69–70.

"Monday, Wash-day." *Ellsworth Journal* (September 1925). In Braithwaite (1926), 214–15.

"The Mould Shade Speaks." *Vagrant* No. 10 (October 1919): 11–12.

"The Musquash." *United Amateur* 19, No. 1 (September 1919): 6.

"My Love's Eyes." *Coyote* (January 1916).*

"Mysteries." *Gypsy* (December 1926). In Braithwaite (1927), 162.

"The Narrow Street." *Coyote* (October 1917):.*

"Nearing Winter." *Boston Transcript*. *United Amateur* 18, No. 2 (November 1918): 23.

"The Night Wind." *Coyote* (January 1916).*

"The Night Wind Bared My Heart." *Conservative* 2, No. 1 (April 1916): 2.*

"The Northwest Corner." *Outlook* 129, No. 13 (30 November 1921): 527. In Braithwaite (1922), 99.

"O Heart of Me." *Vagrant* No. 15 (Spring 1927): 281.

"Oh Rose, Red Rose." *Scot* (May 1916).*

"Oh, She Was Smart." *Maine Bulletin* (September 1928). In Braithwaite (1929), 167–68.

"Oh Where Is Springtime?" *Woodbee* (January 1916).*

"On Ellen Going Wrong." *Gypsy* (Winter 1925). In Braithwaite (1926), 218.

"On Meeting Father Goose." *Maine Bulletin* (November 1925). In Braithwaite (1926), 215–16.

"On Shore." *Conservative* 4, No. 1 (July 1918): 2.*

"On the Road down to Aurora." *Vagrant* No. 9 (September 1919): 38–39.

"Outdoors." *Tryout* 4, No. 12 (December 1918): 15.

"Pardel's Fat Shote." *Maine Bulletin* (September 1928). In Braithwaite (1929), 167.

"Pattern." *Gypsy* (June 1926).

"Pear Seeds." See "Tales of Women."

"Pitch o' Pine Sonnets." *Maine Bulletin*. In Braithwaite (1926), 212–14. Includes: I. John's Mary; II. Quills; III. Clem's Fool.

"The Pool." *Conservative* 2, No. 3 (October 1916): 7.*

"Poor River Drivers." *Maine Bulletin* (August 1924). In Braithwaite (1925), 175–76.

"Pores." *Maine Bulletin* (February 1929). In Braithwaite (1929), 169–70.

"The Purchase." In Braithwaite (1921), 97.

"Quills." *Maine Bulletin* (November 1925). See "Pitch o' Pine Sonnets."

"Red Winds." *Emerson Quarterly*. In *Fellowship Anthology of the New England Poetry Club*. Natick, MA: Suburban Press, 1922. n.p. In Braithwaite (1923), 178–79.

"The Return." *Muses* (February 1925).

"Rigby's Bar." See "Tales of Women."

"The River of Life." *National Magazine* 45, No. 1 (October 1916): 142.

"The Road to the Great Pond." *Bonnet* (January 1920): [5].

"The Rose of Friendship." *Vagrant* No. 15 (Spring 1927): 281.

"Scuffled Dust." *Ellsworth Journal* (1925). *Maine Bulletin* (November 1925). In Braithwaite (1926), 217.

"Sea-Winds." *Crisis* (1920?) p. 76.

"Sevensomeness." See "Tales of Women."

"She Told Mary." *The Book Chat*. In Braithwaite (1924), 132–33.

"Sickle Scythes." *Maine Bulletin* (1927–28). In Braithwaite (1928), 185.

"The Sin." *Lyric* 2, No. 11 (November 1922): 3. In Braithwaite (1923), 179.

"The Singer." *Hub Club Quill* 12, No. 1 (January 1920): 7.

"The Singing Heart." *Weekly Unity* (17 June 1916).*

"Smiles." *Vagrant* No. 15 (Spring 1927): 280.

"The Song of Fair Kate Loring." *United Amateur* 20, No. 4 (March 1921): [47]–48.

"The Song of Johnny Laughlin." *United Amateur* 20, No. 3 (January 1921): [33].

"Song of the North Wind." *Conservative* 1, No. 4 (January 1916): 1.*

"The Song of the Sea Shell." *National Magazine* (September 1916): 936.*

"Strange Paths." *Lyric* 2, No. 11 (November 1922): 8. In Braithwaite (1923), 178.

"Stumps." *Contemporary Verse* (December–January 1927). In Braithwaite (1927), 176.

"Susie." See "Tales of Women."

"The Sweet Today." *Silver Clarion* 2, No. 2 (May 1918): [1].*

"Sunrise at Cooper." *Tryout* 4, No. 3 (March 1918): 1.

"Tales of Women." *Maine Bulletin* (December 1926). In Braithwaite (1927), 162–75.

"Tenants." *Ellsworth Weekly* (7 December 1924). In Braithwaite (1925), 168–69.

"That I Might Be in the Cool Blue Wind." *Voice from the Mountains* (July 1918): 13.*

"There's a Way." *United Co-operative* 1, No. 2 (June 1919): 1.

"Thistles." *Silver Clarion* 2, No. 9 (December 1918): 2.*

"Threads." *Boston Evening Transcript*. In Braithwaite (1923), 177–78.

"'Tis Maytime in the Pine Tree State." *United Amateur* 17, No. 5 (May 1918): [81].

"To a Breeze." *Coyote* (July 1916?).*

"To a Decoy Duck." *Tryout* 4, No. 4 (April 1918): [1].

"To You." *Tryout* 2, No. 3 (February 1916): [11].

"The Tricksy Tune." In Braithwaite (1921), 89–91.

"Trust." *Silver Clarion* 3, No. 6 (September 1919): 2.*

"Under-Currents." *Voices: A Journal of Verse.* In Braithwaite (1922), 99.

"The Vagrant." *Conservative* 2 No. 4 (January 1917): 1.*

"Values." *Crisis* 21, No. 1 (November 1920): 15.*

"The Voice of God." *Silver Clarion* 4, No. 3 (June 1920): 3.*

"Waiting for Betty." *Boston Post* (19 March 1921): 18.

"Weights." *Ellsworth Journal* (1926?), not found. *Maine Bulletin* (April 1926). In Braithwaite (1926), 217–18.

"What More." *Tryout* 2, No. 3 (February 1916): [13].

"When I Sail the Sea." *Voice from the Mountains* (July 1918).*

"When I Wake." *Philosopher* 1, No. 1 (December 1920): 9.*

"When Love Is with You." *Norwich [Connecticut] Bulletin* (21 June 1919): 9.

"When the Sea Calls." *The Amateur Special* (July 1916).*

"When the Woods Call." *Dowdell's Bearcat* (December 1915).* *Sunday Post Sunday Magazine* (12 December 1920): 7.

"White Star of Love." *Vagrant* No. 15 (Spring 1927): 3.

"Who Will Fare with Me?" *Conservative* 5, No. 1 (July 1919): 9.*

"Wimin's Work." *Magnet* (December 1924). In Braithwaite (1925), 172–74.

"A Wind Waif." *Vagrant* No. 15 (Spring 1927): 279.

"A Witch's Daughter and a Cobbler's Son." *Maine Bulletin* (November 1925). In Braithwaite (1926), 216–17.

Poems not located

"Assurance."

"The Call."

"Caza, the Dancer."

"Death Is a Moment."

"Driftwood."

"The Duty."

"The End."

"The Fight."

"Haying."

"I Knew a Tall Lad Once."

"If You But Smile."

"If You Think You Are Beaten, Well, Why?"

"It's Lovetime."

"Joe."

"Larry Gorman, Singer."

"Let Us Dream Again."

"Mary, Queen of Scots."

"The Mirror."

"Red Wings."

"September."

"Smoke."

"Something Back in April."

"The Song."

"The Time of Peach Tree Bloom."

"The Token."

"When You Went."

"Workin' Out."

Fiction

"The Crawling Chaos" (with H. P. Lovecraft). *United Co-operative* 1, No. 3 (April 1921): 1–6 (as by "Elizabeth Berkeley and Lewis Theobald, Jun."). In *CF* 4.

"A Girl to Her Mirror." *All-Story* (8 February 1930).

"The Green Meadow" (with H. P. Lovecraft). *Vagrant* No. 15 (Spring 1927): 188–95 (as by "Elizabeth Neville Berkeley and Lewis Theobald Jr."). In *CF* 4.

"A Parable." *Silver Clarion* 3, No. 2 (May 1919): 4 (as by "Elizabeth Berkley").

"The Slip-Up." *Young's Magazine Snappy Stories* 59, No. 3 (May 1930): 3–18.

F. Arthur Leeds

Fiction

"The Carbon Copy." *Black Cat* 21, No. 7 (April 1916): 55–56; 25, No. 5 (March 1920): 122–23[?].

"He Had to Pay the Nine-Tailed Cat." *Ghost Stories* 1, No. 4 (October 1926): 36–39. In Mara Kirk Hart and S. T. Joshi, ed. *Lovecraft's New York Circle: The Kalem Club, 1924–1927.* New York: Hippocampus Press, 2006. 142–53.

"The Man Who Shunned the Light." *Black Cat* 20, No. 5 (February 1915): 25–30.

"A Mutual Understanding." *Snappy Stories* 31, No. 3 (18 December 1917): 315–21.

"Over the Great Divide." *Black Cat* 19, No. 9 (June 1914): 1–8. *Black Cat* 25, No. 7 (May 1920): 101–7.

"The Return of the Undead." *WT* 6, No. 5 (November 1925): 589–98.

"The Spinning Terror." *Parisienne Monthly Magazine* 9, No. 2 (August 1919): 51–56.

"The Sweetness of the Light." *Lippincott's Magazine* 94, No. 3 (September 1914): 373–79.

Nonfiction

"A. Van Buren Powell—Author, Editor and Photoplay Teacher." *Photoplay Author and Writer's Monthly* 5, No. 4 (April 1915): [104]–6.

"Henry Albert Phillips: An Idealist with a 'Punch.'" *Photoplay Author* 4, No. 3 (September 1914): [69]–74.

"How Much Help Do You Give the Director?" *Photoplay Author and Writer's Monthly* 5, No. 1 (January 1915): [3]–6.

"Photoplay Construction" (with J. Berg Esenwein). *Photoplay Author* 4, No. 1 (July 1914): [14]–22; 4, No. 2 (August 1914): [43]–53; 4, No. 3 (September 1914): [78]–84; 4, No. 4 (October 1914): [106]–16; 4, No. 5 (November 1914): [139]–46; 4, No. 6 (December 1914): [173]–81; 5, No. 1

(January 1915): [15]–21; 5, No. 2 (February 1915): [46]–52; 5, No. 3 (March 1915): [75]–82.

"Preparedness." *Photoplay Author and Writer's Monthly* 5, No. 2 (February 1915): [53].

"Schrock—A Dreamer Who Does Things." *Photoplay Author and Writer's Monthly* 5, No. 1 (January 1915): [9]–12.

"Thinks and Things." *Photoplay Author and Writer's Monthly* 5, No. 3 (March 1915): [90]–92; 5, No. 4 (April 1915): [124]–31; 5, No. 5 (May 1915): [169]–71; 5, No. 6 (June 1915): [206]–09.

Photoplays
The Germinal Element.
The Heart of a Jew.
In the Country God Forgot.
The Man Who Mocked.
A Pearl of Greater Price.
Sun, Sand and Solitude.
Through Another Man's Eyes.
Without Reward.

G. Paul J. Campbell

Prose

"Achievements with Wooden Legs." *Courage: Official Magazine of the Fraternity of the Wooden Leg* 1, No. 4 (September 1940): 21–23.

"Adventures in Amateur Journalism." *Fossil* 102, No. 2 (January 2006): 5–11. An extract from "Adventures in Appreciation" (December 1941–January 1942), q.v.

"Adventures in Appreciation." *Courage: Official Magazine of the Fraternity of the Wooden Leg* No. 1 (January 1940) [10]–18; No. 3 (August 1940): [7]–16; No. 4 (September 1940): [9]–17; No. 5 (October 1940): [7]–12; No. 6 (November–December 1940): [7]–18; No. 7 (January–February 1941): [8]–15; No. 8 (March 1941): [8]–17; No. 9 (April–May 1941): [6]–13; No. 10 June–July 1941): [12]–15; No. 11 (October–November [1941]): [10]–15; No. 13 (December [1941]–January [1942]): 6–20; No. 21 (April–May 1943): [13]–17; No. 22 (June–July 1943) [10]–14; No. 3 (January 1945): 12–15 (rpt. from *The Shut-in Companion*, November 1944).

"After Seven Years." *Invictus* 1, No. 1 (January 1915): 14–16 (under "Amateur Affairs").

"The Age of Accuracy." *Invictus* 1, No. 2 (July 1916): 6–10.

"The Alumni and the United Amateur Press Association." An extract from "Adventures in Appreciation" (April–May 1943), q.v.

"Amalgamation in Amateurdom." *Invictus* 1, No. 1 (January 1915): 16–17 (under "Amateur Affairs").

"Amateur Affairs." *Invictus* 1, No. 1 (January 1915): 14–26; 1, No. 2 (July 1916): 11–30; 1, No. 8 (July 1917): 9–17; 2, No. 1 (April 1920): 8–12.

"Announcement of Appointment." *Courage: Official Magazine of the Fraternity of the Wooden Leg* 1, No. 5 (October 1940): 16–17.

"Around the Circle." *Tryout* 14, No. 1 (May 1931): [11–13].

"The Artistic Sense." *Idle Hours* 4, No. 2 (October 1913): 4–6.

"The Avenue of Approach." *Invictus* 1, No. 8 (July 1917): 6–8.

"Boost for the Boren Bill." *Courage: Official Magazine of the Fraternity of the Wooden Leg* 3, No. 20 [*sic*] (February–March 1943): 25.

"The Comprehensive View." *United Amateur* 9, No. 5 (May 1910): 80–81.

"The Discovery of Columbus." *Invictus* 1, No. 1 (January 1915): 20–21 (under "Amateur Affairs").

"Diverse Desires." *Liberal* 1, No. 3 (February 1923): 18–19.

"Does it Pay?" *United Official Quarterly* 1, No. 2 (February 1915): 3–4.

"Down in Mexico." *Invictus* 1, No. 1 (January 1915): 9.

"Down to the Styx." *Courage: Official Magazine of the Fraternity of the Wooden Leg* 1, No. 4 (September 1940): 19–20.

"Echoes." *Invictus* 2, No. 1 (April 1920): 10–12.

"Editorial." *Liberal* 1, No.1 (February 1921): 26–31.

"Editorial Essentials." *United Amateur* 11, No. 3 (January 1912): 38–39.

"The Era of Equality." *Invictus* 1, No. 1 (January 1915): 17–20 (under "Amateur Affairs").

"The Event of the Season." *Liberal* 1, No. 2 (February 1922): 36 (unsigned).

"The Erford Amateur Press Association." *Liberal* 1, No. 1 (February 1921): 28–31. *Fossil* 103, No. 2 (April 2007): 21–23.

"The Expansionist Party." *Invictus* 1, No. 2 (July 1916): 22–23 (under "Amateur Affairs").

"The Expansionist Ticket." *Invictus* 1, No. 2 (July 1916): 23–26 (under "Amateur Affairs").

"Experience Meeting." *Liberal* 1, No. 3 (February 1923): 11.

"An Experience Meeting." *Liberal* 1, No. 1 (February 1921): 31–2.

"Federal Loans for Limbs." *Courage: Official Magazine of the Fraternity of the Wooden Leg* 1, No. 4 (September 1940): [1] (unsigned).

"The Field of the Future." *United Amateur* 14, No. 4 (March 1915): 70–71.

"Founding the Fraternity of the Wooden Leg." *Courage: Official Magazine of the Fraternity of the Wooden Leg* 1, No. 1 (June 1940): [1]–2.

"The Fremont Experiment." *Invictus* 1, No. 2 (July 1916): 11–12 (under "Amateur Affairs").

"From Shanghai to Cork, the Fraternity Marches On." *Courage: Official Magazine of the Fraternity of the Wooden Leg* 1, No. 4 (September 1940): 2–5.

"The F. W. L. Meets the A. L. M. A. at Chicago Convention." *Courage: Official Magazine of the Fraternity of the Wooden Leg* 1, No. 5 (October 1940): 3–4.

"Girls Are Like Gold." *United Amateur* 16, No. 9 (January 1917): 80.

"Going to a Funeral" [fiction]. *Vagrant* No. 4 (September 1916): [14–22].

"The Good Will of a Dog." *United Official Quarterly* 2, No. 2 (January 1916): [6–8].

"The Harp of Pain." *Courage: Official Magazine of the Fraternity of the Wooden Leg* 1, No. 4 (September 1940): [9].

"Hope and Expectation." *United Amateur* 17, No. 6 (July 1918): 113–14.

"The Ideal Official Organ." *Invictus* 1, No. 2 (July 1916): 18–22 (under "Amateur Affairs").

"Ideals of the Amateur." *United Amateur* 4, No. 3 (January 1915): 49.

"The Impost of the Future." *Invictus* 1, No. 1 (January 1915): 2–3.

"The Joke Was on the White Man." *Texaco Star* 18, No. 10 (December 1931): 25–26, 32.

"Lending a Hand to the Handicapped." *Courage: Official Magazine of the Fraternity of the Wooden Leg* 3, No. 20 [*sic*] (February–March 1943): [1]–4.

[Letter.] *Campaigner* 1, No. 1 (June 1923): 7.

[Letter to the Editor.] *WT* 2, No 4. (December 1923–January 1924): 86.

"The License of Literature." *United Amateur* 10, No. 4 (March 1911): 3–4.

"The Literary Conscience.' *United Amateur* 9, No. 4 (March 1910): [49–50].

"Literature in Amateur Journalism." *United Amateur* 9, No. 3 (January 1910): 41–42.

"The Logic of the Jungle." *Liberal* 1, No. 1 (February 1921): 17–22.

"Lost the Handicap on the Wood Standard." *Courage: Official Magazine of the Fraternity of the Wooden Leg* 1, No. 4 (September 1940): 25 (unsigned).

"Man of Vision." *Courage: Official Magazine of the Fraternity of the Wooden Leg* 4, No. 25 [*sic*] (January 1944): 2–5 (as by "Paul J. Campbell, Jr.").

"Marks Manual of Artificial Limbs." *Courage: Official Magazine of the Fraternity of the Wooden Leg* 4, No. 25 [*sic*] (January 1944): 9–12.

[Miscellany.] *Invictus* 1, No. 1 (January 1915): 21–26.

[Miscellany.] *Liberal* 1, No. 3 (February 1923): 19–20.

"A Misfortune." *Tryout* 11, No. 5 (May 1927): [29–30].

"The Nonparticipants." *Invictus* 1, No. 2 (July 1916): 13–16 (under "Amateur Affairs").

"One Leg Too Many." *Courage: Official Magazine of the Fraternity of the Wooden Leg* 1, No. 5 (October 1940): 5–6.

"The Orthodox View." *Invictus* 1, No. 8 (July 1917): [2–5].

"Pacifists and Patriots." *Invictus* 2, No. 1 (April 1920): 2–6.

"Passing Paragraphs." *Invictus* 1, No. 2 (July 1916): 26–30 (under "Amateur Affairs").

"Patriotism." *Liberal* 1, No. 2 (February 1922): 2–13.

"Paul J. Campbell, the Legal Guardian of Paul M. Campbell, Minor," United States Congress, Senate, 78th Congress, 2nd Session, Report No. 869 (10 May 1944): 1–6. See especially pp. 4–6.

"The Philosophy of Mark Twain." *Liberal* 1, No. 3 (February 1923): 7–11.

"The Price of Freedom." *Excelsior* (March 1917).

"The Procession of Progress." *Invictus* 1, No. 2 (July 1916): 12–13 (under "Amateur Affairs").

"Progress in Artificial Limbs." *Courage: Official Magazine of the Fraternity of the Wooden Leg* 1, No. 1 (June 1940): 19–20.

"The Pursuit of Happiness." *Invictus* 1, No. 2 (July 1916): 2–5.

The Pursuit of Happiness [novel]. Completed c. July 1925. Unpublished.

"The Real Amateur Spirit." *Dowdell's Bearcat* (October 1916).

"A Representative Official Organ." *United Amateur* 15, No. 8 (March 1916): 110.

"Report of the Supervisor of Amendments." *United Amateur* 14, No. 4 (March 1915): 77–79.

"Rubber Shock Absorber Ankle for Tender Stumps." *Courage: Official Magazine of the Fraternity of the Wooden Leg* 2, No. 10 [*sic*] June–July 1941): 19.

"Signals." *Little Budget* (May 1917).

"A Song to the Fallen." *Courage: Official Magazine of the Fraternity of the Wooden Leg* 1, No. 5 (October 1940): [7].

"Staff Contributors." *Invictus* 1, No. 2 (July 1916): 16–18 (under "Amateur Affairs").

"The Sublime Ideal." *Invictus* 1, No. 1 (January 1915): 4–8.

"This Ain't Love." *Ghost* No. 1 (Spring 1943): 33.

"2000 Miles Away." *Liberal* 1, No. 2 (February 1922): 35–36 (unsigned).

"The United Amateur Press Association: An Historical Survey, 1895–1912." *Californian* 4, No. 4 (Spring 1937): [first part by W. Paul Cook, 32–37]; "An Historical Survey, 1915" (by Campbell): 38–39.

"The Vintage of Time" [fiction]. *Monadnock Monthly* (May 1913): 57–61.

"Virtue Avenged" [fiction]. *Californian* 6, No. 1 (Summer 1938): 50–56.

"Visit to Modern Limb Factory." *Courage: Official Magazine of the Fraternity of the Wooden Leg* 1, No. 3 (August 1940): 20–22.

"Whom God Hath Put Asunder." *Invictus* 1, No. 1 (January 1915): 10–13.

"The Woodbee Administration." *Liberal* 1, No. 3 (February 1923): 19.

"You Can't Convince a Scotchman." *The Ideal Politician* 1, No. 1 (1902).

Verse

"Along the Way to Town." *The Decature* 2, No. 2 (June 1905): 21–22.

"Camp Meeting Time." [Original appearance not found.] *National Amateur* 41, No. 6 (July 1919): 155–57.

"Chicago River." *Courage: Official Magazine of the Fraternity of the Wooden Leg* 1, No. 3 (August 1940): [7].

"German Kulture." *Invictus* 1, No. 2 (July 1916): 10.

"The Heritage of Life." *Invictus* 1, No. 8 (July 1917): [1].

"Huerta's Finish." *Emissary* (July 1914): 22.

"Inspiration." *Invictus* 1, No. 1 (January 1915) [1]; *Courage: Official Magazine of the Fraternity of the Wooden Leg* 1, No. 1 (June 1940): [10].

"The Larger Life." *Invictus* 1, No. 1 (January 1915): 3–4.

"The Light That Lingers." *Invictus* 1, No. 8 (July 1918): 8–9.

"The Major Strain." *Invictus* 1, No. 2 (July 1916): 6.

"The Sunshine Girl." *Invictus* 1, No. 2 (July 1916): [1].

[Untitled verse: "The race, it seems, is to the swift;]". *Courage: Official Magazine of the Fraternity of the Wooden Leg* 1, No. 6 (November–December 1940): [7].

[Untitled verse: "The world is not so bad a world . . .]". *Courage: Official Magazine of the Fraternity of the Wooden Leg* 1, No. 9 (April–May 1941): [6].

H. Works by Others

Airne, C[lement] W[allace] (1889–?). *Britain's Story Told in Pictures*. Manchester: Sankey, Hudson & Co., [1935]. (*LL* 18)

———. *The Story of Hanoverian and Modern Britain Told in Pictures*. Manchester: Sankey, Hudson & Co., 1935. (*LL* 19)

———. *The Story of Mediaeval Britain Told in Pictures*. Manchester: Sankey, Hudson & Co., 1935. (*LL* 20)

———. *The Story of Prehistoric & Roman Britain Told in Pictures*. Manchester: Sankey, Hudson & Co., [1935]. (*LL* 21)

———. *Story of Saxon and Norman Britain Told in Pictures*. Manchester: Sankey, Hudson & Co. [1935]. (*LL* 22)

———. *The Story of Tudor and Stuart Britain Told in Pictures*. Manchester: Sankey, & Hudson & Co., 1935. (*LL* 23)

Appleton, John Howard (1844–1930). *The Young Chemist: A Book of Laboratory Work for Beginners*. Providence, RI: J. A. & R. A. Reid, 1876. (*LL* 47)

Bagg, E. N. "Arthur Leeds—Ideal Preparator." *Photoplay Author* 1, No. 12 (1913): 8.

Baudelaire, Charles Pierre (1821–1867). *The Poems of Charles Baudelaire*. Selected and translated from the French by F. P. Sturm (1879–1942). London: Walter Scott Publishing Co., 1906.

Beckford, William (1759–1844). *The Episodes of Vathek*. <1912> Translated from the Original French by Sir Frank T. Marzials. Boston: Small, Maynard & Co., [1922?] or [1924?]. (*LL* 83)

———. *The History of the Caliph Vathek* (1786; rpt. New York: W. L. Allinson, [1868?] or [188-?]). (*LL* 84)

Bierstadt, Edward Hale (1891–1970), *Dunsany the Dramatist,* new and rev. ed. Boston: Little, Brown, 1919. (*LL* 102)

Boswell, James (1740–1795). *Journal of a Tour to the Hebrides with Samuel Johnson, LL.D.* <1785> London: J. M. Dent & Co./E. P. Dutton (Everyman's Library), 1910f. (*LL* 124)

Braithwaite, William Stanley (1878–1962), ed. *Anthology of Magazine Verse for 1921 and Year Book of American Poetry*. Boston: Small, Maynard & Co., 1921.

———, ed. *Anthology of Magazine Verse for 1922 and Year Book of American Poetry*. Boston: Small, Maynard & Co., 1922.

————, ed. *Anthology of Magazine Verse for 1923 and Year Book of American Poetry*. Boston: Small, Maynard & Co., 1923.

————, ed. *Anthology of Magazine Verse for 1924 and Year Book of American Poetry*. Boston: B. J. Brimmer Co., 1924.

————, ed. *Anthology of Magazine Verse for 1925 and Year Book of American Poetry*. Boston: B. J. Brimmer Co., 1925.

————, ed. *Anthology of Magazine Verse for 1926 and Year Book of American Poetry*. Boston: B. J. Brimmer Co., 1926.

————, ed. *Anthology of Magazine Verse for 1927 and Year Book of American Poetry*. Boston: B. J. Brimmer Co., 1927.

————, ed. *Anthology of Magazine Verse for 1928 and Year Book of American Poetry*. New York: Harold Vinal, 1928.

————, ed. *Anthology of Magazine Verse for 1929 and Year Book of American Poetry*. New York: George Sully & Co., 1929.

————, ed. *Anthology of Massachusetts Poets*. Boston: Small, Maynard & Co., 1922. [1922a]

Bulfinch, Thomas (1796–1867). *The Age of Fable; or, Beauties of Mythology*. <1855> Edited by J[ohn] Loughran Scott (1846–1919). Rev. ed. Philadelphia: David McKay, [1898]. (*LL* 142)

Bullen, John Ravenor (1886–1927). *White Fire*. Ed. H. P. Lovecraft. Athol, MA: Recluse Press, 1927 [actually January 1928]. (*LL* 143)

Burroughs, Edgar Rice (1875–1950). *Tarzan of the Apes*. *All-Story* (October 1912). Chicago: A. C. McClurg, 1914.

Charles Francis Adams (1835–1915). *Massachusetts: Its Historians and Its History*. Boston: Houghton Mifflin, 1893.

de Castro, Adolphe (1859–1959). *Portrait of Ambrose Bierce*. With a preface by Belknap Long. New York: Century Co., 1929.

Darwin, Erasmus (1731–1802). *Beauties of the Botanic Garden*. <1791> New York: D. Longworth, 1805. (*LL* 236)

De Quincey, Thomas (1785–1859). *Confessions of an English Opium-Eater and Selected Essays*. <1822> Edited with Notes by David Masson. New York: A. L. Burt, n.d. (*LL* 247)

Dunsany, Edward John Moreton Drax Plunkett, 18th Baron (1878–1957). *The Gods of Pegāna*. <1905> (*LL* 293)

————. *The Last Book of Wonder*. Boston: John W. Luce, [1916]. (*LL* 295)

————. *Plays of Gods and Men*. Boston: John W. Luce, 1917. (*LL* 296) [Contains *The Queen's Enemies*.]

————. *Plays of Near and Far*. New York: G. P. Putnam's Sons, 1923. (*LL* 297)

————. *Time and the Gods*. <1906> In *The Book of Wonder* [and *Time and the Gods*]. New York: Boni & Liveright (Modern Library), 1918. (*LL* 288)

————. *Unhappy Far-Off Things*. Boston: Little, Brown, 1919. (*LL* 300)

Dzwonkoski, Peter, ed. *American Literary Publishing Houses, 1900–1980: Trade and Paperback.* Dictionary of Literary Biography Vol. 46. Detroit: Gale Research Company, 1986.

Edkins, Ernest Arthur (1867–1946). *Amenophra and Other Poems.* Detroit: Edwin B. Hill, 1889.

Emerson, Ralph Waldo (1803–1882). *Culture.* New York: Barse & Hopkins, 1910. (*LL* 313)

Ferber, Edna (1885–1968). *Cimarron.* Garden City, NY: Doubleday, 1930.

France, Anatole (1844–1924). "The Procurator of Judea." In *Mother of Pearl.* Tr. Frederic Chapman. London: John Lane/The Bodley Head; New York: Dodd, Mead, 1922. 3–28.

Gautier, Théophile (1811–1872). *One of Cleopatra's Nights and Other Fantastic Romances.* Tr. Lafcadio Hearn. New York: Worthington, 1882. (*LL* 367)

Gough, John B. (1817–1886). *Sunlight and Shadow; or, Gleanings from My Life Work.* Hartford, CT: A. D. Worthington, 1881.

Grimm, Jakob Ludwig Karl (1785–1863), and W. K. Grimm (1786–1859). *Fairy Tales.* <1812–15> (*LL* 405)

Goodenough, Arthur Henry (1871–1936). *Songs of Four Decades.* Athol, MA, W. Paul Cook, 1927.

Haden, David. *Lovecraft in Historical Context: The Fourth Collection of Essays and Notes.* n.p., 2013.

Haeckel, Ernst (1834–1919). *Die Welträthsel.* <1899> Tr. Joseph McCabe as *The Riddle of the Universe.* New York: Harper & Brothers, 1900.

Haggard, H. Rider (1856–1925). *She: A History of Adventure.* <1887> New York: Gorton & Payne, [19—]. (*LL* 411)

Hale, Susan (1833–1910). *Men and Manners of the Eighteenth Century.* Philadelphia: George W. Jacobs, 1898. (*LL* 417)

Harré, T. Everett (1884–1948), ed. *Beware After Dark! The World's Most Stupendous Tales of Mystery, Horror, Thrills and Terror.* New York: Macaulay, 1929. [Contains HPL's "The Call of Cthulhu."] (*LL* 425)

Harrison, Thomas G. (1860–1911). *The Career and Reminiscences of an Amateur Journalist, and a History of Amateur Journalism.* Indianapolis: Thomas G. Harrison, 1883.

Harrison, William Henry, Jr. *Colored Girls and Boys' Inspiring United States History, and A Heart to Heart Talk about White Folks.* [Allentown, Pa.: Searle & Dressler Co.], 1921.

Hartrampf, Gustavus A. (1875–1934). *Hartrampf's Vocabularies: Synonyms, Antonyms, Relatives.* Atlanta: Hartrampf Co., 1929.

Hawthorne, Nathaniel (1804–1864). *Dr. Grimshawe's Secret.* Ed. Julian Hawthorne. Boston: Houghton, Mifflin, 1882.

Hoag, Jonathan E. (1831–1927). *The Poetical Works of Jonathan E. Hoag.* [New York: Privately printed], 1923. (*LL* 453)

Hodgson, William Hope (1877–1918). *The Boats of the "Glen Carrig."* London: Chapman & Hall, 1907.

Irwin, Virginia. "The Fraternity of the Wooden Leg." *St. Louis Post Dispatch: Everyday Magazine* (18 June 1940): 27.

Johnson, Samuel (1709–1784). *A Journey to the Western Islands of Scotland.* <1775> 1st. American Ed. Baltimore: P. H. Nicklin & Co.; Boston: Farrand, Mallory & Co., 1810. (*LL* 515)

Joshi, S. T., and David E. Schultz, ed. *Ave atque Vale: Reminiscences of H. P. Lovecraft.* West Warwick, RI: Necronomicon Press, 2018.

Joshi, S. T., with David E. Schultz. *Lovecraft's Library: A Catalogue.* 4th ed. New York: Hippocampus Press, 2017.

Level, Maurice (1875–1926). *Tales of Mystery and Horror.* Tr. Alys Eyre Macklin. New York: Robert M. McBride & Co., 1920. (*LL* 565)

Lodge, Sir Oliver (1851–1940). *Raymond, or Life and Death: With Examples of the Evidence for Survival of Memory and Affection after Death.* New York: George H. Doran, 1916.

Long, Frank Belknap (1901–1994). *The Goblin Tower.* Cassia, FL: Dragon-Fly Press, 1935. (*LL* 580).

———. *A Man from Genoa and Other Poems.* Athol, MA: W. Paul Cook, 1926. (*LL* 581)

Loveman, Samuel (1887–1976). *The Hermaphrodite: A Poem.* With a Preface by Benjamin De Casseres. Athol, MA: W. Paul Cook, 1926. (*LL* 593)

———. *Out of the Immortal Night: Selected Works by Samuel Loveman.* Ed. S. T. Joshi and David E. Schultz. Rev. ed. New York: Hippocampus Press, 2020.

Lucretius (T[itus] Lucretius Carus) (98?–50 B.C.E.?). *De Rerum Natura Libri Sex.* Tr. H[ugh] A[ndrew] J[ohnson] Munro (1819–1885). London: George Bell and Sons, 1900.

Ludlow, Fitz Hugh (1836–1870). *The Hasheesh Eater: Being Passages from the Life of a Pythagorean.* New York: Harper & Brothers, 1857. (*LL* 601)

Machen, Arthur (1863–1947). *The House of Souls.* <1906> New York: Alfred A. Knopf, 1923. (*LL* 618)

Mather, Cotton (1663–1728). *Magnalia Christi Americana; or, The Ecclesiastical History of New-England, from Its First Planting in the Year 1620, unto the Year of Our Lord, 1698.* London: Printed for T. Parkhurst, 1702. (*LL* 645)

Milton, John (1608–1674). *Paradise Lost.* <1667> Illustrated by Gustave Doré <1866>. (*LL* 656)

Montgomery, David Henry (1837–1928). *The Leading Facts of American History.* Boston: Ginn & Co., 1887 (rev. ed.).

The New-England Primer: Improved, for the More Easy Attaining the True Reading of English: To Which Is Added The Assembly of Divines, and Mr. Cotton's Catechism. <1760?> Albany, NY: Joel Munsell, 1777. (*LL* 706)

Nixon, John Travis (1867–1909). *A History of the National Amateur Press Association.* Crowley, LA: John T. Nixon, 1900.

O'Brien, Edward J. (1890–1941), ed. *The Best Short Stories of 1928 and the Yearbook of the American Short Story.* New York: Dodd, Mead, 1928. (*LL* 714)

Owings, Mark, and Irving Binkin. *A Catalog of Lovecraftiana: The Grill/Binkin Collection.* Baltimore: Mirage Press, 1975.

Parker, Richard Green (1798–1869). *Aids to English Composition, Prepared for Students of All Grades.* Boston: R. S. Davis; New York, Robinson, Pratt & Co. 1844. (*LL* 738)

Pendergast, Patrick James (1850–?). *Selected Gems.* [Jamaica Plain, MA: Angel Guardian Press, 1917.]

Percy, Thomas (1729–1811), ed. *Reliques of Ancient English Poetry.* <1765> London: J. M. Dent; New York: E. P. Dutton (Everyman's Library), [1906]–[1932]. 2 vols. (*LL* 752)

Renshaw, Anne Tillery (1890–c. 1945). *Well Bred Speech: A Brief, Intensive Aid for English Students.* [Washington, DC: Standard Press, 1936.] (*LL* 796)

Reynolds, George W. M. (1814–1879). *Faust and the Demon: A Romance of the Secret Tribunals.* London: G. Vickers, 1847.

———. *Wagner, the Wehr-Wolf.* London: J. Dicks, 1848, 1857, 1872.

Richardson, Leon Burr (1878–1951). *History of Dartmouth College.* Hanover, NH: Stephen Daye Press, 1932. 2 vols.

[Sargent, Lucius M.] (1786–1867). *Dealings with the Dead.* "By a sexton of the old school." Boston: Dutton & Wentworth, 1856. 2 vols.

Seeger, Alan (1888–1916). *Poems.* New York: Charles Scribner's Sons, 1916.

Shaw, George Bernard (1856–1950). *Back to Methuselah: A Metabiological Pentateuch.* New York: Brentano's, 1921. (*LL* 861)

Shivell, Paul (1874–1968). *Stillwater Pastorals and Other Poems.* Boston: Houghton Mifflin, 1915.

Smith, Russell E. "The Author of the Photoplay." *Book News Monthly* 33, No. 7 (March 1915): 327–32.

Spencer, Truman J. (1864–1944). *A Cyclopedia of the Literature of Amateur Journalism.* Hartford, CT: Truman J. Spencer, 1891. (*LL* 899)

Spengler, Oswald (1880–1936). *Der Untergang des Abendlandes.* <1918–22> Tr. Charles Francis Atkinson as *The Decline of the West.* London: George Allen & Unwin, 1922–26 (2 vols.). New York: Alfred A. Knopf, 1926–28 (2 vols.).

Stoker, Bram (1847–1912). *The Jewel of Seven Stars.* London: Heinemann, 1903. London: William Rider & Son, 1912, 1919.

Taylor, Gregory S. *James Larkin Pearson: A Biography of North Carolina's Longest-Serving Poet Laureate.* Lanham, MD: Lexington Books, 2015.

Thompson, Denman (1833–1911). *Sunshine of Paradise Alley.* [Boston, 1896.]

Thomson, James (1700–1748). *The Seasons; with The Castle of Indolence.* <1726–30; 1748> New-York: Published by W. B. Gilley, . . . Clayton & Kingsland, Printers, 1819. (*LL* 967)

Tromblee, Charles. "Lovecraft Collaborator—Winifred Virginia Jackson." 24 June 2017. winifredvjackson.blogspot.com

Vincennes Fortnightly Club. *Historic Vincennes: Souvenir Tourist's Guide.* Vincennes, IN: Vincennes Fortnightly Club, 1923; 2d edition 1925. (*LL*)

Virgil (P. Vergilius Maro) (70–19 B.C.E.). *The Aeneid.* Tr. [verse] James Rhoades (1841–1923). London: Longmans, Green, 1906. Later included in Rhoades's translation of *The Poems of Virgil.* London: Oxford University Press, 1921.

———. *The Æneid of Virgil.* Tr. [verse] John Conington (1825–1869). New York: Armstrong & Son, 1886.

———.*The Works of Virgil.* Tr. John Dryden (1631–1700) <1697>. London: Henry Frowde/Oxford University Press (World's Classics), 1903–25. (*LL* 1002)

Weigall, Arthur (1880–1934). *Wanderings in Roman Britain.* London: Thornton Butterworth, 1926. (*LL* 1025)

Wescott, Glenway (1901–1987). *The Grandmothers: A Family Portrait.* New York: Harper & Brothers, 1927.

Wetzel, George T. (1921–1983), and R. Alain Everts. *Winifred Virginia Jackson, Lovecraft's Lost Romance.* Madison, WI: Strange Company, 1976.

White, Michael. "The Poetry of Winifred Virginia Jackson." *Hub Club Quill* (June 1920).

Index

www.ingramcontent.com/pod-product-compliance
Lightning Source LLC
Chambersburg PA
CBHW070356030726
47504CB00001B/201